Essential VHDL
RTL Synthesis Done Right

Sundar Rajan

Essential VHDL: RTL Synthesis Done Right by Sundar Rajan

Copyright 1998 ©, by Sundar Rajan and Gennis Lafayette. All rights reserved. Printed in the USA.

Printing History
First Article, June 1998.
Second Article, March 1999.

All trademarks used herein are credited to the respective companies. Trademarked terms used in this book are designated with a trademark (TM) symbol. Neither the author nor publisher are responsible for errors or omissions herein. All simulations and examples in this book were tested by the author but are not guaranteed. Neither the author nor publisher are responsible if the user does not experience the identical results.

Technical illustrations contained in this book were created using Visio® Technical V5.0 by Visio Corporation, Seattle, Washington.

Tri-state is a registered trademark of National Semiconductor Corporation.
pASIC and Quicklogic are registered trademarks of Quicklogic Corporation.
Altera and Flex are registered trademarks of Altera Corporation.
Synplify and Synplicity are registered trademarks of Synplicity Corporation.

ISBN: 0-9669590-0-0

Contents

Preface .... *xxi*
    VHDL Basics xxi
    Design Topics xxi
    Advanced Issues xxi

Acknowledgements .... *xxv*

1 VHDL Basics 1
    What is VHDL? 1
    Black Boxes 1
    Connecting Logic Using Signals 2
    Connecting Black Boxes 3
    Naming and Labeling 5
    Implementing Basic Logic 8
    Ordering of Statements 8
    Design for RTL Synthesis 10
    Different Styles of Design Description 10

2 Getting Your First Design Done 13
    Defining the Black Box 13
    The Entity 14
    The Architecture 16
        Dataflow Design 17
        Structural Design 18
        Behavioral Design 20

3 Gates, Decoders and Encoders 25
    Gates 25
        Gates Using Structural Instantiation 25
        Gates Using Concurrent Assignments 27
    Decoders 28
        Decoders Using Concurrent Assignments 30
        Decoders Within a Process Using the *Case* Statement 31
        Decoders Using *with...select* 35
        Decoders Using *if...then* 37
        The Difference Between *if...then* and *Case* Statements 39
        Factorization: Where the Tool Meets the Road 40
    Encoders 47

4 Registers and Latches 51
Registers 51
Structural Instantiation of Flip-flops 51
Behavioral Inference of Flip-flops 52
Using the *Wait* Statement 53
Flip-flops with Enable 57
Flip-flops with *if...then* and a Sensitivity List 58
Key Difference Between *if...then* and *wait*-Generated Flip-flops 60
Flip-flop Reset and Preset 62
Asynchronous Resets and Preset 62
Synchronous Resets and Presets 65
Notable Issues with Sets and Resets 67
Latches 70
Structural Instantiation of Latches 70
Latches Using Concurrent Assignments 72
Latches Using Processes 73
Key Difference Between Processes and Dataflow Inferred Latches 73

5 Counters and Simple Arithmetic Functions 75
Arithmetic Functions in Predefined Packages 75
Load-able and Enable-able Counters 79
Operator Overloading 83
Vector Direction 83
Functions Available in the Standard Packages 85
Adders and Subtractors 92
Multiplication, Division and Exponentiation 94
Design Example 95

6 Finite State Machines 101
Typical State Machine Blocks 101
State Machine Inputs and Outputs 102
Developing the State Diagram 104
Creating a Type for Your States 105
Coding the Next State Conditioning Logic 106
Registering the Current State Vector 107
Coding the Output Conditioning Logic 108
The Complete PCI Target State Machine Design 109
State Machines as Part of Your System Design 113
   Step 1: Determine the Datapath 113
   Step 2: Determine the Control Algorithm 114
   Step 3: Defining the Black Box 115
   Step 4: Describe the States Using Enumerated Types 116
   Step 5: Code the Next State Conditioning Logic 116

Contents

    Step 6: Code the Current State Register 117
    Step 7: Code the Output Conditioning Logic 117
    Step 8: Integrate with the Datapath 118
  Issues Related to State Machine Design Technique 121

7 Reset, Presets, Tri-state and Bi-directional Signals 123
  Asynchronous Presets and Resets 123
    Structural Instantiation of a Flip-flop with Preset and Reset 123
    Behavioral Coding of a Flip-flop with Preset and Reset 125
    Using Asynchronous Presets/Resets to Load a Flip-flop 127
  Tri-states 131
    Tri-state Buffer Using Structural Instantiation 132
    Tri-state Buffer Using Concurrent Assignment 133
    Tri-state Buffer Using *if...then* Statements 133
    Enabling or Disabling a Bus Using Aggregates 134
  Bi-directional Buffers 136
    Bi-directional Buffer Using Structural Instantiation 136
    Bi-directional Buffer Using Concurrent Assignment 137
    Design Example 138

8 Understanding Hardware Creation 141
  Signals Have Implicit Memory 141
  The Last Signal Assignment is the One that Takes Effect 146
  Implicit Latch Inference 147
    Unwanted Implicit Latches 148
    Completely Specifying *if...then* Statements to Avoid Implicit Latches 149
    Completely Specifying All Outputs of a *Case* Statement
      to Avoid Implicit Latches 151
    Implicit Memory from Lack of Reset or Preset to a Flip-flop 155
  Don't Care Comparisons and Assignments 157
    Don't Cares in Wildcard Comparisons 157
    Don't Care Output Assignment 158
  Resolution Functions, Tri-states and Muxes 161
  Resource Sharing 163

9 Design Partitioning 167
  Design Hierarchy 168
  Hierarchy in VHDL 169
    Positional Versus Named Association for Component Instances 173
    Leaving an Output Port Unconnected 174
  Libraries 176
    Adding Components to Libraries 176
  Packages 179
  Component Configuration 181

Partitioning Techniques that Influence Implementation 185

10 Getting the Most from Your State Machines 191

State Encoding 191
    Sequential State Encoding 192
    Equation 1: Equation for the Number of Encoded States 192
    Explicitly Encoding States Sequentially 192
    Analyzing the Next State Logic 197
    Number and Complexity of Branch Conditions 198
    Number of State Bits 199
    Reducing the Number of State Bit Transitions When Going From
        State to State 200
    One-hot Coded State Machines 201
    Explicit Method for One-hot Coded State Machines 201
    Step 1: Creating the Type for the State Machine 201
    Step 2: Set the Default State for the State Vector 202
    Step 3: Replace Case With *if...then* for the *nextState* Assignment 202
    Step 4: Change the Code for the Idle State Condition in the Current
        State Process 202
    Step 5: Replace Case With *if...then* for the Output Conditioning Logic 203
    State Encoding Guidelines for Performance 207
    Design Implications of State Encoding 208
    Other Issues When Explicitly Assigning State Bits 209
Output Decoding 210
    Default Output Assignment 210
    Registered Outputs 211
    Don't Cares 212
    Directly Encoding Outputs 213
    Design Considerations for Outputs 217

11 Scalable and Parameterizable Design 219

VHDL Facilitates Scalable and Parameterizable Design 219
Unconstrained Arrays 220
Generics 222
Variables 226
Loops 226
Attributes 230
The Generate Statement 232
    Similarity Between *for...loop* and *for...generate* 235
    Conditional Generate Statements 236

12 Enhancing Design Readability and Reuse 241

Functions 241
    Standard Functions 242

Contents   *v*

    User-defined Functions 246
  Procedures 250
    Disadvantage of Using Subprograms 255
  Aliases 255

13 Creative Potpourri *259*
  Aggregates 259
  Concatenation 262
  Records 264
  Multidimensional Arrays 266
  Array Indexing Using Enumerated Types 270
  While Loops 274
  Signal Mode Buffer 279

14 Simulation and Design Verification *281*
  Simulation Modeling 282
  Modeling a Simple Gate 282
  Enhancing the Basic Model 284
  Adding Debug Messages to the Model 287
  Hierarchy and Wire Delays 289
  Design Verification 291
  Basic Anatomy of a VHDL Testbench 292
  Reading and Writing Text 293
  Testbench Incorporating Vectors as an Array 295
  Testbench with Vectors in a Separate Text File 298

Appendix A: Measuring Performance and Utilization *305*
Index *307*
References and Sources *315*

Figures

1 VHDL Basics 1
    Figure 1: Black Box 2
    Figure 2: Mode *in* 4
    Figure 3: Mode *out* 4
    Figure 4: Mode *out* with Readable Intermediate Signal 5
    Figure 5: Mode *inout* 5
    Figure 6: Order Within an Architecture is Unimportant 9
    Figure 7: The Order of Statements Within a Process is Important 9
    Figure 8: RTL Design Description 10
    Figure 9: 3-input XOR Gate 11

2 Getting Your First Design Done 13
    Figure 1: Black Box Representing Logic Function 13
    Figure 2: Labeling and Signal Listing in the Entity Declaration 14
    Figure 3: Port Signal Names, Mode and Type Declaration 15
    Figure 4: Library Statement and *Use* Clause 15
    Figure 5: Format of the Library Statement and *Use* Clause 16
    Figure 6: Entity-architecture Pair 16
    Figure 7: Dataflow Design Implementation of *LogicFcn* 17
    Figure 8: Structure of *LogicFcn* 18
    Figure 9: Format of Component Instantiation 19
    Figure 10: Structural Implementation of *LogicFcn* 19
    Figure 11: Processes in an Architecture 20
    Figure 12: Behavioral Implementation of *LogicFcn* 22
    Figure 13: *LogicFcn* Synthesis Results 22

3 Gates, Decoders and Encoders 25
    Figure 1: AND2, INVERTER and OR2 Gates 25
    Figure 2: Sample Combinational Logic with Few Gates 26
    Figure 3: Few Gates Using Structural Instantiation 27
    Figure 4: Few Gates Using Concurrent Assignments 28
    Figure 5: Subsystem Using Programmable Logic as a Decoder 29
    Figure 6: Decoder Within Programmable Logic 29
    Figure 7: Decoder Using a *Case* Statement 34
    Figure 8: Decoder Using a *with...select* Statement 37
    Figure 9: Decoder with Qualifying *if...then* Inside the Same Process 43
    Figure 10: Decoder with Qualifying *if...then* in a Separate Process 46

  Figure 11: Priority Encoder 49
4 *Registers and Latches*..*51*
  Figure 1: D-type Flip-flop with Synchronous Enable 51
  Figure 2: D-type Flip-flop with Enable 52
  Figure 3: SR-type Flip-flop 56
  Figure 4: D-type Flip-flop Using *if...then* and a Sensitivity List 59
  Figure 5: More Complex Enabled DFF Using *if...then* and a Sensitivity List ... 60
  Figure 6: DFF with Asynchronous Reset 63
  Figure 7: DFF with Asynchronous Expression Reset 64
  Figure 8: DFF with Synchronous Reset 66
  Figure 9: Generic Latch 70
  Figure 10: Transparent Latch Truth Tables 70
  Figure 11: Transparent-High D-type Latch (DLATCHH) 71
  Figure 12: D-type Latch - Structural 71
  Figure 13: D-type Latch with Concurrent Assignments 72
5 *Counters and Simple Arithmetic Functions* *75*
  Figure 1: Simple Up-counter 77
  Figure 2: Counter with Non-zero Asynchronous Reset 78
  Figure 3: Counter Implemented Using an Ascending Range Vector 85
  Figure 4: Equality Compare of Two Unequal Length Vectors 91
  Figure 5: Full Adder Using Unsigned Vectors 93
  Figure 6: Accumulator Example 94
  Figure 7: Programmable Pulse Generator 95
  Figure 8: Programmable Pulse Generator Block Diagram 96
  Figure 9: Programmable Pulse Generator Circuit 99
6 *Finite State Machines*...*101*
  Figure 1: Typical State Machine Structure 102
  Figure 2: PCI Target State Machine Inputs and Outputs 103
  Figure 3: PCI Target State Machine State Transition Diagram 104
  Figure 4: Block Diagram of Programmable Pulse Generator Using a
   State Machine 114
  Figure 5: Programmable Pulse Generator Using a State Machine ... 115
  Figure 6: Programmable Pulse Generator State Machine
   Inputs and Output 115
  Figure 7: RTL View of Programmable Pulse Generator Using
   a State Machine 121
7 *Reset, Presets, Tri-state and Bi-directional Signals*.........................*123*
  Figure 1: D-type Flip-flop with Asynchronous Preset and Reset 123
  Figure 2: DFF with Reset-dominant Asynchronous Preset/Reset 126
  Figure 3: DFF with Preset Dominant Over Reset 127

Figures

- Figure 4: Register with Asynchronous Load 129
- Figure 5: Block Diagram for Counter with Synchronous Load 130
- Figure 6: Block Diagram for Counter with Asynchronous Load 130
- Figure 7: Counter with Asynchronous Load 131
- Figure 8: Tri-state Buffer Symbol and Truth Table 132
- Figure 9: Active High Enabled Tri-state Buffer 134
- Figure 10: Bi-directional Buffer Symbol and Truth Table 136
- Figure 11: Bi-directional Buffer 138
- Figure 12: Block Diagram for Counter with Bi-directional Outputs 138
- Figure 13: Counter with Bi-directional Outputs 140

8 Understanding Hardware Creation 141

- Figure 1: Waveform Demonstrating δdelay of Signals (Listing 2) 143
- Figure 2: Waveform Demonstrating δdelay of Signals (Listing 3) 145
- Figure 3: Gate-Level Representation of a Latch 148
- Figure 4: Elimination of Logic Using Else Statement 149
- Figure 5: Chained *if...then* Representation Using Muxes 150
- Figure 6: Parallel *if...then* Representation Using Muxes 151
- Figure 7: Seven-segment Binary Coded Decimal Display 152
- Figure 8: DFF with an Implicit Latch Caused by a Missing Asynchronous Reset 156
- Figure 9: BCD to Seven-segment Display with Output Pull-ups 159
- Figure 10: Bussed Signal Example 161
- Figure 11: Bussed Drivers Translated to Muxes 163
- Figure 12: Logic Implementation With and Without Resource Sharing 165

9 Design Partitioning 167

- Figure 1: Design Hierarchy Shown in Tree Form 168
- Figure 2: Design Hierarchy Shown in Block Form 168
- Figure 3: Component and Entity-architecture Associations 169
- Figure 4: Combination of Simple Gates 169
- Figure 5: Counter with Terminal Count 174
- Figure 6: Instantiation of Terminal Count, with *TermCnt* Left Unconnected 174
- Figure 7: Component Configuration 182
- Figure 8: Bus with Internal Tri-states 186
- Figure 9: Bus with Tri-states Buried in a Hierarchical Module 186
- Figure 10: Modes Must Propagate Appropriately Through the Architecture 188
- Figure 11: Bi-directional Counter Implemented Using Hierarchy 188

10 Getting the Most from Your State Machines 191

- Figure 1: Logic Affecting Transition to the Backoff State 197

11 Scalable and Parameterizable Design 219
Figure 1: D Flip-flop Scalable to a Width of n 220
Figure 2: Parameterizable Flip-flop and Tri-state Buffer 223
Figure 3: Odd Parity Generation Circuit for an 8-bit Bus 226
Figure 4: Odd Parity Generation Circuit for an 8-bit Bus
  Using 2-input XOR Gates 227
Figure 5: Single Bit Full Adder Element 228
Figure 6: n-bit Wide Adder (0 to n-1) Built Using the Single-bit
  Adder Elements 229
Figure 7: T Flip-flop Symbol and Truth-table 233
Figure 8: n-bit Up-counter Based on a TFF Slice 233
Figure 9: Odd Parity Generator Using a Parallel XOR Tree 238
Figure 10: Scalable, "Parallel" Parity Generator 238

12 Enhancing Design Readability and Reuse 241
Figure 1: Symbol and Truth Table for 2-of-4 Decoder 251

13 Creative Potpourri 259
Figure 1: Simple Logic Using Gates 262
Figure 2: Tri-state Buffer Symbol and Ports 264
Figure 3: 8-bit Register with Tri-state Buffer 265
Figure 4: Divide-by Clock Waveform 267
Figure 5: Pulse Generator State Machine 270
Figure 6: Register File Symbol 274
Figure 7: Interrupt Priority Encoder 277
Figure 8: Simple Counter and its Equivalent Logic 279

14 Simulation and Design Verification 281
Figure 1: OR Gate Symbol, Truth-table and Architecture 282
Figure 2: Propagation Delay for OR Gate 283
Figure 3: Pulse Rejection Example 284
Figure 4: Enhancing the Basic Delay Model 285
Figure 5: 2-1 Mux Symbol and Truth Table 285
Figure 6: Timing Characteristics of a 2-1 Mux 285
Figure 7: DFF Symbol and Timing Waveform 287
Figure 8: Simulation Model Showing Wire Delays 290
Figure 9: Basic Anatomy of a Testbench 292
Figure 10: Sample *read* Procedure Calls 294
Figure 11: Sample *write* Procedure Call 294
Figure 12: Sample Readline and Writeline Procedure Calls 295
Figure 13: Load-able, Reset-able Up-counter 298
Figure 14: Stimulus Application and Response Check for loadCnt 299
Figure 15: Sample Vector File and the VHDL that Reads It 299

Figures

Appendix A *305*
    Figure 1: Sample Table Demonstrating a Particular Coding Technique 305

Tables

1 VHDL Basics 1
- Table 1: *std_logic* Type Values and Their Meanings 3
- Table 2: Reserved Words in VHDL 7
- Table 3: Logical Operators for the *std_logic* type 8

2 Getting Your First Design Done 13
- Table 1: Truth Table for Sample Logic Function 13

3 Gates, Decoders and Encoders 25
- Table 1: Decode Table for Programmable Device Implementation 30

4 Registers and Latches 51
- Table 1: D-type Flip-flop with Enable Truth Table 51
- Table 2: SR-type Flip-flop Truth Table 55

5 Counters and Simple Arithmetic Functions 75
- Table 1: Arithmetic Operators in the Standard Packages 86
- Table 2: Relational Operators in the Standard Packages 87
- Table 3: Shift Operators in the Standard Packages 88
- Table 4: Type Conversion Functions in the Standard Packages ... 89
- Table 5: Other Functions Available in the Standard Packages 89

6 Finite State Machines 101
- Table 1: PCI Target State Machine State Transitions 105

7 Reset, Presets, Tri-state and Bi-directional Signals 123
- Table 1: Truth Table for D-type Flip-flop with Asynchronous Preset and Reset 124

8 Understanding Hardware Creation 141
- Table 1: Improvement in Logic Utilization Using "Don't Cares" in the Seven-segment Design 161
- Table 2: Adder and Multiplier Resource Usage Normalized for a Shift Register 163

10 Getting the Most from Your State Machines 191
- Table 1: Simple Encoding for State Type 192
- Table 2: Ways to Reach the Backoff State 198
- Table 3: Speed Decreases and Utilization Increases Using Four State Bits Versus Three State Bits 199

Table 4: Speed Increase and Utilization Decrease Using Encoding
Option 2 Versus Option 1 200
Table 5: Speed and Utilization Increase Using One-hot
Versus Encoded States 207
Table 6: Speed Increase and Utilization Decrease Using Default
Assignments (Versus Not Using) 211
Table 7: Speed Increase and Utilization Decrease Using "Don't Care"
Defaults Versus Fixed Defaults 213
Table 8: Output Pulse in Each State 214
Table 9: State Encoding Use Pulse and an Extra State Register (*StateReg*) 214

11 Scalable and Parameterizable Design 219
Table 1: Predefined Signal Attributes Useful for
Parameterizable Components 231

12 Enhancing Design Readability and Reuse 241
Table 1: Shift Operators per the VHDL'93 Standard 245
Table 2: Resolution Table for *std_logic* 246

13 Creative Potpourri 259
Table 1: Table Showing Divided Clock Values from Time 0 Through 11 267
Table 2: State Encoding that Incorporates the Outputs 271

14 Simulation and Design Verification 281
Table 1: Truth Table for the OR Operation on Two *std_logic* Inputs 284

Listings

3 Gates, Decoders and Encoders..25
  Listing 1: Structural Description of Few Gates 26
  Listing 2: Few Gates Using Concurrent Assignment 27
  Listing 3: Decoder Using Concurrent Assignments 30
  Listing 4: Decoder Using *Case* Statements 32
  Listing 5: Violation of Locally Static Requirement of a Case Choice 35
  Listing 6: Decoder Using *with...select* Statements 35
  Listing 7: Decoder Using *if...then* Statement 38
  Listing 8: Decoder with Qualified Outputs Using *if* Statements 41
  Listing 9: Decoder with Qualified Outputs Using and External *if* Statements 44
  Listing 10: Encoder Using *if...then* Statements 47
  Listing 11: Encoder Using Concurrent Assignments 48

4 Registers and Latches..51
  Listing 1: Structural Implementation of D-type Flip-flop with Enable 52
  Listing 2: D-type Flip-flop with *Wait* Statement 53
  Listing 3: D-type Flip-flop with Enable Using the *rising_edge* Function 54
  Listing 4: SR Flip-flop Using *Wait* Statement 55
  Listing 5: SR Flip-flop Using *rising_edge* 56
  Listing 6: DFF with Enable Using *Wait* 57
  Listing 7: DFF Using *if...then* and a Sensitivity List 58
  Listing 8: Additional Example of a DFF Using *if...then* and a Sensitivity List 59
  Listing 9: DFF Using *wait...on* 60
  Listing 10: Illegal Coding! DFF with *Wait* and Sensitivity List 61
  Listing 11: DFF with Asynchronous Reset 62
  Listing 12: DFF with Asynchronous Expression Reset 63
  Listing 13: DFF with Asynchronous Reset Implemented as a Local Signal 64
  Listing 14: DFF with Asynchronous Preset 65
  Listing 15: Synchronous Reset with a *Wait* Statement 65
  Listing 16: Synchronous Reset Using *if...then* 66
  Listing 17: Asynchronous Reset with Incorrect Sensitivity List 68
  Listing 18: Assigning Asynchronous Preset and Reset
    with the Same Signal 68
  Listing 19: Assigning Synchronous Preset and Reset with the Same Signal 69
  Listing 20: Structural Instantiation of a D-Latch 71

Listing 21: Concurrent Description of a D-Latch 72
Listing 22: D-Latch Using *if...then* 73

5 Counters and Simple Arithmetic Functions 75
Listing 1: Simple Up-counter 76
Listing 2: Counter with Asynchronous Reset 77
Listing 3: Counter with Synchronous Reset 78
Listing 4: Counter with Synchronous Load 79
Listing 5: Modulo 11 Down-Counter 80
Listing 6: Counter with Synchronous Load and Enable 81
Listing 7: Counter Adding a Vector Constant 82
Listing 8: Counter with Ascending Range Vector 84
Listing 9: Equality Compare with Operands of Different Ranges 90
Listing 10: Use of *to_stdlogicvector* Function 91
Listing 11: Example Using *to_unsigned* Showing Direction Significance 92
Listing 12: Adder Using Unsigned Vectors 93
Listing 13: Accumulator Example 93
Listing 14: Implementation of a Programmable Pulse Generator 96

6 Finite State Machines 101
Listing 1: Entity Declaration for PCI Target State Machine 103
Listing 2: Next State Conditioning Logic for the PCI Target State Machine 106
Listing 3: Current State Vector Register for PCI Target State Machine 107
Listing 4: Output Conditioning Logic Process
    for PCI Target State Machine 108
Listing 5: PCI Target State Machine 109
Listing 6: Programmable Pulse Generator State Machine
    Entity Declaration 116
Listing 7: Programmable Pulse Generator State Machine
    - Next State Conditioning Logic 116
Listing 8: Programmable Pulse Generator State Machine
    - Current State Register 117
Listing 9: Programmable Pulse Generator State Machine
    - Output Conditioning Logic 117
Listing 10: Programmable Pulse Generator Using a State Machine 118

7 Reset, Presets, Tri-state and Bi-directional Signals 123
Listing 1: Structural Description of an Enabled D Flip-flop with
    Asynchronous Preset and Reset 124
Listing 2: Behavioral Description of an Enabled D Flip-flop with
    Asynchronous Preset and Reset 125
Listing 3: DFF with Preset Dominant Over Reset 126
Listing 4: Register with Asynchronous Load 128

Listing 5: Counter with Asynchronous Load 130
Listing 6: Structural Description of a Tri-state Buffer 132
Listing 7: Tri-state Buffer Using Concurrent Assignment 133
Listing 8: Tri-state Buffer Using *if...then* Statements 133
Listing 9: Byte-wide Tri-state Bus Using Concurrent Assignment 135
Listing 10: Byte-wide Tri-state Bus Using a Process 135
Listing 11: Structural Implementation of a Bi-directional Buffer 137
Listing 12: Bi-directional Buffer Using Concurrent Assignments 137
Listing 13: Counter Using Bi-directional Outputs 139

8 *Understanding Hardware Creation* *141*
Listing 1: 2-input AND Gate Using Concurrent Assignment 141
Listing 2: Design Example 1 Showing the Delay Updating Signals Using a Process 142
Listing 3: Design Example 2 Showing the Delay Updating Signals Using a Process 144
Listing 4: Pulse-Generated Model (Not for Synthesis) 145
Listing 5: Design Example Showing that Only the Last Signal Assignment Takes Effect 146
Listing 6: D-type Latch by Implicit Inference 147
Listing 7: Binary Coded Decimal to Seven-segment Display Decoder 153
Listing 8: Flip-flop with Implicit Latch Caused by a Missing Asynchronous Reset 156
Listing 9: Seven-segment Decoder Using Don't Cares 159
Listing 10: Multiple Drivers on a Resolved Signal 162
Listing 11: Design with Common Adders 164
Listing 12: Design with Explicit Resource Sharing 165

9 *Design Partitioning* *167*
Listing 1: Simple Gates Using Component Declaration and Instantiation 171
Listing 2: Counter Instantiation Illustrating the Use of open 175
Listing 3: AND2 Entity-architecture in a Single Design File 177
Listing 4: Simple Gates with Component Entities in Separate Files 178
Listing 5: Package Declaration for *GatesPkg* 179
Listing 6: Simple Gates Design with Components in the *GatesPkg* Package . 180
Listing 7: Configuration Declaration for Simple Gates Design 182
Listing 8: Configuration Declaration Using the for *All* Statement 183
Listing 9: Configuration Specification for Simple Gates Design 184
Listing 10: Counter with Bi-directional Output 188

10 *Getting the Most from Your State Machines* *191*
Listing 1: PCI Target State Machine Using Explicit Sequential State Encoding 193

Listing 2: 3-bit Encoding of the PCI Target State Machine 199
Listing 3: 4-bit Encoding of the PCI Target State Machine 199
Listing 4: 3-bit Encoding for PCI Target State Machine - Option 1 200
Listing 5: 3-bit Encoding for PCI Target State Machine - Option 2 200
Listing 6: PCI Target State Machine Written to Explicitly
         Use One-hot Coding 204
Listing 7: Programmable Pulse Generator Using Direct Encoding 214

11 Scalable and Parameterizable Design 219

Listing 1: Scalable D Flip-flop 221
Listing 2: 8-bit Register Using Scalable D Flip-flop 222
Listing 3: Parameterizable D Flip-flop with Reset and Enable 223
Listing 4: Parameterizable Tri-state Buffer 224
Listing 5: 8-bit Register with Tri-state Using Parameterizable
         Base Components 225
Listing 6: Parameterizable Parity Generator Using a *for...loop* 227
Listing 7: Parameterizable Adder Using the *for...loop* Construct 230
Listing 8: Parameterizable Adder Using Predefined Attributes 231
Listing 9: Scalable Up-counter Using TFFs, Placed in the Scalable Package .. 234
Listing 10: Odd Parity Generator Using *for...generate* 236
Listing 11: Parity Generator Using a Conditional Generate Statement 236
Listing 12: Scalable Parity Generator 239

12 Enhancing Design Readability and Reuse 241

Listing 1: Type Conversion to *std_logic_vector* 242
Listing 2: Type Conversion Using the resize Function 243
Listing 3: Power Function 246
Listing 4: Design to Raise an Input to its 4th Power 247
Listing 5: Using Nested Functions in the PowerOfFour Calculation 248
Listing 6: The *specialFunctions* Package Containing the Pow Function 249
Listing 7: Using Functions in Packages 250
Listing 8: 2-of-4 Decoder Using a Procedure 251
Listing 9: Procedure that Results in a D Flip-flop 253
Listing 10: Decoder Procedures Package 254
Listing 11: 2-of-4 Decoder Using Procedure from a Package 255
Listing 12: Decoder Design Using Aliases 256

13 Creative Potpourri 259

Listing 1: Seven-segment Decoder Using Aggregates 260
Listing 2: Simple Gates Using the Concatenation Operator 262
Listing 3: Overflow Capable Adder Using the + Operator
         and Concatenation 264
Listing 4: 8-bit Register with Tri-state Buffer Using Record Types 265

Listing 5: Divide-by Clock Logic Using Multi-dimensional Arrays 269
Listing 6: Pulse Generator State Machine Using Indexed Arrays
 with Enumerated Types 272
Listing 7: Register File Using *while...loop* for Register Reset 275
Listing 8: Interrupt Priority Encoder Using *while...loop* 278
Listing 9: Counter Using Outputs of Mode Buffer 280

14 Simulation and Design Verification *281*
Listing 1: OR Gate Model with tPD = 10ns 283
Listing 2: Simulation Model for 2-1 Mux 286
Listing 3: Simulation Model for a DFF 287
Listing 4: OR Gate Model in the *simPrimitives* Package 289
Listing 5: Hierarchical Model Using Transport Delays 291
Listing 6: Testbench for BCD-to-seven-segment Display 295
Listing 7: Testbench for Load-able, Reset-able, Up-counter 300
Listing 8: Vector Set to Completely Test Load-able, Reset-able Up-counter 303

Preface

This book provides a simple, hands-on approach to writing VHDL for RTL synthesis. It follows a systematic, "how-to" style and instructs readers on practical VHDL design. Although targeted primarily at programmable logic designers, the techniques presented in this book make it equally useful for those interested in real-world HDL design. I wrote this book to bring awareness two fundamental issues:

- The primary purpose of a VHDL synthesis tool is to create hardware that matches the results of simulation.
- VHDL's rich descriptive capability provides many ways to describe hardware, with varying results when synthesized.

My goal is that soon after reading this book, you will be able to write correct VHDL in a style that will positively impact both the design process and the quality of the end result.

Most other VHDL texts describe VHDL in terms of its grammar and lexical elements. They start from the bottom up, describing types, constructs, identifiers, operators, compilation and elaboration. In this book, however, I have tried to reduce academic language and description as much as possible to focus on design issues and techniques. Syntax and grammar is discussed in the context of design, and language elements are discussed in terms of how they affect the design and synthesis process.

I have relied heavily on both illustrations and design examples to demonstrate key concepts in a step-by-step fashion. Each idea has an example that goes with it, as well as an explanation, its implication, and suggestions on when to use it during design. In addition, where different coding styles exist to implement a particular circuit, each of these styles is shown, and the implications of each is discussed.

The styles and techniques that I have shown in the design examples are independent of the synthesis tool and the target technology/device. They deliberately do not target any specific device/architecture/technology combination. However, some of the issues raised by the examples are comparative in nature, and are best illustrated showing the speed or utilization of the resulting circuit targeted to a device. In such cases, I have taken a ratiometric approach to show the "before v/s after" result. This demonstrates the concept while avoiding the subjective and ever-changing nature of benchmarking programmable logic devices.

I have divided this text into three sections, based on the natural progression of design complexity: VHDL Basics, Design Topics and Advanced Techniques. Each section builds on the one(s) before, further developing previously formulated ideas. However, you can stop and set the book aside at the end of any section, and still be well equipped to tackle everyday design problems.

VHDL Basics

This section begins with a brief overview of VHDL, and explains a few basic terms often used in VHDL. The second chapter implements a simple design, and shows different VHDL coding styles by example. With this introduction, the subsequent chapters discuss simple problems encountered during everyday design. These include memory elements (registers and latches), and various forms of combinational logic (encoders and decoders). This section concludes with an introduction to arithmetic operations, using up and down counters as an example. The *std_logic_1164* and *std_logic_arith* packages are introduced here, in the context of doing simple arithmetic circuits.

Design Topics

The Design Topics section continues by tackling issues that one would encounter during the design process, including synchronous state machines. The basics of state machine implementation are discussed, and a design style is presented that facilitates good partitioning, documentation, and maintenance of state machines. While I have tried to keep the book independent of a target device architecture, some architecture and technology specific issues are discussed here. These include control signals such as resets, presets, tri-states™ and bi-directional signals.

I have devoted one chapter in this section to design partitioning issues in VHDL. Coding style and hierarchy are introduced with respect to how logic is realized during the synthesis process. This includes *libraries*, *packages*, modular design and block level partitioning.

Advanced Issues

I have dealt with advanced issues, once again, in the context of design. State machine encoding and explicit declaration of one-hot-coded state machines are discussed in detail. The flexibility and power of VHDL is demonstrated by writing modules that are parameterizable, such as shifters and counters. Functions and procedures, and their applications in design, are also explained. Finally, to demonstrate the versatility of VHDL, and to encourage you to explore VHDL further, I have included examples that illustrate "clever" VHDL. These designs show ways of visualizing a problem that bring advantages in terms of model reuse, compact design description and modularity.

VHDL has inherent simulation capabilities. As design verification and test are crucial to any design process, I have included a chapter that introduces testbenches and simulation modeling. Examples that illustrate both functional VHDL testbenches and those that incorporate timing are shown.

VHDL has been gaining popularity in the marketplace, and has established itself as a standard HDL for design capture. It allows hardware description at several levels of abstraction, and provides a strong, disciplined framework for structured design. It is my sincere hope that this book will enable you to execute designs successfully, and provide a good foundation for more advanced work with VHDL.

Sundar Rajan
May, 1998

Acknowledgements

Essential VHDL began as a germ of an idea a few years ago, and has been made possible with a great deal of help, encouragement and support. I would like to thank my friends at *Synplicity Corporation*, starting with Bill Cox, who arranged for a loaner copy of *Synplify* when I first began this project. For technical review, prompt bug fixes, and numerous discussions on logic synthesis philosophy, implications and direction, I would like to thank Ken McElvain, Andrew Dauman, Andy Haines, Jeff Garrison, Jim Tatsukawa, Rick Carlson and Suresh Gopalrathnam. I would also like to thank *Visio Corporation* for giving me a copy of *Visio Technical* for all the drawings created in the book.

In addition to the team from *Synplicity*, several people reviewed the draft manuscript. Randy Oyadomari, Brian Small and Stefanka Kitanovska of *Quicklogic Corporation* gave me extensive technical feedback on the book from the perspective of a silicon vendor. Mike Dini and Neal Palmer at the *Dini Group* spent valuable time over several lively telephone discussions recommending changes based on their experiences as leading-edge programmable logic and ASIC designers. A very prompt and thorough review from Bill Billowitch refined several topics presented in the book. I am also grateful to Bill for his help and guidance on the presentation and title of this book. Comments from J. Bhasker resulted in a greater emphasis on the *numeric_std* package throughout the book and clarification of library issues. The viability of this book was confirmed by contributions from Chris MacAskill, Deborah Bohn and Penny Wendland at *Computer Literacy*, who also provided insight into the book publishing world.

It has been a pleasure to work with my friend and colleague Gennis Piazza. Her attention to detail and tireless refinement of the layout created the high quality book format and cover design.

And finally, I would like to thank my wife who shared this endeavor with me every step of the way, and without her unconditional support, this book would not have been possible.

1
VHDL Fundamentals

What is VHDL?

VHDL stands for <u>V</u>HSIC (<u>V</u>ery <u>H</u>igh <u>S</u>peed <u>I</u>ntegrated <u>C</u>ircuit) <u>H</u>ardware <u>D</u>escription <u>L</u>anguage. This language resulted from a United States Government, Department of Defense, sponsored effort to advance and overhaul the way integrated circuits were exchanged between different companies. In 1987, VHDL was adopted by the IEEE as a standard: IEEE Std. 1076-1987.

This original standard is often referred to as VHDL-87, because VHDL is a "living" standard. The IEEE requires that all standards be updated in order to be maintained as an IEEE standard. To comply with this, the IEEE-1076 standard committee convenes every five years to re-ballot the standard. The intent behind the re-ballot is to review the language, enhance it, address its weaknesses, and incorporate feedback from the user community. The first such revision was adopted in 1993. Language elements that were adopted at this time are referred to as IEEE Std. 1076-1993 (VHDL-93) elements. For the purpose of synthesis, VHDL-93 does not present a significant change from VHDL-87. However, these (VHDL-93) elements are noted in this book, where appropriate.

VHDL can be applied throughout the design process: for design capture, verification (simulation), synthesis and documentation. VHDL's chief strength lies in its ability to facilitate design description at a higher level of abstraction than the gate level. It has a wide range of descriptive capability, which is particularly true when using VHDL for logic synthesis.

Like most languages, VHDL balances its flexibility and powerful capabilities by enforcing a certain amount of discipline on the designer. This is done using strictly enforced *type* rules, through several declarative requirements, and other rules on how and when statements need to be completed. While these rules may appear cumbersome at first, their value (especially in complex designs) rapidly eclipses any aspect of the language that might impede the design process.

This chapter introduces VHDL by discussing language fundamentals that enable and influence hardware design.

Black Boxes

For the most part, we visualize hardware as separate blocks, or units. Each of these can be represented figuratively as a "black box". A black box has a visible and well characterized interface, while its inside is invisible, due to the opaque, "black" exterior. The basic element in VHDL is analogous to this black box, and is equivalent to a symbol in a schematic drawing. *Figure 1* shows an example of a symbol, or black box. Although the interface to what is inside the black box is clearly defined, the interior of the box is invisible. In VHDL, this black box is known as an *entity*.

Figure 1: Black Box

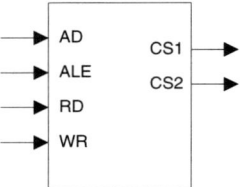

In addition to the black box, VHDL allows you to associate an implementation with the black box that describes the contents of the black box. This is analogous to an underlying schematic associated with the symbol. In VHDL, this implementation is called the *architecture*.

Connecting Logic Using Signals

The second aspect to any hardware description language is the ability to connect different parts of a design. VHDL accomplishes this using *signals*, which move data or information in a design.

In "real" hardware, *signals* can be thought of as wires. In a more abstract sense, they are analogous to data queues. New values assigned to signals may be queued in time order and "scheduled" in time range, from 0ns to the largest time value supported by your VHDL simulator. This abstract model leads to some important properties of signals, which we will discuss later on in the book, most notably in *Chapter 8*.

Every signal has a *type*. A *type* is a collection of values that a signal can take. VHDL inherently supports a type known as bit, which allows signals of this (*bit*) *type* to take the values '0' or '1'. Additionally, VHDL natively supports the integer type, where signals of this type may take integer values between $+(2^{31} - 1)$ to $-(2^{31} - 1)$.

However, wires in real hardware take on values other than the '0' or '1'. We might see the high-impedance value, 'Z', or perhaps we might wish to model an unknown value, 'X'. As such, you will most often use the *std_logic* type, defined in the IEEE 1164 standard, when describing wires as signals. The *std_logic* type has nine values. These values are as shown in *Table 1*.

Table 1: *std_logic* Type Values and Their Meanings

Value	Meaning
U	Uninitialized
X	Forcing (strong driven) unknown
0	Forcing (strong driven) 0
1	Forcing (strong driven) 1
Z	High Impedance
W	Weak (weakly driven) unknown
L	Weak (weakly driven) 0...models a pull-down
H	Weak (weakly driven) 1...models a pull-up
-	Don't Care (wildcard for comparison)

These values have their roots in modeling for simulation. Most synthesis tools will treat these values slightly differently than simulators. For example, if a signal is set to 'L' or 'H', the synthesis tool treats it as if it was set to '0' and '1', respectively. The values '-' and 'X' might be treated as "don't cares". '-' is used as a wildcard for comparisons, while 'X' and '-' are both used for "don't care" output assignment. The similarities and differences between '-' and 'X' are discussed in *Chapter 8*.

Setting values for signals in VHDL is known as *assignment*. In general, when using the *std_logic* type, stick to the values 'X', '0', '1', and 'Z' when making signal assignments. This will make your designs more portable between synthesis tools. In addition to *std_logic*, which is similar to a wire in hardware, you can use the *std_logic_vector*, which is an array, or vector, of the *std_logic* type. It represents a bus, and, as such, has a dimension associated with it, which is known as the *range* of the vector.

Signals are used both within an *architecture* and in the *entity*. When used in the *entity*, a signal functions as the interface to the *entity*, and is known as a *port*. In this way, the *entity*, or black box, can be connected to other parts of a design.

A key concept of signals is that of a driver associated with the signal. This may seem obvious, but it is a departure from some of the older languages that were used to describe small programmable logic designs. We will discuss signals and signal drivers later in this book.

Connecting Black Boxes

VHDL allows black boxes to be connected to each other. For synthesis, the ports of an *entity* usually correspond to the pin interface at the chip level. It is in fact at the *port* of an *entity* that we first encounter the issue of signal drivers.

A signal in the port has not only an associated type, but also a *mode*. The *mode* of a signal indicates its driver direction, and also indicates whether or not the port can be read from within the entity. There are three modes that are most often used in design:

- *in*
- *out*
- *inout*

The mode *in* means that the port signal can be read within the entity, and that the driver for this signal is outside the entity, as shown in *Figure 2*.

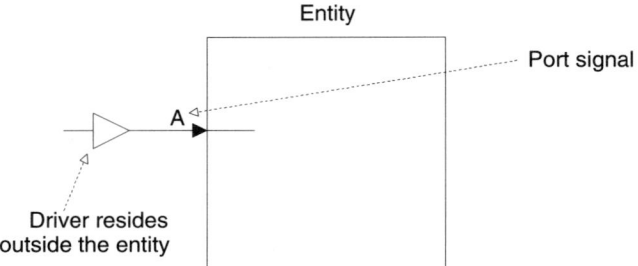

Figure 2: Mode *in*

Mode *out* implies that the port signal driver resides within the black box, but the signal itself cannot be read within the entity, as shown in *Figure 3*.

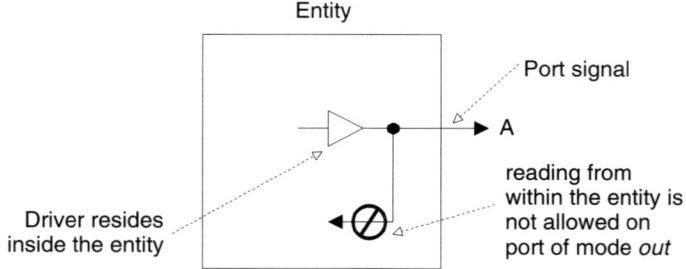

Figure 3: Mode *out*

There are cases where we might want an output signal to be read within the black box (entity). In this case, we create an intermediate signal (internal to the black box) that can be read within the black box, and then connect this signal to the port of mode *out*. This is shown in *Figure 4*, where the signal *Int* is visible only inside the entity, and can be read or fed back. It is then connected to the output *A*, which is of mode *out*.

Figure 4: Mode *out* with Readable Intermediate Signal

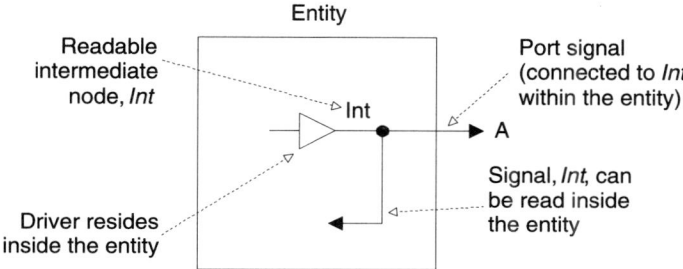

Finally, mode *inout* implies that the signal can be read within the *architecture*, and the driver may be either inside or outside the black box, as shown in *Figure 5*.

Figure 5: Mode *inout*

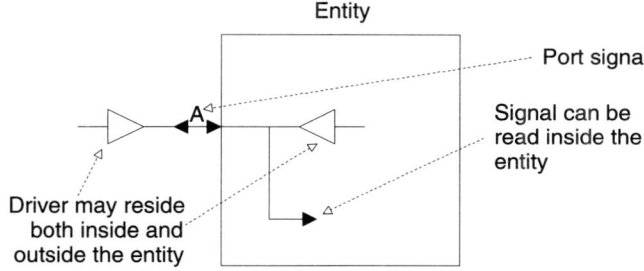

Naming and Labeling

As with any language, VHDL has certain naming rules and conventions that must be followed.

- VHDL is not case sensitive.

So, for example, if we chose the name *DataBus* for a signal, then

```
DataBus
databus
dataBus
Databus
DATABUS
```

will all identify the same signal in a design, within the same entity declaration. The same applies to other labels and names in a design.

- VHDL is "free format".

This means that there are no formatting conventions, such as spacing or indentation, imposed by VHDL on a design. Spaces and carriage returns are treated the same. For example:

```
    if (a = b) then
or
    if       (a = b)         then
or
    if (a =
       b) then
```

will all be interpreted in exactly the same way.

- Comments in VHDL are indicated with a "double-dash", i.e., "--".

The comment indicator may be placed anywhere in a line and any text that follows it on the <u>same line</u> will be treated as a comment. The carriage return terminates a comment. There is no method in VHDL for commenting a block, or series of statements.

```
    -- if (a = b) then not evaluated as line begins with a comment indicator

    if (a = b) then -- this is evaluated as the comment begins after the code
```

- There are certain characters in VHDL that are reserved.

There are several characters that are reserved in VHDL, too, such as +, -, !, &, as these have special meaning. So, rather than list them all, the following are some general rules-of-thumb to follow when naming and labeling in VHDL:

1. All names must start with an alphabet character
2. Use only alphabet characters (a-z and A-Z), digits (0 to 9) and _ (underscore)
3. Do not use any punctuation characters in a name (!, ?, ., ,, etc.)
4. Do not use consecutive _ (underscore) characters. For example, `Sel_A` is a valid label, but `Sel__A` is not
5. All names and labels in a given entity and architecture must be unique

VHDL does not impose any limit on the number of characters in an identifier. Even so, many synthesis tools and simulators limit the length of identifiers, some to as few as 32 characters. So, try to keep identifiers descriptive without making them too long. For example, the identifiers *clock* and *data* are far more meaningful than *c* and *d*. The idea here is to choose a name that will help document the design, and make it easy to maintain in the future.

Chapter 1 - VHDL Fundamentals

- There are certain keywords in VHDL that are reserved.

The language has designated keywords that have a specific meaning, and should be avoided. Some synthesis tools have a good syntax checker, and will provide useful error messages. Others will produce strange error messages, or (in extreme cases) incorrect results if reserved keywords are used as names or identifiers. *Table 2* shows a list of keywords that are reserved by the language.

Table 2: Reserved Words in VHDL

abs	downto	label	port	srl[1]
access		library	postponed[1]	subtype
after	else	linkage	procedure	
alias	elsif	literal[1]	process	
all	end	loop	pure[1]	then
and	entity			to
architecture	exit	map	range	transport
array		mod	record	type
assert	file		register	
attribute	for	nand	reject[1]	units
function		new	rem	unaffected[1]
begin		next	report	until
block	generate	nor	return	use
body	generic	not	rol[1]	
buffer	group[1]	null	ror[1]	variable
bus	guarded			
		of	select	wait
case	if	on	severity	when
component	impure[1]	open	shared[1]	while
configuration	in	others	signal	with
constant	inertial[1]	out	sla[1]	
	inout		sll[1]	xor
disconnect	is	package	sra[1]	xnor[1]

---

1. All reserved words are indicated per the VHDL-87 Standard, except those annotated, which are reserved as stated in the VHDL-93 Standard.

Implementing Basic Logic

Since it is a hardware description language, it is natural that VHDL supports logical operators. Unlike other languages, however, operators in VHDL are associated with a particular type. VHDL supports several operators for the *std_logic* type, as shown in *Table 3*.

Table 3: Logical Operators for the *std_logic* Type

Operator	Meaning
AND	Logical AND Operation
NAND	Logical AND Operation Complemented
OR	Logical OR Operation
NOR	Logical OR Operation Complemented
XOR	Logical XOR Operation
XNOR	Logical XOR Operation Complemented

Using the left-arrow, <=, indicating a signal assignment, we can perform a logic operation on two signals as follows:

```
result <= a AND b;
```

Note, however, that there is no implied precedence among the operators listed in *Table 3*. If there are two or more different operators in an equation, then the order of precedence is from left to right. So, in the assignment

```
result <= a AND b OR c XOR d;
```

the AND operation is executed, followed by the OR, followed by the XOR operation. You can change the order of precedence by using parentheses. So,

```
result <= (a AND b) OR (c XOR d);
```

results in the AND and XOR operations being executed before the OR operation. There are other operators in VHDL, which we will discuss in *Chapter 5*.

Ordering of Statements

VHDL supports the notion of "concurrent execution", or "concurrency", which is very close to the way hardware behaves. Within a VHDL architecture, we implement logic that describes the entity or black box. The architecture may have separate sections of logic that are unrelated in terms of their function and operation. In other words, events that are unrelated may cause separate blocks of logic to change state, or "switch". VHDL supports two methods of describing such concurrence inside a black box: *processes* and *concurrent assignments*.

At a given instant in time, processes and concurrent assignments may be evaluated in parallel. The relative order of concurrent assignments and processes within an architecture is unimportant, as shown in *Figure 6*.

Figure 6: Order Within an Architecture is Unimportant

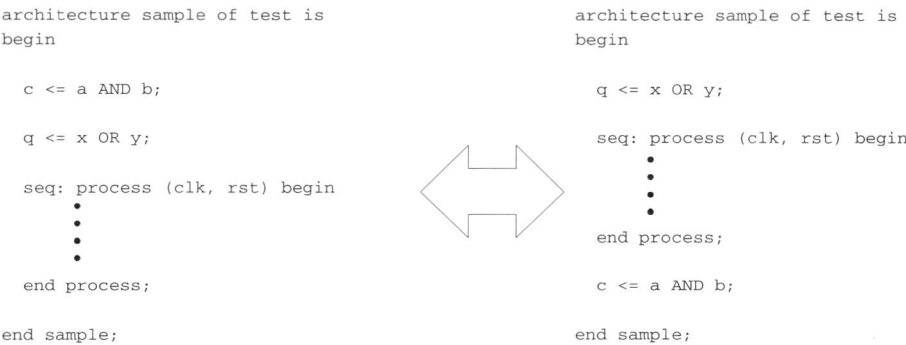

```
architecture sample of test is          architecture sample of test is
begin                                   begin

  c <= a AND b;                           q <= x OR y;

  q <= x OR y;                            seq: process (clk, rst) begin
                                            •
  seq: process (clk, rst) begin             •
    •                                       •
    •                                     end process;
    •
  end process;                            c <= a AND b;

end sample;                             end sample;
```

The most significant difference between them is that processes are a collection of sequential statements, while concurrent assignments may not contain any sequential statements. When evaluating the logic inside a process, each statement is executed in the order, or sequence, that it is written. Hence, inside a process, the order of statements is important, as shown in *Figure 7*.

Figure 7: The Order of Statements Within a Process is Important

```
architecture sample of test is          architecture sample of test is
begin                                   begin

  seq: process (clk, rst) begin           seq: process (clk, rst) begin
    c <= a OR b;                            c <= x AND y;

    c <= x AND y;                           c <= a OR b;
  end process;                            end process;

end sample;                             end sample;
```

Even though statements within a process are evaluated sequentially, the hardware generated after synthesis usually consists of concurrent logic. This concurrent logic has conditions imposed on it that change the outcome of a function to match the logic described by the sequential statements of the process. Hence, the synthesized logic incorporates the intentions of the designer, which were described as a sequential evaluation. This is important to note, the reasons for which will become clearer as we progress through the book.

Design for RTL Synthesis

The focus of this book is design for Register Transfer Level (RTL) synthesis. This means that logic is treated as if it were combinational logic in between registers, as shown in *Figure 8*.

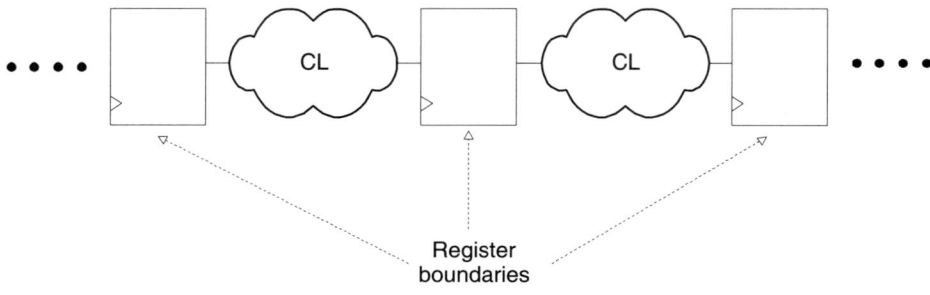

Figure 8:   RTL Design Description

CL = Combinational logic

RTL synthesis optimizes logic between the two register boundaries, which can be implemented in any of the VHDL design styles namely structural, dataflow, or behavioral.

Different Styles of Design Description

Finally, VHDL offers the capability to describe designs in different ways. On one hand, it allows you to describe logic using simple equations, while on the other, it allows you to describe complex algorithms in a clear, succinct way.

There are, broadly speaking, three design styles in VHDL:

- Structural design
- Dataflow design
- Behavioral design

The design style should be chosen depending on what you are trying to describe. We will discuss them briefly, not for the purpose of classifying designs or showing the complete syntax, but rather to illustrate the different styles, and to provide a reference point for terminology used later in this book. To illustrate these different styles, let us consider a very simple piece of logic: a 3-input XOR gate implemented using 2-input XORs, as shown in *Figure 9*.

Figure 9: 3-input XOR Gate

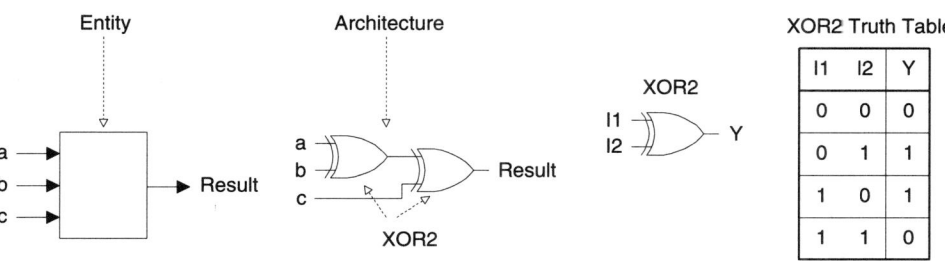

Structural design is the simplest to understand. It is the style closest to schematic capture, where fairly low-level building blocks are used to compose a logic function:

```
architecture structural of gate is
begin

  u1: xor2 port map (a => I1,
                     b => I2,
                     u1_out => Y);

  u2: xor2 port map (u1_out => I1,
                     c => I2,
                     Result => Y);

end structural;
```

Here, we have effectively placed two gates called *xor2* into the architecture, which implements the entity.

Dataflow design refers to an implementation that uses a series of equations to represent a flow of data:

```
architecture dataflow of gate is
begin

  node <= I1 XOR I2;
  I1 <= a;
  I2 <= b;
Result <= node XOR c;

end dataflow;
```

Notice that the equations are not placed in any particular order as they are all executed continuously.

Behavioral design describes the behavior of the black box. It usually incorporates a process, with sequential statements, and describes in algorithmic form the operation of the black box:

```
architecture behavior of gate is
begin

  process (a, b, c) begin
    if ((a XOR b XOR c) = '1') then
      Result = '1';
    else
      Result = '0';
    end if;
  end process;

end behavior
```

2
Getting Your First Design Done

Now that we have been introduced to the basics of VHDL, we are ready to tackle our first design. Our focus in this chapter is to apply the basics of the language covered in *Chapter 1* to a simple, though real, design example, with the intent of getting up-and-running quickly.

Logic functions can be described using a truth table. For illustrative purposes, we will implement the logic function shown in *Table 1*.

Table 1: Truth Table for Sample Logic Function

A	B	C	Y
0	0	X	1
X	X	1	1
others			0

X => "don't care"

others => all other logic combinations

Defining the Black Box

The first step in implementing our design is to define the black box for our logic function. The function shown in *Table 1* has three inputs and one output. Hence, our black box would appear as shown in *Figure 1*.

Figure 1: Black Box Representing Logic Function

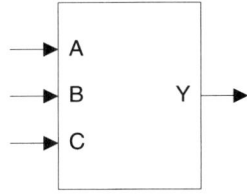

The Entity

We will name our entity *LogicFcn* and declare it as follows:

```
library IEEE;
use IEEE.std_logic_1164.all;

entity LogicFcn is port (
  A: in std_logic;
  B: in std_logic;
  C: in std_logic;
  Y: out std_logic
  );
end LogicFcn;
```

There are three sets of issues to note with the entity declaration:

- Port signal naming and listing
- Port signal *mode* and *type*
- *Library* statement followed by the *use* clause

Let us examine each of these issues.

First of all, note the labeling and signal listing issues, as shown in *Figure 2*.

Figure 2: Labeling and Signal Listing in the Entity Declaration

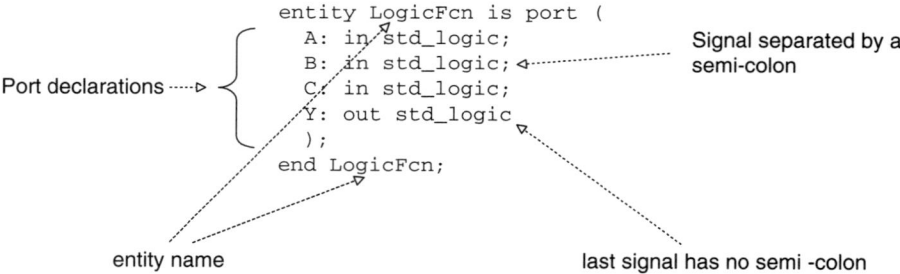

The port declarations are made together and are separated from each other using a semi-colon. Note however, that the last signal in the interface list, *Y*, in our case, does not have a separating semi-colon. Also, the entity name in the opening and closing statements are identical. The entity name chosen follows the labeling guidelines shown in *Chapter 1*. The port signal names and their corresponding mode and type declarations are shown in *Figure 3*.

Figure 3: Port Signal Names, Mode and Type Declaration

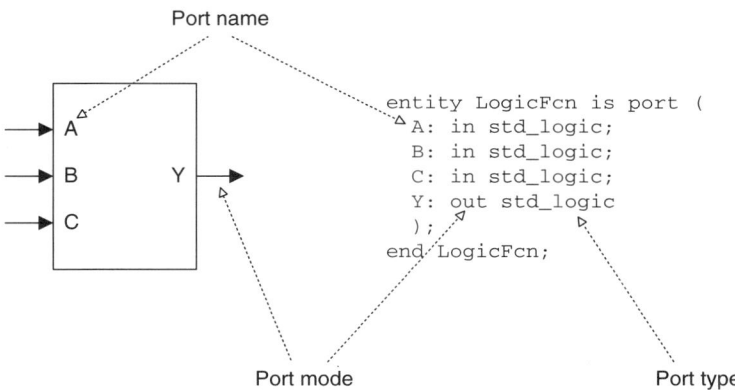

Second, the port signal modes correspond to the direction of the arrows in the black box drawing and the port signal type follows the mode to completely specify the signal in the port list.

Third, there is a *library* statement, followed by the *use* clause, as shown in *Figure 4*.

Figure 4: *Library* Statement and *Use* Clause

```
library IEEE;                        ⎫ Library statement
use IEEE.std_logic_1164.all;         ⎭ and use clause

entity LogicFcn is port (
   A: in std_logic;
   B: in std_logic;
   C: in std_logic;
   Y: out std_logic
   );
end LogicFcn;
```

The *library* statement and *use* clause will be discussed in detail in *Chapter 9*. For the moment, we will consider it sufficient to say that this statement is required in order to use the std_logic type. The *std_logic* type is defined in the *std_logic_1164 package*, which resides in the *IEEE library*. Hence, in order to use it, we first state the library in which it exists (IEEE) and then use it with the *use* clause, separating the *library* and *package* names with a period, as shown in *Figure 5*. The "all" at the end of the *use* clause indicates that the entire contents of the *std_logic_1164 package* are visible, and therefore may be used.

Figure 5: Format of the Library Statement and Use Clause

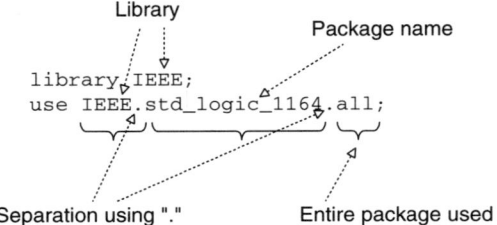

The Architecture

Having defined the black box and its interface, the next step in the design *process* is to describe the contents of the black box. This implementation is performed in the *architecture*. Every entity has an architecture associated with it, so that we often refer to the black box and its implementation as the *entity-architecture pair*.

An architecture is associated with an *entity* by using the *of* clause followed by the entity name, as shown in *Figure 6*.

Figure 6: Entity-architecture Pair

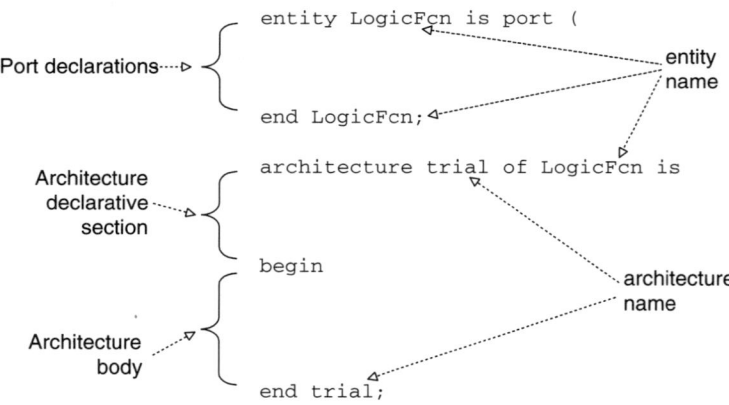

The *architecture* consists of two sections, as shown in *Figure 6*. First, there is a declarative section, located between the *architecture* identification, and the *begin* statement that immediately follows it. In this section, we declare any items that are used within the *architecture*. This includes *local signals* (signals that are only visible inside the architecture), which are used to connect different parts of the design within the *architecture*.

Chapter 2 - Getting Your First Design Done

Second, there is the architecture body, or the main section, where the design is actually implemented. The implementation may use all declarations in the *entity* as well as those in the architecture declarative region.

Recall that there are three styles of implementing designs within the architecture body:

- Dataflow
- Structural
- Behavioral

Each style is useful at different times when expressing logic. The dataflow style is the most useful and compact when implementing Boolean equations. Structural design is useful when expressing a design that is naturally composed of sub-blocks. Behavioral design is best applied to control logic, algorithms, or complex logic functions.

We will begin with a dataflow description of our logic function. While this is the best way to describe the function, *LogicFcn*, structural and behavioral styles will also be shown to illustrate these styles. Logic that is particularly suitable for these styles will be discussed later on in the book.

Dataflow Design

Dataflow design uses a series of *concurrent statements* to express logic. Concurrent statements are so named as they are all evaluated concurrently. As such, the order of these statements does not affect the design. The "left arrow" (<=) indicates a signal assignment. The logic shown in *Figure 7* is expressed using operators built into the *std_logic_1164* package, as we discussed in *Chapter 1*.

Figure 7: Dataflow Design Implementation of *LogicFcn*

```
                    library IEEE;
                    use IEEE.std_logic_1164.all;

     Entity ······▷ entity LogicFcn is port (
                        A: in std_logic;
                        B: in std_logic;
                        C: in std_logic;
                        Y: out std_logic
                        );
                    end LogicFcn;

Architecture ······▷ architecture dataflow of LogicFcn is

                    begin

    Dataflow        { Y <= '1' when (A = '0' AND B = '0') OR
   description ····▷ {              (C = '1')
                    {         else '0';

                    end dataflow;
```

parentheses separating operators

In this style of description, we have more than one operator in the dataflow statement that defines the output, *Y*. The precedence of these operators is defined by the parentheses that separate the operator, as we saw in *Chapter 1*. In our case, the parentheses show that the *AND* function of *A* and *B* will be performed before the *OR* operation.

The keyword *when* indicates all the conditions under which *Y* will take the value '1', and the *else* keyword indicates the value for all other conditions, just as we defined in *Table 1*. The signal assignment shows the "flow" of data that defines the function *Y*, hence the term "dataflow description".

Structural Design

Structural design is analogous to writing a netlist description of a schematic design. In essence, this design is similar to design capture using schematics, where the design is decomposed into small functional boxes, and then connected.

As we will see, this is not an efficient way in which to describe simple functions, such as the one above. However, it very useful in describing the intentional structure or composition of a design, as will be discussed later in this book. For the moment, we will show how to structurally describe our simple logic function to demonstrate the concepts behind structural design.

Before proceeding with capturing the design, we must first understand the structure to be implemented. In this example, we can describe the structure as shown in *Figure 8*.

Figure 8: Structure of *LogicFcn*

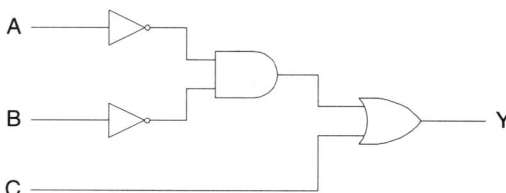

As is shown in our design, we need three types of gates: an *INVERTER*, an *AND* gate and an *OR* gate. Connecting these gates will implement our design. Each gate is laid down, or instantiated in the design, the format for which is shown in *Figure 9*.

Figure 9: Format of Component Instantiation

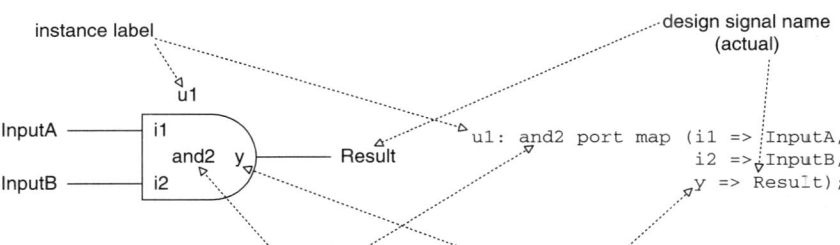

Each occurrence, or instance, of the gate is given a unique label, which is followed by the name of the component being instantiated. This is followed by a list that associates the signal names of the component, or *formal* signals, with the design signals, or *actual* signals. This association is performed with the "=>", or "right-arrow" sign. We will discuss structural design in more detail later on in this book. The complete design is shown in *Figure 10*.

Figure 10: Structural Implementation of *LogicFcn*

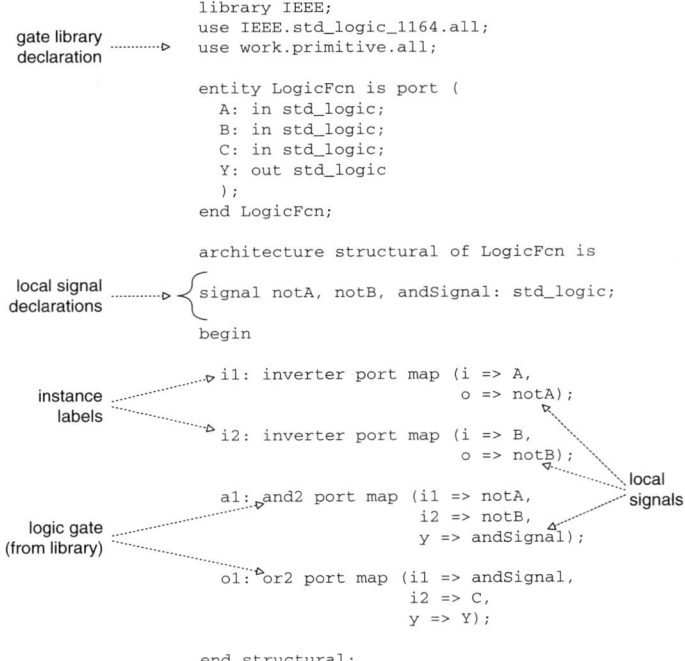

```
library IEEE;
use IEEE.std_logic_1164.all;
use work.primitive.all;

entity LogicFcn is port (
  A: in std_logic;
  B: in std_logic;
  C: in std_logic;
  Y: out std_logic
  );
end LogicFcn;

architecture structural of LogicFcn is

signal notA, notB, andSignal: std_logic;

begin

i1: inverter port map (i => A,
                       o => notA);

i2: inverter port map (i => B,
                       o => notB);

a1: and2 port map (i1 => notA,
                   i2 => notB,
                   y => andSignal);

o1: or2 port map (i1 => andSignal,
                  i2 => C,
                  y => Y);

end structural;
```

There are three things to note about this design. First, the *primitive* library is incorporated into the design with the *use* clause at the beginning of the design. This library contains the gate-level components that are used in the design.

Second, in the architecture declaration section we have declared local signals that are, in effect, wires that connect the different gates together. They are not visible outside the black-box design, since they are local to the architecture and not in the entity port declaration list.

Finally, each gate is given a unique instance label, which is similar to assigning a unique reference designator when capturing a schematic.

As the style of design implements the logic function in terms of its structure, we term this type of design description as "structural description".

Behavioral Design

Behavioral design makes use of the *process* in VHDL. A *process* is a collection of *sequential* statements. *Sequential* statements are those that are evaluated in the sequence, or order, in which they appear in the design. However, *concurrent* statements are evaluated "simultaneously", hence making their order insignificant, as we discussed in *Chapter 1*. Processes are written within the body of an architecture, as shown in *Figure 11*.

Figure 11: Processes in an Architecture

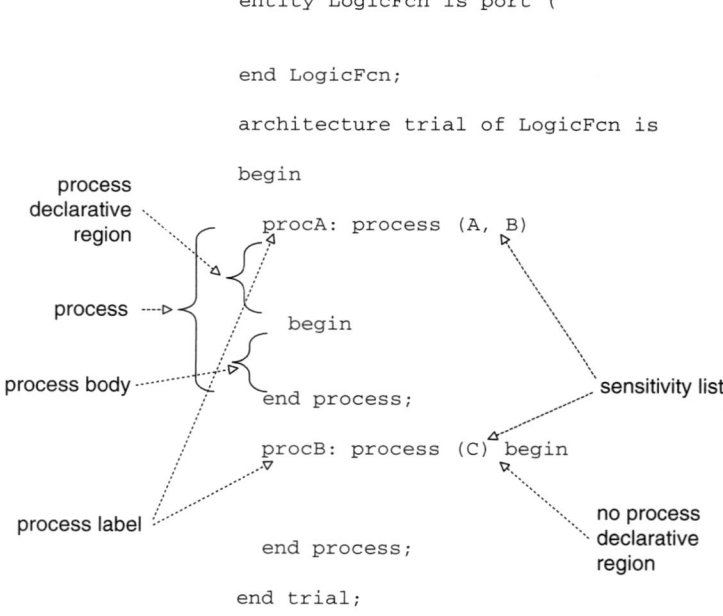

Each *process* should be identified using a unique label, which is optional but good design practice, particularly for synthesis. Signals that are generated by the synthesis tool will often include the name of the *process* they came from, making it easier to track them during design debug.

A *process*, just like an architecture, has a declarative region. Here elements that are local to the *process* may be declared, as shown in *Figure 11*, for the *process procA*. The sequential statements that are executed in the process are written within the *process* body.

A key part of a *process* is the *sensitivity* list. This is the list of <u>all</u> signals that trigger execution of the *process*. In the example, *procA* is sensitive to A and B, and *procB* is sensitive to C. In VHDL, this means that the *process* is not executed unless one (or more) of the signals in the sensitivity list changes in value. While it may seem obvious, it is important to note that one of the primary purposes of a logic synthesis tool is to realize hardware that correctly reflects the logic described. Thus, the behavior of the VHDL design in simulation must exactly match the results of synthesizing the same design. As a result, an incomplete sensitivity list may produce undesirable results, as the synthesis tool may be trying to generate logic that accurately models the incomplete sensitivity list.

We will deal with this subject in greater detail in *Chapter 8*. However, at this time, we will only state that it is essential that the sensitivity list be completely specified. Some synthesis tools make assumptions or ignore the rules about the sensitivity list, which can be misleading when verifying or debugging a design. It is therefore particularly important to specify the sensitivity list correctly.

There are several sequential statements in VHDL. One of the most common is the *if* statement, which we shall use to implement our design. To summarize, the *if* statement:

- is used to test a particular condition before performing an operation
- can test multiple conditions using *elsif*
- is terminated with an *end if*
- should be closed with an *else* to define all the possibilities for that *if* chain

With these features of the *if* statement in mind, we can describe our logic function as shown in *Figure 12*.

Figure 12: Behavioral Implementation of *LogicFcn*

```
library IEEE;
use IEEE.std_logic_1164.all;

entity LogicFcn is port (
  A: in std_logic;
  B: in std_logic;
  C: in std_logic;
  Y: out std_logic
  );
end LogicFcn;

architecture behavioral of LogicFcn is

begin                                    ------- sensitivity list

    fcn: process (A,B,C) begin
    
        if (A = '0' and B = '0') then      -- if statement begun
            Y <= '1';
        elsif C = '1' then                  -- multiple conditions tested using elsif
            Y <= '1';                       -- closing condition
        else
            Y <= '0';
        end if;

    end process;                             -- if statement ended

end behavioral;
```

The circuit that results from synthesizing the VHDL in *Figure 7*, *Figure 10* and *Figure 12* is shown in *Figure 13*.

Figure 13: *LogicFcn* Synthesis Results

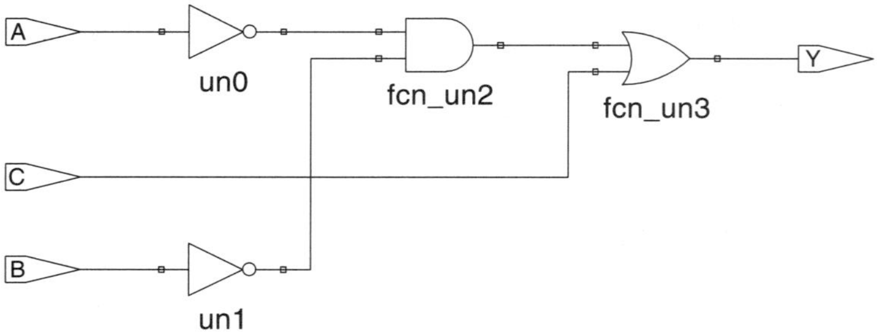

Figure 13 demonstrates that even though we have sequential assignments, we still achieve the same results as the structural or dataflow circuits since the synthesis tools infer the correct behavior. As such, our design implementations are equivalent.

Behavioral design describes how the black box behaves, without any specific data flow or structure associated with the description. Often, a logic synthesis tool infers a particular physical implementation from the behavior to realize a circuit. Hence, this style of design description is known as behavioral description.

The notion of *inference* is an important one, as we will see in the coming chapters. VHDL design descriptions often require a description of a circuit, or template, from which a particular circuit is inferred and created by the logic synthesis tool.

While we have shown dataflow, behavioral and structural styles of describing a design, it is not uncommon to combine more than one style in a given design. In fact, choosing a particular design style for synthesis depends on several factors, as will be demonstrated during the course this book.

3
Gates, Decoders and Encoders

Gates, decoders and encoders are the most common forms of combinational logic encountered in logic design. Combinational logic is a universal term that describes logic functions whose values are dependent only on the current value of their inputs. The simplest form of combinational logic is a gate, such as an *AND* gate or an *OR* gate. More complex forms of combinational logic might be decoders or encoders, where the outputs are a function of several inputs. In addition, you might see combinational logic in the form of signals that qualify other functions, such as the generation of a strobe or chip select.

Gates

Gates Using Structural Instantiation

The simplest way to describe a logic gate would be to instantiate it structurally. To do this, let us assume that we have a library that contains three primitive gates, *AND2*, *OR2* and *INVERTER*. These are a 2-input AND gate, a 2-input OR gate and an inverter, respectively, as shown in *Figure 1*. In our case, let us assume that we have compiled a *package* called *primitive* into the *work* library.

Figure 1: AND2, INVERTER and OR2 Gates

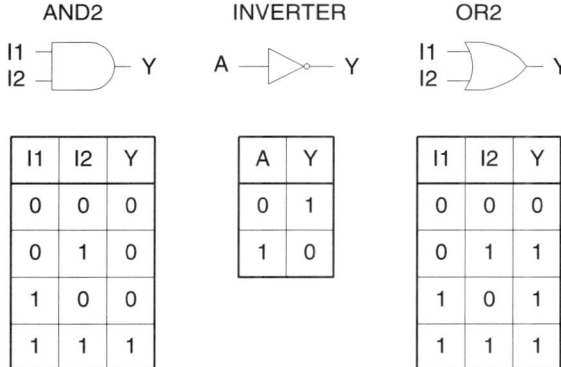

The implementation of the logic function shown in *Figure 2* is in *Listing 1*.

Figure 2: Sample Combinational Logic with Few Gates

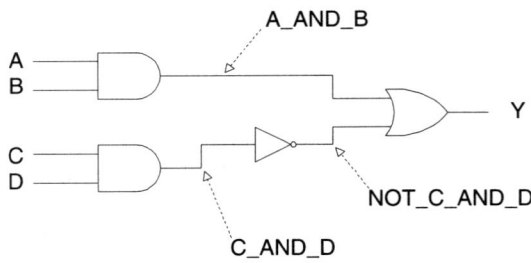

Listing 1: Structural Description of Few Gates

```
library IEEE;
use IEEE.std_logic_1164.all;

use work.primitive.all;

entity FEWGATES is port (
  a,b,c,d: in std_logic;
  y: out std_logic
  );
end FEWGATES;

architecture structural of FEWGATES is

signal a_and_b, c_and_d, not_c_and_d: std_logic;

begin

  u1: and2 port map (i1 => a,
                     i2 => b,
                     y => a_and_b
                     );

  u2: and2 port map (i1 =>c,
                     i2 => d,
                     y => c_and_d
                     );

  u3: inverter port map (a => c_and_d,
                         y => not_c_and_d);

  u4: or2 port map (i1 => a_and_b,
                    i2 => not_c_and_d,
                    y => y
                    );

end structural;
```

gatesstr.vhd

Chapter 3 - Gates, Decoders and Encoders

Following synthesis, the VHDL description in *Listing 1* results in the RTL circuit shown *Figure 3*.

Figure 3: Few Gates Using Structural Instantiation

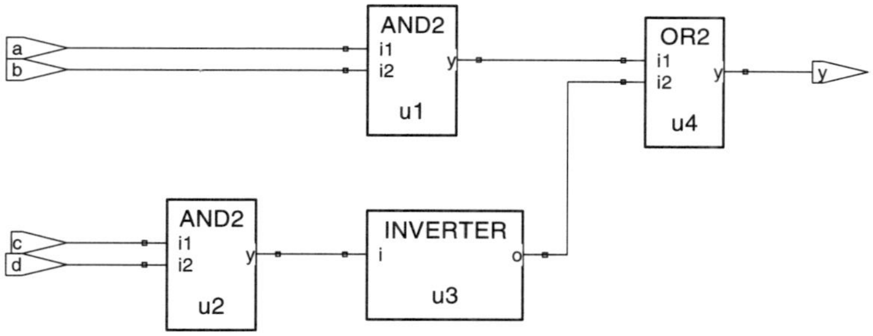

Gates Using Concurrent Assignments

Although structural instantiation of gates has its advantages, it can get cumbersome and may sometimes be difficult to follow. We can use concurrent assignments to model gates, too. Here, we need to rely on the built-in logic functions of the VHDL language, or the library that we are using. Since most designs use the *std_logic* type, this package includes all the standard functions for logic, such as *AND*, *OR*, *NOR*, etc. These functions are visible when you use the *std_logic_1164* package. The combinational logic in *Figure 2* can be implemented using concurrent assignments as shown in *Listing 2*.

Listing 2: Few Gates Using Concurrent Assignment

```
library IEEE;
use IEEE.std_logic_1164.all;

entity FEWGATES is port (
  a,b,c,d: in std_logic;
  y: out std_logic
  );
end FEWGATES;

architecture concurrent of FEWGATES is

signal a_and_b, c_and_d, not_c_and_d: std_logic;

begin

  a_and_b <= '1' when a = '1' and b = '1' else '0';
  c_and_d <= '1' when c = '1' and d = '1' else '0';

  not_c_and_d <= not c_and_d;

  y <= '1' when a_and_b = '1' or not_c_and_d = '1' else '0';

end concurrent;
```

gatescon.vhd

This results in the circuit realization shown in *Figure 4*.

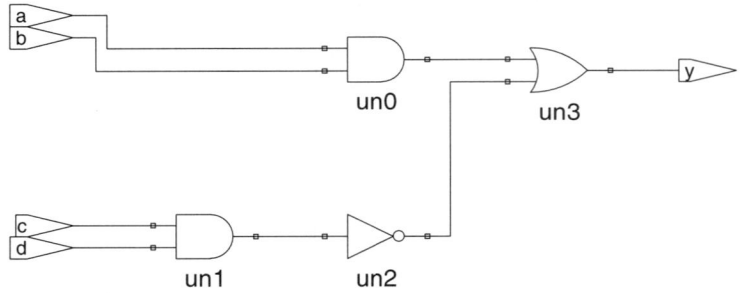

Figure 4: Few Gates Using Concurrent Assignments

Note that there is much similarity between the two circuit realizations shown in *Figure 3* and *Figure 4*. Both require intermediate nodes (signals) that represent the outputs of the gates not visible outside the entity. Structural instantiation is particularly useful when you want to explicitly use a large gate (i.e. one with multiple inputs, and perhaps more than one output), and when the synthesis tool cannot be coaxed into realizing the desired result.

Decoders

Decoders are commonplace in logic design, and are implemented using combinational logic. For the purpose of illustrating different styles of writing decoders, let us consider the design of a typical decoder. Although the decoder is part of a larger design, we will only focus on the decoder for the purpose of illustrating issues and techniques related to decoder design.

In our design, a programmable logic device decodes a device address bus (*DEV_ADR*). It generates a "chip select" for an external I/O controller (SIO Chip), and also generates select signals for four internal registers addressable via the *DEV_ADR* bus. The block diagram for this subsystem is shown in *Figure 5*.

Chapter 3 - Gates, Decoders and Encoders

Figure 5: Subsystem Using Programmable Logic as a Decoder

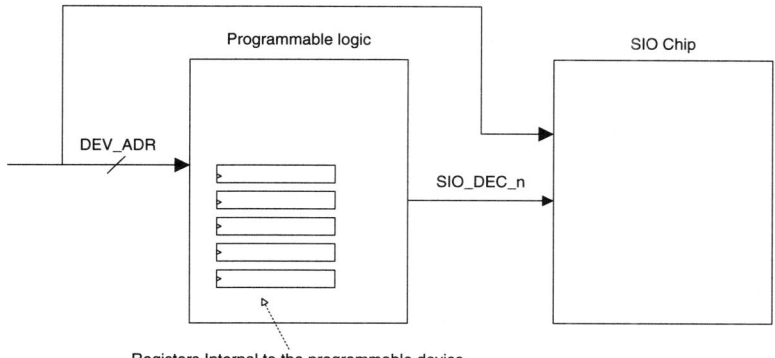

Figure 6 shows our decoder logic generating five signals, seen coming out of the "cloud" that represents the decoder logic. Note that the output signal *SIO_DEC_n* is not relevant to our implementation, since this will be taken care of at a higher level within the programmable logic design hierarchy.

Figure 6: Decoder Within Programmable Logic

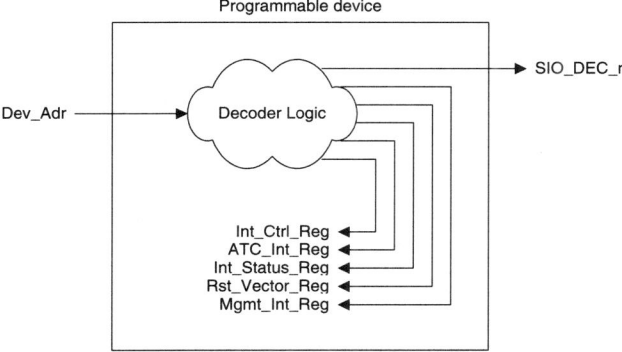

In our design, the address ranges that need to be decoded for the various "select" or "enable" signals are shown in *Table 1*. The decoder takes the three most significant bits of the *DEV_ADR* bus and uses them to determine whether the operation is destined for the SIO chip or one of the internal registers. If this gross decode results in one of the internal control registers, then the lower seventeen bits of the *DEV_ADR* bus are decoded to determine which of the internal registers has been selected.

Table 1: Decode Table for Programmable Device Implementation

DEV_ADR(19 downto 0)	Decode Output
0x4xXXX	SIO_DEC_n
0x80000	Int_Ctrl_Reg
0x80001	Io_Int_Stat_Reg
0x80002	Rst_Ctrl_Reg
0x80003	Atc_Status_Reg
0x80004	Mgmt_Status_Reg

Now that we have defined the decoder, let us take a look at the different ways of implementing it.

Decoders Using Concurrent Assignments

In this case, we use a series of concurrent assignments to implement the decoder shown in *Table 1*. The code for this decoder is shown in *Listing 3*. The gross decode for the internal register versus the external SIO chip is shown using the constant *CtrlRegRange* and *SuperIORange*. These constants are used to compare the three high-order bits in the design. The seventeen lower-order bits of the decode are also compared against constants *IntCtrlReg*, *IoIntStatReg*, *RstCtrlReg* and *AtcStatusReg*. The use of constants helps both design readability and maintenance.

The decoder outputs are all active-low asserted and hence are named with a trailing *_n*. Thus, their default value is '1', i.e. de-asserted.

Listing 3: Decoder Using Concurrent Assignments

```
library ieee;
use ieee.std_logic_1164.all;

entity isa_dec is port
(
  dev_adr:            in std_logic_vector(19 downto 0);

  sio_dec_n:          out std_logic;
  rst_ctrl_rd_n:      out std_logic;
  atc_stat_rd_n:      out std_logic;
  mgmt_stat_rd_n:     out std_logic;
  io_int_stat_rd_n:   out std_logic;
  int_ctrl_rd_n:      out std_logic
  );
end isa_dec;


architecture synthesis of isa_dec is
```

```vhdl
     constant   CtrlRegRange: std_logic_vector(2 downto 0)  := "100";
     constant   SuperIoRange: std_logic_vector(2 downto 0)  := "010";

     constant   IntCtrlReg:    std_logic_vector(16 downto 0) := "00000000000000000";
     constant   IoIntStatReg:  std_logic_vector(16 downto 0) := "00000000000000001";
     constant   RstCtrlReg:    std_logic_vector(16 downto 0) := "00000000000000010";
     constant   AtcStatusReg:  std_logic_vector(16 downto 0) := "00000000000000011";
     constant   MgmtStatusReg: std_logic_vector(16 downto 0) := "00000000000000100";
  begin
    sio_dec_n <= '0' when dev_adr (19 downto 17) = SuperIORange else '1';

    int_ctrl_rd_n <= '0' when (dev_adr (19 downto 17) = CtrlRegRange)
                        and (dev_adr(16 downto 0) = IntCtrlReg) else '1';

    io_int_stat_rd_n <= '0' when (dev_adr (19 downto 17) = CtrlRegRange)
                           and (dev_adr(16 downto 0) = IoIntStatReg) else '1';

    rst_ctrl_rd_n <= '0' when (dev_adr (19 downto 17) = CtrlRegRange)
                        and (dev_adr(16 downto 0) = RstCtrlReg) else '1';

    atc_stat_rd_n <= '0' when (dev_adr (19 downto 17) = CtrlRegRange)
                        and (dev_adr(16 downto 0) = AtcStatusReg) else '1';

    mgmt_stat_rd_n <= '0' when (dev_adr (19 downto 17) = CtrlRegRange)
                         and (dev_adr(16 downto 0) = MgmtStatusReg) else '1';


  end synthesis;
```

dec_conc.vhd

Decoders Within a Process Using the *Case* Statement

Processes are simply a collection of sequential statements. These statements are executed simultaneously, even though they are evaluated sequentially. So, if the process is made sensitive to all the inputs of the decoder, we can realize combinational logic since the process will be executed every time there is a change in one of the inputs. A decoder using the *case* statement that implements *Table 1* is shown in *Listing 4*.

Just as in the example using concurrent assignments, we use constants to perform the gross and fine decodes in the *case* statement implementation. However, the most notable difference between *case* statements and concurrent assignments is the use of default assignments for the outputs. This ensures that the outputs always get assigned to a value before they are set within the *case* statement. Failure to do so will generate inefficient although correct results. The reasons behind this are discussed in *Chapter 8*.

Listing 4: Decoder Using *Case* Statements

```
library ieee;
use ieee.std_logic_1164.all;

entity isa_dec is port
(
  dev_adr:           in std_logic_vector(19 downto 0);

  sio_dec_n:         out std_logic;
  rst_ctrl_rd_n:     out std_logic;
  atc_stat_rd_n:     out std_logic;
  mgmt_stat_rd_n:    out std_logic;
  io_int_stat_rd_n:  out std_logic;
  int_ctrl_rd_n:     out std_logic
);
end isa_dec;


architecture synthesis of isa_dec is

    constant   CtrlRegRange:  std_logic_vector(2 downto 0)    := "100";
    constant   SuperIoRange:  std_logic_vector(2 downto 0)    := "010";

    constant   IntCtrlReg:    std_logic_vector(16 downto 0) := "00000000000000000";
    constant   IoIntStatReg:  std_logic_vector(16 downto 0) := "00000000000000001";
    constant   RstCtrlReg:    std_logic_vector(16 downto 0) := "00000000000000010";
    constant   AtcStatusReg:  std_logic_vector(16 downto 0) := "00000000000000011";
    constant   MgmtStatusReg:std_logic_vector(16 downto 0) := "00000000000000100";

begin

    decoder: process (dev_adr)
      begin
        -- Set defaults for outputs

            sio_dec_n         <= '1';
            int_ctrl_rd_n     <= '1';
            io_int_stat_rd_n  <= '1';
            rst_ctrl_rd_n     <= '1';
            atc_stat_rd_n     <= '1';
            mgmt_stat_rd_n    <= '1';

            case dev_adr(19 downto 17) is

            when SuperIoRange =>
               sio_dec_n <= '0';

            when CtrlRegRange =>

                case dev_adr(16 downto 0) is
```

```vhdl
          when IntCtrlReg =>
            int_ctrl_rd_n <= '0';

          when IoIntStatReg =>
            io_int_stat_rd_n <= '0';

          when RstCtrlReg =>
            rst_ctrl_rd_n <= '0';

          when AtcStatusReg =>
            atc_stat_rd_n <= '0';

          when MgmtStatusReg =>
            mgmt_stat_rd_n <= '0';

          when others =>
            null;

        end case;

      when others =>
        null;

    end case;

  end process decoder;

end synthesis;
```

dec_case.vhd

The *case* statement is essentially a series of "parallel" checks, to determine whether or not a condition has been satisfied. Each choice condition is evaluated in a *when* statement. Since each condition is evaluated in parallel with the others, *case* statements rely on the user for completeness. You will be not be able to simulate or synthesize a *case* statement that is incomplete. In addition to this, each *when* condition must be used only once in the *case* statement, and care must be taken not to duplicate possibilities.

The safest way to ensure that this never happens is to always terminate a *case* statement with a *when others* clause, which will guarantee that all possible *case* conditions are covered. The *when others* clause has to be the last *when* condition in the *case* statement. The *null* statements for both the *case* statements simply mean "do nothing".

Figure 7: Decoder Using a *Case* Statement

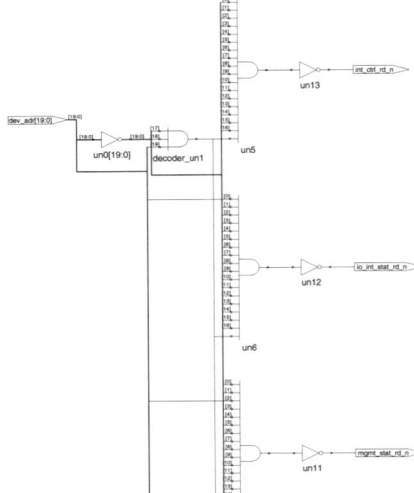

Some rules govern the use of *case* statements. While these are simple, it is possible that your synthesis tool may return a cryptic error message. One error often seen indicates that the synthesis tool requires a particular choice, or *when* branch, to be "locally static". This tells us that the *case* statement must be locally static during the VHDL analysis stage of the synthesis process. So, for example, you cannot have a *when* condition that changes while it is being evaluated. Consider the example shown in *Listing 5*.

Listing 5: Violation of Locally Static Requirement of a *Case* Choice

```
process (inputA, inputB)
  variable localVar: integer;
  begin
    case localVar is
      when localVar + 1 =>
        ..
        ..
        ..
        ..
    end case;
  end process;
```

In this example, notice that *localVar* is a variable and, hence, gets updated instantaneously. As a result, the first *when* condition changes the value of the *case* (*localVar*) while the *case* statement is being executed. This is an example of a choice that is not locally static, and would fail syntax checking.

Decoders Using *with...select*

This implementation could be considered to be a cross between writing concurrent assignments, and using a *case* statement. *With...select* statements are concurrent, in that they are written outside a process and within an architecture. The decoder in *Table 1* would be written as shown in *Listing 6*.

Listing 6: Decoder Using *with...select* Statements

```
library ieee;
use ieee.std_logic_1164.all;

entity isa_dec is port
(
  dev_adr:          in std_logic_vector(19 downto 0);
  sio_dec_n:        out std_logic;
  rst_ctrl_rd_n:    out std_logic;
  atc_stat_rd_n:    out std_logic;
  mgmt_stat_rd_n:   out std_logic;
  io_int_stat_rd_n:out std_logic;
  int_ctrl_rd_n:    out std_logic
  );
end isa_dec;


architecture synthesis of isa_dec is

  constant   CtrlRegRange: std_logic_vector(2 downto 0)  := "100";
  constant   SuperIoRange: std_logic_vector(2 downto 0)  := "010";

  constant   IntCtrlReg:   std_logic_vector(16 downto 0) := "00000000000000000";
  constant   IoIntStatReg: std_logic_vector(16 downto 0) := "00000000000000001";
```

```vhdl
    constant  RstCtrlReg:    std_logic_vector(16 downto 0) := "00000000000000010";
    constant  AtcStatusReg:  std_logic_vector(16 downto 0) := "00000000000000011";
    constant  MgmtStatusReg: std_logic_vector(16 downto 0) := "00000000000000100";

begin
  with dev_adr(19 downto 17) select
     sio_dec_n <= '0' when SuperIORange,
                  '1' when others;

  with dev_adr(19 downto 0) select
     int_ctrl_rd_n <= '0' when CtrlRegRange & IntCtrlReg,
                      '1' when others;

  with dev_adr(19 downto 0) select
     io_int_stat_rd_n <= '0' when CtrlRegRange & IoIntStatReg,
                         '1' when others;

  with dev_adr(19 downto 0) select
     rst_ctrl_rd_n <= '0' when CtrlRegRange & RstCtrlReg,
                      '1' when others;

  with dev_adr(19 downto 0) select
     atc_stat_rd_n <= '0' when CtrlRegRange & AtcStatusReg,
                      '1' when others;

  with dev_adr(19 downto 0) select
     mgmt_stat_rd_n <= '0' when CtrlRegRange & MgmtStatusReg,
                       '1' when others;

end synthesis;
```

dec_with.vhd

The similarities between *with...select* statements and *case* statements extend to the rules that govern *case* statements. Just like case statements, *with...select* statements must cover all possible condition combinations in the select choices. Also, each condition must be covered only once, so an *others* clause at the end of the *with...select* statement is the best way this can be ensured. *Listing 6* results in the circuit shown in *Figure 8*.

Figure 8: Decoder Using a *with...select* Statement

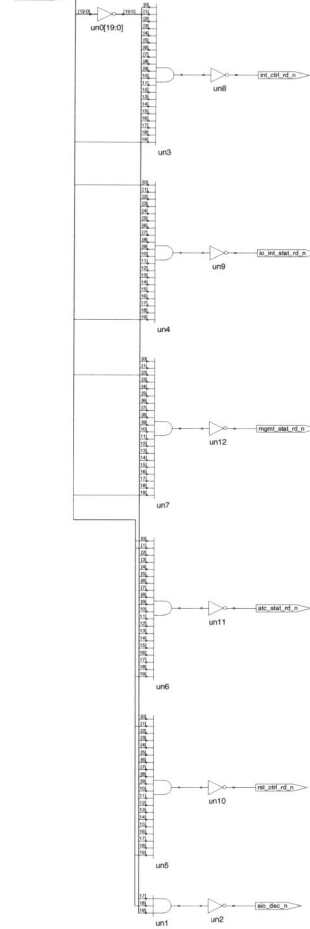

Notice, that unlike *case* statements, there is no need to assign default values to the outputs. These are automatically covered with the *others* clause at the end of the *with...select* statement.

Decoders Using *if...then*

Decoders using *if...then* statements are written with the same ease as *case* statement. Just as in the *case* statement, a sensitivity list is required. The *if...then...elsif...else* statements condition the outputs. The decoder using *if...then* statements would be written as shown in *Listing 7*.

Listing 7: Decoder Using *if...then* Statement

```
library ieee;
use ieee.std_logic_1164.all;

entity isa_dec is port
(
   dev_adr:            in std_logic_vector(19 downto 0);

   sio_dec_n:          out std_logic;
   rst_ctrl_rd_n:      out std_logic;
   atc_stat_rd_n:      out std_logic;
   mgmt_stat_rd_n:     out std_logic;
   io_int_stat_rd_n:   out std_logic;
   int_ctrl_rd_n:      out std_logic
);
end isa_dec;


architecture synthesis of isa_dec is

   constant  CtrlRegRange: std_logic_vector(2 downto 0)   := "100";
   constant  SuperIoRange: std_logic_vector(2 downto 0)   := "010";

   constant  IntCtrlReg:    std_logic_vector(16 downto 0) := "00000000000000000";
   constant  IoIntStatReg:  std_logic_vector(16 downto 0) := "00000000000000001";
   constant  RstCtrlReg:    std_logic_vector(16 downto 0) := "00000000000000010";
   constant  AtcStatusReg:  std_logic_vector(16 downto 0) := "00000000000000011";
   constant  MgmtStatusReg: std_logic_vector(16 downto 0) := "00000000000000100";

begin

   decoder: process ( dev_adr )
     begin
       -- Set defaults for outputs - for synthesis reasons.

       sio_dec_n          <= '1';
       int_ctrl_rd_n      <= '1';
       io_int_stat_rd_n   <= '1';
       rst_ctrl_rd_n      <= '1';
       atc_stat_rd_n      <= '1';
       mgmt_stat_rd_n     <= '1';

       if dev_adr(19 downto 17) = SuperIOrange then

          sio_dec_n <= '0';

       elsif dev_adr(19 downto 17) = CtrlRegrange then

          if dev_adr(16 downto 0) = IntCtrlReg then

             int_ctrl_rd_n <= '0';
```

```
            elsif dev_adr(16 downto 0)= IoIntStatReg then
               io_int_stat_rd_n <= '0';
            elsif dev_adr(16 downto 0) = RstCtrlReg then
               rst_ctrl_rd_n <= '0';
            elsif dev_adr(16 downto 0) = AtcStatusReg then
               atc_stat_rd_n <= '0';
            elsif dev_adr(16 downto 0) = MgmtStatusReg then
               mgmt_stat_rd_n <= '0';
            else
               null;
            end if;
         else
            null;
         end if;
      end process decoder;
   end synthesis;
```
dec_if.vhd

Just as with the *case* statement, the key to successful and efficient results is to set the default values of the outputs in the process. In both the examples of case and *if...then* shown in *Listing 4* and *Listing 7*, the default values are shown at the start of the process statement, before the beginning of the first *if...then* or case statement.

The Difference Between *if...then* and *Case* Statements

There is a significant difference between *case* and *if* statements. In an *if...then* statement, each condition can only be evaluated if <u>all</u> preceding conditions are not satisfied. In other words, in the following pseudo-VHDL

```
if <condition 1> then
   ...
elsif <condition 2> then
   ...
elsif <condition 3> then
   ...
else
   ...
end if;
```

condition 3 will only be evaluated if *condition 1* and *condition 2* are not satisfied. So, the logic that conditions *condition 3* includes the complement of *condition 1* and *condition 2*. This can result in large amounts of logic in *if...then* chains that are deep or nested.

Case statements, on the other hand, are parallel by definition, as we noted earlier. Hence, the logic for each *case* condition does not overlap with any other and is mutually exclusive. In this respect, it is preferable to use the *case* statement over the *if...then* statement. However, in applications where there are several inputs to a sparse logic function, it may be useful to use an *if...then* statement, since it will automatically prioritize conditions without having to decode all inputs to the function.

Note, however, that the implementations of the decoder in *Listing 6* and *Listing 7* produce the same results. Each condition specified in the *if...then* implementation does not overlap with any other condition - they are mutually exclusive to one another. So, while *if...then* and *case* statements are not directly interchangeable, if carefully written *if...then* statements can be as efficient as *case* statements, and produce the same results when synthesized. Other aspects of *if...then* and *case* statements are discussed in *Chapters 7* and *8*.

Factorization: Where the Tool Meets the Road
One step during the synthesis and optimization process is factorization. Prior to factorization, the design is usually flattened. In other words, all hierarchy in the design is removed, and the entire design is transformed into a flat, generic, sum-of-products (AND-OR) form. Factorization does the opposite of flattening. It adds structure to the generic design by extracting common logic factors and representing them as intermediate nodes, to produce smaller, more compact logic. This is part of the process of mapping the design to a specific target device-architecture. However, in many cases, synthesis tools may produce inefficient results after factorization, or they may not have adequate information on the logic that the designer had in mind. This can result in a large or slower circuit (or both). In such cases, a small modification to the design description can give the synthesis tool enough information to improve the results of synthesis.

To illustrate this, let us examine a design where the outputs are qualified by another signal. In other words, the outputs may only be asserted if the qualifier is asserted. Care must be taken when determining where to place qualifying signals in the design, to eliminate the qualifier from the critical path of the design. Consider a slightly extended version of our decoder, where the signal $CS0\_n$ is qualifying the outputs, as shown in *Listing 8*. The *if...then* statement that encapsulates the *case* statement conditions the outputs based on $CS0\_n$ being asserted (set to '0'). Just as with the *case* statement, default values are used to ensure that the outputs are de-asserted unless all conditions that cause them to be asserted are satisfied. Just like the *case* statement, the *null* assignments mean "do nothing".

Listing 8: Decoder with Qualified Outputs Using *if* Statements

```vhdl
library ieee;
use ieee.std_logic_1164.all;

entity isa_dec is port
(
  dev_adr:          in std_logic_vector(19 downto 0);
  cs0_n:            in std_logic;

  sio_dec_n:        out std_logic;
  rst_ctrl_rd_n:    out std_logic;
  atc_stat_rd_n:    out std_logic;
  mgmt_stat_rd_n:   out std_logic;
  io_int_stat_rd_n: out std_logic;
  int_ctrl_rd_n:    out std_logic
);
end isa_dec;


architecture synthesis of isa_dec is

   constant CtrlRegRange: std_logic_vector(2 downto 0)  := "100";
   constant SuperIoRange: std_logic_vector(2 downto 0)  := "010";

   constant IntCtrlReg:    std_logic_vector(16 downto 0) := "00000000000000000";
   constant IoIntStatReg:  std_logic_vector(16 downto 0) := "00000000000000001";
   constant RstCtrlReg:    std_logic_vector(16 downto 0) := "00000000000000010";
   constant AtcStatusReg:  std_logic_vector(16 downto 0) := "00000000000000011";
   constant MgmtStatusReg: std_logic_vector(16 downto 0) := "00000000000000100";

begin

   decoder: process (dev_adr, cs0_n)
     begin
       -- Set defaults for outputs - for synthesis reasons.

         sio_dec_n         <= '1';
         int_ctrl_rd_n     <= '1';
         io_int_stat_rd_n  <= '1';
         rst_ctrl_rd_n     <= '1';
         atc_stat_rd_n     <= '1';
         mgmt_stat_rd_n    <= '1';

         if (cs0_n = '0') then
           case dev_adr(19 downto 17) is

           when SuperIoRange =>
              sio_dec_n <= '0';

           when CtrlRegRange =>
```

```vhdl
            case dev_adr(16 downto 0) is

              when IntCtrlReg =>
                int_ctrl_rd_n <= '0';

              when IoIntStatReg =>
                io_int_stat_rd_n <= '0';

              when RstCtrlReg =>
                rst_ctrl_rd_n <= '0';

              when AtcStatusReg =>
                atc_stat_rd_n <= '0';

              when MgmtStatusReg =>
                mgmt_stat_rd_n <= '0';

              when others =>
                null;

            end case;

          when others =>
            null;

        end case;
      else
        null;
      end if;

  end process decoder;

end synthesis;
```

dec_ifin.vhd

This results in the circuit shown in *Figure 9*.

Chapter 3 - Gates, Decoders and Encoders

Figure 9: Decoder with Qualifying *if...then* Inside the Same Process

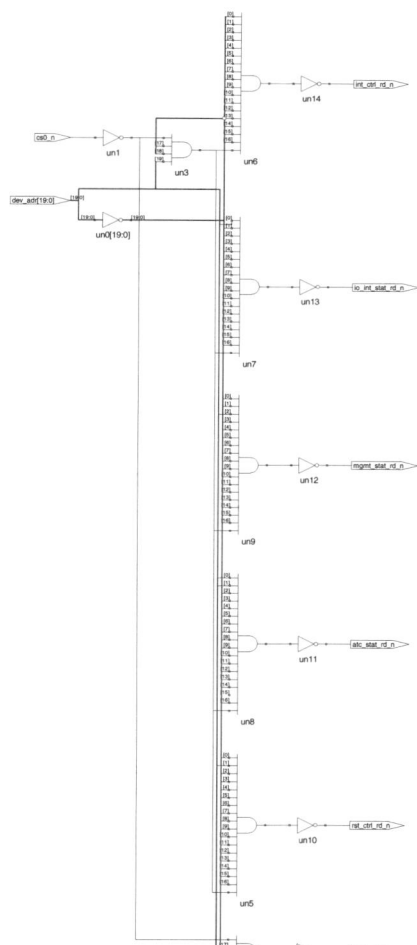

If the design was rewritten so that the qualification occurred after the outputs were generated, instead of before (as shown in *Figure 9*), it would result in the code shown in *Listing 9*. In this example, we have a separate process labeled *qualify* that performs the qualification of the outputs based on *CS0_n* being asserted. We have essentially pulled out the *if...then* statement from the code in *Listing 8* and placed it in the second process. The other notable difference is that in order to do this, we use local signals to determine the decoder outputs, which begin with *L*, and then qualify them with *CS0_n* to become the outputs of the decoder module.

Listing 9: Decoder with Qualified Outputs Using and External *if* Statements

```vhdl
library ieee;
use ieee.std_logic_1164.all;

entity isa_dec is port
(
  dev_adr:           in std_logic_vector(19 downto 0);
  cs0_n:             in std_logic;
  sio_dec_n:         out std_logic;
  rst_ctrl_rd_n:     out std_logic;
  atc_stat_rd_n:     out std_logic;
  mgmt_stat_rd_n:    out std_logic;
  io_int_stat_rd_n:  out std_logic;
  int_ctrl_rd_n:     out std_logic
);
end isa_dec;


architecture synthesis of isa_dec is

    constant  CtrlRegRange: std_logic_vector(2 downto 0)   := "100";
    constant  SuperIoRange: std_logic_vector(2 downto 0)   := "010";

    constant  IntCtrlReg:    std_logic_vector(16 downto 0) := "00000000000000000";
    constant  IoIntStatReg:  std_logic_vector(16 downto 0) := "00000000000000001";
    constant  RstCtrlReg:    std_logic_vector(16 downto 0) := "00000000000000010";
    constant  AtcStatusReg:  std_logic_vector(16 downto 0) := "00000000000000011";
    constant  MgmtStatusReg: std_logic_vector(16 downto 0) := "00000000000000100";

    signal Lsio_dec_n:         std_logic;
    signal Lrst_ctrl_rd_n:     std_logic;
    signal Latc_stat_rd_n:     std_logic;
    signal Lmgmt_stat_rd_n:    std_logic;
    signal Lio_int_stat_rd_n:  std_logic;
    signal Lint_ctrl_rd_n:     std_logic;

begin

    decoder: process (dev_adr)
      begin
        -- Set defaults for outputs - for synthesis reasons.

            Lsio_dec_n          <= '1';
            Lint_ctrl_rd_n      <= '1';
            Lio_int_stat_rd_n   <= '1';
            Lrst_ctrl_rd_n      <= '1';
            Latc_stat_rd_n      <= '1';
            Lmgmt_stat_rd_n     <= '1';

            case dev_adr(19 downto 17) is
```

Chapter 3 - Gates, Decoders and Encoders

```vhdl
          when SuperIoRange =>
            Lsio_dec_n <= ;'0';

          when CtrlRegRange =>

            case dev_adr(16 downto 0) is

              when IntCtrlReg =>
                Lint_ctrl_rd_n <= '0';

              when IoIntStatReg =>
                Lio_int_stat_rd_n <= '0';

              when RstCtrlReg =>
                Lrst_ctrl_rd_n <= '0';

              when AtcStatusReg =>
                Latc_stat_rd_n <= '0';

              when MgmtStatusReg =>
                Lmgmt_stat_rd_n <= '0';

              when others =>
                null;

            end case;

          when others =>
            null;

      end case;

end process decoder;

qualify: process (cs0_n) begin

   sio_dec_n         <= '1';
   int_ctrl_rd_n     <= '1';
   io_int_stat_rd_n  <= '1';
   rst_ctrl_rd_n     <= '1';
   atc_stat_rd_n     <= '1';
   mgmt_stat_rd_n    <= '1';

   if (cs0_n = '0') then
      sio_dec_n         <= Lsio_dec_n;
      int_ctrl_rd_n     <= Lint_ctrl_rd_n;
      io_int_stat_rd_n  <= Lio_int_stat_rd_n;
      rst_ctrl_rd_n     <= Lrst_ctrl_rd_n;
      atc_stat_rd_n     <= Latc_stat_rd_n;
      mgmt_stat_rd_n    <= Lmgmt_stat_rd_n;
   else
      null;
```

```
        end if;
    end process qualify;

end synthesis;
```

dec_ifout.vhd

The resulting circuit, shown in *Figure 10*, will be faster for all paths from *CS0_n* to the outputs. This is beneficial if *CS0_n* arrives later (in time) than the other inputs to the decoder.

Figure 10: Decoder with Qualifying *if...then* in a Separate Process

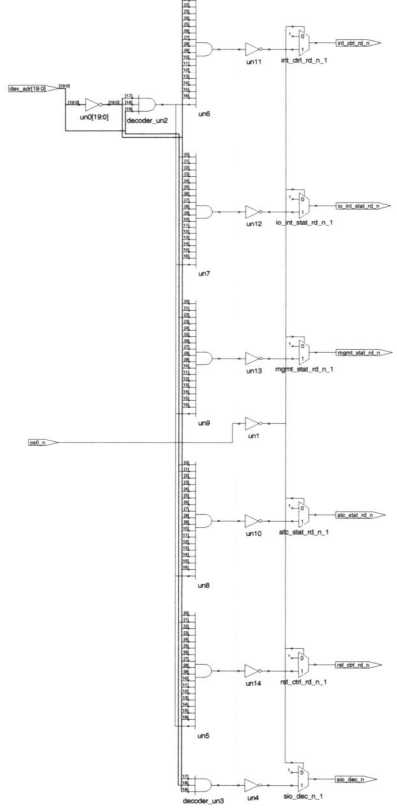

Placing the *if...then* qualifier for *CS0_n* after the decode results in *CS0_n* having less fanout, and no longer being in the critical timing path of the system. This technique has effectively factored out the qualifier and placed it where it is more efficiently used in the design. *Listing 8* is an example of logic that factors well and naturally. If such code is rewritten appropriately to take advantage of this natural factorization (*Listing 9*), it can enhance the size and performance of the circuit realized by the synthesis tool.

Encoders

Encoders, like decoders, can be implemented using different coding styles. We will use an 8-3 priority encoder to illustrate two techniques for implementation. The first technique, shown in *Listing 10*, uses *if...then* statements and the second, shown in *Listing 11*, uses concurrent assignments. A key point in the priority encode when using both the *if...then* technique and the concurrent assignment technique is the issue of precedence. Note that both in the *if* chain and the concurrent assignment, the first choice in the selection has the highest priority. If that condition is satisfied, none of the other conditions are evaluated until the next evaluation cycle. Hence, in our example, the most-significant bit (bit 7) of the input vector *invec* has the highest priority and the least-significant bit (bit 0) has the lowest priority. The resulting circuit is shown in *Figure 11*.

Listing 10: Encoder Using *if...then* Statements

```vhdl
library ieee;
use ieee.std_logic_1164.all;

entity encoder is
  port (invec:in std_logic_vector(7 downto 0);
        enc_out:out  std_logic_vector(2 downto 0)
       );
end encoder;

architecture rtl of encoder is
begin
  process (invec)
    begin
      if invec(7) = '1' then
        enc_out <= "111";

      elsif invec(6) = '1' then
        enc_out <= "110";

      elsif invec(5) = '1' then
        enc_out <= "101";

      elsif invec(4) = '1' then
        enc_out <= "100";

      elsif invec(3) = '1' then
        enc_out <= "011";

      elsif invec(2) = '1' then
        enc_out <= "010";
```

```
      elsif invec(1) = '1' then
        enc_out <= "001";

      elsif invec(0) = '1' then
        enc_out <= "000";

      else
        enc_out <= "000";
      end if;
    end process;
end rtl;
```

encoder2.vhd

Listing 11: Encoder Using Concurrent Assignments

```
library ieee;
use ieee.std_logic_1164.all;
entity encoder is
  port (invec: in std_logic_vector(7 downto 0);
        enc_out: out std_logic_vector(2 downto 0)
        );
end encoder;

architecture rtl of encoder is

begin
  enc_out <= "111" when invec(7) = '1' else
             "110" when invec(6) = '1' else
             "101" when invec(5) = '1' else
             "100" when invec(4) = '1' else
             "011" when invec(3) = '1' else
             "010" when invec(2) = '1' else
             "001" when invec(1) = '1' else
             "000" when invec(0) = '1' else
             "000";

end rtl;
```

encoder3.vhd

Chapter 3 - Gates, Decoders and Encoders

Figure 11: Priority Encoder

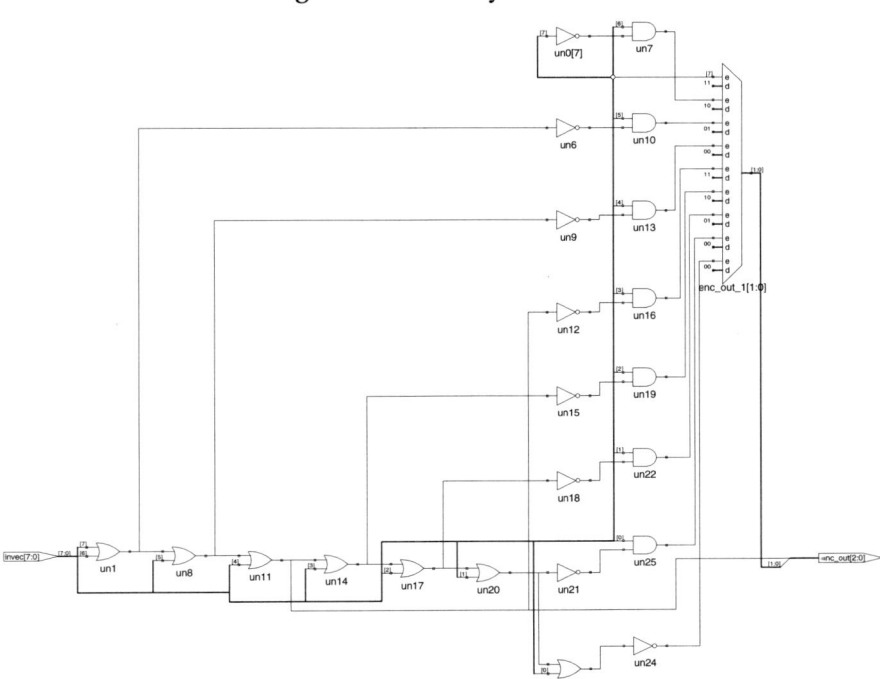

4
Registers and Latches

Registers

Structural Instantiation of Flip-flops

There are two ways of describing memory elements in VHDL: explicitly, and through implicit inference. The explicit method uses structural instantiation, while implicit inference uses behavioral or RTL description. The advantage of the structural instantiation method is that you can access device-specific hardware resources, or implement specific functionality. This method requires a *library* containing these components. You must understand which library the components reside in, and what the port mappings are. This library needs to be compiled and made visible with the *use* clause.

For example, let us assume that we compile a *package* called *primitive* into the *work* library, and it contains a component called *dffe* - a rising-edge-triggered D-type flip-flop with synchronous enable, which would look like *Figure 1*.

Figure 1: D-type Flip-flop with Synchronous Enable

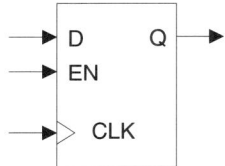

Table 1: D-type Flip-flop with Enable Truth Table

EN	D	CLK	Q
X	X	0	Q'
X	X	1	Q'
1	D	↑	D
0	X	↑	Q'

Q' indicates the value of Q
after the prior clock edge

We could then instantiate *dffe* into our model as shown in *Listing 1*.

Listing 1: Structural Implementation of D-type Flip-flop with Enable

```
library IEEE;
use IEEE.std_logic_1164.all;

entity struct_dffe is port (
  d: in std_logic;
  clk: in std_logic;
  en: in std_logic;
  q: out std_logic
  );
end struct_dffe;

use work.primitive.all;

architecture instance of struct_dffe is

begin

  ff: dffe port map (
  d => d,
  clk => clk,
  en => en,
  q => q
      );

end instance;
```

dffstruct.vhd

This would be synthesized as shown in *Figure 2*.

Figure 2: D-type Flip-flop with Enable

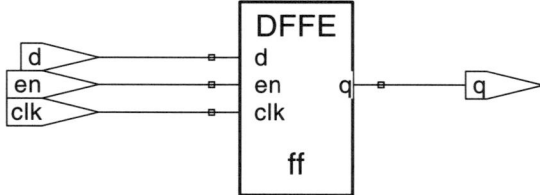

Behavioral Inference of Flip-flops

While it does have its use, the structural approach can get unwieldy. For this reason, registers are typically inferred from higher level statements, the simplest of which uses a *wait* statement. The *wait* statement is a sequential statement, and must be used inside a process. Most RTL synthesis tools accept only one *wait* statement per process, which is

Chapter 4 - Registers and Latches

usually required at the beginning or end of a process. As most tools accept the single *wait* statement at the beginning of a process, our examples will follow this style.

Using the *Wait* Statement

The D-type flip-flop described in *Table 1* is expressed using the *wait* statement as shown in *Listing 2*.

Listing 2: D-type Flip-flop with *Wait* Statement

```
library IEEE;
use IEEE.std_logic_1164.all;

entity DFF is port (
    d: in std_logic;
    clk: in std_logic;
    en: in std_logic;
    q: out std_logic
    );
end DFF;

architecture rtl of DFF is

begin

  process begin
    wait until clk = '1';
      if en = '1' then
        q <= d;
      end if;
  end process;

end rtl;
```

dffwait.vhd

All signal assignments that follow the *wait* statement result in an edge-triggered memory element. In the example shown in *Listing 2*, a rising edge-triggered registered memory element is inferred and generated by the synthesis tool. While it appears as though the *wait* statement describes a level sensitive function, the *wait* statement, in fact, results in an edge-triggered element due to an implied *on* clause. In other words, the line

```
wait until clk = '1';
```

is exactly equivalent to

```
wait on clk until clk = '1';
```

This implies that the process is suspended until there is a change in value of the signal *clk*, and it does not execute the statements after the *wait* statement unless *clk* is also '1'. This change in value represents a signal transition, which corresponds to a rising edge on the signal *clk*.

We could describe the same D-type flip-flop using other forms of the *wait* statement. For example, replacing

```
wait until clk = '1';
```

with

```
wait until clk'event and clk = '1';
```

or

```
wait until clk'last_value = '0' and clk = '1'
```

will <u>all</u> produce exactly the same result during synthesis.

The *std_logic_1164* package includes two functions, *rising_edge* and *falling_edge*, which allow you to describe a rising-edge-triggered and falling-edge-triggered memory element, respectively. These functions may be used as shown in *Listing 3*.

Listing 3: D-type Flip-flop with Enable Using the *rising_edge* Function

```
library IEEE;
use IEEE.std_logic_1164.all;

entity DFF is port (
    d: in std_logic;
    clk: in std_logic;
    end: in std_logic;
    q: out std_logic
    );
end DFF;

architecture rtl of DFF is

begin

  process begin
    wait until rising_edge(clk);
      if en = '1' then
        q <= d;
      end if;
  end process;

end rtl;
```

dffrise.vhd

We can also describe other edge-triggered memory elements using similar methods. For example, let us consider an edge-triggered SR-flop whose behavior is described in *Table 2*.

Table 2: SR-type Flip-flop Truth Table

S	R	CLK	Q
0	0	X	Q'
0	1	↑	0
1	0	↑	1
1	1	X	*

* = Undefined
Q' indicates the value of Q after the prior clock edge

This can be written as shown in *Listing 4* and *Listing 5*. Note that in both these listings, the value of the *Q* output when *S* and *R* are both '1' is in fact *Q*'. This was done for ease of implementation and because the case when S and R are both '1' should never occur, by design.

Listing 4: SR Flip-flop Using *Wait* Statement

```
library IEEE;
use IEEE.std_logic_1164.all;

entity SRFF is port (
    s,r: in std_logic;
    clk: in std_logic;
    q: out std_logic
    );
end SRFF;

architecture rtl of SRFF is

begin

  process begin
    wait until clk = '1';
      if s = '0' and r = '1' then
        q <= '0';
      elsif s = '1' and r = '0' then
        q <= '1';
      end if;
  end process;

end rtl;
```

srffwait.vhd

Listing 5: SR Flip-flop Using *rising_edge*

```
library IEEE;
use IEEE.std_logic_1164.all;

entity SRFF is port (
    s,r: in std_logic;
    clk: in std_logic;
    q: out std_logic
    );
end SRFF;

architecture rtl of SRFF is

begin

  process begin
    wait until rising_edge(clk);
      if s = '0' and r = '1' then
      q <= '0';
      elsif s = '1' and r = '0' then
      q <= '1';
      end if;
  end process;

end rtl;
```

srffrise.vhd

Both of these circuits synthesize as shown in *Figure 3*. The component instance labeled *un7* shows a selector, which places the value of the data, *d*, when the corresponding enable condition, *e*, is '1'.

Figure 3: SR-type Flip-flop

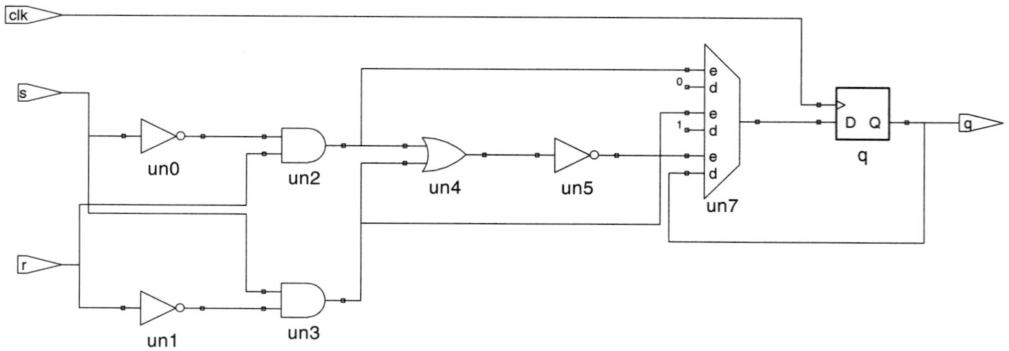

Chapter 4 - Registers and Latches

An important point to note here is that the synthesis tool has created a D-type flip-flop with logic in front of it. This is primarily for two reasons. First, most synthesis tools assume that the fundamental edge-triggered flip-flop is in fact a DFF. The second reason is that *Figure 3* does not show the results of technology mapping. This is the process by which the logic created is mapped to the fundamental logic elements that exist in the target technology, be it a programmable logic device, gate-array or ASIC.

Flip-flops with Enable

In synchronous design, you often need to suspend or "disable" a clock signal. Rather than gate the clock, it is better design practice to use a synchronous clock enable signal, which effectively holds the current value of the flip-flop when asserted. This is not only to create more reliable designs, but also because programmable logic devices have dedicated clock networks to distribute clocks with minimum delays and low skew. These clock networks are a scarce resource that will quickly run out if there are multiple clock sources, resulting in greater clock skew and poor clock distribution. Using a synchronous clock enable also helps reduce the number of clock domains for synthesis, optimization and greatly simplifies timing analysis. Many programmable device architectures (and other semi-custom, and full-custom, target semiconductor technologies for that matter) offer D-type flip-flops with an enable control. As such, many tools are now able to detect and map enable signals to the target logic element.

Hence, it is useful to know how to articulate D-type flip-flops with enables in VHDL so that it is easy for the synthesis tool to recognize them. The simplest form of a D-type flip-flop with enable can be written using *wait* statements as shown in *Listing 6*.

Listing 6: DFF with Enable Using *Wait*

```vhdl
library IEEE;
use IEEE.std_logic_1164.all;

entity DFFE is port (
    d: in std_logic;
    en: in std_logic;
    clk: in std_logic;
    q: out std_logic
    );
end DFFE;

architecture rtl of DFFE is

begin

  process begin
    wait until clk = '1';
      if en = '1' then
        q <= d;
      end if;
  end process;

end rtl;
```

dffenab.vhd

Flip-flops with *if...then* and a Sensitivity List

The most flexible, and preferred way of describing flip-flops is using the *if...then* statement along with a sensitivity list. To see the reason for this, let us begin with the description of a DFF with enable as shown in *Listing 7*.

Listing 7: DFF Using *if...then* and a Sensitivity List

```
library IEEE;
use IEEE.std_logic_1164.all;

entity DFF is port (
    d: in std_logic;
    clk: in std_logic;
    en: in std_logic;
    q: out std_logic
    );
end DFF;

architecture rtl of DFF is

begin

  process (clk) begin
    if clk'event and clk = '1' then
      if en = '1' then
        q <= d;
      end if;
    end if;
  end process;

end rtl;
```

dffif.vhd

Notice that the first *if...then* statement only covers the register inference. This statement makes use an *attribute*. Attributes are properties that are indicated with the ' ' character. In this case, the *event* attribute indicates that there has been a change in the value of the signal *clk*. When this is qualified with *and clk* = *'1'*, a register is inferred for all subsequent signal assignments. The *if...then* enable is nested inside the first *if...then* statement and there is no *else* clause that terminates either *if...then* statement. The logic generated is shown in *Figure 4*.

Figure 4: D-type Flip-flop Using *if...then* and a Sensitivity List

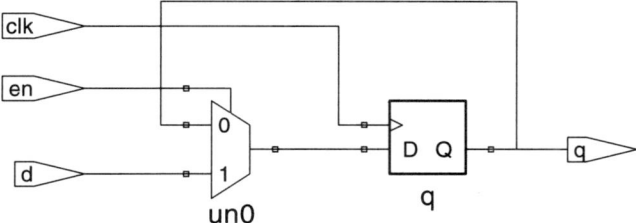

In the strictest sense, the *rising_edge* and *falling_edge* functions are the most accurate representation of edge-triggered memory elements, since they detect the transition from 0 to 1 (and 1 to 0), specifically. Other statements that detect transition (using the '*event* attribute) could potentially detect a transition from some other value (such as 'X') to '1'. The '*event* attribute detects a change in value of a signal. Since one possible value of a *std_logic* is 'X', the *clk'event and clk = '1'* condition will be satisfied, which incorrectly indicates a rising edge.

In many designs, you may come across an enable condition that is more complex than just a single signal. For example, the outputs of a counter could be used to enable a register. *Listing 8* is an example where the enable-inference is a more complex logic function. Note that it follows the same, 2-deep, nested *if...then* statement of the simple D-type flip-flop with enable, shown in *Listing 7*. In this case, the flip-flop is enabled (i.e. passes through the value on the *D* input to the *Q* output) whenever the input vector is "10010111". Otherwise, it holds the value at the *Q* output. The resulting circuit is shown in *Figure 5*.

Listing 8: Additional Example of a DFF Using *if...then* and a Sensitivity List

```
library IEEE;
use IEEE.std_logic_1164.all;

entity DFF is port (
    d: in std_logic;
    clk: in std_logic;
    envector: in std_logic_vector(7 downto 0);
    q: out std_logic
    );
end DFF;

architecture rtl of DFF is

begin

  process (clk) begin
    if clk'event and clk = '1' then
      if envector = "10010111" then
```

```
            q <= d;
         end if;
      end if;
   end process;

end rtl;
```

                                                                    dffif2.vhd

Figure 5: More Complex Enabled DFF Using *if...then* and a Sensitivity List

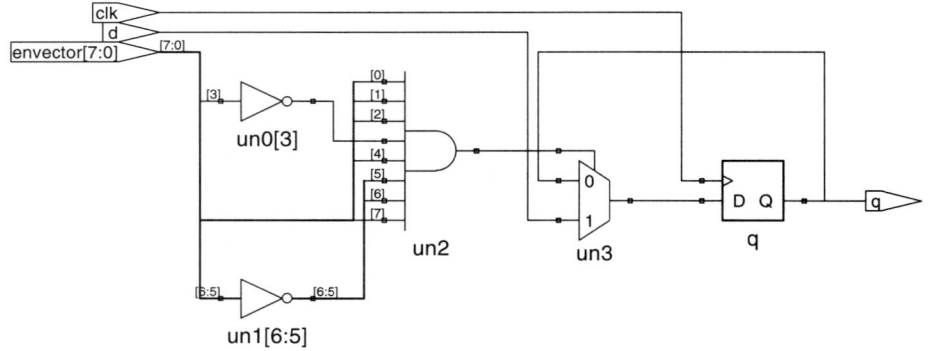

Key Difference Between *if...then* and *wait*-Generated Flip-flops

The most significant difference to note between the description of flip-flops using the *if...then* approach and the *wait* statement is the sensitivity list of the process. Notice that the process with the *wait* statement has no sensitivity list, while the *if...then* process does.

The sensitivity list of a process suspends execution of a process, unless there is a change in value of a signal in the sensitivity list. In other words, in the *if...then* process the process is not executed unless there has been a change in the value of the signal *clk*. This sensitivity list is in fact equivalent to a *wait on* statement at the end of the process. In other words, *Listing 7* could be re-written as shown in *Listing 9*.

Listing 9: DFF Using *wait...on*

```
library IEEE;
use IEEE.std_logic_1164.all;

entity DFF is port (
    d: in std_logic;
    clk: in std_logic;
    en: in std_logic;
    q: out std_logic
    );
end DFF;
```

```
architecture rtl of DFF is

begin

  process begin
    if clk'event and clk = '1' then
      if en = '1' then
        q <= d;
      end if;
    end if;
    wait on clk;
  end process;

end rtl;
```

dff_diff.vhd

While this could be simulated in a VHDL simulator with identical results, it is preferable to write code for synthesis using *Listing 7* rather than *Listing 9*. This is because most synthesis tools do not support register inference from the coding style in *Listing 9*. The *wait* statement, in fact, already contains an implied *on* clause, as we discussed earlier. The *wait on* clause suspends execution of the process until there is a change in the *clk* signal. Processes with a *wait* statement **and** a sensitivity list are **illegal**, and not allowed by VHDL. An example of such code is shown in *Listing 10*.

Listing 10: Illegal Coding! DFF with *Wait* and Sensitivity List

```
library IEEE;
use IEEE.std_logic_1164.all;

entity DFF is port (
    d: in std_logic;
    clk: in std_logic;
    q: out std_logic
    );
end DFF;

architecture rtl of DFF is

begin

  process (clk) begin
    wait until clk = '1';
      q <= d;
  end process;

end rtl;
```

ffwrong1.vhd

Flip-flop Reset and Preset

Flip-flops should be either reset or preset to a value, usually on start-up, or when the system is being initialized. This is done primarily for four reasons:

- The initial state of the flip-flop may not be known after power-up
- The initial state of the flip-flop may not be the desired value after power-up
- You may want to place the system into a known state during operation as a fall-back or recovery feature
- Simulation may require it

There are two kinds of resets (or presets): asynchronous and synchronous. Asynchronous presets and resets can only be described using the *if...then* style of flip-flop coding. Synchronous resets can be described using either the *if...then* or *wait* coding style. Note that the words "preset" and "set" mean the same thing and are used interchangeably. This section serves as an introduction to asynchronous resets and presets. They are discussed in greater detail in *Chapters 7 and 8*.

Asynchronous Resets and Preset

We can express an asynchronous reset to a D-type flip-flop as shown in *Listing 11*.

Listing 11: DFF with Asynchronous Reset

```
library IEEE;
use IEEE.std_logic_1164.all;

entity DFF is port (
    d: in std_logic;
    clk: in std_logic;
    arst: in std_logic;
    q: out std_logic
    );
end DFF;

architecture rtl of DFF is

begin

  process (clk, arst) begin
    if arst = '1' then
      q <= '0';
    elsif clk'event and clk = '1' then
        q <= d;
    end if;
  end process;

end rtl;
```

dffarst.vhd

Notice that the reset condition is described in the first *if...then* statement. The *elsif* condition, that immediately follows, is the description of the register itself. As the reset condition is evaluated before the description of the register, the reset has priority and is, hence, an asynchronous reset. The sensitivity list includes the signal *arst*, since the value of the flip-flop may change at any time irrespective of the clock signal. The rest of the code behaves exactly as a D-type flip-flop described earlier. This code results in the logic shown in *Figure 6*.

Figure 6: DFF with Asynchronous Reset

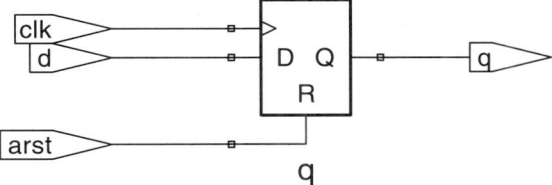

Your reset signal need not be limited to a single signal. It may be an expression or a function of multiple signals as in the example shown in *Listing 13*.

Listing 12: DFF with Asynchronous Expression Reset

```
library IEEE;
use IEEE.std_logic_1164.all;

entity DFF is port (
    d: in std_logic;
    clk: in std_logic;
    a,b,c : in std_logic;
    q: out std_logic
    );
end DFF;

architecture rtl of DFF is

begin

  process (clk, a,b,c) begin
    if ((a = '1' and b = '1') or c = '1') then
      q <= '0';
    elsif clk'event and clk = '1' then
        q <= d;
    end if;
  end process;

end rtl;
```

dffarst2.vhd

This code results in the logic shown in *Figure 7*.

Figure 7: DFF with Asynchronous Expression Reset

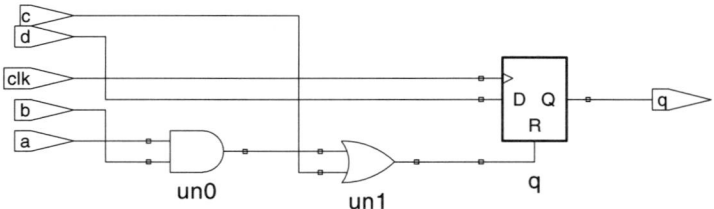

Some logic synthesis tools cannot handle expressions in the reset condition, of the kind shown in *Listing 12*. In this event you will need to create a signal that is local to the architecture, and use this in the process as shown in *Listing 13*.

Listing 13: DFF with Asynchronous Reset Implemented as a Local Signal

```
library IEEE;
use IEEE.std_logic_1164.all;

entity DFF is port (
    d: in std_logic;
    clk: in std_logic;
    a,b,c : in std_logic;
    q: out std_logic
    );
end DFF;

architecture rtl of DFF is

signal localRst: std_logic;

begin

  localRst <= '1' when (( a = '1' and b = '1') or c = '1') else '0';

  process (clk, localRst) begin
    if localRst = '1' then
       q <= '0';
    elsif clk'event and clk = '1' then
         q <= d;
    end if;
  end process;

end rtl;
```

dffarst3.vhd

This produces the result shown in *Figure 7*, which is identical to the logic realized from synthesizing *Listing 12*.

Presets are generated in exactly the same way as shown in the last few examples. The only difference being that instead of the initial *if...then* condition setting the flip-flop output to '0', it is now set to '1', as shown in *Listing 14*.

Listing 14: DFF with Asynchronous Preset

```
library IEEE;
use IEEE.std_logic_1164.all;

entity DFF is port (
    d: in std_logic;
    clk: in std_logic;
    aset : in std_logic;
    q: out std_logic
    );
end DFF;

architecture rtl of DFF is

begin

  process (clk, aset) begin
    if aset = '1' then
      q <= '1';
    elsif clk'event and clk = '1' then
        q <= d;
    end if;
  end process;

end rtl;
```
dffaset.vhd

Synchronous Resets and Presets

Synchronous resets and presets may be written using either a *wait*, or *if...then* statement. In the case of a *wait* statement, the logic that follows the *wait* statement must be encapsulated in an *if...then* statement, as shown in *Listing 15*. The difference between asynchronous and synchronous resets lies in the evaluation of the reset condition. In *Listing 15*, the reset is evaluated after the clock condition (unlike the asynchronous reset) results in a synchronous reset.

Listing 15: Synchronous Reset with a *Wait* Statement

```
library IEEE;
use IEEE.std_logic_1164.all;

entity DFF is port (
    d: in std_logic;
    clk: in std_logic;
    srst : in std_logic;
    q: out std_logic
    );
end DFF;
```

```
architecture rtl of DFF is

begin

  process begin
    wait until clk = '1';
      if srst = '1' then
        q <= '0';
      else
        q <= d;
      end if;
  end process;

end rtl;
```
dffsrst2.vhd

This results in the logic shown in *Figure 8*.

Figure 8: DFF with Synchronous Reset

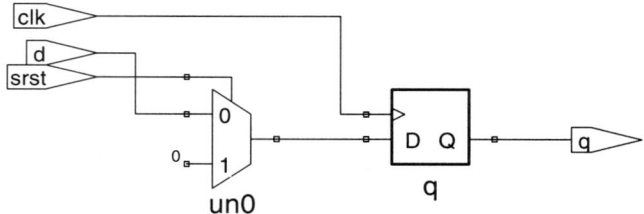

Similar to the *wait* example, we can nest a synchronous *if...then* statement that resets logic as shown in *Listing 16*.

Listing 16: Synchronous Reset Using *if...then*

```
library IEEE;
use IEEE.std_logic_1164.all;

entity DFF is port (
    d: in std_logic;
    clk: in std_logic;
    srst : in std_logic;
    q: out std_logic
    );
end DFF;

architecture rtl of DFF is

begin

  process (clk) begin
    if clk'event and clk = '1' then
```

```
      if srst = '1' then
        q <= '0';
      else
        q <= d;
      end if;
    end if;
  end process;

end rtl;
```

dffsrst.vhd

This description also results in the logic shown in *Figure 8*.

Notice in *Listing 16* that the reset condition is the very first condition that is evaluated in the *if...then* statement. This indicates that the reset condition takes precedence over all other statements when the logic is evaluated and realized into gates. This is an important point to note, since *if...then* statements are "chained". In other words, as you move down the chain of *if* conditions, the first one to be successfully evaluated changes the resulting value of the output logic. All conditions that follow it are never evaluated.

Notable Issues with Sets and Resets

There are two issues to remember when writing code for synchronous versus asynchronous sets and resets.

- The sensitivity lists for asynchronous and synchronous sets and resets are different
- The assignment encompasses all signals within the *if...then* of the reset or preset condition.

The sensitivity list for a *process* where signals have an asynchronous reset includes the clock, and <u>all</u> signals that are part of the reset condition. Note that in the example in *Listing 12*, we had:

```
process (clk, a,b,c) begin
```

However, for a *process* where the signals have a synchronous reset, such as the one in *Listing 16*, the sensitivity list of the process (if it has a sensitivity list, then the *process* <u>cannot</u> have a *wait* statement) only contains the clock signal, just like a process that uses *if...then* to infer a clock:

```
process (clk) begin
```

While this may seem obvious, it is a significant difference. In the case of asynchronous reset and presets, the sensitivity list shows that the process is evaluated whenever there is a change in <u>either</u> the reset condition or the clock. Most good synthesis tools will issue a warning if you write an asynchronous reset without placing the signals that are part of the reset condition in the sensitivity list. For example, the code shown in *Listing 17* should not synthesize to an asynchronous reset, and does not simulate correctly.

Listing 17: Asynchronous Reset with Incorrect Sensitivity List

```
library IEEE;
use IEEE.std_logic_1164.all;

entity DFF is port (
    d: in std_logic;
    clk: in std_logic;
    arst : in std_logic;
    q: out std_logic;
    );
end DFF;

architecture rtl of DFF is

begin

  process (clk) begin
    if arst = '1' then
      q <= '0';
    elsif clk'event and clk = '1' then
      q <= d;
    end if;
  end process;

end rtl;
```

dffarbad.vhd

From time to time, you will come across a design where you may have a process where some of the signals are preset to '1', and some are reset to '0'. This can be handled fairly simply. In the case of asynchronous resets and presets, assign the appropriate signals from the first *if...then* statement, which is the reset/preset condition. An example of this is shown in *Listing 18*.

Listing 18: Assigning Asynchronous Preset and Reset with the Same Signal

```
library IEEE;
use IEEE.std_logic_1164.all;

entity DFF is port (
    d1, d2: in std_logic;
    clk: in std_logic;
    arst : in std_logic;
    q1, q2: out std_logic
    );
end DFF;
```

```
architecture rtl of DFF is

begin

  process (clk, arst) begin
    if arst = '1' then
      q1 <= '0';
      q2 <= '1';
    elsif clk'event and clk = '1' then
      q1 <= d1;
      q2 <= d2;
    end if;
  end process;

end rtl;
```
dffboth.vhd

In *Listing 18*, *arst* is used to reset or preset different registers. Similarly, in *Listing 19*, the signal *srst* performs a synchronous reset and preset on different registers.

Listing 19: Assigning Synchronous Preset and Reset with the Same Signal
```
library IEEE;
use IEEE.std_logic_1164.all;

entity DFF is port (
    d1, d2: in std_logic;
    clk: in std_logic;
    srst : in std_logic;
    q1, q2: out std_logic
    );
end DFF;

architecture rtl of DFF is

begin

  process (clk) begin
    if clk'event and clk = '1' then
      if srst = '1' then
   q1 <= '0';
   q2 <= '1';
      else
        q1 <= d1;
        q2 <= d2;
      end if;
    end if;
  end process;

end rtl;
```
dffsboth.vhd

Using a *wait* statement will result in logic identical to that generated by *Listing 19*. To do so, the outer *if...then* statement would be replaced with a *wait* statement, while the inner *if...then* statement would remain the same.

Latches

Latches are memory elements that are level-sensitive. They typically consist of three signals: an enable, an input and an output signal, as shown in *Figure 9*. The enable signal latches or holds the value of the output.

Figure 9: Generic Latch

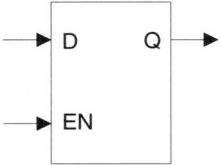

The enable signal may either be active high, or active low. In the former case, we call the latch "transparent-high", and in the latter case, we call the latch "transparent-low". These terms indicate when the latch is in flow-through mode (where the output takes the value of the input), and when the latch is in "recirculate" mode (where it recirculates the output value to the input). The truth-table for these latches is shown in *Figure 10*.

Figure 10: Transparent Latch Truth Tables

D	EN	Q
D	0	Q'
D	1	D

D	EN	Q
D	0	D
D	1	Q'

Latch - Transparent-High   Latch - Transparent-Low
Q' indicates the last value of Q stored in the latch

Structural Instantiation of Latches

Just like registers, latches may be explicitly described by using structural instantiation in a design. For example, let us assume that we compile a *package* called *primitive* into the *work* library, and it contains a component called DLATCHH - a transparent-high level-sensitive latch as shown in *Figure 11*.

Chapter 4 - Registers and Latches

Figure 11: Transparent-High D-type Latch (DLATCHH)

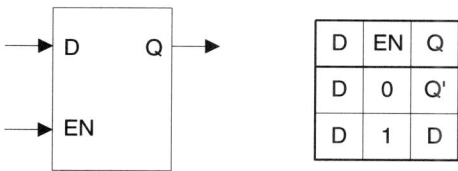

Q' indicates the last value of Q stored in the latch

We could then instantiate DLATCHH into our model as show in *Listing 20*.

Listing 20: Structural Instantiation of a D-Latch

```
library IEEE;
use IEEE.std_logic_1164.all;

entity struct_dlatch is port (
  d: in std_logic;
  en: in std_logic;
  q: out std_logic
  );
end struct_dlatch;

use work.primitive.all;

architecture instance of struct_dlatch is

begin

  latch: dlatchh port map (
  d => d,
  en => en,
  q => q
      );

end instance;
```

clatstruc.vhd

This would be synthesized as shown in *Figure 12*.

Figure 12: D-type Latch - Structural

Just like flip-flops, expressing latches structurally can be cumbersome. Most synthesis tools offer at least one way in which you can describe latches using higher level constructs from which latches can be inferred. We will discuss two common ways of doing this: using concurrent assignments and using processes.

Latches Using Concurrent Assignments

The simplest and shortest way to describe a latch uses concurrent or dataflow assignments, as shown in *Listing 21*. Notice the use of the local signal, *qLocal*, which is necessary as the mode of Q is *out*. Recall that signals of mode *out* cannot be read within the architecture, as we discussed in *Chapter 1*.

Listing 21: Concurrent Description of a D-Latch

```
library IEEE;
use IEEE.std_logic_1164.all;

entity DLATCHH is port (
    d: in std_logic;
    en: in std_logic;
    q: out std_logic
    );
end DLATCHH;

architecture rtl of DLATCHH is

signal qLocal: std_logic;

begin

  qLocal <= d when en = '1' else qLocal;

  q <= qLocal;

end rtl;
```

dlatconc.vhd

This results in the synthesis tool generating a latch circuit as shown in *Figure 13*.

Figure 13: D-type Latch with Concurrent Assignments

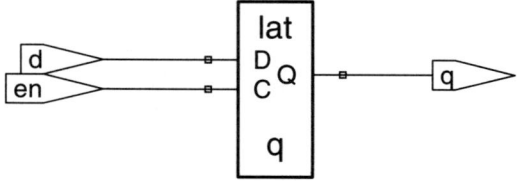

Chapter 4 - Registers and Latches

Latches Using *Processes*

A slightly longer, but equally straight-forward way of describing a latch uses a *process* with a sensitivity list. The main difference between the sensitivity list of a latch and a flip-flop stems from the difference in operation between the two memory elements. In the case of a latch, the value of the output may change depending on either the state of the enable signal or the input(s). When the latch is in transparent mode, the input(s) may be changing. Hence, the process needs to be sensitive to both the enable and the input signals. An example is shown in *Listing 22*.

Listing 22: D-Latch Using *if...then*

```
library IEEE;
use IEEE.std_logic_1164.all;

entity DLATCHH is port (
    d: in std_logic;
    en: in std_logic;
    q: out std_logic
    );
end DLATCHH;

architecture rtl of DLATCHH is

begin

  process (en, d) begin
    if en = '1' then
      q <= d;
    end if;
  end process;

end rtl;
```
dlatif.vhd

When synthesized, *Listing 22* results in a circuit identical to *Figure 13*.

There is an important observation to make when creating latches using a *process* and *if...then* statement. Notice that the latch is created by the *if...then* statement without a closing *else*. The latch is implied or inferred from the lack of the closing *else* prior to the *end if*. This can lead to significant consequences on the logic generated if the *else* is omitted "accidentally", as we will see in *Chapter 8*.

Key Difference Between Processes and Dataflow Inferred Latches

As seen from the examples, when the latch enable signal is asserted, the input value flows through to the output. When it is deasserted, the output value is recirculated, or held to the value it was at when the enable was deasserted. An important issue to note when using concurrent assignments to describe the latch is the use of *qLocal*, an intermediate node in the latch operation. The output of the latch is not only the source or driver for this signal, but it is also read or observed in the process. This can be seen in the *else* condition of the concurrent assignment. As the signal *q* is of mode *out*, it may only be an output and cannot be used as a feedback signal within the architecture. Hence, the need for *qLocal*. The latch inferred from a process, on the other hand, does not require the use of an intermediate node, such as *qLocal*.

5
Counters and Simple Arithmetic Functions

Counters are, perhaps, the simplest and most common arithmetic functions that you will implement in your designs. Most modern synthesis tools apply some form of operator inferencing to counters during the synthesis process, as they are highly regular structures. By this, we mean that modern synthesis tools seldom flatten counters into Boolean equations. Instead, they identify or tag constructs known to result in counters. Substitutions are then performed on these constructs based on optimization objectives. These objectives direct the synthesis tools to generate a solution that achieves a target speed or area, and even timing. Hence, it is important to write VHDL from which compilers can infer these circuits for best results.

Arithmetic Functions in Predefined Packages

VHDL has built-in support for arithmetic operations on integer data types. However, in hardware modeling for synthesis, one typically uses the *std_logic* type that we have been using so far in this book. VHDL allows operations to be defined for any type. Arithmetic operations for the *std_logic* type are defined in the following packages:

- *numeric_std*
- *std_logic_signed*
- *std_logic_unsigned*
- *std_logic_arith*

Broadly speaking, we can describe these packages as follows.

The *numeric_std* package performs arithmetic operations on *std_logic*, *signed* and *unsigned* types, and returns these types from its functions.

The *std_logic_signed* and *std_logic_unsigned* packages perform *signed* and *unsigned* arithmetic, respectively, on *std_logic* types, and return *std_logic* types.

The *std_logic_arith* package contains arithmetic functions that accept *signed* and *unsigned* argument types and can return *std_logic*, *unsigned* and *signed* types.

Due to historical reasons, the *std_logic_signed*, *std_logic_unsigned* and *std_logic_arith* packages are often found in the *IEEE* library. It is important to note, however, that these packages are not standard IEEE packages. For maximum portability, use the *numeric_std* package, especially in new designs. The *numeric_std* package was adopted as the IEEE 1076.3-1997 standard.

These libraries are made visible by the *library* declaration, and the appropriate *use* clause. In most of your designs, you will already be declaring the *IEEE* library, since you are using the *std_logic* type. So, we only need to add the *use* clause for the particular library after this statement. For example, if you wish to use the *numeric_std* package, then the VHDL preamble to the *entity* declaration is as follows:

```
library ieee;
use ieee.std_logic_1164.all;
use ieee.numeric_std;
```

This would be done at the beginning of your design, before the entity declaration.

Numeric_std defines two unconstrained arrays of *std_logic* known as *signed* and *unsigned*, which are vectors that are interpreted as signed and unsigned, respectively. Since virtually all the arithmetic we deal with in RTL synthesis is unsigned, you must use the *unsigned* type with the *numeric_std* package in your designs. In the event that your design is hierarchical, using the *unsigned* type throughout your design, or performing a type conversion at the port level, is required. To illustrate this, let us consider the design of a counter.

The simplest counter that we can write is an up-counter, or incrementing circuit, that increments by one on each clock cycle. This would be written as shown in *Listing 1*.

Listing 1: Simple Up-counter

```
-- Incorporates Errata 5.4
library ieee;
use ieee.std_logic_1164.all;
use ieee.numeric_std.all;

entity counter is port (
  clk: in std_logic;
  count: out std_logic_vector(3 downto 0)
  );
end counter;

architecture simple of counter is

signal countL: unsigned(3 downto 0);

begin

  increment: process (clk) begin
    if (clk'event and clk = '1') then
      countL <= countL + 1;
    end if;
  end process;

  count <= std_logic_vector(countL);

end simple;
```

count1.vhd

Chapter 5 - Counters and Simple Arithmetic Functions

In this example, we have used a local version of the signal *count* called *countL*. This is for two reasons. First, *count* is a port signal whose mode is *out* and, therefore, cannot be read within the architecture. As a result, it cannot be placed on the right-hand side of any signal assignment. Second, the *numeric_std* package supports the "+" function for the *unsigned* and *signed* types, only. So, *countL* must be of the *unsigned* type. Hence, the need to use *countL*, followed by a concurrent assignment with the type conversion to equate the *count* to *countL*. The type conversion can be performed in this way, since the two types are very similar (*signed* and *unsigned* types are arrays of *std_logic*). Notice also that there is no *else* condition that specifies the default operation of *countL* <= *countL* or "hold the current value" when load and enable are deasserted. This condition is not required as it is implied in the *if...then* chain. Synthesizing *Listing 1* results in the logic shown in *Figure 1*.

Figure 1: Simple Up-counter

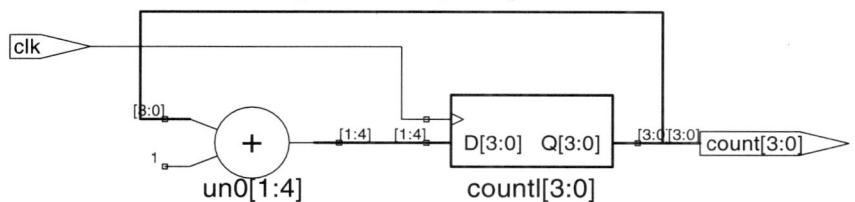

Notice that the counter is simply an adder, where one of the operands happens to be a constant '1'. This is followed by a register, and the output from the register feeds back to the other operand of the adder.

Counters contain registers, and just as with other registered elements in a design, it is sometimes necessary to set the counter to a specific value when the system is initialized. This is usually accomplished with an asynchronous reset, which is implemented in a similar fashion as illustrated in *Chapter 4*, and is shown in *Listing 2*.

Listing 2: Counter with Asynchronous Reset

```
-- Incorporates Errata 5.4

library ieee;
use ieee.std_logic_1164.all;
use ieee.numeric_std.all;

entity counter is port (
  clk: in std_logic;
  reset: in std_logic;
  count: out std_logic_vector(3 downto 0)
  );
end counter;

architecture simple of counter is

signal countL: unsigned(3 downto 0);
```

```
begin

  increment: process (clk, reset) begin
    if reset = '1' then
      countL <= "1001";
    elsif(clk'event and clk = '1') then
      countL <= countL + 1;
    end if;
  end process;

  count <= std_logic_vector(countL);

end simple;
```
count2.vhd

This results in the circuit shown in *Figure 2*.

Figure 2: Counter with Non-zero Asynchronous Reset

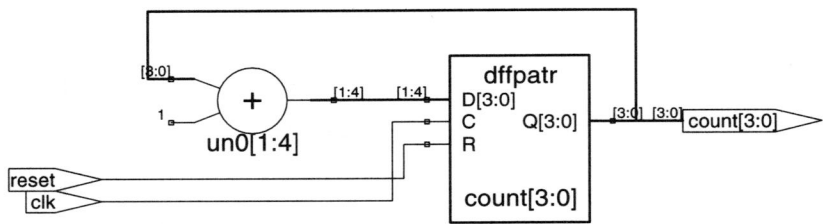

In this example, the 4-bit counter, *count(3 downto 0)* is reset to "1001" when the asynchronous reset is asserted. Note that the "1001" reset value is not visible in *Figure 2*, but would be apparent if you entered the *dffpatr* block.

Synchronous resets for counters work in a similar fashion to synchronous resets for flip-flops as seen in *Chapter 4*. The counter shown in *Listing 2*, with a synchronous reset is shown in *Listing 3*.

Listing 3: Counter with Synchronous Reset
```
-- Incorporates Errata 5.4

library ieee;
use ieee.std_logic_1164.all;
use ieee.numeric_std.all;

entity counter is port (
  clk: in std_logic;
  reset: in std_logic;
  count: out std_logic_vector(3 downto 0)
  );
end counter;
```

Chapter 5 - Counters and Simple Arithmetic Functions

```
architecture simple of counter is

signal countL: unsigned(3 downto 0);

begin

  increment: process (clk) begin
    if(clk'event and clk = '1') then
      if (reset = '1') then
        countL <= "0000";
      else
        countL <= countL + 1;
      end if;
    end if;
  end process;

  count <= std_logic_vector(countL);

end simple;
```
cntsrst.vhd

Load-able and Enable-able Counters

You often come across the need to load a counter, enable a counter or both. An example of a load-able counter is one where an up-counter is free-running, and at certain times gets loaded with a value and continues running. This is shown in *Listing 4*. Notice the use of the *to_unsigned* function to convert the *std_logic_vector* signal *data* to an *unsigned* type.

Listing 4: Counter with Synchronous Load

```
-- Incorporates Errata 5.4

library ieee;
use ieee.std_logic_1164.all;
use ieee.numeric_std.all;

entity counter is port (
  clk: in std_logic;
  reset: in std_logic;
  load: in std_logic;
  data: in std_logic_vector(3 downto 0);
  count: out std_logic_vector(3 downto 0)
  );
end counter;

architecture simple of counter is

signal countL: unsigned(3 downto 0);

begin

  increment: process (clk, reset) begin
    if (reset = '1') then
```

```
      countL <= "0000";
    elsif(clk'event and clk = '1') then
      if (load = '1') then
        countL <= to_unsigned(data);
      else
        countL <= countL + 1;
      end if;
    end if;
  end process;

  count <= std_logic_vector(countL);

end simple;
```

cntload.vhd

Another example of this would be a free-running down-counter that counts down from 11 to 0, and then resets itself to 11, and begins the sequence all over again. In this case, the load is of an internal value or constant. This would be written as shown in *Listing 5*.

Listing 5: Modulo 11 Down-Counter

```
-- Incorporates Errata 5.4

library ieee;
use ieee.std_logic_1164.all;
use ieee.numeric_std.all;

entity downCounter is port (
  clk: in std_logic;
  reset: in std_logic;
  count: out std_logic_vector(3 downto 0)
  );
end downCounter;

architecture simple of downCounter is

signal countL: unsigned(3 downto 0);
signal termCnt: std_logic;

begin

  decrement: process (clk, reset) begin
    if (reset = '1') then
      countL <= "1011";          -- Reset to 11
      termCnt <= '1';
    elsif(clk'event and clk = '1') then
      if (termCnt = '1') then
        countL <= "1011";        -- Count rolls over to 11
      else
        countL <= countL - 1;
      end if;

      if (countL = "0001") then  -- Terminal count decoded 1 cycle earlier
```

Chapter 5 - Counters and Simple Arithmetic Functions

```
          termCnt <= '1';
        else
          termCnt <= '0';
        end if;
      end if;
    end process;

    count <= std_logic_vector(countL);
  end simple;
```

dncnten.vhd

Notice that in *Listing 5*, we have decoded the terminal count one cycle before it is needed. In order to have the counter reload the value "1011" when the counter reaches zero, it is decoded one cycle earlier and registered. The technique of registering the terminal count is a useful one as it helps the counter run faster and more efficiently, especially in programmable logic design. The terminal count is effectively a "load" signal, and decoding one bit for the load is easier than decoding all the bits of the counter at the rollover count.

As we saw in *Chapter 4*, we might need to suspend the updating of a flip-flop, which in the case of a counter is also performed using an enable signal to control when the register is clocked. Just as with a flip-flop, it is better design practice to use a synchronous enable, rather than gate the clock. If we were to extend *Listing 4* to incorporate an enable, it would be written as shown in *Listing 6*.

Listing 6: Counter with Synchronous Load and Enable

```vhdl
-- Incorporates Errata 5.4

library ieee;
use ieee.std_logic_1164.all;
use ieee.numeric_std.all;

entity counter is port (
  clk: in std_logic;
  reset: in std_logic;
  load: in std_logic;
  enable: in std_logic;
  data: in std_logic_vector(3 downto 0);
  count: out std_logic_vector(3 downto 0)
  );
end counter;

architecture simple of counter is

signal countL: unsigned(3 downto 0);

begin
  increment: process (clk, reset) begin
    if (reset = '1') then
      countL <= "0000";
```

```
      elsif(clk'event and clk = '1') then
        if (load = '1') then
          countL <= to_unsigned(data);
        elsif (enable = '1') then
          countL <= countL + 1;
        end if;
      end if;
  end process;

  count <= std_logic_vector(countL);

end simple;
```

cntlden.vhd

If neither the *load* nor *enable* conditions are satisfied, the default behavior of the counter is that no change occurs on the outputs of the counter.

So far, we have implemented all our counters by adding an *integer* type to an *unsigned* type. We could certainly implement these counters by adding the constant "0001", which is in effect the same as adding 1. This can be seen in *Listing 7*.

Listing 7: Counter Adding a Vector Constant

```
-- Incorporates Errata 5.4

library ieee;
use ieee.std_logic_1164.all;
use ieee.numeric_std.all;

entity counter is port (
  clk: in std_logic;
  reset: in std_logic;
  count: out std_logic_vector(3 downto 0)
  );
end counter;

architecture simple of counter is

signal countL: unsigned(3 downto 0);

begin

  increment: process (clk, reset) begin
    if (reset = '1') then
      countL <= "1001";
    elsif(clk'event and clk = '1') then
      countL <= countL + "0001";
    end if;
  end process;

  count <= std_logic_vector(countL);

end simple;
```

count3.vhd

Chapter 5 - Counters and Simple Arithmetic Functions

The synthesis result is identical to that of *Listing 2* as shown in *Figure 2*.

There are two key issues illustrated by the examples shown in *Listing 2* and *Listing 7*:

- Operator overloading
- Vector direction during the arithmetic operation

While our examples have covered only the "+" operator, the above concepts apply universally to all functions in the standard libraries we are dealing with, and as such are important to understand.

Operator Overloading

VHDL has the native capability to handle operator overloading. Simply put, operator overloading allows different argument types for a given function. The VHDL tool resolves which of these functions to select based on the types of the inputs. This is transparent to the user as long as the function has been defined for those argument types.

Listing 2 and *Listing 7* illustrate operator overloading. *Listing 2* shows addition of *unsigned* and *integer* types in the statement

```
countL <= countL + 1;
```

and *Listing 7* shows addition of two *unsigned* types in the statement

```
countL <= countL + "0001";
```

Note that other than these lines, *Listing 2* and *Listing 7* are exactly the same. This is because the package we have used, *numeric_std*, overloads this operator for the two sets of arguments. A quick examination of the function prototypes taken from this *package* shows the two sets of arguments in question.

```
function "+" (L: UNSIGNED; R: NATURAL) return UNSIGNED;

function "+" (L, R: UNSIGNED) return UNSIGNED;
```

The first of these function prototypes adds an *unsigned* and a *natural*, or positive integer. The second adds two *unsigned* types. Hence, the *package* has defined the function "+" for two different sets of operand types, and the correct function has been automatically selected.

Vector Direction

It is important to understand what the input function assumes for vector direction. In other words, you need to know which are the most and least significant bits in a vector, especially when it comes time to use functions from standard packages.

Notice that the function prototypes do not assume an ascending range or descending range for their inputs. Consider the function prototypes from the *numeric_std* package:

```
function "+" (L: UNSIGNED; R: NATURAL) return UNSIGNED;
function "=" (L, R: UNSIGNED) return BOOLEAN;
function "<=" (L, R: UNSIGNED) return BOOLEAN;
```

All functions in the arithmetic packages assume that the left-most bit, in an *unsigned* vector passed to the function, represents the most-significant bit, and the right-most bit is the least-significant bit. So, in our counter example in *Listing 2*, we used

```
countL <= countL + 1;
```

where *count* and *countL* both have a descending range *unsigned(3 downto 0)*. In this case, the least-significant bit is *count(0)*, which toggles most often as the counter counts, and *count(3)* is the most-significant bit that toggles the least often as the counter counts.

Now let us consider rewriting the counter using an ascending range for *count*. This would be done as shown in *Listing 8*.

Listing 8: Counter with Ascending Range Vector

```
-- Incorporates Errata 5.4

library ieee;
use ieee.std_logic_1164.all;
use ieee.numeric_std.all;

entity counter is port (
  clk: in std_logic;
  reset: in std_logic;
  count: out std_logic_vector(0 to 3)
  );
end counter;

architecture simple of counter is

signal countL: unsigned(0 to 3);

begin

  increment: process (clk, reset) begin
    if reset = '1' then
      countL <= "1001";
    elsif(clk'event and clk = '1') then
      countL <= countL + 1;
    end if;
  end process;

  count <= std_logic_vector(countL);

end simple;
```

count2a.vhd

The resulting circuit is shown in *Figure 3*.

Figure 3: Counter Implemented Using an Ascending Range Vector

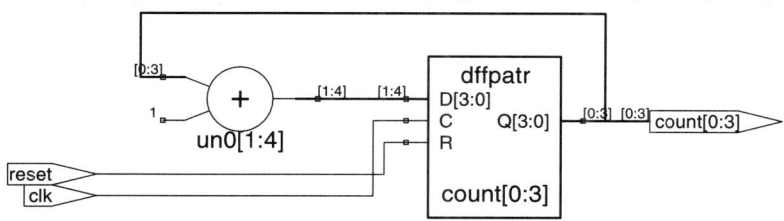

Notice that in this case, the most significant bit is now *count(0)*, since it is the left-most bit, and the least significant bit is *count(3)*, since it is the right-most bit as seen in the inputs to the adder module of *Figure 3*.

Thus, it is always the left-most bit that is the most significant bit, regardless of its label.

Functions Available in the Standard Packages

Most of the functions you will need can be found in the *numeric_std* package, which should be the package of choice, as it a standard package. For reference, the *std_logic_arith* and *std_logic_unsigned* packages are also shown. The functions in these packages can be broadly classified into five categories:

- Arithmetic operators
- Relation operators
- Shift operators
- Type conversion functions
- Others (signed and unsigned extension of vectors and absolute values)

A closer look will reveal that the functions are overloaded and exist in all packages. The choice of package to be used is determined by the type of the operands and the desired type of the result. *Table 1*, *Table 2*, *Table 3*, *Table 4* and *Table 5* summarize the various functions available, their operand types and the result types.

Table 1: Arithmetic Operators in the Standard *Packages*

Function	Operand Types	Result Types	Package
+	signed, unsigned, integer, natural	signed, unsigned	numeric_std
-	signed, unsigned, integer, natural	signed, unsigned	numeric_std
**	signed, unsigned, integer, natural	signed, unsigned	numeric_std
/	signed, unsigned, integer, natural	signed, unsigned	numeric_std
rem	signed, unsigned, integer, natural	signed, unsigned	numeric_std
mod	signed, unsigned, integer, natural	signed, unsigned	numeric_std
+	signed, unsigned, integer, std_logic	signed, unsigned, std_logic_vector	std_logic_arith
-	signed, unsigned, integer, std_logic	signed, unsigned, std_logic_vector	std_logic_arith
*	signed, unsigned	signed, unsigned, std_logic_vector	std_logic_arith
+	std_logic, integer, std_logic_vector	std_logic_vector	std_logic_unsigned
-	std_logic, integer, std_logic_vector	std_logic_vector	std_logic_unsigned
*	std_logic_vector	std_logic_vector	std_logic_unsigned

Example usage for arithmetic operators:

```
sum <= a + b;
```

Table 2: Relational Operators in the Standard *Packages*

Function	Operand Types	Result Types	Package
>	signed, unsigned, integer, natural	boolean	numeric_std
<	signed, unsigned, integer, natural	boolean	numeric_std
=	signed, unsigned, integer, natural	boolean	numeric_std
>=	signed, unsigned, integer, natural	boolean	numeric_std
<=	signed, unsigned, integer, natural	boolean	numeric_std
/=	signed, unsigned, integer, natural	boolean	numeric_std
>	signed, unsigned, integer	boolean	std_logic_arith
<	signed, unsigned, integer	boolean	std_logic_arith
=	signed, unsigned, integer	boolean	std_logic_arith
>=	signed, unsigned, integer	boolean	std_logic_arith
<=	signed, unsigned, integer	boolean	std_logic_arith
/=	signed, unsigned, integer	boolean	std_logic_arith
>	std_logic_vector, integer	boolean	std_logic_unsigned
<	std_logic_vector, integer	boolean	std_logic_unsigned
=	std_logic_vector, integer	boolean	std_logic_unsigned
>=	std_logic_vector, integer	boolean	std_logic_unsigned
<=	std_logic_vector, integer	boolean	std_logic_unsigned
/=	std_logic_vector, integer	boolean	std_logic_unsigned

Example usage for relational operators:

```
if (a >= b) the
  aGreaterEqualb <= '1'
else
  aGreaterEqualb <= '0';
end if;
```

It is important to note that relational operators have a lower precedence than logical operators. So, for example, let assume that *a*, *b*, and *c* are *Boolean* type signals in the assignment:

```
y <= '1' when (a = b and c) else '0';
```

In this assignment, the AND function is evaluated before the equality comparison.

Table 3: Shift Operators in the Standard *Packages*

Function	Operand Types	Result Types	Package
Shift_Left	signed, unsigned, natural	signed, unsigned	numeric_std
Shift_Right	signed, unsigned, natural	signed, unsigned	numeric_std
Rotate_Left	signed, unsigned, natural	signed, unsigned	numeric_std
Rotate_Right	signed, unsigned, natural	signed, unsigned	numeric_std
SHL	signed, unsigned, integer	signed, unsigned	std_logic_arith
SHR	signed, unsigned, integer	signed, unsigned	std_logic_arith
SHL	std_logic_vector, integer	std_logic_vector	std_logic_unsigned
SHR	std_logic_vector, integer	std_logic_vector	std_logic_unsigned

Example usage for shift operators:

```
shiftby2 <= Shift_Left(address, 2);  -- shift "address" left by 2 positions
```

Table 4: Type Conversion Functions in the Standard *Packages*

Function	Operand Types	Result Types	Package
to_integer	signed, unsigned	integer, natural	numeric_std
to_unsigned	natural, std_logic_vector	unsigned	numeric_std
to_signed	natural, std_logic_vector	signed	numeric_std
conv_integer	signed, unsigned, std_ulogic	integer	std_logic_arith
conv_signed	signed, unsigned, std_ulogic, integer	signed	std_logic_arith
conv_unsigned	signed, unsigned, std_ulogic, integer	unsigned	std_logic_arith
conv_std_logic_vector	signed, unsigned, std_ulogic, integer	std_logic_vector	std_logic_arith
conv_integer	std_logic_vector	integer	std_logic_unsigned

Example usage for type conversion functions:

```
dataInt <= to_integer(dataVector); -- converts an unsigned to an integer

dataVector <= to_stdlogicvector(dataInt, 32) -- converts the integer dataInt to
a 32-bit std_logic_vector (31 downto 0), where bit 31 is the MSB.
```

Table 5: Other Functions Available in the Standard *Packages*

Function	Operand Types	Result Types	Package
Resize	signed, unsigned, natural	signed, unsigned	numeric_std
std_match	signed, unsigned, std_logic_vector, std_ulogic_vector	boolean	numeric_std
EXT	std_logic_vector	std_logic_vector	std_logic_arith
SXT	std_logic_vector	std_logic_vector	std_logic_arith
ABS	signed	signed	std_logic_arith

```
longVec <= ext(shortVec, 32); -- unsigned extension of shortVec to a 32-bit
vector, from (31 downto 0), where 31 is the MSB.
```

The +, -, =, /=, >, <, <=, >= are arithmetic and relational operators that are familiar and easy to understand. For example, we saw how to implement a counter by adding two *unsigned* types, as shown in *Listing 7*.

Notice that in the increment statement, the addition constant "0001" is the same range as the signal that represents the counter, *count(3 downto 0)*.

```
countL <= countL + "0001";
```

This was done for good design practice and style. However, an arithmetic or relational operation performed on vector types (such as *unsigned* or *std_logic_vector* types) need not be of the same range when using the *numeric_std* package. The *package* will, in fact, zero-extend the smaller vector to the same size as the larger vector. So, in *Listing 7*, if we were to replace this line with

```
countL <= countL + "001";
```

where *countL* is four bits wide, and is added to a constant, "001", that is three bits wide, the "+"operation would still work. Similarly, *Listing 9* will work, even though the two operands being compared have different ranges.

Listing 9: Equality Compare with Operands of Different Ranges

```
-- includes Errata 5.2
library ieee;
use ieee.std_logic_1164.all;
use ieee.numeric_std.all; -- errata 5.2

entity compare is port (
   ina: in std_logic_vector (3 downto 0);
   inb: in std_logic_vector (2 downto 0);
   equal: out std_logic
   );
end compare;

architecture simple of compare is

begin

  equalProc: process (ina, inb) begin
    if (ina = inb ) then
      equal <= '1';
    else
      equal <= '0';
    end if;
  end process;

end simple;
```
equal1.vhd

In this case, the smaller vector is zero-extended as shown in *Figure 4*.

Chapter 5 - Counters and Simple Arithmetic Functions

Figure 4: Equality Compare of Two Unequal Length Vectors

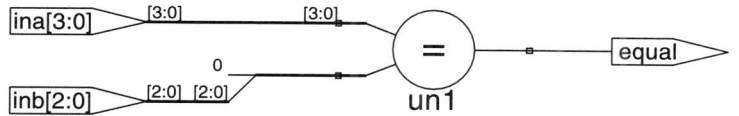

This emphasizes that it is important to know the direction of vectors required by the functions in the standard libraries.

Conversion functions further highlight the importance of ascertaining the vector direction required by standard libraries. For example, one way of resetting an unusually sized register is to use the *to_unsigned* function as in the example shown in *Listing 10*.

Listing 10: Use of *to_unsigned* Function

```
-- Incorporates Errata 5.4

library ieee;
use ieee.std_logic_1164.all;
use ieee.numeric_std.all;

entity counter is port (
  clk: in std_logic;
  reset: in std_logic;
  count: out std_logic_vector(9 downto 0)
  );
end counter;

architecture simple of counter is

signal countL: unsigned(9 downto 0);

begin

  increment: process (clk, reset) begin
    if reset = '1' then
      countL <= to_unsigned(0,10);
    elsif(clk'event and clk = '1') then
      countL <= countL + 1;
    end if;
  end process;

  count <= std_logic_vector(countL);

end simple;
```
cntconv.vhd

The *to_unsigned* function, as shown, takes two parameters, both of which are integers. The first parameter (0 in this case) is the integer that is to be converted to an *unsigned*. The second parameter is the length of the vector to be returned. In our example, the resultant vector has 10 bits. It is assumed that the left-most bit in the vector, *count(9)*, is the most significant bit in the conversion. This is particularly noticeable when the reset value of the counter is non-zero. Let us consider the example in *Listing 11*.

Listing 11: Example Using *to_unsigned* Showing Direction Significance

```
-- Incorporates Errata 5.4

library ieee;
use ieee.std_logic_1164.all;
use ieee.numeric_std.all;

entity counter is port (
  clk: in std_logic;
  reset: in std_logic;
  count: out std_logic_vector(0 to 9)
  );
end counter;

architecture simple of counter is

signal countL: unsigned(0 to 9);

begin

  increment: process (clk, reset) begin
    if reset = '1' then
      countL <= to_unsigned(3,10);
    elsif(clk'event and clk = '1') then
      countL <= countL + 1;
    end if;
  end process;

  count <= std_logic_vector(countL);

end simple;
```

cntconv2.vhd

In this example, the vector *countL(0 to 9)* is reset to 3. Note that the *to_unsigned* function will result in *count(8)* and *count(9)* being set to '1' on reset, while all other bits will be set to '0' on reset.

Adders and Subtractors

The *numeric_std* package make it easy to implement adders and subtractors. A four-bit adder would be implemented as shown in *Listing 12*, with the resulting circuit shown in *Figure 5*.

Chapter 5 - Counters and Simple Arithmetic Functions

Listing 12: Adder Using *Unsigned* Vectors

```
library ieee;
use ieee.std_logic_1164.all;
use ieee.numeric_std.all;

entity adder is port (
  a,b: in unsigned(3 downto 0);
  sum: out unsigned(3 downto 0)
  );
end adder;

architecture simple of adder is

begin

  sum <= a + b;

end simple;
```

adder.vhd

Figure 5: Full Adder Using *Unsigned* Vectors

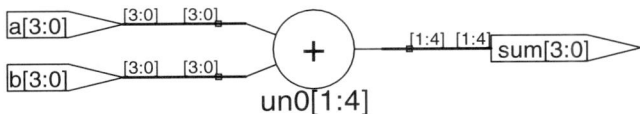

It is important to note, once again, that the "+" function returns a vector whose left-most bit is the most significant. So, in our example, *sum(3)* is the most-significant bit of the design.

Subtractions are equally easy, since you only have to substitute the "+" operator with the "-" operator.

Accumulators are adders where one of the input operands is the current sum, and they usually have a register at their outputs to store the current sum. An accumulator example is shown in *Listing 13*, with its resulting circuit shown in *Figure 6*.

Listing 13: Accumulator Example

```
-- Incorporates Errata 5.4

library ieee;
use ieee.std_logic_1164.all;
use ieee.numeric_std.all;

entity accumulator is port (
  a: in std_logic_vector(3 downto 0);
  clk, reset: in std_logic;
  accum: out std_logic_vector(3 downto 0)
  );
```

```
end accumulator;

architecture simple of accumulator is

signal accumL: unsigned(3 downto 0);

begin

  accumulate: process (clk, reset) begin
    if (reset = '1') then
      accumL <= "0000";
    elsif (clk'event and clk= '1') then
      accumL <= accumL + to_unsigned(a);
    end if;
  end process;

  accum <= std_logic_vector(accumL);

end simple;
```
accum.vhd

Figure 6: Accumulator Example

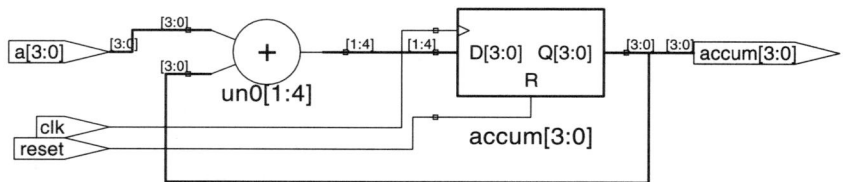

Adders and subtractors can occupy a large amount of a devices' resources, depending on the target device architecture and technology. So, it is a good idea to investigate the efficiency and performance of such circuits before committing to a particular device/technology combination.

Multiplication, Division and Exponentiation

Many synthesis tools can synthesize multipliers from a behavioral description as follows:

```
mult <= a * b;
```

where *a* and *b* can be of *signed*, *unsigned* or other types (as defined in the *numeric_std* package). However, you are probably better off instantiating these structurally if a library component is available. Multipliers are very large, and slow when they are implemented to perform single-cycle operations - which is exactly what an RTL synthesis tool would do. However, a pipelined multiply can dramatically improve the timing of a design. This is very system specific and depends on a whole series of issues including the target technology, which are not covered in this book. It is sufficient to say that if you need to implement a multiplier in your design, then seriously consider the design issues and trade-offs with this function and instantiate it structurally.

Most synthesis tools will only allow division by constants, and some restrict you further to a number that is an integer power of 2. This reduces the division to a simple right-shift operation, which is easily synthesized. A similar restriction is usually applied to the exponentiation functions, where the exponent must be a constant and power of 2. As these circuits are not often found in designs, implementing them using structural instantiation should not be difficult.

Design Example

Let us consider a simple design example to illustrate some of the issues that we have discussed so far. Our objective is to design a programmable pulse generator. When the pulse generator is enabled, it continues to emit a pulse. The delay between pulses, and the length or duration of each pulse is programmable, as shown in *Figure 7*.

Figure 7: Programmable Pulse Generator

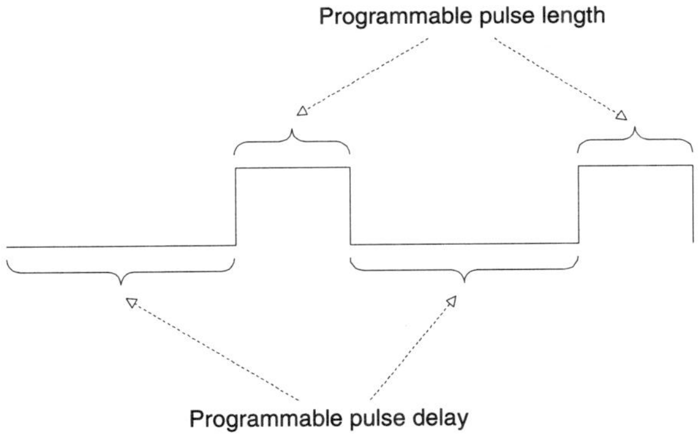

One possible implementation breaks up this design into the following blocks:
- Two holding registers for the pulse delay and pulse length values
- A load-able and enable-able down-counter that delays the initiation of the pulse
- A load-able and enable-able down-counter that generates the pulse width
- An identity comparator that indicates we have reached the pulse-delay limit
- An identity comparator that indicates we have reached the pulse-length limit
- An RS-type flip-flop circuit that controls the pulse output

The block diagram shown in *Figure 8* represents one possible solution for our design. For the sake of clarity, the clock and reset connections are not shown, but are global and noted on each block.

Figure 8: Programmable Pulse Generator Block Diagram

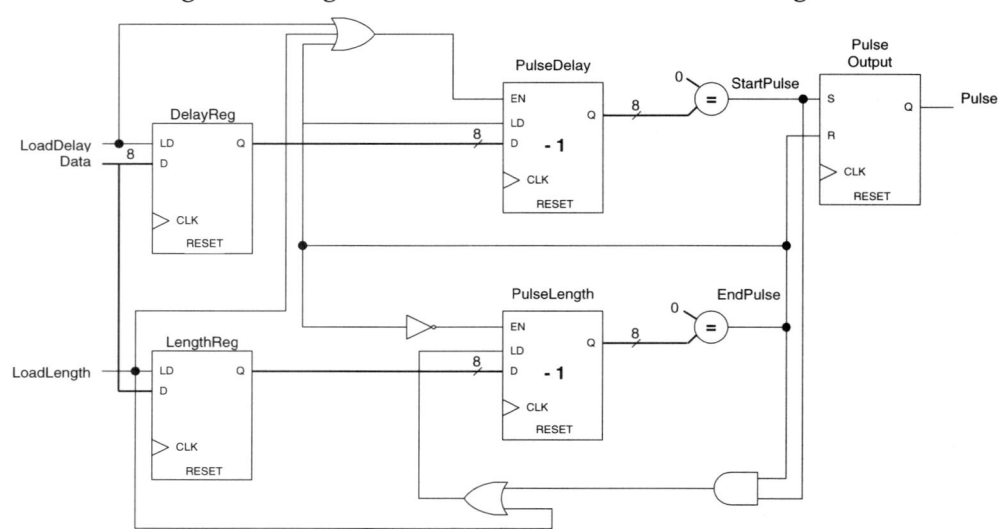

In this design, *data* is loaded into the two holding registers when *loadDelay* and *loadLength* are asserted. At the same time, the two counters, *pulseDelay* and *pulseLength* are also loaded. Note that the pulse-delay counter is also loaded if the *loadLength* signal is asserted. In other words, whenever a new delay value or length value is loaded, we start generating the waveform that relates to these values.

When the counter load signals are deasserted, the respective counters may start down-counting. The delay counter starts down-counting to zero. When it reaches zero, it asserts the *pulse* output, by driving the "set" signal of the RS-type flip-flop. The pulse length timer now begins down-counting and when it reaches zero, the *pulse* output is deasserted. At the same time, the delay counter circuit is reloaded with the delay value, and the delay counter begins down-counting again. The process repeats, so that the pulse waveform is repeated until a new value is loaded into either the pulse-length or pulse-delay registers.

We can implement this block diagram as shown in *Listing 14*.

Listing 14: Implementation of a Programmable Pulse Generator

```
-- Incorporates Errata 5.1 and 5.4

library ieee;
use ieee.std_logic_1164.all;
use ieee.numeric_std.all;

entity progPulse is port (
  clk, reset: in std_logic;
  loadLength,loadDelay: in std_logic;
```

Chapter 5 - Counters and Simple Arithmetic Functions

```vhdl
    data: in std_logic_vector(7 downto 0);
    pulse: out std_logic
    );
end progPulse;

architecture rtl of progPulse is

signal delayCnt, pulseCnt: unsigned(7 downto 0);
signal delayCntVal, pulseCntVal: unsigned(7 downto 0);
signal startPulse, endPulse: std_logic;

begin

  delayReg: process (clk, reset) begin
    if reset = '1' then
      delayCntVal <= "11111111";
    elsif clk'event and clk = '1' then
      if loadDelay = '1' then
        delayCntVal <= unsigned(data);
      end if;
    end if;
  end process;

  lengthReg: process (clk, reset) begin
    if reset = '1' then
      pulseCntVal <= "11111111";
    elsif clk'event and clk = '1' then
      if loadLength = '1' then -- changed loadLength to loadDelay (Errata 5.1)
        pulseCntVal <= unsigned(data);
      end if;
    end if;
  end process;

  pulseDelay: process (clk, reset) begin
    if (reset = '1') then
      delayCnt <= "11111111";
    elsif(clk'event and clk = '1') then
      if (loadDelay = '1' or loadLength = '1' or endPulse = '1')
          then -- changed startPulse to endPulse (Errata 5.1)
        delayCnt <= delayCntVal;
      elsif endPulse = '1' then
        delayCnt <= delayCnt - 1;
      end if;
    end if;
  end process;

  startPulse <= '1' when delayCnt = "00000000" else '0';

  pulseLength: process (clk, reset) begin
    if (reset = '1') then
      pulseCnt <= "11111111";
    elsif (clk'event and clk = '1') then
```

```
        if (loadLength = '1') then
          pulseCnt <= pulseCntVal;
        elsif (startPulse = '1' and endPulse = '1') then
          pulseCnt <= pulseCntVal;
        elsif (endPulse = '1') then
          pulseCnt <= pulseCnt;
        else
          pulseCnt <= pulseCnt - 1;
        end if;
      end if;
  end process;

  endPulse <= '1' when pulseCnt = "00000000" else '0';

  pulseOutput: process (clk, reset) begin
      if (reset = '1') then
        pulse <= '0';
      elsif (clk'event and clk = '1') then
        if (startPulse = '1') then
          pulse <= '1';
        elsif (endPulse = '1') then
          pulse <= '0';
        end if;
      end if;
  end process;

end rtl;
```

design.vhd

This synthesizes to the circuit shown in *Figure 9*.

Chapter 5 - Counters and Simple Arithmetic Functions

Figure 9: Programmable Pulse Generator Circuit

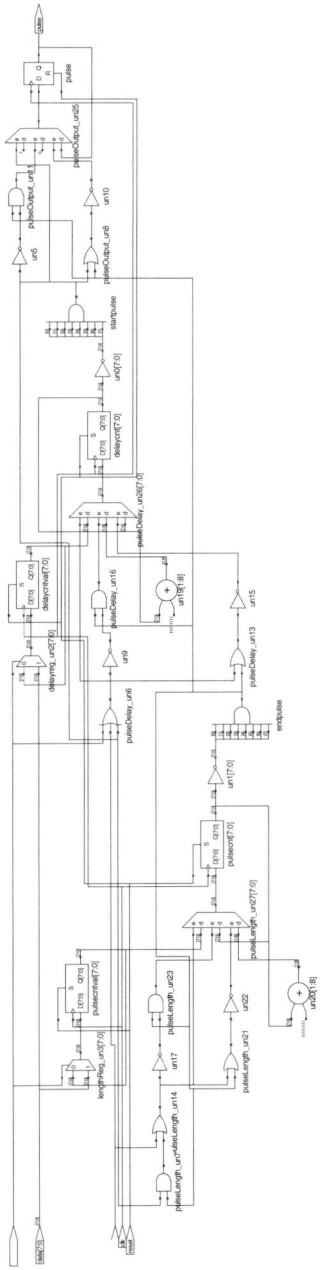

6
Finite State Machines

As your designs start becoming more complex you will inevitably design finite state machines (FSMs), commonly referred to as "state machines". Complex designs usually require logic that sequences through a set of control signals, that in turn cause other logic to perform some algorithm or function. In synchronous designs, the Finite State Machine approach is generally regarded as the best way of expressing such circuits.

Software engineers have used flow charts to describe how algorithms work. While similar to this approach, state machines differ from flow charts in one key respect: the concept of time intervals, almost always based on a synchronous clock. A flow chart only describes the sequence of events as there is no implied time interval. In fact, the very name "state machine" implies that the circuit goes through a series of "states". In each state, the value of the previous state (or states) is known. Using this information, along with various input conditions, the state machine can determine the next state, and transition to it at fixed time intervals.

While state machine design is an art, this chapter presents a style that can be easily and reliably synthesized, and perhaps more importantly, modularly written for maintenance and modification. This style deals with state machines that are triggered by a single clock and develops FSMs from concept to decomposition followed by implementation. We will begin with a discussion of the basic partitioning and structure, followed by a step-by-step implementation of a design that incorporates an FSM. The hardware implications of FSM coding style will be analyzed in *Chapter 10*.

Typical State Machine Blocks

State machines can be divided into three blocks:

- Next state conditioning logic
- Current state vector register
- Output conditioning logic

The next state and output conditioning logic blocks are combinational, while the current state register retains state information, and propagates next state information on each rising clock edge. The block diagram for our state machine is shown in *Figure 1*.

Figure 1: Typical State Machine Structure

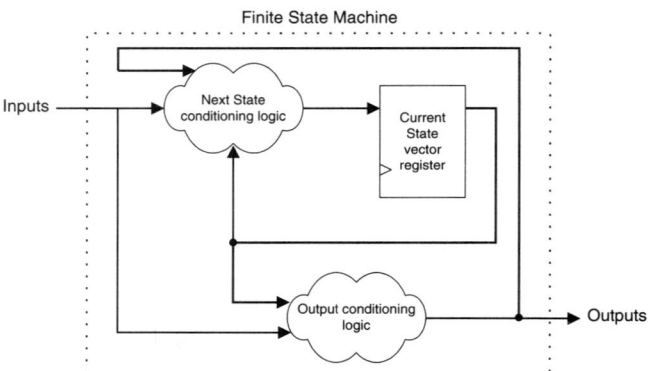

We will use this natural partitioning when describing our state machine in VHDL. Our design will be partitioned into three processes, one for each of the blocks shown in *Figure 1*.

To illustrate the steps in state machine design, let us consider the design of a state machine whose functionality has been clearly defined - the PCI Target Sequencer Machine, as defined in *Appendix B* of the *PCI 2.1 Specification*. For the purpose of simplicity, it is assumed that the Target Lock Machine (referred to in the *PCI Specification* as well) is not required, and no optimizations or application specific modifications are made to the design shown in *Appendix B* of the *PCI Specification*. We also assume that we do not have to deal with a fast decode target. In addition, parity and parity error have not been addressed in this design.

Important Note: It is not required that you be familiar with the *PCI 2.1 Specification*. However, be aware of the disclaimer in *PCI Specification*. This specifically states that *Appendix B* is to help illustrate the PCI protocol, and should not be used directly to implement the state machines. As such, this implementation should not be used directly in any PCI design.

State Machine Inputs and Outputs

Clearly the first step in state machine design is the same as with other logic blocks: determination of the inputs and outputs, as shown in *Figure 2*.

Chapter 6 - Finite State Machines

Figure 2: PCI Target State Machine Inputs and Outputs

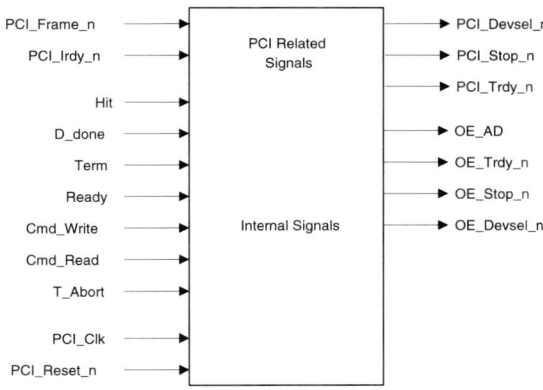

Our state machine has some signals that are connected directly to a PCI bus. These are shown with a "PCI" prefix on the top of the diagram in Figure 2. There are other signals that are internal to our PCI device, which are not visible on the PCI bus, and are as such shown without the "PCI" prefix. This input/output block diagram almost directly translates to the entity declaration of the state machine as shown in *Listing 1*.

Listing 1: Entity Declaration for PCI Target State Machine

```
entity pci_target is port (
  PCI_Frame_n: in std_logic;-- PCI Frame#
  PCI_Irdy_n: in std_logic;-- PCI Irdy#
  Hit: in std_logic;-- Hit on address decode
  D_Done: in std_logic;-- Device decode complete
  Term: in std_logic;-- Terminate transaction
  Ready: in std_logic;-- Ready to transfer data
  Cmd_Write: in std_logic;-- Command is Write
  Cmd_Read: in std_logic;-- Command is Read
  T_Abort: in std_logic;-- Target error  - abort transaction
  PCI_Clk: in std_logic;-- PCI Clock
  PCI_Reset_n: in std_logic;-- PCI Reset#

  PCI_Devsel_n: out std_logic;-- PCI Devsel#
  PCI_Stop_n: out std_logic;-- PCI Stop#
  PCI_Trdy_n: out std_logic;-- PCI Trdy#
  OE_AD: out std_logic;-- PCI AD bus enable
  OE_Trdy_n: out std_logic;-- PCI Trdy# enable
  OE_Stop_n: out std_logic;-- PCI Stop# enable
  OE_Devsel_n: out std_logic-- PCI Devsel# enable

  );
end pci_target;
```

Developing the State Diagram

The next step is to develop the state diagram, or "bubble diagram". This is the core of the state machine. It indicates all the possible state transitions, as well as the conditions under which we will transfer from one state to another. The state transition diagram for our state machine is shown in *Figure 3*. In this diagram, we have assigned a name to each state. We have also assigned a name to each transition condition (C1, C2... etc.). This has been done for the purpose of clarity - you would typically annotate the transition condition on the diagram itself.

Figure 3: PCI Target State Machine State Transition Diagram

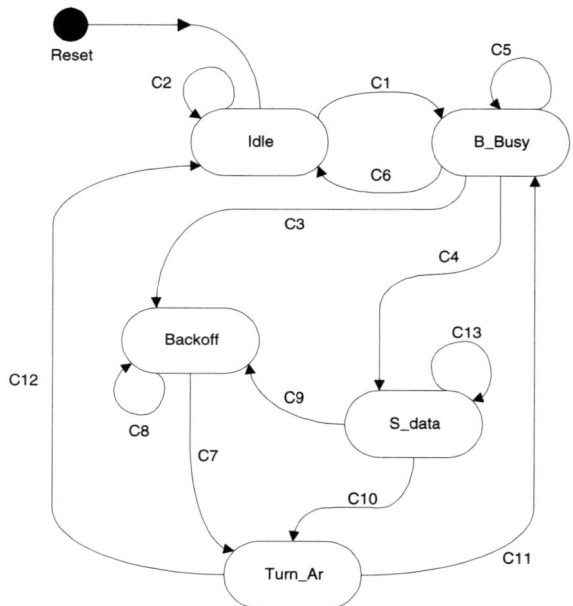

The equation for each transition condition is shown in *Table 1*, along with its transition number as shown in *Figure 3*. The transition equations for each state are shown in priority order, which is significant for the state machine implementation.

Table 1: PCI Target State Machine State Transitions

Current State	Condition	Equation	Next State
Idle, Turn_Ar	C1, C11	PCI_Frame_n	Idle
	C2, C12	!PCI_Frame_n * !Hit then	B_Busy
B_Busy	C6	(PCI_Frame_n * D_Done) + (PCI_Frame_n * !D_Done * !PCI_Devsel_n)	Idle
	C4	(!PCI_Frame_n + !PCI_Trdy_n) * Hit * (!Term + Term * Ready)	S_Data
	C3	(!PCI_Frame_n + !PCI_Irdy_n) * Hit * (Term * !Ready)	Backoff
	C5	else	B_Busy
S_Data	C9	!PCI_Frame_n * !PCI_Stop_n * (PCI_Trdy_n + !PCI_Irdy_n)	Backoff
	C10	PCI_Frame_n * (!PCI_Trdy + !PCI_Stop_n)	Turn_Ar
	C13	else	S_Data
Backoff	C7	PCI_Frame_n	Turn_Ar
	C8	else	Backoff

We are now ready to write VHDL for our state machine. Recall that in *Figure 1*, we saw how a state machine can be naturally partitioned into three blocks. We will use this natural partitioning to write three separate processes in VHDL, each of which will perform one of the three functions as follows:

- Next state conditioning logic (*nxtStProc*)
- Current state vector register (*curtStProc*)
- Output conditioning logic (*outConProc*)

However, just before doing this, we must create the signals and types necessary for us to describe the state machine and the outputs.

Creating a Type for Your States

The state transition diagram indicates all the possible states in the state machine. The first step in coding the architecture of the state machine is to create a type that represents the state values that can be taken by the state machine. VHDL allows you to do this in an abstract fashion, using *enumerated* types. Simply put, an enumerated type allows you to enumerate, or define the values that a particular signal can take. Since our state machine can take the values *Idle*, *B_Busy*, *Backoff*, *S_Data* and *Turn_Ar*, our type can be declared in VHDL as follows:

```
type targetFsmType is (Idle, B_Busy, Backoff, S_Data, Turn_Ar);
```

As signals are the "wires" in our design, we need to declare two signals: one that represents the current state and another that represents the next state for our state machine. This is done by assigning the type for these two signals to the type we just created, as follows:

```
signal currState, nextState: targetFsmType;
```

The type and signal declarations are placed within the architecture, as we will see later in this chapter. State encoding, and its impact on FSMs will be discussed in *Chapter 10*.

Coding the Next State Conditioning Logic

The next state conditioning logic follows the equations in *Table 1*. When coding it in VHDL, we will use a *process* in which the *case* statement is used to select the next state, based on the current state value and the input conditions. Hence, our *case* selects between one of the five possible states, and in each state, an *if...then* statement determines the next state. This is shown in *Listing 2*.

Listing 2: Next State Conditioning Logic for the PCI Target State Machine

```
nxtStProc: process (currState, PCI_Frame_n, Hit, D_Done, PCI_Irdy_n,
                    LPCI_Trdy_n, LPCI_Devsel_n, LPCI_Stop_n, Term, Ready) begin
  case currState is
    when Idle   =>
      if (PCI_Frame_n = '0' and Hit = '0') then
        nextState <= B_Busy;
      else
        nextState <= Idle;
      end if;

    when B_Busy =>
      if (PCI_Frame_n ='1' and D_Done = '1') or
      (PCI_Frame_n = '1' and D_Done = '0' and LPCI_Devsel_n = '0') then
        nextState <= Idle;
      elsif (PCI_Frame_n = '0' or PCI_Irdy_n = '0') and Hit = '1' and
      (Term = '0' or (Term = '1' and Ready = '1') ) then
        nextState <= S_Data;
      elsif (PCI_Frame_n = '0' or PCI_Irdy_n = '0') and Hit = '1' and
      (Term = '1' and Ready = '0') then
        nextState <= Backoff;
      else
        nextState <= B_Busy;
      end if;

    when S_Data =>
      if PCI_Frame_n = '0' and LPCI_Stop_n = '0' and (LPCI_Trdy_n = '1' or
          PCI_Irdy_n = '0') then
        nextState <= Backoff;
      elsif PCI_Frame_n = '1' and (LPCI_Trdy_n = '0' or LPCI_Stop_n = '0') then
        nextState <= Turn_Ar;
      else
        nextState <= S_Data;
      end if;
```

```
      when Backoff =>
        if PCI_Frame_n = '1' then
          nextState <= Turn_Ar;
        else
          nextState <= Backoff;
        end if;

      when Turn_Ar   =>
        if (PCI_Frame_n = '0' and Hit = '0') then
          nextState <= B_Busy;
        else
          nextState <= Idle;
        end if;

      when others =>
        null;

    end case;

  end process nxtStProc;
```

Note that the next state process is sensitive to the current state vector, *currState*, and all the inputs of the state machine module.

Registering the Current State Vector

The register for the current state vector is generated with the technique developed in *Chapter 4* for a simple D-type flip-flop with asynchronous reset, as shown in *Listing 3*. Notice that the asynchronous reset places the state machine into a known *(Idle)* state on reset. This is important for two reasons. First, all synchronous logic (including state machines) should be in a known state on system start-up, which is normally just after the system reset has occurred. Second, the target technology may or may not place registers into a default state on start-up. If it does not, then the state machine may not power-up into a known or desired state. Hence, the necessity to reset the state machine after power-up.

Listing 3: Current State Vector Register for PCI Target State Machine

```
curStProc: process (PCI_Clk, PCI_Reset_n) begin
  if (PCI_Reset_n = '0') then
    currState <= Idle;
  elsif (PCI_Clk'event and PCI_Clk = '1') then
    currState <= nextState;
  end if;
end process curStProc;
```

Coding the Output Conditioning Logic

Just like the next state conditioning logic process, the output conditioning logic is also coded in a single process. This process too is sensitive to the current state vector, *currState*, and all the inputs of the state machine module, as shown in *Listing 4*.

Listing 4: Output Conditioning Logic Process for PCI Target State Machine

```
outConProc: process (currState, Ready, T_Abort, Cmd_Write,
    Cmd_Read, T_Abort, Term) begin
  case currState is
    when S_Data =>
      if (Cmd_Read = '1') then
        OE_AD <= '1';
         else
        OE_AD <= '0';
      end if;

      if (Ready = '1' and T_Abort = '0' and (Cmd_Write = '1' or
         Cmd_Read = '1')) then
        LPCI_Trdy_n <= '0';
      else
        LPCI_Trdy_n <= '1';
      end if;

      if (T_Abort = '1' or Term = '1') and (Cmd_Write = '1' or
         Cmd_Read = '1')  then
        LPCI_Stop_n <= '0';
      else
        LPCI_Stop_n <= '1';
      end if;

      if (T_Abort = '0') then
        LPCI_Devsel_n <= '0';
      else
        LPCI_Devsel_n <= '1';
      end if;

      OE_Trdy_n <= '1';
      OE_Stop_n <= '1';
      OE_Devsel_n <= '1';

    when Backoff =>
      if (Cmd_Read = '1') then
        OE_AD <= '1';
         else
        OE_AD <= '0';
      end if;

      LPCI_Stop_n <= '0';
```

```vhdl
            OE_Trdy_n <= '1';
            OE_Stop_n <= '1';
            OE_Devsel_n <= '1';

            if (T_Abort = '0') then
              LPCI_Devsel_n <= '0';
            else
              LPCI_Devsel_n <= '1';
            end if;

          when Turn_Ar =>

            OE_Trdy_n <= '1';
            OE_Stop_n <= '1';
            OE_Devsel_n <= '1';

    when others =>

            OE_Trdy_n <= '0';
            OE_Stop_n <= '0';
            OE_Devsel_n <= '0';
OE_AD <= '0';
            LPCI_Trdy_n <= '1';
            LPCI_Stop_n <= '1';
            LPCI_Devsel_n <= '1';

      end case;

    end process outConProc;
```

Note that the *when others* clause covers output conditioning for the *Idle* and *B_Busy* states. Output generation will be discussed in greater detail in *Chapter 10*.

The Complete PCI Target State Machine Design

Now that we have shown the various code fragments, we can stitch these together to form the complete design, as shown in *Listing 5*. Notice that the PCI-related outputs, *PCI_Trdy_n*, *PCI_Stop_n* and *PCI_Devsel_n*, are actually generated using signals local to the architecture, which, in turn, are then assigned to the port output. This is because they are not only outputs, but are also read within the architecture.

Listing 5: PCI Target State Machine

```vhdl
library IEEE;
use IEEE.std_logic_1164.all;

entity pci_target is port (
  PCI_Frame_n: in std_logic;      -- PCI Frame#
  PCI_Irdy_n: in std_logic;       -- PCI Irdy#
  Hit: in std_logic;              -- Hit on address decode
```

```vhdl
    D_Done: in std_logic;              -- Device decode complete
    Term: in std_logic;                -- Terminate transaction
    Ready: in std_logic;               -- Ready to transfer data
    Cmd_Write: in std_logic;           -- Command is Write
    Cmd_Read: in std_logic;            -- Command is Read
    T_Abort: in std_logic;             -- Target error  - abort transaction
    PCI_Clk: in std_logic;             -- PCI Clock
    PCI_Reset_n: in std_logic;         -- PCI Reset#

    PCI_Devsel_n: out std_logic;       -- PCI Devsel#
    PCI_Stop_n: out std_logic;         -- PCI Stop#
    PCI_Trdy_n: out std_logic;         -- PCI Trdy#
    OE_AD: out std_logic;              -- PCI AD bus enable
    OE_Trdy_n: out std_logic;          -- PCI Trdy# enable
    OE_Stop_n: out std_logic;          -- PCI Stop# enable
    OE_Devsel_n: out std_logic         -- PCI Devsel# enable
    );
end pci_target;

architecture fsm of pci_target is

signal LPCI_Devsel_n, LPCI_Trdy_n, LPCI_Stop_n: std_logic;

type targetFsmType is (Idle, B_Busy, Backoff, S_Data, Turn_Ar);

signal currState, nextState: targetFsmType;

begin

-- Process to generate next state logic

 nxtStProc: process (currState, PCI_Frame_n, Hit, D_Done, PCI_Irdy_n,
                    LPCI_Trdy_n, LPCI Devsel_n, LPCI_Stop_n, Term, Ready) begin
    case currState is
      when Idle  =>
        if (PCI_Frame_n = '0' and Hit = '0') then
          nextState <= B_Busy;
        else
          nextState <= Idle;
        end if;

      when B_Busy =>
        if (PCI_Frame_n ='1' and D_Done = '1') or
        (PCI_Frame_n = '1' and D_Done = '0' and LPCI_Devsel_n = '0') then
          nextState <= Idle;
        elsif (PCI_Frame_n = '0' or PCI_Irdy_n = '0') and Hit = '1' and
       (Term = '0' or (Term = '1' and Ready = '1') ) then
           nextState <= S_Data;
        elsif (PCI_Frame_n = '0' or PCI_Irdy_n = '0') and Hit = '1' and
       (Term = '1' and Ready = '0') then
           nextState <= Backoff;
        else
```

```vhdl
          nextState <= B_Busy;
        end if;

    when S_Data =>
      if PCI_Frame_n = '0' and LPCI_Stop_n = '0' and (LPCI_Trdy_n = '1' or
         PCI_Irdy_n = '0') then
        nextState <= Backoff;
      elsif PCI_Frame_n = '1' and (LPCI_Trdy_n = '0' or LPCI_Stop_n = '0') then
        nextState <= Turn_Ar;
      else
        nextState <= S_Data;
      end if;


    when Backoff =>
      if PCI_Frame_n = '1' then
        nextState <= Turn_Ar;
      else
        nextState <= Backoff;
      end if;

    when Turn_Ar  =>
      if (PCI_Frame_n = '0' and Hit = '0') then
        nextState <= B_Busy;
      else
        nextState <= Idle;
      end if;

    when others =>
      null;

    end case;

  end process nxtStProc;


-- Process to register the current state

  curStProc: process (PCI_Clk, PCI_Reset_n) begin
    if (PCI_Reset_n = '0') then
      currState <= Idle;
    elsif (PCI_Clk'event and PCI_Clk = '1') then
      currState <= nextState;
    end if;
  end process curStProc;


-- Process to generate outputs

  outConProc: process (currState, Ready, T_Abort, Cmd_Write,
                       Cmd_Read, T_Abort, Term) begin
    case currState is
```

```vhdl
      when S_Data =>
        if (Cmd_Read = '1') then
          OE_AD <= '1';
        else
          OE_AD <= '0';
        end if;

        if (Ready = '1' and T_Abort = '0' and (Cmd_Write = '1' or
            Cmd_Read = '1')) then
          LPCI_Trdy_n <= '0';
        else
          LPCI_Trdy_n <= '1';
        end if;

        if (T_Abort = '1' or Term = '1') and (Cmd_Write = '1' or
            Cmd_Read = '1') then
          LPCI_Stop_n <= '0';
        else
          LPCI_Stop_n <= '1';
        end if;

        if (T_Abort = '0') then
          LPCI_Devsel_n <= '0';
        else
          LPCI_Devsel_n <= '1';
        end if;

        OE_Trdy_n <= '1';
        OE_Stop_n <= '1';
        OE_Devsel_n <= '1';

      when Backoff =>
        if (Cmd_Read = '1') then
          OE_AD <= '1';
        else
          OE_AD <= '0';
        end if;

        LPCI_Stop_n <= '0';

        OE_Trdy_n <= '1';
        OE_Stop_n <= '1';
        OE_Devsel_n <= '1';

        if (T_Abort = '0') then
          LPCI_Devsel_n <= '0';
        else
          LPCI_Devsel_n <= '1';
        end if;

      when Turn_Ar =>
```

Chapter 6 - Finite State Machines

```
                OE_Trdy_n <= '1';
                OE_Stop_n <= '1';
                OE_Devsel_n <= '1';

            when others =>
                OE_Trdy_n <= '0';
                OE_Stop_n <= '0';
                OE_Devsel_n <= '0';
                OE_AD <= '0';
                LPCI_Trdy_n <= '1';
                LPCI_Stop_n <= '1';
                LPCI_Devsel_n <= '1';

        end case;

    end process outConProc;

    -- Assign output ports

    PCI_Devsel_n <= LPCI_Devsel_n;
    PCI_Trdy_n <= LPCI_Trdy_n;
    PCI_Stop_n <= LPCI_Stop_n;

end fsm;
```

target.vhd

There is an important point to note about *Listing 5*. This implementation, while logically correct, may not generate the most efficient results. This has to do with the fact that several signals (such as *LPCI_Devsel_n*) have not been specified in each *when* condition. The reasons for this (and the related solution) will be discussed in *Chapter 8*.

State Machines as Part of Your System Design

You will rarely design a state machine in isolation from the rest of your system. In fact, much of the "art" of logic design lies in the separation of the design into control elements and datapath elements, which can both be subsequently implemented. To illustrate the procedures described using the previous state machine example as part of an overall system design, let us redesign the programmable pulse generator example from *Chapter 5*, step-by-step, to incorporate a state machine.

Step 1: Determine the Datapath

First we need to determine the datapath, which is similar to the implementation in *Chapter 5*. If you look carefully at this design, you will notice that the datapath element (in this case the counter) can be used during both the pulse delay phase and the pulse generation phase, since these are non-overlapping. In other words, we can eliminate one of our counters and replace it (along with its associated conditioning logic) with a state machine that controls the counter, and use it as a countdown timer as shown in *Figure 4*. Thus the state machine lends itself well for use in this application. The two registers that hold the pulse-delay and pulse-length values still exist as before. However, both of their outputs go to the state machine, which controls the down-counter.

Figure 4: Block Diagram of Programmable Pulse Generator Using a State Machine

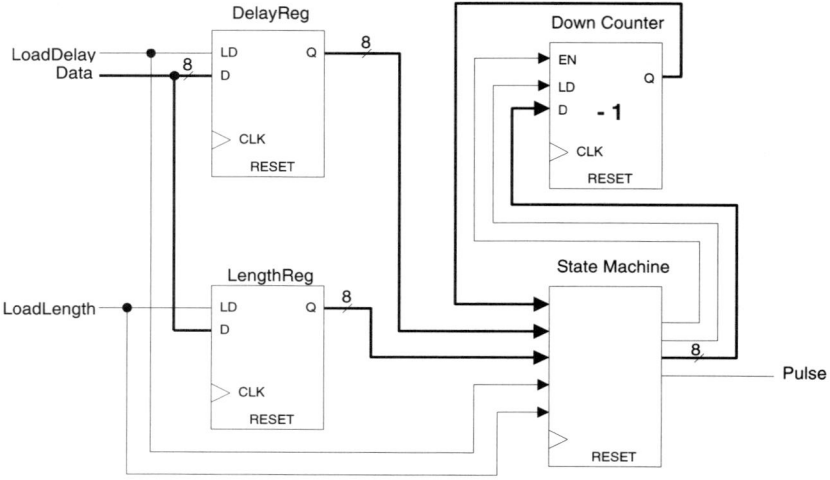

Step 2: Determine the Control Algorithm

Once we have separated the datapath and control path, we need to determine the control algorithm. In our design, the state machine starts by loading the down-counter with the value from the delay register. It then waits until this register has counted down to zero, at which point it loads the counter with the pulse-length value, asserting the *pulse* output at the same time. When the counter reaches zero (i.e. the pulse length has expired), the state machine loads the delay value once again and repeats the process. This is functionally equivalent to the design we saw in *Chapter 5*. The state diagram for our control state machine would be as shown in *Figure 5*. Also shown are the transition conditions for each state.

Chapter 6 - Finite State Machines

Figure 5: Programmable Pulse Generator Using a State Machine

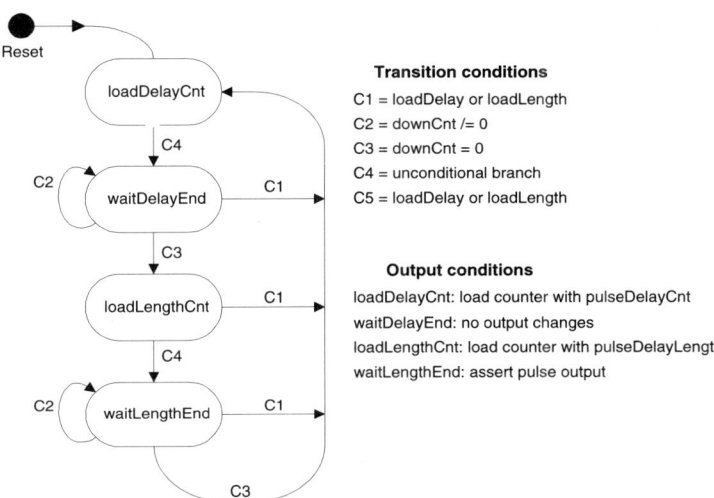

Step 3: Defining the Black Box

The next step in implementing our state machine is exactly as before: determining the inputs and outputs for our state machine "black box", as shown in *Figure 6*. The entity declaration that corresponds to this black box is shown in *Listing 6*.

Figure 6: Programmable Pulse Generator State Machine Inputs and Output

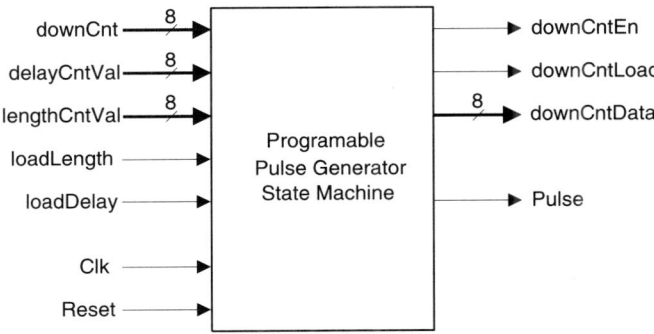

Listing 6: Programmable Pulse Generator State Machine Entity Declaration

```
entity progPulseFsm is port (
  downCnt: in std_logic_vector(7 downto 0);
  delayCntVal: in std_logic_vector(7 downto 0);
  lengthCntVal: in std_logic_vector(7 downto 0);
  loadLength: in std_logic;
  loadDelay: in std_logic;
  clk: in std_logic;
  reset: in std_logic;

  downCntEn: out std_logic;
  downCntLd: out std_logic;
  downtCntData: out std_logic_vector(7 downto 0);

  pulse: out std_logic
  );
end progPulseFsm;
```

Step 4: Describe the States Using Enumerated Types

Just as we did earlier, we define our state type based on names. In addition, we declare the current state and next state vectors that are of this type, as follows.

```
type progPulseFsmType is (loadDelayCnt, waitDelayEnd, loadLengthCnt,
                          waitLengthEnd);
signal currState, nextState: progPulseFsmType;
```

Both these declarations are placed in the architecture section of the design.

Step 5: Code the Next State Conditioning Logic

The next step is to code the next state conditioning logic. This is done using the case statement, as shown in *Listing 7*.

Listing 7: Programmable Pulse Generator State Machine - Next State Conditioning Logic

```
nextStProc: process (currState, downCnt, loadDelay, loadLength) begin
    case currState is
      when loadDelayCnt =>
        nextState <= waitDelayEnd;

      when waitDelayEnd =>
        if (loadDelay = '1' or loadLength = '1') then
          nextState <= loadDelayCnt;
        elsif (downCnt = 0) then
          nextState <= loadLengthCnt;
        else
          nextState <= waitDelayEnd;
        end if;

      when loadLengthCnt =>
```

Chapter 6 - Finite State Machines

```
            if (loadDelay = '1' or loadLength = '1') then
              nextState <= loadDelayCnt;
            else
              nextState <= waitLengthEnd;
            end if;

          when waitLengthEnd =>
            if (loadDelay = '1' or loadLength = '1') then
              nextState <= loadDelayCnt;
            elsif (downCnt = 0) then
              nextState <= loadDelayCnt;
            else
              nextState <= waitDelayEnd;
            end if;

          when others =>
            null;

      end case;

    end process nextStProc;
```

Step 6: Code the Current State Register
The current state register is placed in a separate process, as shown in *Listing 8*.

Listing 8: Programmable Pulse Generator State Machine - Current State Register

```
    currStProc: process (clk, reset) begin
      if (reset = '1') then
        currState <= loadDelayCnt;
      elsif (clk'event and clk = '1') then
        currState <= nextState;
      end if;
    end process currStProc;
```

Step 7: Code the Output Conditioning Logic
Finally, we use a separate process for the output conditioning logic, as shown in *Listing 9*.

Listing 9: Programmable Pulse Generator State Machine - Output Conditioning Logic

```
    outConProc: process (currState, delayCntVal, lengthCntVal) begin
        case currState is
          when loadDelayCnt =>
            downtCntEn <= '0';
            downtCntLd <= '1';
            downtCntData <= delayCntVal;
            pulse <= '0';

          when waitDelayEnd =>
            downtCntEn <= '1';
            downtCntLd <= '0';
```

```
          downtCntData <= delayCntVal;
          pulse <= '0';

        when loadLengthCnt =>
          downtCntEn <= '0';
          downtCntLd <= '1';
          downtCntData <= lengthCntVal;
          pulse <= '1';

        when waitLengthEnd =>
          downtCntEn <= '1';
          downtCntLd <= '0';
          downtCntData <= lengthCntVal;
          pulse <= '1';

        when others =>
          downtCntEn <= '0';
          downtCntLd <= '1';
          downtCntData <= delayCntVal;
          pulse <= '0';

      end case;
   end process outConProc;
```

Step 8: Integrate with the Datapath

The final step for our design is to integrate the state machine with the datapath elements. In our case, each datapath element has its own process. The two delay count holding registers appear just as they did before. Only now we have to integrate a down counter and state machine. The complete listing for our design is shown in *Listing 10*.

Listing 10: Programmable Pulse Generator Using a State Machine

```
library ieee;
use ieee.std_logic_1164.all;
use ieee.numeric_std.all;

entity progPulse is port (
  clk, reset: in std_logic;
  loadLength,loadDelay: in std_logic;
  data: in std_logic_vector(7 downto 0);
  pulse: out std_logic
  );
end progPulse;

architecture rtl of progPulse is

signal downCnt, downCntData: unsigned(7 downto 0);
signal downCntLd, downCntEn: std_logic;
signal delayCntVal, pulseCntVal: unsigned(7 downto 0);
signal startPulse, endPulse: std_logic;

type progPulseFsmType is (loadDelayCnt, waitDelayEnd, loadLengthCnt,
```

```vhdl
             waitLengthEnd);
signal currState, nextState: progPulseFsmType;

begin

  delayreg: process (clk, reset) begin
    if reset = '1' then
      delayCntVal <= "11111111";
    elsif clk'event and clk = '1' then
      if loadDelay = '1' then
        delayCntVal <= to_unsigned(data);
      end if;
    end if;
  end process;

  lengthReg: process (clk, reset) begin
    if reset = '1' then
      pulseCntVal <= "11111111";
    elsif clk'event and clk = '1' then
      if loadDelay = '1' then
        pulseCntVal <= to_unsigned(data);
      end if;
    end if;
  end process;

  nextStProc: process (currState, downCnt, loadDelay, loadLength) begin
    case currState is
      when loadDelayCnt =>
        nextState <= waitDelayEnd;

      when waitDelayEnd =>
        if (loadDelay = '1' or loadLength = '1') then
          nextState <= loadDelayCnt;
        elsif (downCnt = 0) then
          nextState <= loadLengthCnt;
        else
          nextState <= waitDelayEnd;
        end if;

      when loadLengthCnt =>
        if (loadDelay = '1' or loadLength = '1') then
          nextState <= loadDelayCnt;
        else
          nextState <= waitLengthEnd;
        end if;

      when waitLengthEnd =>
        if (loadDelay = '1' or loadLength = '1') then
          nextState <= loadDelayCnt;
        elsif (downCnt = 0) then
          nextState <= loadDelayCnt;
        else
          nextState <= waitDelayEnd;
        end if;
```

```vhdl
      when others =>
        null;
    end case;
  end process nextStProc;

  currStProc: process (clk, reset) begin
    if (reset = '1') then
      currState <= loadDelayCnt;
    elsif (clk'event and clk = '1') then
      currState <= nextState;
    end if;
  end process currStProc;

  outConProc: process (currState, delayCntVal, pulseCntVal) begin
    case currState is
      when loadDelayCnt =>
        downCntEn <= '0';
        downCntLd <= '1';
        downCntData <= delayCntVal;
        pulse <= '0';

      when waitDelayEnd =>
        downCntEn <= '1';
        downCntLd <= '0';
        downCntData <= delayCntVal;
        pulse <= '0';

      when loadLengthCnt =>
        downCntEn <= '0';
        downCntLd <= '1';
        downCntData <= pulseCntVal;
        pulse <= '1';

      when waitLengthEnd =>
        downCntEn <= '1';
        downCntLd <= '0';
        downCntData <= pulseCntVal;
        pulse <= '1';

      when others =>
        downCntEn <= '0';
        downCntLd <= '1';
        downCntData <= pulseCntVal;
        pulse <= '0';

    end case;
  end process outConProc;

  downCntr: process (clk,reset) begin
    if (reset = '1') then
      downCnt <= "00000000";
    elsif (clk'event and clk = '1') then
      if (downCntLd = '1') then
```

```
          downCnt <= downCntData;
       elsif (downCntEn = '1') then
          downCnt <= downCnt - 1;
       else
          downCnt <= downCnt;
       end if;
     end if;
  end process;

end rtl;
```

pulsefsm.vhd

Figure 7: RTL View of Programmable Pulse Generator Using a State Machine

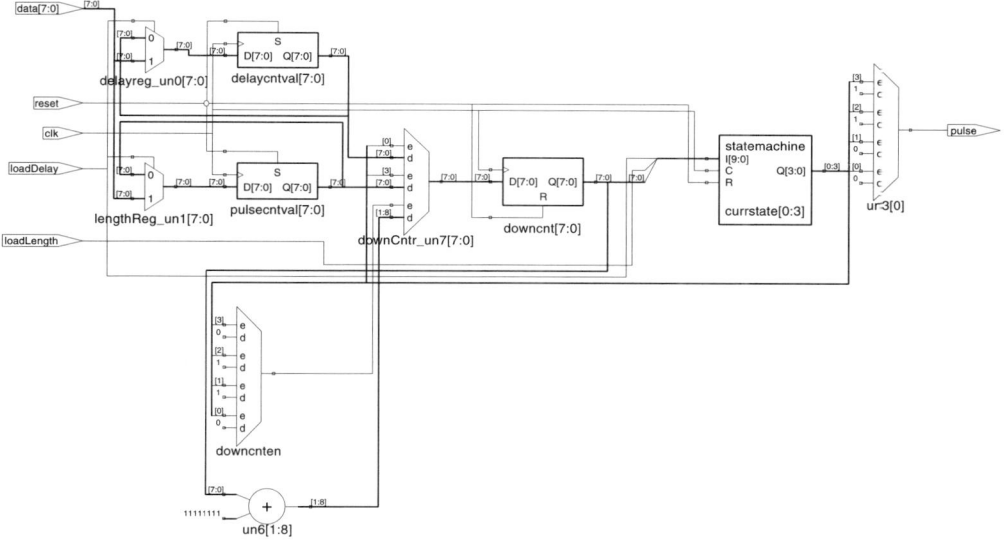

Issues Related to State Machine Design Technique

Eventually, when the synthesis process is complete, our abstract states are mapped to individual registers or state bits. While the approach described in this chapter is a sound technique for describing state machines, it does not cover issues that relate to the hardware created by the synthesis tool. For example, one of the disadvantages of implementing FSMs in such an abstract fashion is the lack of visibility into the current state vector register - you cannot connect them directly to a pin during design debug. Hence, you may want to use *std_logic_vectors* for the state vectors. This and other issues such as state encoding and logic optimization, will be covered *Chapter 10*, leveraging off this basic partitioning and coding style that we have developed here.

7

Reset, Presets, Tri-state and Bi-directional Signals

In this chapter we will discuss four design topics that relate to control signals commonly used in design, which are also influenced by the target technology. The first two, asynchronous presets (set and preset are used interchangeably) and resets, we have encountered earlier in *Chapter 4*, and will revisit in greater detail. In addition, we will discuss tri-state and bi-directional signals. It is important to understand when and why these issues are influenced by the target technology. Ironically, this importance is highlighted when using a logic synthesis tool that is flexible. This is because the synthesis tool will probably allow you to describe logical circuits that do not naturally fit within a target architecture, but can be implemented through "clever" logic mapping.

Asynchronous Presets and Resets

In *Chapter 4*, we saw how to write a simple reset or a preset for flip-flops and registers. Many target architectures and devices available allow both preset and reset to be applied to a flip-flop at the same time. While you will probably not see this often, when it does happen, you need to understand which of these is dominant. When both these signals are applied to the flip-flop, one of them has to "win", or take precedence. This depends on the characteristics of the flip-flop in the device, which may not be accessible via configuration or programming. Let us explore this issue first by examining different ways in which to express flip-flops with both reset and preset.

Structural Instantiation of a Flip-flop with Preset and Reset

It is possible to have access to a library that has a flip-flop with both preset and reset, as shown in *Figure 1*. Asynchronous signals are usually placed at the top edge and bottom edge of the symbol, indicating that they are asynchronous, while synchronous signals are placed on the left and right edges of the symbol, indicating that their characteristics are relative to the edge-triggered clock.

Figure 1: D-type Flip-flop with Asynchronous Preset and Reset

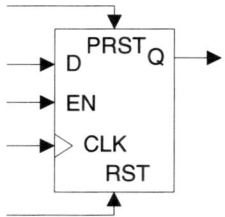

In the event that you are connecting both reset and preset, it is important to understand the issue of preset and reset dominance, since the details of the component (and, hence, its characteristics) provided is not visible. The truth table for the flip-flop in *Figure 1* is shown in *Table 1*. This table describes a flip-flop that is reset-dominant.

Table 1: Truth Table for D-type Flip-flop with Asynchronous Preset and Reset

EN	D	RST	PRST	CLK	Q
X	X	0	0	0	Q'
X	X	0	0	1	Q'
1	D	0	0	↑	D
0	X	0	0	↑	Q'
X	X	1	X	X	0
X	X	0	1	X	1

Q' indicates the value of Q after the prior clock edge

Structural instantiation of the flip-flop is shown in *Listing 1*.

Listing 1: Structural Description of an Enabled D Flip-flop with Asynchronous Preset and Reset

```
library IEEE;
use IEEE.std_logic_1164.all;

entity struct_dffe_sr is port (
  d: in std_logic;
  clk: in std_logic;
  en: in std_logic;
  rst,prst: in std_logic;
  q: out std_logic
  );
end struct_dffe_sr;

use work.primitive.all;

architecture instance of struct_dffe_sr is

begin
    ff: dffe_sr port map   (d => d,
                            clk => clk,
                            en => en,
                            rst => rst,
                            prst => prst,
                            q => q
                            );

    end instance;
```

dffsrstr.vhd

Behavioral Coding of a Flip-flop with Preset and Reset

Behaviorally describing the flip-flop shown in *Table 1* is an extension of the code that we saw in *Chapter 4*. We will use the *if...then* approach to describing this flip-flop. Only here, we will include both the reset and preset conditional statements prior to the statement that describes the edge-triggered clock.

Listing 2: Behavioral Description of an Enabled D Flip-flop with Asynchronous Preset and Reset

```
library IEEE;
use IEEE.std_logic_1164.all;

entity DFFE_SR is port (
    d: in std_logic;
    en: in std_logic;
    clk: in std_logic;
    rst: in std_logic;
    prst: in std_logic;
    q: out std_logic
    );
end DFFE_SR;

architecture rtl of DFFE_SR is

begin

  process (clk, rst, prst) begin
    if (rst = '1') then
      q <= '0';
    elsif (prst = '1') then
      q <= '1';
    elsif (clk'event and clk = '1') then
      if (en = '1') then
        q <= d;
      end if;
    end if;
  end process;

end rtl;
```

dffsrbhv.vhd

The VHDL shown in *Listing 2* illustrates a reset-dominant flip-flop. Note that the sensitivity list includes both the reset and preset conditions. The reset and preset conditions are written before the edge-triggered statement, indicating that they have no relationship to the clock signal.

What is most significant in *Listing 2* is the order in which we have written the preset and reset condition. The reset condition appears first, which indicates that it is the dominant signal when both set and reset occur at the same time. Since most synthesis tools do not make assumptions about the preset/reset dominance, they realize logic that explicitly defines the dominance. A good synthesis tool, however, will have knowledge of the flip-flop characteristics of the target device, and will generate the most efficient logic. For example, *Listing 2* targeted to a device whose flip-flops are reset-dominant will result in the logic shown in *Figure 2*.

Figure 2: DFF with Reset-dominant Asynchronous Preset/Reset

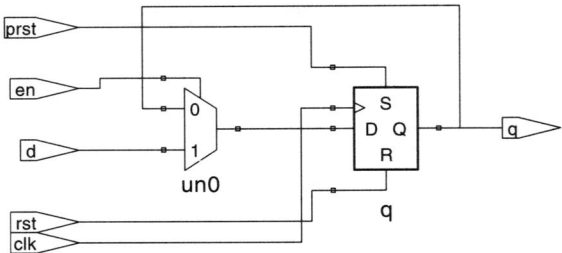

Behaviorally describing the D flip-flop has two advantages over the structural description. First of all, we do not have to worry about the details of preset/reset dominance in the target architecture at this stage of design capture. Second, we can control the dominance of preset or reset in the design. For example, in *Listing 2* the first condition in the *if...then* statement is the reset condition, which made reset dominant. If preset is to be dominant, we simply change the order of evaluation of the first two *if...then* conditions. This is shown in *Listing 3*.

Listing 3: DFF with Preset Dominant Over Reset

```
library IEEE;
use IEEE.std_logic_1164.all;

entity DFFE_SR is port (
    d: in std_logic;
    en: in std_logic;
    clk: in std_logic;
    rst: in std_logic;
    prst: in std_logic;
    q: out std_logic
    );
end DFFE_SR;

architecture rtl of DFFE_SR is

begin

   process (clk, rst, prst) begin
      if (prst = '1') then
```

```
        q <= '1';
      elsif (rst = '1') then
        q <= '0';
      elsif (clk'event and clk = '1') then
        if (en = '1') then
          q <= d;
        end if;
      end if;
    end process;

  end rtl;
```

dffpdom.vhd

Preset dominance, as shown in *Listing 3*, implemented in a device whose flip-flops are naturally reset-dominant can be seen in *Figure 3*.

Figure 3: DFF with Preset Dominant Over Reset

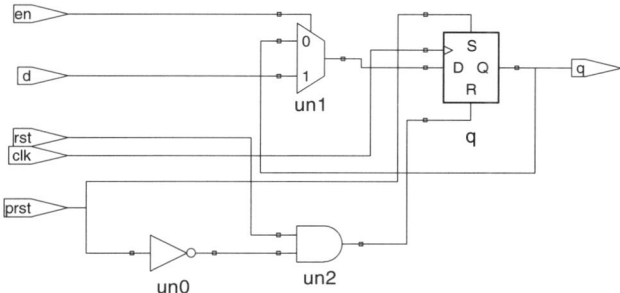

In the event that you know the preset/reset-dominance characteristics of the target device, and your synthesis tool does not recognize this, you may reduce logic utilization by structurally instantiating the flip-flop, similar to that shown in *Listing 1*. Note, however, that this makes your design device-dependent since you are now relying on the target device characteristics in your design description.

Using Asynchronous Presets/Resets to Load a Flip-flop

An asynchronous load to a flip-flop is a creative use of asynchronous presets and resets. However, asynchronous design is not recommended design practice. Not only is the design of reliable asynchronous circuits difficult, but the performance of the logic varies from device to device. Detailed timing analysis of asynchronous circuits can be quite complex, so in order to simplify the design process, it is often preferable to keep the design synchronous. Having said this, you may come across an opportunity to use the asynchronous load technique, in which case, the following two conditions must be satisfied:

- The flip-flop load operation must be slow, allowing it to be executed over a long period of time
- The flip-flop clock is not enabled for some time after the load is deasserted to let the flip-flops recover from the reset

Asynchronous presets and resets are usually not performance critical, and are hence not part of the critical electrical parameters of a flip-flop. This is why the flip-flop load needs to be slow when we are using the preset or reset as a load. Flip-flops also have an asynchronous preset/reset "recovery" time. This refers to the time it takes for the flip-flop to "recover" after it has been preset or reset, before it can be clocked. Thus, the need to wait for a specified time period after the reset and preset have been deasserted before clocking the flip-flop.

To demonstrate the asynchronous load, let us consider the design of a four-bit register. The VHDL for this looks similar to describing an asynchronous reset. In an asynchronous reset, we use an *if...then* statement to assign the value '0' to a register, as follows:

```
process (clk, arst) begin
  if arst = '1' then
    q <= '0';
  elsif clk'event and clk = '1' then
```

With asynchronous loads, the difference is that the output *q* is assigned to a signal and not to a fixed value.

```
process (clk, load, loadVal) begin
  if load = '1' then
    q <= loadVal;
  elsif clk'event and clk = '1' then
```

The VHDL for our asynchronous loading register is shown in *Listing 4*.

Listing 4: Register with Asynchronous Load

```
library IEEE;
use IEEE.std_logic_1164.all;

entity asyncLoad is port (
  loadVal, d: in std_logic_vector(3 downto 0);
  clk, load: in std_logic;
  q: out std_logic_vector(3 downto 0)
  );
end asyncLoad;

architecture rtl of asyncLoad is

begin

  process (clk, load, loadVal) begin
```

```
      if (load = '1') then
        q <= loadVal;
      elsif (clk'event and clk = '1' ) then
        q <= d;
      end if;
    end process;

  end rtl;
```

asyncld.vhd

The logic generated by *Listing 4* is shown in *Figure 4*.

Figure 4: Register with Asynchronous Load

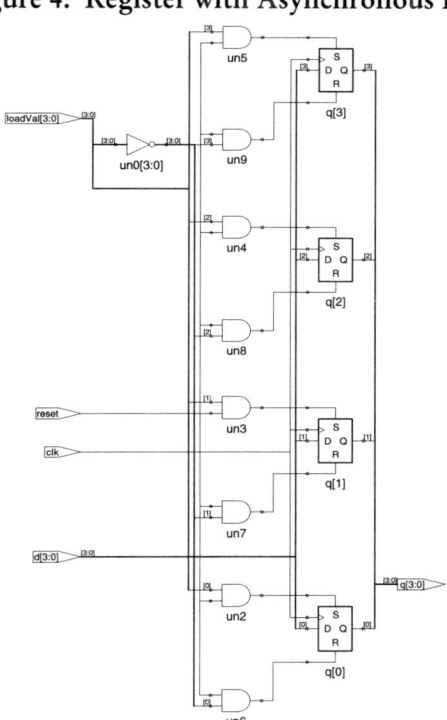

An advantage of the asynchronous load technique is that it reduces the logic that is in front of the register, when compared to a synchronous load. Consider an up-counter with a synchronous load and enable. We could represent this counter as shown in *Figure 5*.

Figure 5: Block Diagram for Counter with Synchronous Load

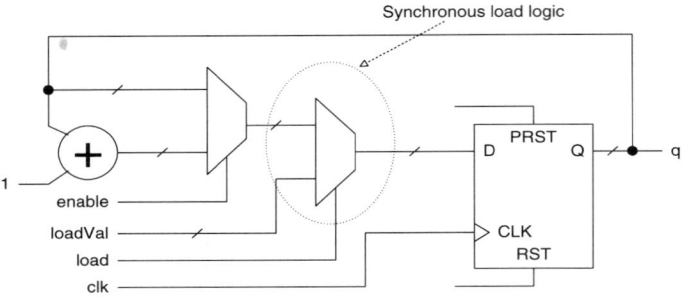

The synchronous load logic is shown circled in the drawing. By placing this logic on the asynchronous reset and preset pins, we can simplify the logic in front of the register. This might result in a faster counter (depending on the target architecture), since the load logic has been removed from the increment path to the register as shown in *Figure 6*.

Figure 6: Block Diagram for Counter with Asynchronous Load

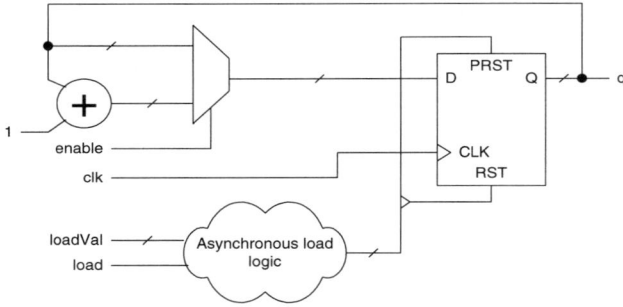

The listing for this counter, excluding the *enable* signal, is shown in *Listing 5* and the logic generated by this counter is shown in *Figure 7*.

Listing 5: Counter with Asynchronous Load

```
library IEEE;
use IEEE.std_logic_1164.all;
use IEEE.numeric_std.all;

entity asyncLdCnt is port (
  loadVal: in std_logic_vector(3 downto 0);
  clk, load: in std_logic;
  q: out std_logic_vector(3 downto 0)
  );
end asyncLdCnt;
```

Chapter 7 - Reset, Presets, Tri-state and Bi-directional Signals

```
architecture rtl of asyncLdCnt is

signal qLocal: unsigned(3 downto 0);

begin

  process (clk, load, loadVal) begin
    if (load = '1') then
      qLocal <= to_unsigned(loadVal);
    elsif (clk'event and clk = '1') then
      qLocal <= qLocal + 1;
    end if;
  end process;

  q <= std_logic_vector(qLocal);

end rtl;
```

ldcnta.vhd

Figure 7: Counter with Asynchronous Load

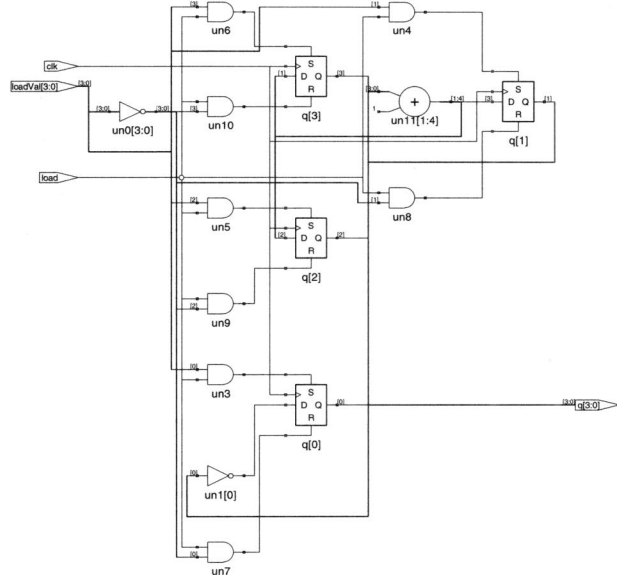

Tri-states

Shared busses are a common occurrence in systems. If the target device has outputs that can drive the bus, you will need to place the output into a high-impedance state to prevent it from driving the bus when it is not supposed to do so (also known as bus contention). Hence, the name tri-state: the output can take three values: logical 0, logical 1 or high-impedance value.

As with other design elements, we can structurally instantiate tri-state buffers. A tri-state buffer exists in the *primitive* package. This buffer is described as shown in *Figure 8*. Recall that the *std_logic* type can take the high-impedance state, which is represented by the value 'Z'.

Figure 8: Tri-state Buffer Symbol and Truth Table

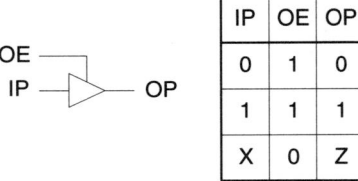

It is important to note that the value of the output port, *op*, assumes that *op* is being driven only by *ip* when *oe* is asserted.

Tri-state Buffer Using Structural Instantiation

Using the component in the *primitive* package, we structurally instantiate our output enable as shown in Listing 6.

Listing 6: Structural Description of a Tri-state Buffer

```
library IEEE;
use IEEE.std_logic_1164.all;

use work.primitive.all;

entity tribuffer is port (
   input: in std_logic;
   enable: in std_logic;
   output: out std_logic
   );
end tribuffer;

architecture structural of tribuffer is

begin

   u1: tribuf port map (ip => input,
                        oe => enable,
                        op => output
                        );

end structural;
```

oe.vhd

There are two common ways of describing tri-state buffers:

- Concurrent assignment
- Sequential assignment using *if...then* statements

Tri-state Buffer Using Concurrent Assignment

With concurrent assignments, we assign the output to 'Z' whenever the output enable is deasserted. This is shown in *Listing 7*.

Listing 7: Tri-state Buffer Using Concurrent Assignment

```
library IEEE;
use IEEE.std_logic_1164.all;

entity TRIBUF is port (
  ip: in std_logic;
  oe: in std_logic;
  op: out std_logic
  );
end TRIBUF;

architecture concurrent of TRIBUF is

begin

  op <= ip when oe = '1' else 'Z';

end concurrent;
```

oecond.vhd

Tri-state Buffer Using *if...then* Statements

Similarly, using the sequential *if...then* statement, the output is placed into a high-impedance state when the *enable* signal is deasserted. This is shown in *Listing 8*.

Listing 8: Tri-state Buffer Using *if...then* Statements

```
library IEEE;
use IEEE.std_logic_1164.all;

entity TRIBUF is port (
  ip: in std_logic;
  oe: in std_logic;
  op: out std_logic
  );
end TRIBUF;

architecture sequential of TRIBUF is

begin
```

```
   enable: process (ip,oe) begin
      if (oe = '1') then
         op <= ip;
      else
         op <= 'Z';
      end if;
   end process;

end sequential;
```
oeseq.vhd

The logic from both *Listing 7* and *Listing 8* results in an active-high enabled tri-state buffer, as shown in *Figure 9*.

Figure 9: Active High Enabled Tri-state Buffer

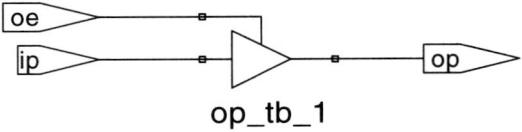

op_tb_1

An active-low enabled tri-state buffer is generated by testing the *oe* condition for '0'.

While the VHDL language is not case sensitive, there is an important point to note with regard to the *std_logic* type. In both behavioral descriptions, the high-impedance assignment is to 'Z', and not to 'z'. *std_logic* is a character-based type and each character value is in this type is in upper case. Hence, the values (or literals) that *std_logic* can take include 'Z' and not 'z'.

Enabling or Disabling a Bus Using Aggregates

It is often necessary to disable (or enable) an entire bus with a single signal. Extending the example shown in *Listing 7*, each element of the bus needs to be assigned to 'Z' for a bus to be disabled. For example, a four-bit bus would be disabled as follows

```
   op <= ip when oe = '1' else "ZZZZ";
```

As the bus width increases, this form of assignment can get unwieldy and rather unreadable. If *op* and *ip* were 32-bit buses, we might have to write

```
   op <= ip when oe = '1' else "ZZZZZZZZZZZZZZZZZZZZZZZZZZZZZZZZ";
```

since each element in the 32-bit takes on the 'Z' value.

Chapter 7 - Reset, Presets, Tri-state and Bi-directional Signals

Fortunately, there is a more compact form in which we can express this, as follows:

```
op <= ip when oe = '1' else (others => 'Z');
```

The reserved word *others* is used to assign the entire vector *op* to the value 'Z'. We can do this because *op* is a *std_logic_vector*, which is an array aggregate of the *std_logic* type. The word *others* assigns all the individual elements in the *std_logic_vector* to 'Z'. Since we have not specified any slice of the vector, the entire vector gets assigned to 'Z'. To further illustrate the concept of aggregates, we could say:

```
op <= ip when oe = '1' else (op(3 downto 0) => '0', others => 'Z');
```

In this example, the slice *op(3 downto 0)* is driven to 0 when *oe* is deasserted, and all other elements in the vector *op* are placed in high impedance.

We can extend our tri-state buffer example in *Listing 7* and *Listing 8* to a byte-wide tri-state buffer, as shown in *Listing 9* and *Listing 10*, respectively.

Listing 9: Byte-wide Tri-state Bus Using Concurrent Assignment

```
library IEEE;
use IEEE.std_logic_1164.all;

entity TRIBUF8 is port (
  ip: in std_logic_vector(7 downto 0);
  oe: in std_logic;
  op: out std_logic_vector(7 downto 0)
  );
end TRIBUF8;

architecture concurrent of TRIBUF8 is

begin

  op <= ip when oe = '1' else (others => 'Z');

end concurrent;
```

oeconbus.vhd

Listing 10: Byte-wide Tri-state Bus Using a *Process*

```
library IEEE;
use IEEE.std_logic_1164.all;

entity TRIBUF8 is port (
  ip: in std_logic_vector(7 downto 0);
  oe: in std_logic;
```

```
    op: out std_logic_vector(7 downto 0)
    );
end TRIBUF8;

architecture sequential of TRIBUF8 is

begin

  enable: process (ip,oe) begin
    if (oe = '1') then
      op <= ip;
    else
      op <= (others => 'Z');
    end if;
  end process;

end sequential;
```

oeseqbus.vhd

Bi-directional Buffers

Bi-directional buffers are simply tri-state buffers where the tri-state port itself also enters the device, as shown in *Figure 10*. This allows the port to be both written to (when the buffer is enabled), and read from (both when the buffer is enabled and disabled). Hence, the term "bi-directional".

Figure 10: Bi-directional Buffer Symbol and Truth Table

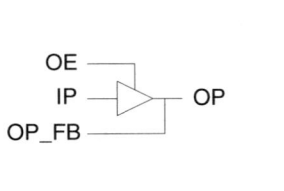

IP	OE	OP	OP_FB
0	1	0	0
1	1	1	1
X	0	Z*	Z*

* indicates a value of 0 or 1 depends on another driver connect to this port

Just like the tri-state buffer, it is important to note that the value of the output port, *op*, assumes that *op* is being driven only by *ip* when *oe* is asserted.

Bi-directional Buffer Using Structural Instantiation

The structural implementation of the bi-directional buffer is shown in *Listing 11*.

Listing 11: Structural Implementation of a Bi-directional Buffer

```vhdl
library IEEE;
use IEEE.std_logic_1164.all;

use work.primitive.all;

entity bidirbuffer is port (
  input: in std_logic;
  enable: in std_logic;
  feedback: out std_logic;
  output: inout std_logic
  );
end bidirbuffer;

architecture structural of bidirbuffer is

begin

  u1: bidir port map (ip => input,
                      oe => enable,
                      op_fb => feedback,
                      op => output
                      );

end structural;
```

bidir.vhd

Bi-directional Buffer Using Concurrent Assignment

The most notable difference between the tri-state and bi-directional buffers is the *mode*, or direction of the output *op*. In the bi-directional buffer, the mode of *op* is *inout*, which indicates that the driver for this port can be inside or outside the entity. We can see this more clearly by describing our bi-directional buffer behaviorally, using concurrent assignments, as shown in *Listing 12*. In this example, *op_fb* is a copy of the port signal.

Listing 12: Bi-directional Buffer Using Concurrent Assignments

```vhdl
library IEEE;
use IEEE.std_logic_1164.all;

entity BIDIR is port (
  ip: in std_logic;
  oe: in std_logic;
  op_fb: out std_logic;
  op: inout std_logic
  );
end BIDIR;

architecture rtl of BIDIR is
```

```
begin

  op <= ip when oe = '1' else 'Z';
  op_fb <= op;

end rtl;
```
bidirconc.vhd

The result of synthesizing this description is shown in *Figure 11*.

Figure 11: Bi-directional Buffer

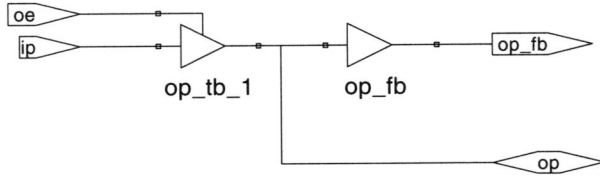

Design Example

To illustrate the use of bi-directional buffers in design, let us consider a simple application: a load-able up-counter. A block diagram for this counter is shown in *Figure 12*.

Figure 12: Block Diagram for Counter with Bi-directional Outputs

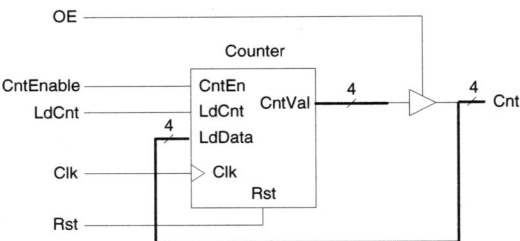

In this counter, the data value that is loaded into the counter is, in fact, on the same pins as the counter outputs. When the counter needs to be loaded, the counter outputs are disabled, and the load value is placed on those outputs. The counter is then synchronously loaded with this value, after which it continues counting when the count is enabled. The behavioral description for this counter is shown in *Listing 13*.

Listing 13: Counter Using Bi-directional Outputs

```vhdl
library IEEE;
use IEEE.std_logic_1164.all;
use IEEE.std_logic_unsigned.all;

entity BidirCnt is port (
  OE: in std_logic;
  CntEnable: in std_logic;
  LdCnt: in std_logic;
  Clk: in std_logic;
  Rst: in std_logic;
  Cnt: inout std_logic_vector(3 downto 0)
  );
end BidirCnt;

architecture behavioral of BidirCnt is

signal CntVal: std_logic_vector(3 downto 0);

begin

  counter: process (Clk, Rst) begin
    if Rst = '1' then
      CntVal <= (others => '0');
    elsif (Clk'event and Clk = '1') then
      if (LdCnt = '1') then
        CntVal <= Cnt;
      elsif (CntEnable = '1') then
        CntVal <= CntVal + 1;
      else
        CntVal <= CntVal;
      end if;
    end if;
  end process;

  bidirBuf: process (oe,CntVal) begin
    if (oe = '1') then
      Cnt <= CntVal;
    else
      Cnt <= (others => 'Z');
    end if;
  end process;

end behavioral;
```
bidircnt.vhd

Listing 13 separates the design into two processes, which is in fact the natural partitioning for the design. One process describes the counter logic, and the other describes the bi-directional buffer. The two processes are connected through the signal *CntVal*, which is local to the architecture. The resulting circuit is shown in *Figure 13*.

Figure 13: Counter with Bi-directional Outputs

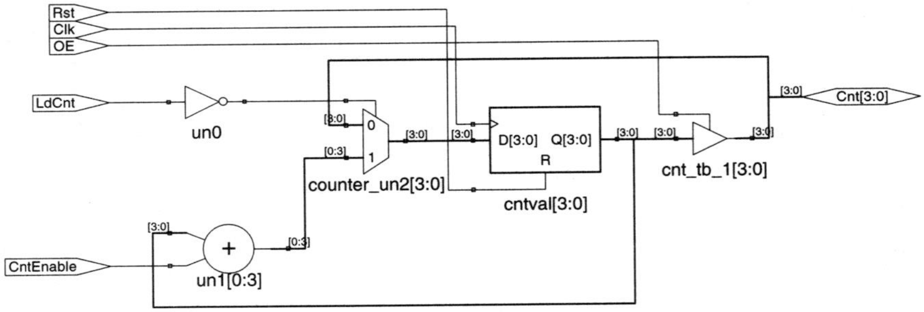

8

Understanding Hardware Creation

In the chapters thus far, we have been primarily concerned with writing VHDL to generate hardware. In this chapter, we will re-examine our approach to writing VHDL with the intention of gaining some insight into the hardware creation process. The details of logic synthesis and technology mapping are beyond the scope of this book. However, we will examine a few properties of the VHDL language and how they influence the process of hardware creation.

The goal is to ensure that the logic creation process does not generate unwanted results. In some cases, the unwanted results may be hard to track down, since the logic might be correct, but slow and inefficient. In other cases, the error messages of the synthesis tool may be cryptic, or perhaps incorrect results may be generated based on aspects of the language that are not obvious. By examining a few key issues that will have a significant impact on the hardware generated by the synthesis tool used, we will develop some simple rules to follow when writing synthesizable VHDL.

This chapter centers around three key issues:

- Signals (and certain variables) in a process have implicit memory
- Setting defaults or initial values for signals in a process
- *std_logic* is a resolved type

Signals Have Implicit Memory

To understand this concept, we need to go back to some of the fundamental properties of a signal. In *Chapter 1*, signals were introduced as "wires", as they are used to communicate information within a design. The more abstract analogy is that of a queue, as assignments to signals are queued in time order. This model of signals is significant, since it means that when a signal is assigned a value, it only takes this value at some point later in time. This is true even of assignments that happen in "zero" time. To illustrate this, and to introduce the concept of delta delays, let us consider a two-input AND gate, whose description is shown in *Listing 1*.

Listing 1: 2-input AND Gate Using Concurrent Assignment

```
library ieee;
use ieee.std_logic_1164.all;

entity and2 is port (
```

```
    a,b: in std_logic;
    a_and_b: out std_logic
    );
end and2;

architecture dataflow of and2 is

begin

  a_and_b <= '1' when a = '1' and b = '1' else '0';

end dataflow;
```
and2.vhd

The single dataflow statement in this design implies that the value of the output, *a_and_b* is updated immediately. There is no delay specified in this case. In fact, this is how most designs for RTL synthesis are written. The delay that results from the combinational logic generated by *signal* assignments is determined by the target device and technology, and is calculated using timing analysis tools after the design has been physically mapped into the target device.

There is a delay, known as δ_{delay}, or a "delta delay" in the assignment of the signal *a_and_b*. δ_{delay} is a delay that does not advance time. We can see this by considering two very basic examples that are only slightly different from each other. While these examples may not make much sense from a design standpoint, they will help demonstrate the implications of δ_{delay} when updating signals from within a process. The first example is shown in *Listing 2*.

Listing 2: Design Example 1 Showing the Delay Updating Signals Using a *Process*

```
library ieee;
use ieee.std_logic_1164.all;

entity signalDemo is port (
  a: in std_logic;
  b: out std_logic
  );
end signalDemo;

architecture basic of signalDemo is

signal c: std_logic;

begin

  demo: process (a) begin

    c <= a;
```

```
        if c = '1' then
            b <= a;
        else
            b <= '0';
        end if;

    end process;

end basic;
```

sigdemo.vhd

When c is assigned to *a* at the beginning of the process, its value is only updated at the end of the execution of the process *demo*. Hence, what we are testing in the *if...then* statement is in fact the value of c at the end of the previous execution of *demo*. This is seen in *Figure 1*.

Figure 1: **Waveform Demonstrating δ_{delay} of Signals (*Listing 2*)**

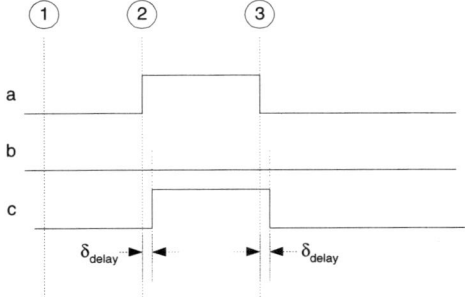

Time ① shows *a* assigned a value '0', after which it transitions to '1' at time ②. At this point, since *a* has changed, and *demo* is sensitive to *a*, we enter the process and start its execution. The signal c is assigned to *a*, and the condition (c = '1') is tested. This condition will be asserted "false", since c is still at '0', and has not been updated to '1' as the signal assignment does not take effect until time ②+ δ_{delay}, which occurs at the end of the process, without advancing time. Hence, at the end of this process execution, *b* is still at '0'.

At time ③, *a* transitions to '0', at which point we once again execute the process *demo*, since there has been a change to *a*. As c is only updated at time ③+ δ_{delay}, it retains its previous value of '1'. The condition (c = '1') is now true, and *b* is assigned the value of *a* at the end of the process - i.e. '0'. Hence, *b* remains at '0' throughout.

Now let us look at a slight variation of this design, as shown in *Listing 2*. Here, the condition that we evaluate is:

```
   if c = '0' then
```

rather than

```
   if c = '1' then
```

Listing 3: Design Example 2 Showing the Delay Updating Signals Using a *Process*

```
library ieee;
use ieee.std_logic_1164.all;

entity signalDemo is port (
  a: in std_logic;
  b: out std_logic
  );
end signalDemo;

architecture basic of signalDemo is

signal c: std_logic;

begin

  demo: process (a) begin

    c <= a;

    if c = '0' then
      b <= a;
    else
      b <= '0';
    end if;

  end process;

end basic;
```

sigdemo2.vhd

The waveform for this, as shown in *Figure 2*, is quite different from *Figure 1*.

Figure 2: Waveform Demonstrating δ_{delay} of Signals (*Listing 3*)

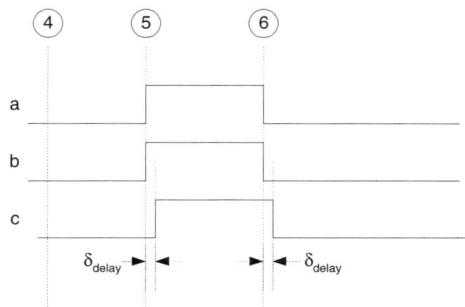

As you can see, *b* essentially tracks *a* (and *c*). Here, time ④ shows *a* with a value of '0', after which it transitions to '1' at time ⑤. At this point, since *a* has changed, and *demo* is sensitive to *a*, we enter the process and start its execution. The signal *c* is assigned to *a*, and the condition (*c* = '0') is tested. This condition will be asserted "true", since *c* is still at '0', as it is only updated at time ⑤ + δ_{delay}. Hence, at the end of this process execution, *b* is assigned the value *a*, which is '1'.

At time ⑥, *a* transitions to '0', at which point we once again execute the process *demo*, since there has been a change to *a*. This time, *c* retains its previous value of '1' as it will not be updated until time ⑥ + δ_{delay}. The condition (*c* = '0') is now true, and *b* is assigned the value of '0'. Hence, *b* now tracks the value of *a* as shown in *Figure 2*.

Thus, we can conclude the following about the nature of signals:

- Signal assignments do not take effect immediately, but at some point later in time.
- Signals "remember" their previous value.

By this we mean that signals have *implicit memory*. They retain their previous value, and are not updated until some later time or event. Although it would seem to follow that we can use this property of signals to determine when a signal is transitioning, this is not true. *Listing 4* is an example of VHDL that would not work for synthesis.

Listing 4: Pulse-Generated Model (Not for Synthesis)

```
library ieee;
use ieee.std_logic_1164.all;

entity pulseErr is port
  (a: in std_logic;
   b: out std_logic
  );
```

```
   end pulseErr;

   architecture behavior of pulseErr is

   signal c: std_logic;

   begin

     pulse: process (a,c) begin
        b <= c XOR a;

        c <= a;
     end process;

   end behavior;
```

pulseerr.vhd

If we analyze *Listing 4* in a similar manner to *Listing 2*, it would appear that this VHDL ought to generate a pulse every time *a* transitions from 0 → 1 or 1 → 0. While this may be true for simulation (you would observe a "spike" whose width is δ_{delay}), it results in a combinational loop for *c*, which is poor design practice. Most synthesis tools will not even attempt to synthesize *Listing 4*. Those synthesis tools that do will simplify the design to *b* = *a*, which is not the desired result.

Hence, if you must generate a pulse for a signal transition, avoid describing the logic as shown in *Listing 4*. Instead, use a memory element, such as a register or a latch to capture the "previous" state of the signal. Then use this to compare with the "current" state of the signal in order to generate the pulse.

The Last Signal Assignment is the One that Takes Effect

There is an important corollary to the fact that signals have implicit memory. When multiple assignments are made to a signal within a process and each assignment has no delay associated with it, then only the last assignment takes effect. To illustrate this, let us consider the example shown in *Listing 5*.

Listing 5: Design Example Showing that Only the Last Signal Assignment Takes Effect
```
   library ieee;
   use ieee.std_logic_1164.all;

   entity lastAssignment is port
     (a, b: in std_logic;
      selA, selb: in std_logic;
      result: out std_logic
     );
   end lastAssignment;
```

```
architecture behavioral of lastAssignment is

begin

  demo: process (a,b,selA,selB) begin
    if (selA = '1') then
      result <= a;
    else
      result <= '0';
    end if;

    if (selB = '1') then
      result <= b;
    else
      result <= '0';
    end if;
  end process demo;

end behavioral;
```

sigassig.vhd

In the process *demo*, the first assignment to the signal *result* is dependent on the signal *selA*. The second assignment to *result* is conditional on the signal *selB*. If both *selA* and *selB* are asserted, then the assignments are queued, in order, to occur after δ_{delay}. Since both occur at the same time, the second assignment, due to the *selB* condition, will take effect because it is the last assignment in the queue.

The *selA* condition has absolutely no impact on the value of the signal *result*, as the behavior of *result* is completely specified in the second *if...then* statement, the last assignment for *result*. In fact, we could completely eliminate the first *if...then* statement (*result* as a function of *selA*), and see no difference in the behavior of the design.

Implicit Latch Inference

In *Chapter 4*, we saw how to create latches by implicitly inferring them from the behavioral description. This required the use of a process and an *if...then* statement to generate a flow-through D-latch as shown in *Listing 6*.

Listing 6: D-type Latch by Implicit Inference

```
library IEEE;
use IEEE.std_logic_1164.all;

entity DLATCHH is port (
    d: in std_logic;
    en: in std_logic;
```

```
      q: out std_logic
      );
end DLATCHH;

architecture rtl of DLATCHH is

begin

  process (en, d) begin
    if en = '1' then
      q <= d;
    end if;
  end process;

end rtl;
```
dlatif.vhd

In this case, we are actually taking advantage of the implicit memory property of signals in VHDL to infer the latch. In the process when the condition (*en* = '*1*') is asserted, we flow the data through the latch. However, if that condition is not satisfied, the signal must hold its value as per the implicit memory requirement of VHDL. Thus we have created a level-sensitive memory element, or a latch, which is why latch inference from the code in *Listing 6* occurs.

Unwanted Implicit Latches

While the explicit generation of latches is sometimes desired, there are times when an implicit latch may be generated "accidentally". By this we mean that the it is not the intention of the designer to create the latch, but it is inferred from the code written. This is undesirable, as an implicit latch can create additional unwanted logic. A latch can be represented using simple gates as shown in *Figure 3*.

Figure 3: Gate-Level Representation of a Latch

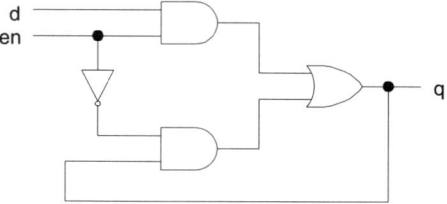

Most often, the resulting logic will be functionally correct, and will simulate correctly. However, it will be slow and result in a much larger circuit than necessary. For example, if what we really meant to say in *Listing 6* was "*q* is *d* qualified by *en*", then we could rewrite our VHDL process as follows:

```
process (en,d) begin
   if en = '1' then
      q <= d;
   else
      q <= '0';
   end if;
end process;
```

This VHDL would result in the logic shown in *Figure 4*.

Figure 4: Elimination of Logic Using *Else* Statement

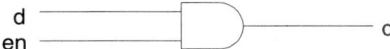

Hence, the completion of the *if* statement with the *else* statement results in significantly less logic, and almost always gives a smaller, faster design. Thus, for the fastest, most efficient designs, we must do the following:

- Completely specify all conditions within a process
- Completely specify all output possibilities within a process

Following these two "rules" also has another benefit: the discipline of specifying all conditions and all output possibilities at the design capture stage, which will simplify debugging later in the design cycle.

Completely Specifying *if...then* Statements to Avoid Implicit Latches

If...then statements are "chained". By this we mean that there is a series, or chain, of conditions, whose order of evaluation, or precedence, is defined by the order the condition appears in the chain. For example, in *Chapter 6*, one of our PCI Target state machine next state transition equations was as follows:

```
when B_Busy =>
    if (PCI_Frame_n ='1' and D_Done = '1') or(PCI_Frame_n = '1' and
       D_Done = '0' and LPCI_Devsel_n = '0') then                    -- [C6]
      nextState <= Idle;
    elsif (PCI_Frame_n = '0' or PCI_Irdy_n = '0') and Hit = '1' and
       (Term = '0' or (Term = '1' and Ready = '1') ) then            -- [C4]
      nextState <= S_Data;
    elsif (PCI_Frame_n = '0' or PCI_Irdy_n = '0') and Hit = '1' and
       (Term = '1' and Ready = '0') then                             -- [C3]
      nextState <= Backoff;
    else
      nextState <= B_Busy;                                            -- [C5]
    end if;
```

The first *if...then* in the chain has the highest precedence (condition C6). If this condition is satisfied, then all the others are ignored. The next *elsif* condition, C4, has the second highest priority, and is only evaluated if the first *if...then* condition is false. And so on down the chain, until the final *else* condition. Chained *if...then* conditions can be thought of as a series of muxes. If we were to represent the above *if...then* chain with muxes, it would appear as shown in *Figure 5*.

Figure 5: Chained *if...then* Representation Using Muxes

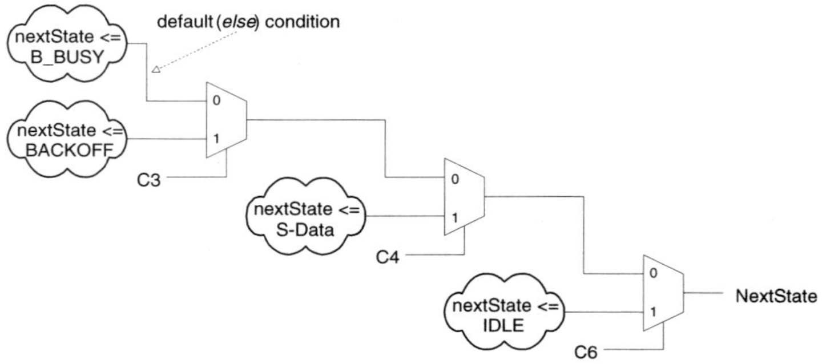

If the *else* condition is not specified, then the output signals within the *if...then* chain will retain their last value due to implicit memory. Hence it is necessary to complete each chained *if...then* statement with an *else* condition.

It is important to note that in VHDL, *if...then* statements are always chained and there is no method of expressing "parallel" *if...then* statements. *If...then* statements can result in large amounts of logic, especially when the chain is long, or nested (*if...then* statements within each *if...then* condition), as was discussed in *Chapter 3*. If (and only if) you can guarantee by design that each of the conditions in the *if...then* statement shown is uniquely asserted, then some synthesis tools will determine by analysis that the logic can be simplified. Each condition does not need to include the complement of all previous conditions. So if, for example, when condition C6 is asserted, we could guarantee that conditions C4 and C3 are not asserted, then the logic generated could be represented as shown in *Figure 6*.

Figure 6: Parallel *if...then* Representation Using Muxes

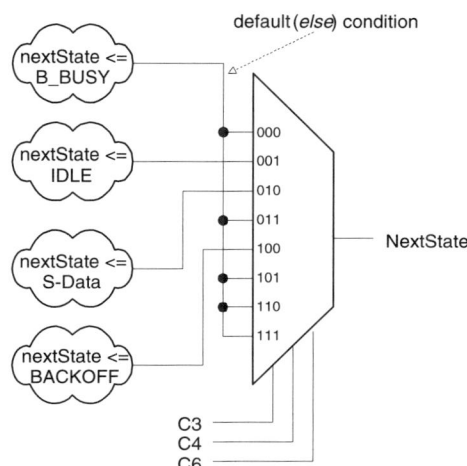

The best way to write your *if...then* statement is to ensure that each of the conditions is mutually exclusive. As there is no overlap, the most efficient implementation possible can be generated by the synthesis tool, just like *case* statements.

Case statements, are truly parallel evaluation of conditions, and the guidelines that we have discussed for *if...then* statements can be applied to *case* statements as well.

Completely Specifying All Outputs of a *Case* Statement to Avoid Implicit Latches

To illustrate the technique with the *case* statement, let us consider the example of a seven-segment display. The seven-segment display takes a binary-coded decimal number as its input, and drives an appropriate combination of seven LED segments, *a* through *g*, to display the corresponding decimal number from 0 to 9. The display, its display combinations and corresponding binary inputs are shown in *Figure 7*.

Figure 7: Seven-Segment Binary Coded Decimal Display

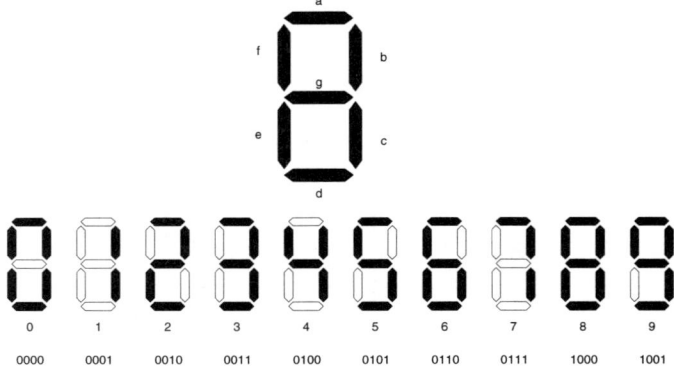

The *case* statement is perfectly suited to this application, since we are selecting one of a possible combination of inputs. However, note that in our case, only ten of the possible sixteen input combinations will result in a valid display output.

The VHDL compiler will require you to specify all combinations of the inputs. Our *case* statements will look something like this:

```
case bcdInputs is =>
  when "0000" =>
    <<condition outputs >>
  when "0001" =>
    << condition outputs >>
  when "0010" =>
    << condition outputs >>
    .
    .
    .
  when "1001" =>
    << condition outputs >>
  when others =>
    << condition outputs >>
  end case;
```

In our application, only the 10 decimal values (0 to 9) will result in a valid display. All others will result in a blank display. However, even if you continue the *case* statement and specify each of the 16 possible binary combinations of four bits, you will still require the *when others* condition to close a *case* statement. The language requires that all possible combinations are taken care of in the set of *when* conditions. Recall that the *std_logic* type can take on nine possible values: U, X, 0, 1, Z, W, L, H, -). So, from a language and type standpoint, we have only described 16 of the possible 6561 values[1] that the four bits can take. Thus the need for the *when others* condition, even if all 16 possible logic combinations of 0s and 1s are shown.

Chapter 8 - Understanding Hardware Creation

The outputs must be specified completely for all selection options in the *case* statement. We can do this by setting the default value to "off" at the beginning of the process. Each of the display driver outputs is active-low asserted, so the signal is labeled with a trailing _n and has a default value of '1'.:

```
process (bcdInputs) begin
  -- Assign default values to the outputs
  a_n <= '1';
  b_n <= '1';
  c_n <= '1';
  d_n <= '1';
  e_n <= '1';
  f_n <= '1';
  g_n <= '1';

  case bcdInputs is =>
    when "0000" =>
      a_n <= '0';
      b_n <= '0';
      c_n <= '0';
      d_n <= '0';
      e_n <= '0';
      f_n <= '0';
    when "0001" =>
      b_n <= '0';
      c_n <= '0';
    when "0010" =>
      .
      .
      .
```

We assert only the outputs necessary within each selection in the *case* statement, as shown. This takes advantage of the fact that VHDL signal values do not get updated until the end of a process. The complete design is shown in *Listing 7*.

Listing 7: Binary Coded Decimal to Seven-segment Display Decoder

```
library ieee;
use ieee.std_logic_1164.all;

entity sevenSegment is port (
  bcdInputs: in std_logic_vector (3 downto 0);
  a_n, b_n, c_n, d_n,
  e_n, f_n, g_n: out std_logic
);
end sevenSegment;
```

---

1. Since each bit position can take 9 values, the four-bit vector may take (9x9x9x9) = 6561 possible values.

```vhdl
architecture behavioral of sevenSegment is

begin

  bcd2sevSeg: process (bcdInputs) begin

  -- Assign default to "off"
    a_n <= '1';      b_n <= '1';
    c_n <= '1';      d_n <= '1';
    e_n <= '1';      f_n <= '1';
    g_n <= '1';

    case bcdInputs is
      when "0000" =>
        a_n <= '0';          b_n <= '0';
        c_n <= '0';          d_n <= '0';
        e_n <= '0';          f_n <= '0';

      when "0001" =>
        b_n <= '0';          c_n <= '0';

      when "0010" =>
        a_n <= '0';          b_n <= '0';
        d_n <= '0';          e_n <= '0';
        g_n <= '0';

      when "0011" =>
        a_n <= '0';          b_n <= '0';
        c_n <= '0';          d_n <= '0';
        g_n <= '0';

      when "0100" =>
        b_n <= '0';          c_n <= '0';
        f_n <= '0';          g_n <= '0';

      when "0101" =>
        a_n <= '0';          c_n <= '0';
        d_n <= '0';          f_n <= '0';
        g_n <= '0';

      when "0110" =>
        a_n <= '0';          c_n <= '0';
        d_n <= '0';          e_n <= '0';
        f_n <= '0';          g_n <= '0';

      when "0111" =>
        a_n <= '0';          b_n <= '0';
        c_n <= '0';

      when "1000" =>
        a_n <= '0';          b_n <= '0';
```

```
                c_n <= '0';          d_n <= '0';
                e_n <= '0';          f_n <= '0';
                g_n <= '0';

            when "1001" =>
                a_n <= '0';          b_n <= '0';
                c_n <= '0';          d_n <= '0';
                f_n <= '0';          g_n <= '0';

            when others =>
                null;

        end case;

    end process bcd2sevSeg;

end behavioral;
```
sevseg.vhd

The *when others* condition performs a *null* operation, which says "do nothing". This will not have any adverse effects, since we have already assigned all segment drivers to "off" at the beginning of the process, which will turn off all segment display drivers for the decimal values 10 through 15.

In our application, the default signal assignment ensures that the decoder works properly. If we did not have this default assignment, the decoder would function incorrectly for the illegal decimal values of 10 through 15 as the display would continue driving the previous valid decimal value. In addition, we would need to manually assign all seven-segment drivers in each selection choice, rather than just the driven segments. Thus the default assignment before the *case* statement not only provides the correct result for this application, but also helps the resulting logic to be efficient and more compact.

Implicit Memory from Lack of Reset or Preset to a Flip-flop

For reasons of implicit memory, it is possible to get a latch inferred when you do not assign a reset or preset to a flip-flop. Recall from *Chapter 4* that we can describe a D-type flip-flop with asynchronous reset using a process, as follows:

```
    process (clk, arst) begin
      if arst = '1' then
        q <= '0';
      elsif clk'event and clk = '1' then
        q <= d;
      end if;
    end process;
```

Let us extend this design where one of the outputs is asynchronously reset, and the other is not, as shown in *Listing 8*.

Listing 8: Flip-flop with Implicit Latch Caused by a Missing Asynchronous Reset

```
library IEEE;
use IEEE.std_logic_1164.all;

entity DFF is port (
    d1,d2: in std_logic;
    q1,q2: out std_logic;
    clk: in std_logic;
    rst : in std_logic
    );
end DFF;

architecture rtl of DFF is

begin

  resetLatch: process (clk, rst) begin
    if rst = '1' then
       q1 <= '0';
    elsif clk'event and clk = '1' then
       q1 <= d1;
       q2 <= d2;
    end if;
  end process;

end rtl;
```

resetlat.vhd

Listing 8 results in the logic shown in *Figure 8*.

Figure 8: DFF with an Implicit Latch Caused by a Missing Asynchronous Reset

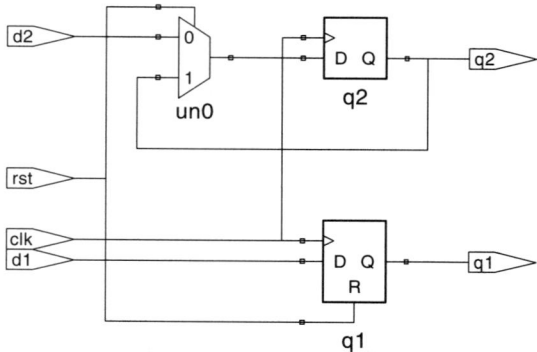

Notice the latch (implemented with a mux) is placed in front of the register for *q2*. When *rst* changes and the process *resetLatch* is executed, there is no change to *q2*. As *rst* is an asynchronous operation, a latch is implied to retain the previous value of *q2*. One way to avoid this implicit latch being created is to reset (or preset) all registers within the process, in other words, reset all signals that are assigned after the clock statement (such as *clk'event and clk = '1'*). Alternatively, use two separate processes, one for signals with reset (or preset) and one without.

Don't Care Comparisons and Assignments

Sometimes the logic circuit designed may take advantage of a "don't care" when evaluating a logic function, or when assigning its outputs. Not all logic synthesis tools support the *std_logic* '-'and 'X' values for "don't cares". In the event that the tool does, there is an important distinction to note between '-' and 'X' when used for comparison and assignment. When using a "don't care" in a comparison, we use the '-'. Here, we mean that the synthesis tool has no hardware choice to make with respect to the bit being compared and that any value will match '-'. When making an assignment, however, you can use either the 'X' or the '-'. In this case, the synthesis tool is allowed to make a choice as to whether the output is driven to a '0' or a '1' for that assignment.

Don't Cares in Wildcard Comparisons

To illustrate these, let us consider a typical example: decoding an address bus to determine whether or not we have an address "hit".

Assume that we have to decode "7ABxxxxx" on a 32-bit address bus to determine if we have an address hit, where 'x' indicates a "don't care" bit. In other words, the twelve most-significant bits must correspond to "7AB" in hexadecimal and the remaining bits are ignored (for the purpose of determining the address decode). It would seem that the following code might work:

```
process (addressBus) begin
  if (addressBus = "011110101011--------------------") then
    addressHit <= '1';
  else
    addressHit <= '0';
  end if;
end process;
```

In fact, this would **not** give the desired result! The '-' in this case is not treated as a "don't care". Hence, the *if...then* condition always returns a result of "false". This stems from the fact that the *std_logic* type is a character-based type. The overloaded "=" operation in the *numeric_std*, *std_logic_unsigned* and *std_logic_arith* packages compares each bit position with the incoming *addressBus* vector character by character. This means that bit positions *(19 downto 0)* must equal the character '-' in order for the comparison to be true. So, the condition always returns "false" and would show *addressHit* being continuously asserted to '0'.

There are two ways of performing the comparison. The first and, perhaps, more obvious way is to compare the appropriate slice of the vector *addressBus*, as follows:

```
compare: process(addressBus) begin
  if (addressBus(31 downto 20) = "011110101011") then
    addressHit <= '1';
  else
    addressHit <= '0';
  end if;
end process compare;
```

This clearly only compares the twelve higher order bits, explicitly. In the event that you do not wish to do this, and if your synthesis tool supports it, you can use the *std_match* function from the *numeric_std* package. This function takes in two *std_logic_vector* types, and compares them, interpreting the "-" as a wildcard. Our VHDL would be written as follows:

```
compare: process(addressBus) begin
  if (std_match (addressBus, "011110101011--------------------") then
    addressHit <= '1';
  else
    addressHit <= '0';
  end if;
end process compare;
```

To use the *std_match* function, make sure that the package *numeric_std* in the *IEEE* library is included in the *use* clause at the beginning of the design.

Don't Care Output Assignment

"Don't cares" can be useful when assigning outputs, to give the synthesis tool some freedom to further optimize the design. They should be used with great care, and only if you are able to guarantee by design that the output is truly "don't care". While the signal takes on the value '-' or 'X' in description and simulation, it will be assigned either '0' or '1' at the end of the logic synthesis process.

For example, in the BCD-to-seven-segment decoder example, we cannot assign the outputs to "don't care" in the *when others* condition, since we want the outputs to be deasserted. However, we could slightly modify this design to use "don't cares", by disabling the outputs whenever an invalid binary value appeared on the inputs. Weak pull-up resistors on the outputs ensure that the LED display pins reached a valid '1' logic level. Our board would thus appear as shown in *Figure 9*. Effectively, for all invalid input conditions, the outputs are now '1', or "off".

Figure 9: BCD to Seven-segment Display with Output Pull-ups

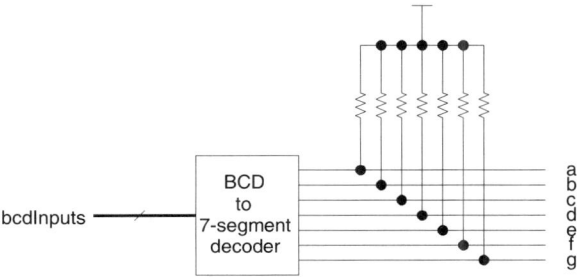

We could rewrite our decoder as shown in *Listing 9*.

Listing 9: Seven-segment Decoder Using Don't Cares

```
library ieee;
use ieee.std_logic_1164.all;
use ieee.std_logic_unsigned.all;

entity sevenSegment is port (
  bcdInputs: in std_logic_vector (3 downto 0);
  a_n, b_n, c_n, d_n,
  e_n, f_n, g_n: out std_logic
  );
end sevenSegment;

architecture behavioral of sevenSegment is

signal la_n, lb_n, lc_n, ld_n, le_n, lf_n, lg_n: std_logic;
signal oe: std_logic;

begin

  bcd2sevSeg: process (bcdInputs) begin

  -- Assign default to "off"
    la_n <= '1';    lb_n <= '1';
    lc_n <= '1';    ld_n <= '1';
    le_n <= '1';    lf_n <= '1';
    lg_n <= '1';

    case bcdInputs is
      when "0000" => la_n <= '0';        lb_n <= '0';
                     lc_n <= '0';        ld_n <= '0';
                     le_n <= '0';        lf_n <= '0';

      when "0001" => lb_n <= '0';        lc_n <= '0';

      when "0010" => la_n <= '0';        lb_n <= '0';
                     ld_n <= '0';        le_n <= '0';
```

```vhdl
                              lg_n <= '0';

           when "0011" => la_n <= '0';        lb_n <= '0';
                          lc_n <= '0';        ld_n <= '0';
                          lg_n <= '0';

           when "0100" => lb_n <= '0';        lc_n <= '0';
                          lf_n <= '0';        lg_n <= '0';

           when "0101" => la_n <= '0';        lc_n <= '0';
                          ld_n <= '0';        lf_n <= '0';
                          lg_n <= '0';

           when "0110" => la_n <= '0';        lc_n <= '0';
                          ld_n <= '0';        le_n <= '0';
                          lf_n <= '0';        lg_n <= '0';

           when "0111" => la_n <= '0';        lb_n <= '0';
                          lc_n <= '0';

           when "1000" => la_n <= '0';        lb_n <= '0';
                          lc_n <= '0';        ld_n <= '0';
                          le_n <= '0';        lf_n <= '0';
                          lg_n <= '0';

           when "1001" => la_n <= '0';        lb_n <= '0';
                          lc_n <= '0';        ld_n <= '0';
                          lf_n <= '0';        lg_n <= '0';

-- All other inputs possibilities are "don't care"

           when others => la_n <= 'X';        lb_n <= 'X';
                          lc_n <= 'X';        ld_n <= 'X';
                          le_n <= 'X';        lf_n <= 'X';
                          lg_n <= 'X';

      end case;

   end process bcd2sevSeg;

   -- Disable outputs for all invalid input values

   oe <= '1' when (bcdInputs < 10) else '0';

   a_n <= la_n when oe = '1' else 'Z';
   b_n <= lb_n when oe = '1' else 'Z';
   c_n <= lc_n when oe = '1' else 'Z';
   d_n <= ld_n when oe = '1' else 'Z';
   e_n <= le_n when oe = '1' else 'Z';
   f_n <= lf_n when oe = '1' else 'Z';
   g_n <= lg_n when oe = '1' else 'Z';

end behavioral;
```

sevseg2.vhd

Notice that in the *when others* condition, all the outputs are assigned to "X" or don't care. Assigning them to "-" will produce the same results as far as synthesis is concerned. The improvement in logic utilization can be significant. *Table 1*[2] shows that the "don't care" logic has considerably reduced the logic utilization of our design. So, while "don't cares" should be used with caution, they can have a significant impact on the resources used by a design.

Table 1: Improvement in Logic Utilization Using "Don't Cares" in the Seven-segment Design

Device	% Improvement
LUT architecture	38%
Mux architecture	23%

Resolution Functions, Tri-states and Muxes

In *Chapter 7*, we implemented tri-state and bi-directional buffers using the *std_logic* type. However, each buffer had only one driver for the signal. Hardware design often involves more than one driver on a given wire or bus, as shown in *Figure 10*.

Figure 10: Bussed Signal Example

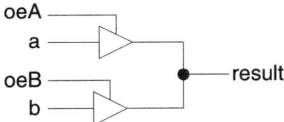

As a hardware description language, VHDL has the capability of allowing multiple drivers on a given wire, or signal. However, when there are multiple drivers you have to determine what the value is on the wire. When modeling hardware in VHDL, this is performed using resolution functions. The resolution function evaluates the value of all drivers that are driving a particular signal, and resolves the final value of that signal. The *std_logic* type is a resolved type. In other words, a resolution function is associated with the type *std_logic* that defines how signals with multiple drivers resolve. In the *std_logic_1164* package, the base type *std_ulogic*, is defined as:

```
TYPE std_ulogic IS ( 'U',   -- Uninitialized
                     'X',   -- Forcing   Unknown
                     '0',   -- Forcing   0
                     '1',   -- Forcing   1
                     'Z',   -- High Impedance
                     'W',   -- Weak      Unknown
                     'L',   -- Weak      0
                     'H',   -- Weak      1
                     '-'    -- Don't care
```

---

2. See Appendix A: Measuring Performance and Utilization

The type *std_logic* is then declared to be:

```
SUBTYPE std_logic IS resolved std_ulogic;
```

A *subtype* is a subset of a base type and is used when additional constraints need to be placed on a base type. In other words, we may want to perform all the operations that the base type is capable of doing, and then place some additional constraints on top of this. In our case, the constraint that we place over and above the *std_ulogic* type is the resolution function, *resolved*. The function is declared as:

```
FUNCTION resolved ( s : std_ulogic_vector ) RETURN std_ulogic;
```

We will take a detailed look at functions in *Chapter 12*. For the moment, we will treat the function *resolved* as a "black box", which determines the final value of a signal driven by multiple drivers.

Thus, in our designs, we can describe bussed signals, as shown in *Figure 10*. The VHDL for *Figure 10* is shown in *Listing 10*.

Listing 10: Multiple Drivers on a Resolved Signal

```vhdl
library ieee;
use ieee.std_logic_1164.all;

entity resFcnDemo is port (
   a, b: in std_logic;
   oeA,oeB: in std_logic;
   result: out std_logic
   );
end resFcnDemo;

architecture multiDriver of resFcnDemo is

begin

   result <= a when oeA = '1' else 'Z';
   result <= b when oeB = '1' else 'Z';

end multiDriver;
```

resfcn.vhd

In many devices, internal buses do not have hardware capability. Hence, our buses need to be mapped to muxes to provide the same logic. Tri-states can be thought of as fully-decoded muxes. In other words, the tri-state enable signal selects which of the drivers has control of the bus. Just as in a system with a shared bus, the design has to guarantee that only one of the enables is asserted, so that there is no bus contention. We can thus map the tri-state enables to select lines for the muxes.

The number of select lines to the mux is exactly equal to the number of tri-state enables, or drivers, in the system. *Figure 10* can be represented using muxes, as shown in *Figure 11*.

Figure 11: Bussed Drivers Translated to Muxes

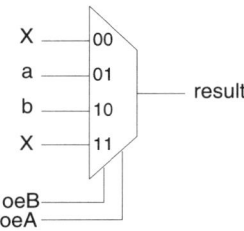

This automatic mapping of tri-states to muxes has its advantages. In particular, it is portable across target architectures, independent of whether or not the target architecture supports muxes or tri-states. Also, the most appropriate logic will be generated, depending on the hardware resources of the target architecture. Note that there are some other considerations that might impact your design. First of all, the values assigned to the mux for the "00" condition shown in *Figure 11* might not be the desired default value for the result. Second, the fanout of the select lines may be affected, since they may go to more cells than the output enables in a tri-state bus. This results in less control over fanout optimization later in the design cycle. And finally, there might be timing considerations, which can cause glitches in the result when transitioning from one driver to another as a result of the mux circuit being (typically) faster than the tri-state. The net result is that if you are concerned about any of these issues and the target device does not support internal tri-state buses, explicitly implement a mux-based selection scheme.

Resource Sharing

Certain types of logic, arithmetic in particular, may consume a large amount of a device's resources, depending on the target device architecture. To illustrate this, consider 16-bit adder and parallel multiplier circuits, implemented using logic elements only. In *Table 2*, these circuits are normalized, for the purpose of comparison to that of a 16-bit shift register, implemented using logic elements in the same device.

Table 2: Adder and Multiplier Resource Usage Normalized for a Shift Register

Device	Shift Register	Adder	Multiplier
LUT architecture	1	1	33.6
Mux architecture	1	1.6	31.1

Table 2[3] shows that 16-bit multipliers can consume over 30 times the resource of a 16-bit shift register, and a 16-bit adder can consume over 1 1/2 times the resource of a 16-bit shift-register. Hence, it is a good idea to conserve these resources where possible. To illustrate this, let us consider the example shown in *Listing 11*.

Listing 11: Design with Common Adders

```
library IEEE;
use IEEE.std_logic_1164.all;
use IEEE.std_logic_unsigned.all;

entity ForceShare is port (
  a,b,c,d,e,f: in std_logic_vector (7 downto 0);
  result: out std_logic_vector(7 downto 0)
  );
end ForceShare;

architecture behaviour of ForceShare is

begin

  sum: process (a,c,b,d,e,f)
  begin

    if (a + b = "10011010") then
      result <= c;
    elsif (a + b = "01011001") then
        result <= d;
    elsif (a + b = "10111011") then
      result <= e;
    else
      result <= f;
    end if;
  end process;

end behaviour;
```

noshare.vhd

As can be seen, the addition operation *a* + *b* is common to the first three conditions in the *if...then* chain. *Figure 12* shows the desirable logic implementation, versus a more wasteful implementation in terms of logic resource.

---

3. See Appendix A: Measuring Performance and Utilization.

Chapter 8 - Understanding Hardware Creation

Figure 12: Logic Implementation With and Without Resource Sharing

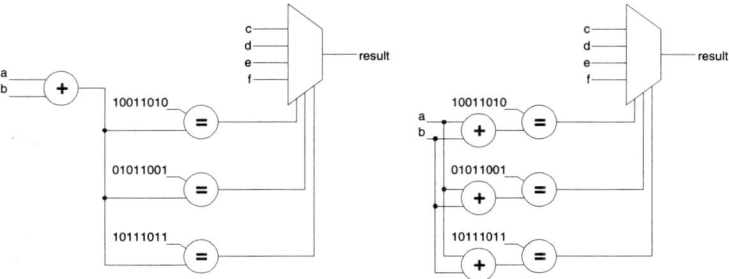

More desirable result using resource sharing   Wasteful result without using resource sharing

In the event that the logic synthesis tool does not generate the more desirable result, you will need to explicitly create a temporary node for the addition operation that is then subsequently used in the *if...then* chain. *Listing 12*, demonstrates the use of variables to take advantage of resource sharing.

Listing 12: Design with Explicit Resource Sharing

```vhdl
library IEEE;
use IEEE.std_logic_1164.all;
use IEEE.std_logic_unsigned.all;

entity ForceShare is port (
  a,b,c,d,e,f: in std_logic_vector (7 downto 0);
  result: out std_logic_vector(7 downto 0)
  );
end ForceShare;

architecture behaviour of ForceShare is

begin

  sum: process (a,c,b,d,e,f)
  variable tempSum: std_logic_vector(7 downto 0);
  begin

    tempSum := a + b; -- temporary node for sum

    if (tempSum = "10011010") then
      result <= c;
    elsif (tempSum = "01011001") then
        result <= d;
    elsif (tempSum = "10111011") then
      result <= e;
    else
      result <= f;
    end if;
  end process;

end behaviour;
```

share.vhd

9
Design Partitioning

Partitioning, prior to implementation, is a very important part of digital design. It is the process of organizing and sub-dividing a design into smaller units for the purpose of:

- Managing design complexity
- Enhancing reliability via design reuse
- Making it easier to maintain a design
- Incrementally synthesizing the design as it is developed

There are several programmable devices available that have the capacity to implement thousands (and in many cases even tens-of-thousands) of equivalent logic gates in a single chip. Many of these devices have heterogeneous architectures, in that they offer both logic elements and RAM elements. This has only increased the importance of design partitioning.

There are three keys to successful design partitioning. First, there is the "art" of partitioning. Logic design involves not only understanding the problem, but also decomposing it into smaller units, or blocks so that they can be implemented. This has as much to do with the aesthetics of design, as it does with logic, since there is seldom only one solution to any given problem. This aspect of design partitioning is beyond the scope of this book.

However, there are some underlying principles that can help the partitioning process. This leads to the second aspect of partitioning: design hierarchy. Hierarchy is a method of modularizing a design at different levels. Each successive level represents modules of lesser complexity than the one above it until, finally, the design is completely specified in terms of relatively simple blocks.

And thirdly, there are issues in partitioning that relate to implementation. Top-down design is perhaps the preferred way of solving the initial logic problem. However, top-down designers make several excursions to low-level implementation during the design process. This ensures that the overall partitioning chosen can be successfully implemented as there are several low-level (or bottom-up) issues that can impact the partitioning of a design.

In this chapter, we will discuss the latter two aspects of design partitioning as tools with which to successfully partition designs. There is, of course, no substitute to the "eye" of experience when performing design partitioning. The techniques and methods in this chapter, however, should provide suggestions not only on how to partition a design, but also on how to avoid some of the device-specific issues that might impact partitioning.

Design Hierarchy

Hierarchy is a key tool when managing design complexity. The idea here is to break up, or decompose, a design into smaller, simpler blocks. This is continued, until finally the blocks at the leaf-nodes of a hierarchy tree are simple, or characterized well enough to be implemented. An example of hierarchy is shown in *Figure 1*. Here the top level of the design is *Bus Interface*, which consists of three blocks. One of the blocks is *Address Decode*, and there are two copies of the block called *I/O Interface*. *I/O Interface* itself consists of two blocks, *Delay Counter* and *Sequencer*.

Figure 1: Design Hierarchy Shown in Tree Form

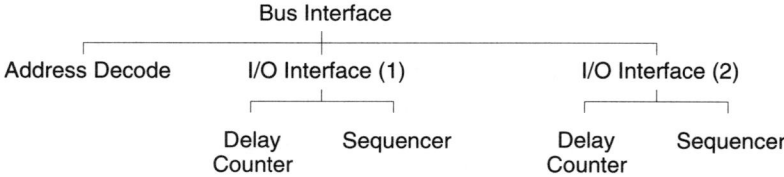

The leaf-node blocks (*Delay Counter*, *Sequencer* and *Address Decode*) are simple to implement. The design has been abstracted in such a way that the two modules for *I/O Interface* are just replicas of each other.

An alternative representation of hierarchy is shown in *Figure 2*. This shows hierarchy in block form, similar to the way in which we draw schematics.

Figure 2: Design Hierarchy Shown in Block Form

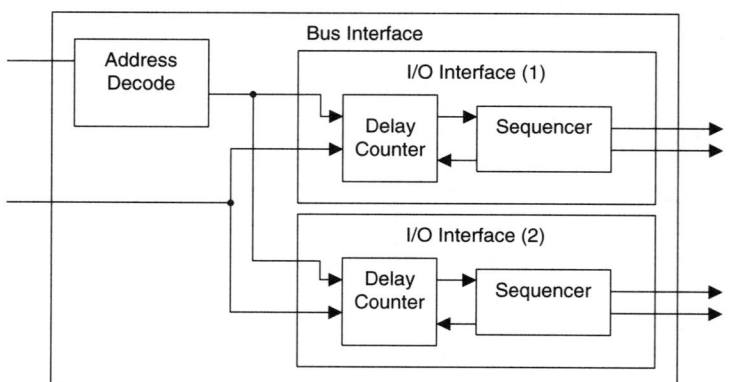

Hierarchy in VHDL

VHDL has the native capability to handle hierarchy. Thus far, we have used the entity-architecture pair to express a "black box", and we now need to place or *instantiate* one or more copies of the black box. In VHDL, the entity itself cannot be instantiated. We must declare a *component* that corresponds to the entity-architecture, which can then be instantiated.

There is a degree of similarity between the entity declaration and the component declaration, in that both describe how the black-box communicates with other black boxes. Components, however, only describe the ports (and *generics*, if they exist) for a given black box. The logical behavior of the component is based on a corresponding entity-architecture pair. For example, *Figure 3*, shows components with two input ports and one output port, which could be associated with entity-architecture pairs for any 2-input, 1-output logic gate.

Figure 3: Component and Entity-architecture Associations

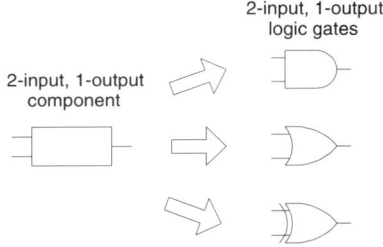

While this is a very powerful feature of the VHDL language, the following rules should be followed when declaring a component for synthesis:

- The component name must match the corresponding entity name
- The signal names in the component should be the same as the signal names in the entity

To illustrate how to create and instantiate components, we will return to the simple gate design of *Chapter 3*, which is illustrated in *Figure 4*.

Figure 4: Combination of Simple Gates

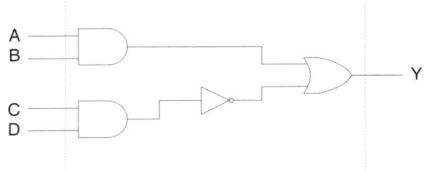

The top level design in *Figure 4* is defined by the box that encapsulates the gates. We first begin our design by defining three entity-architecture pairs for the logic gates in our design.

The next step is just as we have seen before: defining the entity-architecture pair for the top level of the design, as follows:

```
library IEEE;
use IEEE.std_logic_1164.all;

entity FEWGATES is port (
  a,b,c,d: in std_logic;
  y: out std_logic
  );
end FEWGATES;
```

We now begin the architecture declaration of the design. It is here that we define the components for each of the three gates in the design. By giving the components and entity the same labels, the two are associated by default as follows:

```
component AND2 port (
  i1: in std_logic;
  i2: in std_logic;
  y: out std_logic
  );
end component;

component OR2 port (
  i1: in std_logic;
  i2: in std_logic;
  y: out std_logic
  );
end component;

component INVERTER port (
  i: in std_logic;
  o: out std_logic
  );
end component;
```

We can now *instantiate* the components:

```
begin
  u1: and2 port map (i1 => a ,
                     i2 => b,
                     y => a_and_b
                     );
  u2: and2 port map (i1 => c,
                     i2 => d,
                     y => c_and_d
                     );
```

Each component instance has a label (*u1*, *u2*), and has its port association mapped to the appropriate signals in the design. The VHDL for this design is shown in *Listing 1*.

Listing 1: Simple Gates Using Component Declaration and Instantiation

```
library IEEE;
use IEEE.std_logic_1164.all;

entity AND2 is port (
    i1: in std_logic;
    i2: in std_logic;
    y: out std_logic
    );
end AND2;

architecture rtl of AND2 is

begin

  y <= '1' when i1 = '1' and i2 = '1' else '0';

end rtl;

library IEEE;
use IEEE.std_logic_1164.all;

entity OR2 is port (
    i1: in std_logic;
    i2: in std_logic;
    y: out std_logic
    );
end OR2;

architecture rtl of OR2 is

begin

  y <= '1' when i1 = '1' or i2 = '1' else '0';

end rtl;

library IEEE;
use IEEE.std_logic_1164.all;

entity INVERTER is port (
    i: in std_logic;
    o: out std_logic
    );
end INVERTER;

architecture rtl of INVERTER is

begin
```

```vhdl
    o <= not i;

end rtl;

library IEEE;
use IEEE.std_logic_1164.all;

entity FEWGATES is port (
  a,b,c,d: in std_logic;
  y: out std_logic
  );
end FEWGATES;

architecture structural of FEWGATES is

  component AND2 port (
    i1: in std_logic;
    i2: in std_logic;
    y: out std_logic
    );
  end component;

  component OR2 port (
    i1: in std_logic;
    i2: in std_logic;
    y: out std_logic
    );
  end component;

  component INVERTER port (
    i: in std_logic;
    o: out std_logic
    );
  end component;

signal a_and_b, c_and_d, not_c_and_d: std_logic;

begin

  u1: and2 port map (i1 => a,
                     i2 => b,
                     y => a_and_b
                     );

  u2: and2 port map (i1 => c,
                     i2 => d,
                     y => c_and_d
                     );

  u3: inverter port map (i => c_and_d,
                         o => not_c_and_d);
```

```
u4: or2 port map (i1 => a_and_b,
                  i2 => not_c_and_d,
                  y => y
                  );
end structural;
```

gates.vhd

There are three key issues to note about this design:

- The entity-architecture for each component is written before the top level component (*fewgates*). This is due to the top-to-bottom order in which the file is analyzed, which we will discuss shortly.
- Each entity-architecture pair has its own library statement, along with the corresponding *use* clause. This has to do with the *scope* of the *use* clause, which we will also discuss later in this chapter.
- Each component instantiation is done concurrently within the architecture and can never be placed within a process.

Positional Versus Named Association for Component Instances

All the examples we have seen so far, have used what is known as "named association" when instantiating components. By this we mean that each signal in the port list (the *formal* name) of the component is explicitly connected to a signal within the architecture (the *actual* name). The instance *u4*, for example:

```
u4: or2 port map (i1 => a_and_b,
                  i2 => not_c_and_d,
                  y => y
                  );
```

shows the explicit association of *i1*, *i2*, and *y* with their corresponding signals in the structural architecture. Alternatively, we can connect signals in the order, or position, that they appear in the component list, which is known as "positional association". The instance *u4* using position association could be written as follows:

```
u4: or2 port map (a_and_b,
                  not_c_and_d,
                  y
                  );
```

This implies that *a_and_b, not_c_and_d,* and *y* are connected to *i1, i2* and *y* respectively since this is the order in which the latter set of signals have been declared.

It is preferable to use named association, as this method clearly states how component signals are being connected. This is useful when debugging and documenting designs.

Leaving an Output Port Unconnected

Output ports (those of mode *out*) may be left unconnected. This is useful, since we can define components that have multiple outputs, which may or may not be used in a particular instantiation. Most synthesis tools are good at removing unnecessary logic, so you do not have to worry about logic "residue" from unconnected ports. To illustrate this, let us consider the example of a 4-bit counter with an additional output that represents the terminal count of this counter. The terminal count is generated whenever all the counter bits are '1', as shown in *Figure 5*.

Figure 5: Counter with Terminal Count

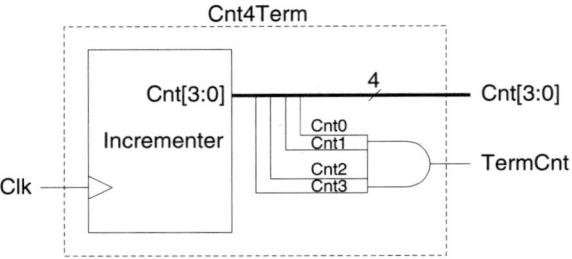

A four-bit counter (*Counter*) can be implemented by instantiating this component and leaving the terminal count port, *TermCnt*, unconnected, as shown in *Figure 6*.

Figure 6: Instantiation of Terminal Count, with *TermCnt* Left Unconnected

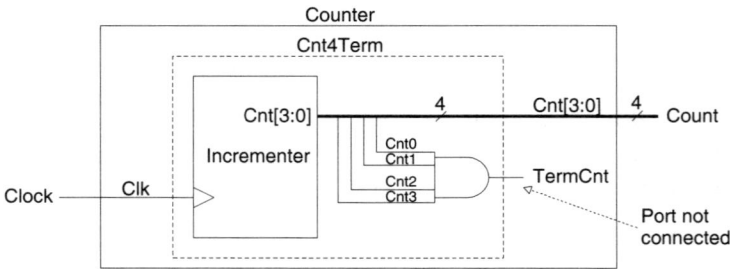

In VHDL, an unconnected output port is indicated with a port assignment of *open*. This is shown in *Listing 2*, which represents the VHDL *Figure 6*.

Listing 2: Counter Instantiation Illustrating the Use of *open*

```vhdl
library IEEE;
use IEEE.std_logic_1164.all;
use IEEE.numeric_std.all;

entity Cnt4Term is port (
  clk: in std_logic;
  Cnt: out std_logic_vector(3 downto 0);
  TermCnt: out std_logic
  );
end Cnt4Term;

architecture behavioral of Cnt4Term is

signal CntL: unsigned(3 downto 0);

begin

  increment: process begin
    wait until clk = '1';
      CntL <= CntL + 1;
  end process;

  Cnt <= std_logic_vector(CntL);

  TermCnt <= '1' when CntL = "1111" else '0';

end behavioral;

library IEEE;
use IEEE.std_logic_1164.all;

entity Counter is port (
  clock: in std_logic;
  Count: out std_logic_vector(3 downto 0)
  );
end Counter;

architecture structural of Counter is

  component Cnt4Term port (
    clk: in std_logic;
    Cnt: out std_logic_vector(3 downto 0);
    TermCnt: out std_logic);
  end component;

begin

  u1: Cnt4Term port map (clk => clock,
                        Cnt => Count,
                        TermCnt => open
                        );

end structural;
```

cntr.vhd

Hierarchical designs can become cumbersome and quite impractical if we place all the entity-architecture pairs in a single file, along with the component declaration in the architecture declaration section, as we did in *Listing 1* and *Listing 2*. We need a better scheme of modularizing the design, especially if we wish to reuse the design elsewhere. VHDL has two such tools to managing hierarchy:

- Libraries
- Packages

Libraries

Libraries are a very important part of VHDL, encountered on several occasions earlier on in this book, which we will now examine in detail.

Designs are stored in libraries, and may be added to, removed from, or just used from the library. It is very important to note that the *physical* implementation of libraries is *not* defined by the VHDL standard. As such, library implementation varies greatly from tool to tool. Libraries are uniquely identified by a label, or name, the *IEEE* library being the most commonly used. While the name of this library is always the same, it may be implemented physically in any way. Most tools use directories to implement libraries. So, for example, the *IEEE* library may reside in the C:\SYNTH\LIBS\IEEE directory. As each tool implements libraries in a different way, you should check the documentation to understand the format and contents of the library.

This brings us to the next aspect of using libraries: visibility. Library names are made "visible" by declaring them using the *library* clause. For example, we might say:

```
library IEEE;
```

There are two libraries that are implicitly visible, and do not need the *library* clause for visibility. These are the *std* library and the *work* library.

The *std* library contains the various types as well as operators that are part of the VHDL standard. For example, the Boolean operators (*and*, *or*, *nor*, etc.), relational operators (>, <, etc.) and the *bit_vector* type all reside in this library.

The *work* library is the default working library. When the design is being analyzed for either synthesis or simulation, this library is used by default.

Adding Components to Libraries

It is often useful to keep logical building blocks of a design in separate files, as this helps manage the size and readability of the design. Most synthesis tools provide support for designs that are implemented using multiple files. For example, we could change *Listing 1* so that each of the components, *AND2*, *OR2* and *INVERTER* are placed in separate files. To do so, however, these lower level design units, or entity-architecture pairs, must be analyzed (into the work library) before the top level of the design is analyzed.

For example, the *AND2* design would appear in a separate file which we might call *and2.vhd* as shown in *Listing 3*.

Listing 3: AND2 Entity-architecture in a Single Design File

```
library IEEE;
use IEEE.std_logic_1164.all;


library IEEE;
use IEEE.std_logic_1164.all;

entity AND2 is port (
    i1: in std_logic;
    i2: in std_logic;
    y: out std_logic
    );
end AND2;

architecture rtl of AND2 is

begin

  y <= '1' when i1 = '1' and i2 = '1' else '0';

end rtl;
```

and2.vhd

The three entity-architecture pairs, once analyzed an placed into the default *work* library, can now be accessed from our top level design. This is done with the *use* clause just before the architecture declaration statement that directly accesses the component from the *work* library, as follows:

```
use work.and2;
use work.or2;
use work.inverter;
```

The complete listing for the new design, with the entity-architecture pairs in separate files, is shown in *Listing 4*.

Listing 4: Simple Gates with Component Entities in Separate Files

```
library IEEE;
use IEEE.std_logic_1164.all;

entity FEWGATES is port (
  a,b,c,d: in std_logic;
  y: out std_logic
  );
end FEWGATES;

use work.and2;
use work.or2;
use work.inverter;

architecture structural of FEWGATES is

  component AND2 port (
    i1: in std_logic;
    i2: in std_logic;
    y: out std_logic
    );
  end component;

  component OR2 port (
    i1: in std_logic;
    i2: in std_logic;
    y: out std_logic
    );
  end component;

  component INVERTER port (
    i: in std_logic;
    o: out std_logic
    );
  end component;

signal a_and_b, c_and_d, not_c_and_d: std_logic;

begin

  u1: and2 port map (i1 => a,
                     i2 => b,
                     y => a_and_b
                     );

  u2: and2 port map (i1 => c,
                     i2 => d,
                     y => c_and_d
                     );

  u3: inverter port map (i => c_and_d,
```

Chapter 9 - Design Partitioning

```
                           o => not_c_and_d);
    u4: or2 port map (i1 => a_and_b,
                      i2 => not_c_and_d,
                      y => y
                      );
end structural;
```
gatecomp.vhd

While this technique does help manage the size of the design, and its readability, it does not help with reuse of the individual modules. To achieve this, VHDL uses packages.

Packages

A *package* is a collection of declarations, which can be accessed by the *use* clause. In its simplest form, a package may be used to declare components, which can then be made visible not only for the current design, but by any design that references the package. Our package, *gatesPkg* is shown in *Listing 5*. While VHDL does not require it to be in a separate file, we will place it in a separate file for the purpose of clarity and maintenance.

Listing 5: Package Declaration for *GatesPkg*

```
library IEEE;
use IEEE.std_logic_1164.all;

package GatesPkg is

  component AND2 port (
    i1: in std_logic;
    i2: in std_logic;
    y: out std_logic
    );
  end component;

  component OR2 port (
    i1: in std_logic;
    i2: in std_logic;
    y: out std_logic
    );
  end component;

  component INVERTER port (
    i: in std_logic;
    o: out std_logic
    );
  end component;

end GatesPkg;
```
gatespkg.vhd

We must first add this package to the *work* library before it can be *use*-ed. For most synthesis tools, this implies that the compilation of the file containing *GatesPkg* must occur prior to that of the top level design that *use*-s the package *GatesPkg*. When used for synthesis, the *use* clause, often has the following syntax:

```
use <library-name>.<package-name>.<component-name>
```

So, for example, we could write:

```
use work.GatesPkg.and2;
use work.GatesPkg.or2;
use work.GatesPkg.inverter;
```

The component name might also be a wild card, which includes all the declarations in the package. This is accomplished using the word "all" in place of the component name, as follows:

```
use work.GatesPkg.all;
```

Thus, with a single *use* clause, we have made all the declarations in the package visible, and available for use within the design. The VHDL implementation of the simple gates design that incorporates the use of the *GatesPkg* package is shown in *Listing 6*. The *use* clause is placed just before the architecture declaration of the design.

Listing 6: Simple Gates Design with Components in the *GatesPkg* Package

```
library IEEE;
use IEEE.std_logic_1164.all;

entity FEWGATES is port (
  a,b,c,d: in std_logic;
  y: out std_logic
  );
end FEWGATES;

use work.GatesPkg.all;

architecture structural of FEWGATES is

signal a_and_b, c_and_d, not_c_and_d: std_logic;

begin

  u1: and2 port map (i1 => a,
                     i2 => b,
                     y => a_and_b
                     );

  u2: and2 port map (i1 => c,
```

```
                    i2 => d,
                    y => c_and_d
                    );

    u3: inverter port map (i => c_and_d,
                           o => not_c_and_d);

    u4: or2 port map (i1 => a_and_b,
                      i2 => not_c_and_d,
                      y => y
                      );
end structural;
```

gatepack.vhd

Placing components into packages facilitates design reuse. It can also be useful for creating implementation-specific packages, which contain component implementations that have been optimized for a particular device or architecture. In addition, types and sub-types may also be placed into packages. The *std_logic_1164* package, for example, defines the *std_logic* and *std_ulogic* types.

As we have noted, the compilation order of packages, entities and architectures is important. This leads to another important issue, the *scope*, or applicability, of the *use* clause. Recall that VHDL does not place any restrictions on how files are associated with design units, packages or libraries. As such, multiple design units may be placed in a single file. A library declaration and *use* clause(s) are only valid for one design unit that follows the clause. Hence, in *Listing 1*, for example, we placed a *library* and *use* clause before *each* entity-architecture pair. Similarly, in *Listing 5*, the *library* and *use* clause is valid only for the package declaration. If there were any entity-architecture pairs that followed the package declaration, they would have to have their own *use* clause preceding the entity declaration.

Component Configuration

VHDL not only allows components to be instantiated multiple times, but also gives the designer the ability to configure each component instance separately. While most synthesis tools do not support component configuration (they only support one default configuration), it is very useful to understand how to configure components, as it can help when simulating and verifying your design.

In VHDL, a component declaration may apply to several entities, which in turn may be expressed using several architectures.

Figure 7: Component Configuration

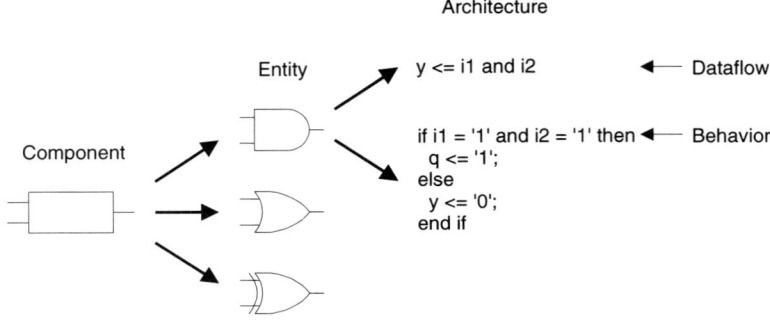

Figure 7 shows how there may be multiple entities for a given 2-input, 1-output component. In addition, each entity may be expressed using different architectures (*Dataflow* and *Behavior*, in this example). The process of associating a specific entity and architecture to a component is known as *configuration*.

There are two kinds of configuration:

- Configuration declaration
- Configuration specification

Configuration declarations bind each component to an entity-architecture pair in a design. They may be hierarchical, in that they may be composed of other configuration declarations. Configuration specifications, on the other hand, are written within an architecture, and only bind components for that architecture.

A configuration declaration for the simple gates design in *Listing 6* might be written as shown in *Listing 7*. Here, a configuration called *SimpleGatesCfg* is created for the top level entity, *FEWGATES*. There is only one architecture for this implementation, called *structural*, which we configure. Each instance of a component is bound to a specific entity-architecture pair from the library.

Listing 7: Configuration Declaration for Simple Gates Design

```
configuration SimpleGatesCfg of FEWGATES is

   for structural

      for u1: and2
         use entity work.and2(rtl);
      end for;

      for u2: and2
```

```
      use entity work.and2(rtl);
    end for;

    for u3: inverter
      use entity work.inverter(rtl);
    end for;

    for u4: or2
      use entity work.or2(rtl);
    end for;

  end for;

end SimpleGatesCfg;
```

gatecfg.vhd

If we chose to bind all instances of a given component to a given entity architecture pair, we can use the *for all* statement in the configuration declaration. For example, all the *and2* gates in our design are bound to the entity-architecture pair *and2(rtl)* in our design. We could thus rewrite our configuration declaration as shown in *Listing 8*.

Listing 8: Configuration Declaration Using the for All Statement

```
configuration SimpleGatesCfg of FEWGATES is

  for structural

    for all: AND2
      use entity work.and2(rtl);
    end for;

    for u3: inverter
      use entity work.inverter(rtl);
    end for;

    for u4: or2
      use entity work.or2(rtl);
    end for;

  end for;

end SimpleGatesCfg;
```

gatecfg2.vhd

As we noted earlier, configuration declarations may be hierarchical. So, each *for* statement may configure the various components instantiated within its corresponding level of the hierarchy.

In the event that the component declarations are local to a given architecture, we need to use configuration specifications, as shown in *Listing 9*. Note that the configuration specification is written just after the components have been declared, and prior to the *begin* statement.

Listing 9: Configuration Specification for Simple Gates Design

```
library IEEE;
use IEEE.std_logic_1164.all;

entity FEWGATES is port (
  a,b,c,d: in std_logic;
  y: out std_logic
  );
end FEWGATES;

use work.and2;
use work.or2;
use work.inverter;

architecture structural of FEWGATES is

  component AND2 port (
    i1: in std_logic;
    i2: in std_logic;
    y: out std_logic
    );
  end component;

  component OR2 port (
    i1: in std_logic;
    i2: in std_logic;
    y: out std_logic
    );
  end component;

  component INVERTER port (
    i: in std_logic;
    o: out std_logic
    );
  end component;

  signal a_and_b, c_and_d, not_c_and_d: std_logic;

  -- Configution specifications

  for all: and2 use entity work.and2(rtl);
  for u3: inverter use entity work.inverter(rtl);
  for u4: or2 use entity work.or2(rtl);

  begin
```

```
u1: and2 port map (i1 => a, i2 => b,
                   y => a_and_b
                   );

u2: and2 port map (i1 => c, i2 => d,
                   y => c_and_d
                   );

u3: inverter port map (i => c_and_d,
                       o => not_c_and_d);

u4: or2 port map (i1 => a_and_b, i2 => not_c_and_d,
                  y => y
                  );
end structural;
```

gateconf.vhd

Since most synthesis tools do not support configuration specifications and declarations, it is advisable to:

- Place component declarations in packages
- Use configuration declarations, and keep them in a separate file for simulation purposes

This helps not only design portability, but also avoids having to modify designs when moving between synthesis and simulation.

Partitioning Techniques that Influence Implementation

Having examined hierarchy and the techniques to manage it, it is useful to know when and how to apply it. While much of design partitioning is an art, there are some things that are worthy of consideration when implementing a design. As there are several issues to consider, we will introduce hints and suggestions that fall broadly into two categories

- Separation of logic
- Port type and mode selection

When separating logic into different entities, try and follow the natural partitioning of the design. While this may seem obvious, it is often overlooked. When describing (for documentation) a design contains several functions, try drawing blocks around the individual functions, as this might naturally result in a good partition. A natural partition is the one that tends to separate datapath from control logic. This is particularly true when there are several arithmetic circuits in a design. It can also help when trying to examine whether or not datapath resources can be shared to reduce the size of the overall design.

This form of partitioning also helps to create blocks that might need optimization as you go further along in the design process.

Another useful technique is to try and separate a design into blocks that might require optimization later on, either for reasons of performance, architecture, or implementation. An example of this might be a design where there is a common internal bus within a programmable device, as shown in *Figure 8*.

Figure 8: Bus with Internal Tri-states

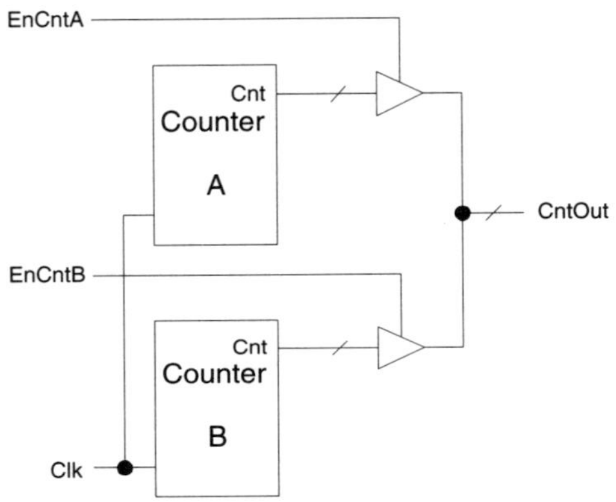

Not all programmable devices are capable of implementing internal tri-state buses. Instead, the tri-state may be converted to a mux, as we saw in *Chapter 7*. If this is the case, it may be desirable to control the implementation and the fanout of the control lines on the mux. Partition the design as shown in *Figure 9*, creating a separate module for the bus implementation.

Figure 9: Bus with Tri-states Buried in a Hierarchical Module

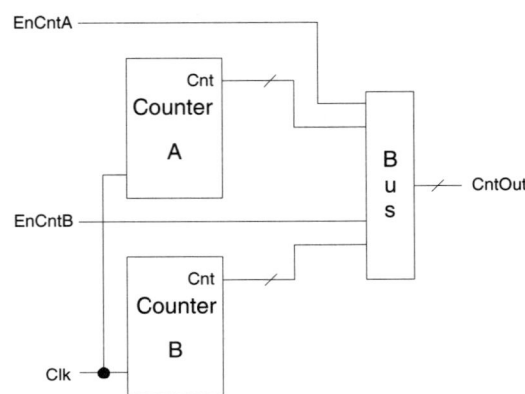

Chapter 9 - Design Partitioning

Within an architecture, processes can be used to separate portions of the design that can be logically grouped together. We took advantage of this in the state machine partitioning used in *Chapter 6*. However, take care when relying too much on processes for partitioning: use components as part of a design hierarchy as we have discussed in this chapter. There is no formula for determining how much logic to place in a design. However, one metric to examine is the ratio of the number of port signals (in the entity) to the amount of logic (in the architecture). If this number is very small, then you have too much logic and should consider partitioning the design. If the number is large, then it is likely that you have too little logic in the architecture. This measure, though by no means foolproof, can offer a clue as to when you should consider sub-dividing the design into smaller blocks.

Finally, another consideration when separating logic is based on the device-specific or architecture specific control signals in the design. The key point here is to consider all features of a design that might impact the post-synthesis process, which would include:

- One tri-state enable signal per entity-architecture pair. The exception to this might be a block that represents a bus, as we saw earlier.
- One clock per entity-architecture pair. This helps separate clock domains, and optimize partitioning, and even floor plan logic based on common clock signals
- One reset (or preset) signal per entity-architecture pair

Signal type and mode selection can play an important role when partitioning a design. In general, the following "rules of thumb" apply when selecting the *mode* and *type* in your designs:

- All port signals should be of type *std_logic* or *std_logic_vector*
- All port modes should be either *in* or *out*
- Only the top level entity should have ports of mode *inout*

As VHDL is strongly typed, we need to be consistent with type selection at the entity ports, since entities are connected via ports. The *std_logic* type is a standard supported by virtually all synthesis tools, and is highly portable. In addition, it also provides the flexibility that one needs in logic design since it allows you to describe not only the logic levels of '0' and '1', but also '-', 'Z' and 'X'.

While it may occasionally be tempting, do not use abstract types, such as enumerated types, or integers in the port map. Keep these types local to the architecture, and use type conversion functions, where appropriate, to convert them to the *std_logic* type at the ports.

The *mode*, or driver direction of a port signal also impacts partitioning. The mode of a signal must propagate throughout the hierarchy of a design. *Figure 10* shows signal *A* passing through three hierarchy levels, *L1*, *L2*, and *L3*. The signal modes at each of these levels must correspond to the mode at *L3*, the level at which the driver resides.

Figure 10: Modes Must Propagate Appropriately Through the Architecture

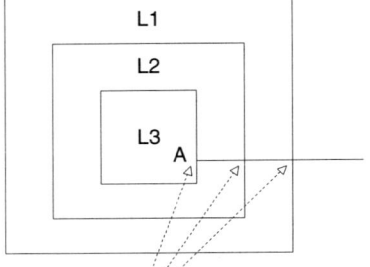

Signal modes must correspond

Using only the modes *in* and *out* (except at the top level of the hierarchy) also helps in the readability and documentation of a design. For example, consider the bi-directional counter that we first saw in *Chapter 7*. A hierarchical implementation of this counter is shown in *Figure 11*.

Figure 11: Bi-directional Counter Implemented Using Hierarchy

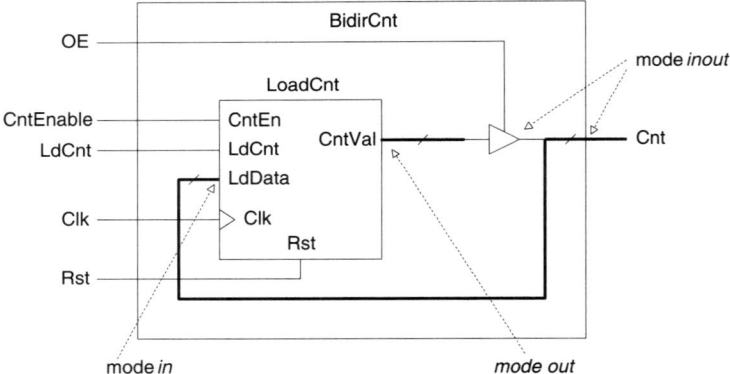

The inner component, *LoadCnt*, has only ports of mode *in* and *out*. Only the topmost component, *BidirCnt*, an *inout* port, since it interfaces at the "chip" level to a bi-directional pin. The listing for the top level, *BidirCnt*, is shown in *Listing 10*.

Listing 10: Counter with Bi-directional Output

```
library IEEE;
use IEEE.std_logic_1164.all;

entity BidirCnt is port (
  OE: in std_logic;
```

```vhdl
    CntEnable: in std_logic;
    LdCnt: in std_logic;
    Clk: in std_logic;
    Rst: in std_logic;
    Cnt: inout std_logic_vector(3 downto 0)
    );
end BidirCnt;

use work.bidirbuf.all;
use work.loadcnt.all;

architecture behavioral of BidirCnt is

  component LoadCnt port (
    CntEn: in std_logic;
    LdCnt: in std_logic;
    LdData: in std_logic_vector(3 downto 0);
    Clk: in std_logic;
    Rst: in std_logic;
    CntVal: out std_logic_vector(3 downto 0)
    );
  end component;

  component BidirBuf port (
    OE: in std_logic;
    input: in std_logic_vector;
    output: inout std_logic_vector
    );
  end component;

signal CntVal: std_logic_vector(3 downto 0);
signal LoadVal: std_logic_vector(3 downto 0);

for all: bidirbuf use entity work.bidirbuf(behavioral);
for all: loadcnt use entity work.loadcnt(behavioral);

begin

  u1: loadcnt port map (CntEn => CntEnable,
                        LdCnt => LdCnt,
                        LdData => LoadVal,
                        Clk => Clk,
                        Rst => Rst,
                        CntVal => CntVal
                        );

  u2: bidirbuf port map (OE => oe,
                         input => CntVal,
                         output => Cnt
                         );

  LoadVal <= Cnt;
end behavioral;
```

bidircnt.vhd

10
Getting the Most from Your State Machines

In *Chapter 6*, we developed a coding style that partitioned state machines into three blocks. This coding style takes advantage of VHDL's capability to abstract logic details, and relies on the synthesis tool to create the hardware. In this chapter, we will take a further look at state machines in order to understand the hardware implications of coding style on state machine design. We will also examine techniques that provide more direct control over the hardware created by logic synthesis tools.

There are two aspects that we will consider when examining state machine coding style:

- State machine performance
- Design implications of a particular coding style

The goal is to develop a grasp of how coding style affects the performance and size of the logic generated. We will also explore system considerations when approaching state machine design. The latter is part of the art of design, and as such is very difficult to completely quantify. However, we will attempt to raise the relevant issues so that they may be taken into account when you are trying to get the most our of your state machine.

There are two factors that govern both the performance, as well as the design implications of a state machine:

- State encoding
- Output generation

State Encoding

In *Chapter 6*, we expressed states using names to focus on algorithm development. This use of enumerated types relies on the logic synthesis tool to perform what is known as state encoding for these types. State encoding refers to the mapping of the abstract type to actual binary values, which are then assigned to each state to uniquely identify that state. This is done to generate next state information, as well as generate outputs based on a current state condition held in flip-flops. Hence, after synthesis, an abstract state encoding such as

```
type targetFsmType is (Idle, B_Busy, Backoff, S_Data, Turn_Ar);
```

will be synthesized as a vector (an array of register bits), where each state in turn is represented by a unique vector value. The technique we have used so far involves the use of enumerated types. However, there are times when you will not want to rely on the logic synthesis tool to assign the state encoding. In these instances, VHDL provides the capability of directly assigning that state encoding.

Sequential State Encoding

The most straight forward way of uniquely encoding states is to simply assign each state a number, represented in binary. In other words, our abstract state type could be assigned values as shown in *Table 1*.

Table 1: Simple Encoding for State Type

State	Number	Binary Value
Idle	0	000
B_Busy	1	001
Backoff	2	010
S_Data	3	011
Turn_Ar	4	100

This form of state encoding is often referred to as "sequential" coding, since the state values are sequentially assigned in an ascending fashion from 0. Notice that the minimum number of bits required to encode the states is n, where n is expressed in *Equation 1*.

Equation 1: Equation for the Number of Encoded States

$$2^n \geq \text{Total number of states}$$

In our example, we had a total of five states, which requires three bits to encode the states (n = 3).

Explicitly Encoding States Sequentially

Let us first take a look at how we might explicitly encode our states using sequential state assignments in the PCI target state machine example, that we saw earlier in *Chapter 6*. Clearly, our entity declaration remains the same. However, we will now use constants to define our state types in the architecture section, rather than enumerated types. As a result, we will replace

```
type targetFsmType is (Idle, B_Busy, Backoff, S_Data, Turn_Ar);

signal currState, nextState: targetFsmType;
```

with
```
    subtype targetFsmType is std_logic_vector(2 downto 0);

    constant Idle:    targetFsmType:= "000";
    constant B_Busy:  targetFsmType:= "001";
    constant Backoff: targetFsmType := "010";
    constant S_Data:  targetFsmType := "011";
    constant Turn_Ar: targetFsmType := "100";

    signal currState, nextState: targetFsmType;
```

From a design modification standpoint, there are two significant things to notice about this change:

- The use of *subtype*
- Minimal change in the design

As we saw in *Chapter 8*, *subtypes* may be thought of as a *sub*set *type*. In other words, they are a subset of a another type that has already been defined and declared in such a way that it is "visible" within the architecture. In our case, *targetFsmType* is a *subtype* of *std_logic_vector*, which has already been defined in the *std_logic_1164* package, and is made "visible" with the *use* clause. Subtypes also make the code much more readable and maintainable. Rather than declare each constant as a *std_logic_vector (2 downto 0)*, we simply define the *subtype* once, and declare the constants to be of this subtype.

Also, note that we have now seen the first benefit of the coding style we developed in *Chapter 6*. The only change we needed to make in our design was to the type declaration and constant definition. The rest of the design remains *entirely* the same. The entire listing of the sequentially coded target state machine can be seen in *Listing 1*.

Listing 1: PCI Target State Machine Using Explicit Sequential State Encoding

```
library IEEE;
use IEEE.std_logic_1164.all;

entity pci_target is port (
    PCI_Frame_n: in std_logic;      -- PCI Frame#
    PCI_Irdy_n:  in std_logic;      -- PCI Irdy#
    Hit:         in std_logic;      -- Hit on address decode
    D_Done:      in std_logic;      -- Device decode complete
    Term:        in std_logic;      -- Terminate transaction
    Ready:       in std_logic;      -- Ready to transfer data
    Cmd_Write:   in std_logic;      -- Command is Write
    Cmd_Read:    in std_logic;      -- Command is Read
    T_Abort:     in std_logic;      -- Target error  - abort transaction
    PCI_Clk:     in std_logic;      -- PCI Clock
    PCI_Reset_n: in std_logic;      -- PCI Reset#
```

```vhdl
    PCI_Devsel_n: out std_logic;    -- PCI Devsel#
    PCI_Trdy_n: out std_logic;      -- PCI Trdy#
    PCI_Stop_n: out std_logic;      -- PCI Stop#
    OE_AD: out std_logic;           -- PCI AD bus enable
    OE_Trdy_n: out std_logic;       -- PCI Trdy# enable
    OE_Stop_n: out std_logic;       -- PCI Stop# enable
    OE_Devsel_n: out std_logic      -- PCI Devsel# enable
  );
end pci_target;

architecture fsm of pci_target is

  signal LPCI_Devsel_n, LPCI_Trdy_n, LPCI_Stop_n: std_logic;

  subtype targetFsmType is std_logic_vector(2 downto 0);

  constant Idle:    targetFsmType := "000";
  constant B_Busy:  targetFsmType := "001";
  constant Backoff: targetFsmType := "011";
  constant S_Data:  targetFsmType := "110";
  constant Turn_Ar: targetFsmType := "100";

  signal currState, nextState: targetFsmType;

begin

  nxtStProc: process (currState, PCI_Frame_n, Hit, D_Done, PCI_Irdy_n,
     LPCI_Trdy_n, LPCI_Devsel_n, LPCI_Stop_n, Term, Ready) begin
    case currState is
      when Idle   =>
        if (PCI_Frame_n = '0' and Hit = '0') then
          nextState <= B_Busy;
        else
          nextState <= Idle;
        end if;

      when B_Busy =>
        if (PCI_Frame_n ='1' and D_Done = '1') or(PCI_Frame_n = '1' and
           D_Done = '0' and LPCI_Devsel_n = '0') then
          nextState <= Idle;
        elsif (PCI_Frame_n = '0' or PCI_Irdy_n = '0') and Hit = '1' and
           (Term = '0' or (Term = '1' and Ready = '1') ) then
          nextState <= S_Data;
        elsif (PCI_Frame_n = '0' or PCI_Irdy_n = '0') and Hit = '1' and
           (Term = '1' and Ready = '0') then
          nextState <= Backoff;
        else
          nextState <= B_Busy;
        end if;

      when S_Data =>
```

```vhdl
        if PCI_Frame_n = '0' and LPCI_Stop_n = '0' and
          (LPCI_Trdy_n = '1' or PCI_Irdy_n = '0') then
          nextState <= Backoff;
        elsif PCI_Frame_n = '1' and (LPCI_Trdy_n = '0' or LPCI_Stop_n = '0') then
          nextState <= Turn_Ar;
        else
          nextState <= S_Data;
        end if;

      when Backoff =>
        if PCI_Frame_n = '1' then
          nextState <= Turn_Ar;
        else
          nextState <= Backoff;
        end if;

      when Turn_Ar   =>
        if (PCI_Frame_n = '0' and Hit = '0') then
          nextState <= B_Busy;
        else
          nextState <= Idle;
        end if;

      when others =>
    null;
    end case;
end process nxtStProc;


curStProc: process (PCI_Clk, PCI_Reset_n) begin
  if (PCI_Reset_n = '0') then
    currState <= Idle;
  elsif (PCI_Clk'event and PCI_Clk = '1') then
    currState <= nextState;
  end if;
end process curStProc;

outConProc: process (currState, Ready, T_Abort, Cmd_Write,
                     Cmd_Read, T_Abort, Term) begin
  case currState is
    when S_Data =>
      if (Cmd_Read = '1') then
        OE_AD <= '1';
      else
        OE_AD <= '0';
      end if;

      if (Ready = '1' and T_Abort = '0' and (Cmd_Write = '1' or
          Cmd_Read = '1')) then
        LPCI_Trdy_n <= '0';
      else
```

```vhdl
      LPCI_Trdy_n <= '1';
    end if;

    if (T_Abort = '1' or Term = '1') and (Cmd_Write = '1' or Cmd_Read = '1') then
      LPCI_Stop_n <= '0';
    else
      LPCI_Stop_n <= '1';
    end if;

    if (T_Abort = '0') then
      LPCI_Devsel_n <= '0';
    else
      LPCI_Devsel_n <= '1';
    end if;

    OE_Trdy_n <= '1';
    OE_Stop_n <= '1';
    OE_Devsel_n <= '1';

  when Backoff =>
    if (Cmd_Read = '1') then
      OE_AD <= '1';
    else
      OE_AD <= '0';
    end if;

    LPCI_Stop_n <= '0';

    OE_Trdy_n <= '1';
    OE_Stop_n <= '1';
    OE_Devsel_n <= '1';

    if (T_Abort = '0') then
      LPCI_Devsel_n <= '0';
    else
      LPCI_Devsel_n <= '1';
    end if;

  when Turn_Ar =>

    OE_Trdy_n <= '1';
    OE_Stop_n <= '1';
    OE_Devsel_n <= '1';

  when others =>

    OE_Trdy_n <= '0';
    OE_Stop_n <= '0';
    OE_Devsel_n <= '0';
    OE_AD <= '0';
    LPCI_Trdy_n <= '1';
    LPCI_Stop_n <= '1';
```

```
            LPCI_Devsel_n <= '1';

      end case;

  end process outConProc;

  PCI_Devsel_n <= LPCI_Devsel_n;
  PCI_Trdy_n   <= LPCI_Trdy_n;
  PCI_Stop_n   <= LPCI_Stop_n;

end fsm;
```

tar_seq.vhd

As we noted earlier, the explicit encoding of states not only affects the performance, but also the hardware implications of the state machine. We will begin by first considering how the next state logic influences performance.

Analyzing the Next State Logic

To analyze how the next state logic is generated, we will use the example of the PCI Target State machine developed in *Chapter 6*. In this design, the *Backoff* state can be entered from either the *B_Busy* state, or the *S_data* state, as shown in *Figure 1*. In addition, we can remain in the *Backoff* state if the condition C8 is satisfied.

Figure 1: Logic Affecting Transition to the Backoff State

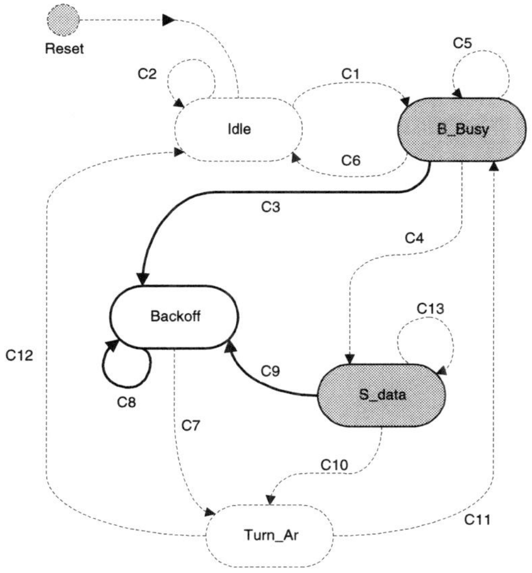

Table 2 shows the various ways in which we can enter the *Backoff* state.

Table 2: Ways to Reach the Backoff State

Current State	Condition	Next State
B_Busy	!C6 * !C4 * C3	Backoff
S_Data	C9	Backoff
Backoff	C8	Backoff

Since we know the encoding for *B_Busy*, *S_data* and *Backoff*, we can rewrite *Table 2* as equations by substituting the state encoding values as follows:

```
nextState <= Backoff when
   (currState = "001" AND (NOT(C6) AND NOT(C4) AND C3)) OR
   (currState = "011" AND (C9) OR
   (currState = "010" AND (C8);
```

We can continue our expansion by substituting the various condition equations. For example, to remain in the *Backoff* state, we must satisfy:

```
currState = "010" AND (NOT(PCI_Frame_n))
```

As the equations are expanded, the state transition logic can get quite complicated. This is true especially when the branch conditions are complex, such as C4 which itself has OR terms in the condition. This leads us to conclude that there are three factors that impact the performance of the next state logic generation, which in turn impacts the performance of the state machine. These are:

- The number and complexity of branch conditions from each state
- The number of state bits to be decoded to determine which state we are in
- Transitions of state bits from (0 to 1 and vice versa) from state to state

Number and Complexity of Branch Conditions

The number and complexity of branch conditions depend on what is being controlled. It may be very difficult to change or modify this, especially in our case, where we are dealing with a state machine that describes the behavior of an industry standard. Methods to tackle the number and complexity of branch conditions would include changing the number of states, or perhaps splitting the state machine into two or more state machines that run parallel to each other.

Chapter 10 - Getting the Most from Your State Machines

Number of State Bits

The number of state bits, on the other hand, is certainly within our control. Clearly, the more state bits we have, the wider the decode for determining which state we are in. To illustrate this, let us consider the same PCI state machine using three bits and four bits to encode the five states of the design. Both approaches result in identical logical behavior, and the state encoding for each approach is shown in *Listing 2* and *Listing 3*. The results show the 4-bit encoding to be less desirable than the 3-bit encoding as shown in the comparison table, *Table 3*[1].

Listing 2: 3-bit Encoding of the PCI Target State Machine

```
constant Idle:      targetFsmType := "000";
constant B_Busy:    targetFsmType := "001";
constant Backoff:   targetFsmType := "010";
constant S_Data:    targetFsmType := "011";
constant Turn_Ar:   targetFsmType := "100";
```

Listing 3: 4-bit Encoding of the PCI Target State Machine

```
constant Idle:      targetFsmType := "0000";
constant B_Busy:    targetFsmType := "0001";
constant Backoff:   targetFsmType := "0011";
constant S_Data:    targetFsmType := "1100";
constant Turn_Ar:   targetFsmType := "1101";
```

Table 3: Speed Decreases and Utilization Increases Using Four State Bits Versus Three State Bits

Device	Speed Decrease	Utilization Increase
LUT architecture	2%	19%
Mux architecture	7%	20%

Table 3 also shows an interesting phenomenon of FPGAs. Control circuits that are smaller, are often faster. This is because a large amount of logic typically results in additional "levels of logic" needed for the function. The number of "levels of logic" refers to the number of logic element levels that a signal has to go through as part of a function computation. Each level represents the basic logic element that the device has, along with interconnect to the next level. Thus, the greater the number of levels of logic for a function, the slower its performance.

Having a large number of state bits does not automatically mean that performance and utilization decreases, as we will see when we discuss one-hot coded and directly encoded state machines later in this chapter.

---

1. See Appendix A: Measuring Performance and Utilization.

Reducing the Number of State Bit Transitions When Going From State to State

Another factor that affects the size and efficiency of logic generated is the number of state bits that transition as we move from state to state. This is because each bit in the state vector that changes, when we move from one state to another, requires conditioning logic to effect that change. In other words, the state encoding itself plays a major part in the logic that is generated.

The basic technique to reduce the logic generated by state transitions is to chose a state encoding that minimizes the number of bits that have to transition when moving from one state to another. To explore this further, let us consider encoding the state machine with three state bits. The two encoding schemes we have used are shown in *Listing 4* and *Listing 5*.

Listing 4: 3-bit Encoding for PCI Target State Machine - Option 1

```
constant Idle:      targetFsmType := "000";
constant B_Busy:    targetFsmType := "101";
constant Backoff:   targetFsmType := "010";
constant S_Data:    targetFsmType := "011";
constant Turn_Ar:   targetFsmType := "110";
```

Listing 5: 3-bit Encoding for PCI Target State Machine - Option 2

```
constant Idle:      targetFsmType := "000";
constant B_Busy:    targetFsmType := "001";
constant Backoff:   targetFsmType := "011";
constant S_Data:    targetFsmType := "010";
constant Turn_Ar:   targetFsmType := "110";
```

Table 4: Speed Increase and Utilization Decrease Using Encoding Option 2 Versus Option 1

Device	Speed Increase	Utilization Decrease
LUT architecture	14%	7%
Mux architecture	0%	5%

Table 4[2] shows that the encoding scheme in *Listing 5* produces better results for this particular state machine. In fact, the state encoding scheme used in this listing is often termed "Gray Coding". It is important to note, however, that Gray coding may not necessarily result in better performance than binary coding. Gray codes work best when they follow the same order as the state transitions. If applied randomly, they are likely to produce results similar to those obtained with binary encoding.

---

2. See Appendix A: Measuring Performance and Utilization.

One-hot Coded State Machines

Recall that there are two factors under our control that influence state machine performance:

- The number of state bits to be decoded to determine the current state
- Transitions of state bits from (0 to 1 and vice versa) from state to state

In certain programmable logic architecture, these factors have lead to the use of "One-hot" coding style for state assignment. One-hot state machine encoding implies that there is only one bit that is set (or "hot") *per* state. This means that we need n registers for our state vector, where n is the number of states in the state machine.

This method uses more registers than an encoded state machine. For instance, our PCI target state machine with five states now takes five registers to represent the state vector, rather than three using an encoded state vector. However, even though the number of state bits is greater, note that we only need to decode one bit to determine which state we are in. This almost always reduces the number of levels of logic in the design, as compared to encoded state machines.

Some synthesis tools will automatically select this state encoding style where appropriate. "Appropriate" refers to those device architectures that have a high register-to-logic ratio. In these device architectures, registers are "cheap" since they are built into each logic element. If unused, they are "wasted" since they still physically exist on the chip. If used, they may be combined with combinational logic and packed into a single logic element. Sometimes, however, the synthesis tool will not generate a one-hot coded state machine, or will be incapable of doing so. As such, we need to develop a coding style that will explicitly result in a one-hot coded state machine during the synthesis process.

Explicit Method for One-hot Coded State Machines

Once again, we will use our PCI target state machine to demonstrate the one-hot coding style for state machines. Changes to the design style developed in *Chapter 6* can be described in five steps.

Step 1: Creating the Type for the State Machine

Here, we declare a *std_logic_vector* whose width is the number of states in the design, as follows:

```
subtype targetFsmType is std_logic_vector(4 downto 0);

constant Idle:      integer := 0;
constant B_Busy:    integer := 1;
constant Backoff:   integer := 2;
constant S_Data:    integer := 3;
constant Turn_Ar:   integer := 4;

signal currState, nextState: targetFsmType;
```

Because our design has five states, we declare a *std_logic_vector* whose range is *(4 downto 0)*. In addition, we declare five constant integers, each of which represents the state. This is done solely to make the design readable, as the integers are used as an index into the state vector, which is of the *std_logic_vector* type.

Step 2: Set the Default State for the State Vector

At the beginning of the next state conditioning process, set the default next state vector to zero as follows:

```
nxtStProc: process (currState, PCI_Frame_n, Hit, D_Done, PCI_Irdy_n, LPCI_Trdy_n,
                LPCI_Devsel_n, LPCI_Stop_n, Term, Ready) begin

    nextState <= (others => '0');
```

This is done to ensure that only one bit is set per state. By completely specifying all states and transition conditions in the subsequent *if...then* statements, we can ensure that only one of the bits in the state vector is always set, representing our one-hot coded state machine.

Step 3: Replace Case With *if...then* for the nextState Assignment

Now, substitute an *if...then* for each *case* condition. For example, the *case* condition for the *Idle* state:

```
case currState is
    when Idle =>
      if (PCI_Frame_n = '0' and Hit = '0') then
        nextState <= B_Busy;
      else
        nextState <= Idle;
      end if;
```

is rewritten as:

```
if currState(Idle) = '1' then
    if (PCI_Frame_n = '0' and Hit = '0') then
      nextState(B_Busy) <= '1';
    else
      nextState(Idle) <= '1';
    end if;
end if;
```

Step 4: Change the Code for the *Idle* State Condition in the Current State Process

On reset, we need to explicitly set the bit in the state vector that represents the *Idle* state, as follows:

```
curStProc: process (PCI_Clk, PCI_Reset_n) begin
    if (PCI_Reset_n = '0') then
      currState(Idle) <= '1';
```

Chapter 10 - Getting the Most from Your State Machines

Step 5: Replace *Case* With *if...then* for the Output Conditioning Logic

Finally we need to replace the *case* statement in the output conditioning logic process with *if...then* statements, similar to the change made to the next state conditioning process. As an example, the output conditioning for the *Backoff* state:

```
when Backoff =>
      if (Cmd_Read = '1') then
   OE_AD <= '1';
  else
    OE_AD <= '0';
  end if;

         LPCI_Stop_n <= '0';

         OE_Trdy_n <= '1';
         OE_Stop_n <= '1';
         OE_Devsel_n <= '1';

         if (T_Abort = '0') then
           LPCI_Devsel_n <= '0';
         else
           LPCI_Devsel_n <= '1';
         end if;
```

is rewritten as:

```
     if (currState(Backoff) = '1') then
          if (Cmd_Read = '1') then
    OE_AD <= '1';
  else
    OE_AD <= '0';
  end if;

         LPCI_Stop_n <= '0';

         OE_Trdy_n <= '1';
         OE_Stop_n <= '1';
         OE_Devsel_n <= '1';

         if (T_Abort = '0') then
           LPCI_Devsel_n <= '0';
         else
           LPCI_Devsel_n <= '1';
         end if;
      end if;
  end if;
```

The complete design, when coded to explicitly describe a one-hot coded state machine, is shown in *Listing 6*.

Listing 6: PCI Target State Machine Written to Explicitly Use One-hot Coding

```vhdl
-- Incorporates Errata 10.1

library IEEE;
use IEEE.std_logic_1164.all;

entity pci_target is port (
  PCI_Frame_n: in std_logic;     -- PCI Frame#
  PCI_Irdy_n: in std_logic;      -- PCI Irdy#
  Hit: in std_logic;             -- Hit on address decode
  D_Done: in std_logic;          -- Device decode complete
  Term: in std_logic;            -- Terminate transaction
  Ready: in std_logic;           -- Ready to transfer data
  Cmd_Write: in std_logic;       -- Command is Write
  Cmd_Read: in std_logic;        -- Command is Read
  T_Abort: in std_logic;         -- Target error - abort transaction
  PCI_Clk: in std_logic;         -- PCI Clock
  PCI_Reset_n: in std_logic;     -- PCI Reset#

  PCI_Devsel_n: out std_logic;   -- PCI Devsel#
  PCI_Trdy_n: out std_logic;     -- PCI Trdy#
  PCI_Stop_n: out std_logic;     -- PCI Stop#
  OE_AD: out std_logic;          -- PCI AD bus enable
  OE_Trdy_n: out std_logic;      -- PCI Trdy# enable
  OE_Stop_n: out std_logic;      -- PCI Stop# enable
  OE_Devsel_n: out std_logic     -- PCI Devsel# enable
  );
end pci_target;

architecture fsm of pci_target is

signal LPCI_Devsel_n, LPCI_Trdy_n, LPCI_Stop_n: std_logic;

subtype targetFsmType is std_logic_vector(4 downto 0);

constant Idle:    integer := 0;
constant B_Busy:  integer := 1;
constant Backoff: integer := 2;
constant S_Data:  integer := 3;
constant Turn_Ar: integer := 4;

signal currState, nextState: targetFsmType;

begin

 nxtStProc: process (currState, PCI_Frame_n, Hit, D_Done, PCI_Irdy_n,
    LPCI_Trdy_n, LPCI_Devsel_n, LPCI_Stop_n, Term, Ready) begin

   nextState <= (others => '0');

   if currState(Idle) = '1' then
      if (PCI_Frame_n = '0' and Hit = '0') then
        nextState(B_Busy) <= '1';
      else
        nextState(Idle) <= '1';
```

```vhdl
         end if;
      end if;

      if currState(B_Busy) = '1' then
         if (PCI_Frame_n ='1' and D_Done = '1') or
          (PCI_Frame_n = '1' and D_Done = '0' and LPCI_Devsel_n = '0') then
            nextState(Idle) <= '1';
         elsif (PCI_Frame_n = '0' or PCI_Irdy_n = '0') and Hit = '1' and
      (Term = '0' or (Term = '1' and Ready = '1') ) then
            nextState(S_Data) <= '1';
         elsif (PCI_Frame_n = '0' or PCI_Irdy_n = '0') and Hit = '1' and
      (Term = '1' and Ready = '0') then
            nextState(Backoff) <= '1';
         else
            nextState(B_Busy) <= '1';
         end if;
      end if;

      if currState(S_Data) = '1' then
         if PCI_Frame_n = '0' and LPCI_Stop_n = '0' and
             (LPCI_Trdy_n = '1' or PCI_Irdy_n = '0') then
            nextState(Backoff) <= '1';
         elsif PCI_Frame_n = '1' and (LPCI_Trdy_n = '0' or LPCI_Stop_n = '0') then
            nextState(Turn_Ar) <= '1';
         else
            nextState(S_Data) <= '1';
         end if;
      end if;

      if currState(Backoff) = '1' then
         if PCI_Frame_n = '1' then
            nextState(Turn_Ar) <= '1';
         else
            nextState(Backoff) <= '1';
         end if;
      end if;

      if currState(Turn_Ar) = '1' then
         if (PCI_Frame_n = '0' and Hit = '0') then
            nextState(B_Busy) <= '1';
         else
            nextState(Idle) <= '1';
         end if;
      end if;

   end process nxtStProc;

   curStProc: process (PCI_Clk, PCI_Reset_n) begin
      if (PCI_Reset_n = '0') then
         currState(Idle) <= '1';
      elsif (PCI_Clk'event and PCI_Clk = '1') then
         currState <= nextState;
      end if;
   end process curStProc;
```

```vhdl
outConProc: process (currState, Ready, T_Abort, Cmd_Write,
                     Cmd_Read, T_Abort, Term) begin
  OE_Trdy_n <= '0';OE_Stop_n <= '0';OE_Devsel_n <= '0';-- defaults per
  Errata 10.1
  OE_AD <= '0';LPCI_Trdy_n <= '1';LPCI_Stop_n <= '1';
  LPCI_Devsel_n <= '1';

  if (currState(S_Data) = '1') then
    if (Cmd_Read = '1') then
      OE_AD <= '1';
    else
      OE_AD <= '0';
    end if;

    if (Ready = '1' and T_Abort = '0' and (Cmd_Write = '1' or
      Cmd_Read = '1')) then
        LPCI_Trdy_n <= '0';
    else
      LPCI_Trdy_n <= '1';
    end if;

    if (T_Abort = '1' or Term = '1') and (Cmd_Write = '1' or
      Cmd_Read = '1')  then
      LPCI_Stop_n <= '0';
    else
      LPCI_Stop_n <= '1';
    end if;

    if (T_Abort = '0') then
      LPCI_Devsel_n <= '0';
    else
      LPCI_Devsel_n <= '1';
    end if;

    OE_Trdy_n <= '1';
    OE_Stop_n <= '1';
    OE_Devsel_n <= '1';
  end if;

  if (currState(Backoff) = '1') then
    if (Cmd_Read = '1') then
      OE_AD <= '1';
    else
      OE_AD <= '0';
    end if;

    LPCI_Stop_n <= '0';

    OE_Trdy_n <= '1';
    OE_Stop_n <= '1';
    OE_Devsel_n <= '1';
```

```
      if (T_Abort = '0') then
        LPCI_Devsel_n <= '0';
      else
        LPCI_Devsel_n <= '1';
      end if;
    end if;

    if (currState(Turn_Ar) = '1') then
      OE_Trdy_n <= '1';
      OE_Stop_n <= '1';
      OE_Devsel_n <= '1';
    end if;

    if (currState(Idle) = '1' or currState(B_Busy) = '1') then
      OE_Trdy_n <= '0';
      OE_Stop_n <= '0';
      OE_Devsel_n <= '0';
      OE_AD <= '0';
      LPCI_Trdy_n <= '1';
      LPCI_Stop_n <= '1';
      LPCI_Devsel_n <= '1';
    end if;

  end process outConProc;

  PCI_Devsel_n <= LPCI_Devsel_n;
  PCI_Trdy_n <= LPCI_Trdy_n;
  PCI_Stop_n <= LPCI_Stop_n;

end fsm;
```

tar_ohot.vhd

The comparative results of an encoded state machine using the state assignments in *Listing 2*, and the one-hot coded state machine in *Listing 6* are shown in *Table 5*.

Table 5: Speed and Utilization Increase Using One-hot Versus Encoded States

Device	Speed Increase	Utilization Increase
LUT architecture	29%	15%
Mux architecture	-10%	15%

State Encoding Guidelines for Performance
As can be seen from *Table 5*[3], the size of the state machine and the target device/ technology greatly influence the type of state encoding used for performance

---

3. See Appendix A: Measuring Performance and Utilization.

considerations. *Table 5* shows that for the LUT-based device, the increase in size is accompanied by a significant increase in performance, as was the premise behind one-hot coding. However, note that for the Mux architecture device, the one-hot coding, while increasing the number of logic elements used, in fact degraded the state machine performance for this particular state machine.

For LUT and Mux based programmable logic architectures, we can use simple rules of thumb to determine the state encoding. Small state machines, with two to four states should always be encoded, and larger state machines (those which have more than ten to twelve states) should be one-hot coded. However you need to perform some analysis or experimentation with state machines that fall between these two sizes, or those that are significantly larger (in the region of thirty states). This can be seen in *Table 5*, for the Mux architecture device, where the state machine with five states has better utilization and performance characteristics when the states are encoded, as opposed to one-hot coding. For devices with a sum-of-product architecture, it is often best to encode state machines with two to sixteen states. This is generally true of ASICs and gate-arrays too.

For large state machines, especially those that have long chains of unconditional branches interspersed with a few states with conditional branches, consider using a combination of one-hot and sequential coding. The states with conditional branches should be "one-hot coded", while the remaining states should be encoded. This means that the detection of state transitions with conditional branches is dependent on only a single bit decoding while the remaining state transitions rely on decoding the entire state vector. The state assignment should be chosen carefully, to avoid spurious state transitions.

Design Implications of State Encoding

There are two very important design consideration when choosing a particular state encoding. They are:

- Default or power-up state
- Recovering from a transition into an unknown state

The default or power-up state relates to the current state of the state machine when the device first powers up in your system. In general, it is desirable for the state machine to power-up into a known state, as the state machine is connected to other logic that should not be spuriously triggered. For this reason, encoded states with a default state encoded as all zeros are useful, as many devices power-up with their registers in a reset state. Devices whose registers do not power-up into a known state require an additional reset signal to place state machines into the default state. The default or power-up state is a design consideration when choosing the one-hot coding style for state machines. One-hot state machines need to be reset to be placed into the default state, where one bit is set (or hot), and the others are reset. In such case, care must be taken to ensure that the reset skew between state registers does not impact the operation of the state machine.

Events that are outside your control (and sometimes external to the system) might cause an inadvertent change in the state of a register. This could result in the state machine going into an unknown or unassigned state. As such, it is important to design state machines that can recover from being placed into an unknown state. One technique for this would be to decode unassigned states and reset the state machine whenever it enters one of these states. However, you can readily see that one-hot coded state machines will require more decoding logic (as compared to encoded state machines) to determine when the state machine is in an unknown state. This aspect of one-hot coded state machines makes them undesirable when designing a state machine that has illegal-state recovery as a requirement.

There is also a subtle, but important, side-effect of state encoding when it comes to simulation. As per the language specification, a signal defaults to the left-most of the possible assigned values. For example, the default value of a *std_logic* signal is 'U', as *std_logic* may be assigned ('U', 'X', '0', '1', 'Z', 'W', 'L', 'H', '-'). This is significant, since your target device may not power-up into the default state. This discrepancy between simulation and the physical device is even more noticeable when using enumerated types. Let us consider the following type and signal declaration:

```
type targetFsmType is (Idle, B_Busy, Backoff, S_Data, Turn_Ar);

signal currState: targetFsmType;
```

In this case, *currState* always defaults to *Idle* when the simulation begins. The hardware, however, will reflect this default state only if all of the following are satisfied:

1. The state machine is encoded
2. The *Idle* state has all registers in the encoded state vector set to '0'
3. The device powers-up with all registers reset

Thus, simulation, especially of the pre-synthesis behavioral model, should be performed with particular attention to the power-up state and must comprehend differences between the behavioral description and the hardware synthesized.

Other Issues When Explicitly Assigning State Bits
While explicitly assigning state bits will certainly give you more control over the result, there are a few side effects that should be noted.

The first, perhaps most obvious, consequence is that we lose the abstraction of enumerated types when we explicitly encode states using *std_logic_vectors*. The abstract type allows the synthesis software to choose the best state encoding based on the target device/architecture. The explicit state encoding is just that: explicit. It will make the tool produce the same logic equations regardless of the target device, as a result of which the design may not be as portable as it is with the abstract enumerated types.

Secondly, by using *std_logic_vector* to explicitly encode the state bits, we can easily bring this vector out to pins and examine the state bits while debugging the design. However, with enumerated types we need to decode each state and bring it out to a pin. For state machines with a large number of states, this can be difficult, since there may not be enough pins left on the device to bring all the decoded states to pins.

Finally, synthesis tools are getting better at assigning states. Some even include the capability of inferring state machines from logic, and then reassigning the state encoding for best results. If you choose to use this capability, make sure that you follow the state machine partitioning guidelines developed in *Chapter 6*.

Output Decoding

So far, we have only examined how state encoding affects state machine performance. However, the state machine has outputs which feed other logic in the design. Part of the output generation logic is the next state generation logic. These could easily become the bottlenecks for performance. There are four approaches to improving output decoding performance:

- Set a default condition for the output and next state conditioning logic
- Register the outputs
- Use "don't cares" for the outputs where possible
- Directly encode the outputs as part of the state vector

Default Output Assignment

The default output conditions must be assigned at the beginning of the output decode process due to implicit latch generation as described in *Chapter 8*. Recall that if you do not assign each output in all stages of output generation, then the output generation process will generate implicit latches to hold or recirculate the value. For both the one-hot and encoded versions of our PCI target state machines, we only need to add the default case at the beginning of the process for each of the outputs, as follows:

```
outConProc: process (currState, Ready, T_Abort, Cmd_Write,
                     Cmd_Read, T_Abort, Term) begin

   -- Set default output assignments
   OE_Trdy_n <= '0';
   OE_Stop_n <= '0';
   OE_Devsel_n <= '0';
   OE_AD <= '0';
```

Chapter 10 - Getting the Most from Your State Machines

```
   LPCI_Trdy_n   <= '1';
   LPCI_Stop_n   <= '1';
   LPCI_Devsel_n <= '1';

   case currState is
```

In addition, in the *nxtStProc* process, instead of the default assignment

```
when others =>
  null;
```

send the next state to *Idle*, as follows:

```
when others =>
  nextState <= Idle;
```

These two changes can have a dramatic impact on the number of logic elements used in the design, and also the performance, just as we saw in *Chapter 8*. The results for the PCI target state machine, with the states encoded as in *Listing 2* are shown in *Table 6*.

Table 6: Speed Increase and Utilization Decrease Using Default Assignments (Versus Not Using)

Device	Speed Increase	Utilization Decrease
LUT architecture	38%	11%
Mux architecture	6%	25%

An interesting point to note in *Table 6*[4] is that the Mux architecture device only shows a 6% performance improvement over the implementation without defaults. This might be attributed to the fact that the mux-based logic element of this device inherently supports latches well, which is why we do not see such a significant performance improvement in that device.

Registered Outputs

Performance of the outputs can be improved by registering them, rather than making them just combinational outputs of the state machine. This method not only gives good performance, but also avoids glitches in the design caused by state vector and input signals propagating through the output conditioning logic. Performing a "lookahead" on the outputs and then registering them will ensure that they appear on the correct cycle. Effectively, the lookahead decodes each output presented one clock cycle before it is needed, after which it is registered so that is the output on the correct cycle. Given the way we partitioned our state machine from the start, it is in fact quite easy to make this change.

---

4. See Appendix A: Measuring Performance and Utilization.

Note that the output conditioning logic process begins with

```
outConProc: process (currState, Ready, T_Abort, Cmd_Write,
                    Cmd_Read, T_Abort, Term) begin
    case currState is
```

We need to make two changes. The first is to change the *case* statement so that selection is based on the *nextState* vector instead of *currState*. Secondly, we need to register all outputs in the process, as follows:

```
outConProc: process (PCI_Clk, PCI_Reset_n) begin
    if PCI_Reset_n = '0' then
        OE_Trdy_n <= '0';
        OE_Stop_n <= '0';
        OE_Devsel_n <= '0';
        OE_AD <= '0';
        LPCI_Trdy_n <= '1';
        LPCI_Stop_n <= '1';
        LPCI_Devsel_n <= '1';
    elsif (PCI_Clk'event and PCI_Clk = '1') then
        case nextState is
```

The remainder of the process stays the same. There are two side effects of doing this, which should be noted. Firstly, the state machine timing changes and the delays through the input-to-output functions need to meet the timing parameters of the flip-flop (set-up time and hold-time). Secondly, if there are output functions that can change while the state machine is in a given state, then our registering scheme will clearly not work. This is because we have now registered the outputs, which can only change on the subsequent rising clock edge.

Don't Cares

Finally, another way to reduce logic and improve the performance of the design is to use a 'X' or "don't care", similar to what we saw in *Chapter 8*. "Don't cares" should be used with caution. Make sure that the logic is truly a "don't care" for that given condition (or conditions). Pay close attention to this during system simulation, and attempt to apply a stimulus that will cover these conditions.

In the PCI target state machine design, we have two opportunities to use "don't cares". The first is in *nxtStProc*, the next state output conditioning process, and the second is in *outConProc*, the output conditioning logic process. On further examination, we really cannot use don't cares in the output conditioning logic. This is because some of the outputs are control signals for tri-state buffers which are connected to the shared system PCI bus. Hence, a don't care on these enables might result in the buffers being driven when they are not supposed to be driven.

Chapter 10 - Getting the Most from Your State Machines

This leaves the default case for next state conditioning. By adding the constant

```
constant Dont_Care: targetFsmType := "XXX";
```

at the beginning of the architecture specification, and by changing the default case for the next state conditioning logic to

```
when others =>
    nextState <= Dont_Care;
```

we can give further room to the compiler to optimize the next state conditioning logic. As a side note, the use of "XXX" as the default case can also be useful for simulation debug purposes.

Table 7[5] shows the advantage of using "don't cares" as the default condition, as opposed to no default conditions for the PCI state machine design. The source code uses the state encoding in *Listing 2*.

Table 7: Speed Increase and Utilization Decrease Using "Don't Care" Defaults Versus Fixed Defaults

Device	Speed Increase	Utilization Decrease
LUT architecture	11%	15%
Mux architecture	4%	15%

Directly Encoding Outputs

State encoding and output generation can be combined in a coding style that directly encodes the outputs as part of the state vector. This method can result in a more compact and better performing state machine, and should be considered when explicitly coding a state machine. To use this technique for state assignment and output generation, we need to take the following steps:

1. Determine which of the state machines outputs are set in each of its states
2. Note these output combinations as part of the state vector
3. Add a sufficient number of bits to the state vector to uniquely encode the states

To illustrate this, let us consider the example of the programmable pulse generator state machine implemented in *Chapter 6*. Following the first step, we can see that the state machine has only one output, *pulse*, that is driven as shown in *Table 8*.

---

5. See Appendix A: Measuring Performance and Utilization.

Table 8: Output Pulse in Each State

State	Pulse
loadDelay Cnt	0
waitDelayEnd	0
loadLengthCnt	1
waitLengthEnd	1

Thus, following steps 2 and 3, if we directly encode the *pulse* output as part of the state, it is clear that we only need one more register to uniquely encode the state vector, as shown in *Table 9*.

Table 9: State Encoding Use Pulse and an Extra State Register (StateReg)

State	Encoding (StateReg, Pulse)
loadDelayCnt	0,0
waitDelayEnd	1,0
loadLengthCnt	1,1
waitLengthEnd	0,1

We can now code our state machine as shown in *Listing 7*.

Listing 7: Programmable Pulse Generator Using Direct Encoding

```
library ieee;
use ieee.std_logic_1164.all;
use ieee.numeric_std.all;

entity progPulse is port (
  clk, reset: in std_logic;
  loadLength,loadDelay: in std_logic;
  data: in std_logic_vector(7 downto 0);
  pulse: out std_logic
  );
end progPulse;

architecture rtl of progPulse is

signal downCnt, downCntData: unsigned(7 downto 0);
signal downCntLd, downCntEn: std_logic;
signal delayCntVal, pulseCntVal: unsigned(7 downto 0);
signal startPulse, endPulse: std_logic;

subtype fsmType is std_logic_vector(1 downto 0);
constant loadDelayCnt : fsmType := "00";
constant waitDelayEnd : fsmType := "10";
```

```vhdl
  constant loadLengthCnt : fsmType := "11";
  constant waitLengthEnd : fsmType := "01";

  signal currState, nextState: fsmType;

begin

  delayreg: process (clk, reset) begin
    if reset = '1' then
      delayCntVal <= "11111111";
    elsif clk'event and clk = '1' then
      if loadDelay = '1' then
        delayCntVal <= to_unsigned(data);
      end if;
    end if;
  end process;

  lengthReg: process (clk, reset) begin
    if reset = '1' then
      pulseCntVal <= "11111111";
    elsif clk'event and clk = '1' then
      if loadDelay = '1' then
        pulseCntVal <= to_unsigned(data);
      end if;
    end if;
  end process;

  nextStProc: process (currState, downCnt, loadDelay, loadLength) begin
    case currState is
      when loadDelayCnt =>
        nextState <= waitDelayEnd;

      when waitDelayEnd =>
        if (loadDelay = '1' or loadLength = '1') then
          nextState <= loadDelayCnt;
        elsif (downCnt = 0) then
          nextState <= loadLengthCnt;
        else
          nextState <= waitDelayEnd;
        end if;

      when loadLengthCnt =>
        if (loadDelay = '1' or loadLength = '1') then
          nextState <= loadDelayCnt;
        else
          nextState <= waitLengthEnd;
        end if;

      when waitLengthEnd =>
        if (loadDelay = '1' or loadLength = '1') then
          nextState <= loadDelayCnt;
        elsif (downCnt = 0) then
          nextState <= loadDelayCnt;
```

```vhdl
          else
            nextState <= waitDelayEnd;
          end if;

        when others =>
          null;
      end case;
    end process nextStProc;

    currStProc: process (clk, reset) begin
      if (reset = '1') then
        currState <= loadDelayCnt;
      elsif (clk'event and clk = '1') then
        currState <= nextState;
      end if;
    end process currStProc;
    outConProc: process (currState, delayCntVal, pulseCntVal) begin
      case currState is
        when loadDelayCnt =>
          downCntEn <= '0';
          downCntLd <= '1';
          downCntData <= delayCntVal;

        when waitDelayEnd =>
          downCntEn <= '1';
          downCntLd <= '0';
          downCntData <= delayCntVal;

        when loadLengthCnt =>
          downCntEn <= '0';
          downCntLd <= '1';
          downCntData <= pulseCntVal;

        when waitLengthEnd =>
          downCntEn <= '1';
          downCntLd <= '0';
          downCntData <= pulseCntVal;

        when others =>
          downCntEn <= '0';
          downCntLd <= '1';
          downCntData <= pulseCntVal;

      end case;
    end process outConProc;

    downCntr: process (clk,reset) begin
      if (reset = '1') then
        downCnt <= "00000000";
      elsif (clk'event and clk = '1') then
        if (downCntLd = '1') then
          downCnt <= downCntData;
```

Chapter 10 - Getting the Most from Your State Machines

```
      elsif (downCntEn = '1') then
        downCnt <= downCnt - 1;
      else
        downCnt <= downCnt;
      end if;
    end if;
  end process;

  -- Assign pulse output
  pulse <= currState(0);

end rtl;
```

pulsedir.vhd

An important point to note about directly encoded state machines is that they might require more bits to encode than sequential or Gray-coded state machines. This does not necessarily imply that the overall state machine results in greater logic utilization. In fact, in many cases, it will occupy less logic. This issue needs to be determined on a design-specific basis.

Design Considerations for Outputs

Just like with state-encoding, the default or power-up values for the outputs are important design considerations. This is true for both registered, as well as combinational outputs. Pay particular attention to outputs that directly (or in combination with other signals) drive output pins. This is because they should always power-up in a state that will not adversely affect the system on power-up. Consider, for example, a state machine whose outputs are connected to pins that select one of several devices that reside on a shared bus. If the power-up condition results in more than one device being selected and driving the bus, this could easily damage the system.

In closing, there are no firm rules for state machine design. The issues are more complex than just optimizing the number of state bits, or choosing a particular state encoding, as we saw in *Table 5*. We also need to examine, for example, the complexity of the transition conditions. Several theses have been written on state machine design, and it continues to be a subject for research and development. Even so, keep in mind the overall concepts and approach discussed so far. They should produce favorable results, and will at the very least give you more insight into results that you obtain at the end of the synthesis process.

11
Scalable and Parameterizable Design

Design reuse is an integral part of successful design, and this is particularly true as designs get more complex. In *Chapter 9*, we discussed packages and library management as a means of facilitating design reuse. In this chapter, we will discuss a powerful concept: design modules that are written in such a way that they can automatically scale to different sizes, widths or even implementations. Scalable design can be very useful, for instance, to scale the datapath width of a design. This is beneficial not only for the reuse of a scalable component from design to design, but also within a design, where operations may be performed on different slices of the datapath.

Scaling or parameterizing a design can be done with or without scaling parameters passed to the design module. Scalable and parameterizable designs have several benefits for design reuse, as follows:

- Each module is well understood as it behaves the same way, regardless of how it scales
- Simplifies the design process by reducing the number of items for design capture (for example, we do not need a different component for each bus width)
- Modules can be improved/added over time, if they are placed in packages
- Since most scalable modules are datapath elements, the designer can focus on the control path

The modules that we generate can, of course, be placed into a library just as we saw in *Chapter 9*.

VHDL Facilitates Scalable and Parameterizable Design

Several features built into VHDL make it easy to scale and parameterize designs. In this chapter we will focus on the following features:

- Unconstrained arrays (arrays of unspecified size) passed to a component
- *Generics*, or parameters passed to configure an entity
- Variables
- Loops
- Predefined attributes
- *for-generate* and *if-generate* statements to generate logic

Unconstrained Arrays

So far, we have only dealt with constrained *std_logic_vector* signal. By this we mean that the size of the vector is defined, and it can be declared in either the entity declaration or in the signal declaration. For example, we can declare signals as follows:

```
entity adder is port
  a: in std_logic_vector(15 downto 0);
  b: in std_logic_vector(15 downto 0);
  sum: out std_logic_vector(15 downto 0)
  );
end adder;
```

or

```
signal result: std_logic_vector(7 downto 0);
```

In both the entity and signal declaration examples, we have specified the size *(range)* of each signal. As VHDL allows port signals to be declared unconstrained, we can declare signals using two methods, as follows:

```
entity adder is port (
  a: in std_logic_vector;
  b: in std_logic_vector;
  sum: out std_logic_vector
  );
end adder;
```

or

```
signal result: std_logic_vector;
```

Let us first consider the entity declaration. Here, the unconstrained array is very useful in creating a scalable D-type flop, as shown in *Figure 1*.

Figure 1: D Flip-flop Scalable to a Width of n

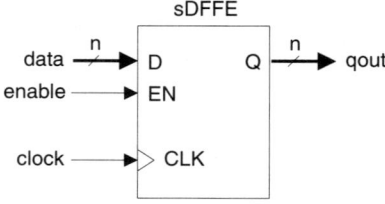

Our base component, *sDFFE*, describing the flip-flop is shown in *Listing 1*. It is a scalable D type flip-flop with synchronous enable and asynchronous reset. The signals *clk* and *en* are common to all flip-flops, regardless of their width.

Listing 1: Scalable D Flip-flop

```vhdl
library IEEE;
use IEEE.std_logic_1164.all;

entity sDFFE is port (
    d: in std_logic_vector;
    en: in std_logic;
    clk: in std_logic;
    q: out std_logic_vector
    );
end sDFFE;

architecture rtl of sDFFE is

begin

  process begin
    wait until clk = '1';
      if (en = '1') then
        q <= d;
      end if;
  end process;

end rtl;
```

Note that this implementation assumes that d and q have the same dimension, which is why we can assign $q <= d$ in the design. The rest of the VHDL looks very much like the description of the D-type register that we saw in *Chapter 4*.

To instantiate this entity-architecture pair, we must create a corresponding component declaration, as follows:

```vhdl
component sDFFE port (
  d: in std_logic_vector;
  en: in std_logic;
  clk: in std_logic;
  q: out std_logic_vector
  );
end component;
```

After placing this component declaration into the primitive package, we can then instantiate our scalable flip-flop into a design. An example implementing an 8-bit register is shown in *Listing 2*.

Listing 2: 8-bit Register Using Scalable D Flip-flop

```vhdl
library IEEE;
use IEEE.std_logic_1164.all;

use work.primitive.all;

entity scaleDFF is port (
  data: in std_logic_vector(7 downto 0);
  clock: in std_logic;
  enable: in std_logic;
  qout: out std_logic_vector(7 downto 0)
  );
end scaleDFF;

architecture scalable of scaleDFF is

begin

  u1: sDFFE port map (d => data,
                     clk =>clock,
                     en => enable,
                     q => qout
                     );

end scalable;
```

scaledff.vhd

Here we have created an 8-bit register from our base, scalable component. By changing only the size of the input and output vectors (*data* and *qout*) the design is automatically scaled. In addition, this design is independent of the range direction (*downto* or *to*) of the input and output vectors. It is the responsibility of the designer to ensure that either the direction of both of these vectors are the same, or intentionally different by design.

The second use of unconstrained signal declaration is when it is declared local to the architecture. However, most synthesis tools will not support unconstrained signal declarations within the architecture, the reasons for which are beyond the scope of this book. As such we have to explore different ways of developing parameterizable components when intermediate signals are required.

Generics

Generics are constants that are passed into the entity declaration. They can never be outputs from an entity, and are always declared before the port declaration in the entity. They are not only used to pass information to an entity, but are useful when sizing an array in the port declaration, and even within the architecture. For example, we might declare an entity as follows:

Chapter 11 - Scalable and Parameterizable Design

```
entity adder is
  generic (size: integer);-- number of bits in operands and result
  port (
  a: in std_logic_vector(size - 1 downto 0);
  b: in std_logic_vector(size - 1 downto 0);
  sum: out std_logic_vector(size -1 downto 0)
  );
end adder;
```

or within an architecture:

```
signal result: std_logic_vector(size - 1 downto 0);
```

Most synthesis tools will accept *generics* in this fashion. Let us consider slightly extending the flip-flop in *Figure 1* to incorporate a tri-state buffer, as shown in *Figure 2*.

Figure 2: Parameterizable Flip-flop and Tri-state Buffer

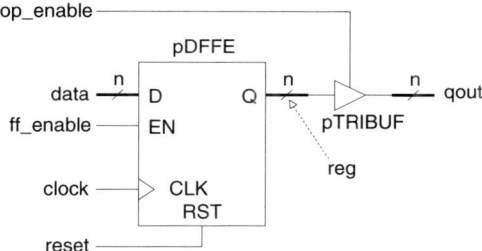

In this case, we create two base components, *pDFFE* and *pTRIBUF*, which are a parameterizable DFF (with enable) and parameterizable tri-state buffer, respectively. The VHDL to do so is shown in *Listing 3* and *Listing 4*.

Listing 3: Parameterizable D Flip-flop with Reset and Enable

```
library IEEE;
use IEEE.std_logic_1164.all;

entity pDFFE is
  generic (n: integer := 2);
  port (
  d: in std_logic_vector(n - 1 downto 0);
  en: in std_logic;
  clk: in std_logic;
  rst: in std_logic
  q: out std_logic_vector(n - 1 downto 0);
  );
end pDFFE;
```

```
architecture rtl of pDFFE is

begin

  process (rst, clk) begin
    if (rst = '1') then
      q <= (others => '0');
    elsif (clk'event and clk = '1') then
      if (en = '1') then
        q <= d;
      end if;
    end if;
  end process;

end rtl;
```

Listing 4: Parameterizable Tri-state Buffer

```
library IEEE;
use IEEE.std_logic_1164.all;

entity pTRIBUF is
  generic (n: integer := 2);
  port (
  ip: in std_logic_vector(n - 1 downto 0);
  oe: in std_logic;
  op: out std_logic_vector(n - 1 downto 0)
  );
end pTRIBUF;

architecture rtl of pTRIBUF is

begin

  op <= ip when oe = '1' else (others => 'Z');

end rtl;
```

Note that these two base components have a default width of two, which is indicated in the generic declaration. This is not only good design practice, but is also required by most synthesis tools. VHDL does not *require* that the generic be passed to the component. In order to determine what hardware to create, the synthesis tool must determine the width of a parameterizable component in the event that the generic is not passed to the component when it is instantiated.

As before, if the component declarations for these two design units are placed in the *primitive* package, then the VHDL that describes *Figure 2* is as shown in *Listing 5*.

Listing 5: 8-bit Register with Tri-state Using Parameterizable Base Components

```
library IEEE;
use IEEE.std_logic_1164.all;

use work.primitive.all;

entity paramDFF is
  generic (size: integer := 8);
  port (
  data: in std_logic_vector(size - 1 downto 0);
  clock: in std_logic;
  reset: in std_logic;
  ff_enable: in std_logic;
  op_enable: in std_logic;
  qout: out std_logic_vector(size - 1 downto 0)
  );
end paramDFF;

architecture parameterize of paramDFF is

signal reg: std_logic_vector(size - 1 downto 0);

begin

  u1: pDFFE generic map (n => size)
           port map   (d => data,
                       clk =>clock,
                       rst => reset,
                       en => ff_enable,
                       q => reg
                      );
  u2: pTRIBUF generic map (n => size)
             port map    (ip => reg,
                          oe => op_enable,
                          op => qout
                         );

end paramterize;
```

paramdff.vhd

There are a few things to note in *Listing 5*. First, the entity *paramDFF* has a generic *size* that controls the width of the input and output vectors. Second, the signal *reg* to be scaled is based on the generic *size*. This is useful since we need the intermediate signal *reg*, and most synthesis tools need to determine the size of the local signals before proceeding with synthesis. Finally, the *size* generic is passed to each of the parameterizable base components, *pDFFE* and *pTRIBUF* via the generic map.

Variables

We can also use *variables* when designing parameterized modules. *Variables*, like signals, have a given type, and can be assigned values. Also, variables may be subject to implicit memory behavior, depending on how they are used. However, they are notably different to signals in that:

- They may only be declared within a process (or a *subprogram* such as a *function* or a *procedure* as we will see in *Chapter 13*)
- When assigned, they take on the assigned value immediately, and not at the end of the process (or subprogram).

As such, variables should be used only for compilation control (such as loop counters in scalable control structures), and not for logic nodes.

Loops

It is often useful to iterate through a set of statements to create logic. The number of iterations dictates how the statements produce logic, effectively scaling the design. Loop constructs in VHDL allow you to iterate through sequential statements. There are two kinds of loops in VHDL: *for...loop* and *while...loop*. *For...loop* control structures are useful when designing scalable components, and this is what we will focus on.

To illustrate the use of variables and *for...loop*, let us consider the example of an odd parity generator. Parity is odd when there are an odd number of bits in a bus that are '1'. Hence, for an 8-bit bus, *D0...D7*, odd parity can be represented by the XOR of *D0...D7*, as shown in *Figure 3*.

Figure 3: Odd Parity Generation Circuit for an 8-bit Bus

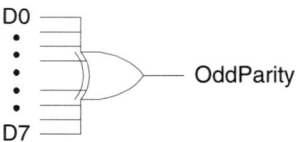

This is equivalent to the logic shown in *Figure 4*. What we have done is decompose the 8-bit wide XOR into a series of 2-bit wide XORs.

Figure 4: Odd Parity Generation Circuit for an 8-bit Bus Using 2-input XOR Gates

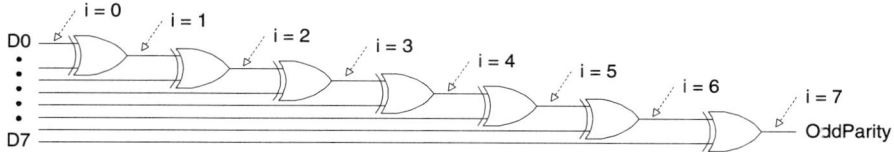

If we wrote this using *for...loop*, we can iterate through the input vector *D0...D7*. At each iteration, *i*, we use a variable to store the XOR value. Also, at each iteration, the XOR value is updated, so that when we have reached the last bit in the vector, *D7*, we are left with the cumulative XOR value, which is the odd parity. The code for this is shown in *Listing 6*.

Listing 6: Parameterizable Parity Generator Using a *for...loop*

```
library ieee;
use ieee.std_logic_1164.all;

entity oddParityLoop is
  generic ( width : integer := 8 );
  port (ad: in std_logic_vector (width - 1 downto 0);
        oddParity : out std_logic ) ;
end oddParityLoop ;

architecture scaleable of oddParityLoop is
begin

  process (ad)
    variable loopXor: std_logic;
  begin
    loopXor := '0';

    for i in 0 to width -1 loop
        loopXor := loopXor xor ad( i ) ;
    end loop ;

    oddParity <= loopXor ;

  end process;

end scaleable ;
```
oparity.vhd

There are three things to note about the *for...loop* implementation shown in *Listing 6*. First, we have explicitly declared the variable *loopXor* in the process. This is the temporary place holder for the parity calculation, and is always initialized to '0' at the beginning of the process, before the *loop* is begun. Second, the loop variable, *i*, is implicitly declared.

VHDL does not require loop variables to be declared at the beginning of a process. Finally, loops must be inside a process because they are control structures that are wrapped around sequential statements and cannot be placed outside a process.

While VHDL has powerful capabilities to describe algorithms, the preceding parity generation example demonstrates a very important design consideration:

> The key to writing scalable and parameterizable VHDL is that you must determine the slice of logic that repeats, and the algorithm for repetition.

We can further illustrate this by examining a parameterizable full adder. We will start by examining a single-bit full adder element. The symbol for this element, its truth-table and corresponding logic equation are shown in *Figure 5*.

Figure 5: Single Bit Full Adder Element

Full Adder Element

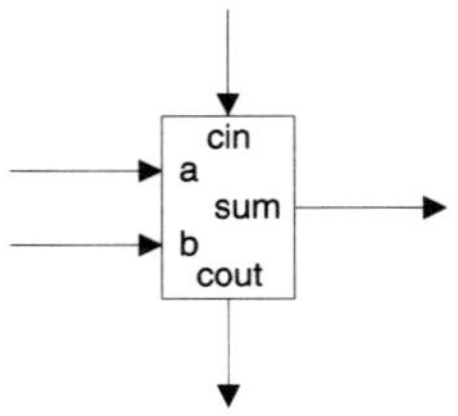

Full Adder Truth Table

cin	a	b	sum	cout
0	0	0	0	0
0	0	1	1	0
0	1	0	1	0
0	1	1	1	1
1	0	0	1	0
1	0	1	0	1
1	1	0	0	1
1	1	1	1	1

Full Adder Equations

sum = a XOR b XOR cin

cout = (a AND b) OR (a AND cin) OR (b AND cin)

We can build an *n*-bit adder by cascading *n* one-bit full adders (from *Figure 5*), as shown in *Figure 6*.

Figure 6: n-bit Wide Adder (0 to $n-1$) Built Using the Single-bit Adder Elements

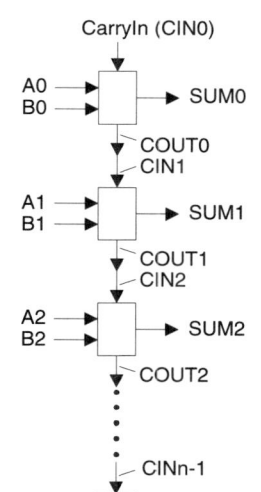

We can see the makings of an iterative algorithm here. Notice that n^{th} carry-in (*cin*) is in fact the $n-1^{th}$ carry-out (*cout*). *Sum* is a function of each pair of *a* and *b*, as well as the corresponding *cout*. Substituting this into the equations for each full-adder in *Figure 5*, we can write our equations for sum as follows:

$$sum_i = a_i \text{ XOR } b_i \text{ XOR } cin_i$$
$$cout = (a_i \text{ and } b_i) \text{ or } (a_i \text{ and } cin_i) \text{ or } (b_i \text{ and } cin_i)$$

and, since $cout_i$ is the same as the following *cin*, or cin_{i+1}, we can rewrite the equations for *cout* as follows:

$$cin_{i+1} = (a_i \text{ and } b_i) \text{ or } (a_i \text{ and } cin_i) \text{ or } (b_i \text{ and } cin_i)$$

This is well suited for a *loop*. The only corner case that we have to take care of is the case where $i=0$, since the carry-in to this element is in fact the carry-in to the *pAdder* entity. The adder is parameterizable using the generic n to size the input operands and the output result. Our adder in VHDL is written as shown in *Listing 7*.

Listing 7: Parameterizable Adder Using the *for...loop* Construct

```vhdl
library IEEE;
use IEEE.std_logic_1164.all;

entity pAdder is
  generic(n : integer := 8);
  port (a    : in std_logic_vector(n - 1 downto 0);
        b    : in std_logic_vector(n - 1 downto 0);
        cin  : in std_logic;
        sum  : out std_logic_vector(n - 1 downto 0);
        cout : out std_logic);
end pAdder;


architecture loopDemo of pAdder is

begin

  process(a, b, cin)
    variable carry: std_logic_vector(n downto 0);
    variable localSum: std_logic_vector(n - 1 downto 0);

  begin

    carry(0) := cin;

    for i in 0 to n - 1 loop
      localSum(i)  := (a(i) xor b(i)) xor carry(i);
      carry(i + 1) := (a(i) and b(i)) or (carry(i) and (a(i) or b(i)));
    end loop;

    sum  <= localSum;
    cout <= carry(n - 1);

  end process;

end loopDemo;
```

adder.vhd

As we enter the process, the corner case when the loop variable *i* is 0 is assigned to the carry-in value, *cin*. Note that the signals are assigned to the local variables at the end of the process, and that the signal *cout* is the carry-out generated by the last stage of the logic, as shown in *Figure 6*.

Attributes

Properties that describe certain characteristics in VHDL are called *attributes*. Attributes can be associated with types, signals, entities and architectures and other elements of

Chapter 11 - Scalable and Parameterizable Design

VHDL. In fact, we have already seen a signal attribute in *Chapter 4*, the *'event* attribute, when describing a flip-flop. The statement

```
if clk'event and clk = '1' then
```

uses the attribute *'event* to determine if there has been a change in value of the signal *clk*. This is an example of what is known as a *predefined attribute*, or an attribute that is already defined in VHDL standard. VHDL does allow user-defined attributes as well, and you might see these as a means of passing hints or directives to the synthesis tool. Predefined attributes are more commonly used for simulation, but there are some that can be quite useful for synthesis, especially when trying to create scalable and parameterizable components. *Table 1* shows a few such attributes, which can be applied to signals.

Table 1: Predefined Signal Attributes Useful for Parameterizable Components

Attribute	Property	Example Use
'range	range of array	determine bounds of a std_logic_vector
'reverse_range	reverse range of array	if an ascending or descending range is required by the algorithm and the input signal has the opposite range
'left	left-most bound of array	determine the first element in the array
'right	right-most bound of array	determine the last element in the array
'high	highest index value in an array	determine high index count independent of the range direction
'low	lowest index value in an array	determine low index count independent of the range direction
'length	number of elements in array	determine iteration count

To illustrate the use of predefined attributes, we will re-write the parameterizable adder in *Listing 7*. The entity declaration remains the same, but the intermediate variables, and loop index are determined by using predefined signal attributes, as shown in *Listing 8*.

Listing 8: Parameterizable Adder Using Predefined Attributes

```
library IEEE;
use IEEE.std_logic_1164.all;

entity pAdderAttr is
  generic(n : integer := 8);
  port (a    : in  std_logic_vector(n - 1 downto 0);
        b    : in  std_logic_vector(n - 1 downto 0);
        cin  : in  std_logic;
        sum  : out std_logic_vector(n - 1 downto 0);
        cout : out std_logic);
```

```
  end pAdderAttr;

  architecture loopDemo of pAdderAttr is

  begin

    process(a, b, cin)
      variable carry: std_logic_vector(sum'length downto 0);
      variable localSum: std_logic_vector(sum'high downto 0);

    begin

      carry(0) := cin;

      for i in sum'reverse_range loop
        localSum(i)  := (a(i) xor b(i)) xor carry(i);
        carry(i + 1) := (a(i) and b(i)) or (carry(i) and (a(i) or b(i)));
      end loop;

      sum <= localSum;
      cout <= carry(carry'high - 1);

    end process;

  end loopDemo;
```

adderatt.vhd

For the variable *carry*, we have used the *'length* attribute, since it is one bit longer than the result (to ensure that the loop index does not go out of range). The intermediate result, *localSum*, has the same dimension as the final output, *sum*. In the *for...loop*, we have used the attribute *'reverse_range*. The algorithm requires that the carry term be calculated from the least significant bit onwards, and our input vectors (and result) use the descending range.

The Generate Statement

The *generate* statement in VHDL generates logic by repeating a slice of logic. Like the *for...loop*, it is very useful in creating regular structures. Furthermore, just like the *for...loop*, the key to using the *generate* statement is in identifying the slice of logic that is to be replicated. Unlike the *for...loop*, however, the *generate* statement encapsulates concurrent statements. These concurrent statements can be either concurrent assignments, or component instances.

To illustrate the *generate* statement, let us consider an up-counter, similar to the kind we saw in *Chapter 5*. Our goal is to create a scalable counter, that will scale to *n* bits. For our example, our base element will be the toggle flip-flop, or TFF, as shown in *Figure 7*. A T-flip-flop toggles the output whenever the input is '1', and holds the output value when the input is '0'.

Figure 7: T Flip-flop Symbol and Truth-table

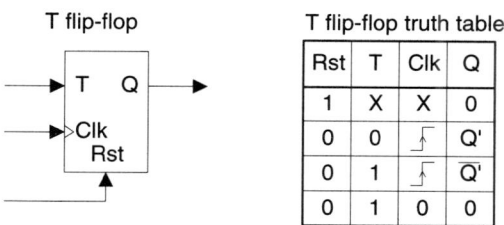

Using the TFF as the slice, we can represent an *n*-bit up-counter as shown in *Figure 8*. For the sake of clarity, the clock and reset signals are not shown connected.

Figure 8: n-bit Up-counter Based on a TFF Slice

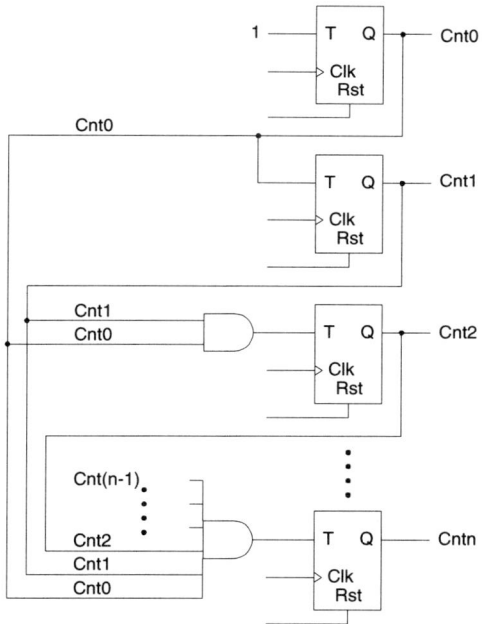

As we can see, each bit in the counter toggles when all lower bits are '1', which is represented by the AND gates. The only special case we need to deal with is the least significant bit, *Cnt0*, which has its input always set to '1', since it always toggles. Our iterative equations would be as follows:

```
for Cnt0: toggle input = 1
for Cnt(1..n): toggle input = AND of all lower order bits
```

In order for us to instantiate the scalable counter, we will need to create a component declaration for the parameterizable counter. Since our counter is scalable, we will use an unconstrained array for the output, as follows:

```
component scaleUpCnt  port (
  clk: in std_logic;
  reset: in std_logic;
  cnt: out std_logic_vector
  );
end component;
```

Next, we must build the entity-architecture pair for *scaleUpCnt*. Let us assume that the TFF exists in the *primitive* package. We will place this component into a package called *scalable*, so that it can be used later, as shown in *Listing 9*.

Listing 9: Scalable Up-counter Using TFFs, Placed in the Scalable Package

```
library IEEE;
use IEEE.std_logic_1164.all;

package scaleable is
  component scaleUpCnt port (
    clk: in std_logic;
    reset: in std_logic;
    cnt: in std_logic_vector
    );
  end component;
end scaleable;

library IEEE;
use IEEE.std_logic_1164.all;

use work.primitive.all;

entity scaleUpCnt is port (
  clk: in std_logic;
  reset: in std_logic;
  cnt: out std_logic_vector
  );
end scaleUpCnt;

architecture scaleable of scaleUpCnt is

signal one: std_logic := '1';
signal cntL: std_logic_vector(cnt'range);
signal andTerm: std_logic_vector(cnt'range);

begin

-- Special case is the least significant bit
```

```
   lsb: tff port map (t => one,
                      reset => reset,
                      clk => clk,
                      q => cntL(cntL'low)
                     );

   andTerm(0) <= cntL(cntL'low);

-- General case for all other bits

   genAnd: for i in 1 to cntL'high generate
     andTerm(i) <= andTerm(i - 1) and cntL(i);
   end generate;

   genTFF: for i in 1 to cntL'high generate
     t1: tff port map (t => andTerm(i),
                       clk => clk,
                       reset => reset,
                       q => cntl(i)
                      );
   end generate;

   cnt <= CntL;

end scaleable;
```

supcnt.vhd

The implementation of the counter shown in *Listing 9* highlights three important points that we need to note when using the *generate* statement to create scalable designs:

- Special case
- Generation of concurrent statements
- Generation of components

First, the special case was bit zero (least significant bit) of the counter, which is the T flip-flop labeled *lsb*, along with the concurrent assignment of *andTerm(0)* to 1. Second, the *generate* statement is used to repeat a concurrent assignment representing the *and* gate in the statement labeled *genAnd*. And finally, we also use the *generate* statement to create multiple instances of the T flip-flop in the statement labeled *genTFF*.

Similarity Between *for...loop* and *for...generate*

For simple slices of logic there is a lot of similarity between the *for...loop* statement and the *for...generate* statement. For example, the odd parity generator in *Figure 4* expressed using the *for...loop* in *Listing 6* can also be written using *for...generate*. In this case, the replicated structure is a 2-input XOR gate, and the code for this is shown in *Listing 10* (it is assumed that the *xor2* component is in the *primitive* library).

Listing 10: Odd Parity Generator Using *for...generate*

```vhdl
library ieee;
use ieee.std_logic_1164.all;

use work.primitive.all;

entity oddParityGen is
  generic ( width : integer := 8 );
  port (ad: in std_logic_vector (width - 1 downto 0);
        oddParity : out std_logic ) ;
end oddParityGen;

architecture scaleable of oddParityGen is

signal genXor: std_logic_vector(ad'range);

begin

  genXOR(0) <= '0';

  parTree: for i in 1 to ad'high generate
    x1: xor2 port map (i1 => genXor(i - 1),
                       i2 => ad(i - 1),
                       y  => genXor(i)
                       );
  end generate;

 oddParity <= genXor(ad'high) ;

end scaleable ;
```

oparityg.vhd

Conditional *Generate* Statements

It is possible in VHDL to create logic conditionally. The conditions must be static, such as a generic or a constant, at the time of synthesis (or simulation). For example, in our parity generator the first XOR generated is a special case, as we saw in *Listing 10*. In this listing, the *parTree generate* statement loop begins at 1. This *generate* statement could be across the entire range of *ad*, and within it we could test for a special case. This is shown in *Listing 11*.

Listing 11: Parity Generator Using a Conditional Generate Statement

```vhdl
library ieee;
use ieee.std_logic_1164.all;

use work.primitive.all;

entity oddParityGen is
  generic ( width : integer := 32 );
  port (ad: in std_logic_vector (width - 1 downto 0);
```

Chapter 11 - Scalable and Parameterizable Design

```
              oddParity : out std_logic ) ;
end oddParityGen;

architecture scaleable of oddParityGen is

signal genXor: std_logic_vector(ad'range);

signal one: std_logic := '1';

begin

  parTree: for i in ad'range generate
    g0: if i = 0 generate
      x0: xor2 port map (i1 => one,
                         i2 => one,
                         y  => genXor(0)
                         );
    end generate;

    g1: if i > 0 and i <= ad'high generate
      x1: xor2 port map (i1 => genXor(i - 1),
                         i2 => ad(i - 1),
                         y  => genXor(i)
                         );
    end generate;

  end generate;

  oddParity <= genXor(ad'high) ;

end scaleable ;
```

paritygc.vhd

Listing 6, *Listing 10* and *Listing 11* all produce identical logic - a series of 2-input XOR gates. This raises a very important issue when writing scalable and parameterizable design:

> The algorithm used to generate the logic has a profound impact on the end result.

The reasons for this are clear: the slice of logic being replicated is fairly small, and the algorithm for replication creates specific circuits. For instance, in the parity generation examples, the logic produced might be slow, since what has been implemented is a series of XOR gates, as shown in *Figure 4*. The signal *ad(0)* might have to propagate through several levels of logic before it changes the output, *oddParity*.

An alternate method of representing this logic would be to calculate as many XORs in parallel, as shown in *Figure 9*.

Figure 9: Odd Parity Generator Using a Parallel XOR Tree

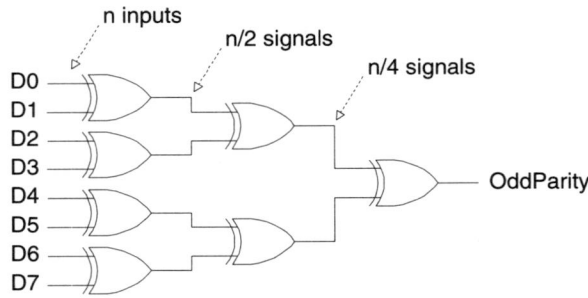

A closer look at *Figure 9* reveals that at each XOR stage we have half the number of inputs than at the previous stage. In other words, the number of XORs and signals feeding them grow in powers of 2. We will take advantage of this when creating the algorithm for the *generate* statement.

For the scalable "parallel" parity generator, we will assume that there are a maximum of n inputs, where n is an integer power of 2. If we also assume that $2 \leq n \leq 32$, we can make some simplifying assumptions that allow us to build a faster parity generator. In this case, since $n<=32$, we know that there will never be more than five stages of XORs in calculating the output. We can thus represent our alternative implementation of the parity generator as shown in *Figure 10*.

Figure 10: Scalable, "Parallel" Parity Generator

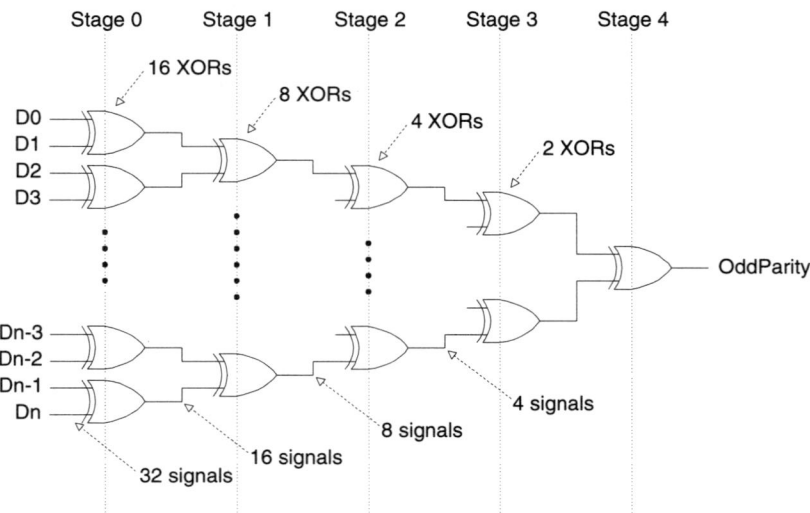

Chapter 11 - Scalable and Parameterizable Design

As such, we can declare four sets of intermediate signals that will capture the intermediate XOR terms. Using conditional *generates*, we can now build our scalable parity generator very quickly. The algorithm representing *Figure 10* is as follows:

```
for all XOR stages:
  for all signals in each stage:
    XORn output = last Stage Outputn XOR last Stage Outputn + m
```

  n = index representing signal output for the current state
  m = total number of signals output in the current stage

In addition to this, depending on the number of inputs to the generator (2,4,8,16 or 32), we need to conditionally assign the bus input signals to the correct XOR stage, in order to calculate parity. The VHDL for this is shown in *Listing 12*.

Listing 12: Scalable Parity Generator

```
library ieee;
use ieee.std_logic_1164.all;

use work.primitive.all;

entity oddParityGen is
  generic ( width : integer := 32 );  -- (2 <= width <= 32) and a power of 2
  port (ad: in std_logic_vector (width - 1 downto 0);
        oddParity : out std_logic ) ;
end oddParityGen;

architecture scaleable of oddParityGen is

signal stage0: std_logic_vector(31 downto 0);
signal stage1: std_logic_vector(15 downto 0);
signal stage2: std_logic_vector(7 downto 0);
signal stage3: std_logic_vector(3 downto 0);
signal stage4: std_logic_vector(1 downto 0);

begin

  g4: for i in stage4'range generate
    g41: if (ad'length > 2) generate
        x4: xor2 port map (stage3(i), stage3(i + stage4'length), stage4(i));
    end generate;
  end generate;

  g3: for i in stage3'range generate
    g31: if (ad'length > 4) generate
        x3: xor2 port map (stage2(i), stage2(i + stage3'length), stage3(i));
    end generate;
  end generate;
```

```
        g2: for i in stage2'range generate
          g21: if (ad'length > 8) generate
              x2: xor2 port map (stage1(i), stage1(i + stage2'length), stage2(i));
            end generate;
        end generate;

        g1: for i in stage1'range generate
          g11: if (ad'length > 16) generate
              x1: xor2 port map (stage0(i), stage0(i + stage1'length), stage1(i));
            end generate;
        end generate;


        s1: for i in ad'range generate
          s14: if (ad'length = 2) generate
              stage4(i) <= ad(i);
            end generate;

          s13: if (ad'length = 4) generate
              stage3(i) <= ad(i);
            end generate;

          s12: if (ad'length = 8) generate
              stage2(i) <= ad(i);
            end generate;

          s11: if (ad'length = 16) generate
              stage1(i) <= ad(i);
            end generate;

          s10: if (ad'length = 32) generate
              stage0(i) <= ad(i);
            end generate;

        end generate;


        genPar: xor2 port map (stage4(0), stage4(1), oddParity);

      end scaleable ;
```

parityp.vhd

The resulting circuit usually runs faster, though it occupies more logic cells than the serial parity generation approach. We could take the parameterization a step further by creating a component that combines the serial and parallel versions of the parity generator and is selected using a *generic*.

Using conditional *generate* statements can also be useful when creating a set of technology specific scalable designs for a library, since the granularity can go right down to the most fundamental logic element of the device architecture.

12
Enhancing Design Readability and Reuse

In *Chapter 9*, we discussed how partitioning, packages and a modular approach helps design readability and reuse. We drew on these concepts in *Chapter 11*, where we developed scalable designs. In fact, VHDL provides several mechanisms that facilitate design readability and reuse and in this chapter, we explore this further by introducing the following features of the language:

- Functions
- Procedures
- Aliases

Functions and *procedures* are both VHDL elements known as subprograms. In addition to making designs more readable, they are used to:

- Abstract operations that are repeatedly performed
- Perform type conversion

Subprograms are assigned names, which help to understand and document the design, and can be used repeatedly in a design (or multiple designs for that matter). Much like functions and procedures in software programming languages, *functions* and *procedures* are passed parameters when they are *called*. *Calling* a function or procedure is analogous to instantiating a component, in that it is being incorporated into a design. The function or procedure performs an operation on the parameters to generate a result.

Aliases are alternative labels or identifiers. They allow you to use a more convenient (or relevant) name for documentation or readability purposes.

Functions

Functions have the following key characteristics:

- They never modify the parameters passed to them
- They always return a single value as a result
- They are always used in some expression, and not called on their own

As early as *Chapter 4*, we encountered our first function, *rising_edge*, when describing flip-flops. Recall that this function checks to see if a 0 →1 transition has occurred on a signal, and might be used as follows:

```
process begin
  wait until rising_edge(clk);
    q <= d;
end process;
```

In the *std_logic_1164* package, this function is defined as

```
FUNCTION rising_edge (SIGNAL s : std_ulogic) RETURN BOOLEAN;
```

Here, the function accepts a *std_ulogic* type signal (or any of its subtypes), and determines if it has just transitioned from 0 → 1, in which case it returns a single value: the Boolean TRUE. If not, it returns FALSE. The input signal, *s*, is not modified. Furthermore, the function *rising_edge* is used in the expression *wait until...*, and not on its own, since it is returning a value (a Boolean in this case).

Functions are only used as part of expressions in a concurrent statement, or inside a process, because they always return a value. They are never *called* "stand-alone".

Standard Functions

You will almost always use one or more standard functions in your designs. There are several functions that have been defined in packages that we are already familiar with, such as *std_logic_1164* and *numeric_std*, many of which were introduced in *Chapter 5*. If you are not familiar with what these are, check the help files or directory structure of the synthesis tool you are using. There should be a file defining the functions and what parameters they are passed.

One of the most common uses for standard functions is in type conversion. VHDL is a strongly typed language, and signals must be converted from one type to another before they can be assigned. For example, let us consider the example in *Listing 1*.

Listing 1: Type Conversion to *std_logic_vector*

```
-- incorporates Errata 12.1

library IEEE;
use IEEE.std_logic_1164.all;
use IEEE.numeric_std.all;

entity typeConvert is port (
  a: out unsigned(7 downto 0)
  );
end typeConvert;

architecture simple of typeConvert is

constant Const: natural := 43;

begin

  a <= To_unsigned(Const,8);

end simple;
```

convert.vhd

Here, we have used the function *to_unsigned* that is in the *numeric_std* package. While it would seem like the assignment

```
a <= Const
```

ought to work, it does not, since the types do not match. Hence the need to convert *Const* to a *unsigned* type.

Just like the operators we saw in *Chapter 5*, functions can be overloaded. For example, the function *to_unsigned* may be overloaded as follows:

```
FUNCTION TO_UNSIGNED (ARG, SIZE: NATURAL) return UNSIGNED;
FUNCTION TO_UNSIGNED (ARG: STD_LOGIC_VECTOR) return UNSIGNED;
```

We can call the function with either a non-negative integer (natural) or a *std_logic_vector* and the correct one will be picked, depending on the type of the argument passed. Most standard functions, like *to_unsigned*, accept unconstrained arrays as their inputs. In the case of a *std_logic_vector* argument, the result returned is of the same dimension and bit-ordering as the argument(s) passed to it.

The *numeric_std* package provides a function called *resize* with the following parameters:

```
FUNCTION resize (ARG: SIGNED; NEW_SIZE: NATURAL) return SIGNED;
FUNCTION resize (ARG: UNSIGNED; NEW_SIZE: NATURAL) return UNSIGNED;
```

These functions require not only the argument, *ARG*, but also an integer, *NEW_SIZE*, which indicates the size of the vector being returned. There are three important points to remember when using this function:

- If the input argument is smaller than the result, then the result is either zero-extended (*unsigned*) or sign extended (*signed*)
- If the result is bigger in size than the vector being passed to it, it is truncated
- The result is a descending range vector (from *NEW_SIZE - 1 downto 0*)

To illustrate this, let us consider the example shown in *Listing 2*.

Listing 2: Type Conversion Using the *resize* Function

```
library IEEE;
use IEEE.std_logic_1164.all;
use IEEE.numeric_std.all;

entity convertArith is port (
  truncate: out unsigned(3 downto 0);
  extend: out unsigned(15 downto 0);
```

```
       direction: out unsigned(0 to 7)
       );
  end convertArith;

  architecture simple of convertArith is

  constant Const: unsigned(7 downto 0) := "00111010";

  begin

     truncate  <= resize(Const, truncate'length);
     extend    <= resize(Const, extend'length);
     direction <= resize(Const, direction'length);

  end simple;
```

conarith.vhd

The result of this design is as follows:

```
  truncate  (3 downto 0)  = 1010
  extend    (15 downto 0) = 0000000000111010
  direction (0 to 7)      = 00111010
```

The *resize* function shows us the importance of understanding what the function is doing. In this case, the direction is particularly significant when converting an *integer* type to an *unsigned* type, or during operations (relational and arithmetic), as we saw in *Chapter 5*.

Just as with instantiating components (*Chapter 9*), we can use either positional or named association when calling functions. In *Listing 2*, we used positional association when calling the function *resize*:

```
     truncate  <= resize(Const, truncate'length);
```

We could certainly have written:

```
     truncate  <= resize(new_size => truncate'length, arg => Const);
```

Here, since we are specifically assigning the formal parameters (*new_size* and *arg*) to the actual parameters (*truncate'length* and *Const*), we do not need to maintain the order in which we list the parameters.

In addition to carefully understanding the size, type and direction of the parameters passed to a function, you must be aware of which functions are synthesizable, and under what conditions. For example, let us consider the standard shift functions that were included as part of the VHDL'93 standard, as shown in *Table 1*.

Table 1: Shift Operators per the VHDL'93 Standard

Function	Input Parameter Types	Result Type	Description
sll	a: BIT_VECTOR; d: INTEGER	BIT_VECTOR	a logically shifted left d bit positions.
srl	a: BIT_VECTOR; d: INTEGER	BIT_VECTOR	a logically shifted right d bit positions
sla	a: BIT_VECTOR; d: INTEGER	BIT_VECTOR	a arithmetically shifted left d bit positions
sra	a: BIT_VECTOR; d: INTEGER	BIT_VECTOR	a arithmetically shifted right d bit positions
rol	a: BIT_VECTOR; d: INTEGER	BIT_VECTOR	a rotated left d bit positions
ror	a: BIT_VECTOR; d: INTEGER	BIT_VECTOR	a rotated right d bit positions

Most synthesis tools will only support these functions if the shift or rotation amount (*d* in *Table 1*) is a constant at synthesis time. In other words, the parameter *d* should be either a *constant* or a *generic* in your design. Similarly, there are some operators whose usage is even more restricted than the shift operators in synthesis. For example, the division or '/'operator is usually required to be not only a constant at the time of synthesis, but an integer power of 2. Other than the standard arithmetic and relational operators, use operators in your design for synthesis with great care. This is for both VHDL compatibility (across tools) reasons, and also because not all tools will perform high quality optimization of such circuits.

Functions are also used to resolve signals that have multiple drivers. Synthesis tools invariably do not support resolution functions, with the exception of the *resolved* function for the *std_logic* type. Even so, it is useful to understand what resolution functions do. We will take a look at the *resolved* function, and understand how this behaves, more for the purposes of simulation and modeling, rather than synthesis.

In the *std_logic_1164* package, the base type *std_ulogic* is declared. This type is unresolved, and may take one of nine values:

```
TYPE std_ulogic IS ('U','X','0','1','Z','W','L','H','-' );
```

subsequently, *resolved* is declared:

```
FUNCTION resolved (s : std_ulogic_vector) RETURN std_ulogic;
```

and the subtype *std_logic* is declared with *resolved* as the resolution function:

```
SUBTYPE std_logic IS resolved std_ulogic;
```

In the event that there are multiple drivers on the signal, the function *resolved* uses a look-up table to determine the value of the signal, as follows:

Table 2: Resolution Table for *std_logic*

		Signal A								
		U	X	0	1	Z	W	L	H	-
Signal B	U	U	U	U	U	U	U	U	U	U
	X	U	X	X	X	X	X	X	X	X
	0	U	X	0	X	0	0	0	0	X
	1	U	X	X	1	1	1	1	1	X
	Z	U	X	0	1	Z	W	L	H	X
	W	U	X	0	1	W	W	W	W	X
	L	U	X	0	1	L	W	W	W	X
	H	U	X	0	1	H	W	H	H	X
	-	U	X	X	X	X	X	X	C	X

In this table, there are two signals, A and B. When signal A is 0, and signal B is 1, the result is a forcing unknown, or 'X', as can be seen by looking up the corresponding row and column for A and B. The resolution function loops through all drivers on the particular signal to determine what the resulting value of the signal is.

User-defined Functions

While standard functions are more or less sufficient, from time to time you will come across the need to define your own functions. There is considerable similarity between the declaration and use of components (*Chapter 9*) and functions:

- Functions are declared between the architecture declaration statement and the *begin* statement of that architecture, just like components
- Function declaration and calling follows the *formal* and *actual* parameters we saw with components
- Functions may be placed in packages

To illustrate these aspects of using functions, let us implement a function that calculates raising an integer to a given power. VHDL does include such a function, '**', but most synthesis tools require that both operands are constants. So in this case, we will build our own logic.

Our function would be as shown in *Listing 3*:

Listing 3: Power Function

```
function Pow( N, Exp : integer )  return integer is

    Variable Result   : integer := 1;
```

Chapter 12 - Enhancing Design Readability and Reuse

```
  begin

    for i in 1 to Exp loop
      Result := Result * N;
    end loop;
    return( Result );

end Pow;
```

The function is labelled *Pow*, and accepts two integer parameters. *N* is the value of the integer to be exponentiated and will be raised to the power of *Exp*. The function returns an unconstrained value of type *integer*. Just as a *process*, local variables are declared right after the function declaration statement, and before the *begin* statement that indicates the beginning of the function.

Our function uses a *for...loop* statement to calculate the result, which is returned using the *return* statement. All statements within the function are executed sequentially. An important point to note is that functions always use variables to store intermediate values. Variables, unlike signals, are updated "immediately" after assignment, so that the value can be returned to the function caller.

The function can now be incorporated into a design, as shown in *Listing 4*. This design takes an input value, and raises it to the power of four. Since the largest value that the input, *inputVal*, can take is 15 (4 bits), the output, *power*, needs to be a 16-bit value.

Listing 4: Design to Raise an Input to its 4th Power

```
library IEEE;
use IEEE.std_logic_1164.all;
use IEEE.numeric_std.all;

entity powerOfFour is port(
  clk      : in  std_logic;
  inputVal : in  unsigned(3 downto 0);
  power    : out unsigned(15 downto 0)
  );
end powerOfFour;

architecture behavioral of powerOfFour is

  function Pow( N, Exp : integer )  return integer is
    Variable Result     : integer := 1;

  begin
    for i in 1 to Exp loop
      Result := Result * N;
    end loop;
    return( Result );
```

```
      end Pow;

   signal inputValInt: integer range 0 to 15;
   signal powerL: integer range 0 to 65535;

begin

   inputValInt <= to_integer(inputVal);
   power <= to_unsigned(powerL,16);

   process begin
     wait until Clk = '1';

       powerL <= Pow(inputValInt,4);

   end process;

end behavioral;
```

powerfcn.vhd

There are a few things to note in *Listing 4*. First of all, the function declaration is done inside the architecture, just before the *begin* statement. This makes the function visible within the architecture only, and not outside the entity. Secondly, there are two intermediate signals, *inputValInt* and *powerL* that are integer representations of the unsigned input and output respectively. Finally, the *to_integer* and *to_stdlogicvector* functions are found in the *numeric_std* package.

Functions can also be 'nested'. We can eliminate the local signals for type conversion by nesting the functions, as shown in *Listing 5*.

Listing 5: Using Nested Functions in the PowerOfFour Calculation

```
-- Incorporate errata 5.4

library IEEE;
use IEEE.std_logic_1164.all;
use IEEE.numeric_std.all;

entity powerOfFour is port(
  clk      : in  std_logic;
  inputVal : in  std_logic_vector(3 downto 0);
  power    : out std_logic_vector(15 downto 0)
  );
end powerOfFour;

architecture behavioral of powerOfFour is

   function Pow( N, Exp : integer )  return integer is
      Variable Result   : integer := 1;

   begin
```

Chapter 12 - Enhancing Design Readability and Reuse

```
         for i in 1 to Exp loop
            Result := Result * N;
         end loop;
         return( Result );
      end Pow;

   begin

      process begin
        wait until Clk = '1';

            power <= std_logic_vector(to_unsigned(Pow
                    (to_integer(to_unsigned(inputVal)),4),16));

      end process;

   end behavioral;
```

pwrnest.vhd

Functions can also be placed in a package, just like components, for reuse and visibility to other entities. There is one key difference, however, and that is the use of the *package body* declaration. The "body" of a component declaration is its associated entity-architecture pair, as we saw in *Chapter 9*. However, the body of a function must be declared inside a *package body*. For example, if we wish to place our function *Pow* in a package called *specialFunctions*, we would need to place the *function body* inside the *package body*, as shown in *Listing 6*.

Listing 6: The *specialFunctions* Package Containing the Pow Function

```
library IEEE;
use IEEE.std_logic_1164.all;

package specialFunctions is

   function Pow(N, Exp : integer) return integer;

end specialFunctions;

package body specialFunctions is

   function Pow(N, Exp : integer) return integer is
      Variable Result    : integer := 1;
   begin
      for i in 1 to Exp loop
         Result := Result * N;
      end loop;
      return( Result );
   end Pow;

end specialFunctions;
```

specfcn.vhd

As seen in *Listing 6*, the function *Pow* is declared in the package header, while the body is placed in the package body. The *package body* and package declaration must have the same identifier. Our *powerOfFour* design now becomes very compact, as re-written in *Listing 7*.

Listing 7: Using Functions in Packages

```vhdl
-- Incorporates errata 5.4

library IEEE;
use IEEE.std_logic_1164.all;
use IEEE.numeric_std.all;

use work.specialFunctions.all;

entity powerOfFour is port(
   clk      : in  std_logic;
   inputVal : in  std_logic_vector(3 downto 0);
   power    : out std_logic_vector(15 downto 0)
   );
end powerOfFour;

architecture behavioral of powerOfFour is

begin

   process begin
     wait until Clk = '1';

        power <= std_logic_vector(to_unsigned
        (Pow(to_integer(unsigned(inputVal)),4),16));

   end process;

end behavioral;
```

pwrnestp.vhd

Procedures

Procedures are similar to functions, in that they are called, and passed, various parameters. Statements within a *procedure* are also evaluated sequentially, just like functions. However, they are markedly different from functions in the following characteristics:

- They may modify the parameters passed to them
- They may calculate and modify several parameters as a result of being called
- They may be called on their own

Procedures calls occur in sequence within a process. When called outside a process, *procedure* calls occur concurrently. When called from within a process, it is as if the statements within the *procedure* are substituted within the process. Hence, *procedures* are effective in enhancing the readability of a design, whether called from inside a process or concurrently. To illustrate this, let us consider the design of a 2-of-4 decoder. The logic for this is as shown in *Figure 1*.

Figure 1: Symbol and Truth Table for 2-of-4 Decoder

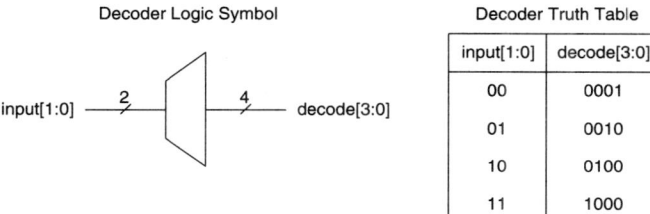

Our 2-of-4 decoder, written as a *procedure* would appear as shown in *Listing 8*. Like functions, procedures may be declared within an architecture body, just before the begin keyword. And as with functions, this makes the procedure visible only within that architecture.

Listing 8: 2-of-4 Decoder Using a Procedure

```
library IEEE;
use IEEE.std_logic_1164.all;

entity decoder is port (
  decIn: in std_logic_vector(1 downto 0);
  decOut: out std_logic_vector(3 downto 0)
  );
end decoder;

architecture simple of decoder is

  procedure DEC2x4 (inputs: in std_logic_vector(1 downto 0);
                    decode: out std_logic_vector(3 downto 0)
                   ) is
  begin
    case inputs is
      when "11" =>
        decode := "1000";
      when "10" =>
        decode := "0100";
      when "01" =>
        decode := "0010";
      when "00" =>
        decode := "0001";
```

```
          when others =>
            decode := "0001";
        end case;
    end DEC2x4;

begin

    DEC2x4(decIn,decOut);

end simple;
```

dec2x4P.vhd

We could call the procedure *DEC2x4* sequentially from within a process by replacing the architecture body in *Listing 8* as follows:

```
begin

  process (decIn) begin

    DEC2x4(decIn,decOut);

  end process;

end simple;
```

Both schemes of calling the *procedure* produce identical results. This illustrates an important point to note when calling *procedures* concurrently: there is an implied sensitivity list (to *decIn* in this case) when calling a *procedure* concurrently, and none when calling it from within a process.

As *procedures* can modify the parameters passed to them, it is very important to ensure that the parameter being passed has either a mode *out* or *inout*. A careful examination of the *procedure* in *Listing 8* shows that the parameters passed, *inputs* and *decode*, are both variables. They are **copies** of the signals *decIn* and *decOut* that are local to the *procedure*, and are used to update the *procedure* when it has finished execution.

We could certainly pass signals to the *procedure* by explicitly declaring the *procedure* as follows:

```
      procedure DEC2x4 (signal inputs : in std_logic_vector(1 downto 0);
                        signal decode: out std_logic_vector(3 downto 0)
                       ) is
    begin
      case inputs is
        when "11" =>
          decode <= "1000";
        when "10" =>
```

```
        decode <= "0100";
      when "01" =>
        decode <= "0010";
      when "00" =>
        decode <= "0001";
      when others =>
        decode <= "0001";
    end case;
  end DEC2x4;
```

Naturally, all variable assignments to *decode* are changed to signal assignments. However, what is significant from a modeling standpoint is the fact that the signal itself has been passed, and not the copy. As such, if the *procedure* was called from within a process, then you would need to take into account the properties of the signal when assigning values to, or reading values from the signal.

In addition, do not call a *procedure* that has a statement that results in a flip-flop from within a process, since this may cause undesired results. To illustrate this, let us consider the example of a *procedure* that creates a D-type flip-flop similar to the one we saw in *Chapter 4*. This is shown in *Listing 9*.

Listing 9: Procedure that Results in a D Flip-flop

```
library IEEE;
use IEEE.std_logic_1164.all;

entity flipFlop is port (
  clock, input: in std_logic;
  ffOut: out std_logic
  );
end flipFlop;

architecture simple of flipFlop is

  procedure dff (signal clk: in std_logic;
                 signal d: in std_logic;
                 signal q: out std_logic
                ) is
  begin
    if clk'event and clk = '1' then
      q <= d;
    end if;
  end procedure dff;

begin

  dff(clock, input, ffOut);

end simple;
```

dffproc.vhd

If we called this *procedure* from within a process, any concurrent assignments that followed the *procedure* within the same process would also get registered, which may not be desired. Furthermore, if there is another statement from which a clock can be inferred, it will result in an error from most RTL synthesis tools, since they typically handle only one clock inference statement per process.

Just like functions, *procedures* may be placed in packages for use elsewhere in a design, or in other designs. This requires the use of the *package body* statement, as shown in *Listing 10*, which places the 2-of-4 decoder *procedure* into the package *decodeProcs*.

Listing 10: Decoder Procedures Package

```
library IEEE;
use IEEE.std_logic_1164.all;

package decProcs is

  procedure DEC2x4 (inputs : in std_logic_vector(1 downto 0);
                    decode: out std_logic_vector(3 downto 0)
                   );
end decProcs;

package body decProcs is

  procedure DEC2x4 (inputs: in std_logic_vector(1 downto 0);
                    decode: out std_logic_vector(3 downto 0)
                   ) is
  begin
    case inputs is
      when "11" =>
        decode := "1000";
      when "10" =>
        decode := "0100";
      when "01" =>
        decode := "0010";
      when "00" =>
        decode := "0001";
      when others =>
        decode := "0001";
    end case;
  end DEC2x4;

end decProcs;
```
decprocs.vhd

By using this package, we can rewrite our decoder as shown in *Listing 11*.

Listing 11: 2-of-4 Decoder Using Procedure from a Package

```
library IEEE;
use IEEE.std_logic_1164.all;

use work.decProcs.all;

entity decoder is port (
  decIn: in std_logic_vector(1 downto 0);
  decOut: out std_logic_vector(3 downto 0)
  );
end decoder;

architecture simple of decoder is

begin

  DEC2x4(decIn,decOut);

end simple;
```

dec2x4pr.vhd

Procedures can also be made parameterizable by using unconstrained arrays in their parameters, and can be overloaded for different types, just like functions.

Disadvantage of Using Subprograms

While subprograms can be very useful, they should be used with great care in designs. Make sure you understand not only their hardware implications, but also the details of the parameters passed, their size and direction. In addition, subprograms may not result in resource sharing as we saw in *Chapter 8*, and as such might result in a larger circuit than necessary.

Aliases

Another capability of VHDL to enhance the readability of a design is the aliasing of signals. An *alias* is simply an alternative label or identifier. They are most commonly used to create names that are readable for signals, and to illustrate this, let us consider a modified version of the address decoder that we saw in *Chapter 3*, as shown in *Listing 12*. In this listing, the signals in the entity declaration are of the *std_logic_vector* type. However, the input signal *dev_adr* is decoded in two slices - the upper three bits, and the lower seventeen bits. Furthermore, the array *decOut_n* has individual bits in the vector asserted (or deasserted) under specific input conditions. These signals are aliased to make the design easier to read.

Listing 12: Decoder Design Using Aliases

```vhdl
library ieee;
use ieee.std_logic_1164.all;

entity isa_dec is port
(
  dev_adr:          in std_logic_vector(19 downto 0);

  decOut_n:         out std_logic_vector(5 downto 0)

);
end isa_dec;


architecture synthesis of isa_dec is

  constant   CtrlRegRange: std_logic_vector(2 downto 0)     := "100";
  constant   SuperIoRange: std_logic_vector(2 downto 0)     := "010";

  constant   IntCtrlReg:   std_logic_vector(16 downto 0) := "00000000000000000";
  constant   IoIntStatReg: std_logic_vector(16 downto 0) := "00000000000000001";
  constant   RstCtrlReg:   std_logic_vector(16 downto 0) := "00000000000000010";
  constant   AtcStatusReg: std_logic_vector(16 downto 0) := "00000000000000011";
  constant   MgmtStatusReg:std_logic_vector(16 downto 0) := "00000000000000100";

  alias sio_dec_n: std_logic is          decOut_n(5);
  alias rst_ctrl_rd_n: std_logic is      decOut_n(4);
  alias atc_stat_rd_n: std_logic is      decOut_n(3);
  alias mgmt_stat_rd_n: std_logic is     decOut_n(2);
  alias io_int_stat_rd_n: std_logic is decOut_n(1);
  alias int_ctrl_rd_n: std_logic is      decOut_n(0);

  alias upper: std_logic_vector(2 downto 0) is dev_adr(19 downto 17);
  alias CtrlBits: std_logic_vector(16 downto 0) is dev_adr(16 downto 0);

begin

  decoder: process (upper, CtrlBits)
    begin
      -- Set defaults for outputs - for synthesis reasons.

        sio_dec_n         <= '1';
        int_ctrl_rd_n     <= '1';
        io_int_stat_rd_n <= '1';
        rst_ctrl_rd_n     <= '1';
        atc_stat_rd_n     <= '1';
        mgmt_stat_rd_n    <= '1';

        case upper is

        when SuperIoRange =>
```

```
              sio_dec_n <= '0';

      when CtrlRegRange =>

        case CtrlBits is

          when IntCtrlReg =>
            int_ctrl_rd_n <= '0';

          when IoIntStatReg =>
            io_int_stat_rd_n <= '0';

          when RstCtrlReg =>
            rst_ctrl_rd_n <= '0';

          when AtcStatusReg =>
            atc_stat_rd_n <= '0';

          when MgmtStatusReg =>
            mgmt_stat_rd_n <= '0';

          when others =>
            null;

        end case;

      when others =>
        null;

    end case;

  end process decoder;

end synthesis;
```
decalias.vhd

Aliases are declared in the architecture body, along with constants and other local signal declarations, before the *begin* statement. Within the process *decoder*, we use aliases to determine the outputs. The aliases make the design clearer and easier to understand and debug.

13
Creative Potpourri

Pot-pour-ri: A general mixture of often disparate or unrelated materials or subject matter.[1]

This chapter contains a creative assortment of some advanced features of VHDL that should be kept in your "bag of tricks" to use some day. This chapter is also intended to serve as a launching pad for further exploration: VHDL is a rich and powerful language, with the capability to abstract hardware descriptions in a manner that greatly eases design capture, documentation and maintenance.

In this chapter, we will introduce:

- Aggregates
- Concatenation
- Records
- Multi-dimensional arrays
- Array indexing with enumerated types
- While-loops
- Signals of mode buffer

Do keep in mind that not all synthesis tools will support these language features. However, there is almost always an alternative method for describing the same logic using the techniques described in earlier chapters of this book.

Aggregates

We first encountered aggregates in *Chapter 7*, with the *others* clause. Aggregates are a group or collection of elements. The most common aggregate we have used in the book so far are array types, such as *std_logic_vector*. So, if *op* is a *std_logic_vector(7 downto 0)*, then the assignment:

```
op <= (op(3 downto 2) => '0', op(1 downto 0) => '1', others => 'Z')
```

results in

```
op = "ZZZZ0011"
```

Note that the *others* clause must be the last in the aggregate assignment.

---

1. Defined as listed in Webster's Third New International Dictionary.

Aggregates can also be used to gather two or more *std_logic* type signals into a *std_logic_vector* type. To illustrate this, let us revisit the seven-segment decoder in *Chapter 8*. In this design, each segment had to be turned either on or off in each *case* condition. We could assign the outputs as an aggregate, as shown in *Listing 1*.

Listing 1: Seven-segment Decoder Using Aggregates

```
library ieee;
use ieee.std_logic_1164.all;

entity sevenSegment is port (
  bcdInputs: in std_logic_vector (3 downto 0);
  a_n, b_n, c_n, d_n,
  e_n, f_n, g_n: out std_logic
  );
end sevenSegment;

architecture behavioral of sevenSegment is
-- LED segment.........................................abcdefg
constant DefaultValue: std_logic_vector(6 downto 0) := "1111111";
constant zero        : std_logic_vector(6 downto 0) := "0000001";
constant one         : std_logic_vector(6 downto 0) := "1001111";
constant two         : std_logic_vector(6 downto 0) := "0010010";
constant three       : std_logic_vector(6 downto 0) := "0000110";
constant four        : std_logic_vector(6 downto 0) := "1001100";
constant five        : std_logic_vector(6 downto 0) := "0100100";
constant six         : std_logic_vector(6 downto 0) := "0100000";
constant seven       : std_logic_vector(6 downto 0) := "0001111";
constant eight       : std_logic_vector(6 downto 0) := "0000000";
constant nine        : std_logic_vector(6 downto 0) := "0000100";

begin

  bcd2sevSeg: process (bcdInputs) begin

  -- Assign default to "off"
  (a_n, b_n, c_n, d_n, e_n, f_n, g_n) <= defaultValue;

    case bcdInputs is
      when "0000" =>
        (a_n, b_n, c_n, d_n, e_n, f_n, g_n) <= zero;

      when "0001" =>
        (a_n, b_n, c_n, d_n, e_n, f_n, g_n) <= one;

      when "0010" =>
        (a_n, b_n, c_n, d_n, e_n, f_n, g_n) <= two;

      when "0011" =>
        (a_n, b_n, c_n, d_n, e_n, f_n, g_n) <= three;
```

```
        when "0100" =>
          (a_n, b_n, c_n, d_n, e_n, f_n, g_n) <= four;
        when "0101" =>
          (a_n, b_n, c_n, d_n, e_n, f_n, g_n) <= five;
        when "0110" =>
          (a_n, b_n, c_n, d_n, e_n, f_n, g_n) <= six;
        when "0111" =>
          (a_n, b_n, c_n, d_n, e_n, f_n, g_n) <= seven;
        when "1000" =>
          (a_n, b_n, c_n, d_n, e_n, f_n, g_n) <= eight;
        when "1001" =>
          (a_n, b_n, c_n, d_n, e_n, f_n, g_n) <= nine;
        when others =>
          null;
      end case;
    end process bcd2sevSeg;
  end behavioral;
```
sevseg.vhd

The aggregate is represented in parentheses on the left hand side of the <= signal assignment. Notice that we used constants (*one, two, three,.....,nine*) to assign to the outputs, rather than using double-quotes, as follows:

```
    (a_n, b_n, c_n, d_n, e_n, f_n, g_n) <= "0000100";
```

This assignment using constants is required because VHDL is strongly typed. The value "0000100" might be a *std_logic_vector*, *unsigned* or *string* type, for example. Hence, the result type of the aggregate is ambiguous if it is assigned "0000100".

An alternative to using constants would be to typecast the value on the right hand side of the signal assignment to be a *std_logic_vector*. This is done using what is known as a *qualified expression*, which qualifies an expression to be a certain type. To do this, we would declare the desired subtype as follows:

```
    subtype sevenBit is std_logic_vector(6 downto 0);
```

In the signal assignment, we would now write:

```
    (a_n, b_n, c_n, d_n, e_n, f_n, g_n) <= sevenbit'("0000000");
```

Aggregates may also be used on the right hand side of the <= signal assignment, and not just on the left hand side of an assignment, as shown in *Listing 1*.

Concatenation

Concatenation is similar to aggregation, in that it allows you to group signals together. It is performed using the '&' operator on array types, or elements of array types (such as *std_logic_vector* and *std_logic* respectively).

Concatenating signals is useful in making expression evaluations easier to read. For example, in *Chapter 3*, we described a few simple gates shown in *Figure 1* using concurrent assignments. In *Listing 2*, we see how we can describe the same logic using the concatenation operator.

Figure 1: Simple Logic Using Gates

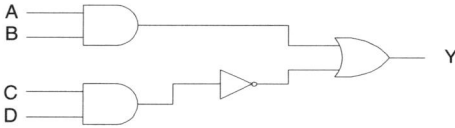

Listing 2: Simple Gates Using the Concatenation Operator

```
library IEEE;
use IEEE.std_logic_1164.all;
use IEEE.numeric_std.all;

entity FEWGATES is port (
  a,b,c,d: in std_logic;
  y: out std_logic
  );
end FEWGATES;

architecture concurrent of FEWGATES is

constant THREE: std_logic_vector(1 downto 0) := "11";

begin

  y <= '1' when (a & b = THREE) or (c & d /= THREE) else '0';

end concurrent;
```

concat.vhd

Chapter 13 - Creative Potpourri

When gathering slices of an array to construct a bigger array, note that concatenation will gather elements of the array in their bit order. For example, if we have three vectors

```
a(1 downto 0)
b(2 to 3)
c(2 to 5)
```

and we wish to concatenate them to *y(7 downto 0)* as follows:

```
y <= a & b & c;
```

This would be exactly the same as saying:

```
y(7) <= a(1);
y(6) <= a(0);
y(5) <= b(2);
y(4) <= b(3);
y(3) <= c(2);
y(2) <= c(3);
y(1) <= c(4);
y(0) <= c(5);
```

The left-most bit in the concatenation *(a(1))* is assigned to the left-most bit of *y (y(7))*.

Concatenation is also useful for "padding" an array to extend its length. Let us consider the *sll* operator that we discussed in *Chapter 12*. If the signals *shift* and *value* are both *bit_vector(7 downto 0)*, then the operation:

```
shift <= value sll 2
```

could be re-written as

```
shift <= value(5 downto 0) & "00";
```

Where the '&' operator is being used to pad the slice *value(5 downto 0)* to eight bits, so that the assignment to *shift* is valid.

Another example where concatenation for padding can be useful is in the usage of standard arithmetic operators. In *Chapter 5*, the "+" operator is defined for the *std_logic_vector* type. However, when performing a sum of two vectors, it might be useful to know if the result overflowed, but the "+" operator does not inherently facilitate this. One way to address this is to pad the operands by one bit, and calculate the sum extended by one bit. The most significant bit is now the overflow bit, and the remaining bits are the sum. This example is shown in *Listing 3*.

Listing 3: Overflow Capable Adder Using the + Operator and Concatenation

```
library ieee;
use ieee.std_logic_1164.all;
use ieee.numeric_std.all;

entity adder is port (
  a,b: in std_logic_vector(3 downto 0);
  sum: out std_logic_vector(3 downto 0);
  overflow: out std_logic
  );
end adder;

architecture concat of adder is

signal localSum: std_logic_vector(4 downto 0);

begin

  localSum <= std_logic_vector(unsigned('0' & a) + unsigned('0' & b));

  sum <= localSum(3 downto 0);
  overflow <= localSum(4);

end concat;
```

overflow.vhd

In the example, the local signal *localSum* holds the result that has been extended by one bit. Slices of *localSum* are then assigned to the port outputs using concurrent assignments.

Records

Records are characterized by individual elements of different types. This feature makes them very useful when trying to associate related elements of different types. Records are not often supported in synthesis tools, and are more frequently used in simulation than synthesis. Records can, however, be very useful during synthesis, if only for documentation and readability reasons. For example, in *Chapter 7*, we showed how to structurally instantiate a tri-state buffer, *tribuf*, located in the *primitive* package.

Figure 2: Tri-state Buffer Symbol and Ports

We can express this using records as follows:

Chapter 13 - Creative Potpourri

```
type tribufType is record
  ip: std_logic;
  oe: std_logic;
  op: std_logic;
end record;
```

We could then declare a signal to be of this type:

```
signal tri: tribufType;
```

Each element within this type is now accessible via a "dot-extension". In other words, the signal *tri* has three elements, which can be accessed as follows:

```
tri.ip
tri.oe
tri.op
```

To illustrate this, let us consider the design of an 8-bit tri-state buffer, similar to the one we saw in *Chapter 11*, as shown in *Figure 3*. This uses the tri-state buffer in *Figure 2*, and the primitives for *dffe* and *tribuf* in the *primitive* package.

Figure 3: 8-bit Register with Tri-state Buffer

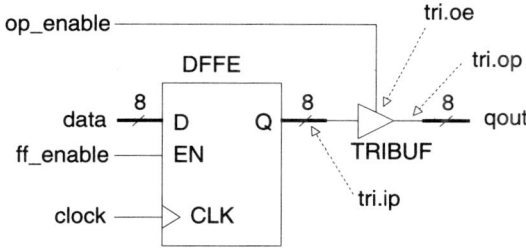

The VHDL implementation, in parameterizable form, for *Figure 3* is shown in *Listing 4*.

Listing 4: 8-bit Register with Tri-state Buffer Using Record Types

```
library IEEE;
use IEEE.std_logic_1164.all;

use work.primitive.all;

entity dffTri is
  generic (size: integer := 8);
  port (
  data: in std_logic_vector(size - 1 downto 0);
  clock: in std_logic;
```

```
    ff_enable: in std_logic;
    op_enable: in std_logic;
    qout: out std_logic_vector(size - 1 downto 0)
    );
end dffTri;

architecture parameterize of dffTri is

type tribufType is record
  ip: std_logic;
  oe: std_logic;
  op: std_logic;
end record;

type tribufArrayType is array (integer range <>) of tribufType;

signal tri: tribufArrayType(size - 1 downto 0);

begin

  g0: for i in 0 to size - 1 generate
    u1: DFFE port map (data(i), tri(i).ip, ff_enable, clock);
  end generate;

  g1: for i in 0 to size - 1 generate
    u2: TRIBUF port map (tri(i).ip, tri(i).oe, tri(i).op);
    tri(i).oe <= op_enable;
    qout(i) <= tri(i).op;
  end generate;

end parameterize;
```
dfftri.vhd

There are three important things to note about *Listing 4*. First, the unconstrained array type, *triBufArrayType*, is declared. This is not essential as we could have simply declared *tri* to be an array of *triBufType* as follows:

```
signal tri is array (size - 1 downto 0) of tribufType;
```

Second, we have used positional notation when instantiating *DFFE* and *TRIBUF*. These components are declared in the *primitive* package that we have used before. And finally, we use the *generate* statement labeled *g1* to assign the output enable, *op_enable*, and tri-state output, *qout*, to the intermediate signals.

Multidimensional Arrays

So far, we have been dealing with one-dimensional arrays, such as *std_logic_vector*. For applications where one needs a lookup table, it is useful to have a multidimensional table where the table consists of a series of *std_logic_vector* constants. VHDL supports multidimensional arrays, which is accomplished by declaring an array of another array, and then indexing into the second array to locate a value. To illustrate this, let us consider the example of a clock divider circuit.

In several synchronous applications, it is useful to divide down the reference, or master, clock into sub-multiples. Let us assume that for our sample application, we need to generate the waveforms for divided clocks as shown in *Figure 4*. The master clock, *Clk*, is divided by 2, 4, 6 and 8.

Figure 4: Divide-by Clock Waveform

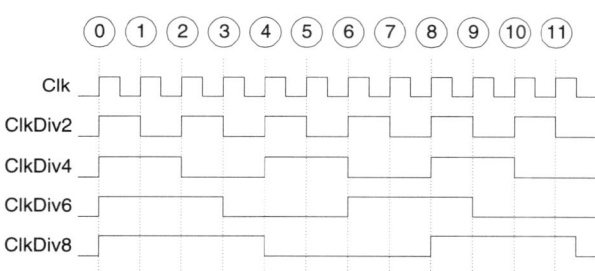

One approach to solve this would be by using counters. However, since this is a repetitive waveform, we could express a table, where each index in the table (0 through 11) corresponds to the time at the rising edge of *Clk* in *Figure 4*. The table would be as shown in *Table 1*.

Table 1: Table Showing Divided Clock Values from Time 0 Through 11

Time	ClkDiv2	ClkDiv4	ClkDiv6	ClkDiv8
0	1	1	1	1
1	0	1	1	1
2	1	0	1	1
3	0	0	0	1
4	1	1	0	0
5	0	1	0	0
6	1	0	1	0
7	0	0	1	0
8	1	1	1	1
9	0	1	0	1
10	1	0	0	1
11	0	0	0	1

We must first declare our multidimensional array. We will use subtypes, the first of which is a subtype of *std_logic_vector*, while the second indicates the array range of the subtype.

```
subtype numClks is std_logic_vector(1 to 4);
subtype numPatterns is integer range 0 to 11;
```

As we have four clocks, the *std_logic_vector* subtype is from 1 to 4. Since we have twelve sets of patterns, our tables contains twelve entries of *numClks*. Note that one of the reasons that we number the array entries from 0 onwards is because this simplifies the counter index that steps through the waveform.

The two dimensional array now looks almost exactly like *Table 1*.

```
constant clkTable: clkTableType := clkTableType'(
-- ClkDiv8_____
-- ClkDiv6_____ |
-- ClkDiv4____ ||
-- ClkDiv2 __ |||
--            ||||
            "1111",
            "0111",
            "1011",
            "0001",
            "1100",
            "0100",
            "1010",
            "0010",
            "1111",
            "0001",
            "1001",
            "0101");
```

Next, we need a simple counter that allows us to index each clock "tick" into this table. When this index reaches the maximum number of patterns (*numPatterns*), it wraps around and starts counting all over again.

Finally, we use an aggregate to assign each of the divided clock outputs:

```
(ClkDiv2,ClkDiv4,ClkDiv6,ClkDiv8) <= clkTable(index);
```

The complete VHDL for this design is shown in *Listing 5*.

Listing 5: Divide-by Clock Logic Using Multi-dimensional Arrays

```
library IEEE;
use IEEE.std_logic_1164.all;

entity clkGen is port (
  clk: in std_logic;
  reset: in std_logic;
  ClkDiv2, ClkDiv4,
  ClkDiv6,ClkDiv8: out std_logic
  );
end clkGen;

architecture behav of clkGen is

subtype numClks is std_logic_vector(1 to 4);
subtype numPatterns is integer range 0 to 11;

type clkTableType is array (numpatterns'low to numPatterns'high) of numClks;

constant clkTable: clkTableType := clkTableType'(
-- ClkDiv8_____
-- ClkDiv6_____ |
-- ClkDiv4____ ||
-- ClkDiv2 __ |||
--            ||||
           "1111",
           "0111",
           "1011",
           "0001",
           "1100",
           "0100",
           "1010",
           "0010",
           "1111",
           "0001",
           "1001",
           "0101");

signal index: numPatterns;

begin

  lookupTable: process (clk, reset) begin
    if reset = '1' then
      index <= 0;
    elsif (clk'event and clk = '1') then
      if index = numPatterns'high then
        index <= numPatterns'low;
      else
        index <= index + 1;
      end if;
```

```
    end if;
  end process;

  (ClkDiv2,ClkDiv4,ClkDiv6,ClkDiv8) <= clkTable(index);

end behav;
```
                                                                clkgen.vhd

Array Indexing Using Enumerated Types

Another application of multidimensional arrays is array indexing using enumerated types. One possible application of such a feature is when each bit in a state vector is an output of the state machine. Indexing with enumerated types gives us the flexibility and readability of enumerated types, while at the same time allows us control over the state assignment.

To illustrate this, let us recall the example of the pulse generation state machine from *Chapter 6*, as shown in *Figure 5*. A closer look at this design reveals that the outputs can, in fact, be expressed as a function of the state vector, as shown in the output conditions table in *Figure 5*. Hence, we could define a state vector, where the pulse output, *pulse*, the counter enable, *downCntEn*, and the counter load, *downCntLd*, are all part of the state vector. This is shown in *Table 2*.

Figure 5: Pulse Generator State Machine

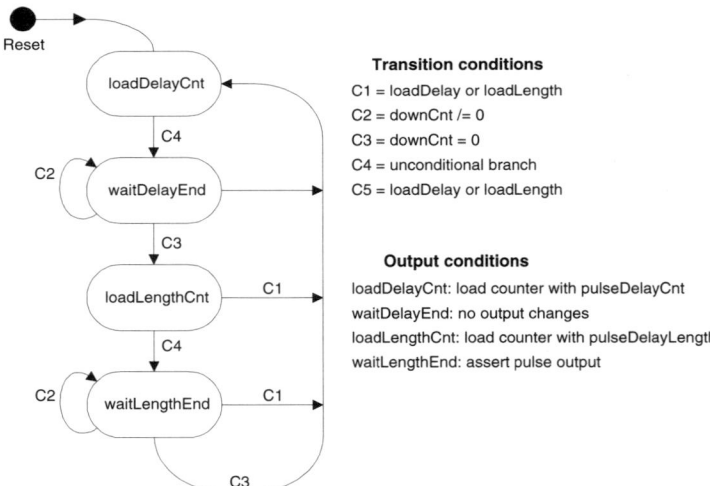

Chapter 13 - Creative Potpourri

Table 2: State Encoding that Incorporates the Outputs

State \ Outputs	pulse	downCntEn	downCntLd	loadVal
loadDelayCnt	0	0	1	0
waitDelayEnd	0	1	0	0
loadLengthCnt	0	0	1	1
waitLengthEnd	1	1	0	1

Note that the output *loadVal* indicates whether we should load either the delay value or the length value into the counter. Hence, it is essentially the select line of a mux that selects the delay value (*loadValue* = '0') or the length value (*loadValue* = '1').

To start, we create an enumerated type that represents our state vector. This is just as we did before:

```
type progPulseFsmType is(loadDelayCnt, waitDelayEnd, loadLengthCnt, waitLengthEnd);
```

The next step is to create a vector that represents the state vector. In our example, we need four bits,

```
type stateVec is array (3 downto 0) of std_logic;
```

We now declare a 2-dimensional array type, which is array *stateVec* bits wide, and is indexed by the enumerated type:

```
type stateBits is array (progPulseFsmType) of stateVec;
```

We must now set up the table with the vectors shown in *Table 2*:

```
constant stateTable: stateBits := (
   loadDelayCnt  =>   "0010",
   waitDelayEnd  =>   "0100",
   loadLengthCnt =>   "0011",
   waitLengthEnd =>   "1101" );
--                     ^^^^
--                     ||||__ loadVal
--                     |||___ downCntLd
--                     ||____ downCntEn
--                     |_____ pulse
```

The rest of the state machine stays the same, in that we still have one process that generates the next-state conditioning logic, and one process that generates the current state. However, we can now replace the output generation process by a straightforward index into the table using the enumerated type:

```
pulse      <= stateTable(currState)(3);
downCntEn  <= stateTable(currState)(2);
downCntLd  <= stateTable(currState)(1);
loadVal    <= stateTable(currState)(0);
```

The complete VHDL for this design is shown in *Listing 6*.

Listing 6: Pulse Generator State Machine Using Indexed Arrays with Enumerated Types

```
library ieee;
use ieee.std_logic_1164.all;
use ieee.numeric_std.all;

entity progPulseFsm is port (
  downCnt: in std_logic_vector(7 downto 0);
  delayCntVal: in std_logic_vector(7 downto 0);
  lengthCntVal: in std_logic_vector(7 downto 0);
  loadLength: in std_logic;
  loadDelay: in std_logic;
  clk: in std_logic;
  reset: in std_logic;

  downCntEn: out std_logic;
  downCntLd: out std_logic;
  downCntData: out std_logic_vector(7 downto 0);

  pulse: out std_logic
  );
end progPulseFsm;

architecture fsm of progPulseFsm is

type progPulseFsmType is (loadDelayCnt, waitDelayEnd, loadLengthCnt,
   waitLengthEnd);
type stateVec is array (3 downto 0) of std_logic;
type stateBits is array (progPulseFsmType) of stateVec;

signal loadVal: std_logic;

constant stateTable: stateBits := (
  loadDelayCnt   => "0010",
  waitDelayEnd   => "0100",
  loadLengthCnt  => "0011",
  waitLengthEnd  => "1101" );
--                   ^^^^
```

```vhdl
  --                  ||||__ loadVal
  --                  |||___ downCntLd
  --                  ||____ downCntEn
  --                  |_____ pulse

  signal currState, nextState: progPulseFsmType;

begin

  nextStProc: process (currState, downCnt, loadDelay, loadLength) begin
    case currState is
      when loadDelayCnt =>
        nextState <= waitDelayEnd;

      when waitDelayEnd =>
        if (loadDelay = '1' or loadLength = '1') then
          nextState <= loadDelayCnt;
        elsif (to_unsigned(downCnt) = 0) then
          nextState <= loadLengthCnt;
        else
          nextState <= waitDelayEnd;
        end if;

      when loadLengthCnt =>
        if (loadDelay = '1' or loadLength = '1') then
          nextState <= loadDelayCnt;
        else
          nextState <= waitLengthEnd;
        end if;

      when waitLengthEnd =>
        if (loadDelay = '1' or loadLength = '1') then
          nextState <= loadDelayCnt;
        elsif (to_unsigned(downCnt) = 0) then
          nextState <= loadDelayCnt;
        else
          nextState <= waitDelayEnd;
        end if;

      when others =>
        null;

    end case;

  end process nextStProc;

  currStProc: process (clk, reset) begin
    if (reset = '1') then
      currState <= loadDelayCnt;
    elsif (clk'event and clk = '1') then
      currState <= nextState;
    end if;
```

```
    end process currStProc;

    pulse      <= stateTable(currState)(3);
    downCntEn  <= stateTable(currState)(2);
    downCntLd  <= stateTable(currState)(1);
    loadVal    <= stateTable(currState)(0);

    downCntData <= delayCntVal when loadVal = '0' else lengthCntVal;

end fsm;
```

pulseidx.vhd

Indexing arrays with enumerated types reduces the amount of code written in the design, as shown in *Listing 6*, and retains the readability of enumerated types while allowing you to effectively assign the states for the design.

While Loops

In *Chapter 11*, we introduced the *for...loop*. This is useful when we wish to control the number of iterations for which the loop must be executed. The *while...loop*, on the other hand, continues to be executed, until the loop condition is satisfied. *While* loops can be used in different ways for synthesis. For example, we can use *while* loops to initialize an array.

To illustrate this, let us consider the example of a register file. A register file is often encountered in computer architecture. It is a set of registers that is used to hold data that is being operated on. Our example register file is shown in *Figure 6*. It consists of four 32-bit registers. These registers can be written using the *wrEnable* signal. This signal, when asserted, writes the value *data* into the selected register. The register to be read or written is selected using the *regSel* signal.

Figure 6: Register File Symbol

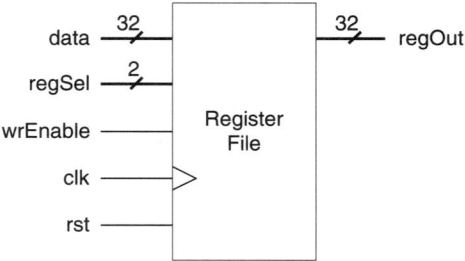

In this design, we must first declare the 4x32 array of registers. We will do this by declaring a subtype, *reg*, for each 32-bit register, and then declaring a type, *regArray*, as an unconstrained integer array of *reg*, as follows:

Chapter 13 - Creative Potpourri

```
subtype reg is std_logic_vector(31 downto 0);
type regArray is array (integer range <>) of reg;
```

Our register file consists of a set of four registers, so we declare the signal *registerFile* to be a 4-element array of *regArray*:

```
signal registerFile: regArray(0 to 3);
```

Registers typically need to be reset on system start-up, which is accomplished by the *rst* signal. We use a *while loop* to loop through the array, resetting each flip-flop when *rst* is asserted:

```
regProc: process (clk, rst)
  variable i: integer;

  begin
    i := 0;

    if rst = '1' then
      while i <= registerFile'high loop
        registerFile(i) <= (others => '0');
        i := i + 1;
      end loop;
```

Note the significant difference between *for...loop* and *while...loop* in this code fragment. First, in a *for...loop*, the loop index is implicitly declared, while it has to be explicitly declared in the *while...loop*. Furthermore, the *for...loop* index has to be initialized each time the process runs. Second, the *while...loop* requires the counter, *i*, to be explicitly incremented at the end of each loop iteration, unlike the *for...loop*. The complete VHDL design for the register file is shown in *Listing 7*.

Listing 7: Register File Using *while...loop* for Register Reset

```
library IEEE;
use IEEE.std_logic_1164.all;

entity regFile is port (
  clk, rst: in std_logic;
  data: in std_logic_vector(31 downto 0);
  regSel: in std_logic_vector(1 downto 0);
  wrEnable: in std_logic;
  regOut: out std_logic_vector(31 downto 0)
  );
end regFile;

architecture behavioral of regFile is

subtype reg is std_logic_vector(31 downto 0);
type regArray is array (integer range <>) of reg;
```

```vhdl
  signal registerFile: regArray(0 to 3);

begin

  regProc: process (clk, rst)
  variable i: integer;

  begin
    i := 0;

    if rst = '1' then
      while i <= registerFile'high loop
        registerFile(i) <= (others => '0');
        i := i + 1;
      end loop;

    elsif clk'event and clk = '1' then
      if (wrEnable = '1') then
        case regSel is
          when "00" =>
            registerFile(0) <= data;
          when "01" =>
            registerFile(1) <= data;
          when "10" =>
            registerFile(2) <= data;
          when "11" =>
            registerFile(3) <= data;
          when others =>
            null;
        end case;
      end if;
    end if;
  end process;

  outputs: process(regSel, registerFile) begin
    case regSel is
      when "00" =>
        regOut <= registerFile(0);
      when "01" =>
        regOut <= registerFile(1);
      when "10" =>
        regOut <= registerFile(2);
      when "11" =>
        regOut <= registerFile(3);
      when others =>
        null;
    end case;
  end process;

end behavioral;
```

regfile.vhd

Another example illustrating the use of *while..loop* is the exponentiation function we saw in *Chapter 12*. The function *Pow* was implemented using *for...loop*:

```
function Pow( N, Exp : integer )  return integer is
     Variable Result   : integer := 1;

  begin
     for i in 1 to Exp loop
        Result := Result * N;
     end loop;
     return( Result );
  end Pow;
```

We could also express it using the *while...loop* as follows:

```
function Pow( N, Exp : integer )  return integer is
     Variable Result   : integer := 1;
     Variable i        : integer := 0;
  begin
     while( i < Exp ) loop
        Result := Result * N;
        i      := i + 1;
     end loop;
     return( Result );
  end Pow;
```

In both these examples, the *while...loop* can, in essence, be substituted with the *for...loop*, and vice-versa. However, the *while...loop* is particularly useful if one needs to exit the loop when a condition is achieved, without looping through all the options. While this is possible using the *exit* statement in VHDL, many synthesis tools do not support the *exit* statement for synthesis. To demonstrate this strength of the *while...loop*, let us consider the example of an interrupt priority encoder, as shown in *Figure 7*.

Figure 7: Interrupt Priority Encoder

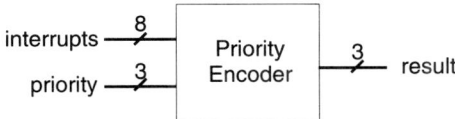

This encoder takes eight inputs, *interrupts*, and determines which one has the highest priority (*result*). The highest priority interrupt is set using the *priority* input. The priorities are searched in descending order, and when we reach *interrupt(0)*, we wrap around to *interrupt(7)*. So, for example, if *priority* is set to the decimal value 5, or binary 101, then the highest priority interrupt is *interrupt(5)*, followed by *interrupt(4)*, and so on until *interrupt(6)*, which is the lowest priority interrupt. The core loop is as follows:

```vhdl
      while (LoopCount <= 7) and (interrupts(selectIn) /= '0') loop

        if (selectIn = 0) then
          selectIn := 7;
        else
          selectIn := selectIn - 1;
        end if;

        LoopCount := LoopCount + 1;

      end loop;

      result <= std_logic_vector(to_unsigned(selectIn,3));
```

The *loop* condition determines whether we have checked a total of eight interrupts, as *LoopCount* performs eight loops from 0 to 7. The priority checking is begun at the highest priority, where *selectIn* is the integer representation of the signal *priority*. The loop also checks to see if the interrupt currently selected is asserted before entering the loop *(interrupts(selectIn) /= '0')*. The loop is exited whenever this condition is satisfied. This results in the highest priority interrupt being asserted on *result*. *SelectIn* is finally converted back to a *std_logic_vector* so that it can be assigned to *result*. The VHDL for this design is shown in *Listing 8*.

Listing 8: Interrupt Priority Encoder Using *while...loop*

```vhdl
library ieee;
use ieee.std_logic_1164.all;
use ieee.numeric_std.all;

entity priority_encoder is port
  (interrupts : in  std_logic_vector(7 downto 0);
   priority   : in  std_logic_vector(2 downto 0);
   result     : out std_logic_vector(2 downto 0)
  );
end priority_encoder;

architecture behave of priority_encoder is
begin

  process (interrupts)
     variable selectIn  : integer;
     variable LoopCount : integer;
  begin

    LoopCount := 1;
    selectIn  := to_integer(to_unsigned(priority));

      while (LoopCount <= 7) and (interrupts(selectIn) /= '0') loop

        if (selectIn = 0) then
          selectIn := 7;
```

Chapter 13 - Creative Potpourri

```
      else
        selectIn := selectIn - 1;
      end if;

      LoopCount := LoopCount + 1;

    end loop;

    result <= std_logic_vector(to_unsigned(selectIn,3));

  end process;

end behave;
```

prienc.vhd

Finally, we will discuss an aspect of VHDL that relates to signal drivers: signals of mode *buffer*.

Signal Mode Buffer

So far, we have used signals that have mode *in*, *out* and *inout*. There is an additional mode known as *buffer*. This mode implies that the driver(s) of the signal are located inside the entity, and are not outside. However, the value of the signal may be read inside the entity as well. This concept is easily demonstrated using the example of a counter. The basic counter symbol is shown in *Figure 8*.

Figure 8: Simple Counter and its Equivalent Logic

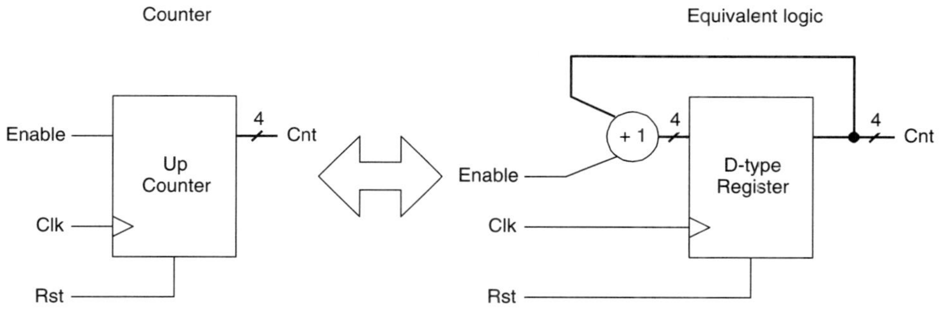

The equivalent logic shows that the *Cnt* outputs feed back into the increment logic. Hence, the signal *Cnt* is not only an output, but is also "read" by the increment logic within the design. In *Chapter 5*, the counter outputs were declared to be of mode *out*. We hence needed to create an intermediate signal local to the architecture, and assign this to the output. If we declare *Cnt* to be of mode *buffer* in the port declaration, then we need not use the intermediate signal. We can write the VHDL as shown in *Listing 10*.

Listing 9: Counter Using Outputs of Mode Buffer

```
library ieee;
use ieee.std_logic_1164.all;
use ieee.numeric_std.all;

entity counter is port (
  clk: in std_logic;
  enable: in std_logic;
  reset: in std_logic;
  count: buffer unsigned(3 downto 0)
  );
end counter;

architecture simple of counter is

begin

  increment: process (clk, reset) begin
    if reset = '1' then
      count <= "0000";
    elsif(clk'event and clk = '1') then
      if enable = '1' then
        count <= count + 1;
      else
        count <= count;
      end if;
    end if;
  end process;

end simple;
```

cnt4.vhd

While this is certainly a clean description, mode *buffer* should be used with care (recall the related issues that we noted in *Chapter 9*). The *mode* of a port signal needs to propagate all the way up the hierarchy, which will impact various choices including library components.

14
Simulation and Design Verification

VHDL modeling can be broadly classified into two areas:

- Modeling for synthesis
- Modeling for simulation and design verification

This book focuses specifically on VHDL modeling for RTL synthesis. However, it is very difficult to discuss hardware design without mentioning verification. Verification is the means by which we can ensure that the original design objectives have been met. There are several aspects to verification, some of the more basic of which are:

- Functionality: does it operate as expected?
- Timing analysis: does it meet the electrical timing requirements?
- Power consumption: has the power budget been met?
- Performance: have the throughput/bandwidth/latency objectives been met?

As can be seen, this is a subject of great depth and complexity. While the book concentrates on RTL synthesis, this chapter introduces VHDL for simulation and design verification.

Verification is quickly being regarded as an art in its own right, and is a crucial part of any design methodology. As designs get more complex:

- Design schedules are dominated by the verification process
- "Soft" verification must be performed prior to hardware debug
- Design must be performed with verification in mind

One of the great strengths of VHDL is its dual application for synthesis and simulation. All models written for synthesis can be simulated using a VHDL simulator. As such, the VHDL language can be used for both design description and verification.

This chapter emphasizes correctness and ease of use over model and simulation performance. It should be treated as a brief introduction, or launching pad from which to explore VHDL further for simulation and verification. A few simple concepts and techniques will be presented, the focus of which are:

- Simulation models and modeling
- Functional verification
- Simple timing verification
- Highlighting the differences between RTL synthesis and simulation modeling

Simulation Modeling

The purpose of a model is to accurately describe the behavior of your design. This is true for both simulation and synthesizable models. However, there are several differences in simulation models, when compared to synthesizable VHDL models, that we have seen thus far in the book. The most notable of these differences are:

- The notion of time
- Messages for information or debug while the model is running
- Availability of the full complement of VHDL constructs

For the most part, you will use simulation models that have been automatically generated by software. With programmable logic tools, "post-layout" models are generated when the back-end tools have successfully run. These tools use well-characterized models of the electrical properties of the device to generate timing models, which are written in the form of a VHDL netlist. Even though these models are automatically generated, we will discuss the basic elements of simulation modeling.

Modeling a Simple Gate

To begin with, let us consider the model of an OR gate, as shown in *Figure 1*.

Figure 1: OR Gate Symbol, Truth-table and Architecture

Symbol	Truth Table			RTL Synthesis VHDL
I1, I2 → Y	I1	I2	Y	`architecture simple of OR2 is`
	0	0	0	`begin`
	0	1	1	`  Y <= I1 OR I2;`
	1	0	1	`end simple;`
	1	1	1	

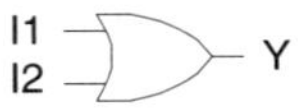

The design description for RTL synthesis shown in *Figure 1* assigns the value of *Y* in zero time. For the purposes of simulation, we must incorporate the notion of time, or propagation delay, associated with the gate. The time it takes to propagate the signal, or t_{PD} is shown in *Figure 2*.

Figure 2: Propagation Delay for OR Gate

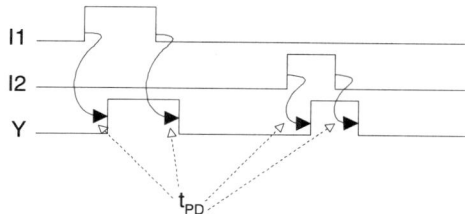

The VHDL shown in *Figure 1* shows a "zero-delay" gate. In other words, Y changes at the same instant in time that *I1* or *I2* changes. We can insert a delay into this assignment by using the word *after* as shown in *Listing 1*, where t_{PD} is assumed to be 10ns.

Listing 1: OR Gate Model with t_{PD} = 10ns

```
library IEEE;
USE IEEE.std_logic_1164.all;


entity OR2 is port (
  I1, I2: in std_logic;
  Y: out std_logic
  );
end OR2;

architecture simple of OR2 is

begin

  Y <= I1 OR I2 after 10 ns;

end simple;
```

orgate.vhd

There are two important points to note about the model shown in *Listing 1*:

- The OR operator will propagate 'X's for any input combination that is not valid
- Pulses are "swallowed", or rejected, for any pulse width less than the propagation delay

The first point is based on the OR function that is defined in the *std_logic_1164* package. Recall that the *std_logic* type can be assigned one of nine values: U, X, 0, 1, Z, W, L, H and -. The result, Y, can only be a valid '1' if one of the inputs is a valid '1'. The *std_logic_1164* OR function truth table for two inputs of the *std_logic* type is shown in *Table 1*.

Table 1: Truth Table for the OR Operation on Two *std_logic* Inputs

	U	X	0	1	Z	W	L	H	-
U	U	U	U	1	U	U	U	1	U
X	U	X	X	1	X	X	X	1	X
0	U	X	0	1	X	X	0	1	X
1	1	1	1	1	1	1	1	1	1
Z	U	X	X	1	X	X	X	1	X
W	U	X	X	1	X	X	X	1	X
L	U	X	0	1	X	X	0	1	X
H	1	1	1	1	1	1	1	1	1
-	U	X	X	1	X	X	X	1	X

The second point to note is that any pulse that is less than the propagation delay specified by *after* will be rejected by the OR gate. In our example, any pulse that is less than 10ns will be rejected. This behavior is shown in *Figure 3*, where a 5ns pulse on the input *I2* is rejected, and does not appear on the output *Y*.

Figure 3: Pulse Rejection Example

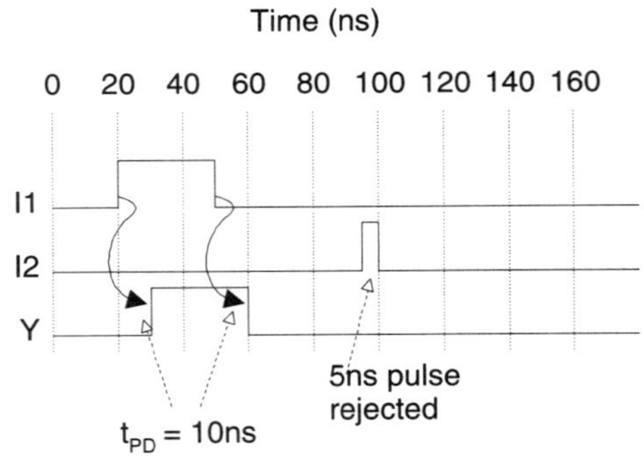

Enhancing the Basic Model

It is often useful to describe a model that shows more detailed timing information. For example, we may wish to show a different propagation delay for a high-to-low transition than a low-to-high transition. Or perhaps, we might wish to show different propagation delays, depending on which inputs are switching. One technique to implement this is to create a "zero-delay" model (just as if we were writing a model for RTL synthesis), that describes functionality, and then assign delays based on signal transitions, as shown in *Figure 4*.

Figure 4: Enhancing the Basic Delay Model

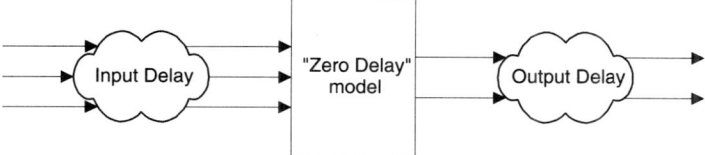

To demonstrate this, let us consider the model of a mux, as shown in *Figure 5*.

Figure 5: 2-1 Mux Symbol and Truth Table

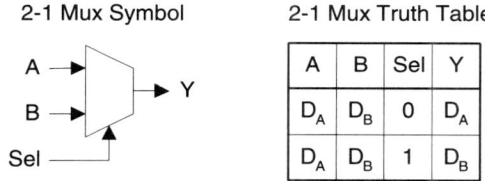

This mux may exhibit different timing characteristics, depending on which input (*A*, *B* or *Sel*) is changing. We will call these delays t_{PD_A}, t_{PD_B} and t_{PD_Sel} respectively, and define them as shown in *Figure 6*.

Figure 6: Timing Characteristics of a 2-1 Mux

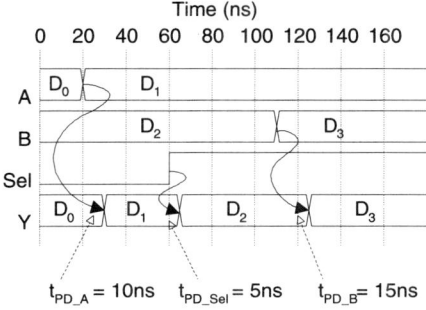

We will model this as a "zero-delay" mux, followed by delay conditioning logic that determines which signal is transitioning. Since the slowest transition is t_{PD_B}, this will take precedence over t_{PD_A} and t_{PD_Sel} in determining when the output *Y* is valid. The VHDL for this model is shown in *Listing 2*.

Listing 2: Simulation Model for 2-1 Mux

```vhdl
library IEEE;
use IEEE.std_logic_1164.all;

entity mux is port (
  A, B, Sel: in std_logic;
  Y: out std_logic
  );
end mux;

architecture simModel of mux is

-- Delay Constants
constant tPD_A:   time := 10 ns;
constant tPD_B:   time := 15 ns;
constant tPD_Sel: time := 5 ns;

begin

  DelayMux: process (A, B, Sel)

  variable localY: std_logic; -- Zero delay place holder for Y

  begin

  -- Zero delay model
    case Sel is
      when '0' =>
        localY := A;
      when others =>
        localY := B;
    end case;

  -- Delay calculation
    if (B'event) then
      Y <= localY after tPD_B;
    elsif (A'event) then
      Y <= localY after tPD_A;
    else
      Y <= localY after tPD_Sel;
    end if;

  end process;


end simModel;
```

mux.vhd

Note the use of constants of type *time* in the model to define the three propagation delays. The type is native to VHDL, and no special package needs be used to make this type

Chapter 14 - Simulation and Design Verification

available. While the use of constants is not required, it is good design practice for reasons of documentation and readability. The delay calculation uses the *'event* attribute, which checks to see if there has been a change in the value of an input signal.

Adding Debug Messages to the Model

Having added more detail to the timing characteristics of a model, it is useful to add messages to the model that will appear when one or more of the timing parameters have been violated. This is particularly true in synchronous design to determine if the timing parameters of a register have been violated. These messages may have different levels of severity, ranging from purely informational to catastrophic when the simulation is halted.

To illustrate the use of such messages, let us consider a rising-edge triggered D flip-flop, whose timing characteristics are shown in *Figure 7*.

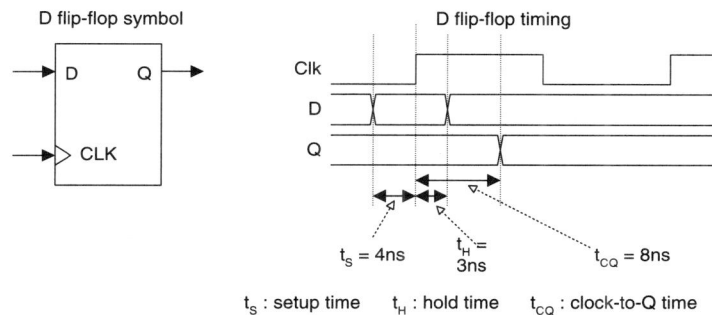

Figure 7: DFF Symbol and Timing Waveform

Our goal is to correctly model the timing characteristics of the flip-flop, and to provide messages when either the set-up time or the hold time are violated. This check is performed in VHDL using the *assert* statement. When the *assert* condition is false, the assertion will *report* a particular message that may be associated with a *severity*. Severity can take one of four values, *Note, Warning, Error* and *Failure*, as defined in the *standard* package.

Our simulation model for the flip-flop that includes timing checks is shown in *Listing 3*.

Listing 3: Simulation Model for a DFF

```
library IEEE;
use IEEE.std_logic_1164.all;

entity SimDFF is port (
  D, Clk: in std_logic;
```

```vhdl
    Q: out std_logic
    );
end SimDff;

architecture SimModel of SimDFF is

constant tCQ: time := 8 ns;
constant tS:  time := 4 ns;
constant tH:  time := 3 ns;

begin

  reg: process (Clk, D) begin

    -- Assign output tCQ after rising clock edge
    if (Clk'event and Clk = '1') then
      Q <= D after tCQ;
    end if;

    -- Check setup time
    if (Clk'event and Clk = '1') then
      assert (D'last_event >= tS)
        report "Setup time violation"
        severity Warning;
    end if;

    -- Check hold time
    if (D'event and Clk'stable and Clk = '1') then
      assert (Clk'last_event > tH)
        report "Hold Time Violation"
        severity Warning;
    end if;

  end process;

end simModel;
```
ff.vhd

There are four significant issues to note with this model. First, note that the process is sensitive to both *Clk* and *D*. Just as in the RTL synthesis model, *Clk* must be placed in the sensitivity list as all timing and functionality of the flip-flop is dependent on the rising edge of *Clk*. However, unlike the synthesis model, we also make the process sensitive to *D* so that we can check for a hold time violation.

Second, the output of the flip-flop is assigned in a similar fashion to the synthesis model. The only difference is that the simulation model assigns *D* to *Q* after time t_{CQ}.

Third, we have used two attributes, *'stable* and *'last_event*. The *'stable* attribute is asserted whenever a signal is not changing. The *'last_event* attribute indicates how much time has elapsed since the last change in value of the signal. We can use these built-in attributes to determine whether or not there has been a timing violation.

Finally, notice that the hold time check assumes that the clock high time is in fact greater than the hold time of the flip-flop. While this is often a reasonable assumption, it serves to show that it is important to understand the bounds of a model so that the reported messages are consistent and accurate.

Hierarchy and Wire Delays

Hierarchy and module reuse are as applicable for simulation models as they are for synthesis. Simulation models can be placed in a library, and instantiated in a design. There are two notable issues when creating hierarchical simulation models:

- Delay characteristics should be passed as instance-specific *generics*, making the models reusable
- Just as in a real system, wires that connect different blocks may have a delay associated with them that needs to be modeled

Instance specific generics should be created for the delay constants, and passed to the model using the *generic map*. For example, the OR gate shown in *Listing 1* may be placed in a package called *simPrimitives* as shown in *Listing 4*. The generics are initialized to a default nominal value, which may be overridden when the component is instantiated.

Listing 4: OR Gate Model in the *simPrimitives* Package

```
library IEEE;
USE IEEE.std_logic_1164.all;

package simPrimitives is

  component OR2
    generic (tPD: time := 1 ns);

    port (I1, I2: in std_logic;
      Y: out std_logic
      );
  end component;

end simPrimitives;


library IEEE;
USE IEEE.std_logic_1164.all;
```

```
entity OR2 is
  generic (tPD: time := 1 ns);

  port (I1, I2: in std_logic;
    Y: out std_logic
    );
end OR2;

architecture simple of OR2 is

begin

  Y <= I1 OR I2 after tPD;

end simple;
```
orpkg.vhd

There are two kinds of delays in VHDL: *inertial* and *transport* delay. Inertial delay is the default delay type. It is used to model component delays, where there is a component "inertia" that needs to be overcome before an output will take the assigned value. Transport delays are delays that are propagated regardless of their duration. In other words, there is no "inertia" to overcome, and the delay is always "transported". Hence, *transport* delays are used to model wires and are denoted by using the word *transport* in the signal assignment:

```
dataInLocal <= transport dataIn after 5 ns;
```

We can now combine these two concepts to create hierarchical simulation models. To illustrate this, we will combine the OR gate and flip-flop developed in this chapter, as shown in *Figure 8*. Each bubble in *Figure 8* represents the delay associated with the corresponding wire.

Figure 8: Simulation Model Showing Wire Delays

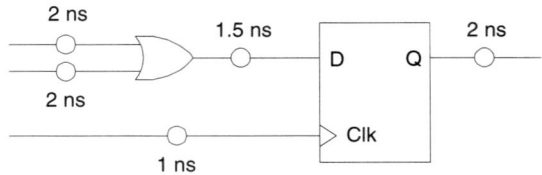

Hence, our model uses intermediate nodes on which we apply the wire delays, as shown in *Listing 5*.

Listing 5: Hierarchical Model Using Transport Delays

```vhdl
library IEEE;
use IEEE.std_logic_1164.all;

use work.simPrimitives.all;

entity simHierarchy is port (
  A, B, Clk: in std_logic;
  Y: out std_logic
  );
end simHierarchy;

architecture hierarchical of simHierarchy is

signal ADly, BDly, OrGateDly, ClkDly: std_logic;
signal OrGate, FlopOut: std_logic;

begin

  ADly <= transport A after 2 ns;
  BDly <= transport B after 2 ns;
  OrGateDly <= transport OrGate after 1.5 ns;
  ClkDly <= transport Clk after 1 ns;

  u1: OR2 generic map (tPD => 10 ns)
         port map ( I1 => ADly,
                    I2 => BDly,
                    Y => OrGate
                  );

  u2: simDFF generic map ( tS => 4 ns,
                           tH => 3 ns,
                           tCQ => 8 ns
                         )
            port map ( D => OrGateDly,
                       Clk => ClkDly,
                       Q => FlopOut
                     );

  Y <= transport FlopOut after 2 ns;

end hierarchical;
```

hiermod.vhd

Design Verification

The importance of design verification cannot be overemphasized. It includes ensuring that we have met the logical functionality of the design requirements, as well as important timing parameters. In VHDL, logical verification is performed using a testbench.

At the very minimum, a testbench applies stimulus to the design being tested. The response is either written to a file, or viewed in a simulation console or waveform window. This "manual" checking of the results may work well for very small designs, since it allows you to write the testbench quickly. However, it is labor intensive, and prone to errors as designs get more complex.

A better way of writing testbenches is in a self-checking or self-verifying manner. By this we mean that the testbench not only applies the stimulus, but also verifies that the outputs of the design are as expected. Note that "expected response" could be a failure condition that is being tested.

We will explore two styles of writing testbenches:

- Embedding the stimulus and response into the testbench in the form of a table
- Using a separate text file that contains the stimulus and response

Basic Anatomy of a VHDL Testbench

A VHDL testbench is implemented using an entity-architecture pair. The design being tested is placed within the testbench architecture, along with any other components, processes, procedures, etc., that make up the verification environment. The basic anatomy of a testbench is shown in *Figure 9*.

Figure 9: Basic Anatomy of a Testbench

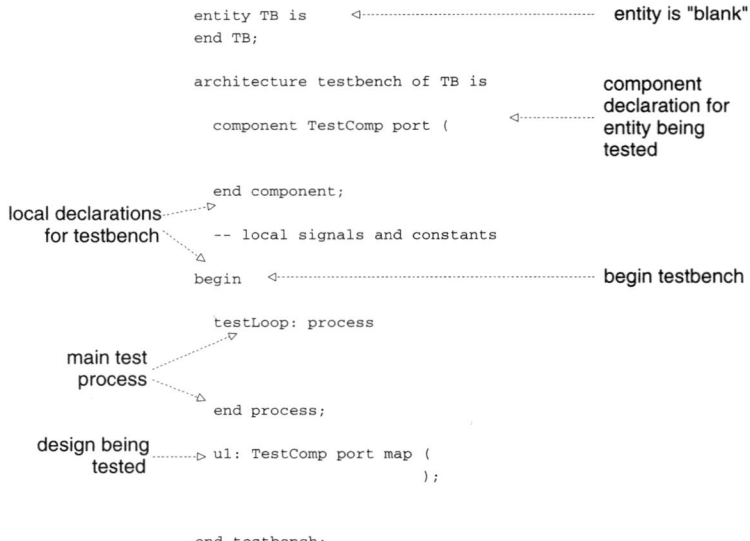

The are no ports in the testbench entity declaration, as the testbench itself does not interface with or connect to any other components. Most often, you will test the top level entity-architecture pair of your design, in which case there is no component declaration for this entity-architecture pair. Hence, a component must be declared for this entity-architecture pair so that it can be instantiated in the testbench. Along with the component declaration are various signal and constant declarations that are used in the testbench. The design being tested is instantiated in the architecture of the testbench, which also contains a process that is the main test process to verify the design being tested. In some cases, the main test process is best separated into two or more processes or even replaced with a component to provide the same functionality, as this may be easier to manage in terms of complexity.

Along with these basic elements, we should also include some basic messages that indicate whether the vectors passed or failed, along with a time stamp that will help us locate the point in time when the error occurred.

There are two important points to note when writing vectors for a testbench:

- The concept of delay in a model
- What will adequately test the design

Part of the attraction of a VHDL testbench is that we can use the same testbench to perform verification of the RTL synthesis model, as well as the "post-layout" model generated by the back-end tools. However, our RTL synthesis model does not have any timing information, and, from a simulation standpoint, is a "zero-delay" model. As such, when writing a testbench, we must incorporate the notion of timing into the testbench, and test the model for the final objectives, which include delays associated with the end result.

Another very important aspect of writing the testbench is determining what conditions will adequately test the design. This is particularly true as designs get more complex, where exhaustive testing of all input combinations is not feasible, if only from the point of view of the time it would take to complete the simulation. To a large extent, understanding the design and how to test it, is the "art" of logical design verification.

Reading and Writing Text

Before illustrating sample testbenches, we will discuss the generation of messages that need to be reported during simulation. We have already discussed one mechanism: the *assert* statement and the optional *report* and *severity* that are associated with an *assert* statement.

In addition to this, VHDL provides some standard routines to read and write text files, and also the simulation console. These procedures are located in the *std* library, and are in the *textio* package. They are overloaded to handle virtually all the types that you will come across during simulation. These functions have been overloaded for the *std_logic* type in the *io1164* package that resides in the *UTILS* library.

The *read* and *write* procedures read or modify a *line*. The read procedure continues to read characters until it encounters a "space", "tab" or "end-of-line" character. It is overloaded for many types including *bit*, *std_logic*, *std_logic_vector* and *integer* types, as shown in *Figure 10*. The *read* procedure can be optionally called with a Boolean parameter that indicates if what was read was valid, in terms of the type passed to it. In other words, if we called the procedure *read* with a *std_logic* type, the *good* Boolean parameter indicates whether the character read from the line is a valid *std_logic* value.

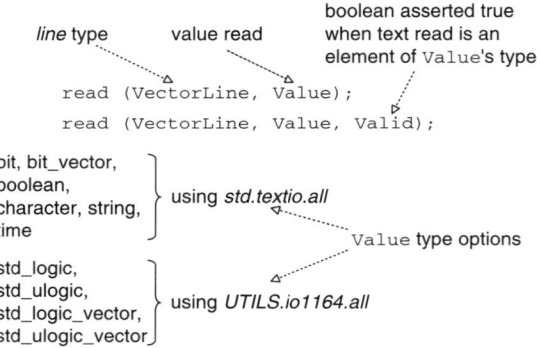

Figure 10: Sample *read* Procedure Calls

The *write* procedure is similar to *read*, as shown in *Figure 11*, except that there is no optional Boolean flag, since this is not necessary.

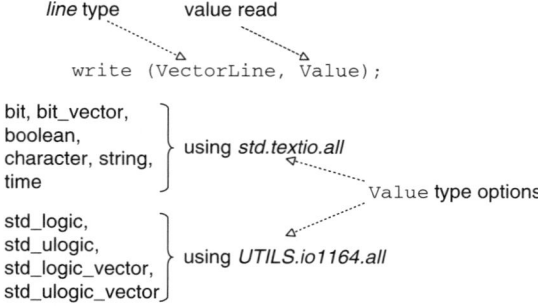

Figure 11: Sample *write* Procedure Call

Chapter 14 - Simulation and Design Verification

As the *read* and *write* procedures operate on a *line*, we must use another procedure (or procedures) to read and write lines. These are the *readline* and *writeline* procedures, and are called as shown in *Figure 12*.

Figure 12: Sample Readline and Writeline Procedure Calls

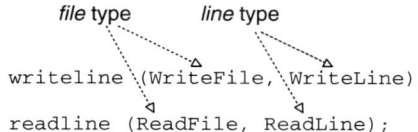

The two files indicated in the sample procedure calls are ASCII files. In addition to ASCII files, there are two special files called *input* and *output*. These represent the standard input and standard output respectively, and allow us to interact with the simulation console, rather than just read and write from text files.

Testbench Incorporating Vectors as an Array

The first approach to writing a testbench incorporates the test vectors directly into the testbench in the form of a 2-dimensional array, or table. To illustrate this approach, we will write a testbench for the BCD-to-seven-segment display decoder that we developed in *Chapter 8*. This testbench is shown in *Listing 6*, and follows the format of the testbench anatomy discussed earlier.

Listing 6: Testbench for BCD-to-seven-segment Display

```
library ieee;
use ieee.std_logic_1164.all;

use std.textio.all;

entity sevenSegmentTB is
end sevenSegmentTB;

architecture testbench of sevenSegmentTB is

component sevenSegment port (
  bcdInputs: in std_logic_vector (3 downto 0);
  a_n, b_n, c_n, d_n,
  e_n, f_n, g_n: out std_logic
  );
end component;

type vector is record
  bcdStimulus: std_logic_vector(3 downto 0);
  sevSegOut: std_logic_vector(6 downto 0);
```

```
end record;

constant NumVectors: integer:= 17;
constant PropDelay: time := 40 ns;
constant SimLoopDelay: time := 10 ns;

type vectorArray is array (0 to NumVectors - 1) of vector;
constant vectorTable: vectorArray := (
  (bcdStimulus => "0000", sevSegOut => "0000001"),
  (bcdStimulus => "0001", sevSegOut => "1001111"),
  (bcdStimulus => "0010", sevSegOut => "0010010"),
  (bcdStimulus => "0011", sevSegOut => "0000110"),
  (bcdStimulus => "0100", sevSegOut => "1001100"),
  (bcdStimulus => "0101", sevSegOut => "0100100"),
  (bcdStimulus => "0110", sevSegOut => "0100000"),
  (bcdStimulus => "0111", sevSegOut => "0001111"),
  (bcdStimulus => "1000", sevSegOut => "0000000"),
  (bcdStimulus => "1001", sevSegOut => "0000100"),
  (bcdStimulus => "1010", sevSegOut => "ZZZZZZZ"),
  (bcdStimulus => "1011", sevSegOut => "ZZZZZZZ"),
  (bcdStimulus => "1100", sevSegOut => "ZZZZZZZ"),
  (bcdStimulus => "1101", sevSegOut => "ZZZZZZZ"),
  (bcdStimulus => "1110", sevSegOut => "ZZZZZZZ"),
  (bcdStimulus => "1111", sevSegOut => "ZZZZZZZ"),
  (bcdStimulus => "0000", sevSegOut => "0110110") -- this vector fails
  );

for all : sevenSegment use entity work.sevenSegment(behavioral);

signal StimInputs: std_logic_vector(3 downto 0);
signal CaptureOutputs: std_logic_vector(6 downto 0);

begin

  u1: sevenSegment port map (bcdInputs => StimInputs,
                             a_n => CaptureOutputs(6),
                             b_n => CaptureOutputs(5),
                             c_n => CaptureOutputs(4),
                             d_n => CaptureOutputs(3),
                             e_n => CaptureOutputs(2),
                             f_n => CaptureOutputs(1),
                             g_n => CaptureOutputs(0));

  LoopStim: process
    variable FoundError: boolean := false;
    variable TempVector: vector;
    variable ErrorMsgLine: line;
  begin

    for i in vectorTable'range loop
      TempVector := vectorTable(i);
```

Chapter 14 - Simulation and Design Verification

```
            StimInputs <= TempVector.bcdStimulus;

        wait for PropDelay;

        if CaptureOutputs /= TempVector.sevSegOut then
            write (ErrorMsgLine, string'("Vector failed at "));
            write (ErrorMsgLine, now);
            writeline (output, ErrorMsgLine);
            FoundError := true;
        end if;

        wait for SimLoopDelay;

      end loop;

      assert FoundError
        report "No errors. All vectors passed."
        severity note;

      wait;

    end process;

  end testbench;
```

sevsegtb.vhd

There are several things to make a note of in this testbench implementation. First of all, we have defined a *record* type for the test vector that consists of a stimulus vector and response vector. The test vectors are defined as an array of this type, very similar to what we saw in *Chapter 13*. For a design with a small vector set, the use of such a test vector table is easy, and can be written quickly. To make the design a little more readable, we could place the vectors in a separate package and *use* this package in the testbench.

Second, we have implemented seventeen test vectors in our example of which sixteen exhaustively cover all possible input combinations, and one indicates "failure". The exhaustive approach works well here, since we have a simple design to test.

Third, we have used a configuration specification that specifically identifies the behavioral entity-architecture pair for simulation. This configuration could be modified with the name of the post-layout entity architecture pair (to perform a post-layout simulation), assuming that it has the same entity port declarations as the behavioral entity.

Fourth, we have two delay constants, *SimLoopDly* and *PropDly*, which together ensure that the logic works within a 50 ns delay budget. The reason that the 50 ns delay budget has been separated this way, while somewhat arbitrary, is to demonstrate the use of incremental delays when applying a stimulus and checking the response within a loop. Notice that the vectors are applied at the beginning of the loop, and checked after *PropDly*. We then wait for *SimLoopDly* to make it easy to identify an error reported by the *assert* statement. The *assert* statement includes the time-stamp of the failed vector, which is the one applied *SimLoopDly* before the next transition of the inputs.

Next, we have used the message reporting technique that was described earlier. *ErrorMsgLine* is a temporary variable that gathers the message to be printed. The message "Vector failed at" is typecast to a string type using *string'*. In addition, we use the special function *now* to indicate how much time has elapsed since the start of the simulation. This gives us a time-stamp that indicates when a failure occurred so that we can locate the problem vector easily. The message is written to the standard output (the simulation console) in the *writeline* procedure.

Finally, we use a Boolean error flag, *FoundError*, that is initialized to *True* at the start of the simulation. This flag is asserted *False* whenever a vector fails. Recall that the assert statement tests for a *False* condition, so the "successful simulation" message will only appear if all vectors pass. In our simulation example, this message will never appear, unless we change the last vector in our vector table.

Testbench with Vectors in a Separate Text File

Vector tables can become unwieldy as the number of vectors increase. Furthermore, note that it is possible that a VHDL simulator would try and hold the entire table in memory, which could significantly limit the size of the vector table. This brings us to the second approach to writing testbenches: placing the vectors in a separate file. This method is very similar to the 2-dimensional array approach, in that it follows the same basic testbench anatomy. The core difference is that the vectors reside in a file, which has been formatted so as to follow the algorithm that reads and parses the vectors from the file. To illustrate this, we will write a testbench for a load-able, reset-able up-counter, as shown in *Figure 13*.

Figure 13: Load-able, Reset-able Up-counter

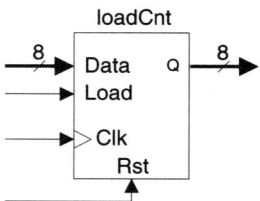

As this is a synchronous design, we need to determine when to apply the stimulus and when to check the result. Let us assume that the design objective is to meet a 10 MHz clock frequency. One approach is to apply the stimulus with adequate set-up time before the clock, and to verify the results at an appropriate time after the rising edge of the clock. For our implementation, we will apply the stimulus at 1/4 the clock period before the rising edge of the clock, and verify the results at the falling edge of the clock, as shown in *Figure 14*.

Figure 14: Stimulus Application and Response Check for *loadCnt*

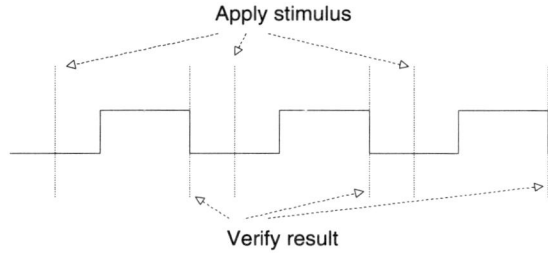

There are three differences in this testbench implementation, as compared to the table approach:

- The stimulus application is placed in its own, separate, process
- Output verification is performed in its own, separate, process
- The clock is applied as a "free running" clock using a concurrent assignment

Having noted this, the next step in our testbench implementation is to define the file format, and the VHDL that will read this file format. Also, we will place both the file reading and the stimulus application in the same process. A sample vector file, and the corresponding VHDL that reads this file is shown in *Figure 15*. The vector file does not contain any spaces, since the *read* routine in the *io1164* package does not allow them.

Figure 15: Sample Vector File and the VHDL that Reads It

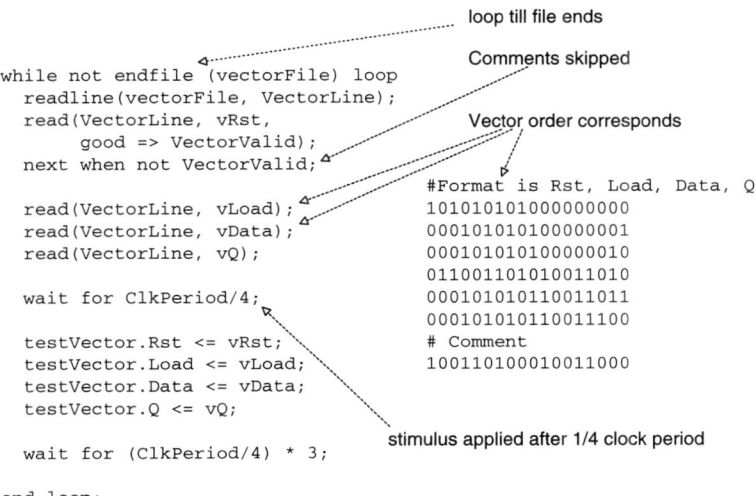

The use of *VectorValid* gives us the ability to place comments in the file, and skip these comments as necessary. It is important to choose the file format carefully, as any change will require you to rewrite the VHDL that reads and interprets it. The VHDL for the entire testbench is shown in *Listing 7*. Notice that this testbench reads a file called "vectorfile", where the vectors reside. This file usually resides in the same "project" directory as the VHDL source files for the testbench.

Listing 7: Testbench for Load-able, Reset-able, Up-counter

```vhdl
library IEEE;
use IEEE.std_logic_1164.all;
library UTILS;
use UTILS.io1164.all;
use std.textio.all;

entity loadCntTB is
end loadCntTB;

architecture testbench of loadCntTB is

  component loadCnt port (
    data: in std_logic_vector (7 downto 0);
    load: in std_logic;
    clk: in std_logic;
    rst: in std_logic;
    q: out std_logic_vector (7 downto 0)
    );
  end component;

file vectorFile: text is in "vectorfile";
type vectorType is record
  data: std_logic_vector(7 downto 0);
  load: std_logic;
  rst: std_logic;
  q: std_logic_vector(7 downto 0);
end record;

signal testVector: vectorType;
signal TestClk: std_logic := '0';
signal Qout: std_logic_vector(7 downto 0);

constant ClkPeriod: time := 100 ns;

for all: loadCnt use entity work.loadcnt(rtl);

begin

-- File reading and stimulus application
  readVec: process
    variable VectorLine: line;
    variable VectorValid: boolean;
```

Chapter 14 - Simulation and Design Verification

```vhdl
      variable vRst: std_logic;
      variable vLoad: std_logic;
      variable vData: std_logic_vector(7 downto 0);
      variable vQ: std_logic_vector(7 downto 0);

    begin
      while not endfile (vectorFile) loop
        readline(vectorFile, VectorLine);

        read(VectorLine, vRst, good => VectorValid);
        next when not VectorValid;
        read(VectorLine, vLoad);
        read(VectorLine, vData);
        read(VectorLine, vQ);

        wait for ClkPeriod/4;

        testVector.Rst <= vRst;
        testVector.Load <= vLoad;
        testVector.Data <= vData;
        testVector.Q <= vQ;

        wait for (ClkPeriod/4) * 3;

      end loop;

    assert false
      report "Simulation complete"
      severity note;

    wait;

    end process;

  -- Free running test clock
    TestClk <= not TestClk after ClkPeriod/2;

  -- Instance of design being tested
    u1: loadCnt port map (Data => testVector.Data,
                          load => testVector.Load,
                          clk => TestClk,
                          rst => testVector.Rst,
                          q => Qout
                          );

  -- Process to verify outputs
    verify: process (TestClk)
    variable ErrorMsg: line;
    begin
      if (TestClk'event and TestClk = '0') then
        if Qout /= testVector.Q then
          write(ErrorMsg, string'("Vector failed "));
```

```
            write(ErrorMsg, now);
            writeline(output, ErrorMsg);
         end if;
      end if;
   end process;


end testbench;
```

loadcnttb.vhd

Another advantage of using vectors in a separate text file is that you only need to change the text file when you want to change the vectors. This is easy, and does not require the entire testbench to be recompiled. The downside is that you need to write VHDL that performs file I/O that adds to the testbench complexity, but this needs to be done only once.

Before closing this chapter, it is important to touch briefly on two issues: the choice of vectors for simulation and the time to run a simulation.

It is clear that an exhaustive simulation of the load-able counter would require an unreasonably large number of vectors. It would require the load, reset and increment functions of the counter to be tested over each count, over the entire count range, from 0 to $2^8 - 1$. However, this is unnecessary as a complete set of vectors to test the counter would verify the following:

- On reset assertion, all counter outputs go to a logical zero
- Each bit of the counter can be loaded with either a '0' or '1'
- Each bit in the counter can toggle from '0' to '1' and vice-versa

We can satisfy these objectives with the following vectors:

- Load the counter so that all counter outputs are '1', assert reset, and verify that all the outputs are '0'
- Load the counter with a pattern that has only one bit set to '0', and all the others set to '1', and then perform an increment. This verifies that all the outputs can be loaded with either '0' or '1', as well as transition from both '0' to '1' and '1' to '0' when counting begins
- Load the counter with all '1's, and then increment to verify that it rolls-over to all '0's.

Hence, with twenty vectors, we can completely test our design, as shown in *Listing 8*.

Listing 8: Vector Set to Completely Test Load-able, Reset-able Up-counter

```
#Format is Rst, Load, Data, Q
#load the counter to all 1s
011111111111111111
#reset the counter
101010101000000000
#now perform load/increment for each bit
011111111011111110
001111111011111111
#
011111110111111101
001111110111111110
#
011111101111111011
001111101111111100
#
011111011111110111
001111011111111000
#
011110111111101111
001110111111110000
#
011101111111011111
001101111111100000
#
011011111110111111
001011111111000000
#
010111111101111111
00 0111111110000000
#
#check roll-over case
011111111111111111
001111111100000000
#
# End vectors
```

vectorfile

Finally, do not be surprised if your post-layout simulation takes significantly longer to run than the simulation using the synthesis model. The more complex the simulation model, the longer it will take to run. Post-layout models incorporate not only delays, but almost always include resolution functions, detailed timing checks, along with error and warning messages that take long to process. The value of a compact, efficient testbench will be particularly noticeable when verifying the post-layout model.

Appendix A: Measuring Performance and Utilization

Essential VHDL focuses on techniques and coding styles that are independent of both the synthesis tool and target device-architecture. However, some aspects of design are best understood by synthesizing to a target device, as shown by some of the examples. These examples are not benchmarks but demonstrate application of a particular design technique or coding style. As such, the synthesis outputs have been tabulated using a ratiometric comparison of the "before versus after" result for the same device.

Results using two popular programmable device architectures are shown in the tables: LUT, or Lookup Table, and Mux, or multiplexer. LUT architectures are those that use an SRAM lookup table as the basis for the fundamental logic cell, while Mux architectures use one or more multiplexers as the basis for the fundamental logic cell, as shown in *Figure 1*.

Figure 1: Sample Table Demonstrating a Particular Coding Technique

$$\text{Utilization} = \frac{\text{logic cells before}}{\text{logic cells after}} \%$$

Altera EPF10K10-3

Device	Speed Decrease	Utilization Increase
LUT architecture	2%	19%
Mux architecture	7%	20%

Quicklogic 2003-2

$$\text{Speed} = \frac{\text{speed (MHz) before}}{\text{speed (MHz) after}} \%$$

Results for the LUT architecture are based on the *Altera*™ *EPF10K10-3* device, while those for the Mux architecture are based on the *Quicklogic*™ *2003-2* device. VHDL designs were synthesized to these devices using Synplicity's *Synplify*™ logic synthesis tool, and all analyses were based on Synplify's results. The results are shown as a percentage change rather than as absolute cell utilization or speed change. This emphasizes that the change being discussed is independent of the target device/architecture, for a given set of synthesis settings, thus avoiding a benchmark comparison of two FPGA architectures. Benchmarking is a much more complex issue worthy of a separate effort.

Index

Symbols

- 86
+ 86
* 86
/ 86
/= 87
= 87
> 87
>= 87
<= 87
& operator 262

Numerics

2-1 mux 285
2-input AND gate 25
2-input OR gate 25, 282
2-input XOR 227
2-of-4 decoder 251
7-segment display 152
8-3 priority encoder 47

A

ABS 89
accumulator 93
actual
   component 19, 173
   function 246
adder 220, 92, 164
   parameterizable 228
   with overflow 264
after 283
aggregate 134, 259
   using parentheses 261
algorithmic state machine (*see also* state machine)
aliases 241, 255, 256

all
   use clause 180
AND gate 25
AND operator 8
architecture 2, 16
architecture name 16
arithmetic 75
   adder 92 (*see also* "+")
   division 94 (*see also* "/")
   exponentiation 94
   multiplication 94 (*see also* "*")
   subtractor 92 (*see also* "-")
   vector direction 83
array indexing 259
arrays
   array or vector 3
   indexing using enumerated types 270
   multi-dimensional 259, 266
   range 83
ascending range 84, 231
ASMs (*see also* state machine)
assert statement 298
assignment 3
   signal 3
   variable 226
asynchronous load 127
asynchronous reset
   (*see also* reset, asynchronous)
asynchronous preset
(*see also* preset, asynchronous)
attribute 58, 219, 230
   'range 231
   'reverse_range 231
   'event 54, 231
   'last_event 289
   'last_value 54
   'high 231
   'left 231

'length 231
'low 231
predefined 231
'right 231
'stable 289

B

base type 161
BCD-to-seven-segment display 151
behavioral design 10, 12, 20
bi-directional buffer
    concurrent 137
bit type 2
black box 1, 13
    state machines 115
bubble diagram 104
buffer
    bi-directional 136
    see also tri-state 131
buffer mode (see also mode buffer) 259
bus
    as a mux 163
    hierarchy 186

C

call, function and procedure 241
case statement 31, 32
    difference from if...then 39
    locally static 34
character
    literal 134
comment 6
comparator (see also "=", ">", "<", "<=", and "=>")
component
    actual 19
    adding to libraries 176
    association with entity-architecture 169
    configuration 181
    declaration 170
    formal 19
    function, actual 246
    instantiation 19, 25, 170
concatenation 259, 262
concurrent statement 17, 27
conditional generate 236
configuration 181
    declaration 182
    for all 183
    specification 182
constant 30, 192, 193
conv_integer 89
conv_signed 89
conv_std_logic_vector 89
conv_unsigned 89
conversion (see also type conversion)
counter
    adding a vector 82
    ascending vector 84
    asynchronous reset 77
    bi-directional outputs 137, 188
    loadable 79, 137, 188
    modulo 11 80
    scalable 233
    synchronous enable 81
    synchronous reset 78
    terminal count 81, 174
    testbench 300
    up 76
    using mode buffer 280
    using TFF 233
    vector direction 83
current state 101, 107

D

dataflow design 10, 11, 17
debug messages 287
decoder 25, 28, 251
    if...then 37
    process 35

Index 309

using procedures 254
default assignment 31
default state 208
default value 209
delay
    inertial (*see also* inertial delay)
    transport (*see also* transport delay)
delta delay 141
Department of Defense 1
descending range 231, 243
design hierarchy 168
design verification 281
DFF
    asynchronous expression reset 63
    asynchronous reset 62
    difference between if...then and wait 60
    if...then 59
    wait on 60
    write enable 51
direct encoding 213
divide-by clock 267
division 94
don't care 157, 158, 161
    using '-' 157
driver
    multiple drivers 162
    notion of 3
D-type flip-flop
    DF, wait statement 53
    parameterizable 223
    scalable 220
    simulation model 287
    using a procedure 253
    write enable 51

E

edge-triggered 53, 59
else statement 149
elseif 37
encoders 25, 47
entity 2, 14

entity name 14
enumerated types 105, 270
equality compare 90
error severity level 297
event 54, 231
exit statement 277
exponentiation 94
expression
    qualified (*see also* qualified expression)
EXT 89

F

factorization 40
factors 40
falling_edge 54
file 299, 300
file format 299
finite state machine (*see also* state machine)
flattening 40
flip-flop 52
    behavioral 52
    if...then 58
    sensitivity list 58
    structural 51
flip-flop with enable 57
flip-flops with if...then 58
for all 183
for...generate 219
    similarity to for...loop 235
for...loop 226, 230
formal
    component 19, 173
    function 246
FSM (*see also* state machine)
function 241
    now 298
    resolution 245
    nested 250
    others 89
    overloading 243
    standard 85

type conversion 89

G

gate 282
   AND 25
   INVERTER 25
   OR 25
generate 232
   conditional 236
generics 219, 222, 289
Gray Coding 200

H

hold time 287

I

I/O buffer
   see also, buffer, bi-directional 136
IEEE 1076.3-1997 75
IEEE Std. 1076-1987 1
if
   else 21
   elseif 21
   endif 21
if statement 21
if...else 37
if...generate 219, 236
if...then 37, 58
   avoiding implicit latches 149
   chained 40, 150
   decoder 37
   difference from case 39
   difference from wait 60
   encoders 47
   flip-flop 58
   nested 40
   parallel 150
implicit latch 141, 147, 155
implicit memory 141, 147, 155

inertial delay 290
inference 23
inferred latch 141, 147
instance label 19
   see also label, instance
instance name (see also label, instance)
instantiation 169
   component 19, 170
interrupt priority encoder 278
inverter 25

L

label
   architecture 16
   entity 14
   instance 19
   process 20
last_value 54
latch 70
   concurrent assignment 72
   if...then 73
   using processes 73
   structural 70
levels of logic 199
library 15, 176
   std 176
   work 176
line 294
load
   asynchronous 127
locally static (see also case statement,
   locally static)
loops 219, 226

M

mathematic operators
   see also "+", "-", "*", "/"
mod 86
mode 4
   buffer 259

Index

in 4
inout 5
out 4
selection 185
mode buffer 279
modeling
   simple gate 282
multi-dimensional arrays 259, 266
multiplexer (*see also* mux) 161
multiplication 94
mux
   for tri-state 163
   simulation model 285

N

named association 173
naming 5
NAND operator 8
next state 101, 106, 197
NOR operator 8
now, predefined function 298
null 33
numeric_std 75

O

on clause 53
one-hot coding 201
operator
   logical 8
   overloading 83
   vector direction 83
   arithmetic 85
   logical 8
   relational 87
   shift 88
   std_logic 8
OR gate 25
OR operator 8
others 135
   array aggregate 135

case statement 33
others clause 259
output conditioning logic 101, 108
overloading 83, 157
   functions 243

P

package 176, 179
package body 249
parameterizable
   adder 229
   DFF 223
   parity generator 227
   tri-state 224
parameterizable full adder 228
parity generator 226
   using for...loop 227
   using if...generate 236
   using parallel XORs 238
partitioning 167, 185
PCI
   one-hot coding 204
   state machine 109
   target state machine 104
port 3, 14
   actual 19, 173
   association 19
   buffer 279
   formal 19, 173
   in 4
   inout 5
   mode 4
   out 4
   unconnected 174
port map 11, 171
positional association 173
power-up state 208
predefined attribute 231
preset 62, 65
   asynchronous 62, 123
   dominance 126

implicit memory 155
important issues 67
synchronous 65
priority encoder 278
procedures 241, 250
process 20, 31
    body 20, 21
    decoder 35
    label 20
    reset, asynchronous 62
    reset, sensitivity list 21
propagation delay 283
pulse generator 95
    black box 115
    block diagram 114
    complete design 118
    direct encoded 214
    using indexed arrays 272
pulse rejection 284

Q

qualified expression 261

R

range 2, 3, 231 (*see also* ascending range, descending range)
read procedure 294
reading text 293
record type 297
records 259, 264
register 222, 265
register file 275
registers 51
relational operators 87
rem 86
report 297
reserved words 7
reset 62
    asynchronous 62, 63, 123
    asynchronous expression 64

dominance 126
if...then precedence 67
implicit memory 155
important issues 67
synchronous 65
synchronous, if...then 66
synchronous, wait 65
resize 89, 243
resolution function 161, 246
    muxes 161
    tri-state 161
resource sharing 163, 165
    explicit 165
reverse_range 231
rising_edge 54, 56, 242
rol 245
ror 245
rotate_left 88
rotate_right 88
RTL 10

S

scalable
    DFF 220
    parity generator 239
scope 173
sensitivity list 21
sequencer (*see also* state machine)
sequential encoding 192
sequential statements 20
set
    if...then precedence 67
    see also, preset 123
set-up time 287
seven-segment decoder
    using aggregates 260
seven-segment display 151
    test bench 295
severity 287
severity note 297
shift_left 88

shift left arithmetic (*see also* sla)
shift left logical (*see also* sll)
shift_right 88
shift right arithmetic (*see also* sra)
shift right logical (*see also* srl)
SHL 88
SHR 88
signal 2
   assignment 17, 146
   declaration 14, 16
   driver 3
   last assignment 146
   queue model 141
   vs. variable 226
signed type 75
simulation 281, 282
sla 245
slice 255
sll 245
SR flip-flop 54, 56, 95
sra 245
SRFF (*see also* SR flip-flop)
srl 245
state diagram 104
state encoding 191
   binary 192
   direct 213
   gray 200
   guidelines 207
   implications 208
state machine
   black box 115
   don't care 212
   encoding 191
   one hot 201
   output encoding 210
   pulse generator 118
   registered outputs 211
   sequential encoding 192
   system considerations 113
state transition diagram 104

statement
   concurrent 17
   if 21
   order 9
   sequential 20
std library 176
std_logic 2
   logical operators 8
std_logic_1164 161
std_logic_arith 75
std_logic_signed 75
std_logic_unsigned 75
std_match 89
std_ulogic 161
structural design 10, 11, 18, 25
subprograms 241
subtractor 92
subtype 162
   in state machines 193
SXT 89

T

test bench 292
   basic anatomy 292
   using a text file 298
   using an array 295
text
   reading and writing 293
textio package 294
TFF (*see also* toggle flip-flop) 232
three-state 131
   (*see also* tri-state)
to_integer 89
to_signed 89
to_stdlogicvector 76, 89, 91, 243
to_unsigned 80, 89
   showing direction significance 92
toggle flip-flop 232
transport delay 290
tri-state 131
   aggregate 134

concurrent 133
hierarchy 186
if...then 133
parameterizable 224
structural 132
using record types 265
two dimensional array 268
type conversion 89
std_logic_vector 76
unsigned 80
type selection 185
typecast 261

U

unconstrained arrays 76, 219
unsigned type 75
unwanted latch 141, 147, 155
use clause 177, 180
scope 173, 181

V

variables 35, 219
vs. signals 226
vector direction 83
to_unsigned 92
verification 291
VHSIC 1

W

wait 53
difference from if...then 60
wait on 60
wait statement 55
warning
severity level (*see also* severity)
when others 33
while loops 259, 274
while...loop 274
wild card 157

wire delay 290
with...select 35, 36
others 36
work library 176
write procedure 294
writing text 293

X

XNOR operator 8
XOR operator 8

Z

zero-delay model 283
zero extension (*see also* EXT or resize)

References and Sources

1. Ashenden, Peter. The Designer's Guide to VHDL. San Francisco, CA: Morgan Kaufmann, 1995.
2. Bhasker, J. A VHDL Primer. Revised Edition. Englewood Cliffs, NJ: Prentice Hall, 1992.
3. Brown, Stephen et al. Field Programmable Gate Arrays. Norwell, MA: Kluwer, 1992.
4. Cohen, Ben. VHDL Coding Styles and Methodologies. Norwell, MA: Kluwer, 1995.
5. Lipsett, Roger et al. VHDL: Hardware Description and Design. Norwell, MA: Kluwer, 1989.
6. Prosser, Franklin et al. The Art of Digital Design. Englewood Cliffs, NJ: Prentice Hall, 1986.
7. Solari, Ed et al. PCI Hardware and Software. San Diego, CA: Annabooks, 1995.
8. IEEE Standard VHDL Language Reference Manual: IEEE Std. 1076-1987: New York, NY, 1988.
9. IEEE Standard VHDL Language Reference Manual: IEEE Std. 1076-1993: New York, NY, 1994.
10. IEEE Standard Multivalue Logic System for VHDL Model Interoperability. IEEE Std. 1164-1993: New York, NY, 1993.
11. PCI 2.1 Specification. Portland OR: PCI SIG, 1995.

Library of
Davidson College

TEACHER EDUCATION IN THE UNITED STATES

TEACHER EDUCATION IN THE UNITED STATES: THE RESPONSIBILITY GAP

A Report By

The Study Commission on Undergraduate Education

and the Education of Teachers

University of Nebraska Press – Lincoln and London

Copyright © 1976 by the University of Nebraska
Copyright is claimed until 1981. Thereafter all portions of this work covered by this copyright will be in the public domain.
Library of Congress Catalog Card Number 75-34710
International Standard Book Number (cloth) 0-8032-0875-8
International Standard Book Number (paper) 0-8032-5839-9

In the interest of timeliness and economy, this work was printed directly from camera-ready copy prepared by the Study Commission on Undergraduate Education and the Education of Teachers. This training document was developed under a grant from the U.S. Office of Education, Department of Health, Education, and Welfare. However, the content does not necessarily reflect the position or policy of that Agency, and no official endorsement of these materials should be inferred.

Manufactured in the United States of America.

TABLE OF CONTENTS

  Page

Letter of Introduction..................................vii
  Virginia Trotter, Assistant Secretary for Education,
  Department of Health, Education and Welfare

Preface and Summary...................................ix
  Paul A. Olson, Director, Study Commission on
  Undergraduate Education and the Education of Teachers

Acknowledgments.....................................xix
  List of Study Commission Members..................xxi
  Members Attending Wingspread Meeting, 1972.........xxix
  Members Attending Wingspread Meeting, 1974..........xxx
  Study Commission Committee Members................xxxi
  List of Study Commission Publications...............xxxv

Chapter I.   The Future of Schools and Children:
      Education of Teachers as a Community Activity......1

Chapter II.   Teacher Education in America Now..............39

Chapter III.   Legal Constraints: Licensing, Accreditation
      and Equity in Teacher Education...............101

Chapter IV.   Gathering Information on the
      Process of Educating Teachers..................155

Chapter V.   The Federal Role in Teacher Education..........189

Chapter VI.   An Alternative Report........................211
      George Denemark, Dean of Education,
      University of Kentucky

Appendix   Definition of Cultural Pluralism................219

LETTER OF INTRODUCTION

The Study Commission on Undergraduate Education and the Education of Teachers was established by the Office of Education to review and make recommendations about federal efforts in the area of teacher preparation at the undergraduate level. Between one fourth and one third of American undergraduate education is concerned with preparing teachers for elementary and secondary schools. Of the many things which influence learning in schools—as well as the failure to learn—the quality of new teachers entering the schools is one of the most important. The Study Commission has evaluated the overall quality of undergraduate teacher preparation and has made recommendations to improve it. It has also evaluated other factors which influence the quality of teachers, including accreditation and licensing, governance and management of schools and colleges, and the federal role in teacher education.

This work endeavors to focus on the impact, in these areas, of recent legal decisions, the growth of citizen participation in teacher preparation, and recent efforts to more closely integrate work and education. It is also concerned with the problem of educating the proper number and kinds of teachers for the diverse clientele of children and parents in America's schools.

No doubt this report will be controversial. It is concerned precisely with those educational issues which are being debated most vigorously throughout this land. Certainly, the extent of local control of schools is the hottest issue. Specifically, the Commission report addresses the issues of who should have control over the selection of teaching personnel for the schools, the extent to which communities should be responsible for the content of pre-service and in-service preparation of teachers, and the extent to which the desire for cultural pluralism should influence the number of acceptable curricular options for training teachers.

Another key issue concerns the licensing of teachers and the accreditation of teacher training institutions. The report raises the question whether or not there should be local licensing procedures for teachers as an alternative to state and national procedures, and whether temporary or provisional licenses should be given to beginning teachers. It discusses the issue of whether eligibility for federal funds should be linked to an institution's accreditation by private, voluntary regional and national associations of the institutions themselves. In addition, it examines the feasibility and desirability of establishing an independent occupational licensing institute which would take over a number of licensing functions and take legal action to mandate reform where hiring practices have badly served particular individuals or groups.

Finally the report addresses the issue of whether and to what extent the present mix of student aid programs helps assure access of diverse ethnic and cultural groups to the teaching profession.

Most of the Commission's recommendations were formulated in 1972 and have been refined since. Because the recommendations are not entirely new in 1975 and because some of them parallel those of other groups, they have been partially implemented already. Other recommendations have proved so controversial that they are still being discussed and debated and therefore are far from the implementation stage. We in the Department of Health, Education, and Welfare are endeavoring through various research and demonstration and statistical collections programs to contribute to the state of knowledge of alternative forms and environments for teacher preparation. In so doing, we are hopeful that new and better teacher preparation programs will emerge that will keep pace with the technological and social demands of the future.

I commend the Study Commission for its comprehensive analysis of the issues concerning teacher preparation. Hopefully, their persistent labors over the last few years will contribute to improved teaching and learning in our nation's schools.

Virginia Trotter
Assistant Secretary for Education
Department of Health, Education and Welfare

PREFACE AND SUMMARY

We believe that our present and future concerns require a diverse pattern of education systems that emphasize man's different capacities to live under the limitations of differentiated environments, to live with scarcity, to limit the technology on which he depends, and to escape anomie by finding a human community to which he can belong—one that serves his sense of need for roots, norms, identity, and mutual giving and receiving. The national interest as it was seen in the past—being served by the mechanisms of standardization and indirect national control through devices such as testing, accreditation, national licensing, and standard curricula—is opposed to our goals. *The burden of this book is that, given the widespread anomie among youth, given the economy that we have, given the spirit of the law itself, the national interest in the future will be better served by putting the weight of the federal government behind the individual in the local cultural group, behind the community, behind the sensitive and differentiated response to local people, languages, physical environments. Virtually all our arguments derive from this position.*

This book examines the balance, in the education of teachers, between the federal and state interest and parent, community, and individual interest. The original Department of Education bill (1867) rejected language which would have created a national system of education, subject to national norms ("to enforce education, without regard to race or color, upon the population of all such states as shall fall below a standard to be established by Congress") and retained language which made of the department a service to the "people of the United States."[1] The people are not the states; they are "the people" in their local natural communities.[2] Commonly this view of the Office of Education function has been retained by the Congress (consider for example the recent debate over the Quie amendments), and the courts have tended to regard education as properly an extension of childrearing, necessarily beginning with the natural development and informal education of children in the immediate environments of their birth and nurture. Eventually, of course, education will in most circumstances make it possible for children to move into the larger world. The notion of preserving citizen contact, responsibility, and choice in education appears to underlie the recent Detroit Supreme Court decision. Consider this section of the majority decision:

> No single tradition in public education is more deeply rooted than local control over the operation of schools; local autonomy has long been thought essential both to the maintenance of community concern and support for public schools and to quality of the educational process. See *Wright v. Council of the City of Emporia,* 407 U.S. 451, 469. Thus, in *San Antonio School District v. Rodriguez,* 411 U.S. 1, 50, we observed that local control over the educational process affords citizens an opportunity to participate in decision-making, permits the structuring of school programs to fit local needs, and encourages "experimentation, innovation and a healthy competition for educational excellence."³

Without debating the merits of the majority or dissenting opinions in the Detroit case, it is possible to argue that, if the majority opinion of the court is to be followed in matters so grave as segregation-desegregation policy, its spirit ought to be followed in other matters such as policy for the education of teachers.

But the court's description of "what ought to be" is not a description of "what is" in American education. The reality of American education and American teacher education is described succinctly by Stephen Bailey of the American Council on Education, formerly of the New York State Department of Education.

> The language [of local control] falls pleasingly on the ears of local school board members, superintendents, teachers and parents; and it may well be a barrier to arbitrariness at higher levels. But the term "local-control"—powerful as it is as a political shibboleth—flies in the face of the fiscal and administrative realities of state and federal grants in aid and the standardizing effect of professionalism upon public education across the land. This struggle between shibboleth and reality is one of the political anomalies of educational finance. Part of the political tension which surrounds and infuses contemporary educational finance controversies derives from the fact that in a highly interdependent, technological world, the myth of local control of educational policy is increasingly unrealistic.⁴

While Mr. Bailey's description may be an accurate characterization of the state of education and teacher education, we cannot accept this picture as fated.

In Chapter I, "The Future of Schools and Children," we offer arguments defining the need to pay close attention to the health of our communities and recommend that:[5]

I. Policy planning for future education be closely related to planning for health, housing, highways, use of resources, and other components of community living. For this reason, futures studies and the resulting decisions or non-decisions must be conducted with inter-agency "cross-impact" emphasis. The Department of Health, Education and Welfare, in cooperation with other government agencies, should establish a method of coordinating the work and distributing the information of planning groups, perhaps through the National Center for Education Statistics and similar organizations. The meshing of the work of these diverse groups with educational planning (in the past, "cross-impact" planning which did occur often omitted the educational component) might lead to (a) alternative forecasts while decisions can still be made; (b) long-term consequences and "collision courses" which can be altered or avoided; (c) information packaged in useable form and made available to Congress, governmental agencies and private groups along with well-publicized goals of various groups. Clients whose lives are affected by future studies and planning should be given the resources to explore various planning strategies and training should be provided for developing planning skills among local personnel.

Education Planning Related to Other Community Systems

II. Educational authorities should foster a multitude of alternatives in and out of the public schools which can be recognized as

counting toward a student's education, and work spaces should be opened up as much as possible to youth, so that living and learning are not separated. Care must be taken here to avoid any implication of tracking students into various social or economic roles.

Alternative Learning Spaces Opened Up

In Chapter II, "Teacher Education in America Now," we argue that the process of teacher education has always been underfunded and has become too often a standardized, insensitive, and alienating process, and that federal money has too seldom improved matters. We recommend that:

I. With the concurrence of Congress, the Department of Health, Education and Welfare [NIE, OE (BEPD), FIPSE] should be responsible for supporting the development of a permanent community-responsive system for educating teachers. By promoting culture- and environment-responsive programs, HEW could assist communities in rebuilding institutions suited to their particular needs.

Permanent Community-Responsive Systems

II. New developments in teacher training should be supported by HEW if they are characterized by relatedness to the community and full use of community resources including extended apprenticeships for new teachers.

New Resources For In-Community Apprenticeships

III. All teacher education programs should exist in a culturally-pluralistic atmosphere—that is in a system which accepts and encourages differences. It is important that acceptance of minority status not prevent an individual or group from sharing in the resources and goods that the system has to offer.

Cultural Differences Encouraged

IV. Local or regional examining schools should be considered as an alternative licensing procedure for teachers. After a needs assessment conducted in an identifiable cultural or geographical region, a set of educational needs and their related skills, competencies and resources should be developed. The examining school, against this framework and with power delegated by the states, would license candidates who met the various standards and would retrain or prescribe retraining for those who did not meet the standards. Specific tasks of the licensee would be negotiated, as in a contract, between the licensee and the potential and actual clients, along with school administrators. Assessment procedures would be based on the outcome of this negotiation.

Regional Examining Universities to Determine if Teachers Have Skills Needed

V. State Boards of Higher Education and the various higher education associations should encourage institutions of higher education to form regional partnerships with local education agencies and the communities they serve. The nature of school-community-based teacher education requires that a relationship between pre-service and in-service education be developed. Federal programs should be aware that both the technical (methods) and critical (theory—more specifically, theory challenging conventional theory) elements of teacher education must utilize the resources of practicing teachers to train prospective teachers and must utilize the resources of the community to train both teachers and future teachers; a continuing facility should be available within the community—either a formal teacher center, a center within a school or a cluster of schools, or a community center which also serves teachers and students.

Regional Partnerships To Be Developed

In Chapter III, "Legal Constraints: Licensing, Accreditation, and Equity in Teacher Education," we argue that homogenization and standardization of teacher training have in part been created by the federal and state governments through the use of the ultimate legitimization mechanisms available to them, legitimization devices increasingly challenged under the law. We recommend that:

I. **Eligibility for federal funds should not be linked to an institution's accreditation by private, voluntary regional and national associations of the institutions themselves.** The Study Commission joins the earlier Newman Commission in recommending that funding possibilities be separated from accrediting. Another desirable end would be to separate licensing of teachers from the accreditation of the institute they attend. Institutions should be judged able to receive federal funds by an open and appealable assessment of (a) their financial responsibility in handling student resources and public funds; (b) their recruitment and public information policies as honest representations of their educational programs; (c) their prospectuses of financial and educational status.

Eligibility For Funds Should Be Separated From Accreditation

II. **If the accrediting group, whether regional or national, is freed of the additional judgment of institutional eligibility for funds, it can truly function as a voluntary association that establishes criteria for entrance into its ranks.** The process of self-study and evaluation by outside teams has become a valuable method of institutional improvement and it should be continued and made as public and community-specific as possible.

Accreditation to Assess Institutional Quality in Relation To Mission

III. **Teacher licensing should remain a state responsibility, but the Commission recommends a provisional license preceding the regular license.** During the provisional period, the future teacher would receive additional training and would demonstrate the capacity to teach with sensitivity. Though most teacher candidates will continue to come from formal teacher training institutions, there should be a continued recognition by licensing agencies of the validity of alternative experiences which can also produce qualified teachers.

Experience suggests that community groups will be most likely to identify and sponsor individuals who exhibit teaching aptitude despite the absence of formal training.

An emphasis on cultural pluralism should pervade selection of teachers—including recruitment, training and licensing of teacher education students. The Commission specifically urges culture-specific education—training for competent teaching, with the competence identified as being appropriate to the communities served, and community participation in the educational decision-making process.

Two-Step Licensing Proposed: One Step in Subject Matter and One Step in Client Needs

IV. An Independent Occupational Licensing Institute, encompassing all fields which require credentials for practicing certain occupations, should be established to make hiring criteria more rational. In the case of teacher education, the Institute should undertake research to identify hiring criteria based on specific groups of students and should be prepared to bring legal action to mandate reform where hiring practices have badly served particular individuals or groups.

Occupational Licensing, Including Teacher Licensing, Should be Subject To Public Scrutiny

In Chapter IV, "Gathering Information on the Process of Educating Teachers," we argue that the measuring procedures used in education and teacher education, which are based on the structures legitimized by accreditation and licensing, pursue things too late, often measure the wrong things and leave out some of the most important things—the consumer perspective, the fieldwork perspective, and the change-oriented perspective. We recommend that:

I. The National Center for Higher Education Management Systems (NCHEMS) and Higher Education General Information Systems (HEGIS) should work with student and citizen participant groups having strong bases in black, Chicano, Native American and other prime American communities to develop priorities for data schedules so that client issues

Management Instruments Should Develop Information For the Public and From A Client Perspective become a matter of public discussion. In fact, we recommend that both licensing and information gathering become two-tier concerns, reflecting general and community-specific perspectives.

II. **NCHEMS should be encouraged to develop management instruments that assess what students have learned in relation to community-articulated needs.** The effects of conventional management systems—using departments, credit hours and full-time equivalent (FTE) mechanisms—and their possible handicaps for non-traditional institutions and teacher education fieldwork should be studied to verify or refute Newman Commission and Study Commission assertions.

Non-traditional Measures for Non-traditional Education Must Be Developed

In Chapter V, "The Federal Role in Teacher Education," we suggest that the role of the federal government is a role of direct service to the people of the United States, a role best fulfilled in counteracting standardization in the development of teachers *and* in counteracting the separation of teachers and schools from the people. In carrying out this work, we recommend that:

I. **A multiple system of funding for student aid**—including basic opportunity grants, state scholarship funds, federally guaranteed student loans, work-study programs and cooperative education—is most likely to promote a measure of equality of access to teacher education programs and to encourage a culturally diverse student body. Such diversity should continue, with the emphasis on grant programs rather than loans.

Pluralistic Student Access to the Teaching Vocation Will be Encouraged By Direct Support To Students

II. **A centralized developmental grant program,** operated by the U.S. Office of Education and given adequate and stable funding, would permit the widest possible range of traditional and alternative institutions of higher education, schools, communities, and other agencies to demonstrate effective training of pre-service and in-service school personnel. Exemplary projects should be widely varied in thrust and subject to careful evaluation. Results of these efforts should be widely disseminated.

Proposal for Federal Developmental Funding as Opposed to Training Grant Funding

III. A comprehensive education law reporter system is needed which would encompass issues from early childhood, elementary, secondary and postsecondary education for use by participants and decision-makers in education. If the federal government provided support for such a system, it could build on existing law reporter systems addressing more limited audiences.

Response to Recent Litigation Could be Heightened By a Law Reporter System

FOOTNOTES

[1] Cf. Donald R. Warren, *To Enforce Education: A History of the Founding Years of the United States Office of Education* (Detroit, Michigan: Wayne State University Press, 1974), pp. 78, 204-05, and 58-97 *passim*.

[2] Cf. Lawrence D. Freeman, "Legal Barriers," *Study Commission Newsletter* (May, 1974), pp. 10-12; cf. also the decisions cited in footnote 84, Chapter II, *infra*.

[3] *Millikin v. Bradley*, quoted in *Education Daily*, July 29, 1974.

[4] Joel S. Berke and Michael W. Kirst, *Federal Aid to Education: Who Benefits? Who Governs?* (Lexington: Lexington Books, 1972), pp. 22-23.

[5] This is an abbreviated summary of the recommendations. Complete recommendations are listed at the ends of Chapters I through V.

ACKNOWLEDGMENTS

The Study Commission began writing its final report three years before the deadline. In fact, at the suggestion of Commission member **Leo Shapiro**, a market researcher in Chicago, the group began to formulate its final recommendations shortly after it came into existence under a grant from the U.S. Office of Education in January, 1972. That way, criticism of the major ideas could be considered early, and the final draft could attempt to answer the arguments or reflect the changes in Commission members' thinking on controversial issues.

Nowhere does the final document purport to represent, word for word, the diverse views of all members of the Commission. As **Robert MacVicar**, president of Oregon State University and Study Commission member, wrote to Director **Paul A. Olson**, about the final report: "Everyone would use his own language, and everyone has his own ideas on this as on any other subject. In general, however, it seems to me it says the matter adequately."

General agreement by most members was reached on the major viewpoints after the Commission staff wrote a first draft of the final report—informally called the August Document—for discussion purposes. Members who attended the first general meeting of the Commission at Wingspread at Racine, Wisconsin, in August, 1972, were asked to discuss and suggest changes for the major recommendations only. Prose style and minor arguments were to be refined after agreement was reached on the main arguments—some of them obviously controversial. Members argued and rewrote for several days before the group voted to support the general recommendations for each chapter. (See list of members who attended the 1972 Wingspread meeting on page xxix.)

All Chapters Needed Rewriting

Though agreeing with the main points, Commission members at Wingspread strongly recommended that each of the original chapters be rewritten throughout the life of the Commission as new research surfaced and arguments were bolstered or torn apart.

After the August, 1972, meeting, summaries of the early text and the main recommendations agreed upon were widely distributed to the news media and education organizations and individuals throughout the United States and Canada. Taking note of responses from members and others who commented on the first draft of the document, staff members continually revised the text during the two-year period following the 1972 Wingspread meeting. Books being written from Study Commission research and printed through the Nebraska Curriculum Development Center were a valuable source of information and ideas. (See list of Study Commission publications and their authors on page xxxv.)

At the second Wingspread meeting—in October, 1974—members again revised the chapters' recommendations and discussed the issues and prose style of the various arguments. (See list of members who attended the 1974 Wingspread meeting on page xxx.) Again, most chapters needed major rewriting, the members agreed. The chapter on educational futures (now Chapter I) was redrafted by **Charles Case**, associate dean of the College of Education at Cleveland State University. **Tom Pace,** of Wrightsville, N.C., former coordinator of the Commission's Network for Alternatives in Undergraduate Education, rewrote the chapter on present teacher education (now Chapter II). Chapter III, on accrediting and the licensing process, was reworked by **Michael Rebell,** a lawyer from White Plains, N.Y. The chapter on information systems and governance (now Chapter IV) was revised and edited by Study Commission staff members, and Chapter V, about the federal role in teacher education, was shortened and revised by **Lew Pino,** director of research and instructional service and professor of chemistry at Oakland University at Rochester, Mich., and **Don Smith,** professor of education at Bernard Baruch College in New York, N.Y. Each of the chapters was then further expanded and edited again by Study Commission staff members, including **Paul A. Olson, James Bowman, Lorna Carter, Larry Freeman, Betty Levitov, Jan Pieper,** and **Les Whipp.**

Suggested Revisions Incorporated

In the final writing and editing process, all revisions suggested by members of the Commission or committee members (and in some cases outside researchers) were incorporated unless the changes conflicted strongly with viewpoints approved at the Wingspread meetings. Unless otherwise noted (by minority report), the ideas and recommendations were agreed upon by the Commission members.

Most of the Commission members either sent specific corrections and new ideas or approved the document in writing or by telephone in its "close-to-final" form in May and June, 1975. Commission members are:

> **Victor Alicea,** chancellor of Universidad Boricua, Washington, D.C., the only Puerto Rican higher education institution in the continental USA.
>
> **Luis Alvarez,** administrator of ASPIRA of America, New York City Puerto Rican community participation organization.
>
> **William Arrowsmith,** classics professor and proponent of reform in teaching in higher education, Boston University.
>
> **Mario Barrera,** political science professor at Muir College, University of California at San Diego; formerly a faculty member at the experimental Third College, UCSD.
>
> **Sam Baskin,** president of Union of Experimenting Colleges and Universities, Yellow Springs, Ohio.
>
> **Eli Bower,** dean of Allied Health Services at the University of California at Berkeley.
>
> **Alfredo Castaneda,** professor of education at Stanford University and former coordinator of the Chicano bilingual-bicultural Follow Through program at the University of California at Riverside.
>
> **Ann Cook,** administrator of the Community Resources Institute which offers teacher education and in-community work to open classroom teachers in New York City; author or co-author of several books dealing with British infant school education and teacher education.

Dean Corrigan, dean of the College of Education and Social Sciences of the University of Vermont at Burlington, a college which includes a number of alternative models for educating teachers, combines education and human service training, and works intensively at various forms of in-community work in Vermont.

George Denemark, dean of education at the University of Kentucky, Lexington, Ky. (Denemark does not wish to be listed as a member who endorses the report. His statement appears as Chapter VI, beginning on page 211.)

James Dixon, president of Antioch College, Yellow Springs, Ohio, and former medical school administrator.

Patrick Dolan, education consultant and author of *The Ranking Game: The Power of the Academic Elite,* an analysis of the conventional ratings of institutions of higher education.

Eleanor Duckworth, professor at the Ecole de Psychologie et Science de l'Education, Université de Genève, Geneva, Switzerland; former elementary school teacher and educator of teachers at the Atlantic Institute of Education, Halifax, Nova Scotia; has also been a translator of the writings and speeches of Jean Piaget.

Jeanette Feeley, former teacher and AFT leader in Washington, D.C., public schools.

David Gipp, executive director of American Indian Higher Education Consortium (AIHEC), a consortium of predominantly American Indian universities, colleges, and community colleges.

Marilyn Gittell, presently professor of political science and associate provost, Brooklyn College of the City University of New York; formerly of the Ford Foundation project on the decentralization of the New York City schools.

Joan Goldsmith, co-director of the Institute of Open Education at Cambridge, Mass.

Charles Hall, student at Howard University, Washington, D.C.

Ken Haskins, professor of education, Harvard School of Education, Cambridge, Mass.; formerly administrator of the Adams-Morgan school in Washington, D.C., and associate superintendent of the Washington, D.C., public schools.

David Hawkins, professor of philosophy with specialties in the philosophy of science and mathematical and scientific learning; head of the Mountain View Center for Environmental Education, Boulder, Colo.

Diane Lewis, professor of anthropology, women's studies and studies in colonialism at Oakes College, University of California at Santa Cruz.

Charles Leyba, education professor and director of Project MAESTRO, one of the earliest of the Career Opportunities Programs—a predominantly Chicano COP—at California State University at Los Angeles.

Robert MacVicar, president of Oregon State University at Corvallis, the institution of which Adams High School and other school community centers are a part.

Larry Magid, presently a student and staff member of the Department of Higher Education at the University of Massachusetts at Amherst, Mass.; formerly editor of *Edcentric* magazine, an education reform publication.

Carol Ohmann, professor of English and women's studies at Wesleyan University, Middletown, Conn., and former chairwoman of the MLA Commission on the Status of Women.

Antonia Pantoja, presently administrator and professor, the School of Social Work, San Diego State College at San Diego; formerly chief administrator of the Puerto Rican Research and Resources Center, Washington, D.C., and of the Universidad Boricua.

Vito Perrone, dean of the Center for Teaching and Learning, a component of the University of North Dakota, Grand Forks, formerly called the New School of Behavioral Studies in Education, a federally subsidized in-service and pre-service teacher education program stressing the fusion of the liberal arts and teacher education, open classrooms, and parent participation in teacher education.

Anita Pfeiffer, presently director of cross-cultural Indian education, University of New Mexico, Albuquerque, N.M.; formerly in charge of staff development and curriculum development at Rough Rock Demonstration School, Rough Rock, N.M.

Lew Pino, director of research services and a chemistry professor at Oakland University, Rochester, Mich.; formerly head of several segments of National Science Foundation (NSF) programs involving the improvement of teacher training and curriculum.

Harry Rivlin, professor of education at Fordham University, New York, N.Y.; former dean of the School of Education at Fordham University, and director of the Leadership Training Institute of the Trainers of Teacher Trainers program.

Edward Rose, professor of sociology at the University of Colorado, Boulder; student of sociolinguistics and ethnomethodology, including the ethnography of schools and other human service institutions.

David Rosen, student and student advocate, historian of education reform in New York City and Cambridge, Mass.; chairman of the Study Commission's student committee; works in various tutoring and education projects in New York City and was recently associated with the editing of an education research journal in Israel.

Leo Shapiro, head of market research firm in Chicago.

Mal Shaw, head of education reform training firm.

Barbara Sizemore, superintendent of Washington, D.C., public schools; former chief administrator, Woodlawn Experimental School District, Chicago, and former associate executive secretary, American Association of School Administrators (AASA).

Donald Smith, professor of education at Bernard Baruch College, City University of New York, and chairman of a CUNY committee to examine the CUNY "open admissions" program; former director of Chicago's Center for Inner City Studies.

David Spencer, active in securing increased parent participation and control in the New York City public schools; presently administrator of the CONTACT program, a penal complex educational program, Poughkeepsie, N.Y.

Maria Gutierrez Spencer, former teacher and now administrator of a bilingual institute and school-community-based teacher training center in the Deming Public Schools, Deming, New Mexico.

Robert Spillane, superintendent of the New Rochelle Public Schools, New Rochelle, N.Y.; former leader in the School Management Study Group.

Murray Wax, chairman of the sociology department, Washington University at Saint Louis. **Rosalie Wax,** professor of anthropology at Washington University. The Waxes have worked as a research team on questions having to do with the relationship between culture and education, particularly on Native American reservations; more recently, they have examined the educational meaning and content of fieldwork.

Jerry Witherspoon, administrator with Universidad Boricua, Washington, D.C.; former president of Goddard College at Plainfield, Vt.

Other Valuable Contributions Recognized

The Study Commission gratefully acknowledges also the specific suggestions for revision sent by these persons, some of whom have been formally associated with the Commission as committee members or as authors of training documents:

Seth Brunner, director of the Experimental College of the University of California at Davis.

Fritz Edelstein, intern for the National Institute of Education's Education Equity Task Force, Washington, D.C.

Jeanne Guertin, associate director of Project MAESTRO, California State University at Los Angeles.

George Kaplan, Institute for Educational Leadership, Washington, D.C.

Max Larsen, interim dean of the College of Arts and Sciences at the University of Nebraska, Lincoln.

Paul Mohr, dean of the College of Education at Florida A&M University at Tallahassee.

Layton Olson, National Student Education Fund, Washington, D.C.

Michael Rebell, White Plains, N.Y., lawyer.

Edythe Stanford, former network coordinator for the Study Commission, Chicago, Ill.

Armando Valdez, former network coordinator for the Study Commission, Hayward, Calif.

David White, Childhood and Government Project, School of Law, University of California at Berkeley.

Frank Wuest, director of Change in Liberal Education, Washington, D.C.

Others who have not been formally associated with the Study Commission but whose research and advice have been invaluable are:

Michael Annison, Denver, Colo.; **Cathy Bernard,** Washington, D.C.; **Howard Bowen,** Claremont, Calif.; **Joel Burdin,** Washington, D.C.; **Audrey Cohen,** New York, N.Y.; **Marty Corey,** Washington, D.C.; **Ivan Dahl,** Grand Forks, N.D.; **Don Davies,** Boston, Mass.; **Manly Fleischmann,** New York, N.Y.; **Ida Fletcher,** Chicago, Ill.; **Jeanne Frein,** Grand Forks, N.D.; **Hector Galicia,** Stanford, Calif.; **Hendrik Gideonse,** Cincinnati, Ohio; **Phyllis Hamilton,** Menlo Park, Calif.; **Joel Henning,** Chicago, Ill.; **Don Hillman,** Burlington, Vt.; **Harold Hodgkinson,** Washington, D.C.; **Sheila Huff,** Syracuse, N.Y.; **Arnold Jirik,** Stillwater, Minn.; **Mohammed Khan,** Albany, N.Y.;

Wallace Maurer, Harrisburg, Pa.; **Alexander Mood**, Irvine, Calif.; **Frank Newman**, Stanford, Calif.; **Richard Nichols**, Denver, Colo.; **Richard Ohmann**, Middletown, Conn.; **Harold Orlans**, Washington, D.C.; **William Robinson**, Washington, D.C.; **Joseph Rosen**, Chicago, Ill.; **Phil Scribner**, Washington, D.C.; **A.W. Van der Meer**, University, Ala.; **Brenda Watkins**, Washington, D.C.; and **John Wish**, Eugene, Ore.

U.S. Office of Education personnel who have served the Study Commission in an official or advisory capacity include:

Gerald Elbers, Donald Bigelow, Tom Carter, Russ Egerton, Bruce Gaarder, Marty Kramer, Freddie Liebermann, Chuck Lovett, Robert Miller, Helen O'Leary, Mary Jane Smalley, William Smith, and **Shirley Steele.**

The support of the Johnson Foundation of Racine, Wis., has been a major factor in the preparing of the Study Commission's final report, since both meetings of the full membership were held at the Wingspread Conference Center. Johnson Foundation staff members who helped plan the conferences and made Study Commission members welcome at Wingspread were **Leslie Paffrath**, president; **Henry Halstead**, vice president and program director; **Rita Goodman**, vice president and area program director; and **Kay Mauer**, conference coordinator.

The directorate of the Study Commission thanks these other staff members (and former staff members) for their contributions toward the final printing of this report:

Rosemary Bergstrom, Jeanne Bishop, Ree Bombach, Kathy Dickson, Karen Hanshew, Isabel Harm, Bill Larson, Rich Rolfes, David Schadt, Nena Shanks, Lisa Temple, Anetta Young, and **Joe Young.**

                                    Paul A. Olson, Director
                                    Larry Freeman
                                    Jim Bowman
                                    Jan Pieper

MEMBERS AND CONSULTANTS ATTENDING WINGSPREAD MEETING
August, 1972

Victor Alicea, Washington, D.C.
Luis Alvarez, Kensington, Md.
Mario Barrera, LaJolla, Calif.
Samuel Baskin, Yellow Springs, Ohio
Barbara Blourock, LaJolla, Calif.
Ree Bombach, Phoenix, Ariz.
Eli Bower, Berkeley, Calif.
James Bowman, Lincoln, Nebr.
Ann Cook, New York, N.Y.
Dean Corrigan, Burlington, Vt.
Kathy Dickson, Lincoln, Nebr.
James Dixon, Yellow Springs, Ohio
Pat Dolan, LaJolla, Calif.
Fred Erickson, Cambridge, Mass.
Angelo Falcon, New York, N.Y.
Jeanette Feeley, Washington, D.C.
Larry Freeman, Springfield, Ill.
Harold Garfinkel, Los Angeles, Calif.
Marilyn Gittell, Brooklyn, N.Y.
Joan Goldsmith, Cambridge, Mass.
Jeanne Guertin, Los Angeles, Calif.
Charles M. Hall, Washington, D.C.
Isabel Harm, Lincoln, Nebr.
George Kaplan, Washington, D.C.
Diane Lewis, Santa Cruz, Calif.
Robert MacVicar, Corvallis, Ore.
Larry Magid, Amherst, Mass.

Robert Miller, OE, Washington, D.C.
Berny Morson, Boulder, Colo.
Nancy Mullen, Philadelphia, Pa.
Carol Ohmann, Middletown, Conn.
Helen O'Leary, OE, Washington, D.C.
Paul Olson, Lincoln, Nebr.
Antonia Pantoja, LaJolla, Calif.
Vito Perrone, Grand Forks, N.D.
Jan Pieper, Lincoln, Nebr.
Lewis Pino, Rochester, Mich.
Harry Rivlin, New York, N.Y.
Ed Rose, Boulder, Colo.
David Rosen, Culver City, Calif.
Edgar Sagan, Lexington, Ky.
Phillip Scribner, Washington, D.C.
Malcolm Shaw, LaJolla, Calif.
Barbara Sizemore, Washington, D.C.
Donald Smith, New York, N.Y.
William Smith, OE, Washington, D.C.
David Spencer, Poughkeepsie, N.Y.
Dolores Spencer, Poughkeepsie, N.Y.
Maria Spencer, Silver City, N.M.
Jerry Witherspoon, Washington, D.C.
Anetta Young, Lincoln, Nebr.

MEMBERS AND CONSULTANTS ATTENDING WINGSPREAD MEETING
October, 1974

Victor Alicea, Washington, D.C.
Jeanne Bishop, Lincoln, Nebr.
Barbara Blourock, LaJolla, Calif.
James Bowman, Lincoln, Nebr.
Charles Case, Cleveland, Ohio
Dean Corrigan, Burlington, Vt.
George Denemark, Lexington, Ky.
Kathy Dickson, Lincoln, Nebr.
Pat Dolan, LaJolla, Calif.
Eleanor Duckworth, Geneva, Switzerland
Frederick Edelstein, Washington, D.C.
Larry Freeman, Springfield, Ill.
Joan Goldsmith, Cambridge, Mass.
Jeanne Guertin, Los Angeles, Calif.
John Hopkins, New York, N.Y.
George Kaplan, Washington, D.C.
Diane Lewis, Santa Cruz, Calif.
Robert MacVicar, Corvallis, Ore.
Larry Magid, Amherst, Mass.
Paul Mohr, Tallahassee, Fla.
George Morales, New York, N.Y.
Richard Nichols, Denver, Colo.
Layton Olson, Washington, D.C.
Paul A. Olson, Lincoln, Nebr.
Tom Pace, Wrightsville Beach, N.C.

Antonia Pantoja, LaJolla, Calif.
Vito Perrone, Grand Forks, N.D.
Anita Pfeiffer, Albuquerque, N.M.
Jan Pieper, Lincoln, Nebr.
Lewis Pino, Rochester, Mich.
Michael Rebell, White Plains, N.Y.
Ed Rose, Boulder, Colo.
David Rosen, Culver City, Calif.
David Schadt, Lincoln, Nebr.
Don Smith, New York, N.Y.
William Smith, OE, Washington, D.C.
Maria Spencer, Silver City, N.M.
Robert Spillane, New Rochelle, N.Y.
Edythe Stanford, Chicago, Ill.
Armando Valdez, Hayward, Calif.
David White, Berkeley, Calif.
Frank Wuest, Washington, D.C.

STUDY COMMISSION COMMITTEE MEMBERS

Evaluation of Impact of Federal Intervention on Higher Education

CHARLES LEYBA, Los Angeles, Calif., chairman; **Jose Cardenas**, San Antonio, Tex.; **Charles DeCarlo**, Bronxville, N.Y.; **Jeanne Guertin**, Los Angeles, Calif.; **Bob Hogan**, Urbana, Ill.; **Richard Longaker**, Los Angeles, Calif.; **Ruth MacFarlane**, Laguna Hills, Calif.; **Charles Wilson**, New York, N.Y.

Academic Disciplines

EDWARD ROSE, Boulder, Colo., chairman; **Kenneth Boulding**, Boulder, Colo.; **David Denton**, Lexington, Ky.; **Linda Ehrlich**, Baltimore, Md.; **Harold Garfinkel**, Los Angeles, Calif.; **Robert Hanson**, Boulder, Colo.; **David Hawkins**, Boulder, Colo.; **Peter Ossorio**, Boulder, Colo.; **David Sudnow**, Irvine, Calif.; **Murray Wax**, St. Louis, Mo.; **Rosalie Wax**, St. Louis, Mo.

Evaluation of Higher Education

BILL ARROWSMITH, Bristol, Vt., and **PAT DOLAN**, LaJolla, Calif., co-chairmen; **Alfredo Castaneda**, Riverside, Calif.; **Herbert Holloman**; **Alistair McIntyre**; **Larry Magid**, Amherst, Mass.

School Administrators

ROBERT SPILLANE, New Rochelle, N.Y., and **BARBARA SIZEMORE**, Washington, D.C., co-chairpersons; **Jose Cardenas**, San Antonio, Tex.; **Richard Foster**, Berkeley, Calif.; **Ken Haskins**, Cambridge, Mass.; **Anita Pfeiffer**, Albuquerque, N.M.; **Vaughn Phelps**, Omaha, Neb.; **Robert Schwartz**, Newtonville, Mass.

Deans of Education

ALFREDO CASTANEDA, Stanford, Calif., and **DEAN CORRIGAN**, Burlington, Vt., co-chairmen; **Nancy Arnez**, Washington, D.C.; **George Denemark**, Lexington, Ky.; **Robert Egbert**, Lincoln, Neb.; **Joan Goldsmith**, Cambridge, Mass.; **William R. Hicks**, Baton Rouge, La.; **Paul Orr**, Tuscaloosa, Ala.; **Vito Perrone**, Grand Forks, N.D.; **Harry Rivlin**, New

York, N.Y.; **Milton Schwebel**, New Brunswick, N.J.

Learning Contexts

JERRY WITHERSPOON, Washington, D.C., chairman; **Samuel Baskin**, Yellow Springs, Ohio; **James Dixon**, Yellow Springs, Ohio; **Allen Graubard**, Cambridge, Mass.; **Colin Greer**, New York, N.Y.; **Charles Hurst**, Chicago, Ill.; **John Sullivan**, Yellow Springs, Ohio.

Cultural Pluralism

ANTONIA PANTOJA, LaJolla, Calif., chairwoman; **Joseph Aguayo**, New York, N.Y.; **Victor Alicea**, Washington, D.C.; **Barbara Blourock**, LaJolla, Calif.; **Edwin Claudio**, Chicago, Ill.; **Robert Dumont**, Chicago, Ill.; **Mario Fantini**, New Paltz, N.Y.; **Jeanette Feeley**, Washington, D.C.; **Marilyn Gittell**, Brooklyn, N.Y.; **A. Reyes Mazon**, Austin, Tex.; **Orlando Taylor**, Washington, D.C.; **Cyril Tyson**, New York, N.Y.

Professional Societies

ELI M. BOWER, Berkeley, Calif., chairman; **Alfredo Castaneda**, Stanford, Calif.; **Al Hollingsworth**, East Lansing, Mich.; **Richard Jones**, Olympia, Wash.; **Diane Lewis**, Santa Cruz, Calif.; **Andre Pacquette**, New York, N.Y.; **Vito Perrone**, Grand Forks, N.D.; **Richard Snyder**, Columbus, Ohio; **Henry Winkler**, New Brunswick, N.J.; **Deborah Wolfe**, Flushing, N.Y.

Student Reference Group

DAVID ROSEN, Culver City, Calif., chairman; **Warren Blumenfeld**, Washington, D.C.; **Edwin Claudio**, Chicago, Ill.; **Rosilyn Curry**, Akron, Ohio; **Deborah Daniels**, Mountain View, Calif.; **Linda Ehrlich**, Baltimore, Md.; **Angelo Falcon**, New York, N.Y.; **Charles Hall**, Washington, D.C.; **Nesta King**, Tallahassee, Fla.; **Larry Magid**, Amherst, Mass.; **Bert Marian**, North Liberty, Ia.; **Eduardo Pardo**, Claremont, Calif.; **Nancy Ryan**, Staten Island, N.Y.; **Jose Sanchez**, New York, N.Y.; **Joe Velasco**, Long Beach, Calif.; **Bert Whitaker**, Pippa Passes, Ky.; **Barbara Yates**, Ames, Ia.

Teachers Reference Group

JEANETTE FEELEY, Washington, D.C., chairwoman; **Anne Burdick**,

Monterey Park, Calif.; **Smith Cliffton**, Mt. Airy, Md.; **Eleanor Duckworth**, Geneva, Switzerland; **Pete Ferry**, Granada Hills, Calif.; **Mildred Gladney**, Chicago, Ill.; **Vivian Hawkins**, Frankfort, Ky.; **Twila Martin**, Syracuse, N.Y.; **Mark Milleman**, Lincoln City, Ore.; **Garrison Nelson**, Burlington, Vt.; **Carol Ohmann**, Middletown, Conn.; **James Olivero**, Hillsborough, Calif.; **Vivian One Feather**, Pine Ridge, S.D.; **Maria Spencer**, Silver City, N.M.; **Laura Wallace**, Chinle, Ariz.

Information System

LEO SHAPIRO, Chicago, Ill., chairman; **Philip Hauser**, Chicago, Ill.; **Harold Hodgkinson**, Washington, D.C.; **John Seaver**; **Joost Yff**, Washington, D.C.

Strategies and Communications

MALCOLM SHAW, LaJolla, Calif., chairman; **William Birenbaum**, Staten Island, N.Y.; **James Doherty**, Wilton, Conn.; **Fred Fisher**, Washington, D.C.; **Marilyn Gittell**, Brooklyn, N.Y.; **Ben Kubasick**, New York, N.Y.; **Michael Moore**, Evergreen, Colo.; **Wallace Wohlking**, New York, N.Y.

Nebraska Internal Reference

Harry Allen, Ted Beck, Donald Costello, Howard Eckel, Robert Egbert, Melvin George, Erwin Goldenstein, Norman Hostetler, Dorothy Kozak, Max Larsen, all of Lincoln, Nebr.

GOVERNANCE COMMITTEES

Membership

KEN HASKINS, Cambridge, Mass., chairman; **William Arrowsmith**, Bristol, Vt.; **Alfredo Castaneda**, Stanford, Calif.; **Joan Goldsmith**, Cambridge, Mass.; **Lew Pino**, Rochester, Mich.; **David Rosen**, Culver City, Calif.

Budget

JAMES DIXON, Yellow Springs, Ohio, chairman; **Larry Magid**, Amherst, Mass.; **Antonia Pantoja**, LaJolla, Calif.; **Paul Salmon**, Washington,

D.C.; **Malcolm Shaw**, LaJolla, Calif.; **Barbara Sizemore**, Washington, D.C.; **Jerry Witherspoon**, Washington, D.C.

Meetings and Agendas

LEO SHAPIRO, Chicago, Ill., chairman; **Eli M. Bower**, Berkeley, Calif.; **George Denemark**, Lexington, Ky.; **Vito Perrone**, Grand Forks, N.D.; **Murray Wax**, St. Louis, Mo.

NETWORK COORDINATORS and STAFF MEMBERS

East Coast

GEORGE MORALES, New York, N.Y., coordinator; **Cheryl Tilghman**, Brooklyn, N.Y., staff member.

Chicago and Southern Colleges

EDYTHE STANFORD, Chicago, Ill., coordinator; **Gwyndolin Carter**, Chicago, Ill., staff member.

Southwest Network

ARMANDO VALDEZ, Hayward, Calif., coordinator; **Rosita Horseley, David Martinez, Gloria Chacon**, all of Hayward, Calif., staff members.

Network for Alternatives in Undergraduate Education (NAUTE)

TOM PACE, Wrightsville Beach, N.C., coordinator; **Charlotte West**, Grand Forks, N.D., staff member.

American Indian Higher Education Consortium (AIHEC)

DAVID GIPP, Denver, Colo., executive director.

STUDY COMMISSION PUBLICATIONS

Academic Disciplines Committee:

Adjustments of Colorado School Districts to Declining Enrollments, by Mark Rodekohr, with an introduction by Kenneth Boulding.

The Structure of the Academic Disciplines and the Structure of Schooling, edited by Edward Rose.

Evaluation of Higher Education:

The Ranking Game: The Power of the Academic Elite, by Pat Dolan.

School Administrators:

The University Can't Train Teachers, edited by Larry Freeman, James Bowman, Paul A. Olson and Jan Pieper.

What is School-Community-Based Education and Why Should School Administrators Be Interested in It?, by Fritz Edelstein.

Deans of Education:

Education for 1984 and After, edited by Paul A. Olson, Larry Freeman and James Bowman.

The Future: Create or Inherit, edited by Charles Case and Paul A. Olson.

Learning Contexts:

Of Education and Human Community, edited by James Bowman, Larry Freeman, Paul A. Olson and Jan Pieper.

Cultural Pluralism:

The Badges and Indicia of Slavery: Cultural Pluralism Redefined, edited by Antonia Pantoja, Barbara Blourock and James Bowman.

Professional Societies:

A Nation Half-Dead at the Top, by Rosemary Bergstrom and Paul A. Olson, based on research by Eli Bower and Diane Savage.

Student Reference Group:

Open Admissions: The Promise and the Lie of Open Access in American Higher Education, by David Rosen, Seth Brunner and Steve Fowler.

Education By, For and About African Americans: A Profile of Several Black Community Schools, by Deborah Daniels.

We'll Do It Ourselves: Combatting Sexism in Education, edited by Barbara Yates, Steve Werner and David Rosen.

How to Research the Power Structure of Your University or College, by Bert Marian.

How to Research the Power Structure of Your Secondary School System, by Bert Marian, David Rosen and David Osborne.

Mini-Manual for a Free University, by Larry Magid with Nesta King.

Wheeling and Dealing in Washington: A Student's Guide to Federal Educational Politics and Resources, by Seth Brunner.

Some New Ways of Learning and Teaching, compiled by Nena Shanks.

Information Committee:

The Supply and Demand of Teachers and Teaching, by Leo Shapiro and Evelyn Zerfoss.

Special Committee on Federal Funding:

Nothing But Praise: Thoughts on the Ties Between Higher Education and the Federal Government, by Lew Pino, with an essay by Kenneth Boulding.

East Coast Network:

Basic Legal Issues in New York State on Teacher Certification, by John O. Hopkins.

Teacher Credentialling Reform in New York State: Critique and a Suggestion for New Directions, by Michael Rebell.

Chicago and Southern Colleges Network:

The Law and the Unitary System of Higher Education: A Discussion of the Impact of Title VI, U.S. Civil Rights Act on Selected Black Public Colleges and Universities, by Paul Mohr and Adelbert Jones.

Problems, Issues and Priorities of Black Colleges and Universities, by Paul Mohr and Adelbert Jones.

Black Colleges and Equal Opportunity in Higher Education: A Variety of Papers Advocating the Retention of Black Colleges and Universities, compiled and edited by Paul Mohr.

Southwest Network:

Parameters of Institutional Change: Chicano Experiences in Education.

Chicano Alternative Education, by Homero Galicia, Clementina Almaguer and others.

Casa de la Raza.

The Education Voucher Intrigue: An Analysis of its Impact on the Alum Rock Community, by Felix Gutierrez and Gloria Chacon.

Education Alternativa: On the Development of Chicano Bilingual Schools, prepared by Reynaldo Macias, Carolyn Webb de Macias, William De La Torre and Mario Vasquez.

The Recruitment, Channeling, and Placement of Chicano Teachers, edited by Gloria Chacon and James Bowman.

STUDY COMMISSION NEWSLETTERS

January, 1973—Deals with higher education institutions which appear to be moving in directions consonant with Study Commission values.

March, 1973—Continues with descriptions of colleges and universities begun in January, 1973, issue.

December, 1973—Contains manpower information data on teachers and on various states' efforts to assess and deal with needs and surpluses.

May, 1974—Tells about legal barriers to possible improvement of teacher education programs and efforts being made to examine relevant court cases.

January, 1975—Contains a re-analysis of the Carnegie Commission survey data on higher education which covered 70,000 undergraduates, 60,000 faculty members, and 33,000 graduate students.

October, 1975—Reports on the Study Commission's site visits to teacher training programs which have been making efforts to work with the schools and communities, thus increasing fieldwork experiences for future teachers and drawing community members and university personnel into the schools.

(For information on any of these publications, write to the **Nebraska Curriculum Development Center, Andrews Hall, University of Nebraska, Lincoln, Nebraska 68588.**)

CHAPTER I

THE FUTURE OF SCHOOLS AND CHILDREN:

EDUCATION OF TEACHERS AS A COMMUNITY ACTIVITY[1]

The Study Commission Value Statement

After Study Commission members had been working together for about a year (1972), gathering information on the state of undergraduate education for teachers, we came to the conclusion that our future assessment of information and our own future action needed to be guided by some sort of value statement. Committee chairmen met at the Belmont Conference Center outside of Washington for several days. They were joined by several officials of the Office of Education and by members of citizen groups interested in the future of education. The "Value Statement" which emerged from the meeting was subsequently adopted by the full Study Commission and has guided our research, educational efforts and action in the field since. We think that it may be a useful general introduction to our conceptions of planning for the future in the spheres of undergraduate education and the education of teachers, both pre-service and in-service. The part of the statement which deals with the concept of "community" and "education" [edited slightly to omit references to UPEP (Undergraduate Preparation for Educational Personnel), a planned federal program which was never funded] reads as follows:

> Education is a personal process. It implies an acquisition of self knowledge and of what is generally called abstract learning. But it is also a social and political process, wherein people organize themselves into groups and endeavor to communicate the skills necessary to their own survival or the survival of the next generation. It is, in fact, a community enterprise when rightly conducted. By a community we mean a group which thinks of itself as having

shared neighborhood or regional responsibilities and interests: a county, an educational service unit, a township, a political or educational subdivision. We also mean a group tied together by a shared system of usages the boundaries of which may or may not coincide with a political subdivision: usages such as those of a language, dialect, ethnic tradition, religious tradition, custom, racial identity, expressive form, or pattern of family and precept for rearing children. It is probable that such an entity can function best if the political lines and lines of group custom are essentially congruent and if the group is not divided by political or "educational subdivision" lines or essentially governed and told how to educate its children by others whom it perceives to be alien, having interests opposed to its interests.

In defining the concept of "community" in relation to "education," we tried to describe why we thought small units including many ages and types of activity were important both to the creation of healthy communities and of humanly productive education:

Recent research in the social sciences suggests that, in general, the healthiest communities, those which are most supportive of intellectual and emotional growth in the young, are those in which the important groups to which the individual looks are small, groups in which youth and age, work and play, education and vocation are not neatly separated. In such communities, competition among the members is not the dominant reason for acting. No young person feels that he stands alone. Indeed, such a supportive community in school and outside of school often seems to be basic to growth in knowledge and skills. If a young person is to feel that he/she belongs to a significant group, both the school and the community must have an authority structure which is not disrupted by, or made dependent on, "outside" authority structures.

In the context of this definition of education "when it works best," we also tried to describe the teacher's responsibility in the furtherance of community health and integrity where it exists, and in its development where it does not exist.

The Study Commission has asked, throughout the last year, whether the education offered in school and college—particularly to those who are preparing to be teachers—is an appropriate means of preparing them for the community which they are entering. It has argued that the teacher should have some capacity and desire to change things when the community which the teacher enters or serves is not a humane community. Since it is education's job both to foster learning and to develop people who can learn and work together, the goal of educating teachers who can promote individual development and the goal of finding and encouraging teachers who can encourage growth toward healthy community are probably equally important.

Future teachers and other education personnel will perform a broad range of human services operating from community-school centers: they may often be street workers; they may offer a variety of medical and community health services; they may assist in developing intellectual and emotional growth in both children and parents; they will, as school-related personnel, relate to other human service agencies and civil agencies; and they will work to create a healthy professional community within the school and assist the community around it in organizing and developing its resources. Indeed, the range of personnel educated by the reformed programs will probably be as broad as the needs of the communities served. It is likely that the matter of the appropriate responsibilities and relationships among the home and educational and community service groups will have to be explored. What future education personnel will regard as appropriate places for assisting young people to learn, to work, to play, and to act, will largely depend on the range of experiences and the contexts which have been central to their education. If teachers-to-be are to regard education as an enterprise which extends beyond the school door, their own intellectual, vocational, and social life at the college or institution of higher education ought to form a single continuum so that this intellectual life does not stop when they go to their living unit.

The education provided should be as open and many-sided as possible, and the institution which offers the education should answer to a fairly specific autonomous culture and its authority system. A variety of ages and stages of growth should be present.[2]

When the "Value Statement" was set down early in 1972, the Study Commission had no idea of how much legal validity it would have, but recent legal decisions appear to be moving in directions to which the statement points. The courts have moved to exempt members of at least two culture groups, the Wisconsin Amish and the Florida Miccosukee, from compulsory school attendance on the grounds that compulsory schooling interfered with their religious exercise, and was not requisite inasmuch as the informal education of children in these communities was adequate to the continuation of satisfactory community life (*State of Wisconsin v. Jonas Yoder,* decided by the Supreme Court, May 15, 1972; the *State of Florida v. Bobby Clay,* decided in the Collier County, Florida, courts, July 24, 1972). The courts have ruled that the initial education of children must be in the language of their nurture and that their people and culture must somehow be visibly present in the ordering of the schools which they attend (*Lau v. Nichols,* decided by the Supreme Court, January 21, 1974; *Serna v. Portales,* decided in district court of New Mexico, 1972, with follow-up memos by Judge Edwin L. Mechan, August 3, 1973; *United States v. State of Texas,* concerning the San Felipe Independent School District, decided in U.S. district court, December 6, 1971, follow-up memorandum by Judge William Wayne Justice). The courts have extended the implications of *Pierce v. Society of Sisters, Meyer v. Nebraska,* and *Farrington v. Tokushige* which "exclude any general power of the state to standardize its children by forcing them to accept instruction from public teachers only." These decisions deny the right of the state to treat its children as school chattel to be placed in "Plato's pen or fold [to] deposit them with certain nurses who dwell in a separate quarter." They defy any effort to make compulsory education limit the parents' right to "direct the education of their own child without unreasonable restriction . . ." (cf. footnote 84, Chapter II). Any continuation of these trends and of certain other legal trends described in Chapter III will do much to make future common school education in this country more sensitive to differences in culture and environment from community to community than past education has been.

Survival Needs and Centralized Institutions

The Study Commission "Value Statement" encourages a certain kind of education as part of a larger effort to visualize the future. What anyone thinks should happen in education will in large part depend on what he or she thinks future societies must look like. We believe that the industrial vision of the recent past—which created the schools of today—may have reached the limits of its effectiveness. Many of its assumptions—ecological and social, as well as educational—are now being questioned.[3] As the Study Commission's Deans Committee, paraphrasing the Club of Rome's sentiments, has said in one of its books, "The principal defect of the industrial way of life with its ethos of expansion is that it is not sustainable. . . . If the present growth trends in world population, industrialization, pollution, food production, and resource depletion continue unchanged, the limits to growth on this planet will be reached sometime within the next hundred years."[4] Whereas the pessimistic projections of the first Club of Rome report have been modified somewhat, the second report still suggests that industrialization and the rapid exhaustion of fossil fuels require education toward the establishment of a new relationship between nature and culture of many, perhaps of all, human communities[5] — communities that by design or necessity exercise population limits and exhibit a clear sense for the necessity of living within the constraints set by the natural system. The necessity of working toward global equilibrium or "organic growth" in capital-in-circulation, population,[6] input and output, is now fairly widely accepted by many nations (Brazil is a notable exception), and the fundamental questions have to do with how life with "limited growth" will serve the third world and how it will affect its relationship to non-socialist and socialist countries.[7] The new style of living will require a distinctly reduced consumption of fossil fuels and a different style of living and acting from that developed by many cultures which have depended on highly centralized structures and rapid growth and industrialization as adaptive mechanisms. The example of decentralized cultures which have traditionally lived in equilibrium with natural forces—the concept of "organic growth"—is coming to be significant for reasons which are neither sentimental nor based on yearnings to perpetuate the skin-deep cultural-pluralism which we have had. Rather, the present interest is based on a policy concern to find the best decentralized societies and equilibrium economies.

Jacques Ellul has pointed out that past societies began their processes of disintegration at the point where they no longer shared a collective image of what they could be. He cautions that motivating images of the sort that can be shared collectively must meet three conditions to be socially effective. First, an image of the future must be based on the real experience of a people, on their feelings, and on the manner in which they represent those feelings.[8] Second, the range of realization lies somewhere between the desirable and the scientifically calculated possibility. And, third, the commonly held values of the group must be determined; the shared values are the starting point for collective action.[9] It is clear that our American society does not share a common image of the future, common goals, or a common culture. The Cultural Pluralism Committee of the Study Commission has called this vividly to the Study Commission's attention in its statement about what people and cultures are preferred and unpreferred in present systems of social and economic development.[10] It has also shown something about how this continuing bias has impoverished our economy, our potential for a common culture, our education, and our sense of community cohesion.

Recent years have witnessed a rapid decline in the prestige of the large, collective centralized institutions which our society has created: international corporations, national churches, the federal Congress and a variety of other agencies. Some of this decline in respect may derive from the extent to which such institutions try to develop a common policy where commonly held values do not exist. We are not under any delusions that there exists a real nation-wide consensus with respect to American education. Indeed, the litigation with respect to the equalization of taxes suggests that there is not a perceived national interest with respect to adequate support of education and, in most states, little perceived state-wide interest: adequate support, if it comes at all, will probably have to be mandated by the courts in the respective states. However, if America no longer possesses clear national visions, we do believe that at the community level there still exist perceived common images of the world, perceived common futures, and perceived cultural identities which can be made the basis of educational policy in the respective American communities. These images, including all the historical and natural constraints which go with them, may be the centers around which to plan the community schools of the future. Both urban and rural areas can foster "healthy human communities" that integrate all aspects of life, each with its own uniqueness, communities wherein social "belonging" is automatic and social groupings are small. To hold up such an integrated community image for social planning plots a direction and says, further, that any effort to affect future teacher training which does not anticipate its effect on the whole of the neighborhood, region, or culture-community is likely to intensify, not alleviate, education's problems.

The internal signs that our centralized human service institutions may have reached a situation parallel to that of other over-centralized institutions—what Ivan Illich calls the "second watershed" of institutions—also tell us that a new educational ethos is needed along with a new industrial ethos. The process of growth and centralization which

Illich describes is a familiar one:

> In the first stage [watershed], there is [in institutions] a direct positive relationship between resources expended and services provided. New knowledge is applied to specific problems and desirable effects are produced. Simple habits and tools become widespread. However, as the modern institution grows, it reaches its second watershed and increases in resources expended actually decrease services.

Illich characterizes the "second watershed" as a series of steps toward system maintenance as an end in itself, with a resulting decrease in services:

1. **Bureaucratization.** An emphasis on rational, efficient management; hierarchal, impersonal, specialized division of labor and assembly line production. Human values become institutionalized and transformed into technical tasks.

2. **Survival and growth become primary goals.** The institution becomes an end in itself whose purposes are indefinite expansion and unlimited creation of new but unrealizable needs.

3. **The institution develops a radical monopoly.** There is a dominance of one type of product rather than one brand. Acceptable alternatives decline. For example, private transportation becomes identified with high speed vehicles. Schools monopolize education by legitimating a particular kind of socially acceptable learning. Medicine becomes the exclusive definer of what constitutes disease and its treatment.

4. **Self-serving elites take control.** These elites define basic needs of people in terms professionals can meet. In medicine, ever more conditions are defined as needing treatment by the creation of new specialties under direct control of the guild. The tools of health care are jealously guarded to prevent their widespread use by the general public.

5. **Services become compulsory.** The outputs of institutions become socially obligatory and defined as basic necessities only large institutions can provide. Services become commodicized— turned into engineered social habits fitting the logic of large scale

production. People end up being exploited by the demands of their tools.

6. **Consumers become addicted to institutional products.** Alternative ways of doing things cannot be imagined. Thus, medical care can only be visualized in terms of doctors and hospitals, and education becomes identified with schools, curricula and teachers. People become classified by their level of consumption.

7. **Services become scarce.** Professionals create a deliberate scarcity. The practice of general medicine declines, health costs soar, and hospitals become a person's contact with a doctor. There are insufficient numbers of doctors, though thousands are turned away from medical schools. In education, more time and resources are spent getting ready to teach than in actually teaching. In transportation, the utility of the car is diminished because more time is spent in traffic jams, accidents and traffic court. Cars also make space scarce and prevent people from the right to walk or ride a bicycle. So, people pay more and get increasingly less. Only the very wealthy can afford access to and autonomous use of industrial tools.

8. **Natural competence is restricted.** Many ancient privileges are lost; healing and consoling one another, burying one's dead, building a shelter, innate mobility and abundant opportunities for learning. Increasingly the individual must rely on the experts because he is told the tools of his society are too complex to understand.

9. **Self-defeating escalation occurs.** Institutional elites announce a crisis because of the growing gap between consumer expectations and actual services. But the elites are locked into one approach to problem solving: more of what is currently offered. The cure for illiteracy is more teachers, books and behavioral engineers.

10. **Finally, the institution becomes a social danger.** Professional medicine becomes a major threat to health as medicine itself creates new kinds of diseases. Huge amounts of money are spent to deal with the irresponsible use of drugs, extend sick life and keep people functioning in inhospitable cities and sickening jobs. Schools become a major threat to education, professional law a

threat to justice, and professional government a threat to continued existence. As these institutions pass their second watershed, people need to be protected from them.[11]

One need not agree with the whole of Illich's social and educational analysis to recognize the cogency of his picture of what too often happens to human service institutions as they grow. If the schools as institutions are not in the "second watershed," they are perilously close. Fed intellectually by the systematic mushrooming of scientific knowledge and guided practically by the need to serve an endlessly mobile and fluctuating population, the schools have developed a standardized education—a standard balanced diet. To serve up this prescribed fare to the young people who pass by, the schools have recruited a special class of mentors, a group no longer expected **to do**, but only expected **to teach**. Indeed, upon certification these teachers are no longer expected to demonstrate even the capacity to learn. The intellectually competent scholar and discoverer of knowledge of the late medieval school has now been replaced in all too many cases by the pedagogue, skilled in drill and in the handling of systematic aids to learning.[12]

History of Educational Centralization

The human service institutions which are experiencing the "second watershed" and the industrial institutions experiencing large-scale worker alienation ("blue collar blues") are similar in form. Both are intensely hierarchic, routinized, and massive in organization. Both tend to make the participants—whether students, teachers, or workers—feel that they are cogs in a machine and not part of a community of persons who care for one another. Both often require waiting in line, sitting or standing at the right station, doing tasks which one has not defined for oneself, and working competitively. Both have created a milieu whose inhabitants engage in a fair amount of deliberate vandalism. That industrial and educational institutions should have had parallel histories in our culture is understandable, since centralized compulsory schools and assembly line factories and other large-scale growth-oriented institutions arose simultaneously. The nineteenth and twentieth century history of the *compulsory* school in the West parallels the history of assembly line industrialization and post-Napoleonic nationalism. The rise of the routinized school (seventeenth and eighteenth century), with its age-grade lockstep, parallels the rise of the middle classes and the development of science as a collective enterprise and with these, of the competitive ethic, individualism, personal profit, and consumption as enviable and prestigious attributes.[13] These in turn produced what has been called "the technological superiority of the West" and prompted the conquest and oppression of other lands, cultures, and peoples.

The school which was very like a factory appeared and grew for the best of reasons: to insure the intellectual growth of groups, and to transmit the growing scientific understanding and capacity to control aversive natural processes. It arose and took its shape in cultures long in skills and short in information.[14] But the creation of the school, a special and separate agency for the education of the young, also entailed unsought consequences. The child no longer worked as an apprentice to an adult who knew what he was doing and regarded the transmitting of his adult skills to the younger craftsman as a major responsibility. School became the instrument whereby work and study, work and recreation, youth and adulthood were separated from each other.[15] Education which theoretically existed to create the possibility of laying hold on the future, both for individuals and for society, became, in fact, schooling which made regimentation its primary activity. For too many children, neither crucial knowledge nor crucial responsibility schemes were shared or developed in the new schools. (The need for "crucial knowledge" to be returned to the curriculum is being recognized in Oregon's "competency-based" education system for ninth graders, which teaches, among other things, skills in "filling out accident reports, writing advertisements for household objects, balancing checkbooks and listing tax-financed and private agencies to demonstrate reading, writing, computation and social responsibility skills," according to *The New York Times* news service.)

In the English-speaking countries, the public school was supposed to serve very local needs, and it was not supposed to preclude the private school. The promise of the early New England school was that it would serve local people and local cultural and economic constraints. In fact the Boston Irish fought the creation of the public schools as efforts by an industrial elite to control education and uproot communities. The Irish wanted their own schools, and they accepted public schools only after promises were made that local autonomy would be respected. The same history has been repeated nation-wide.[16] And when the British first considered "public" schooling in 1870, provisions were made (they are now long forgotten) to maintain the competition between the public and private sectors to keep teachers on their toes. The early economists argued that fee paying as exclusive or partial support for some schools "was the one instrument with which parents could keep desirable competition alive between teachers and schools."[17] If some aspect of parental choice (preferably parental choice of where to spend their education money) could be maintained, the nineteenth century economists argued, teachers would be saved from becoming "petty bureaucrats" whose jobs were protected no matter what degree of competency they possessed. The emphasis here is on parental choice and options rather than simply on production economics. Good teaching would be promoted, the British lawmakers hoped, by continued competition from institutions outside the public schools. It was assumed by the drafters of the 1870 act—because what they intended was "compulsory education," not "compulsory schooling"—that much education would continue to be gained outside the school setting.[18]

John Stuart Mill, who hesitantly came to accept the need to maintain competition in schools, based his case on the desire for liberty—not as an end in itself but as a producer of spontaneity, variety and experiment—which a completely state-controlled system lacking alternatives would tend to squelch. For all his identification with poor people, and his desire to see them freed from the ignorance and misery of the nineteenth century British industrial system, Mill "eventually confined his proposal to a law rendering only education (not schooling) compulsory," and looked to public examinations to discover the efficacy of the education—however done.[19] In the present context, this would allow for people self taught, taught at home, taught by their peers or adults, taught by media or experience, and taught by the authoritative intellectuals of their own community. Mill, with his nineteenth century belief in the universality of intellectual norms, did not prescribe differentiated tests for different cultures and communities. The concept of culture was not as important to him as it is to the Study Commission and to other groups studying education in 1975. However, as things presently stand in many parts of this country, as well as in England, we have neither alternative routes to one educational goal for communities having the same needs nor alternative routes to different goals for those having differentiated educational needs.

In this country, as education became more and more centralized in the schools—and mostly in the "public" schools—it is perhaps not surprising that teaching also tended to become somewhat "lifeless" as well as standardized. The vision of the good society dominant in American education from the beginning gradually came to include centralization not only of political power, and technological and economic resources, but also of educational policy. The proliferation of universal tests, of rules for curriculum, for accreditation and for certification, the control of American education by national educational and professional societies, and the effective control of schools by the white middle-class majority are part of the fulfillment of that vision.[20] Further evidence comes from Coleman's research to show that the aspects of the schools (and teaching) which we have looked at carefully enough to "test" have become more and more homogenized. Even when schools are different, the results are discouragingly equal—and ineffective. Christopher Jencks' re-examination of the Coleman Report compared large urban districts with small suburban and town districts. Taking into account racial and socio-economic factors, Jencks found little variation in academic performance. In checking through such variables as pupil turnover rate, physical facilities, length of school day or school year, teacher salaries, place of teacher preparation, manner of teacher selection, race and education of teachers, whether or not pupils had attended kindergarten, all findings turned out equal—dreary to relate.[21] But where the relationship of education to community planning and hope is not clearly visualized—as it is not, in the main, in this country—it is not surprising if all results look equal.

Jencks' argument has led some to the conclusion that there is no teaching function for the schools, and hence no need for teachers but only for custodians. Moynihan and Mostetler similarly conclude that teachers make no difference.[22] However, the Study Commission believes that if teachers make too little difference now, it is because the content which they teach, and the achievement which their standardized tests measure, makes no social difference—has no importance. The limit of effectiveness of the standardized curriculum has been reached: designed to offer equal educational opportunity for all, it now provides equal irrelevance to all.

"Integrative" Education: Toward Community Goals

In planning for a new kind of future for the schools and society, we cannot choose whether or not to build according to a blueprint for survival. We can only exercise some choice as to which blueprint we choose to use. As Julius Nyerere has observed, "Only when we are clear about the kind of society we are trying to build can we design our educational service to serve our goals."[23] As the "school" in which many ages worked side by side—the community—was replaced by the age-grade-curriculum lockstep which has constituted the school in Western societies from the seventeenth century to the present, the new industrial growth society arose. As we have recounted, schools have been an embodiment of its vision of the "good society," as well as the agent for the fulfillment of that vision. Many a textbook on education still proclaims that the primary purpose of public education is to transmit "the culture." The "culture" transmitted has assumed environmental resources to be limitless, economic expansion to be inherently desirable and endless, technological conquest to be inevitable, and racial and cultural domination by Western society to be part of the natural order. But if we turn from relating this industrial society to the earth and begin to consider the relationship of "person to person" in our society, we may feel that the limit of the old vision of the future has long since been reached. Jan van den Berg characterizes the present industrial "golden age" as the experience of a severe social sickness of long standing. His study cites the rates of anginal complaints in European and American societies, which are considerably higher than in Chinese and black African societies; it cites the widespread appearance in Western societies of anomic complaints—"suicide, divorce, criminality and psychosomatic diseases," all evidence that the sense of bondedness of man to man is declining, partly because of the unnecessary emphasis on mobility in our society, and partly because even those communities which are somewhat stable are, in fact, disintegrated by the divisions among "work and play, work and religion, work and sexuality, faith and desire, life and death, young and old," a description which fits our schools and our system for educating teachers.[24] Until very recently Indian teachers hired by the Bureau of Indian Affairs (BIA) could not teach their own people on their own reservations; county superintendents of schools made it a policy to keep ethnic groups from hiring their own people, and mobility was a principle of success both for principals and superintendents, however provincial their movement might be. Attempts of the education establishment to remedy some of the deficiencies caused by separating children from adults and from younger children may be illustrated by special programs like OE's recent Education for Parenthood course, now being offered in 600 schools. The OE also had plans in early summer, 1975, to award a contract for the "development of an educational television series with lessons in parenthood and plans for organizing community groups to learn how to be better parents," according to the *Omaha World Herald's* Washington Bureau (June 15, 1975).

In a society faced with limited growth—a society that increasingly needs institutions that band people together for mutual support—the institution of education may have to cease to represent itself primarily as the agent of upward mobility (which it is for few in any case) and to begin to act as the agent of a particular people in a particular environment as they seek to come to a very specific analysis and transformation of that environment. If we are to put education back at the center of a community's self-direction and the direction of its young, we will require three things: (1) the **decentralization** of education structures so that the communities themselves can hold responsibility for their children; (2) the **demythologizing** of teaching so that it is seen not as a job for a specialist alone, but as the natural result of constant interaction between children and their peers, their relatives, and other adults with skills or knowledge to communicate; (3) the **acculturation** of the school to the free community outside the school, so that what the school does fits community goals. The "decentralization" proposed should open up educational institutions; the "demythologizing" should open up professional people and clients to each other; and the "acculturation" should assist in putting our divided professional and lay worlds back together.

Decentralization of Educational Structures

The increasing centralization of the structures governing American life—political, economic, intellectual and educational—has ironically, in the individual experience of American life, been accompanied by increasing fragmentation and separation. The social sicknesses which van den Berg describes are being experienced with a special severity in our schools and society. We experience social antagonisms of unprecedented intensity and frequency—of white against black and red and yellow, of rich against poor, of young against old, of male against female. The solution to these antagonisms appears to lie, in part, in the decentralization of many institutions of society—particularly the decentralization of schools. Decentralization is proposed not only as a resolution of the malaise experienced by many individuals in our society, but also as a resolution of educational questions:

> The small community is not only the organizational structure in which internal or systemic controls are most likely to operate effectively, but its dynamic is an essential source of stimulation and pleasure for the individual. Indeed it is probable that only in the small community can a man or woman be an individual. . . . [C]ertain individual aspirations may have to be repressed or modified for the benefit of the community—yet no man controls

another and each has very great freedom of action. . . . At the same time they enjoy the rewards of the small community, of knowing and being known, of an intensity of relationships with a few, rather than urban man's variety of innumerable, superficial relationships.[25]

If the new small communities are not to be produced and regulated by alien coercive forces and if they are not to become too "provincial, conservative, fanatic, or prejudiced," as some critics fear, they will have to be in large measure developed by the education process—small group culture having largely been destroyed or caught up in the larger culture in our nation in many areas. As a community chooses directions for a future based on its culture, it must develop and intertwine educational processes that provide all people with the opportunity to gain the knowledge, skills, and attitudes necessary for healthy change within their community and for change in relationships with other communities and societies. The success of the small community might require a new movement to the rural areas and the redevelopment of smaller communities within existing urban communities; it might also require special problem-solving mechanisms to work out the conflicts in values and interests with other areas.[26]

Many futurists and planners indicate the need for smaller and more autonomous communities to restore health to individuals. For many such planners the solution is a return to rural areas. While our country could support a flow of the population from the urban to the rural areas, a great population shift is not entirely desirable. Too rapid a shift might create or recreate further ecological imbalances between man and nature. But we still have vast land areas that are presently underdeveloped because of our last great migration to the cities. We have the knowledge and means, if we use them with care, to restore such areas. A migration back to rural areas could certainly be a viable option; there is a need for public and private resources and policy to facilitate such migration for those who want it. Equally important is the need for decentralization and redevelopment of subcommunities within urban areas. There are many people at all levels of economic sustenance who deliberately choose to live in urban areas. Our historical drive for homogeneity and uniformity has pushed the dominant ideology of many urban areas toward the "melting pot" view. Many ethnic communities within those areas resisted the "melting." Areas such as Cleveland and Chicago include ethnic groups—both "visible" minorities and "white" minorities—that maintain their culture and heritage in specific geographic subcommunities. Such communities are not likely to welcome urban renewal, government housing which ignores organic community ties, or planned cracker box apartment house "communities" empty of space for community activities or group informal education. The redevelopment we call for is not this type of "urban renewal." It does not disregard older human and community ties. Nor is it a plea to return to the past. It rather seeks to restore the essence of "community" for people, in either a rural or an urban context, and to do so in population units of a size where healthy human interaction is possible and where group identity can be expressed in diverse ways. The establishment of such a policy will require varying educational processes based both on the internal uniqueness of a specific community and on the ability to interact with other communities regionally and globally.

National standardized curricula do not readily lend themselves to decentralization. Neither do national accrediting standards and the present managing of the teacher education process. In Chapter III there are references to the accrediting agencies which approve state programs which in turn rely on regional or national accrediting agencies for their approval. Making accrediting agencies more answerable to the citizenry —by forcing lay participation on governing boards, for example—will require less nationalization of norms and more room for individuality of cultural and educational styles for institutions. Similarly, patterns of education which stress small, self-regulating communities—decentralization—will require different forms of curricula, teacher licensing, testing, information circulation, and assessment (discussed in Chapters II, III and IV).

Demythologizing the Teaching Office and Developing
Small Group Control of Human Services Institutions

The literature of teaching is full of laments that teachers are not expected to be human beings who feel joy and sorrow, who love and become parents, and who occasionally are bored or angry. The image expected has been like that projected for the nurse—the image of an antiseptic, always smiling, disengaged professional. In the past, the price of this canonization was low salaries, and a not altogether comfortable pedestal—one which lawsuits having to do with a teacher's private rights have partially done away with. The demythologizing of the teacher's office and that of other academics may occur as a result of smaller group control. The deprofessionalization of skilled work— posited and fostered now by a large number of human service institutions—will probably continue (1) as no-growth or limited growth production, recycling, and other changes throw the burden for social continuance on labor which serves human needs; (2) as aesthetic or expressive activity is, more and more, seen as crucial to the work of society; and (3) as people increasingly use the consumer movement and licensing challenges to restore to themselves the sense that they can, in fact, attend to some, perhaps many, of their own health needs and that they can teach their own children a good bit (the same observation can be made of some of the trades).[27]

Smaller units of control will, if properly developed, lead to a situation where parents can select the kind of teachers and principals they want for their schools and select the individuals they need.[28] No one expects that teachers will again live with the families whose children they teach, or that parents will hire individual tutors, but certainly the relationship between the teacher and the parent will begin to be closer again. It is interesting that attempts to establish open classrooms in rural areas of North Dakota were accompanied by many explicit comparisons between the open schools and the old one-room school houses. The emphases on individual attention, multi-age grouping, and diversity of activities were not convincing to "modern" rural parents who may have seen the past as something to get away from. Evidence shows that the more "sophisticated" urban dwellers were easier to convince; their tolerance for being "centralized" and removed from decision-making appears to be eroding. Indeed, the control of the schools slipped away from parents so gradually that the present generation of parents hardly seems to realize how powerless they are. When they do realize it, they have a tough time using the present awkward tools:

> The promotion of conflict appears to be another consequence of the erosion of lay control. Parents' and other citizens' inability to make their wishes heard provides an incentive to aggregate demands until complaints are sufficiently loud and pressing to be heard. Moreover, because individual teachers and administrators frequently have no power to alter the situation, it may be necessary to escalate the demand all the way to the school board in order to have it acted upon. Small wonder that the media increasingly portray parents petitioning and picketing board members. Citizens fear that they will go unnoticed otherwise.[29]

Most parents would no doubt prefer making enlightened choices based on accurate information to picketing and sitting-in in order to obtain quality education for their children. But where are they to get the kind of accurate information they need? From the schools themselves? The information will have to be consumer information of both a negative and positive "advertising" sort, information that expresses the confidence that "education consumers" can become well-informed and enlightened consumers, can and will differentiate between the relative "goodness" and "badness" of public and private institutions, and can detect propaganda when they see it. Choices based on such information may well become the basis both of community control of the schools and of the teacher education process.[30] The demythologizing of the teaching office will then require more than parent control and choice; it will require better information, more consumer advocacy work, trials of vouchers and Basic Opportunity Grants (BOG's) as free choice mechanisms, the development of real alternatives so that people have something to choose among, and a recognition of the community's "paracurricular" teaching function. If parents are to have real input, these five conditions must be met:

—Choice Must Be Based on Adequate Information

A group of British investigators ten years ago surveyed the "advertising" literature sent to parents by schools and found evidence of considerable propaganda—often designed to placate disappointed parents whose children's "11 plus" examination grades did not enable them to avoid the "secondary modern schools." The investigators also asked parents what kind of information they really wanted, and found that they wanted a prospectus which would go to all parents stating the aims of the school, its staff and qualifications, "subjects taught and examinations taken, facilities for games, languages and outside activities, library, laboratory and workshop space, with the actual numbers of pupils in each class and the numbers taking certain courses and going on to certain careers. . . ."[31]

—Consumer Advocacy Must Exist

Pehaps this is where the state or federal agencies (which already set educational standards) can be helpful to parents and students. Colleges are now spending from $100 to $1,000 per freshman to recruit, using brochures increasingly competitive, increasingly slick and increasingly lacking solid information, according to a recent *Chronicle of Higher Education*. A giant "Consumer Guide" for all kinds of schooling is not impossible. Attempts are already being made in Oregon to provide a consumer guide for future college students. The National Student Educational Fund's Information Gap project is presently conducting postsecondary education consumer-oriented research in six states. In each state a case study is being conducted on the agencies and offices responsible for information dissemination on admission requirements, academic programs, costs of education at institutions, and available financial aid, including criteria for qualifying for financial aid. Information could be made available to parents and other community members who would want it through consumer guides oriented to specific states, institutions, regions or occupation preparation programs. The Fund for the Improvement of Postsecondary Education (FIPSE) in HEW will be funding for the year 1975-76 a national project entitled "Better Information for Student Choice" to bring together ten to twelve examples of postsecondary educational institutional prospectuses designed to give "full disclosure" of the types of information that prospective students have been determined to need. This project by FIPSE takes place at a time when the Office of Education through its regulations of the Guaranteed Student Loan Program has moved to require disclosure to all prospective students of a "complete and accurate statement (including printed materials) about the institution, its current academic or training programs, and its faculties and facilities, with particular emphasis on those programs in which the prospective student has expressed interest. In the case of an institution having a course or courses of study, the purpose of which is to prepare students for a particular vocation, trade or career field, such statement shall include information regarding the employment of students enrolled." And, Congress is now considering enacting such "full disclosure" requirements for all institutions receiving student financial assistance (currently about 5,500). The exact definitions of "what should be disclosed" will evolve over the next few years, based on the experience of individual institutions and the capability of "outside" data collection sources to report "comparable data" in order to allow "for more reasoned choices."

Such information of the type being gathered on higher education by the project on "Better Information for Student Choice" could be gathered on common school education and made available to parents and other community members who want it. And as the escalating "demands" of parents who make themselves informed about the schools begin to be heard and heeded—with a regaining of some public control of education—changes will start to affect higher education also. We may see a move away from huge centers of teacher training and back toward local colleges or satellites which are part of the local community and culture. Enrollment trends for the past several years seem to indicate a move in that direction already. If "smallness" becomes fashionable once again, the "liberal arts" might again become an integral part of the future teacher's technical training, rather than a separate set of courses taught in a separate college within the university, a development which will require significant changes in both the liberal arts and in professional education. Both will need to build upon the uniqueness of a specific community's culture, the images of the future held by that community, and the knowledge and skills needed for a consciousness of global problems. Far too often our current institutions of higher education provide neither a liberating education nor a training relevant to the needs of the people in a locale. What they do provide is education for alienation (see Chapter II).

—New Free Choice Mechanisms for Common School and Higher Education Students Must Be Tried

The federal government's Basic Opportunity Grant (BOG) plan for higher education—similar to the voucher plans being tested in elementary and secondary schools—may help to reestablish some of the competitive atmosphere which the British, as mentioned above, never intended to take away from the school system. Others see the voucher plan as one way of increasing community involvement by "injecting an element of the market place into school decisions."[32] Under the voucher plan, some schools might emphasize Freire-style education; others, open classrooms; others, "fundamentals"; and still others, "learning networks" and other arrangements congenial to the language, style of learning, authority system, and future plans of the people being served. If the voucher system is to work, it will have to allow for a full range of alternatives desired by parents—not simply for those conceptualized by public officials or the profession.

It is conceivable that, in some areas, current large institutions could, within themselves, be restructured to provide diverse options or clusters to meet a variety of sub-community needs in their locale and/or provide alternative programs based on different philosophies of education. In other areas, new community-specific and culture-specific institutions may need to be created. Such a restructuring, in addition to providing diversity and choice, would provide for smaller clusters of students, faculty, and community. It would provide an educational and training process that in itself allows for a sense of community and personal identity.

Given a commitment to a free choice system, skill-specific vouchers could also be developed—for example, reading vouchers to agencies which really can improve reading skills. If the central educational institutions were relieved of their classical functions, and if basic skill training were allowed to take place outside schools, schools themselves could concentrate on new goals: "to integrate the young into functional community roles that move them into adulthood"[33] and to transform those roles into roles which allow people to take charge of their own lives. Community participation in school life may very well increase in direct proportion as student participation in community life increases—another move toward parental involvement.

The administrative procedures used to implement and maintain any choice system need to be consistent with the purposes of a "free choice" or "voucher-related" plan. Choices need to be real choices, rather than different labels for the same thing. Community participation needs to be real participation, not some form of tokenism. The money should not be allocated in such a way as to make wealthy schools wealthier, and, thereby, further alienate the poor. If these goals are possibly antithetical to the nature and behavior of some portions of the private enterprise system as presently constructed in this country, then the inevitable political difficulties facing such a real free choice system need to be squarely faced at the beginning.

—Wider Choices Among Institutions Must Be Available

The creation of "free choice" community based schools will require new kinds of teachers, and institutions educating teachers will need to reflect the wider choices coming to be available to parents and children, such as the variety listed by the Deans Committee:

> Perhaps the most clearly defined group of schools are those that have emerged in the inner cities. They are predominantly black, with high proportions of children from welfare families. They teach heavy doses of black culture and are controlled by parents.
>
> A second type are set in rural areas and sometimes are run on self-sustaining farms. Some operate along commercial lines and are often counter-cultural. Some have ecological slants or survival slants. As with many other schools except the ethnic based ones, many of the rural alternative schools appeal to wealthy white

parents who see them as a last resort for children who are totally alienated from conventional public and private schools.

A third kind are clustered around university centers and often serve sons and daughters of liberal-minded professors and administrators and graduate students. Like many of the rural schools, they model themselves on Summerhill, A.S. Neill's famous school in England, where freedom for students is the guiding principle. Some others pattern themselves on another British model, the Leicestershire infant schools, where students are allowed to choose their learning activities from a wide range of possibilities carefully planned by adults. The approach is often called the "open classroom."

Still another group are alternative schools set up within public school systems as experimental projects. The Philadelphia Parkway School Project; John Adams High in Portland, Oregon; the Murray Road School in Newton, Massachusetts; John Dewey High School in New York City; and the World of Inquiry School in Rochester, New York, are somewhat better known nationally.[34]

—Paracurricular Education Must Be Recognized

That teacher training must respond to all of these various alternatives and others by educating teachers to work with them is obvious. But teachers must also be educated to work outside the schools, since there are some options in education that can never be offered exclusively through the schools. There is a growing realization that education outside the school setting (which has always taken place) should be officially recognized as education. If education is seen as a lifelong "continuum," then education in the world outside the schools can become part of an official "paracurriculum," operating with full educational "credit," giving students full access to an understanding of labor laws, employee rights, and the function of legal counsel. Two notions— the notion of work within the community as brokered by the schools, and the notion of exposure to theory which has valuable work or reform content, as monitored by the community—become feasible. One proposal for making both notions work goes as follows:

(1) **Deprofessionalize the tools for learning.** Ask first what people need if they want to learn and then make the tools widely

available for all who wish to use them. In other words, open up access to the stored memories of the community in terms of people, places and things and then bet on people's natural curiosity and imagination. (2) **Help match those who want to share what they know with those who want to learn, regardless of age, degree or background.** The school could become a broker to bring together or make contact between responsible people who want to share mutual interests, enthusiasm and ignorance. (3) **Provide abundant opportunities for self-defined and self-initiated learning, which break the tyranny of the expert, addiction to institutions and the mystification of tools (and thus bring into perspective the value of specialized knowledge**—see Illich's description of the "second watershed" of institutions earlier in this chapter); at the same time create numerous opportunities for people to care for and depend on each other. (4) **Enhance the integration of learning with the life of the community.** Schools could become, in James Coleman's terms, an "action space" for young people to engage in and be an integral part of real community problems, work and creativity. To accomplish this, schools would have to become catalytic agents for forcing access to business and government which now shut their doors on young people.[35]

Such a diversity of educational "ways of going" in diverse communities would require that specific institutions attend to their area—to the kinds of special work needed there—to a special and unique kind of pedagogy, culture, or institutional format, or to a carefully delineated range of these.

Education set in the context of work and community activity, paracurricular education, already exists for the 14.5 million people in business, government and military training, in on-the-job informal classes sponsored by an organization itself, or other institutions; for the 7.8 million people enrolled in trade or proprietary schools; for the 2.8 million people in anti-poverty programs; for the 10 million people taking courses by ETV or correspondence schools; and for the about 9.1 million persons taking some form of adult education, including programs conducted by core institutions, libraries, churches, Red Cross, Great Books groups, community centers, and the like. In all, about 44.2 million people in the U.S. are taking one form or another of "in community" peripheral education as contrasted with 56.3 million in conventional "within-walls" formal education in school and college. Educators have tended to ignore this vast access to education in their conventional deliberations; this part of the educational scene is not, however, ignored by the economists. For example, George J. Stigler "measured the kind of education which leads to increases in income-earning power of the individual" and concluded that, in 1940, as much as two thirds of it was acquired not in colleges or schools but by experience and instruction within the factory or office.[36] What is unfortunate is that the paracurricular education tends to work well for those already acculturated to "efficient systems," and not so well for those who live in impoverished or disorganized communities which may require a "paracurriculum" for the oppressed, such as Paolo Freire has proposed, based on pedagogy which supports the desire for freedom and responsibility.

Increasingly, teacher training for those who intend to educate (in and out of schools) in the future will need to depend on fieldwork experiences. Teachers need to be able to move easily into industrial and office settings to teach, then back into the schools or churches or homes. With "task-oriented" jobs for teachers rather than "role-oriented" jobs, a teacher might work part of the year in a school—in the fall when demand is greatest, perhaps. If the teacher is contracted to the school, he or she may be subcontracted to an industrial setting for part of the year, to teach certain skills to workers, to a community organization, a tribal council or a day care center another part of the year. With schools open year around and during the evenings, the teacher may have an adult education class which meets evenings all year or for a shorter intensified period. For a portion of the year, he or she may do private tutoring or have only a series of "after-school" and evening responsibilities at the local youth center or with civil service employees teaching certain skills. Teaching could also occur in social agencies, community centers, courts, correctional institutions, and neighborhood parent education groups. In short, there will be a greater flexibility in scheduling and a greater variety in responsibility.

Acculturating the Schools to the Community Setting and to Community Directions

As teachers work outside the schools and begin to take a more active part in community planning and decision-making, they will also be expected to work in settings that reflect a specific culture or cultures. Present legal theories make abundantly clear that teachers will have to know the language and culture of the children and youth they teach. Ultimately, the rights of communities to education which reflects their language and culture may rest on the Ninth Amendment, which reserves to the people and the states power not conferred on the federal government, on the treaties with the Indian and Hispano people which recognize the force of custom, customary law, and customary corporations in their community, on the specific Supreme Court decisions, arguing for neighborhood schools, and on decisions requiring bilingual education such as the recent *Lau* decision which required the San Francisco schools to provide initial instruction in Chinese for Chinese-speaking children. Although this is not the place to tie community-based and community-specific education to a legal theory, it may be useful to observe that nothing in recent legal decision-making runs contrary to what we are saying. And the Supreme Court decision on Mennonite education (*The State of Wisconsin v. Jonas Yoder*) captures the spirit of what we are saying about culture and education in general. The testimony of Dr. Donald A. Erickson, an "expert witness" on education in that case, showed that the Amish succeed in preparing their high-school-age children (who do not attend public schools) to be productive members of the Amish community. He described their system of learning-through-doing the skills directly relevant to their adult roles in the Amish community as "ideal" and perhaps superior to ordinary high school education. The evidence also showed that the Amish have an excellent record in creating an orderly society for themselves and bringing up the members of that society to be self-sufficient. In such a society, "equality" is defined as a group-life which extends self-sufficiency.[37] It has been argued by the members of the Study Commission staff that culture-specific education is required by legal theories expressing the notion that the state must be neutral with respect to its citizens. The decisions in *San Felipe del Rio* and the recent *Lau* and *Portales* cases seem to give some weight to that notion (cf. Chapter III text and notes for additional discussion). Whether the notion is ultimately upheld in its full range of legal implications attributed to it by Study Commission staff is really irrelevant. It is clear that many people want and must have culture-specific education. Justice William O. Douglas' dissenting opinion in a case having to do with the right of a law school to admit minority students on bases other than that offered by taking first the highest scorers in the Law School Admissions Test (*DeFunis v. Odegaard*) suggests that the educational process should be judged not on the basis of "organization man" criteria, but rather on the basis of a person's relationship to his group.[38]

The vision of an education community responsive to a wide range of cultural entities may be fulfilled sooner than the cynics expect.

Those who have observed the slowness with which the educational bureaucracy responds to mandates for change may be encouraged by the National Institute of Education's recent funding of a proposal from the Indiana University Foundation. In an effort to determine why results of meaningful educational research so seldom (and so slowly) result in changes in the educational institutions, David L. Clark and Egon G. Guba, chief investigators for the new study, will make an assessment of where educational research is being conducted in the schools, colleges and departments of education. Then they will make site visits to check on the accuracy of information collected by questionnaires, recheck their assumptions by input from client groups, and write scenarios for the future. What is interesting is that the scenarios will be of two kinds: (1) "a predicted 'natural' future for such agencies . . . based upon the identification of critical trend determinants [that is, **non-interventionist future scenarios**]" and (2) "a set of **alternative, more effective future scenarios** representing potential, achievable roles for such agencies as derived from various models of the educational change process and empirical studies of the production and utilization of knowledge network in the field of education." These will be accompanied by a "set of recommendations which would be required to mount the intervention necessary to effect the alternative futures." What may make these scenarios more useful than the usual set of "broad policy recommendations" is that they will be divided into two sets—those which "reflect modifications that are feasible on the local, self-contained basis for school, college, or department of education, and those that would require policy modifications at a state, regional, or national level." Thus the recommendations "will be tied to the interventions necessary to move from where the school, college, or department of education is currently to desirable alternatives other than the most likely future."[39]

Summary

But changes in the schools and in teacher training institutes will not be enough. If these visions of the future are to approach reality, there is no way to escape the changes that must take place in the larger society. Many of the changes will be fought by the labor unions, by businessmen—and even by parents. But if the "new goal" of schools—as Coleman suggests—is to train the young for competent adulthood, the changes will be inevitable:

To accomplish this goal requires fundamental changes in the

relation of the young to the community. Practices currently barring young people from productive activity in many areas—such as minimum wage laws and union-imposed barriers against the young—must be relaxed. The school must be integrated with service organizations, such as those providing medical services, so that the young can help in them. Since the school's function will no longer be to protect the child from society but rather to move him into it, the school must be integrated with these other organizations of society and not insulated from them.[40]

We want the schools to be so integrated provided that the society to which they are integrated is a good society.

SPECIFIC RECOMMENDATIONS

Recommendation I:

Plans and studies for the future are, because of the authority they carry as "objective professional" documents, social facts with implications for policy making. They are not neutral management mechanisms. They have large influence on the way things will be.

Because the decisions and non-decisions of the present do affect the future, it is essential that national policies and plans for education identify and publicize: possible consequences of alternative plans, impact of educational decisions on other sectors; effects on local, regional, national and international value systems; the epistemological bases for decisions; degrees of open-endedness provided for in each plan (with encouragement for maximum open-endedness).

Therefore the Study Commission recommends that an Office of the Department of Health, Education and Welfare be established as an alternative futures studies center that integrates plans from sectoral agencies and conducts "cross impact" studies nationally and internationally. Representatives from agencies working with labor, welfare, health, highways, housing, and community planning must be included. Cooperative planning, when it has taken place in the past, has often failed to include educational representation. *There should be an education component for any social plan.* Some of the advantages of such an office would be:

(1) Alternative forecasts—where real choices are still possible—could be widely distributed at the pre-planning stage.

(2) Long-term consequences could be assessed and "collision courses" predicted while they can still be altered or avoided altogether.

(3) Facilities and resources could be exchanged at all levels, even internationally; such exchanges should involve groups who have similar challenges to create education programs germane to the local natural and economic scene and to legitimize the efforts of local people to plan for themselves.

(4) Goals of planning agencies and private sources could be widely publicized and assessed. Private enterprise, when it does not anticipate excessive profit and does not conflict with community goals, could be encouraged in directions which those affected perceive to be right.

(5) Information could be written up and represented in a readable and succinct form and made available to Congress, to government agencies at any level, and to interested private groups.

(6) Development and training of personnel to assist community and area groups to plan could be undertaken. (It is expected that this could be done through universities and other agencies and not done directly by the HEW office described. The training arm, however, would need to include training in architecture, health, law, human services and other related fields, as well as in education.)

Recommendation II:

Since people's and communities' lives might be adversely affected by futures studies which exclude their interests in their execution, clients should be given the wherewithal to trace out the implications of these studies and the resources to construct alternative plans which might insure more favorable outcomes for themselves. The resources made available should be both fiscal and intellectual. Intellectual resources might include supports which would help a group to plan the coordination of various social activities in a community—education, housing, welfare, health, law; they might also include tools for allowing communities to get clear about the values underlying different courses of community action, to envisage alternative modes of teaching and learning which might serve their plans, to predict "collision courses," and to develop congenial patterns of reconciling different social interests.[41]

Recommendation III:

The HEW futures policy office and other futures groups should be encouraged to make explicit how their recommendations for education relate to the establishment of long-term national goals. USOE should perform the following functions with regard to futures planning:

(1) Collation of futures plans and other long range plans as they pertain to education and the education of teachers, including plans which indeed affect the context of educational planning, which are not specifically labelled as future studies; education should be a component in all comprehensive plans.

(2) Identification of needed plans for education and teacher education components.

(3) Commissioning of various plans to fill gaps in current studies such as:

  a. those plans without educational projections; the "structure of vocations" plans; land use and urban planning policy plans; community organizing and community-building policy plans.

  b. those plans which ignore legitimate assumptions, both growth and non-growth orientations, client and cultural orientations.

Recommendation IV:

This resolution is directed to the future restructuring of schools. A multiple of alternatives in education should be fostered, in areas of content and message (curriculum, culture), organization and governance (openness, decentralization), and support (voucher, school or system support). Teachers and teachers of teachers should be conceived of as working in a variety of settings, both in-school settings and non-school settings, e.g., workspaces, prisons. The role of vouchers should be recognized as multiple and flexible. Diverse role possibilities exist, such as community aides, paraprofessionals, and community development facilitators.

The Study Commission recommends the opening of workspaces to children in an effort to bridge the gap between living and learning. Children need to approach the organization of work with considerable critical vision vis-a-vis organizations and the processes of education. Part of their work experience should be creating alternative methods of organization.

Care must be taken here, however, that the opening of such workspaces is not done at the cost of tracking children into designated social roles, nor at the cost of removing "troublesome" children from the classroom.

Recommendation V:

A new role for education in futures planning will necessitate curriculum changes aimed at new kinds of competencies. Research, though incomplete and imperfect, needs to be continued regarding which competencies are desirable. Some research that has been done points the way to developing these competencies. In short, we need to begin to develop ways of teaching the competencies we already consider important. Skills and techniques important for students and their teachers may include the following:

For the individual:

(1) Value clarification which encourages a strong feeling of identity and an awareness of differences in cultural identities—clarification which permits the student to be clear about what his choices mean and, yet, to relate to others;

(2) Continuous experiences in taking social responsibility for problems in one's own family, block, or neighborhood; risk-taking experiences that stress independence, perseverance, and control of one's own destiny;

(3) Periodic value clarification confrontations; experiences

which support flexibility and tentativeness in thinking and feeling;

(4) Problem solving experiences using a "holistic" technique: for example, experiences using the techniques of Gestalt psychology; opportunities to develop group-dynamics skills; learning processes which emphasize the integration of the bodily, mental and emotional life of students.

For groups of people:

(1) Group experiences in formulating and achieving consensus on goals, objectives, and priorities; frequent opportunities to plan, design, initiate, and evaluate activities collaboratively;

(2) Simulations and games that provide residence-work in coping with unexpected emergencies, particularly emergencies which commonly disrupt the life of the specific group to which the student belongs.

For the vocational life of individuals and groups:

(1) Stress on a wide range of general, transferable skills that can be utilized in a variety of vocations and avocations: manual skills, aesthetic skills, and communication skills;

(2) Emphasis on a generalist's, rather than a specialist's, approach to knowledge and skills.

For planning for the future:

(1) Methods and techniques of futures forecasting to probe the possible consequences of alternative actions;

(2) Experimentation with creating alternative futures using imagination, fantasy, and inventiveness: for example, early introduction of such concepts as "infinity" or the "expanding universe" to provide a sense of the vastness of the universe and the multitude of options which man has;

(3) Education in altruistic behavior, the sense of global community, and the importance of cooperation rather than competition;

(4) Experiences which examine not only the first order, intended effects of actions, but also their unintended, second order effects;

(5) Training in the skills required to handle systems analysis and a variety of other information-processing and planning systems.[42]

Recommendation VI:

Children and adults, in an increasingly complex technological age, need to learn information-processing skills to avoid becoming overwhelmed by the flood. We emphasize that while such skills are needed, the implicit support they tend to give technological values is inclined to overshadow more humanitarian and community-building skills. With this in mind, the following long-range principles regarding futures planning need to be asserted:

(1) The context in which teachers should be educated should be the community.

(2) The location of institutions educating teachers should be decentralized as other institutions are decentralized.

(3) The skills and knowledge expected of teachers should include community-building skills.

(4) The ethos developed by the education of teachers and by teachers in the schools should point toward small group values and interactive stances toward nature.

(5) The distinctions between school and community, work and play, and industry and school should be blurred through continuing cooperative endeavors among all sectors of a community.

(6) Education should emphasize differentiation and complementarity of social role rather than an equality based on sameness.

FOOTNOTES

[1] Most of the work in this area has been done for the Study Commission by its Deans Committee, which recently published a book entitled *The Future: Create*

or Inherit, edited by Charles Case and Paul A. Olson (hereafter referred to as Deans Committee, *The Future*). Committee members, led by co-chairmen Dean Corrigan and Alfredo Castaneda, stressed a "created" future—one which involves input from all levels of the education system, including "consumers" of or participants in education—instead of an "inherited" future dictated by natural factors or events caused by forces outside of education. It is especially important, in the committee's thinking (and in that of the Study Commission), that communities whose futures are being debated be informed of alternative possibilities and have a say about which direction their educational futures take.

[2] Excerpt from Study Commission value statement; for the full value statement, see the Study Commission's Learning Contexts Committee's book, *Of Education and Human Community* (Lincoln, Nebraska: Study Commission Publication, 1972), pp. 128-35. The statement cites Jan van den Berg, *The Changing Nature of Man* (New York: W.W. Norton, 1961); Philippe Aries, *Centuries of Childhood* (New York: Knopf, 1962); and Jerome F. Scott and R.P. Lynton, *The Community Factor in Modern Technology* (Paris: UNESCO, 1952), *passim*, for research and bibliography concerning the nature of healthy human community. The research evidence on the need for smallness, cross generational work, and openness in education includes Roger G. Barker and Paul V. Gump, *Big School, Small School* (Stanford: Stanford University Press, 1964), which shows that student participation in extra curricular activities, student satisfaction with *doing* as opposed to *watching*, student participation in community activities, and student participation in a variety of education activities were greater in smaller schools (50-150 students as opposed to the common 2,000+ of the urban high school). This finding is reinforced by parallel findings in Seymour Sarason, *The Culture of the School and the Problems of Change* (Boston: Allyn and Bacon, 1971), pp. 94-109 and James S. Coleman, *et al., Youth: Transition to Adulthood* (Chicago, 1974), pp. 127-44, 76-84, and 151-52. For world of work analogies to the "small" school having an open organization, see James O'Toole, *Work in America* (Cambridge: MIT Press, 1973), pp. 96ff. This emphasis is borne out at the higher education level by a number of further studies: e.g. Harold Hodgkinson, *Institutions in Transition* (New York: McGraw-Hill, 1970), pp. 256-57 and pp. 71ff; cf. Arthur Chickering, *Education and Identity* (San Francisco: Jossey Bass, 1969) and Alan E. Bayer and Alexander Astin, "Faculty Influences in the College Environment," mimeographed, p. 18.

[3] Lester Brown and other futurist authors at a World Future Society assembly in Washington, D.C., June 2-5, 1975, continued to stress the need for abandoning the "pursuit of super-affluence" and for emphasizing "accommodation" and "simplification."

[4] Charles W. Case, "Educational Research and Development Priorities to Create the Future," in Deans Committee, *The Future*, p. 45; Cf. Edward Goldsmith, *et al.*, "A Blueprint for Survival," *The Ecologist* (January, 1972), II, 1, p. 2; Donella H. Meadows, *et al., The Limits to Growth* (New York: Universe Books, 1972), p. 23.

[5] Mahajlo Mesarovic and Eduard Pestel, *Mankind at the Turning Point: The Second Report to the Club of Rome* (New York: Dutton/Reader's Digest Press, 1974), *passim*.

[6] At the recent World Future Society assembly in Washington, D.C. (June 2-5, 1975), Lester Brown noted that the UN is now receiving numerous requests for information on controlling population from countries all over the world, and he predicts a rather dramatic slowing of growth which is not in all the official forecasts. Jay Forrester, though he doesn't entirely share Brown's optimism, said he believes growth will be slowed through involuntary physical pressure (hunger, for example), involuntary social pressure (war, for instance), and perhaps through voluntary social pressure (such as national laws).

[7] According to Charlotte Waterlow, a member of the Club of Rome research group which reported to members of the World Future Society in Washington, D.C., June 2-5, 1975, the Third World nations are naturally suspicious of "no-growth" philosophies espoused by highly developed nations which appear to have their affluence well secured already. The developing nations are eager to modernize, but not to "Westernize," she said, because their egos have been cut down repeatedly by Western imperialism and by Western missionaries. They wish to keep the best of their traditional ways and incorporate them with "the best of the West."

[8] Ervin Laszlo, director of the Club of Rome's *Goals for a Global Society* research project which is just beginning, told members of the World Future Society at its recent assembly (June 2-5, 1975), that writing a report for the future is "very much a participating sport—not a spectator sport." He said futurists—in some previous reports—have "even left themselves out" of the thinking process.

[9] Jacques Ellul, "Search for an Image," *The Humanist*, Vol. 33, No. 6 (Nov./Dec., 1973), pp. 22-25.

[10] Antonia Pantoja, Barbara Blourock and James Bowman, eds., *Badges and Indicia of Slavery: Cultural Pluralism Redefined* (Lincoln, Nebraska: Study Commission Publication, 1975), pp. vi-xi.

[11] Robert Bundy, "Riding the Apocalypse: Education and the Future of Humanity," in Deans Committee, *The Future*, pp. 73-75, based on Ivan Illich, *Tools for Conviviality* (New York: Harper and Row, 1973), pp. 1-83.

[12] Philippe Aries, *Centuries of Childhood*, tr. Robert Baldick (New York: Alfred A. Knopf, Inc., 1962), pp. 137-40 and p. 152.

[13] See chiefly Philippe Aries, *Centuries of Childhood*, pp. 137-336 and pp. 411-15. But also see George Boas, *Cult of Childhood* (London: Warborg Institute, 1966); Philippe Muller, *The Tasks of Childhood* (New York: McGraw Hill, 1969);

Ivan Illich, *Deschooling Society* (New York: Harper and Row, 1970).

[14] See James S. Coleman, "The Children Have Outgrown the Schools," *Of Education and Human Community*, pp. 69-71.

[15] See Jan van den Berg, *The Changing Nature of Man (Metabletica)* (New York: W.W. Norton and Co., 1961), pp. 80-84, 96-102, and Aries, pp. 411-15. The school has strikingly continued as social scalpel into the twentieth century: communities in the rural Midwest in which adults participated in community bands, choruses, theatricals, and dramatic readings now experience these art forms only as audiences of student performances in the schools.

[16] See Michael Katz, *Class, Bureaucracy, and Schools* (New York: Praeger, 1971), pp. 110-11 and 3-55; Joel Spring, *Education and the Rise of the Corporate State* (Boston: Beacon Press, 1972), pp. 22-90, esp. p. 51-52 and pp. 62-63; and Colin Greer, *The Great School Legend* (New York: Basic Books, 1972), *passim*.

[17] E.G. West, *Education and the State* (London: Institute of Economic Affairs, 1970), pp. 120-21.

[18] West, pp. 82-86 and p. 121.

[19] West, pp. 124-25.

[20] See Chapters III and IV of this report and the Study Commission's book on professional societies, Rosemary Bergstrom, *et al., A Time Half Dead at the Top* (Lincoln, Nebraska: Study Commission Publication, 1975), *passim*, but especially pp. vii-xxxviii.

[21] Christopher Jencks, *Inequality: A Reassessment of the Effect of Family and Schooling in America* (New York/London: Basic Books, Inc., 1972), pp. 84-110 and pp. 253-65.

[22] Daniel P. Moynihan and Frederick Mostetler, *On Equality of Educational Opportunity* (New York: Random House, 1972), *passim*, especially pp. 104-05.

[23] Julius Nyerere, "Education for Self-Reliance," *African Report*, 1967, reprinted in *Of Education and Human Community*, pp. 47-67. "Education for Self-Reliance" is the official policy statement on education of the Tanzanian government; the analysis given there of the contrast between the schools appropriate to Tanzania's colonial past and the schools appropriate to Tanzania's healthy future is a surprisingly illuminating way to view the history of American education.

[24] van den Berg, *The Changing Nature of Man*, p. 162; compare Snell Putney and Gail J. Putney, *The Adjusted American: Normal Neuroses in the Individual*

and Society (New York: Harper and Row, 1964), *passim.*

[25] Goldsmith, *et al.,* "A Blueprint for Survival," p. 15.

[26] It is obvious that means would need to be employed to avoid recreating rural and urban ghettos, provincialism, and hostility among diverse groups. But such a task also faces us now, and our current community disorganization results in personal and group impotence and often violence:

> ... smaller, cluster-groupings of population with communications networks that interface the clusters when necessary for larger decision-making purposes [will be required]. Smaller communities will enhance the possibility to achieve internal growth constraints through public participation in decision-making, rather than arbitrary restrictions imposed by a remote and unsympathetic government (Deans Committee, *The Future,* p. 52).

On the relationships between community groups and teachers unions in public participation schools, see Marilyn Gittell, *et al., Local Control in Education: Three Demonstration School Districts in New York City* (New York: Praeger Publishers, 1972), pp. 89-97; cf. Gittell, "Chronicle of Conflict," *Saturday Review* (March 15, 1969), pp. 73-74; and Gittell, "Public Employment and Public Service," (unpublished paper), pp. 31-36 and *passim.*

[27] See the discussion of the education professions and their differences from "true" professions in Amitai Etzione, *Semi-Professionals and Their Organization* (Riverside, New Jersey: Free Press, 1969), pp. 1-54 and 197-247; pp. 197-247 also give an excellent account of the prevalance of male administrators, female work forces and authoritarian administrative styles in the semi-professions.

[28] Maria Spencer, a Chicano educator and teacher educator from Silver City, New Mexico, and member of the Study Commission observes, "I have been struck by the fact that so many parents who themselves hated school and failed want exactly the same kind of schooling for their children, only more of it. Obviously the academic community has not fulfilled a role of leadership in informing the parents of alternatives."

[29] James Guthrie, *Public Affairs Report* (Bulletin of the Institute of Governmental Studies, University of California, Berkeley, June, 1974), p. 4. [See also the NEA's *Inquiry Report, Kanawha County, West Virginia: A Textbook Study in Cultural Conflict* (Washington, D.C.: NEA Teacher Rights Division), February, 1975.]

[30] See comments on information gathering in Chapter IV of this report.

[31] West, p. 194.

³²E.G. West, who distinguished between "public enterprise" and "public financing" (*Education and the State,* p. xxxvii), sees the voucher system as perhaps the only way to avoid destroying parental choice, since it represents a "compromise between complete parental choice and complete government direction" (p. xlii). Though lay people and educators seem to take parental powerlessness for granted, economists, according to West, have stressed all along "the distinction between intervention via the provision of public finance to individuals (or schools) and intervention via the provision of the ('nationalized') education service." He quotes Professor P. Samuelson's remark as typical of the economists' view: "For the (n + 1)th time, let me repeat the warning that a public good should not necessarily be run by public rather than private enterprise" (p. xxxvii). Kenneth Boulding, in an essay in the Study Commission's *Nothing But Praise,* defends the American public education system as "certainly more humane than the British system in which I grew up, which is a (fortunately inefficient) design for the narrowing of the personality into a straight-jacket of arbitrary propriety"; nevertheless, Boulding favors moving more of the educational enterprise into the "exchange" economy and out of the "grants" economy:

> As an economist, I do not believe that anything that is costly should be free and I don't think any of the best things in life are free. Then, where it is necessary to subsidize education—as it is—we should subsidize the *student* not the school.
> This logic also suggests that private and public education institutions should be free to compete on equal terms. There is no reason why education should be a public monopoly. I am in favor of having public enterprise in education. I am not in favor of abolishing the public schools (i.e., presently tax supported) as some of my more extreme colleagues on the Left (or Right) are. There is a great deal to be said for a system in which one can have a variety of education institutions that can compete with one another, and under an educational bank proposal this could be done (from Lewis N. Pino, *Nothing But Praise,* Study Commission, p. 67, cf. pp. 63-67).

³³Coleman, "The Children Have Outgrown the Schools," *Of Education and Human Community,* p. 74; compare Coleman, *Youth: Transition to Adulthood* (Report of the Panel on Youth of the President's Science Advisory Committee, Office of Science and Technology, Executive Office of the President, June, 1973), pp. 145-75.

³⁴Deans Committee, *The Future,* p. 129.

³⁵Deans Committee, *The Future,* p. 91.

³⁶West, p. 90.

³⁷*The State of Wisconsin v. Jonas Yoder,* reprinted in *Of Education and*

Human Community, pp. 107-19.

[38]*Study Commission Newsletter,* May, 1974 (Supplement).

[39]"A Futures Analysis of Teacher Education Institutions as Innovators, Knowledge Producers, and Change Agencies in the Nation's R and D System," NIE Research Proposal No. 51-R1031, Prospectus 400038, on "Production and Utilization of Knowledge."

[40]Coleman, "The Children Have Outgrown the Schools," *Of Education and Human Community,* p. 74.

[41]A group of Swedish researchers have recently pointed to the adverse effects of futures studies which only serve to "optimize the operational environment for multinational companies." In a review of *To Choose a Future* (Swedish Royal Ministry for Foreign Affairs in Cooperation with the Secretariat for Future Studies, Stockholm, 1974), published in the Summer, 1975, edition of the *Journal of World Education,* Thomas Carleton quotes the Swedish group's views that such futures studies "are liable to come into conflict with the legitimate aspirations of people in a developing country to have a say in shaping public policy for the country's independent development . . . it is the citizens themselves who can and must determine the future development of their society" (p. 8). The same caveat is also relevant to developing institutions and groups within the United States.

[42]Adapted from list in Deans Committee, *The Future,* pp. 64-65.

CHAPTER II

TEACHER EDUCATION IN AMERICA NOW

People at many income and age levels of American society are discovering the need for roots, for a sense of community, for taking personal responsibility for their own lives and futures. As they do so, they are asking that the schools be organized differently to guarantee them influence in the schools as parents, as members of neighborhoods, and as members of ethnic groups having separate power bases, customs, and work structures. The parents, the neighborhoods, the distinctive cultural communities which make up the country—the clients of education—are asking to take an active part in making their schools and their teachers effective. Not only the clientele but also the personnel of many of our schools feel that the schools presently fail to facilitate an integrated vocational, intellectual, social, and community life. Education personnel in training and in the field are often unsatisfied with their education environments. Parents want more control of their communities and of the education of their children. Teachers want to feel that they are an organic part of the community in which they are placed. And few people *want* to be part of institutions in which they do not feel a stake or which do not clearly serve their and their clients' emotional and intellectual needs as well as their financial interest.

Dissatisfaction as Grounds for Change in Teacher Education

This chapter attempts to lay the groundwork for a vision of a new educational institution, organic to local communities. Any new vision, any proposed structures, must be constructed to respond to present attitudes of people in or served by education. Particularly crucial are the attitudes of education personnel toward the training that they receive and the attitudes of clients of education toward what they see going on in the schools (Our representation of education personnel attitudes derives from our study of the data collected by the 1969-70

Carnegie Survey of Higher Education[1] and from a variety of other more recent and older studies.)

Attitudes of Teachers-to-be

Undergraduate students in teacher education indicate they are not fully satisfied with their training. On a very basic level, students who are teachers-to-be do not seem to regard their college education as markedly enhancing themselves as people. For example, almost two thirds of the senior teacher candidates in the Carnegie survey agreed strongly or with reservations with the statement: "Most American colleges reward conformity and crush creativity."[2] Almost 50 per cent of these seniors said that it was usually true or almost always true that they found themselves bored in class. More than three fourths of the seniors said that it was usually true or almost always true that "the best way to make it" was to tell professors what they wanted to hear. More than 42 per cent of the seniors agreed that it was difficult both to get good grades and really learn something.

The lack of a sense of personal growth apparent in the survey was accompanied by a disappointment with what colleges and universities were giving as professional training. While 63 per cent of the seniors believed that it was essential that they get a detailed grasp of a specific field, only 27 per cent said that they had received much of a detailed grasp of *their* field. While 60 per cent said it was essential that they get training and skills for an occupation, 20 per cent said that they had received no training and skills for an occupation (only 27 per cent believed that they had received *much* training). Almost 50 per cent of the students agreed strongly or with reservations with the statement: "Much of what is taught at my college is irrelevant to what is going on in the outside world." More than 50 per cent of the student teacher candidates disagreed strongly or with reservations that "Most faculty at my college are strongly interested in the academic problems of undergraduates." Perhaps even more alarming was the fact that 64 per cent, almost two thirds of the senior teacher candidates, said that they had not received enough advice and guidance from faculty and staff.

These statistics would not be so alarming in the context of this study if all other undergraduate students preparing to go into the human services fields chosen for comparison were equally critical. They were not. For instance, 74 per cent of architecture students said it was essential to get training and skills for an occupation, and 48 per cent said they had received *much* training (compared to teacher candidates' 27 per cent). Only 14 per cent of the architecture students said they had received *none*. The teacher candidate group contained a higher percentage of students than all other undergraduate professional and preprofessional areas tabulated, save that of social work and criminology, who said they had received *no* training and skills for an occupation (that is, a higher percentage of *no's* than in health technology, nursing, pharmacy, occupational and physical therapy, and home economics). Also, fewer teacher candidates said they had received *much* training and skills for an occupation than in these other fields. A higher percentage of teacher candidates than of undergraduate students in general or majors in architecture, social work, and nursing said that it is "hard to get good grades and really learn something." Teacher candidates felt more strongly than candidates in other preprofessional areas, save social work and criminology and architecture, that much of what is taught at their college is irrelevant to the outside world, and senior teacher candidates felt so more strongly than architecture majors. The 52 per cent of senior teacher candidates who disagreed with the notion that "faculty at my college are strongly interested in the academic problems of undergraduates" is much higher than the figure for all undergraduates (38.1 per cent) and higher than the figure for all preprofessional or professional areas other than social work and criminology. The 64 per cent of senior teacher candidates who said they had not received enough advice and guidance from faculty and staff was higher than the percentage in any other group tabulated, and teacher candidates in general complained about this more than did candidates in other professional and preprofessional areas aside from social work and criminology and occupational and physical therapy. Generally most preprofessional and professional undergraduate areas outside of teaching, with the notable exception of social work and criminology, gave more satisfaction to their students, in the students' own perceptions, than did preprofessional and professional preparation for teaching.

The undergraduate teachers-to-be had some notion of what would make things better. Ninety-six per cent of the senior teacher candidates said course work should be more relevant to contemporary life and problems. Almost 85 per cent said that more attention should be paid to the emotional growth of the student. Fifty-six per cent of the seniors believed that they had not had enough freedom in course selection and more than three fourths of the seniors agreed that students should have a major role in specifying the college curriculum. Forty-six per cent of the seniors said there was no professor in their major field with whom they often discussed topics in that field, and almost two thirds said that there was no professor in their major field with whom they often discussed other topics of intellectual interest. Furthermore, the students were asked to think about the course that they took during their most recent college term which was most clearly related to their primary field of interest and to state whether they sometimes openly argued with their instructor. Almost two thirds of the senior teacher candidates replied that they did not. The recommendations of the students which can be abstracted from the computer print-out sheets of Carnegie data are brought to life by the recommendations for teacher training of the leadership of the Student National Education Association (SNEA) adopted in 1975. We outline these recommendations later in this chapter. Throughout the Carnegie data and the SNEA statements, there appears to be a close connection between the sense of discouragement with what is being offered and a sense of a lack of freedom, flexibility, field contact, and rigorous intellectual paradigms for analyzing field experiences. In fields where preprofessional education offered people real problems and real tools for handling the problems, respect for the education offered appears to have gone up markedly.[3]

While the data lend themselves to various interpretations, they in no way indicate that teacher candidates are getting the individual education they deserve, the connectedness to field experiences they want, the respect and openness they need, or the teaching skills and power they require to help improve things that concern them closely. While the candidates express reservations about their professional training, it is unclear whether they feel that they are unprepared for today's schools or unprepared to use strategies for changing them. Given their political vagueness and highmindedness (which we discuss later), we suspect that a little of each is involved.

Practicing Teachers

Like the college students' responses, practicing teachers' statements about their teacher education single out the need for fieldwork, individualization, mutual respect between professor and student and an education which, in general, gives one some confidence that one can teach well. A recent survey of new teachers in a South Carolina city is abstracted as follows by its authors:

> The authors thought it desirable to survey new teachers because they most directly experience the adequacies or inadequacies

of their college of education curricula. . . . Over half of all new teachers in the survey rated their teacher education as poor to fair. More than two thirds of the high school teachers indicated dissatisfaction with their teacher education courses. . . . The ten classroom problems which were rated to occur most frequently would be classified into three categories: (1) dealing with individual and group differences, (2) coping with student emotions, (3) and organizing worthwhile activities for all students. . . .[4]

The abstract goes on to suggest that the new teachers, in recommending improvements in teacher education, were almost unanimous in recommending earlier and more field experience. In addition, nearly all respondents said they needed better guidelines for individualizing instruction, and for helping slow learners. This conclusion is strongly reinforced by the Study Commission's School Administrators Committee: all of the teachers and prospective teachers interviewed during the site visits sponsored by that committee concurred with the notion that earlier and more field experiences are needed. The implication is that people are being placed in roles defined as professional or "expert" roles without having had the experience or having been given the intellectual tools which would make them confident in such roles.

Clients of the Schools

The constituents of the schools, the parents and communities they serve, express related dissatisfactions with what happens in schools and with the ways teachers perform in them. For many years blacks, Chicanos, Puerto Ricans, and Native Americans have said that they see their cultures as endangered by current systems of education and teachers who command "the latest methods." But other groups—in Appalachia, in the white ethnic enclaves of the country, and even in the suburbs— feel similarly endangered, which seems to have caught us by surprise. The disappointed minority cultures include ethnic groups of the white world—what Michael Novak has called "the world of Poles, Italians, Greeks, and Slavs (PIGS)." These groups early resisted the "progressive industrialist" expansion of the common schools to include their children,[5] processes which moved their children away from their roots, their indigenous cultural communities, and the informal education which went with these to place them in "efficient" schools which were "perfect anticipatory mirrors" of the assembly line factory needed in a rapid growth economy. The patterns of school behavior which were set up for Eastern European and visible minority communities were too often parodies of patterns implied by a Puritan ethic. Having accepted the schools, these groups are now beginning to stake a claim on them.[6] Parents in rural West Virginia and in South Boston, parents in Alum Rock, California, and on the Pine Ridge in South Dakota—all feel a similar lack of power over their children's lives and education. The issues are not simply "racism in Boston," "textbook selection in West Virginia," "the voucher system in Alum Rock," or "non-Indian teachers on the Pine Ridge." Don Davies' recent annotated bibliography, *Citizen Participation in Education,* shows that many parents in all economic, racial and cultural circumstances are disappointed with the schools' lack of attention to their special concerns.[7] Part of the problem, as several Study Commission reports have shown, is that white middle class (and aspirant) teachers, and minority teachers strongly acculturated to a professional ethos, no matter what their intention, transmit a favoritism toward white middle class values. George Spindler's "The Transmission of American Culture" has compellingly urged the same conclusion;[8] over and over, Spindler found teachers who, in their unconscious behavior, communicated "approval of most of what children of middle class origins said, and of what they were reading," a pattern of "bias and selective perception" in the relationship with students.[9] The antagonism that schools which show such favoritism generate in parents and children by their disrespect for indigenous cultures, by their ignorance of a *genius loci,* and by their mechanical imposition of the values of the school culture, can hardly be overestimated—and this when the school should be a primary upholder of a community's culture and a primary contributor to the idea of learning as a satisfying life-long process.

Outdated Organizational Models

When the classroom life of a school, dependent on static staffing and management structures, in no way fits with the rapidly evolving, hungry world outside, both teachers and students are placed in impossible positions.

Their dilemma may be exemplified in the following descriptions by Rosalie Wax and Roselyn Holyrock of a classroom on the Pine Ridge Reservation in South Dakota:

(First day of academic year; Seventh and Eighth Grades combined in one room; there followed a session on rules:)
Teacher: "What do we do while we are in line?"

(Silence)

Teacher: "Do we push; do we try to trip somebody?"

(Silence to my ears, but visibly to her some of the pupils must have indicated the sought for negative.)

Teacher: "No, we don't push. . . . If you spill something (on cafeteria floor) what do you do? Do you just leave it there? . . .

(Again, silence to my ears, but teacher carries on:)

"No, you are responsible for cleaning up what you spill. So we write: 'Carry trays carefully.' "

She now asked for a volunteer to write the rules on the board and stood there at the front of the room with chalk in hand, pleading for one. Half the boys at the rear of the room raised the tops of their desks, some making a pretense of looking for materials, others just plain hiding behind them, while other boys tried to make themselves invisible. . . .

By a process of pseudo-interrogation which may have yielded some class response I could not detect, the following rules were written on the board:

1. Don't run.
2. Sharpen pencils before school time.
3. Go to the bathroom as we go out.
4. Walk to the right.
5. Come in when the bell rings.
6. Play safely.
   Etc. . . .

(I felt that the absence of the kind of response white kids would have given, must have been a great irritation to the teacher.) (Aug. 27)

(Same class, Feb. 8, Indian observer.) They were having Reading Skills when I went in—they were reading something called "Atomic Submarines." When she asks them questions about it, I don't see none of them answer. But she says they answer . . . maybe she's a lip reader. Out of the whole room no one made a sound except one boy. He barely whispers to her. He sits in the back of the room. But she says: "That's right. That's right." But I can't hear what they're saying. . . . Maybe he whispers. . . . When I couldn't see who was answering, I moved to the other side of the room to watch. But even then I couldn't see anybody's lips move. I even watched here (pointing to juncture of jaw bone and skull) because that way you can see if somebody is talking—but nobody moved there. . . . It was just awful. . . . It reminded me of when I went to visit Pierre and there were some blind and deaf there. They were quiet but they made signs, and at least you could see them make signs. But in this class they didn't even make signs. . . . It was like she had a room full of dead people and she was trying to talk to them.[10]

The classroom described appears at first thought to be simply a place where a dull teacher drones on and passive children seek diversion. But, the conclusion of the researchers, after much puzzling over this classroom and others at various grade levels, was that the Anglo-oriented rules (language, behavior, cognitive system) imposed were so alien to the children forcibly brought into the artificial school community that the children were constrained to exercise a species of community control through passive resistance: ". . . the children simply organize themselves so that the effective control of the classroom passes in a subtle fashion into their hands. . . . The teacher has become defined by the children as an outsider, an intrusive, meddlesome authority; and the school children respond by encasing themselves in the armor of the peer society. They organize themselves to resist the pressures of the educator, so that in confronting the children, he finds himself facing a blank wall."[11] For these Oglala Sioux classrooms and for their teachers the "efficient school" is not efficient. While the "efficient school" may work for some children whose world is highly oriented to middle class codes, for millions of other children, it does not.

At best the result for such alienated children is the covert injustice of boredom and wasted time; at worst it is overt injustice. The following report by a U.S. Civil Rights Commission staff describing a classroom of Anglo and Chicano students is a kind of symbol for what the Civil Rights Commission found in systematic observation of 494 classrooms in which Chicano and Anglo students were placed together:

> There were several Chicanos who kept raising their hands eagerly at every question. Mrs. G. would frequently look right over their heads, and called on some of the same Anglo students over and over. In some cases she would call on the Chicanos only because the Anglos stopped raising their hands. After a while the Mexican children stopped raising their hands.[12]

The behavioral system in the Anglo-oriented school does not respond to the organic or indigenous needs and interests of these Chicano children, and indeed systematically deprives them. Such injustice, though poignant, may appear atypical. Perhaps closer to the typical is the situation described by a Harvard study team which looked at the schools in Watertown, Massachusetts:

> Watertown's young people do not find school an intellectually exciting place. Although the Study Staff observed some good schools staffed in part by able, hard-working, creative teachers, instructing youngsters who were happy, vibrant, and actively engaged in the learning process, these bright spots are over-shadowed by evidence that too often Watertown students look without enthusiasm upon their schools and the learning required in them. In many of the classes observed by the Study Staff, students remain passive and uninvolved in their own education. Watertown's schools do not give the student many opportunities to assume responsibility for his own learning. The student is not encouraged to explore, to stretch his thinking, to pursue an independent line of inquiry. The program of studies is defined by the school, and the student is expected to learn what the school decides he should learn. Rarely does the student in Watertown have the chance to make meaningful decisions; rarely does he have a chance to discover for himself what learning is all about.[13]

How can such enormous expenditure of educational effort and energy on the part of school systems like Watertown's give students so little opportunity for real learning? Why has the "efficient" school system come to bore children in Massachusetts, alienate them in South Dakota, and exclude them in Chicano communities? Perhaps because they are imposed rather than collaborative ventures. Why they are so Procrustean may in part be answered by a closer look at the role systems which make up the schools, the people who occupy them now, and the people newly recruited to these role systems—to change or continue them.

The Staffing of the Schools

Everyone knows that the problems which our school systems have go beyond the individual problems which people have in performing their jobs in them. Yet, the role sets which exist in the schools and the people who presently occupy them must surely be critical, the role sets now assigned being conditioned by hierarchical management and evaluation notions and a segmented and somewhat solipsistic and unsituated notion of how either work or education gets done. These roles affect pre-service teachers as well as teachers in service. That the drama played out by present teachers is the drama for which new teachers are rehearsed is suggested by the fact that the Carnegie statistics on future teachers and administrators in 1970 draw the same profile as Coleman's 1965 statistics on in-service teachers and administrators. Existing school staffs present an image to the teacher-to-be of what teaching is. They conduct a good portion of the student's "professional" or "in-field" training and determine classroom ratings, recommendations, and even the right to student-teach. As such, they are a fundamental hidden curriculum in teacher training for the person who wants to "get into the schools." The network of relations which bind administrators, teachers, and student teachers to each other and permit them to deal with the external pressures on their system is worth exploring. In the case of present administrators and present teachers, the relationship which comes to mind is captured in caricature by the relationship between Lewis Carroll's magisterial Humpty Dumpty, who talks to kings, discourses learnedly, and makes up the rules as he goes along, and his Alice, who, placed in a strange world where she does not know the rules, and hearing the commands of the nursery rhyme potentate, can only shake her head and puzzle and follow directions.

Present Teachers as a Curriculum for the Teacher-to-be

Like Alice in Carroll's book, the teachers of American children are represented by several well-known studies as female (87 per cent of the elementary teachers and 46 per cent of the secondary ones),[14] somewhat passive and alienated in civic areas,[15] and placed in a world which they do not entirely comprehend. When they went to college, they were a little below average among college students in academic attainment.[16] According to one study, they experienced growth in teaching proficiency during their first five teaching years and a fairly strong decline thereafter.[17] Coleman in 1965 found future teachers to be interracially inexperienced persons, and those educated before then would be even more so; predictable numbers of elementary teachers in service in 1965 admitted that they preferred to teach the children of white, "Anglo-Saxon," and white collar groups (31 per cent, 30 per cent, and 12 per cent).[18] They were likely to support their church but unlikely to show much interest in civil rights groups or political groups which asked that they do more than vote.[19]

The picture of the present teacher drawn by these demographic data is an abstract of a person having little realization of the organic links between the school and the "muck-and-mire" world surrounding the school. This abstract is fleshed out vividly in the self portrait of a Chicago teacher who describes herself in Studs Terkel's *Working*. Rose Hoffman is bothered by the Spanish-speaking children in her classes and by the parents who "hang around the school":

> I have eight-year-olds. Thirty-one in the class and there's about twenty-three Spanish. I have maybe two Appalachians. The twenty-three Puerto Ricans are getting some type of help. The two little Appalachians, they never have the special attention these other children get. Their names aren't Spanish. My heart breaks for them. . . .
>
> I see these parents here all the time. A father brings his kids to school and he hangs around in the hall. I think it's dangerous to have all these adults in the school. You get all these characters. I'm afraid to stay in my room unless I lock the door.
>
> We see them at recess. They're there at lunch time. These people, they have a resentment that everything is coming to them. Whereas the Polish people worked their way out of the Depression. They loved property. They loved houses. My father loved his little house and if anyone would step on the grass, he would kill them. (Laughs.) He'd say, "Get out of here! This is mine!" (Softly.) There was a great pride. These people, they have no pride in anything, they destroy. Really, I don't understand them. . . .

[She is also disturbed by the shift in school population, from Polish to Puerto Rican:]

> There were middle- and upper-class people in this neighborhood when I first came. They were very nice people and their children were wonderful. There was an honor system. You'd say, "I'm going to the office for a moment. You may whisper." And they would obey. I was really thrilled. I don't dare do that now. I don't even go to the toilet. (Laughs.) I'm a strong teacher, but I'm afraid to leave them.

In the old days, kids would sit in their seats. If I had to leave the room for a few minutes, I'd say, "Will you please be good?" And they were. These kids today will swear, "We'll be good, we'll be good." I don't know what it is, their training or their ethnic background—or maybe it goes back to history. The poor Spanish were so taken they had to lie and steal to survive. . . .

[Rose Hoffman is proud of her capacity for routine, the passivity and neatness of her students:]

I start with arithmetic. I have tables-fun on the board—multiplication. Everything has to be fun, fun, fun, play, play, play. You don't say tables, you say tables-fun. Everything to motivate. See how fast they can do it. It's a catchy thing. When they're doing it, I mark the papers. I'm very fast. . . .

The next thing I do is get milk money. That's four cents. I have change. I'm very fast. Buy the milk for recess and we have cookies that I bring. To motivate them, to bribe them. . . . On Mondays I write beautifully, "If we go to an assembly, we do not whistle or talk, because good manners are important. If our manners are good, you'll be very happy and make everyone happy, too." On Friday we give them a test. They adore it. Habit, they love habit. . . .

These children baffle me. With the type of students we had before, college was a necessary thing, a must. They automatically went because their parents went. The worship of learning was a great thing. But these children, I don't know . . . I tell them, "Mrs. Hoffman is here, everybody works." . . . The first rule of education for me was discipline. Discipline is the keynote to learning. Discipline has been the great factor in my life. . . . When someone comes in and says, "Oh, your room is so quiet," I know I've been successful.

There is one little girl who stands out in my mind in all the years I've been teaching. She has become tall and lovely. Pam. She was not too bright, but she was sweet. She was never any trouble. She was special. I see her every once in a while. She's a checker at Treasure Island [a "super" supermarket in the community]. She gives no trouble today, either. She has the same smile for everyone.[20]

Rose Hoffman, as she presents herself, lives in an ugly Wonderland where an unintelligible language is used and "she doesn't quite understand." Locked into a structure of white middle-class-aspirant values, a narrow view of "getting ahead in the American way," she cannot adapt herself to different values in a changing community.[21] The changes in behavior and attitudes, as well as the change in skin color, bother her. Unequipped to change her approach, she reacts by intensifying the "standardized" teaching approach, talking, keeping busy—all to keep away the disturbing realities outside. The result seems to be an alienated classroom where "learning" is forced and unsituated, and a frustrated, dissatisfied and lonely teacher. The living children surrounding her hardly exist, save as sources of irritation; and she, like Alice, can only puzzle, be thoughtful, and try to follow directions.

Present Administrators

What teachers do is also dictated by what those who have more power and experience in the school system hierarchy than they have, want them to do. This picture may have been modified by unionization in some places, but many locals have further rigidified teaching and administrative roles rather than softening the hierarchical structure.[22] Administrators too have been acculturated to a role not too different from that of Carroll's Humpty Dumpty, who sits on such a narrow perch that people wonder how he can keep his balance, boasts that he has spoken to a king, offers to shake Alice's hand to show he is not proud, and watches the words "come round me of a Saturday night . . . for to get wages, you know."

Present administrators, as characterized by the Coleman report and *Leadership in Public Education Study*, appear to be somewhat prejudiced, uninterested in social change, and uncommitted to reform, particularly the sort of reform in tough areas which draws on the roots and resources of the areas. They are on the contrary increasingly committed to service to and protection of the centralized hierarchical system in which they will "rise" or "fall" and not to people in the neighborhoods, particularly if they are minority people. For example, elementary school principals surveyed by Coleman (1965) favored "neighborhood elementary schools" regardless of the racial imbalances created (62 per cent of all pupils' principals as contrasted with much smaller percentages in groups favoring other solutions); secondary school principals took the same position (52 per cent of all pupils' principals).[23] Most principals are white (95.6 per cent white, 4.3 per cent black, and less than .1 per cent other minorities in Michigan, where the most comprehensive statistics have been gathered);[24] in a period of white domination of school staffs, the largest elementary principal group believed in selecting white and non-white staff for minority schools (44 per cent) but the largest group also thought that white schools should have all or predominantly white staff (39 per cent). Secondary school principals believed in white and non-white staff for minority students (54 per cent) and in "selecting staff without regard to race" (40 per cent) for white students; 13 per cent believed that white children should have all or predominantly white staff whereas 1 per cent believed that minority children should have all or predominantly minority staff.[25]

But if the principals are committed to neighborhood schools, they are not strongly committed to particular neighborhoods. Whereas 50 per cent of the 1968 principals belonged to civic and fraternal groups and 87.3 per cent belonged to religious groups or churches, only 6.6 per cent belonged to a civil rights organization (only 2.7 per cent were active); only 12.4 per cent belonged to an intercultural group of some sort (6.6 per cent were active); and only 14.9 per cent participated actively in local political parties.[26] Principals have been characterized as localists in the sense that most have received their experience and education within a fairly circumscribed geographic area, have little experience or knowledge of ecumenical perspectives, and depend for their power on who they know rather than what they know.[27] At the same time they are uncommitted to local communities' people:

> The principal is usually promoted from small to larger schools, from inner-city schools to more prestigious ones. These hierarchical considerations do not always correspond to the needs either of the school or the particular principal. What is important in the first place is to catch the eye of the right person in central office and then stay in his good graces.[28]

Even within the schools, an increasingly high percentage of principals (41 per cent) are themselves "followers" or "supporters" of the central administration rather than leaders,[29] perhaps a corollary of the pool from which administrators are drawn. For the pool for school administrators is primarily the pool of "men entering education," and *Leadership in Public Education Study* characterizes this pool in 1969 as follows:

... they were less prone to take an activist role in protesting U.S. military policy, college administration policy, or racial policy. The future educators also more heavily favored mandatory approval of student publications by college officials as well as the banning of extremist speakers on campus. They had larger percentages agreeing that colleges are too lax on student protesters and that the courts give too much concern to the rights of criminals. In other words, the men indicating their career choice as education tended to assign institutions more power in controlling societal problems and individuals than men planning to go into all other fields.[30]

Most principals are male (in Michigan, over 75 per cent) in a profession increasingly male-dominated since the 1920's, and despite the evidence that women administrators are more likely to work on cultural, intercultural, and health and welfare problems, male dominance persists.[31] Neil Gross examined the relationship between training and success as a principal and on the basis of a variety of tests, concluded that "the less extensive the formal preparation of principals, the greater was their staff leadership"[32]—that is, *more* training resulted in *less effective* leadership. If present principals have little faith in education, if their staff leadership is not strong and viable, it may be because, as Gross' study indicates, they themselves are the products of a dysfunctional professional education system.

We emphasize present principals and teachers as a factor in the education of future teachers so much because we believe that both should have a role in the education of future teachers and that both now have a system-defined rather than an experience-defined role. Both must change if teacher education is to change. Principals and other administrators, by virtue of their supervisory positions and the notion of supervisors in our society, have a considerable influence on the behavior and attitudes of elementary and secondary school teachers. The principal's position has evolved from that of a "principal teacher"—a classroom teacher whose responsibilities included that of aiding other teachers—toward that of a behind-the-desk administrator, disciplinarian (of both students and teachers), and sanctioning supervisor, a position with considerably more coercive power over teachers. Such a role is not easy in any institution, providing as it does, little opportunity to try out other people's roles, to work in community with them, or to learn what excites oneself and others. Given the statistical suggestions above as to the administrators' attitudes on public policy matters and motives for human and career action, we can suggest that many administrators push teachers further along toward standardized reactions to students, or at the least that a large number of administrators do not know how to, are not provided a role which allows them to, reverse such trends in the classroom behavior of teachers. At the end of the Humpty Dumpty-Alice scene, the eggking dismisses Alice because she is "so exactly like other people" and asks her to try to put her mouth at the top of her face. This is not the task which we are asking of teachers. What *is* required is that they be more themselves, more an organic part of the constituent community. The pressure of the 60's—when a massive effort to change the education of teachers was mounted, partly to make them more sensitive to their environments, and when the whole legal framework surrounding the schools was changed so as to assert parent rights—should logically have changed things in the direction of allowing teachers and teachers-to-be to enter into a more convivial relationship with parents. But it did not change things.

Future Teachers

Early 70's data, collected after these reform energies of the 60's were at their peak—after almost a decade of the most massive sort of federally-funded assault on problems in teacher education, after sincere efforts on all sides to answer the demands of the civil rights movement—tell us that future teachers and administrators (as represented in the 1970 Carnegie statistics) probably will not have changed much from those present teachers and administrators just described. The "teacher surplus years" in which we should have had time to initiate counseling-out procedures for some of the people who "want to go into teaching," to remove or revamp ineffectual teacher training programs, and to re-tool teacher training structures and their priorities to direct people into areas of need both in schools and in higher education institutions and away from areas where the greatest surpluses have occurred, have almost gone by. We are, according to a recent Rand report,[33] only five or six years from the end of the teacher surplus, and we have not made these changes in teacher education. The same surpluses continue to build up, and the same geographical need areas, subject matter need areas, and human need areas continue to suffer lack of trained personnel. For example, less than 3 per cent of the non-English speaking students who need bilingual-bicultural teachers have them;[34] many vocational education, rural, and Indian reservation areas continue to suffer real shortages of competent teachers. Either people going into teaching did not wish to learn what was needed in the shortage areas or the institutions channeling them did not have the tools to fill the shortages.

That future teachers have not been eager to enter some of the "tough" shortage areas is not surprising. The data of the Carnegie study suggest that teacher education candidates are ordinary middle-class people pushed by the weight of institutional inertia into the roles which schooling demands. It is true that most of the new teacher candidates are idealistic, lower middle-class people,[35] Alice-like in their willingness to oblige and their desire to serve. The answers to the Carnegie questions related to the general topic of idealism and willingness to serve and help others tell us that 54.5 per cent of the education majors agreed strongly or with reservations that all undergraduate students should be required to spend a year in community service in the United States or abroad; two thirds of the future teachers said it was essential to them to work with people rather than things; only 26.3 per cent said it was very important or essential to be very well off financially. More than 50 per cent disagreed with the statement that the chief benefit of a college education is that it increases one's earning power, and 75 per cent thought it was very important or essential to help others who were in difficulty. Two thirds of the future teachers said they had worked or would like to work in the Peace Corps or VISTA, and more than 80 per cent said they would like to tutor or had tutored minority students.[36] All of this is encouraging and promises that future teachers will have the courage to engage community realities. Yet, when one gets to more minute questions relating to attitudes and commitment to the content of education beyond the classroom walls, the results are more discouraging.

For instance, in matters of race and culture, the responses of teachers-to-be appeared either naive or bigoted. Students who were going to be teachers disagreed with reservations or strongly disagreed— by a 3 to 2 margin—with the use of busing to achieve integration in public schools. By about the same margin they disagreed with the statement that the main cause of Negro riots in the cities is "white racism." Yet they did not agree by the same margin that, where *de facto* segregation existed, black people should be assured control over their own schools. It is striking that black teachers-to-be as a group took dramatically different positions on questions of education, the social order, and civil rights.[37]

The teachers-to-be also gave responses which seemed to confine education to its institutionalized form. Two thirds or more said that they did not often discuss topics of intellectual interest with either professors in their major field or professors in other fields. We expect people who are "educators" or "teachers" to consider themselves intellectuals or to express in some form a definite commitment to a life of the mind. But considerably more than 50 per cent of the students who were intending to be teachers disagreed with the statement, "I consider myself an intellectual." Some analysts of the data have suggested that "being an intellectual" is equated in the minds of present students with "living in an ivory tower," but when the notion was rephrased as "living and working in the world of ideas," only a little more than one third of future teachers considered it essential.

In fact, future teachers' answers did not suggest a focused engagement with the real world—which education ostensibly serves—either. Almost 90 per cent of the 1970 future teachers considered it "not important" or only "somewhat important" for them to ever influence the political structure. Approximately 60 per cent said it was "not important" or "only somewhat important" to influence social values. Somewhat over 50 per cent did consider it important to keep up with political affairs, and more than two thirds thought it was important to have friends with different backgrounds and interests than their own.[38] In summary, teachers-to-be, from the distance of the data, appear to be, like Auden's "unknown citizen" and like many of us, somewhat vague, high-minded people who would not go to the wall or understand how to do so for parents and children very different from themselves.

Future Administrators

Future administrators in the 1970's are as much like 1965's on-the-job administrators as 1970 future teachers are like their 1965 counterparts. Almost by definition, one would think that persons recruited to be principals or administrators in the 1970's would have shed the Humpty Dumpty image, would be persons especially committed to the life of the mind, service to the community, respect for the growth and development of children's powers in relation to both local community needs and aspirations. But 1970 school administrators in graduate school were almost 15 per cent lower than the average graduate student in considering themselves intellectuals.[39] They felt more strongly than any other group that the doctorate was mainly a union card enabling them to get the kind of jobs they wanted; they took the most restrictive view of academic freedom of any higher education group or administrative group save the "self employed in business" and "home economics" candidates. Whereas almost 60 per cent of graduate students in general "agreed" or "strongly agreed" that they "do a lot of serious reading outside [their] field of study," less than 50 per cent of education administrators "agreed" or "strongly agreed" (two thirds of college teachers in preparation and of aspiring executives or administrators in government "agreed" or "strongly agreed" with the statement). When asked to rate motives for entering graduate school, they identified as motives which did not mean a great deal to them: "studying [their] field for its intrinsic interest," "serving mankind better," or "engaging in political activity." The motives they did ascribe to themselves had to do with *sustaining prestige, earning money,* and *preserving status relationships.* Using O'Toole's framework of the state of present American corporate organizations, would-be administrators seem to want to become executives of large stratified human groups, and to wield the power which accrues to a carefully controlled or protected hierarchical level.[40] At a time when integration of public schools by busing had already been ordered by many district and circuit courts, only one third of the future school administrators thought that such integration should take place, and long after the Kerner report had presented overwhelming evidence that the main cause of urban black riots was white racism, only 29 per cent of the school administrators-to-be agreed. The administrators did not favor integration by busing; 40 per cent of them did not favor black community control, even in segregated situations.[41] We can add to this the notorious sexism that continues to exist in the selection of principals and administrators in public education.[42]

Teacher Education for the "Efficient School"

We contend that teachers-to-be are educated or selected for a management mode unfortunate both in factories and schools and disastrous in non-industrialized communities. In 1924 when "school administration" as a "profession" first arose with the centralization of vast school systems and the election of "at large" school boards, William Bagley remarked on the diminution of responsibility and of organic community which was occurring as the factory analogy was pursued in the organization of schools. Bagley wrote:

> [What characterizes the new system is a] "hierarchy" of authority and responsibility which makes the school board a "board of directors," the superintendent a "general manager," the assistant superintendents so many "foremen," and the principals

equivalent to "bosses," while the teachers, to complete the picture, have the status of "hands" or routine workers.[43]

It appears, a little over fifty years later, that a winnowing of school personnel designed to perpetuate this form of school management still prevails. It remains to be seen whether higher education and the school can collaborate to create other forms.

A promising direction which might be taken is to look at alternative ways of organizing work outside the schools in various factories, cultures, and neighborhoods. The Taylorite management system emphasizes the isolation of the worker, the segmentation of his work, the application of strict numbers/time indices to his production, and the routinization and simplification of procedures so that each worker does one simple thing obediently and swiftly. Such work requires a clear management hierarchy which implies clear *actives* and *passives* and drives an additional "artificial wedge between classes of workers."[44] The effect of such management has been, usually, an initial upsurge in work accomplished followed by the appearance of conditions which go with employment in meaningless work: "worker alienation, alcoholism, drug addiction, and other symptoms of poor mental health"; "low worker productivity and high rates of sabotage, absenteeism, and turnover."[45]

O'Toole's study, *Work in America,* makes it clear that while work as a daily activity is necessary to most Americans, the Taylorite scheme for organizing, managing, distributing and rewarding work is outdated, in a society whose labor force is predominantly native-born, high school-educated (and more), and ambitious to "get somewhere" in life. To be satisfying, meaningful, and sustainable over long periods, a worker's daily task needs to give him or her some sense of autonomy and of personal dignity and integrity, to entail some continuity, variety, and a sense of completion of a whole useful unit, and not a sense of fragmentation. O'Toole cites numerous examples of factories in the United States and abroad which have increased productivity and decreased employee turnover, absenteeism, waste, and sabotage by instituting worker (or worker team) autonomy (letting teams manage their work, design their tasks and learn more and more skills within an area of work), and by profit sharing which is based on productivity and which is immediate, tangible, and protected by contract. O'Toole's version of how work is rendered rewarding and meaningful could be modified in minority cultural contexts where any periodic reorganization and redivision of labor would also have to take cognizance of traditional family structures for organizing work, traditional values which relate to the sense of craft, older sanctions against forbidden work, and so forth. However that may be, the relevance of the new literature on work to the organization of schools and the education of teachers cannot be denied. A growing literature suggests that the centralization of authority in the schools and the employment of fragmented and isolating work procedures for teachers is precisely what encourages them to erect professional walls against the community of parents around the school, to feel isolated, frightened and in need of union support to protect both their present fragile status in the hierarchy and to maintain clear wage, hour, and working condition arrangements without seeking fundamental reforms.[46]

If work in the schools and the work force in the schools are to be restructured, higher education will have to change too, for higher education and teacher education today are both characterized by many Taylorite structures: the homogeneous departmental arrangement, the standardized credit hour, and the now-standardized performance and accountability schemes. These features are part of higher education's and teacher education's response to continued pressure to achieve production in terms of norms conformable to industry-oriented conceptions of productivity and efficiency. Particularly is this the case of much of the movement in many of America's colleges of education toward "competency-based teacher education" as a recent USOE study has shown.[47] If such notions of efficiency, management, and accountability are outdated even so far as industrial management is concerned, they have no intrinsic place in education. The basic units in higher education, the credit hour and departmental structure, were developed early in this century by the Committee on the Efficient College (sponsored by the Association of American Universities) and related enterprises as part of the effort to construct workable pension plans and establish higher education's relationships to the secondary schools and to the rapid expansion of assemblyline industry.[48] Once the notion of these educational divisions developed, there quickly followed the creation of departments in colleges of education (and also colleges of arts and sciences) to produce personnel which served standard levels of teaching or teaching systems, and upheld the standard mastery and subordination systems in the schools which we have described above. Subordinate teachers were "trained" in elementary and secondary education departments; administrators were given separate school administration degrees by graduate departments, having generally much better funding and staff conditions than undergraduate departments. Presently the conventional teachers colleges include departments in elementary and secondary education, social foundations, educational psychology, special education, educational administration, vocational education and their subcategories.

Divisions like these receive a measure of legitimization from the National Commission on the Accreditation of Teacher Education (NCATE) standard, from the National Association of State Directors of Teacher Education and Certification (NASDTEC) standard criteria (Chapter III), and from the common data-gathering taxonomies (the Higher Education General Information Systems [HEGIS] and the National Center for Higher Education Management Systems [NCHEMS], Chapter IV). It would be difficult to prove that these national standards and taxonomies are exclusive causes of the almost identical structuring of colleges of education, but it is clear that they add their considerable weight to the maintenance of common organizational schemes producing standardized products. If one adds to this the almost universally regularized taxonomy of departments giving general education to teachers in the colleges of arts and sciences, where 75 per cent of the future teacher's education takes place, one has a fairly clear picture of the organizational reasons for things turning out as they do.

The missions of the departments most active in educating teachers-to-be in colleges of arts and sciences and in education are determined by two main considerations (neither of which provides a very specific sense of the needs of the audiences of education). These considerations are (1) the provision of the broad base of general knowledge (considered necessary to the maintenance of the mode of the schools) and (2) the provision of introductions to classroom direction (considered necessary to consensus-based notions of professionalism), e.g., a semester or a few semesters of practice teaching. California and a few other states have recently asked colleges and departments educating teachers to broaden and diversify their mission—to consider seriously distinctions in the audiences and regions which they serve. Most states, however, act as if all institutions educating teachers should be preparing them for all schools.

That the structures described above, reinforced by the legitimization tools described in Chapters III and IV, are in fact standard throughout the range of ordinary teacher education institutions is displayed in a recent American Association of Colleges of Teacher Education-Educational Testing Service (AACTE and ETS) study. It shows that colleges of education almost universally use the same array of departmental structures which teacher education in general used ten years ago; the credit hours required in each curriculum area are almost the same as they were. The advising systems apparently vary little from institution to institution and the degree requirements remain virtually the same.[49] Thus, new and unique organizations to fulfill new and unique missions serving people and environments ignored ten years ago have not evolved. Nor has the ethnic composition of the group seeking to become teachers become more representative of the total population mix. To their credit, the education professions have always encouraged a substantial number of minority people to become teachers, particularly to serve the needs of *de jure* segregated systems in the South. It does not appear that the decade of the sixties markedly changed the composition of the group aspiring to be teachers. For whereas the population of visible minorities in the country is more than 20 per cent[50] and whereas 11 per cent of the in-service teachers in the country in 1965 were minority people (10 per cent black and 1 per cent Mexican American),[51] the AACTE-ETS study found that less than 10 per cent of the present undergraduates who are teacher candidates are minority people: the percentage of minority teachers in the total teacher pool will be going or has gone down. The average teacher education institution in 1973-74 had 1,075 committed undergraduate teacher candidates. Of these, an average of 103 (less than 10 per cent of the total) were minority candidates (of these about 5 per cent were American Indians, 12 per cent Mexican Americans, 70 per cent blacks, 12 per cent Puerto Ricans, and 4 per cent Asian Americans).[52] Of the approximately 75,000 minority undergraduate teacher candidates in 1974, a great many were in college on specially subsidized federal programs directed toward minorities. The Career Opportunities Program must have accounted for almost 10 per cent of these people.[53] In the light of such stepping backward, the "forward" changes which the AACTE-ETS study shows appear to be relatively insignificant. There were changes in training to utilize various dramatic representations of teaching (these are now in use in over 50 per cent of the 719 institutions surveyed, and include microteaching, videotaping, simulation, interaction analysis).[54] And the report indicates some increase in formal training in the field (though hours of field experience still represent a very small percentage of the curriculum).

This maintenance of static structures and relationships—and certainly the decline in percentage of minority teacher candidates—in the midst of an unprecedented civil and cultural rights ferment manifests that the present machinery for governing higher education does not ask people in it to make an analysis of their unique environment or of the requirements of the mixed cultures and economies in the area where a particular college places its teachers.

The Cost of Present Teacher Education and the Failure of Reform

A reward system is desperately needed for supporting the work we shall describe, which says that teaching and teacher education *are* important, and also that the learning climates of both undergraduate education and the schools as related to the home are important. Unfortunately, many college professors see the teaching of undergraduates as of trivial consequence, and most college of education professors see "teaching teachers to teach" as a second-level priority both for themselves and for their colleges.[55] To have a better teacher education, we shall have to have a real rethinking of the learning which makes up higher education, of the social structures which go with the intellectual discipline and action which any particular institution envisages as proper to its environment.[56] And it is not enough to have token projects or token time or token federal money dedicated to what is proposed here. The low support given present "efficient" teacher education structures makes the transition to new structures more difficult and contributes to the assumption that teacher education, no matter how difficult the circumstances to which it is directed (with the exception of teacher education for the handicapped), can be done on a limited budget. Every history of teacher education has pointed to the low level of support received by the normal schools educating the teachers of the nineteenth century industrial classes.[57] Now a low level of support is attached both to the teacher education segments of higher cost institutions and to those institutions having the education of teachers as a primary mission. If one compares full education programs for teachers with programs for students in other areas, the cost per full-time equivalent (FTE) in education programs is lower than that in most other professional sequences. Among the complicated statistics on these matters, some salient features stand out.[58]

Sixty-five per cent of 1970 teachers in training went to institutions which, according to the Gourman quality ratings and the College Ratio quality ratings, were low quality institutions; only 28.6 per cent went to middle quality, and 5.4 per cent to high quality institutions. These ratings are based on a variety of factors which suggest a level of support for the total institution, such as scholarships, fellowships, salaries, and library; some other factors in the Gourman and College Ratio ratings such as board of directors and faculty morale may not reflect fiscal support. This is significant because we now have clear evidence that, even where cultural factors are ignored, Gourman "high quality" institution teachers produce better results with children than the teachers who come from institutions receiving lower Gourman ratings.[59]

As noted above, even within institutions of higher education which are well supported, education sequences and education-related sequences tend to be less well supported than other comparable disciplinary areas (National Center for Higher Education Management Systems-reported institutions).

For example, where History and Philosophy of Education departments existed in the 52 NCHEMS institutions examined, they invariably received less money per student credit hour than either the History or Philosophy departments in colleges of arts and sciences. At the same institutions, field or practicum courses in education were less well supported at 75 per cent of the institutions than were fieldwork or practicum courses in social work, nursing or engineering. Only in special education, where massive federal support has helped and where the giant "handicapped" lobby has intervened, have colleges of education received support on a parity with that for clinical areas outside education, such as speech pathology or audiology.[60] Even institutions distinguished for creative teacher education presently give education short shrift in their budgets. North Dakota's Center for Teaching and Learning, which has been regarded as a highly imaginative program, has one of the lowest allocations of dollars to FTE's of any college in that university. Imagination in teacher education has never attracted large sums of money to support it. Moreover, money alone will not *create* a good teacher education, and imagination cannot be bought simply with big budgets. However, ghettoizing over a long period of time can destroy the imagination of an area of intellectual enterprise and leave it filled with functionaries. Commentators have indicated that even North Dakota has suffered some constraining of its imagination, because of its limited financial support.

Across the 52 institutions examined, the cost of education programs for each FTE in most institutions appears to be about $1,300-$1,500 per year for all four undergraduate years. Cost in other human services professional or preprofessional areas tend to be considerably higher: $1,300-$1,800 per FTE major in the freshman-sophomore courses and $2,000-$2,800 in junior-senior ones. The real costs of the education of a teacher-to-be may be a little higher in the junior and senior years; but, since hardly any of the costs of practical work in the field, school, or community are represented in present data-gathering arrangements (see Chapter IV for more detail), the special costs of junior-senior professional training appear to be mostly borne by the school system, by the cooperating teacher, or by the community.

Were we to decide that we really want teachers for areas which have presently unmet needs, were we to put money into small or nested institutions having clear constituencies and missions, were we to insist that teacher trainers really know the educational needs of the constituencies of their institutions and educate teachers to fit those needs, we might gradually achieve a prouder, more parti-colored teacher education. What we have now are a limited number of token structures, largely federally supported, endeavoring to meet the needs of differentiated environments and producing about "3 per cent" of what they should. One program which has received prizes from the teacher education profession has emphasized exposing its teachers-to-be to minority cultures in a live-in practice teaching experience lasting from twelve weeks to one semester. The program is based on a righteous impulse, but it is not likely, given the brevity of the field experience, to permit the novice teachers to master the behavioral, linguistic, and cultural styles of the community, and at the same time to learn how to be an educator.[61] In effect, the institution (a medium-sized state college) has limited its program dealing with differentiated environments to a nugatory structure. Part of the problem is that the conventional institutional structure does not easily tolerate new situations: for example, the University of California at Riverside "Follow Through" federal project, a well-known and respected project serving Chicanos, appeared to the Study Commission site visitors to have no structured power in the university, to have only a minimal academic relationship to its education segment, and to maintain its effectiveness only by splitting off from the university.[62] The Study Commission examined several projects which originated with federal "soft" money and made an attempt to do a better job of preparing the teachers for minorities or for communities formerly isolated from the "efficient" college. The projects, in most cases, were kept off to the side in their sponsoring institutions, had no tenure to their faculties,[63] and were no threat at all to the home place's ongoing structure, reward system, or ways of recruiting and educating teachers. Such projects will not be real harbingers of change until they receive "hard" money, a tenured faculty, and a system of authority based on norms specific to their group, one which allows them to report primarily to their communities or constituencies. Communities not presently being served should not have to beg service from conventional colleges. They should either get service, or get their own institutions.

Toward a Solution: Changing Models

Were we to pick up on modern post-Taylorite notions of what makes a good workspace and apply them to schools and the education of teachers, we would recognize that education is a collaborative venture between home and school (or other outside agencies), which is designed specifically to meet some idea of the future which a community has. We would provide for periodic reorganization of the work shared by parents and teachers, and for some exchanges of their roles; we would encourage the people involved with the children in a neighborhood to share responsibility for the whole venture of education—not just for an hour, a class, or an age-grade level. We would encourage parents and teachers together to design the educational tasks, since education is a process requiring continued adult learning and experience of the street-community-work world. We would also hope to provide for a sense of completion—such as rural elementary teachers had when "their" students graduated from high school or college or made a distinguished contribution to the community. The educational equivalent of profit sharing is, of course, the pride which accrues to parents or teachers or any other teaching persons when a child nurtured by them serves the community and makes it, however plainly, on his own and his parents' terms. One may illustrate this sense with the talk of a Chicago teacher about what goes with the sort of "profit-sharing" which begins with children and parents' dreams in a wrecked Chicago neighborhood composed of many ethnic groups:

> I don't think they [the students] want to be doctors or lawyers. It's not because they don't know. It's that they have no expectations. Some have vague feelings of wanting to be teachers. They aren't interested in professional roles. See? They just want the security of working—a steady job. Something their parents haven't had in Chicago. These kids are living out their parents' hopes.

. . . .

> I think the parents are glad we're around. We take a great deal of pressure off them. We give them a chance to get on with other things in their lives. We've had a lot of families move back South. A great deal of our neighborhood has gone under the bulldozer of urban renewal. Families who haven't done so well after eight, nine years have now decided they'll give the South another try. Kids are getting in neighborhood trouble. City life may be just a bit too hard.
>
> We're really content when our students get a full-time, good paying job. We're always around for him to learn if he wants to . . . it's something beautiful to me.[64]

The school in which this teacher works has only 68 students, is run by the teachers, and includes some very subtle but clear-headed work with the families of the children. Such collaboration, if it is to become a major feature of American education generally, will obviously require new roles for parents and communities, for learners, for teachers, and most of all for the institutions recruiting and preparing teachers themselves.

Concerning Roles of Parents and Communities in New Models

Albert Nieto of Universidad de Aztlan, speaking for education in Chicano communities, has described the purpose of schools as he sees it and as the school clients with whom he works see it:

> We are concerned that schools "liberate" people rather than domesticate them. We agree that a teacher is accountable to the community (not the school) that employs him. We believe his commitment includes living in the school district and participating in its social and service activities. Educators exist as a resource to the community that employs them. We agree that knowledge should not be partitioned off into separate disciplines, but that it exists as a whole. However, we would add that knowledge should not exist isolated on a campus either, but should be integrated into and be relevant to the community the institution serves. To summarize, we believe that the present educational system miseducates. Therefore, we support all efforts in experimental education that are parent-controlled, provide for total family involvement, are low-cost, and are bilingual/bicultural.[65]

Clients ought to be asked: "What is the potential here in this town, in this neighborhood; what does your community want? What do you plan for or see as possible, given the population, the history, the environment of the place—the tasks that human beings can do together to make it habitable and congenial? What do your children want and deserve from their education and for their future?"

In place of these questions, lay people have often been asked in impersonal surveys: "What are your main concerns with the schools?" This question almost invariably elicits "discipline" as the most common response checked off on an included list of choices, or filled in as a single response. Perhaps people tend to identify symptoms rather than causes as their concerns, when they are asked to respond to such general questions. Clearly the *actions* of many community groups which have become excited about the quality of teaching indicate that discipline is not the root issue. The groups are asking: "What is happening to our children?" "What kind of childhood and adulthood are they going to have?" and "on whose terms?" Other communities' questions are: "What are we planning for our neighborhood?" "What kind of development do we want?" "On what terms are we going to live with each other in the months or years ahead?"

Even without very many adult education or data resources on which to base choices, many communities have acted. Alberto Nieto's push has been supported in many Chicano communities by efforts to create alternative schools or parent-guided public schools. For black Americans, clearly the push of the last decade has been for parent responsibility and control. This push has resulted in different staffing arrangements, different licensing requirements in a few cases, different curricula, different styles of conducting schools, and more effective education in most places—despite the early press representations making black community schools appear counterproductive.[66] ASPIRA and other organizations in the Puerto Rican communities have sought similar ends. Some Native American communities—for example, the Navajo—have begun to ask that the Bureau of Indian Affairs (BIA) stop taking their children away to dormitories in the fall and that the white BIA teachers in their fenced enclaves be replaced by Native American teachers who live in the community and are licensed by the tribes.[67]

A failure to respect the right of parents to have a strong voice and some control of the education of their children, their right not to have their cultural and religious beliefs assaulted, is one of the causes of the current controversy in Appalachia, as Commissioner Terrell Bell pointed out in a speech which was unfortunately widely misrepresented or misunderstood. The NEA's inquiry panel—which sought to enumerate the dynamics of the Appalachian conflict—wrote: "In their varying analyses of the textbook controversy, the Kanawha County citizens who met with this panel conveyed the clear impression of a climate, a public mood, and a pattern of circumstance that have converged to create almost a classic setting for convulsive social conflict. All of the elements of such conflict appear to be present: *A community long divided within itself along lines of class, urban and rural life style, religious belief, and cultural value . . . [and a] school system that, in its liberal educational philosophy and apparent domination by the higher status groups within the city, has grown remote from and alien to its conservative rural communities.*"[68]

Parents in communities who have come together ideologically to form their own schools, select and hire their own teachers, and provide an education which reflects their own epistemology and mind-set may be dismissed as dangerous radicals or as faddists. But to dismiss them as such is to fail to come to grips with people's need to feel that they have some influence over what their own children will become, the future of their communities, and the terms on which they will relate to the generation which succeeds them. James Guthrie has written of the failure of the schools to acknowledge citizens' interests and rights: "Schools are in effect monopolies, whose customers are guaranteed by compulsory attendance laws . . . the price of depoliticization of the schools appears to have been uniformity. Under the aegis of professionals—teachers and administrators—schools have become standardized to a remarkable—some say oppressive—degree. Seldom do schools admit the real diversity of tastes and values among clients. . . ."[69] This failure lies at the root of efforts of parents to resume their responsibilities. When community groups rise up and demand parity and/or control, they are often seen as trying to use the schools as tools for racism or other forms of bigotry and anti-intellectual prejudice. Let us state emphatically that we do not support racist or closed-town educational policies or the deliberate teaching of religious or cultural bias in the interest of community power. We *are* urging a return to general local control over the lives of community members. We specifically urge this in education and teacher education because we think such control is important to sensitive education. We do not deny problems inherent in such proposals—possibilities for racist, sexist, and culturally discriminatory policies. The efficient school has not precluded such policies in the past; nor has its group of professionals, isolated as they often are from the constituent community. People whose world view is utterly denied by the form and substance of the schools they attend and the teachers and administrators they face will control what they can of the integrity of their world view by silent classrooms or overly noisy ones. (See Chapter I, p. 17, for Guthrie's analysis of why *parents* sometimes resort to violence.)

Recently the federal government has commissioned a number of documents in connection with the Career Education Program which suggests that school and community must be fused with one another in ways different from those of the past. Some of these leave out the important element of control by parents and the community over their own affairs and over the conditions of their work and learning. Others include it. To the authors of Coleman's *Youth: Transition to Adulthood,* formal control of the schools by the community is not enough. The school must be controlled by and "become" the community so that parents are at home there with adult education, with credit unions, with community meetings, with political organizing meetings. The community must know that it can serve on the educational staff. It must be willing to make itself an adjunct to the school. This kind of direction cannot but be helpful wherever it appears, whether it is encouraged at the federal level, at the state level, or in the local areas where people are trying to recover from the effects of alienation from their own institutions.[70]

Concerning Learners

New roles for learners will require that they be more active and learn to take responsibility for their own learning earlier. The construction of less-alienated education must also reflect what is known about how human beings learn (little enough is known). What we think we know suggests that what we have said about how a productive work space in learning institutions is organized and how people learn productively are not incompatible. Our present picture of how children learn derives from the close study of linguistics and language learning, Jean Piaget's discoveries over the last fifty years, and the work of some behavioral psychologists who have dealt with handicapped learners. These studies tell us:

(1) That learners' abilities are greatly affected by their feelings

about themselves and that their feelings about themselves are greatly affected by the attitudes of teachers toward them. We think that teachers need to learn how to help learners develop a strong sense of self. If learners' ways of thinking are respected and they are able to feel that respect, they will tend to live up to the level of respect given them. (In his presidential address at the 1974 meeting of the American Psychological Association, learning theorist Albert Bandura stated, "Most people value their self-respect above commodities." Bandura strongly agrees with many principles of behavioral learning theory; yet, he maintains the need to recognize the influential role of "inner" forces such as self-approval. He goes on to say, "Although the empirical issue is not yet completely resolved, there is little evidence that rewards function as *automatic* strengtheners of human conduct. Behavior is not much affected by its consequences without awareness of *what is being reinforced*" [emphasis ours]. And he says external consequences have the greatest influence when "rewardable acts are a source of *self-pride* . . ." [emphasis ours].)[71]

(2) That children learn oral language without explicit teaching, by hearing the mother tongue spoken for a sufficient amount of time so that the rule structures governing the formation of the sounds, sentences, and propositions are internalized. It is clear that children learn most easily when taught in the language of their nurture and when taught in the dialect and gestural systems of their homes. Therefore it is crucial that the first years of schooling be carried out in the language of the child by teachers from the community of the child.

(3) That learners are active organizers of their own learning; each learner apprehends or organizes his knowledge in his own way according to the way of thinking that has already developed. Therefore, we believe that teachers need to be aware of differences in ways of thinking, especially in ways that characterize children as opposed to adult groups and in ways that characterize specific cultural groups.

(4) That some of the most complex and significant of human learning takes place without formal teaching. The child's acquisition of language is an obvious example. The development of basic logical, mathematical and scientific notions as traced by Piaget is equally impressive. Perhaps most compelling of Piaget's findings is that every child constructs these notions for himself. Children in many societies learn the details of intricate and demanding work in informal apprenticeship; indeed most adults in our society maintain that what they

learned through formal education is only a small part of what is significant in their knowledge. Organized education should seek to develop informal apprentice-type approaches to learning in the community as much as possible.[72]

Of course, we need much further research on how children learn. As Barbel Inhelder has written:

> We must determine more of the developmental laws . . . how the child is able to assimilate through his own schemes the knowledge we try to pass on. . . . We need the help of good mathematicians or good physicists or good linguists . . . [to give] us a sense of a heuristic for our research . . . [which we can pass on to the teachers]. We can train the teachers to make curriculum studies . . . but the educators themselves must work out their curricula. The other essential for introducing basic scientific ideas early is that they must be studied through materials which the child can handle himself. . . . Through games, for example, we can teach probabilistic reasoning long before the child can learn . . . the formal expressions of probability theory.[73]

Research may help us to learn what different childhood activities represent to children as they create their own devices for learning.

Good teachers and good teacher educators may use a variety of devices to embody the principles of respect for the learners' ways of organizing their learning, for their feelings about themselves, for learning done through informal apprenticeships, and for the idioms of the learners. The laboratory where teachers must learn to teach must be the living and learning environments of the children themselves. Teachers, of course, need propositional knowledge; they need to know how to do mathematics if they teach math. But they also need "skill mastery"—how to think alongside the child at his level, given his idiom, offering him the next thing that he needs to learn given his environment and community. This has been put more elegantly by David Hawkins in a letter to the Commission about what education for teachers must be—if it is to be anything worth doing:

> Field-based work with teachers-to-be needs to explore in depth what I call the spontaneous educational potential of a given human and material environment. What does this mean?

It means (a) the search for strengths of children already living in that environment—skills and aptitudes it fosters, whether or not these have any presently recognized relation to "the curriculum"; (b) the search for features of that environment itself which would be worthy of further development and exploration—its work-a-day aspects, its geographic and historical character, its riches as input to the expressive and scientific talents of children; (c) a linking of (a) and (b) to curriculum in the sense of a general outline of worthy educational aims, including not only those connected with knowing how to live in the environment, but equally those connected with the big ecumenical world of arts, politics, science, the professions.[74]

Concerning Staff

Finally, new roles for teachers and administrators will be required. A teacher education which starts with what communities and parents want is conceivable despite what we have said of the "teacher-to-be" pool. Teachers assessing their previous education indicate they want to develop a sense of audience, to deal with individual and group differences, to relate to students' emotions, to work with slow learners in an effective way, and to learn to organize worthwhile activities for their students. They do not relish either the silent or the disruptive classroom. They also urge that they get more differentiated field experience as part of their education.

Considering how cut off the "Rose Hoffmans" of teaching are, the research studies synthesized by Henry Hector show a *predictably* steady slow decline in the in-service teacher's performance after the first five years of work.[75] The typical educational format used in the common schools requires the teacher to talk two thirds of the time, to quiz the students two to three times a minute, and to ask fact questions almost all of the time. Student responses average about eleven words. Within these eleven words questions from the students rarely appear.[76] The emotionally debilitating character of a profession so constructed is at least in part contingent on the requirement of a role which now demands almost constant verbal *giving* as part of holding attention and allows for virtually no *getting*.[77] Anyone placed in such a role would tend to create styles, routines, rationalizations such as Rose Hoffman has to reduce guilt arising from not being able to meet the constant demands to *give*. In many schools, nothing leads out to the places where teachers can see fully and pridefully what has happened as a culmination of their work. The poor pay that teachers in some areas of the country get does encourage them to moonlight in the community, but not in a way which provides for intellectual renewal or understanding of the community, and not in a way which allows them to follow their students.[78] There is a compelling need for in-service education which moves the teacher beyond the school into the world which the school is intended to serve.

If teachers are to design or encourage students to design meaningful learning spaces either in the community or the schools, they will have to have adequate help toward role restructuring, help to select moonlighting work which contributes to renewal for them, help to find opportunities for work and study in their teaching capacities, help, most of all, to take responsibility for themselves, their institutions, and their relation to the outside world. For example, political science or civics teachers might well, in some areas, become legislative apprentices on released afternoons or during semester sabbaticals. Vocational education teachers might well be encouraged to work half days or one semester out of every four in the factories or farms or shops or craft places for which they educate young people. New administrators might learn aspects of administration in a prison program, a Volvo-style factory, a manpower program, or a program in community psychology. Native American teachers may wish to learn reservation-specific skills by working for a tribal council or undertaking a course in traditional medicine.[79] Ultimately we shall have to entertain the notion that some people may, through counseling or other experiences, discover for themselves that teaching young people or teaching in a specific community is not what they are best suited for. We shall also require relicensing processes which allow teachers, working with parents and students in a supportive atmosphere, to discover what sorts of experiences they need, both of an intellectual sort and an experiential sort, if they are to be the most effective possible agents of the community's wishes for its children.

Teacher education of the general sort envisaged here appears to be like that also advocated by the leadership of the present teachers-in-training: the Student NEA. The Student NEA suggests goals for reform in teacher education under several headings, including knowledge/theory/practice, internships, field experience and human relations, student input and uses of resources. Student NEA reform criteria include support for the student's right to evaluate the education curriculum and its faculty and to seek the views of other students, teacher organizations in the community, the State Board of Education, and other groups. In reforming the curriculum the group urges that intense fieldwork be continuous across the undergraduate years: that at the beginning students be involved in community exploration with exposure to teaching centers varying in location, size, culture, and grade level; that this be followed by work as tutors, teacher aides, social agency aides; that later the students be involved in small group instruction and other community and administrative aspects of teaching; and that students be involved in student teaching. In short, the Student NEA says that it wants the repertoire of exposure in the community and the school to be as wide as possible. The Student NEA criterion statement also says that teacher education programs must deal with the parent-teacher relationship by developing a whole range of experiences to bring the teacher-to-be, teacher, community, parent, and school together and to enhance community-school involvement, cooperation, and relationships.

[In the same statement, more intensive human relationship training is proposed: sensitivity training, interpersonal communication, group dynamics, ethnic cultural studies, studies in sexism. Further, the group advocates that professors of education and liberal arts get a good dose of school and community experience themselves to "Make the content of their courses and their teaching practice relevant to the contemporary setting."][80]

Concerning New Sorts of Institutions of Higher Education and New Schools Which May Help

The kind of teacher education we advocate is possible. New institutions and roles are emerging. Much of the work of the Study Commission over the past three years has been to identify places where its theoretical statements about what education ought to be like have some visible correlative in real-world practice. This approach has led to the creation of several communications networks which have brought reforming and alternative institutions into contact with each other in a legitimizing and strengthening process. These places differ greatly from each other and cannot be easily categorized. But they are all alike in having a clear sense of what it is they want to do and being close enough to a people to know what the people in a specific community want. They have some of the flavor one would seek in a meaningful work space. The institutions are small, or they are small subcomponents of a larger institution. For example, consider the colleges represented in the American Indian Higher Education Consortium: (includes

Navajo Community College, Standing Rock Community College, Sinte Gleska, D-Q, Oglala Community College, and other newly formed institutions), and in the Chicano network: (includes Universidad de Aztlan, D-Q, Colegio Cesar Chavez, Colegio Jacinto Treviño [Mercedes and San Antonio, Texas], Colegio Tlatelolco, Academia de la Nueva Raza, Juarez-Lincoln Center). Some of the black and Puerto Rican colleges (e.g., Universidad Boricua) and a few of the newer institutions focusing on a specific kind of teaching and learning environment also point the way (such as University of Wisconsin—Green Bay College of Creative Communications, Evergreen State, Thomas Jefferson, Johnston College, The University of North Dakota Center for Teaching and Learning, the Louisville Urban Rural Project). These institutions wish to focus their missions or were created to have focused missions, with clear senses of (1) audience and environment, and (2) organization and reward system which support missions.

The sense of audience and environment at these institutions may include many things. Sense of audience includes attention to what parents and children in the region or cultural constituency of the institution are saying that the community plans mean for the education of children. Sense of environment will include a sense of history, as well as attention to such matters as: observing the symbolism of the four sacred directions in laying out the architecture of a place (Navajo Community College); asking that teacher trainers also teach in homes and rural buildings; knowing about car repair and veterinary science where long distances between communities exist or where there is a heavy dependence on cattle (Sinte Gleska); requiring teacher trainers to live in a barrio and participate in its socio-political activities; requiring that the local voc-ed teacher trainer know both the science and technology of the local group and conventional science and technology; asking teacher trainers and teachers-to-be to do a job of documentation (or "oral history") on an area which begins with the strengths of the local environment and leads out to the ecumenical world of politics, art, and society-organizing (Academia de la Nueva Raza and Center for Inner City Studies). Teacher training activities such as are envisaged may also include work with the common schools, alternative schools or informal educational networks, pushing together home, community, informal learning (Parkway, Metro, Career Education experience-based model).[81]

In almost every case mentioned, the place where the learning takes place is small to protect the sense of mission, the sense of individuality of the people involved, and the sense of informal community of the members. In nearly every case, the practical-action center or centers for educating teachers rely on intensely theoretical knowledge based in the intellectual disciplines often taught in arts and sciences colleges, but the theory emphasized is almost always the theory which has transformative potential for the community's autonomy and well-being. The institution or "center" described is related to a range of like institutions having similar missions; in almost every institution we found useful parent and community people—particularly in those from "left-out" communities—who collaborate with the institution on teaching resources and also sit on its governing and assessing boards. Generally people work in teams, in more open spaces, between the IHE and the community.

In our effort to build institutions to provide teachers less isolated from diverse American communities, we will waste time and money if we simply create new experiments or new "demonstration models" at established and conventional institutions where the weight of numbers and tradition may preclude the effects of new developments. We will also waste money if we only fund "demonstrations from scratch." What is required is expenditure in conventional institutions where sufficient momentum exists to justify supporting new nuclei within them and expenditure for new arrangements, even new institutions where necessary. The same is true of the practice teaching center. Some of the movement toward team work and open spaces has helped to turn a few schools away from the old hierarchical model. But we are talking about a more drastic change—a new place to learn. For instance, the John F. Kennedy Middle School and Community Center in Atlanta appears to be close to the kind of school that Coleman talks about in *Youth: Transition to Adulthood,* a school which reaches into the community. The site includes fourteen health, education, and social service units under one roof, a day care center, vocational training, and places for hobbies. The school is open from 7:30 a.m. until 10:30 at night. Over 500 adults from the community come into the school weekly to be involved in its agency-adult education-community planning programs (contrast Rose Hoffman's feelings about adults in the schools, p. 49). Children and youth are taught not only the conventional subjects, but also how to work in the community. Many of the instructors are "professional" people—doctors, lawyers, nurses, or whatever. Thus the teaching staff represents in nucleus the services that the community offers and needs. Community input in the training of teachers includes work with in-service teachers (though not with pre-service ones yet). The work includes not only education about such matters as the neighborhood and the aspirations of the parents; it also includes value clarification, human relations, and staff adaptations to non-traditional building uses. The building itself is a model of what is to be learned there and in the neighborhood around. It is full of identity-building mosaics taken from black history. The school is controlled by a parent board and has a decentralized governance pattern.[82]

Such schools or school community centers, when linked with the higher education institutions named above or with institutions like those, and provided with a management, licensing, and accreditation structure that supports their unique sense of what their environments are about, can do much toward making education and teacher education once more belong to the people of the United States. Such efforts do not have to be funded from scratch. They only have to be fostered. If they are to be fostered, however, we may have to ask questions different from those we traditionally ask about "what makes a good teacher." The best research on teachers-in-general—and what qualities make good ones—is summarized in Alexander Mood's book, *Do Teachers Make a Difference?* Fluency appears to be a crucial variable in the identification of the good all-purpose teacher. Fluency certainly should not be overlooked in any general recruitment policy. But it is the Study Commission's argument that the search for the good teacher-in-general is not the most meaningful search and will almost invariably produce only the conclusion that teachers must know how to talk articulately. We contend that teachers must know how to act. To put it in other words, teachers are "good teachers" of some thing, to some one, acting and asking others to act in some *environment,* and in the *specific idiom* of that environment. The identification of who can do such a job is a *situated* kind of task. It cannot be done by "experts somewhere else." It must be done by institutions or subcomponents of institutions which are committed to community-building in the same way that we would expect parents and teachers to be committed.

Conclusion

When college of education faculties speak as individuals, as in the Carnegie Survey, they approve of the creation of more humane learning communities. They say that they want to give more power to students in setting requirements and admissions policy; they advocate more student access to the field, more attention to student emotional growth, and more relevancy.[83] Why then do the standardized teacher educator and standardized teacher education program, the standardized teacher and the alienated classroom, still exist? Partly because money is not available for creating change and developing new institutions or new subcomponents of institutions. Partly because our present standardized management and testing devices and other devices for organizing and clarifying the work of the schools still reflect an outmoded sense of industrial efficiency and a need to make all communities and people alike. Partly because of inertia. Partly because school administrators, teachers, and parents are what they are. But if education is to participate in giving children and youth what they deserve—movement from childhood to adulthood as whole persons, a growing sense of self, the capacity to understand and influence the physical and social forces affecting their lives, a job worth doing in a community worth living for —then we shall have to take seriously at every level in our educational ideology the implications of the Supreme Court's continuing commitment to the local, the locally responsive, and the principle of "experimentation, innovation and a healthy competition." Recall the strength of the courts' affirmation of this commitment in *Milliken v. Bradley* (July, 1974):

> No single tradition in public education is more deeply rooted than local control over the operation of the schools; local autonomy has long been thought essential both to the maintenance of community concern and support for public schools and to the quality of the educational process. See *Wright v. Council of the City of Emporia,* 407 U.S. 451, 469. Thus, in *San Antonio School District v. Rodriguez,* 411 U.S. 1, 50, we observed that local control over the educational process affords citizens an opportunity to participate in decision-making, permits the structuring of school programs to fit local needs, and encourages "experimentation, innovation and a healthy competition for educational excellence."[84]

The position of the court in this case, a position encouraging education which fits local needs, is part of an eloquent line of Supreme Court decisions recognizing that education is an extension of childrearing and that it must protect the rights of parents and community to foster the intellectual and vocational growth of children in a fashion congenial not simply to the interests of the state, but more basically to the interests of their own culture. We can create a teacher education adequate to this charge.

SPECIFIC RECOMMENDATIONS

Recommendation I:

The Recruitment of Teachers

At the time of recruitment or early in training, teachers-to-be should select one or more culture-specific areas in which they plan to master such teaching crafts as meet community needs. Candidates to the profession, where admission is not automatic, should be chosen on the basis of their living experience appropriate to the kinds of communities in which they plan to teach (cf. proposals for two-tier licensing in Chapter III). Recruitment criteria should be related to community needs, and should include counseling-out procedures. This would require periodic assessment of the teachers' performance both during training and on the job (cf. Chapter III for the legal framework in which the right to a job must be set).

Recommendation II:

The Location of Programs

Teacher education program developers, whether working in local, state, or federal agencies, must respect the notion that programs should be authorized, funded, and installed only after a particular community has defined a program: the need for it, its content, and the terms on which it will be acceptable. Processes for making citizen participation central in the development of community educational plans are described in Donald Davies' bibliography, *Citizen Participation in Education* (cf. footnote 84 for the legal spirit which informs this recommendation).

Recommendation III:

The Examining School

The Study Commission recommends that the federal government (together with the Education Commission of the States, the Chief State School Officers, the National Citizens Committee on Education, local community groups, and the Commission on Uniform State Laws) undertake an effort to develop a new entity (the "regional examining school") for the selecting and licensing of education personnel. In an identifiable culture district (a geographical region may be appropriate where distinguishable childrearing practices, audiences, and the cultures cannot be clearly separated out), a needs assessment involving the interaction of community, schools, education personnel, and where relevant, institutions of higher education (IHE's), would be undertaken. This needs assessment, based on a prior description of the status quo, would envisage a set of educational needs together with a set of necessary skills, competencies, and resources. Against this framework, the examining school, under power delegated by the states, would examine candidates to determine licensure. The specific tasks to be performed by persons so licensed as well as by persons conventionally licensed might be negotiated, as in a contract, among the licensee, the clients of the institution, and school administrators. Teaching jobs where service and communications are crucial should be distinguished from those where technical skills dominate (e.g., certain sorts of special education). Where service and communication appear to dominate, the community's informal assessment of a person's capacity to communicate with and serve adults and children in it should be a crucial element in the examining process. Assessment procedures would be based on the outcomes of this negotiation and might also be conducted by the examining school (this is only one model of what might be done; cf. the Mansfield memos recorded in Chapter III for an example of an effort to use community validation).

Recommendation IV:

The Reform of Present Institutions and the Creation of New Ones

The Study Commission supports legislation which has as its goal education tempered to its surroundings and to the strengths of the cultural and environmental differences inherent in the surroundings—such legislation as the Ethnic Heritage Act, the Bilingual Education and Career Education Acts. We particularly support programs including community control or parity in the program development and community needs assessments prior to program establishment. Furthermore, we believe, as we indicate in Chapter V, that such community activity needs to become part of a flexible national strategy to secure permanent institutional change. We believe that the Office of Education should direct its support of teacher education to programs which have the following characteristics:

(1) A clear sense of responsibility to life-long education of a region's people.

(2) A general education component taught jointly by faculty members of schools of education and colleges of arts and sciences, integrating the content and methods of the disciplines with the technique and theory of education and relating what is known about human learning to the specific needs of target communities.

(3) A staff which includes excellent teachers from the common schools as well as from higher education and the community, for education of pre-service and in-service teachers.

(4) Teaching apprenticeships in the community and community school across the four undergraduate years with gradually increasing responsibilities.

(5) Learning and education in anthropological models that assist prospective teachers to view the specific community or region in which they are teaching or intending to teach without ethnocentric bias, or more positively, with the eye of the citizen who has the interest of the area and its children at heart.

(6) Education which offers experience with a range of cultural institutions other than schools and which is designed to develop understanding of the ways in which these institutions clash with one another and the community, or the ways in which they act cooperatively toward realization of commonly shared goals.

(7) Education which offers experience leading to acquisition of skills to deal with discontinuities and alienation, probably in the form of working with exemplars, families, or societies that have successfully overcome these sorts of difficulties.

(8) Education which provides for assistance in attending to the private and shared mythologies held by members of the community, which underlie their education, work, and play. This would involve careful work analyzing the rule structures and value postulates implicit in community activities in these areas.

Appropriate federal and state agencies should encourage the notion that the institution of higher education's role in teacher education should have a local habitation and a name—a specific region and mission. The institution of higher education (or several of them together) and the local education agency (or several of them) could, for example, be encouraged to develop a pre-service/in-service partnership with a community or range of local communities in their area such that each institution would work with specific clients/consumers in the area in the total educative process, defining an alternative or range of alternatives for satisfying the educational needs articulated by the communities.

Recommendation V:

Costs

The Study Commission encourages the federal government through the Office of Education and related agencies and appropriate state agencies to develop adequate support for teacher education, beginning with a minimum of $50 per in-service teacher per year and moving eventually across the next ten years to a figure which is the purchasing equivalent of $500 per teacher per year (the present cost of offering in-service support to a teacher in an adequate teacher center). The federal government should take the lead in encouraging the states to limit the recruitment and education of pre-service undergraduates so that a figure bearing a reasonable relationship to the demand is arrived at, and to concentrate on persons having the strengths needed, or having prospects of gaining the strengths needed, in present areas of educational neglect or shortage (cf. Chapter IV for some discussion of the information requirements of such an effort). Simultaneously, we would urge the federal government and appropriate state agencies not to cut present appropriations for teacher education. If anything, we should expand the appropriations to make possible the systems envisaged here and to bring the support level for teacher education as high as or higher than that for other human services professional training areas. Extending the Fleischmann Commission estimates to the country as a whole, we estimate that the cost of the institutional, as opposed to the student support, part of such a system would be about a billion dollars per year. This money could be obtained from a combination of federal funds in present programs and state funds freed for new purposes, were the state teacher education allocation not to be cut during the surplus (cf. Chapter V).

Recommendation VI:

Research

To enable higher education and schools to get in touch with their environments, the National Institute of Education should support:

(1) Policy studies and research and development on the creation of learning opportunities for college, university, and common school faculty members, starting with an identification of future needs of the common schools and IHE's. These studies should include efforts to arrive at:

a. definitions of criteria of effectiveness and quality of teaching which go beyond conventional, quantitative, cost accounting methods;

b. parallel definitions of methods for assessment and facilitation of individual growth;

c. methods for involving faculty in continuous renewal of self and of one's institution.

(2) Research and development on human learning, particularly in regard to bilingual, bicultural, interdisciplinary, future-responsive learning.

(3) Studies directed toward the creation of public learning, consumer-based networks. These demonstration networks would be designed to link the proposed community-based learning environments (community teacher education centers), institutions of higher education which are funded to provide the desired teacher training, centers which provide learning opportunities for faculty of institutions of higher education, and research centers on human learning. They would be based on an open-flow of evaluative and other information and responsiveness to consumer needs.

FOOTNOTES

[1] See January, 1975, issue of *Study Commission Newsletter*.

[2] *Study Commission Newsletter* (January, 1975), pp. 9-13. Cf. Item 41, p. 2 of tables included with newsletter, along with other items of these tables.

[3] A higher respect appears in the following areas: Architecture, Health Technology, Nursing, Pharmacy, and Occupational Therapy. Home Economics majors generally display about the same satisfaction with the college preparation offered

them as do teachers-to-be.

[4] Study cited in *Study Commission Newsletter* (January, 1975), p. 23; complete study available from Study Commission files.

[5] Cf. Michael Novak, *The Rise of the Unmeltable Ethnics* (New York: The Macmillan Company, 1971), pp. 72-115. Also see Michael Katz, *Class, Bureaucracy, and Schools* (New York: Praeger Publishers, 1971), pp. 3-104, 111-13.

[6] Katz, *Class, Bureaucracy, and Schools,* pp. 130-32, 105-53. Cf. *Inquiry Report: Kanawha County, West Virginia: A Textbook Study in Cultural Conflict* (Washington, D.C.: NEA Teacher Rights Division, 1975), *passim:* this traces the history of an attempt by Fundamentalist Scottish-Irish in Appalachia to have an influence in their schools. Cf. Novak, *The Rise of the Unmeltable Ethnics,* pp. 136-66, 214ff., 280-84. Efforts of Eastern European ethnics to achieve a degree of control of the schools their children attend or to protect separate ethnic schools have been particularly marked in Eastern and Midwestern industrial cities, such as Cleveland.

[7] Don Davies and others, *Citizen Participation in Education* (New Haven: Institute for Responsive Education, December, 1973), *passim.* Cf. *The Condition of Education* (Washington, D.C.: Government Printing Office, 1975); page 73 indicates that 31 per cent of parents say that they are becoming less favorable in their views of the schools in recent years, and 27 per cent have no change of opinion.

[8] George Spindler, "The Transmission of American Culture," in *The University Can't Train Teachers* (Lincoln, Nebraska: Study Commission Publication, 1972), p. 49 and *passim,* pp. 41-52.

[9] Spindler, "The Transmission of American Culture," p. 49.

[10] Rosalie and Murray Wax, Roselyn Holyrock and Gerald One Feather, "Formal Education in An American Indian Community," *Social Problems* (Spring, 1964), XI, 4, p. 99.

[11] Murray Wax, "How Should Schools Be Held Accountable?" in Paul A. Olson, Larry Freeman, James Bowman, editors, *Education for 1984 and After* (Lincoln, Nebraska: Study Commission Publication, 1972), p. 63. For an account of the situation of black and Puerto Rican students in New York, which applies Wax's analysis of Indian situations to New York, see Miriam Wasserman, *The School Fix: NYC: USA* (New York: Outerbridge and Dienstfrey, 1970), pp. 185ff, 428-508.

[12] Cecilia Cosca and others, *Teachers and Students* (Washington, D.C.: Government Printing Office, U.S. Commission on Civil Rights: Mexican American Education Study, March, 1973), p. 38.

[13] Charles Silberman, *Crisis in the Classroom* (New York: Vintage Books, 1971), pp. 149-50.

[14] Olson, Freeman, and Bowman, eds., *Education for 1984 and After*, pp. 31-32; John K. Folger and others, *Human Resources and Higher Education* (New York: Russell Sage Foundation, 1970), pp. 75, 108. Slightly different figures are given in *The Condition of Education* (p. 72), which shows teaching staffs to be 70 per cent female.

[15] Cf. Frank Hubbard, *The Elementary School Principalship in 1968: A Research Study* (Washington, D.C.: National Education Association, 1968), p. 95. Only 22 per cent of 1968 teachers participated in political organizations, and only 5.5 per cent in civil rights groups; cf. *Education for 1984 and After*, pp. 30-31.

[16] Folger and others, *Human Resources and Higher Education*, pp. 111-14; *Education for 1984 and After*, pp. 28-29.

[17] Henry Hector, *Teacher Depreciation*, unpublished doctoral dissertation (New York: Columbia University Teachers College, 1972), *passim*. Cf. Seymour Sarason, *The Culture of the School and the Problem of Change* (Boston: Allyn and Bacon, Inc., 1971), p. 163.

[18] James Coleman, *Equality of Educational Opportunity* (Washington, D.C. Government Printing Office, 1966), p. 365, pp. 167, 169, 364-65.

[19] *Education for 1984 and After,* pp. 30-31; cf. Hubbard, p. 93.

[20] Studs Terkel, *Working* (New York: Pantheon Books, 1972), pp. 484-88.

[21] Cf. Sarason, *The Culture of the School and the Problem of Change;* pp. 152-69 provide an excellent analysis of why people come to behave and feel as Rose Hoffman does.

[22] Cf. Stanley Aronowitz, *False Promises: The Shaping of American Working Class Consciousness* (New York: McGraw Hill, 1973), pp. 312-13, p. 434.

[23] Coleman, *Equality of Educational Opportunity,* pp. 171 and 174.

[24] Donald P. Mitchell and others, *Leadership in Public Education Study: A Look at the Overlooked* (Washington, D.C.: Academy for Educational Development, 1972), p. 19.

[25] Coleman, *Equality of Educational Opportunity,* pp. 177 and 181.

[26] Hubbard, *The Elementary School Principalship in 1968: A Research Study,* pp. 93-96.

²⁷Mitchell, *Leadership in Public Education Study,* pp. 40-42.

²⁸Mitchell, *Leadership,* p. 43.

²⁹Hubbard, *The Elementary School Principalship,* p. 143; the number of principals thinking of themselves as leaders declined 10 per cent from 1958-68 and the number thinking of themselves as supporters or followers expanded commensurately.

³⁰Mitchell, *Leadership,* p. 22.

³¹Mitchell, *Leadership,* p. 19, and Hubbard, *The Elementary School Principalship,* p. 95.

³²Mitchell, *Leadership,* pp. 32-33.

³³Stephen G. Carroll, *Analysis of the Educational Personnel System: VIII. The Market for Teachers,* prepared for the Department of HEW (Santa Monica, California: The Rand Corporation, 1974), pp. vii, 1-3, *passim.*

³⁴The NEA estimates that recent legal decisions on bilingual education would require that at least five million American children be provided bilingual teachers, and estimates further that only 3 per cent of these children have such teachers. Cf. *Study Commission Newsletter* (December, 1973), pp. 1-2.

³⁵Cf. Martin Haberman, *Guidelines for the Selection of Students into Programs of Teacher Education* (Washington, D.C.: Association of Teacher Educators and ERIC Clearinghouse on Teacher Education, 1972), pp. 10-13, which suggests that colleges' new student bodies are containing larger percentages of blue-collar family young people—with authoritarian ideas. Sing Nan Fen and Keith Pritchard, in "Social Class Backgrounds of College Teachers of Education," *Journal of Teacher Education* (Summer, 1971), point out that teachers of teachers themselves stem in large per cent from blue-collar origins, often becoming teacher trainers after a teaching career in the schools. (This is interesting to compare with Haberman's comment on the intolerance toward working class people among college faculties.)

³⁶See *Study Commission Newsletter* (January, 1975), pp. 5-6. Also see tables accompanying this newsletter.

³⁷For example, 62.1 per cent of white education majors at four-year colleges disagreed or disagreed strongly with the statement, "There should be integration in elementary schools, even by busing," whereas 80.7 per cent of black education majors agreed or strongly agreed with the statement; black education majors agreed (76.0 per cent) that black education programs should be administered by blacks whereas white education majors disagreed (57.8 per cent); 78.2 per cent of black education majors felt that blacks should control black segregated schools and

70.1 per cent of white education majors agreed, but 59.5 per cent of blacks agreed strongly whereas only 25.0 per cent of whites strongly agreed (45.1 per cent agreeing with reservations and 30 per cent disagreeing). In 1970, 80.3 per cent of black education majors at four-year colleges said that the "main cause of Negro riots is white racism" (53.3 per cent strongly agreed) whereas 58.6 per cent of white education majors disagreed or strongly disagreed. These statistics are taken from Section 4G of the Study Commission analysis of the Carnegie Study (these particular statistics are previously unpublished).

[38] These conclusions appear to be generally confirmed by other surveys of the characteristics of the people recruited to teaching in America; see the studies cited in *Education for 1984 and After,* pp. 30-31; cf. Martin Haberman, *Guidelines for the Selection of Students into Programs of Teacher Education,* pp. 9-10; see also Folger and others, *Human Resources,* pp. 111-14, 119 (chart), 197-216. It may be inappropriate to expect that the large and often underrewarded group which makes up the teaching force in this country should, in a general sense, be an elite group. However, we do argue for careful work to find out which specific qualities and traits, linguistic skills, and teaching, craft or work skills are needed for which particular community environments.

[39] This is taken from *Carnegie Response* (No. 92) in the graduate student survey (previously unpublished): "I consider myself an intellectual": all graduate students, agree or strongly agree, 55.1 per cent; graduate students aspiring to be executives or administrators in education, 42.5 per cent. A lower percentage of would-be education executives agreed or strongly agreed that they considered themselves intellectuals than did any other graduate administrative group in training. Figures for other graduate administrative groups in training are: self-employed in business, 54.1 per cent "intellectuals," executives in government, 47.2 per cent, executives or administrators in private industry, 46.3 per cent. Graduate students preparing to be education administrators generally thought that Ph.D.'s in their field required "much real scholarly" ability (70.3 per cent) and hoped themselves to make a real contribution to knowledge (71.7 per cent) [survey numbers 94 and 97]; yet, less than half (44.1 per cent) saw their field as "getting a good share of the best students." A majority of graduate students in general (65.2 per cent) saw their own field as getting "a good share of the best students" [survey number 117]. Executives or administrators in education had the lowest percentage of persons who regarded "recognition as a good student by my professors" as very important (45.5 per cent so regarded it; 48 per cent of graduate students in general regarded such recognition as important and other administrative groups were particularly high in this area [survey number 126]). Fewer future educational administrators (32.1 per cent) than other future administrators marked "recognition for my academic abilities from my fellow students" as very important (self-employed in business, 49.0 per cent, executive or administrator in government, 35.9 per cent, executive or administrator in private industry, 37.2 per cent [survey number 127]). Almost 10 per cent fewer of the group seeking to be executives or administrators in

education than of the general graduate group claimed to "do a lot of serious reading outside my field of study" (48.5 per cent to 57.9 per cent) [survey number 252].

[40]The following survey numbers, in addition to those summarized in footnote 39, are relevant:

(1) Graduate Student Survey No. 123—"Doctorate is mainly a 'union card' enabling me to get the kind of job I want": 63.5 per cent of would-be executives or administrators in education agreed or strongly agreed as contrasted with 50.9 per cent of graduate students in general, 51.7 per cent of graduate education students planning to teach, and under 57 per cent figures in all other graduate categories including other administrative categories (most of these are under 50 per cent).

(2) Graduate Survey No. 120—"Faculty members should be free to present in class any idea they feel relevant": only 73.9 per cent of would-be executives or administrators in education who were graduate students agreed or strongly agreed (35.6 per cent strongly agreed), whereas 81.7 per cent of all graduate students agreed (45.7 per cent strongly agreed). Other groups having higher percentages of agree or strongly agree answers included graduate students planning careers in elementary or secondary teaching, college teaching, government administration (60 per cent strongly agreed), and executives or administrators in private industry; higher percentages of strongly agree or agree with reservations appeared in the biological and physical science graduate group (86.2 per cent), the social sciences graduate group (93.1 per cent), liberal arts (92.1 per cent), architecture and design (95.8 per cent), social work and welfare (90.7 per cent), physical and health education (85.5 per cent) and law (89.1 per cent).

(3) Graduate Survey No. 89—"I'm in graduate school to better serve mankind": 36.2 per cent of would-be executives or administrators in education strongly agreed, only slightly more than graduate students in general (32 per cent) and considerably fewer than graduate students planning careers in college teaching (48.7 per cent) and somewhat fewer than the average graduate education major (38.8 per cent).

(4) Graduate Survey No. 88—Only 22.3 per cent of would-be executives or administrators in education said strongly that they were in graduate school "to study their field for its intrinsic interest" as contrasted with 29.8 per cent of graduate students in general, 30.7 per cent of graduate elementary or secondary teacher candidates, and 33.4 per cent of graduate candidates for university teaching.

(5) Graduate Survey No. 90—"I'm in graduate school to engage in political activities": only 6.3 per cent of future executives or administrators in education agreed or strongly agreed as contrasted with 12.4 per cent of graduate students in general, 14.2 per cent of graduate candidates to be self-employed in business, 32.1 per cent of graduate candidates to be executives or administrators in government, and 10 per cent of candidates to be executives or administrators in private industry.

(6) Graduate Survey No. 81—69.1 per cent of would-be executives or

administrators in education agreed or strongly agreed that they were in graduate school "in order to obtain an occupation with high prestige," 10 per cent higher than graduate students in general, 16 per cent higher than graduate education majors, 33 per cent higher than graduate students preparing to be elementary or secondary teachers and higher than all but one of eight graduate categories analyzed.

(7) Graduate Survey No. 82—91.4 per cent of would-be executives or administrators in education in graduate school agreed or strongly agreed that they were in graduate school "to increase [their] earning power," 15 per cent higher than graduate students in general and again higher than all but one of eight graduate categories analyzed.

(8) There were no questions that directly concerned "preserving status relationship"; however, though 64.6 per cent of graduate students planning to be administrators agreed or strongly agreed that they were in graduate school "to contribute to [their] ability to change society" (27.5 per cent strongly agreed), future executives or administrators in education generally did not agree or strongly agree with items which asked that the respondent favor strategies commonly used to change society (No. 55, 56, 57, 58, 120), while 87.3 per cent (the highest percentage) agreed or strongly agreed with the statement, "I am as strict about right and wrong as most people" (No. 249); 10 per cent more than graduate students in general agreed or strongly agreed that "there is too much concern in the courts for the rights of criminals" (No. 254); 48.7 per cent, about average for graduate students, agreed that "most poor people could help themselves if they really wanted to" (No. 255).

For present corporate management values, see James O'Toole and others. *Work in America* (Cambridge: MIT Press, 1973), Chapter 4, "The Redesign of Jobs," pp. 93-120, especially p. 106.

[41] See *Study Commission Newsletter* (January, 1975), p. 2.

[42] Mitchell, *Leadership,* p. 19. Only 739 of the 3,288 principals in Michigan are women. At the secondary level, 95.1 per cent of the principals are men.

[43] William Bagley, *et al., An Introduction to Teaching* (New York: The Macmillan Company, 1924), p. 379.

[44] O'Toole, *Work in America,* p. 106.

[45] O'Toole, *Work in America,* p. 186.

[46] *Work in America,* pp. 141-52. Harold Sheppard and Neal Herrick, *Where Have All the Robots Gone?* (New York: The Macmillan Company, 1972), pp. 43-95 suggest what the main factors making for alienation and meaningless work are for all jobs; see also Stanley Aronowitz, *False Promises,* pp. 249-50, 312, 15.

[47] Phyllis D. Hamilton, "A Comparison with Historical Antecedents," in

Competency-Based Teacher Education, USOE-OPPE report, published by Stanford Research Institute (April, 1973), pp. 31-41.

[48] Lawrence Freeman, "The Management of Knowledge," *Journal of Higher Education*, XLV, 2 (1974), p. 84 and *passim*.

[49] Susan S. Sherwin, *Teacher Education: A Status Report* (co-sponsored by ETS and AACTE, 1974), p. iii and pp. 37-38.

[50] 1970 census figures taken from George Delory, *The World Almanac* (New York, 1973), pp. 135, 141, 151, 492, 749. This figure does not include Cuban Americans.

[51] Coleman, *Equality*, p. 127.

[52] Sherwin, *Teacher Education: A Status Report*, p. 8; the charts are not totalled in the AACTE-ETS report.

[53] For example, the Career Opportunities Program, with its 8,000 undergraduate trainees in 1972, included 97.3 per cent low income trainees and several thousand minority trainees. Since the total minority undergraduate training group in the early 70's was about 70,000 per year, it is clear that special federal programs accounted for a sizable proportion of the minority trainees. The percentages of 1972 COP trainees who were members of a minority group were: black, 53 per cent; American Indian, 5 per cent; Chicano and Puerto Rican, 16 per cent. Since many COP people are freshmen and sophomores in college, it is hard to determine the precise overlap between AACTE-ETS and COP figures. These figures are supplied by George Kaplan, of the Institute for Educational Leadership, who is preparing a study of COP. Cf. *The Condition of Education*, p. 71, for state-by-state listing of per cent of minority students and minority teachers in 1972.

[54] Sherwin, *Teacher Education: A Status Report*, p. 38.

[55] One curious feature of the typical education faculty is that many members do not see "professional preparation" as their prime job (*Study Commission Newsletter*, January, 1975, p. 16). In all education institutions, including those which have no graduate programs or limited ones (four-year colleges), almost 30 per cent of the faculty (28.1) listed the training of graduate students "as of first importance to [me] personally." Surprisingly, 18.4 per cent of four-year college education faculty listed this as their first priority. A second large group of education faculty see their priorities as duplicating those of the liberal arts faculties; 36.9 per cent of all education faculty see the need to "provide undergraduates with broad liberal education" as their first priority. Research commands a first priority rating with only 5.6 per cent of all education faculty. However, this leaves only 29.4 per cent of education faculty seeing the need to "prepare undergraduates for their chosen occupation" as their first priority activity. Only slightly more (37 per

cent) education faculty see their institution placing first priority on undergraduate teacher education, the activity which furnishes almost all of America's teachers. The following chart from the *Study Commission Newsletter,* January, 1975, p. 16, shows how faculty members ranked their priorities:

Item 201. According to their importance to you personally—(Percentages rated "of first importance," excluding those who marked two activities first).

Items ranked:
1. Provide undergraduates with broad liberal education
2. Prepare undergraduates for their chosen occupation
3. Train graduate or professional students
4. Engage in research

	All Faculty		University		Four-Year Colleges		Junior Colleges	
	Gen.	Ed.	Gen.	Ed.	Gen.	Ed.	Gen.	Ed.
1. (Lib. Ed.)	47.1	36.9	32.1	22.5	62.5	48.9	57.5	63.7
2. (Occupation)	26.4	29.4	20.2	28.5	28.7	29.7	41.0	36.3
3. (Grad. Students)	15.1	28.1	27.1	40.3	5.0	18.4	0.6	0.0
4. (Research)	11.5	5.6	20.6	8.7	3.7	3.0	0.8	0.0

Item 202 (same items ranked). According to your understanding of what your institution expects of you—(Percentages rated "of first importance," excluding those who marked two activities first).

	All Faculty		University		Four-Year Colleges		Junior Colleges	
	Gen.	Ed.	Gen.	Ed.	Gen.	Ed.	Gen.	Ed.
1. (Lib. Ed.)	40.6	30.2	23.4	15.3	60.4	40.8	45.5	60.9
2. (Occupation)	32.1	37.0	24.0	29.0	34.6	44.2	52.7	39.1
3. (Grad. Students)	11.6	19.9	21.6	29.4	3.2	13.0	0.3	0.0
4. (Research)	15.8	13.0	31.1	26.3	1.8	1.9	1.6	0.0

⁵⁶The need for new kinds of institutions as suggested by the Study Commission's argument is supported by Frank Wuest, director of Change in Liberal Education. He notes: (1) Frequently, new institutions must, in order to obtain accreditation, demonstrate their effectiveness with "scientific" rigor that no existing institution has been forced to match. (2) There is a body of data including work by Newcomb, Sanford, D. Brown, Chickering, Perry and others which suggests that most students in institutions learn *in spite of* the "community" created by faculties and administrations, that is, primarily by and because of the effects of peer groups. (3) Colleges and universities as institutions serve multiple purposes. A study by Gross and Grambsch, *University Goals and Academic Power,* indicates that the creation of a learning community is not a high-ranking priority. On a list of 47 possible goals, "training students for scholarship/research" ranked sixth in perceived importance; "prepare students for useful careers" ranked thirteenth; "cultivate students' intellect" ranked fourteenth. In the top twenty priorities, the majority had to do with the maintenance or increase of prestige and power of the faculty member or were directed toward the advancement of faculty research and scholarship. (4) Works by C. Robert Pace, *Demise of Diversity* (Berkeley, California: Carnegie Commission, 1974) and W.B. Martin, *Conformity* (San Francisco, California: Jossey-Bass Inc., 1969) point to the pattern of similarity in organization, values, goals and teaching/learning practice in most colleges and universities. This lack of diversity can be taken as an indication that modeling on the prestigious university remains the practice for any institution of higher education to adopt. (This research has been confirmed in large part by an analysis of the meaning of the Cartter report. See W. Patrick Dolan, *The Ranking Game: The Power of the Academic Elite,* to be published soon by the Study Commission.) (5) The range of directions of academic reform is quite limited. The Winter, 1975, *Daedalus* included an article by G. Grant and David Riesman which identified only five clear models of academic reform in existence in U.S. higher education. The "academic revolution" model, identified by Riesman and Jencks, includes Evergreen, Hampshire, and Green Bay and a number of other experimental institutions. These are classified as a subcategory of the "academic revolution" model which they call the "adaptation of means." Grant and Riesman mean by this that these institutions follow the academic model, differing solely in the means of achieving the desired goals. The other four alternative models are distinctive in that they represent consistent institutional patterns of reform. Very few institutions, however, fit these categories. (6) Given the limited range of alternative reform models which have developed and given the present need for reform, institutions which begin with a different cultural, philosophical, perceptual, motivational base hold some promise for developing new models of educational reform and assisting conventional institutions in finding new directions for themselves.

⁵⁷For example, see Martin Haberman and T.M. Stinnett, *Teacher Education and the New Profession of Teaching* (Berkeley, 1973), pp. 29-39. This pattern continued into the 60's. In the early 60's "normal schools" received less than half the support per student that typical universities received. See also Paul A. Olson,

"The Preparation of the Teacher: An Evaluation of the State of the Art," *Education for 1984 and After,* pp. 33-34.

[58]The Study Commission, using Carnegie indices, examined the NCHEMS/FTE reports on institutions, looking at the support given to teacher education at the various levels. Carnegie indices rank colleges as "high quality," "middle quality" and "lower quality," using the Gourman indices (supported by several other "quality indices") which rate quality of academic departments in terms of quality of instruction, proportion of students receiving scholarships and fellowships and quality of non-departmental features (e.g., administration "commitment to excellence," level of financial aid, board of trustees, faculty morale). Another quality index which the Carnegie group found to support Gourman was the Gross-Grambsch index, which includes fiscal features. Carnegie "Quality I" institutions scored 580 on Gourman; Quality II scored 477-579; Quality III had less than 477. According to Study Commission calculations, the average FTE cost per education major is about $1,500 at Carnegie I universities; $1,300 at Carnegie III universities; $2,100 at Carnegie I colleges, $1,200 at Carnegie II, and about $1,300 at Carnegie III. The lower the Carnegie rating of NCHEMS-analyzed institutions, the larger the percentage of education undergraduates. Except for the Class I colleges, all Carnegie levels appear to spend about $1,300-$1,500 per FTE undergraduate in education ('72-'73). This is lower than the cost for other undergraduate professional or preprofessional areas. In the other areas (engineering, nursing, social work, audiology, etc.), lower division costs tend to be around $1,300-$1,800 per FTE major and upper division around $2,000-$2,800.

Average tuition at public colleges in '72-'73 was about $500 and in private colleges about $2,200; education students appear to have paid about $650 average tuition or about half their full annual FTE cost per major. On the average, American students at all levels pay 1/5 of their full FTE costs (5.9 billion out of 29.5 billion). Moreover, it seems highly unlikely that any other professional area educates 65 per cent of its professionals at Carnegie Quality III colleges and universities. Most important, even the Carnegie I and II "quality" universities and the Carnegie II colleges do not spend much on educating teachers.

In 1969-70 about 30 per cent of all undergraduates were in education or planned a teaching career. There were 6 million undergraduates in 1969-70—about 1,800,000 potential teachers or 450,000 for each college year. In 1970, about 880,000 degrees were conferred, and about 1.8 million students started college. Dropouts reduced the number of education graduates to around 300,000 of the 880,000, or well over 30 per cent of the undergraduates graduating. Undergraduate education witnesses a drifting phenomenon—out of hard science and engineering areas into education. The total cost of undergraduate teacher education in 1970 at $1,300 per FTE and 1,800,000 students would have been about 2 billion, 340 million dollars. Total expenditure for higher education in the year was 24.7 billion dollars, of which the 2 billion+ dollars for teachers seems a remarkably small sum. Medical education and graduate education are included in the $24.7 billion figure.

When one puts this in "campus-by-campus" terms, comparing costs for courses in education-fieldwork courses with other fieldwork courses (i.e., elementary and secondary education with social work, nursing, or engineering), and when one compares education "clinical" courses with other field clinical courses (pathology, audiology, etc.), or education "liberal studies courses" (foundations) with comparable "liberal studies courses" (history, philosophy) in arts and sciences, education comes out on the short end of the stick 75 per cent of the time. Costs per credit hour and per FTE are lower 75 per cent of the time in fieldwork areas and 100 per cent of the time in foundation areas; only in clinical areas—educational psychology and special education—are they equal, and these areas have had heavy federal support. Education people are also being "educated" in less costly "arts and sciences" courses, and the ratio of education faculty to credit hours generated are high within the institutions. Even what many critics have regarded as the best and most exciting of places in education seems to have poor resources. The Center for Teaching and Learning at the University of North Dakota, praised by Silberman in *Crisis in the Classroom,* receives $36 per lower-division credit hour and $51 per upper-division, has a very high faculty-to-FTE credit hour ratio and receives about $1,500 annual support per FTE major. Thus, teacher education is not only primarily placed in the bottom-of-the-heap institutions, but when it is placed in the "quality institutions," it is given less than quality treatment. The areas chosen for comparison as requiring roughly comparable support (e.g., "history and philosophy of education" in education colleges to be compared with "history" and "philosophy" in arts and sciences colleges) were chosen by Vito Perrone, George Denemark, and Dean Corrigan—all deans of colleges of education. The figures were obtained from the forty NCHEMS model institutions (Cost Data and Descriptive Information booklets) and calculated by Gary Rex of the Study Commission staff. NCES has no statistics available in this area, but a recent calculation of "instructional program cost" in FTE majors in elementary education and special education using the most recent NCHEMS data shows basically the same pattern described here, with a few exceptions (Fisk, Shippensburg, SUNY at Plattsburgh, University of New Mexico "special ed"). This calculation was done by Lewin & Associates, *Design Study for a National Survey of the Preparation of Education Personnel* (Study Review Panel Book, June 3, 1975), pp. 13-16.

[59] The percentage of teacher candidates attending institutions at each of the Gourman levels was obtained by David Schadt from runs of the Carnegie study data. Cf. Anita A. Summers and Barbara L. Wolfe, "Which School Resources Help Learning? Efficiency and Equity in Philadelphia Public Schools," unpublished article available from the Philadelphia Federal Reserve Bank, p. 9 and *passim.*

[60] These calculations were done by Gary Rex and David Schadt of the Study Commission. The full calculations of NCHEMS statistics are available from Study Commission files.

[61] Antonia Pantoja, Barbara Blourock, James Bowman, editors, *Badges and*

Indicia of Slavery (Lincoln, Nebraska: Study Commission publication, 1975), p. 53.

[62]Pantoja, "University Based Training and Cultural Pluralism," *Badges and Indicia of Slavery,* pp. 50-53, 55-57.

[63]This is based on the Marilyn Gittell and Frederick Edelstein site visits done by the Cultural Pluralism and School Administrators Committees. Cf. Gittel, *Badges and Indicia of Slavery,* pages 64-117; cf. also the recent study of school-based teacher education by the School Administrators Committee, site visits by Frederick Edelstein and written by Lorna Carter and Edelstein. See also the Federal Role Committee's study of the Career Opportunities Program. Less than 50 per cent of the COP-IHE coordinators (or the chief-IHE officer, in this joint IHE-school program) have tenure at the IHE (47 per cent); only 57 per cent of the IHE's consider the COP director's work "deserving of consideration for promotion or salary increase." Between 30 per cent and 45 per cent of the COP "higher education" institutions (depending on who is reporting) have extended COP "admission modifications" to assist low-income or minority candidacy in teacher education. Only a little over 50 per cent of the COP institutions would recognize transfer courses from other COP programs as applying to a degree. And after several years of project operation, only 37.7 per cent of the faculty have tenure.

Jeanne Guertin, who conducted much of this COP research, wrote in explanation of the sentence beginning, "Less than 50 per cent . . .": "Fewer of the IHE coordinators were selected only for the duration of the project in comparison to the COP directors. Also fewer of the IHE coordinators had tenure (47 per cent). At the four-year institutions 64 per cent of the respondents felt, however, that participation in the COP program would be favorably looked upon for promotion. Since 57 of the 82 faculty members (70 per cent) who became IHE coordinators had not reached the full professor rank, the coordinator's job offered possible upward mobility at a later date. At the two-year institutions only 23 per cent of the respondents felt their COP positions would influence their position and/or compensation in the future. Both the 64 per cent and 23 per cent response to this question of promotion/compensation may well represent only faculty responses, as the percentage of administrators holding the coordinator's position is 40 per cent (four years) and 89 per cent (two years) respectively.

On the 34 per cent (two years) to 42 per cent (four years) extending admission modifications to other students, it should be remembered that most of the two-year colleges already had open admissions and some of the state universities which were selected for COP sites also had a form of open admissions prior to COP funding."

[64]Terkel, *Working,* pp. 490-93.

[65]Letter to the Study Commission from Alberto Nieto, Universidad de

Aztlan, July, 1972, Study Commission files.

[66] See, for example, the various essays in Nathan Wright, Jr., *What Black Educators Are Saying* (New York, 1970), pp. 231ff; cf. Davies' bibliography, pp. 85-123.

[67] This is a primary goal of the Coalition of Indian-Controlled School Boards, Suite 4, 811 Lincoln, Denver, Colorado 80203.

[68] *Inquiry Report: Kanawha County, West Virginia: A Textbook Study in Cultural Conflict,* p. 37.

[69] James Guthrie, *Public Affairs Report,* Bulletin of the Institute of Governmental Studies (Berkeley: University of California, June, 1974), pp. 1-4.

[70] James S. Coleman, *et al., Youth: Transition to Adulthood,* Report of the Panel on Youth of the President's Science Advisory Committee (Chicago, Illinois: University of Chicago Press, 1974).

[71] Albert Bandura, unpublished text, presidential address of the American Psychological Association, 1974. This set of learning postulates was drawn up by Frank Wuest (who works with a national project called Change in Liberal Education, supported by AACJC, AASCU, AAUP, AAC, and NASULGC) and Eleanor Duckworth, of the Ecole de Psychologie et Science de l'Education, Université de Génève. A series of profoundly significant experiments bearing on these questions are described in Jean Piaget and Barbel Inhelder, *The Growth of Logical Thinking from Childhood to Adolescence* (New York: Basic Books, 1958), *passim;* ideas particularly useful to education translated by Duckworth and others are contained in Vernon Rockcastle and Ripple, *Piaget Rediscovered* (Ithaca, New York: Cornell University School of Education Conference on Cognitive Studies and Curriculum Development publication, 1964). In addition, the following researches may be helpful: Noam Chomsky, review of B.F. Skinner's "Verbal Behavior," reproduced in Jerry A. Fodor and Jerrold J. Katz, *The Structure of Language* (Englewood Cliffs, New Jersey: Prentice Hall, 1964), pp. 547-79; cf. Ruth Weir, *Language in the Crib* (The Hague: Mouton, 1970); and Roger Brown and Ursula Bellugi, "Three Processes in the Child's Acquisition of Syntax," *Harvard Education Review* (Spring, 1964), xxxiv, 2, pp. 133-51. Cf. the testimony in the case of *Lau v. Nichols; ASPIRA; Serna v. Portales,* etc. Cf. the testimony of Bruce Gaarder, Joshua Fishman and others delivered in connection with the passage of the first Bilingual Education bill. Cf. Michael Cole and others, *The Cultural Context of Learning and Thinking* (New York: Basic Books, 1971), *passim;* cf. Michael Cole and Sylvia Scribner, "Cognitive Consequences of Formal and Informal Education," *Science* CLXXII, pp. 553-57. Cole and Scribner's work was carried out with the Kpell people of West Africa, but has analogues in the work of Murray and Rosalie Wax and others in this country. The research on the education of teachers is summarized

in Steve Hartman and Michael Simon, "The Effects of Teacher Training"; this is a review of research in the so-called "Merrow Report," an evaluation of BEPD policy and practice for the National Advisory Council on Education Profession Development, Appendix A, pp. 360-429; the "Merrow Report" is officially titled David Cohen, John Merrow, Ann Taylor, and Walter McCann, *The Role of Evaluation in Federal Education Training Programs,* Center for Educational Policy Research (Harvard University, 1971, mimeo).

[72] Apprenticeship learning is often recommended for skills teaching; it has an equally significant role in advanced scientific enterprises; cf. Stephen Toulmin, *Of Human Understanding* (Princeton, 1973), pp. 159-60. The different organizations of learning implied by various scientific disciplines and the varying student-teacher relations implied by various "disciplines" or "paradigm studies" is examined by Janice Beyer Lodahl and Gerald Gordon, "The Structure of Scientific Fields and the Functioning of University Graduate Departments," *American Sociological Review,* XXXVIII (1972), pp. 57-72. The Study Commission's Academic Disciplines Committee has been studying the relationship between paradigms for learning and the organization of schools and universities (in press).

[73] Elizabeth Hall, "A Conversation with Jean Piaget and Bärbel Inhelder," *Psychology Today*, III, 12 (May, 1970), p. 56.

[74] Letter to the Study Commission from David Hawkins, November 18, 1974, Study Commission files.

[75] Hector, *Teacher Depreciation,* pp. 73-90; cf. pp. 112-14. *The Condition of Education* chart, p. 73, says that in 1971, 29.6 per cent of America's teachers thought the teaching profession was getting worse, whereas in 1964-65 only 13.1 per cent thought the profession was getting worse. In 1965-66, 70.2 per cent of teachers thought the profession was getting better, a figure which in 1971 was down to 34 per cent.

[76] James Hoetker and William P. Ahlbrand, Jr., "The Persistence of Recitation," *AER Journal* (March, 1969), pp. 145-67.

[77] Sarason, *The Culture of the Schools and the Problem of Change,* pp. 167-69.

[78] In the recent past, during the summer, 58.1 per cent of the men and 20.4 per cent of women teachers moonlighted; during the winter, 57.3 per cent of the men and 15.1 per cent of women teachers moonlighted, according to the Research Division, National Education Association, in *The American Public School Teachers: 1965-66* (Washington, D.C., 1967), pp. 21, 24-26, 32-33.

[79] For general suggestions as to the need for change in the sense of the teachers' relationship to society, see O'Toole, *Work in America,* pp. 141-45. Coleman's

Youth: Transition to Adulthood, pp. 151-57, conceptualizes a changed role for the school which would change the whole of the teachers' relationship to the world of work. Coleman also calls attention to the whole tradition of research on smallness, pp. 154-55 and pp. 9-126, and recommends the development of small institutions or small subsets within institutions.

[80]The Student NEA, "Essential Criteria for Teacher Preparation Programs," adopted by the Student NEA (February, 1975), pp. 1-11.

[81]Cf. the Study Commission site visit reports on school-based teacher training at Parkway, Metro, and Shanti, available Study Commission files.

[82]Study Commission School Administrators Committee site visit report, available Study Commission files.

[83]*Study Commission Newsletter* (January, 1975), pp. 14-15.

[84]The quote is from Mr. Justice Burger's majority opinion in *Milliken v. Bradley,* quoted in *Education Daily,* July 29, 1974. Cf. the following quotes from Supreme Court opinions germane to the relation between state interest and parent and community rights:

> The fundamental theory of liberty upon which all governments in this Union repose excludes any general power of the state to standardize its children by forcing them to accept instruction from public teachers only. The child is not the mere creature of the state; those who nurture him and direct his destiny have the right, coupled with the high duty, to recognize and prepare him for additional obligations. *Pierce v. Society of Sisters,* 268 U.S. 510, 534-35.
>
> That the state may do much, go very far, indeed, in order to improve the quality of its citizens, physically, mentally, and morally, is clear; but the individual has certain fundamental rights which must be respected. . . . For the welfare of his Ideal Commonwealth, Plato suggested a law which should provide: "That the wives of our guardians are to be common, and their children are to be common, and no parent is to know his own child nor any child his parent. . . . The proper officers will take the offspring of the good parents to the pen or fold, and there they will deposit them with certain nurses who dwell in a separate quarter; but the offspring of the inferior, or of the better when they chance to be deformed, will be put away in some mysterious, unknown place, as they should be." In order to submerge the individual and develop ideal citizens, Sparta assembled the males at seven into barracks and intrusted their subsequent education and training to official guardians. Although such measures have been deliberately approved by men of great genius, their ideas touching the relation between individual and state were wholly different from those upon which our institutions rest; and it

hardly will be affirmed that any legislature could impose such restrictions upon the people of a state without doing violence to both letter and spirit of the Constitution. *Meyer v. Nebraska,* 262 U.S. 390, 401-02.

The foregoing statement is enough to show that the School Act and the measures adopted thereunder go far beyond mere regulation of privately supported schools where children obtain instruction deemed valuable by their parents and which is not obviously in conflict with any public interest. They give affirmative direction concerning the intimate and essential details of such schools, intrust their control to public officers, and deny both owners and patrons reasonable choice and discretion in respect of teachers, curriculum and textbooks. Enforcement of the act probably would destroy most, if not all, of them; and, certainly, it would deprive parents of fair opportunity to procure for their children instruction which they think important and we cannot say is harmful. The Japanese parent has the right to direct the education of his own child without unreasonable restrictions; the Constitution protects him as well as those who speak another tongue. *Farrington v. Tokushige,* 273 U.S. 284, 293-94.

The history and culture of western civilization reflect a strong tradition of parental concern for the nurture and upbringing of their children. The primary role of the parents in the upbringing of their children is now established beyond debate as an enduring American tradition. . . . However read, the court's holding in Pierce stands as a charter of the rights of parents to direct the religious upbringing of their children. And, when the interests of parenthood are combined with a free exercise claim of the nature revealed by this record, more than merely a "reasonable relation to some purpose within the competency of the state" is required to sustain the validity of the state's requirement under the First Amendment. To be sure, the power of the parent, even when linked to a free exercise claim, may be subject to limitation under *Pierce* if it appears that parental decisions will jeopardize the health or safety of the child, or have a potential for significant social burdens. *Wisconsin v. Yoder,* 406 U.S. 205.

This is interpreted by Attorney Gerrit H. Wormhoudt as meaning that parental decisions must prevail unless the government can show that parents have jeopardized the health and safety of the child or created a potential for significant social burdens ("Supreme Court Decisions," in William F. Rickenbacker, editor, *The Twelve-Year Sentence,* Lasalle, Illinois: Open Court, 1974, pp. 61-94).

CHAPTER III

LEGAL CONSTRAINTS: LICENSING, ACCREDITATION, AND EQUITY IN TEACHER EDUCATION

There is an old medicine man at Zuni who has agreed to take three of the primary children out for a walk each day; in the process, they talk about the vegetation and its significance in the older culture, its name both in English and in the older language. It is a very good experience. I was describing that to someone who told me, "But you know that's against the state law. The school is liable. He is not a certified teacher." And it is at this point that you really have to ask the question about who is the teacher. Not only legally, but morally, who is the teacher? . . .

A Sioux woman who teaches Sioux language and culture at the University (North Dakota) probably managed to finish the ninth grade; she is one of the finest teachers I have ever seen; her work with undergraduate students is exemplary. Could she teach at the high school? No. She couldn't teach at the high school because she lacks all of the certification to teach in that setting. Yet, she has more to contribute to the study of the history, language, culture of her own community than anyone else in the school.[1]

Licensing and Public Protection

The erosion of local cultural authority over education, of local community responsibility and will, begins with actions of the basic mechanisms legitimizing teaching as a profession: licensing and the related processes for accrediting institutions. These determine who—which institution's graduates—will be eligible for a license. Licensing, in its present state, is essentially a national process, unconcerned with such matters as which people are the constituents of the educational processes in this country, what sorts of communities are involved and what futures they project for themselves. As a consequence of the failure of licensing to protect people who have diverse needs, children in classrooms suffer or erect blank walls between themselves and their teachers. We should expect from any future licensing process that it will be just and that it will serve the purposes of education as envisaged by its constituents. As regards licensing processes, justice and service to constituents have received preliminary legal definitions.

A long line of court cases has established that as a general matter an individual cannot be hired and paid as a teacher or supervisor by a local school system without prior certification or licensing.[2] Courts consistently tend to uphold the state's prerogative to exercise its police power and limit the profession of teaching to those who meet prescribed criteria. Presumably, the establishment of such policies by states, and the courts' affirmation of such policies as state responsibility, are intended to protect the general welfare. The point of the courts' decisions—as far as they concern this Commission—is that licensing is a state responsibility, undertaken to insure high teaching standards at the local level—on the assumption that state officials know what constitutes good teaching at the local level. The licensing of teachers and other education personnel would appear to protect state and local interest by guaranteeing the professional competence of those who face children.

But like most other occupational licensing mechanisms, those developed for the teaching profession appear to have emerged haphazardly. Before the creation of public education systems in the United States, teachers were licensed in effect by being hired. The first statewide certification system emerged in Ohio in 1825; this system empowered county officers to examine candidates and issue certificates. Later New York State and Vermont placed this responsibility on county superintendents of schools. Generally, procedures of certification under these and later systems came to employ standardized examinations or preparation requirements. During the past seventy-five years a system which originally placed responsibility for licensing of teachers in some three thousand local licensing authorities has been reduced to the fifty state systems and a handful of large city school districts, such as New York City and Chicago, which retain special authority.

The present general or qualitative requirements for licensure as a teacher (elementary or secondary) appear to be simple enough. They are threefold: (1) typically, the states have citizenship, health, age, and moral requirements; (2) all states minimally require a bachelor's degree for certification; (3) about eight states also require specialized courses in state history, state and federal governments, agriculture and conservation (however, several of these states allow substitution of acceptable scores on proficiency exams in lieu of courses).

The quantitative requirements for licensure also appear at first sight to be straightforward. In 1973, the most common credit hour requirements for licensure among the various states were as follows: 40 to 48 semester hours in "general education" for elementary as well as secondary teachers; 18 to 24 semester hours in professional education for elementary teachers and between 18 and 21 semester hours for secondary teachers.[3]

The seemingly straightforward nature of these requirements may be misleading, however. Most states have adopted an "approved program" approach to the licensing procedure to replace licensure by a state department transcript analysis to see if one has taken the right courses for a license. Program approval is essentially state accreditation. State accreditation is, in turn, related to national accreditation. Hence, this chapter focuses on the legal footing on which both houses, that of accreditation and that of licensing, are erected.

The paths to licensure are in fact complex and crooked. In New Jersey, for instance, one can qualify for a regular certificate by a successful following of one of several routes. Most turn on the completion of one form or another of an accredited program. One can get a certificate if one completes: a state-approved teacher education program, a National Association of State Directors of Teacher Education and Certification (NASDTEC)-approved program accepted in the state licensing officers' list of institutions whose graduates are reciprocally accepted by other states, an elementary teacher education program in Delaware, Maryland, or Pennsylvania which meets state compact conditions, a National Council for the Accreditation of Teacher Education (NCATE)-approved program and several other sorts of "approved programs" or mixtures of approved programs, successful teaching experience or certificate, credit hours and teaching experience.[4]

These various procedures for qualifying for a license in New Jersey are not unusual reciprocal mechanisms; they represent a fairly typical attempt to establish means by which persons educated as teachers in one state can become licensed in another state. It is significant that no substantive reason is given for, for example, including Delaware, Maryland, and Pennsylvania in the elementary teacher compact and leaving out other states, and that no reference is made to what training in these states would do for people's unique talents for working with New Jersey children. Despite the arbitrariness of state rules for accepting licenses given in other states, certain articles of faith run through almost all of the statements as to interstate reciprocity mechanisms. These "articles of faith" mostly refer one back to the authority of NASDTEC and NCATE.

NCATE is a national profession-oriented accrediting body which accredits teacher education throughout the nation. NASDTEC is an organization of state licensing officers which has developed a common standard for approving programs whose graduates will upon recommendation of the program automatically receive certificates from the states. NASDTEC officer-developed "state approval" mechanisms *essentially constitute state accreditation of teacher education* in education *and* arts and science. They are subject to the same limitations as NCATE and regional accreditations and have the additional feature of being entangled with NCATE and professional society accreditation procedures.

For example, the NASDTEC Standards contain notes pertaining to interstate reciprocity, which begin by advising that "state department of education procedures for the approval of teacher education should take into account relationships with accrediting groups," and so on to cite important groups and discuss their relationships to state agencies:

> Of major importance in this regard are the National Council for Accreditation of Teacher Education (NCATE) and the six regional accrediting agencies: Middle States Association of Colleges and Secondary Schools, New England Association of Colleges and Secondary Schools, North Central Association of Colleges and Secondary Schools, Northwest Association of Secondary and Higher Schools, Southern Association of Colleges and Schools, and Western Association of Schools and Colleges. Each of these bodies has certain unique functions, but in general their purposes and procedures are similar.
>
> It would appear to be advantageous to state education

agencies to adopt policies which would permit maximum cooperation with NCATE and coordination of state approval and accreditation functions wherever possible. In organizing visiting committees, it would be desirable to establish cooperative arrangements which facilitate working relationships. Accreditation by NCATE represents a degree of quality in teacher education programs in a general and basic sense. Therefore, if an institution is NCATE-accredited, the state department of education may be able to place less emphasis on reviewing the over-all, general characteristics of a teacher education program (faculty, resources, policies for students, library, performance of graduates), and devote more attention to the review of specific programs. In certain instances, it may be desirable to conduct a cooperative comprehensive evaluation including a concurrent on-site visit by both state and NCATE teams.

It is also important that each state department of education coordinate its work insofar as possible with the regional association functioning in the state. As with NCATE, state departments may find it desirable to establish certain policies jointly with the regional association so that visiting committees of both groups can work within a framework of mutual understanding and with certain common objectives and procedures.

There are also groups concerned with the accreditation of various specialties, such as business, chemistry, and music. State departments of education need to be aware of the work of these groups and of their visitation schedules in the state's universities and colleges.

States in their approval procedures should take into consideration specialty, regional or national accreditation including the utilization of materials and information prepared for other accrediting groups in an effort to avoid unnecessary duplication of effort on the part of the institution being evaluated.[5]

NASDTEC suggests that various states' education departments should coordinate their licensing policies as much as is feasible, through their affiliations within regional associations or with NCATE; this would presumably aid reciprocity and ease the difficulties of transfer of certified teachers between states. However, NASDTEC essentially sidesteps the character of the precise relationships between regional accreditation and state approval. And individual states have varying policies. The Middle States Association requested the Pennsylvania State Board of Education to remove the general reciprocity requirement that an outside applicant for a Pennsylvania certificate be a graduate of a four-year, degree-granting accredited institution of higher education. Middle States Accreditation continues to be relied upon in lieu of state department accreditation, although where institutions do not voluntarily seek Middle States accreditation, the state department performs a Middle States Association-type evaluation.[6] Nebraska, on the other hand, explicitly requires at least candidate status with the North Central Association;[7] Illinois does not require or depend in any way on regional accreditation.[8] Thus no single characterization of the relationship between regional accreditation, NCATE accreditation, and NASDTEC accreditation will do for all states. And nothing in the reciprocity guidelines promises that children will be protected from boredom or unjust treatment, let alone harsher evils. The main protection for children which is supposed to exist is the authority conveyed by an institution which, by recommending its graduates to the state for a certificate, supposedly warrants their capacity to teach.

Character and Effects of Accreditation by NCATE and Regional Associations

But accreditation does not guarantee the quality of the graduates recommended for a license—at least not in any straightforward way. The present accrediting system for teachers in the U.S. is not set up to guarantee the quality of individual graduates, and it is very complex. A program for prospective teachers is "approved" by an institution; but this approval must be sanctioned by several accrediting systems—state and national—if a school's graduates are to be licensed: by national NCATE accreditation, national regional accreditation, and state program approval, and, indirectly, by professional society accrediting.

Four-year or graduate degree-granting institutions in teacher education are eligible for an accreditation evaluation by the national association, NCATE, if they offer programs for the preparation of teachers and/or other professional school personnel and if they fulfill the following prerequisites:

1. They are approved by the appropriate State Department

of Education at the degree levels and in the categories for which the accreditation is sought.

2. They are fully accredited by the appropriate regional accrediting association.

3. Students have been graduated from the program to be accredited so that an evaluation may be made of the quality of the preparation.

The NCATE Council regards accreditation by a regional accrediting association as *reasonable assurance of the overall quality* of an institution, including its general financial *stability,* the *effectiveness* of its administration, the *adequacy* of its general facilities, the *quality* of its student personnel program, the *strength* of its faculty, the *adequacy* of its faculty personnel policies, the conditions of faculty service, and the *quality* of instruction [emphasis added].[9]

One need not be a specialist in semantic nuances to observe that the italicized words are words more easily used by insiders to judge comers than they are by outsiders to identify failed responsibility on the part of established institutions and people.

NCATE regards accreditation by a regional accrediting association as "reasonable assurance of the overall quality of an institution." And in turn NASDTEC observes that "accreditation by NCATE represents a degree of quality in teacher education programs in general and basic sense." The process is circular. Somewhat arbitrarily, we have to begin with regional accreditation since it is the initial accreditation required in most states of an institution on the route to the status of an "approved teacher education institution."

Historically regional accreditation associations first performed analysis of secondary schools for the purpose of insuring that graduates of secondary schools had adequate background to be admitted into colleges. The main reason that regional associations later became involved in accreditation of higher education was to insure that graduates of undergraduate programs would be acceptable potential graduate students.

The regional associations can be viewed as growing out of efforts developed in the first two decades of the twentieth century and initiated by the Rockefeller-funded General Education Fund, the Fund for the Advancement of Teaching established by Andrew Carnegie, and the Association of American Universities (particularly its Committee on the Efficient College). It was during this period of efforts to establish the function of the regional associations, that formalized notions of what constitutes an American college and university came into being. Standards emerged for finance, faculty, physical facilities, admissions standards, and curriculum; and so far as can be discerned at the distance of sixty years, these standards were almost totally accepted by the regionals. Most of these standards were created in response to particular and unique historical circumstances and developed in response to management rather than educational problems and ideology. The standards for constitution of a college as presently enforced by the associations appear to be less mechanical and rigid than those originally established; one or another of the associations has, for instance, accredited a cluster college located in a university (Johnston College, University of the Redlands), accredited a consortium comprised of a number of institutions (University Without Walls and Union Graduate School), and granted candidate status to D-Q University, an Indian-Chicano institution in California. Whether these instances of accrediting action were in response to "political" pressure (Johnston College was well known; University Without Walls and Union Graduate School had its source in Antioch circles and had illustrious educators associated with it and its leadership was well-wired into foundations and USOE; and D-Q's history was stormy) or represent a shift in the association's practices is unclear.

In any case, the divorce between accreditation visitations and serious examinations of the process of education at an institution still exists. Harold Orlans, who has studied the regional associations for the Brookings Institute, sees them as failing to enforce their standards and as responding to political problems and pressure:

> A weakness of regional accreditation is that it has, for most practical purposes, stopped making quality distinctions. That will be denied, but we believe it is true and even axiomatic, for how can distinctions be drawn when all, or virtually all, eligible institutions are accredited?[10]

The implicit assumption in Orlan's position—that the regional associations *ought to make,* or *can make,* meaningful quality distinctions—is open to serious question. After studying North Central Association accrediting reports, Paul Dressel observed that "the examiners' reports coming in were notably weak in comments on evidence of institutional quality as reflected in the achievement of students."[11] Further, Frank Dickey and Jerry W. Miller argue:

> Lacking adequate indices and proven techniques of measurement, and occasionally lacking adequate concepts of educational effectivensss or excellence, accrediting agencies have been forced to rely more than is ideally desirable both on personal judgments which are fallible and on quantitative factors which do not always have a direct or proven correlation with excellence.[12]

No discussion of regional accrediting agencies would appear in this document if they merely engaged in making judgments about institutions *voluntarily* submitting to assessment and if they were in fact—as in name—voluntary associations. The formal relationship between NCATE and the regionals, and the formal or informal arrangements between the regionals and state agencies licensing teachers, indicate that, so far as teacher education is concerned, relationship to the regionals cannot be accurately described as voluntary. If the process is not a voluntary process, it should exhibit the characteristics which we expect of state actions in other spheres: equity and due process. But as Dressel and Miller and Dickey have suggested, the evaluations and determinations performed by accrediting agencies viewed as "technical" evaluations are severely deficient in that they employ largely unvalidated standards and procedures. As to the justice of the procedures as actually carried out, the recent North Central visit to Southwestern Michigan college was sufficiently lacking in *prima facie* impartiality to encourage an investigation by the staff of the Commission on Accreditation and Eligibility, as cited in *Chronicle of Higher Education:*

> ... The complaint filtered down to the Office of Education's Accreditation and Institutional Eligibility staff, headed by John R. Proffitt. Initially, Mr. Proffitt's office routinely accepted the complaint and sent off a letter to North Central asking it to cooperate in a joint assessment of the Anderson team's performance, and another to Mr. Mathews urging the trustees to go through North Central's appeal process. North Central, to Mr. Proffitt's surprise and anger, refused to cooperate.
>
> That was in August of last year. Over the next several

months, North Central and Mr. Proffitt went round and round arguing over the proper relationship between the federal government and privately controlled accrediting agencies, especially in messy situations like the one at Southwestern Michigan.

North Central said it would not submit to a federal review of an examining team's performance in any case where the aggrieved college had ignored the association's appeal process. Its final position then was that it would have nothing to say to Mr. Proffitt's office—or anyone else—about the details of the Southwestern Michigan case.

Mr. Proffitt, in turn, argued that the federal government had a public duty to check out all serious complaints about the impartiality of examining teams (which indirectly bore the government's approval), even if the appeal process of the accrediting agency had not been exhausted. He also privately and unofficially had reason to believe that Mr. Mathews' complaint might be legitimate and that a few other colleges had experienced similar problems with North Central. Last April, therefore, he put together a fact-finding team of six administrators and professors from around the country and asked them to look into the Anderson Team's performance. After talking with Mr. Mathews, trustees, administrators, faculty members, and students in Dowagiac—and getting a continued cold shoulder from North Central—the fact-finders submitted a report criticizing the team's behavior. . . . They agreed with Mr. Mathews that the North Central team had been guilty of sloppy procedures and that Mr. Anderson appeared to have been "inexperienced" in chairing such an examination.

The fact-finders said that Mr. Anderson and Mr. Fischer (but not Mr. Taibl) had been heard on several occasions to utter indiscreet remarks that were bound to raise questions about their impartiality, especially on a campus torn by tension over collective bargaining. It was unacceptable, the fact-finders said, for the examiners to say things like: "Do you know about the faculty getting screwed around here?" or "Why do you stay at this lousy school?" or "We've turned states around, we can turn this board [of trustees] around too." The two examiners, since they were covered by North Central's official blanket of silence on the issue, were not contacted by the fact-finders for their rebuttal, and they told *The Chronicle* last week they did not want to comment on the matter.

In May the fact-finders' report was considered in a public hearing by a fifteen-member committee of educators and laymen that oversees Mr. Proffitt's office and advises the Commissioner of Education on accreditation matters. North Central sent no one, but Mr. Mathews and the other trustees went to Washington to press their case. For the most part they restated their position, but Mr. Mathews also revealed a piece of recently discovered circumstantial evidence he considered important to his conspiracy theory. Mr. Anderson, he reported, was a former president of the Iowa Higher Education Association, with which Southwestern Michigan's union is connected.[13]

Orlans argues that "The public strength of accreditation rests on its mystique, and on the allegiance of precisely more eminent schools which have least need of it and whose presidents are most inclined to scorn it."[14] Such schools are also most likely to benefit from homeostasis and emulation. The Southwestern Michigan case suggests that it may be appropriate to regard the judgments of accreditors as providing a *social* acceptance or rejection as in a club or fraternity, rather than a *technical* acceptance or rejection.

If it were possible to argue that the regionals provide sound technical evaluations and that they enforced clearly articulated "standards of quality" that had been shown to be related to the provision of "quality" undergraduate education, even if these conditions prevailed (and they do not), the positive impact of the regionals on teacher education would still be unclear. For as long as the regionals accredit "institutions in general" and the so-called "general education" component of teacher education, the focus and purpose of the regionals are not sufficient to insure that the "work in the disciplines" required of teachers will be an adequate preparation for their teaching career in a particular community.

The second party in the accrediting-licensing processes, NCATE, unlike the regionals, is a "profession-oriented accrediting program," not an "institutional" accrediting body. The two parts of the accreditation system in higher education, the part conducted by NCATE and that conducted by the various regional accreditation agencies, are both parts of a total system which may impose sanction on, and otherwise influence, the program planning of an institution of higher learning. Neither part makes an analysis of the institution in relationship to environment-specific needs which the institution might serve—needs in its local area and culture. NCATE's purposes are:

1. To assure the public that particular institutions—those named in the annual list—offer programs for the preparation of teachers and other professional school personnel that meet national standards of quality;

2. To insure that children and youth are served by well-prepared school personnel;

3. To advance the teaching profession through the improvement of preparation programs;

4. To provide a practical basis for reciprocity among the states in certifying professional school personnel.[15]

Perhaps the most serious question raised by NCATE's declaration of purposes and standards grows out of the notion that there are identifiable and defensible "national standards of quality"; on its face, the Supreme Court's description of a national standard for pornography as "unascertainable and hypothetical" would appear to apply equally to "national standards of quality" in education. Moreover, the court decisions cited earlier in Chapters I and II seem to indicate that *national* standards (of the inflexible rubber stamp variety) would be inconsistent with the need for a continuing evolution of community-oriented education systems. Consider in this matter of "national standards" the implications for community-based education of the list of prerequisites to be fulfilled by an institution to be eligible for evaluation by NCATE (quoted earlier on pages 106 and 107), and especially the implications of the sentence about "reasonable assurance of . . . quality." Consider also the effect of the description of the preferred departmental structure:

I. *Content for the Teaching Specialty:* [i.e., common school departmental specialties plus elementary education as a "teaching specialty":]

. . . The instruction in the subject matter for the teaching specialties is the basic responsibility of the respective academic departments; the identification and selection of courses and other learning experiences required for a teaching specialty, however, are the joint responsibility of appropriate members of the faculty in the teaching specialty concerned and members of the teacher education faculty. . . . "Teaching specialty" as used in the standard includes elementary education as a specialized field as well as the various specializations offered in the secondary school. . . .

II. *Humanistic and Behavioral Studies:* [i.e., Foundations and Educational Psychology and related studies:]

. . . In the following standard it is assumed that problems concerning the nature and aims of education, the curriculum, the organization and administration of a school system, and the process of teaching and learning can be studied with respect to their historical development and the philosophical issues to which they are related. These studies are referred to hereafter as the humanistic studies. The problems of education can also be studied with respect to the findings and methods of psychology, sociology, anthropology, economics, and political science. Such studies are referred to as behavioral studies. These humanistic and behavioral studies differ from the usual study of history, philosophy, psychology, sociology, anthropology, economics, and political science in that they address themselves to the problems of education. . . .

. . . The standard does not imply that instruction in the humanistic and behavioral studies should be organized or structured in a particular way. Instruction in these studies may be offered in such courses as history and/or philosophy of education, educational sociology, psychology, sociology, or as topics in foundation courses, problems in education courses, or in professional block programs; or as independent readings.

III. *Teaching and Learning Theory with Laboratory and Clinical Experience:* [i.e., Curriculum and Instruction:]

. . . Much of what has been called "general methods" and "special methods" can therefore be taught as the application of teaching and learning theory.

Whereas the study of teaching and learning theory provides the prospective teacher with principles of practice, and the laboratory exercises illuminate and demonstrate these principles, clinical experience confronts the student with individual cases or problems, the diagnosis and solution of which involve the application of principles and theory. . . .

IV. *Practicum:* [i.e., Practice Teaching:]

. . . "Practicum" refers to a period of experience in professional practice during which the student tests and reconstructs the theory which he has evolved and during which he further develops his own teaching style. It provides an opportunity for the student to assume major responsibility for the full range of teaching duties in a real school situation under the guidance of qualified personnel from the institution and from the cooperating elementary or secondary school.[16]

The standard—both in what it says directly and in what the bland tone implies—suggests that NCATE does not seek to guarantee environment-specific quality, the quality appropriate to local community-sensitive education. Chapter II of the present report says that the "efficient" standardized training program turns out the "efficient" standardized teacher, highly qualified for alienation from students and communities. The more "qualified" the teacher trainers and trainees are in terms of this NCATE standard, we submit, the more alienated common school classrooms, children, and some communities are likely to be from each other.[17] The procedures of the NCATE standard suggest equally vividly that it lacks the formal mechanisms required for effective consumer protection. With the organization in the last year of the Commission on Postsecondary Education the point was made that accreditation is a consumer protection function. But little provision is made for that function. For example, the standard requests no educational analysis of what is happening in the schools where graduates of the institution are placed, no judgment by parents or children or students in the IHE. Some members of the Student National Education Association (NEA) report that NCATE enforcement of "student participant" rubrics in the guidelines is without teeth. "In-service assistance" is treated as a regional matter, but nothing is stated about how the special needs of the area are to be envisaged and served. When the Study Commission wrote to NCATE as a "protective" or "regulatory" agency asking for the data on effectiveness of recent graduates which it had collected under its evaluation standard from institutions recently accredited, the reply signed by Doran Christensen, associate director, indicated that "we are sorry to inform you that the documents used in NCATE evaluation and accreditation activities are considered confidential" and invited the directorate to "please call on us if you would be interested in the list of institutions or any other information which we can *legitimately* provide" [emphasis added].[18] Normative national judgments as apart from some thoughtful consideration of what the judgments are for or some careful validation of them move institutions toward national norms. They do not assure quality.

It may be that these limitations are what Commissioner Terrell Bell is pointing to in a recent letter extending NCATE's position on the Commissioner's list of accrediting agencies for only one year. The substantive part of the Bell letter, which makes a rather harsh judgment on NCATE, reads as follows:

> The Advisory Committee's recommendation for a one-year extension of recognition is based upon the Committee's judgment that the Council has failed to address substantively the Criteria for Recognition. The Committee also judged that the accreditation policies and procedures of the Council do not comply satisfactorily with criteria (b)(2)(iv) (complaint review procedures); (b)(4) (ethical practices); and (c)(4) (reflects community of interests) of the Criteria for Recognition. Other special concerns of the Advisory Committee relate to the adequacy of the Council's staff and financial resources to carry out its accreditation program effectively, the length of time between regularly scheduled onsite evaluations of accredited programs, the training and competency of visiting teams, and the Council's encouragement of new and innovative programs. The Committee has requested that, at the end of one year, the Council submit a petition for continued recognition which responds especially to the concerns cited by the Committee.[19]

We would suggest, with respect to national accrediting associations engaged in accrediting teacher education institutions:

1. That their procedures should be straightforward and not circular (i.e., one accreditation depending on and reinforcing another).

2. That "total" teacher training programs should be accred-

ited—within arts and science and education, and wherever else teacher education is done—in terms of a total institutional "mission statement," generally tied to the in-service and pre-service region that the school serves.

3. That the accreditation visitation should look first at how children and parents are being served in the area of expertise which the college or university defines as "its mission." This information could be obtained by getting structured direct and indirect feedback from students and parents, through visits to schools in the region—particularly those least likely to be well served—to see if they are places where children should be, as well as through examining achievement based on criterion-referenced instruments, reflecting community planning and culture-based norms.

4. That the notion of "consumer protection" basic to recent defenses of state program approval and regional and NCATE action would, to be meaningful, have to include several features:

a. Parent, common school student and IHE student would have to have access to all information gathered by the school for the accrediting association on its fulfillment of mission and the performance of its graduates. In developing modes of access, accrediting agencies may profit from the model of constituency-based evaluation now used in California for approved programs. The first four pilot evaluations have been completed. Whereas some higher education institutions and schools of education have not been particularly pleased with the procedures, they are a first attempt to gather information on institutions' fulfillment of mission and the performance of graduates, and as such should instruct others endeavoring to do similar things.[20]

b. Wherever licensing is tied to accreditation and parents and students are not meaningfully part of the accreditation and validation processes attached to accreditation, parents would have to have the right to sue the IHE which gives the degree and recommends for the license if the teacher cannot perform the job for which he/she is licensed. Graduates would have to have the right, if recommended for a license, to sue the recommending institutions if they cannot perform adequately in jobs for which their license and course of study have putatively prepared them.

Professional Societies and Their Influence on Teacher Education

Though NCATE and the regionals constitute the recognized national groups having a prescribed role in national accreditation related to teaching, the professional societies also have a strong role. Pervasive throughout the standards of NCATE, NASDTEC, and individual state approval systems is their strong reliance on curriculum guidelines or advice proffered by "national learned societies and professional associations" for application in teacher training procedures. These tend to reduce the autonomy of the IHE or IHE-school consortium creating teacher education and to make planning less a matter of finding and fulfilling a mission than going by the book. The NCATE standards explicitly provide that "in planning and developing curricula for teacher education, the institution gives due consideration to guidelines for teacher preparation developed by national learned societies and professional associations." The NASDTEC standards on curriculum development include "cooperation and participation of professional associations [and] appropriate committees and commissions," among other groups. Illinois and Nebraska state standards, for example, include similar provisions.

The extant advice, recommendations, and guidelines from professional societies have their primary source in federally-funded projects dating from the 1960's in which, for the most part, NASDTEC worked with a number of professional societies to develop guidelines for teacher education in various discipline-oriented specialties. The advice which is professional society-oriented almost always has to do with courses taken by teachers in arts and sciences to fulfill so-called "teaching majors." Some societies come perilously close to listing not only what departments must be present but what courses must be offered: e.g., English requires phonology, morphology, syntax, metalinguistics, adolescent literature, English literature, American literature, contemporary literature, and "major works," all features of standard pre-graduate school training in English and sliced as in the most standard curricula. Such prescription not only has a strong effect on what courses will be offered within a "discipline" or department—and therefore also on what courses will be left out; the suggestion or prescription of what courses are to be offered inhibits, if it does not absolutely prohibit, interdisciplinary developments, particularly efforts to create some organic merging of the traditional functions of departments or of colleges of arts and sciences and colleges of education as they undertake task-oriented activities to meet the needs of clients in the field.[21]

One Michigan school reports that its programs "follow," "meet," or "surpass" the guidelines or recommendations of the following organizations: National Art Education Association, Committee on Undergraduate Education in the Biological Sciences, National Business Education Association and Delta Pi Epsilon National Communication Association, American Economics Association, Joint Council on Economic Education, NASDTEC Committee on English, American Council on Teaching of Foreign Languages, Commission on College Geography of Association of American Geographics, American Home Economics Association; as well as National Council of Family Relations, American Council on Industrial Arts Teacher Education, National Association of Industrial Teacher Educators, American Vocational Association, American Technical Association, Committee on Undergraduate Education Program of Mathematics Association of America, American Association for Health, Physical Education and Recreation, and the Council for Exceptional Children. Further, it reports that four programs are accredited or approved by the American Chemical Society, the American Library Association, National Association of Schools of Music, and American Speech and Hearing Association. Clearly the influence of these national societies and associations is pervasive at this particular institution, an institution ranking second nationally in the number of teaching certificates issued annually.

Certain NCATE reports illustrate the position of professional societies in teacher training institutions; in one report a major urban university spokesman comments that "The professional societies and associations *important to teacher preparation* have found a number of their leaders and innovators in this School of Education" [emphasis added], and calls attention to the fact that "in most of the individual departmental reports, mention is made of liaison activities with professional organizations of national and international scope."[22] If "leaders and innovators" of certain professional societies also have influence in a school of education, the strong possibility exists that the interests of those professional societies will be well served there; the resulting increase in standardization of teacher education will likely be to the detriment of community-based and local culture-based approaches to teacher education.

The NCATE standard regarding professional associations and learned societies has in effect made even non-accrediting associations and societies *de facto* accrediting ones. A departure from the guidelines and recommendations apparently requires a substantial rationale, while their acceptance requires very little explanation or defense, if any. The guidelines and recommendations (and the teacher programs based on them) which have emerged from national bodies, the states, and from professional societies remain to be validated as having positive effects on the skills, the knowledge, and the competence of prospective or of in-service teachers. It has also not been demonstrated that completion of such a program will cause a teacher to have a "benign" (positive) effect on the achievement or the well-being of the children whom he or she teaches.[23] This absence of validation suggests once again that accreditation and approval mechanisms could, and probably should, be challenged; if accreditation systems rely strongly on the recommendations of professional societies, and the programs based on those recommendations do not meet the needs of children, then the accreditation systems and their reliance on professional societies appear to need amendment.

Profession-Controlled Standards for Licensing

State accreditation which determines precisely which institutions may recommend teachers for licenses and which may not is, in most places, conducted using the same logic as national accreditation and also using many of its determinations. However, state accreditation also requires attention to professional society guidelines developed in consort with NASDTEC. This state licensing system does not now effectually protect the average parent or child from meeting bad teachers and does not protect whole communities from encountering teaching forces not prepared to relate to their designs and customs. Why this is the case is suggested by a report entitled National Policy and Higher Education, by a special task force to the Secretary of HEW (the so-called Second Newman group). The Newman group presents this statement on organized professions as a whole:

> Standards of training and competency in many occupations are essential for consumer protection. All too often, however, such standards become the means for limiting entry to careers.[24]

According to Benjamin Shimberg, it is occupational groups or professions themselves who tend to approve and strongly recommend standardized, restrictive licensing of their prospective new members:

> Pleas for licensing a new occupation have seldom come from

the public or in response to a clearly demonstrated need. More usually the legislative bodies of the states and even of municipalities have heeded the special pleas of the practitioners that public harm might result if steps were not taken to regulate the occupation. Legislation has often been passed with little thought to the conflict of interest created by placing controls in the hands of the very group that was to be regulated.[25]

If, as Shimberg and others suggest, licensing practices for a particular occupation are established by those practicing and wishing to practice that occupation at the time licensing becomes desirable, then it is questionable whether states are indeed protecting either the public interest or the general welfare of their citizens.

But even if the myriad professional licensing boards at the state and local levels were always created in response to identifiable and specific public interests or to public welfare that needed protection and required licensing, it remains questionable whether licensing procedures and criteria as presently conceived and employed—a sort of police power for the state—are capable of providing that protection.

Albert Maslow, Chief of the Personnel Measurement Research and Development Center, U.S. Civil Service Commission, had this to say to a group of state licensing officials:

> I am convinced that we need to sharpen our ability to develop and demonstrate the *rational* relationship between the job requirements and the measurement *system* used to certify or qualify people for an occupation.... The entire decision-making process, from setting minimum standards to making final certification on the basis of appraisal data, must be very carefully analyzed step by step to make sure that it does not inadvertently lock out certain segments of our population.[26]

Vulnerability of Licensing Systems: Emerging Legal Doctrines

An important series of recent court cases, decided under or in conjunction with Title VII of the Civil Rights Act of 1964, have specifically held that large segments of the population have in fact been illegally "locked out" of teaching and other professions by present certification procedures. These cases have required licensing officials to revamp their methods and assure that all job requirements are demonstrably related to attributes actually needed to perform well on the job. It appears that state licensing requirements may be challenged on two fronts:

    1. The procedures themselves may be questioned as racially or sexually discriminatory.

    2. The accreditation system which is the foundation for licensing may be questioned as, in effect, *state action* (that is, an action of a body politic) placing involuntary burdens on certain citizens and institutions without proper safeguards and under monopolistic conditions.

Title VII of the Civil Rights Act of 1964 came about in response to a perception that then-existing employee selection procedures discriminated against minority group applicants on the basis of non-job-related selection criteria. The Title broadly prohibits discriminatory practices in hiring policies. It also empowers the Equal Employment Opportunity Commission (EEOC) to promulgate detailed guidelines to ensure effective enforcement of the Act.

The EEOC guidelines establish three specific methods for providing assurance that an employee selection system is "validated" and non-discriminatory: (1) "criterion-related" or "predictive" validation, which involves a demonstration that high test scores actually correlate to superior on-the-job performance, as measured by definable performance criteria; (2) "content validation," which involves a demonstration that the content of a testing device appears on its face to be directly related to the particular job under consideration; and (3) the rather obscure technique of "construct validation," which involves a demonstration that physical or mental traits (constructs) needed on a job correlate with a test which purports to measure those traits.

While most discussions of Title VII focus on "testing," it is important to note that the EEOC guidelines interpret the statutory provisions of Title VII as prohibiting the use of discriminatory "tests" or the discriminatory use of "tests" rather broadly to include, in addition to "all formal scored, quantified or standardized techniques of assessing job suitability," all "specific educational . . . requirements." The rigorous EEOC guidelines were specifically upheld by the U.S. Supreme Court in its landmark decision in *Griggs v. Duke Power Company*.[27] There the Court held to be invalid for the job under consideration not only certain standardized tests (the Wonderlic Personnel Test and the Bennet Mechanical Aptitude Test) but also the requirement for a high school diploma, stating:

> The facts of this case demonstrate the inadequacy of broad and general testing devices as well as the infirmity of using diplomas or degrees as fixed measures of capability . . . diplomas and tests are useful servants, but Congress had mandated the common-sense proposition that they are not to become masters of reality.[28]

Although Title VII as originally enacted applied basically to private employers, its precepts (and the thrust of the EEOC guidelines) were enforced by the courts against discriminatory hiring and licensing practices of state and local governments through the Fourteenth Amendment; in 1972, Congress specifically amended Title VII to apply directly to local government employment practices. The range of local governmental licensing practices held invalid by the courts have included examinations for police officers, transit workers, firefighters— and written examinations used to screen applicants for public school teaching and supervisory positions such as the National Teachers Examination and the New York City Board of Examiners tests.[29]

The manner in which the courts have applied the Title VII standards to school licensing situations is illustrated by Judge Mansfield's decision in *Chance v. Board of Examiners*. Having determined that the New York City Board of Examiners tests for supervisors (which resulted in a situation where only about 1 per cent of the system's principals were black or Puerto Rican) appeared to have a discriminatory impact upon minority group applicants, the judge required that the defendants make "a strong showing" that this type of examination measures "abilities essential to performance of the supervisory positions for which they are given."[30]

Analyzing in detail the actual examinations given by the Board, the court found that no meaningful predictive validation studies had been undertaken and that even on the less stringent "content validation" standard, the tests could not qualify as being reasonably related to actual job requirements. For example, many of the questions appeared to be "aimed at testing the candidate's ability to memorize rather than the qualities normally associated with a school administrator." Other questions appeared to be totally irrelevant to success on the job as indicated by the following examples cited in the judge's opinion:

I've Got a Little List from *The Mikado* is sung by: (1) Nanki-Poo, (2) Pish-Tush, (3) Ko-Ko, (4) Pooh-Bah;

Which one of the following violin makers is not of the great triumvirate of Cremona? (1) Amati, (2) Stradivarius, (3) Guarnerius, (4) Maggini.[31]

Having found that "the Board has not in practice achieved the goals of constructing examination procedures that are truly job-related," the court issued an injunction banning the continued use of the traditional licensing system. As a result of this injunction, the plaintiffs and the Board are in the process of implementing a new licensing system based upon detailed descriptions of actual job requirements and an extensive on-the-job evaluation process geared to the specific criteria set forth in the job descriptions.

The court's conclusions concerning the New York City supervisors' examinations in *Chance* have been found by a number of other federal courts to apply also to the widely used National Teachers Examination (NTE). For example in *Walston v. Nansemond County School Board,* the court held:

Here the tests measure the person in the abstract. . . . If these questions are a fair example of the remainder of the examination, any connection between the examination and effective teaching is purely coincidental. The NTE, as used by the Board, does not purport to measure the teacher's actual knowledge of the subject matter assigned to be taught or his performance in the classroom, but places primary emphasis on general education and professional training.[32]

The circumstances in which the National Teachers Exam was used in Nansemond County are not unlike the circumstances in which teachers are asked to take "general education" courses as part of the process of fulfilling requirements for a license. First grade teachers were asked as a possible condition of employment to tell who Lucasta, Corinna, Althea, and Julia were (they were 17th century minor Cavalier poets' imaginary mistresses, a bit of information few graduate level English literature departments would regard as crucial). Such a question was asked of teacher applicants in Nansemond County, while no questions appeared which related to "playing the dozens" or to black or other folk literary traditions. A series of English usage discriminations rooted neither in professional writing nor in black dialect were also asked for. The architectural style of St. Basil's Cathedral was asked about, but nothing was asked about the plumbing or housing in Nansemond County or the political forces that shape them. In a brilliant brief, to which the Circuit Court of Appeals paid special attention when it threw out the NTE as discriminatory and non-job-related, National Education Association (NEA) lawyer David Rubin noted that the test, given to high school physics teachers as well as to second grade teachers, carried no evidence that "it tested for knowledge which the job analysis showed to be essential to the job." The test also carried no evidence that it avoided testing "knowledge that might be unrelated to the job."[33]

Title VII-related challenges to current teacher licensing procedures can be expected to increase dramatically in the near future.[34] And it is likely that not merely written examinations but also degree requirements and "approved" program credentialling will be subjected to close judicial scrutiny.[35]

Under existing laws or regulations in most states, when a teacher is licensed, he or she is declared ready to teach on the basis of having completed an approved educational program—not on the basis of an assessment of personal competence. In effect, it is the *program that is certified, not the teacher.* It is becoming increasingly evident, in light of the above court precedents, that such certification by total "program approval" will be legally vulnerable.

According to the Standards for State Approval of Teacher Education set up by NASDTEC, "each State Department of Education is involved directly or indirectly in the accreditation or approval of teacher education programs within both public and private colleges and universities in the State." Under the "approved program" approach, teacher education institutions develop programs of teacher education in accordance with departmentally generated standards. The state education department then reviews, evaluates, and if the program is adequate, approves it. Involved in the program approval approach is "the understanding that the teacher candidate, upon completion of a program thus approved, as attested by the institution, will be entitled to official recognition [i.e., certification] by the State Education Agency." So far as can be determined there are no provisions for judging the effects of the programs or for measuring an increment of achievement and state of well-being in children taught from these programs. It is highly doubtful that these programs could satisfy the vigorous validation requirements of the EEOC guidelines.

The "program approval" approach to the licensing of teacher program graduates appears to be vulnerable to attacks on Title VII-type grounds involving sexual and racial discrimination in the granting of jobs (and possibly also vulnerable to consumer-initiated action[36]) because:

1. No predictive or criterion-related validity has been demonstrated (there are almost no adequate measures currently in existence to ascertain whether people who finish a certain "approved" training do a superior or even an adequate job of teaching real students in real communities).

2. Content validity probably cannot be demonstrated because program approvals are made without prior analyses of the jobs which persons certified upon completion of the program will be entitled to hold or will have to fill.

3. Program approvals by one state are frequently relied on by another state for issuance of certificates, even though the job of teaching may vary radically because of the differences in the communities and students in the two states.

In light of these indications of legal vulnerability of "approved programs," one can only question what a dean or chairman of education may be certifying or what he may believe he is certifying when he signs the statement on a state application form for certification which says, "I certify that the applicant has completed an *approved program* of teacher education and recommend the applicant as being competent in the program of study." In direct contrast to this reassuring affirmation of the competence of approved program graduates, note this statement from the extensive study of the University Council for Educational Administration, Commission on Certification:

With respect to legal and quasi-legal constraints . . . we do not have adequate evidence to justify, particularly with reference to performance criteria, typical existing state certification requirements, university division standards or preparatory programs in educational administration.[37]

While Title VII and EEOC challenges may correct a number of situations where present licensing creates demonstrable racist or sexist effects on the pool of available personnel, they may not inspire a full legal review of present licensing for teachers. Michael A. Rebell, a New York attorney experienced in education law matters, has analyzed the Title VII precedents and has articulated a number of specific legal theories that might provide grounds for extending the precedents established in the cases invalidating special written examination requirements to the broader context of the overall teacher credentialling systems.[38]

First, Rebell argues along the same lines previously mentioned—that present credentialling practices and even many proposed Competency Based Teacher Education reforms would probably be invalidated if subjected to rigorous scrutiny under the EEOC guidelines. However, as indicated in the above discussion of the *Chance* case, in order to directly invoke the EEOC guidelines, a showing must be made of racial or sexual discrimination. Attempting to base a legal attack directly on Title VII alone would be problematic as a practical matter because of the difficulty of obtaining "discriminatory impact statistics on state credentialling laws and practices." Showing a discriminatory impact in approved program credentialling would in essence invoke an analysis of admission and fail-out policies at all colleges in the state (and possibly at all out-of-state colleges which are granted reciprocity privileges).

Rebell's second theory seeks to base a challenge to present teacher credentialling laws on general Constitutional principles which would apply even if there is no strict showing of racial discrimination. This approach works off what he calls "the basic irrationality of perpetuating requirements which have no demonstrable predictive or content validity." A number of recent cases—in the employment discrimination area and elsewhere—indicate that the courts may be moving toward a revitalization of the traditional "compelling interest" or a stronger "rational relationship test," a revitalization that would place a burden on the state to justify types of regulatory actions which for the past few decades have been considered immune from judicial scrutiny. The availability of the EEOC guidelines and other validation measures may provide the necessary tools that would persuade the courts that workable standards are now available for assessing the rationality of vague, invalidated credentialling requirements and that these issues are justiciable.

In addition to equal protection and due process arguments which might be raised on behalf of prospective teachers who are denied employment, Rebell proposes an additional legal approach which could be presented by representatives of aggrieved children and parents. Part of his argument here is that:

> Enforcement of irrational teacher credentialling laws which deny ghetto communities the full ability to hire creative teachers sensitive to their needs could be cited as specific, discriminatory state action. If discriminatory impact could be shown by proving that teachers currently working in ghetto communities are less capable of meeting local performance needs than teachers in middle class communities, the likelihood of rigorous judicial scrutiny of present credentialling laws, whether under the "compelling state interest" or the re-vitalized "rational relationship" rubric, would be enhanced. Of equal importance is the fact that a community perspective might insure that any ultimate relief ordered by a court would take full cognizance of the need to fashion a credentialling sytem that is directly responsive to *local* needs.[39]

New Efforts and Cultural Neutrality in Licensing

Efforts exist to create new sorts of preparation for education personnel, and new ways of assessing them for licensure: in general these are "competency" or "performance"-based systems, advocated in such books as *The Power of Competency-Based Teacher Education* (a report of the Committee on National Program Priorities in Teacher Education). At least seventeen states have taken steps to incorporate aspects of this new approach into their laws and regulations. However, such systems may not be the adequate solution that their advocates claim. William L. Robinson's commentary, "The Power of Competency-Based Teacher Education: Views of a Civil Rights Lawyer,"[40] is instructive, arguing for a more rigorous criterion-referenced or predictive validation of teacher education and licensing. This would require establishing validity not only in terms of the effects of a teacher education program on the *competencies of a prospective teacher in a discipline area* but also in terms of *the effects of the teacher on student achievement and well-being*. Robinson therefore proposes a two-prong test of the validity of teacher licensing practices—in both competence and effect on the student. It is this sort of licensing, tempered not only to subject matter area and grade levels but also to the differing needs of differing children, parents and communities, which we advocate.

The latter test, the test of effect on students, is particularly interesting to the Study Commission in that it recalls the relationships between education, especially education personnel, and the communities in which education takes place. A long line of court cases, some of which we have mentioned in Chapters I and II, has brought education squarely before the eye of the courts and has indicated growing judicial sensitivity to the need to protect the rights in education processes of diverse communities, cultures, and students. When students come to school, they come replete with all the culture patterns they have learned: linguistic, cognitive, affective, gestural, kinesic, social. The direction and import of these patterns need to be caught by and responded to by a teacher in ways which will pass Robinson's proposed second test for licensing and increase the achievement and well-being of the student.[41] The most vital, most sensitive, most visible and useful aspect of their culture that students bring to school with them is their language.

A policy statement adopted by the Executive Committee of the Conference on College Composition and Communication (Spring, 1972) supports the view that students have a right to their language and dialect and to the rest of the world in which they find their identity and style. The statement begins:

> We affirm the student's right to his own language—the dialect of his nurture in which he finds his identity and style. . . .

and goes on to affirm the desirability of preserving the great cultural variety still extant in America—a variety which includes that of dialects. The final comment of the statement is:

> We affirm strongly the need for teachers to have such training as will enable them to support this goal of diversity and this right of the student to his own language.[42]

This is a professional society speaking. If we choose to attend to this particular professional society, as opposed to some others, and attend also to the words of the courts regarding the student's right to his own language and to a teacher who speaks it, we may see beneath the superfices of the position the assertion of a basic principle of benign effect in the relationship between teacher and student. This "principle of benign effect" requires strict neutrality in attitude toward all students in the matter of language, calling upon teachers, administrators, and others not to deny to any students their language and not to disparage the language or dialect of any student. This principle appears to have been directly accepted in the consent decree recently entered by the court in *ASPIRA v. Board of Education.* That order requires the school officials not only to provide intensive English language instruction to Spanish-speaking pupils but also to adopt a "planned and systematic program designed to reinforce and develop the child's use of Spanish."[43] The existence of linguistic imperialism such as that reprimanded in the *ASPIRA* decision has been strongly documented.[44]

The Supreme Court's decision in *Lau v. Nichols* (Supreme Court, 1973) and the other bilingual education cases discussed earlier have clear consequences for the certification and hiring of teachers: teachers in schools attended by students whose linguistic and cultural attributes are not those of the dominant culture should be required to be fluent in the proper non-English language or languages, and should be fully attuned to the students' cultures as well. Specific criteria for such linguistic and cultural proficiency should appear in the detailed job descriptions required under the EEOC guidelines. The significance of this problem cannot be overstated. **In 1969** it was estimated that some three million children were speaking non-English languages as their native tongue and that 75 to 80 per cent of all black children of school age commanded a southern rural or northern urban dialect of English which their teachers in most cases did not know. At that time, USOE argued that approximately six *million* American children "are taught by people who 'do not know their language'."[45] Title VII ESEA officials **in 1975** placed the number of limited-English and no-English children in the United States at between eight million and twelve million (eight million was the Bureau of Census estimate and ten to twelve million was the National Urban Coalition estimate).[46] Licensing as presently conducted clearly is not even guaranteeing children teachers who can speak their language—let alone the other more subtle qualities needed in their teachers.

Justice William O. Douglas, in his dissent to the Supreme Court's refusal on technical grounds to consider the constitutionality of an affirmative action law school admissions policy in *De Funis v.*

Odegaard (1974), elaborated at length on the need for clear understanding of cultural or "racial neutrality" in our diverse society. In arguing for cultural sensitivity in admissions policies, Douglas stated:

> The Indian who walks to the beat of Chief Seattle of the Muckleshoot Tribe in Washington has a different culture than Examiners at Law Schools. I do know, coming as I do from Indian country in Washington, that many of the young Indians know little about Adam Smith or Karl Marx but are deeply imbued with the spirit and philosophy of Chief Robert B. Jim of the Yakimas, Chief Seattle of the Muckleshoots and Chief Joseph of the Nez Perce which offer competitive attitudes towards life, fellow man, and nature. . . .
>
> The key to the problem is consideration of such applications *in a racially neutral way.* Abolition of the LSAT test would be a start. The invention of substitute tests might be made to get a measure of an applicant's cultural background, perception, ability to analyze, and his or her relation to groups. They are highly subjective, but unlike the LSAT they are not concealed but in the open.[47]

The logic of Douglas' argument would seem to apply not only to professional school admission standards, but also to the licensing and certification of such professionals after they graduate from the universities. Just as admissions selection procedures should be attuned to the "beat" of diverse cultural heritages, licensing standards, especially for teachers, should encourage—and require—a manifestation of a professional ability to relate to the cultural realities of the diverse communities in which the teacher will actually work. In short, the basic licensing process must be "wholesomely" neutral with respect to language and culture, just like the teachers themselves in their classrooms. Obviously, a requirement of neutrality cannot be imposed only at the levels of a specific school in a particular community; a requirement for and spirit of "cultural neutrality" (and flexibility) must be implemented at the state level. State licensing must be devised which can insure access to teaching roles in the common schools by people capable of responding to the personhood of the student and to community standards—to traditions, collective conscience, mores, and habit. Otherwise meaningful education may be impossible.

The implications of the above argument for the conduct of

education personnel licensing appear to be profound. Recall the obscenity case heard by the Supreme Court, which decided that questions of obscenity should be ascertained at the local level, by application of community standards. The court further held that national standards for obscenity were "hypothetical and unascertainable." Detailed, across-the-board standards for teaching qualifications are also unascertainable; consequently, reasonable state licensing regulations must be flexible and allow maximum feasible diversity at the local community level.

Vulnerability of Accreditation Systems: Emerging Legal Doctrines

The precedents established by the Title VII cases and the EEOC guidelines may provide a basis for challenging not only the certification practices of the various states but also the standards of the accrediting associations to which most state "approved program" and reciprocal licensing systems are directly linked. As indicated earlier in this chapter, it seems clear that the accrediting agencies conduct "technical evaluations" concerned with measuring physical facilities, faculty size, number of library books, etc. The agencies lack adequate indices for measuring educational quality, and to the extent that the evaluations consider non-technical aspects of curriculum and educational excellence, their considerations appear to be based on unvalidated, "personal" or "social impressions."

The incompatibility of these evaluation standards with the rigorous EEOC guidelines is clear. The accrediting agencies do not attempt to analyze the content of the jobs for which the schools they accredit are preparing their students. Nor do they purport to validate the accrediting criteria they apply according to predictive validation or content validation models. For example, the regional accrediting agencies appear to apply broad and nebulous requirements for required courses in "general education" without attempting in any way to pinpoint the relevance of these specific courses to effectiveness as a teacher. The accrediting agencies and the professional associations also appear to lack the capability to undertake responsible encouragement and accreditation of non-traditional programs, especially those of culture-based institutions designed explicitly to serve the needs and aspirations of identifiable ethnic and cultural groups.[48]

Courts in the past have tended to defer to the educational

"expertise" of the officers of the accrediting agencies because judges had no objective basis for determining whether evaluation criteria were vague or inappropriate.[49] Plaintiffs in future cases can be expected to cite the specific EEOC guidelines as reasonable, objective standards to which courts can readily refer in determining the validity of accrediting agency determinations. Application of such standards may require a total revamping of traditional accrediting practices.

Recent legal developments also indicate that accrediting agencies will be subject to increasing challenges based upon anti-trust and/or broad due process considerations. There can be no doubt that accrediting associations on a regional basis (or through their interlocking relationships and organizations even on a national basis) have achieved a monopoly status. Those schools which are denied membership or accreditation by these agencies suffer substantial competitive disadvantages in their ability to attract students and continue to exist as viable institutions.[50]

In the context of this study, the monopoly achieved is interpreted as a monopoly over the provision of educational services to candidates for the teaching profession, and, in certain instances, over access to jobs in the profession. This tendency toward monopolization has increased since the formation of the National Commission on Accrediting. The Constitution of the Commission explicitly charges that body with responsibility to coordinate "the activities of the approved accrediting agencies in order to avoid duplication and overlapping of functions."[51] And since its creation NCA appears to have been successful in keeping down the number of associations. Recently the National Commission on Accrediting has been superseded by the Council on Postsecondary Accreditation, a combination of the NCA and the regional accrediting agencies (FRACHE, Federation of Regional Accrediting Commissions of Higher Education) which now includes all postsecondary accrediting associations under a single mantle.

The fact that accrediting agencies have achieved monopoly status does not *per se* render them in violation of the anti-trust laws. Liability under the Sherman Act requires a showing that one who alleges a violation must be engaged in a "trade" which the defendant's conduct is "restraining." But numerous Supreme Court cases have held that cooperative associations can be held in violation of the anti-trust laws,[52] and that "It is not necessary, in order to constitute trade or business, that it shall be carried on for profit."[53]

The only reported case to date in which an accrediting agency was accused of violating the anti-trust laws was *Marjorie Webster v. Middle States Association*.[54] In this case Marjorie Webster, a proprietary school, sought to force the Middle States Association to accept its application for accreditation and to evaluate it. Middle States rejected the application solely on the basis that Marjorie Webster was a for-profit institution. The lower court found that education was "trade and commerce" within the regulatory scope of the Sherman Act.

> The myriad financial considerations involved in building programs, teachers' salaries, tuitions, and miscellaneous operating expenses attest to the commercialization which necessarily exists in the field of higher education. . . . Also there is a commercial aspect to the sharp competition for government and private contracts and the quest for research grants. In 1967-68 institutions of higher education expended more than $17 billion dollars. . . . Higher education in America today possesses many of the attributes of business . . . the question is not whether the defendant is engaged in trade but whether plaintiff's trade has been restrained.[55]

The court found that Middle States had achieved a monopoly over regional accreditation and that its exclusion of Marjorie Webster illegally restrained its trade in that its ability to attract students and carry out its educational purposes was substantially handicapped.

However, the Appeals Court reversed the lower court. Applying a narrow interpretation of the attributes necessary to constitute a "restraint of trade," and noting "the historic reluctance of Congress to exercise control in educational matters," the court held that "the Sherman Act is not applicable to Middle States conduct." The Supreme Court later refused to hear the case.

The Appellate Court ruling in *Marjorie Webster v. Middle States* appears to have applied very stringently, and perhaps incorrectly, the Supreme Court precedents in *AMA* and other anti-trust cases. It is not inconceivable that the courts would hold differently in another case, especially if plaintiffs were able to establish a stronger showing of a "restraint of trade," as, for example, a denial of accreditation status to a fledgling institution seeking to offer a unique program of culture-specific studies. In this connection, Donald Baker, Director of Policy Planning for the Antitrust Division of the Department of Justice, writes:

I personally think that this case [*Marjorie Webster*] was decided wrongly, even on its own facts. To the extent that it rests on judicial deference to the nature of the underlying subject matter—education—it is a unique little aberration in the law. Secondly, the association's *flat* refusal to *consider* Marjorie Webster for membership seems entirely inconsistent with the Supreme Court's decision in *Silver v. New York Stock Exchange,* which required procedural due process for exclusion. Thirdly, the court's analysis of economic effects was inconsistent with the rationale of *Associated Press* and *Silver.* The test has never been whether an enterprise could survive without membership, but whether membership was an "important business advantage." . . . The court's argument that Marjorie Webster could go out and form its own association was the very argument that had been flatly rejected by the Supreme Court in *Associated Press.*[56]

Although the possibilities of challenging the practices of accrediting associations under the anti-trust laws are intriguing, the more likely direction of court attacks in the near future will be under the due process clause of the Fourteenth Amendment and analogous state constitutional provisions. Such cases would be based upon allegations of unfair procedures in evaluating applicants for accreditation or upon allegations of arbitrariness in the basic standards themselves.

Traditionally, courts have tended to accept accrediting agencies' self-definition as voluntary associations whose procedures and exclusionary actions would be reviewed by the courts only if they failed to adhere to the minimal procedural requirements set forth in their own by-laws.[57] Occasionally, even under the common law standards, courts have struck down exclusionary practices of similar associations where their actions appeared to flagrantly violate principles of natural justice and public policy.[58]

The increasing quasi-official role of accrediting agencies whose evaluations are widely relied upon by state education departments and the federal Office of Education has tended to undermine their traditional status as private associations and render their activities as "state action" which can be challenged under the more vigorous standards of the due process clause.

The doctrine of "state action" has been conveniently discussed in terms of two primary categories: "quasi-governmental functions" and "government contacts."[59] Accrediting associations can be said to engage in state action of a "quasi-governmental" nature because:

    1. State approval agencies or accrediting agencies frequently rely on standards developed by private accrediting associations or rely directly on private accrediting association actions in lieu of independent state determinations.

    2. By granting or denying accreditation to an educational institution the accrediting association is, in effect, carrying out basic governmental responsibilities.

Under the "governmental contacts" heading, accrediting associations can be said to engage in state action because:

    1. Much of the power and influence exercised by the associations derives from official status and recognition in statutes or regulations.

    2. State tax funds indirectly support accrediting associations.

    3. State departments of education or departmental officials are often eligible for membership and/or hold office in the agency.

    4. State disbursement of federally allotted funds is in part affected by the actions of accrediting agencies.

The extent to which the six regional associations listed above (page 104) have engaged in "state action" vis-á-vis the federal government is delimited and described by John Proffitt:

> Accreditation has become, fundamentally speaking, a service aspect of the Federal Government. . . . [Before 1965-66] Most of the major pieces of legislation provided that . . . an institution shall be accredited or that it shall have reasonable assurance of accreditation [if it were to receive federal funds]. . . .
>
> Now in 1965 and '66 and the early part of '67 the Office of Education sought to implement the "reasonable assurance" provision of the major pieces of legislation. . . .
>
> An agreement was arrived at between the Office of Education

and the six regional associations that . . . [they] would provide . . . a letter . . . regarding an institution which the accrediting association found to have reasonable assurance that it would become accredited within a reasonable period of time.

Proffitt's perceptions are corroborated by an internal FRACHE statement:

> For the past two and one half years, the six regional accrediting associations have operated as service agencies for the U.S. Office of Education in helping to determine the eligibility for participation in federal aid programs for newly founded institutions. The decisions involved in these cases have been made with the USOE through correspondence related to teach institution considered. In effect, it may be construed that the regional accrediting associations have broken with their tradition of complete autonomy and have become party to an implied contract with the USOE.
>
> This relationship with the USOE appears to have seriously altered the philosophical and operational independence of the regional associations from government entanglements.[60]

This web of quasi-governmental functions and governmental contacts led the lower court in considering the allegations of violations of due process in the second count of the *Marjorie Webster* case to unreservedly hold that the association was engaged in state action, despite apparently contrary holdings in earlier cases. The Court of Appeals, although reversing the lower court's substantive holdings on the due process as well as the anti-trust count, "assume[d] without deciding" that state action had been established. The court cited in this context a number of recent U.S. Supreme Court decisions that had found state action in analogous contexts. A finding of state action is, of course, merely a threshold requirement for further judicial scrutiny; in order to establish the invalidity of the relevant regulatory provisions or statutes it would need to be shown that the association in question operates in an arbitrary, capricious and unreasonable manner which is inconsistent with the due process requirements of the Fourteenth Amendment.

Like "state action," "due process" is not a precisely defined notion. It is a rule of "fundamental fairness" in its procedural context and of fundamental values in its substantive context, which depends at times on the nature and importance of the competing individual and governmental interests at issue. Recognizing the centrality of due process rights for a society governed by the rule of law, the U.S. Supreme Court has in recent years expanded traditional concepts and "put flesh upon the due process principle."[61]

William Kaplin suggests that in the case of accrediting associations, procedural "due process" would minimally require administrative regularity, reasonable relationships between the decision-making process and the stated purpose of the agency, and opportunities for affected parties to present their views in a manner commensurate with the interest which they have to protect. To ensure due process in accrediting, established standards and procedures should be followed; schools should be given adequate notice and explanation of adverse action, an opportunity to show cause why it should not be taken, and the opportunity to obtain a hearing and (should adverse action be taken) an appeal; the accrediting body should be free to act without conflict of interest, pursuant to the evidence and in accord with established standards and procedures.[62]

As the example of the Southwestern Michigan case cited earlier in this chapter makes clear, present practices of the accrediting agencies often fall far short of compliance with these fundamental criteria. One questions whether a one- to three-day visit of an inspection team can provide a reasonable basis for assessing the overall educational value of an institution's offerings, even if it is assumed that valid evaluative standards are being applied. The inherent potential conflict of interest created by current practices which call for officials of established institutions to evaluate potential competitors also raises serious due process problems which are likely to be aggravated if new schools or programs which are created because of a felt need to experiment with innovative educational approaches are denied accreditation by practitioners of the old ways.

Although a number of due process cases have been brought against accrediting associations in recent years, few reported decisions appear on the books, largely because in many cases the issues have been settled out of court after the complaint has been filed.[63] The current link between accreditation and eligibility for federal funds and the precedential impact of the doctrines being established in the Title VII cases indicate, however, that a greater magnitude of such cases can be expected to arise in the years to come.

Accrediting agencies have not been oblivious to these developments. Some have begun to strengthen their procedures and hearing and appeal rights. The threat of litigation has led many agencies to take out libel insurance for the first time or to become incorporated in an attempt to insulate association officers from personal liability.[64] A basic question remains, however, as to whether anything short of a total revamping and rationalization of accrediting agencies' traditional procedures—and the substantive standards applied in their evaluations—can immunize them to successful court attacks.

New Directions for Accreditation and Their Implications for Licensing

What is most important in all of this discussion are the numerous implications for the conduct of education personnel licensing and the whole conduct of state-supported education in this argument about the function and position of accrediting agencies. If the total accreditation system is not fair, the licensing based on it cannot be fair. If it cannot make precise quality distinctions, then candidates for licensing are included or excluded on bases other than quality. It appears that accreditation needs to be defined as what it is, an analytic system for an educational community. It may be argued that this analytic system can best serve institutions if it can judge them in terms which respect their unique circumstances and missions, the regions and cultures to which they are primarily responsible and whatever pride of individual teaching and tradition the institution has. **Accreditation ought never to be regarded as a surrogate for a clear and validated assessment of individuals in relation to the jobs they wish to hold.**

Under the conditions established by our argument, an adequate licensing system would almost of necessity be comprised of two tiers, along the lines laid out by William Robinson in his review of "The Power of Competency-Based Teacher Education," as discussed earlier in this chapter.[65] The first tier or step would be providing a prospective teacher with a provisional license on the basis of demonstrated competence in an intellectual, cultural or vocational area. This permission on the part of the state would enable an individual to teach something of conceivable worth and value to someone or some group, with the notions of worth and value broadly interpreted, and would conform to the general criteria of EEOC and *Griggs* as these might apply to job descriptions having to do with level, subject, teaching or administering style and so forth. At the second tier of licensing, the crucial principle is that of "benign influence or effect," which includes the enhancement of the decency and humaneness of the community. This interpretation of "benign influence" is consistent with the Supreme Court's considerations in *Wisconsin v. Yoder,* which relied heavily on the self-sufficient character of the Amish community and its effects on the young. The second licensing tier would certify that a person has demonstrated on-the-job competence in teaching children in a specific kind of neighborhood or community.

Any educational program leading to the acquisition of "first tier" skills need not be, indeed ought not to be, conceptualized as separate from any program leading to "second tier" skills. Many persons, including those cited in Chapter II, have advocated that both general course work about learning to teach and experience in the field be included throughout the four-year teacher training program. The validation of the capacity to teach could be separated into the "general" and the "environment specific" without necessarily requiring that the study be neatly layered sequentially into two segments.

Procedures for Meeting New Licensing Criteria

We may now turn to the question of how education personnel might be prepared to produce this "benign effect" required as part of the second licensing tier. There is no instant procedure to be discovered, for American communities presently appear to be characterized not by the cohesiveness and self-sufficiency of the Amish community, but by various sorts of alienation, by discontinuities and incompatibilities disrupting significant segments of their primary activities—discontinuities between and among work, education, and the expressive and imaginative life. Thus the character of education personnel training has to be such that it enables them to assist and participate in community building or sustaining. It seems clear that considerable reconstruction is needed in the education process for education personnel. The use by some states of national institutional accreditation by private agencies (on the basis of "approved programs" whose effects cannot be clearly validated at the community level) is not enough. Under such a system, a conventional degree in education becomes an automatic guarantee of a license to teach almost anywhere—in any community. Such state sanction for homogenized teacher education unrelated to job descriptions does not conform to Title VII, to the EEOC guidelines, or to the spirit of the court decisions we have described. National accrediting agencies judge institutions largely on a national basis. They seldom seriously look at the differentiated capacities of individuals to fulfill specific jobs within local common school institutions. The degree, as presently conceived, guarantees nothing. By contrast, pre-service and in-service education for local circumstances, and affirmation of continuing competency and effectiveness to serve an area's people based on EEOC guidelines, might proceed as follows:

The second step of the licensing process outlined above (the step particularly related to community-based education), and the recurrent licensing and evaluation of teachers, might well require a context in which the individual would be evaluated from several perspectives—those of administrators, peers, parents, and community people—for competency to teach in a specific kind of neighborhood or culture area. This context would probably best be regarded as the community school itself if it included the formal and informal evaluations from the perspective of all concerned parties which it could provide. This school could also be the examining school for persons taking other "alternative routes" such as are discussed in Chapter II.

In order to assist candidates to prepare for this level of certification, special programs might be developed and perhaps conducted by the community school or the "examining school." These programs would provide for an in-depth understanding of, and supportive relation to, the community in which the program was located (Recommendation IV of Chapter II describes such a program).

The Pursuit of "Equal Educational Opportunity"

We have outlined a set of legal constraints which must surely shape the future of teacher education; it remains to discuss a basic issue growing out of *Brown v. Board of Education*'s articulation of the right to "equal educational opportunity"—the problem of how to secure "equal educational opportunity" and at the same time initiate a community-building education process in which teachers can increase the achievement and growth of students. What makes this issue a problem is in part the inappropriate notion of "equality" which many of us have, which assumes that "equal to" can only be considered in the sense of "identical to." Such a notion is inadequate for a variety of reasons, whether one seeks to measure "equality" in terms of input measurements such as expenditures undertaken in a process of education (such as are examined in accrediting visitations) or in terms of output measurements which look at the outcomes of the process (as in standardized testing). Our experience with "remedial" or "compensatory" education suggests that the current concept of "equality" at a practical level is unworkable, if not destructive. Instead of employing this traditional notion of equality in our education systems we might well, following the lead of David Hawkins, employ instead a more sophisticated analogy, that of "commensurability." Recognizing that human beings are congenitally incommensurable—never indistinguishable or identical—Hawkins argues for "local and dependent curricula and instructional choices, to make the curricular spiral tangible at many points to the individual lives of children, to the educative resources of *their* total environment which *they* know or can be helped to discover. . . . This proposition is no less important for the education of 'advantaged' children; it is only at present less in the political focus."[66]

Hawkins continues:

> But the meaning of incommensurability is that diverse children can attain to a common culture—a common world of meanings and skills, of intellectual tools, moral commitments, and aesthetic involvements. Individual development *can* complement individual differences, but only through a matching diversity of learning styles and strategies. Children can learn equally, in general, only as they learn differently. The more constraints there are toward single-track preprogrammed instruction, the more predictably will the many dimensions of individual variety—congenitally and individually evolved—express themselves as a large rank-order variance in learning.

He concludes his exploration of the notion of incommensurability in the following way:

> Human beings are valued within a community for their useful differences . . . as sources or resources of skill, of aesthetic expression, or moral or intellectual authority. It is not difference as such which we value, but individuality—the unique personal style and synthesis which interests us in each other as subjects of scrutiny, of testing, of emulation, or repudiation. Recognition of individuality completes what I mean by the postulate of incommensurability. The character which members of our own species possess— what we term individuality—implies neither dominance nor identity, but equivalence within a domain of relations sustained by

individual diversity. If the old word *equality* should be used in this sense, it is the equality of craftsmen working at different tasks and with different skills, but with plans and tools congruent enough to provide endless analogies and endless diversions. Or, it is the equality of authors who read other authors' books but must each, in the end, write his own.

"Equal opportunity," in light of the postulate of incommensurability, requires providing a wide range of diversity in that opportunity. Thus, judgment concerning "equality" among institutions (determination of bases for "accrediting" institutions for purposes of federal funding eligibility) and the competency of individual teachers (licensing and evaluation) cannot be formulated against mere hypothetical and unascertainable national or statewide standards of "equality" of inputs or outputs. Such formulations must, rather, be made against the prerequisites for the sufficiency of the individual and decent and humane communities.

SPECIFIC RECOMMENDATIONS

Recommendation I:

Eligibility

The present system of distribution of federal funds to educational institutions depends upon a judgment of eligibility. In practically every case, the federal legislation requires the Commissioner of Education to make that judgment; the G.I. Bill is a typical case in point. As discussed above, through historical accident, the determination of eligibility became linked to the on-going process of accreditation of institutions of higher education.

One of the unintended effects of this coupling of two decisions in one process is that new institutions and/or innovative departures from the traditional higher education models are not eligible for federal funds at the very time that monetary aid is of greatest importance. (Cf. Chapter V, Recommendations.) In an effort to open up this determination of eligibility for federal funds, and to distinguish criteria for eligibility from criteria for accreditation, we recommend the following:

(1) That the Commissioner of Education review the present

arrangement allowing private associations in effect to decide federal eligibility and that he require the Office of the Commissioner to determine, independent of the action of private associations, whether an institution is eligible for federal funds; and

(2) That on the model of the FTC and the SEC, the Commissioner of Education provide a mechanism that would establish and enforce minimal national standards for eligibility including such determinations as:

a. the financial responsibility of an institution—that it can be held accountable for investment of student resources and public funds;

b. the recruitment and public information policies of an institution—that it presents an honest and accurate picture of its educational programs; and that it makes available a prospectus of its financial and educational status, so that prospective students and other interested parties can determine whether the institution meets their needs and interests.

The intent of this recommendation is to separate the question of eligibility from credentialling and accreditation, and in this process to open and simplify the process of obtaining federal funds. We recognize that the Office of Education would need to undertake significant new responsibilities in order to implement this recommendation, and this Commission is prepared to consider in further detail the question of how such functions might be organized. We also recommend that there be a complete appeals process related to the foregoing recommendation.

Recommendation II:

Accreditation

If the accreditation process at both the regional and national levels is freed of the additional burden of weighing institutional eligibility for federal funds, it can then more truly function as an instrument for educational evaluation. The process of self-study and evaluation by outside teams, which has developed over the years, has become a valuable resource in institutional improvement. Traditionally, the criteria for self-study, and the visiting teams themselves, have tended to mirror the interests and concerns of the established academic profession. This entire accreditation process has also taken place outside the public view, and often with decisions being made without full disclosure to the affected institution itself.

This Commission, concerned with opening educational institutions to the public (cf. sections on access in Chapter V), and establishing structures which are representative of the diversity of groups and values prevalent in American society, therefore makes the following recommendations:

(1) Accreditation inspection teams ought to have broader-based membership including strong representation of students, diverse communities and minority groups.

(2) Existing evaluation criteria should be re-examined, and new, more substantive and more relevant standards should be developed that are concerned with the relationship of the IHE to its clientele defined as both the individual students and the general community to which the institution should relate.

(3) The results of both the self-study and the visiting team report should be published and disseminated for public use.

(4) Opportunities for a complete appeals process to an independent outside arbitrator selected by both the accreditation agency and the aggrieved IHE ought to be available.

Recommendation III:

Licensing

As discussed earlier in this chapter, the federal courts have indicated a willingness to enjoin unconstitutional and irrational hiring practices and to mandate new licensing and credentialling approaches. Judges, however, are not educators and judicial involvement in this process can become cumbersome and time consuming. The Commission believes that the profession itself must immediately begin a process of thorough-going structural reform. Present "reforms" in the direction of competency-based teacher education and the NEA-inspired professional practices boards do not address the fundamental problems. Therefore, the Commission recommends the following changes in teacher licensing:

(1) The licensing of competent teachers should remain a state responsibility. Demonstrable teaching competence should be a prerequisite for permanent licensure and such competence should include the demonstrated ability to teach with sensitivity to particular student and community values and needs.

(2) Regular licensure should be preceded by a provisional licensure period during which time a candidate would receive supportive training and would be expected to demonstrate a capacity to teach with sensitivity. The evaluation of the provisional licensure experience should be conducted by teacher training experts, local school administrators, teachers, community, parent and student representatives, acting on a joint committee.

(3) The Commission expects teaching candidates to continue to be drawn from formal teacher training institutions, but encourages an expanded recognition of the validity of alternative experiences which can also produce qualified teachers. For example, talented people lacking a formal teaching degree might be permitted to demonstrate their skills on a provisional licensure basis. Experience suggests that community groups will be able to identify and sponsor individuals who exhibit teaching aptitude despite the absence of formal training. State licensing agencies should give great weight to such community recommendations. The state should also publicize the opportunity for diverse candidates to obtain provisional licensure.

Recommendation IV:

Occupational Licensing Institute

The Commission endorses the establishment of an Occupational Licensing Institute to undertake the necessary research to identify rational hiring criteria for teachers. The competent teacher must know how to teach and what to teach. Developing case law in the wake of the Supreme Court opinion in *Griggs v. Duke Power Co.* indicates that, if necessary, judicial authority can be invoked to rationalize hiring criteria for all segments of the economy. Where demonstration of alternative hiring criteria is insufficient to prompt reform of hiring criteria, the Institute should be prepared to bring legal action to mandate such reform. As a central focus for research and litigation, the Institute should be a source of information, advice and advocacy for individuals or groups badly served by current hiring criteria.

FOOTNOTES

[1] Vito Perrone, *Education for 1984 and After,* eds. Paul A. Olson, Larry Freeman and James Bowman (Lincoln, Nebraska: Nebraska Curriculum Development Center, 1972), p. 191.

[2] See, for instance, *Stetson v. Board of Education of the City of New York,* 218 N.Y. 301 (1916).

[3] Martin Haberman and T.M. Stinnett, *Teacher Education and the New Profession of Teaching* (Berkeley: McCutchan Publishing Corporation, 1973), pp. 20-21.

[4] From New Jersey State Department of Education Regulations:

(1) A state-approved teacher education program;

(2) A college teacher education program included in the annual List of Approved Programs in the National Association of State Directors of Teacher Education and Certification (NASDTEC) Certification Reciprocity System;

(3) An elementary teacher preparation program in the New England States, Delaware, Maryland, and Pennsylvania that meets the criteria set forth in the Northeastern States Elementary Reciprocity Compact;

(4) National Council for the Accreditation of Teacher Education (NCATE—i.e., nationally accredited) approved program;

(5) Completion of a teacher education program approved by the State Department of Education in the state in which the college is located (but not appearing on NCATE or NASDTEC approved program lists), provided that the program meets the minimum standards outlined in the New Jersey *Instructional Supplement to the Standards for State Approval of Teacher Education* (NASDTEC);

(6) Completion of a teacher education program in a state party to the Interstate Agreement on Qualification of Educational Personnel; the college and program must be approved by the other state's department of education and the other state would issue applicant a comparable certificate;

(7) Completion of 27 months of appropriate teaching experience in states party to the Agreement, within seven years prior to application for license in another state in the Agreement, plus a comparable valid (in-force) regular or advanced certificate issued by one of the states in the Agreement, and the appropriate degree required for the certificate in the state where received;

(8) Completion of three years' successful teaching experience in the appropriate field in another state, provided that the applicant presents a standard teacher's certificate in the appropriate field and currently in force in the other state, plus the appropriate college degree, and preparation equivalent in total semester hours—but not necessarily identical in specific content—to the minimum preparation in general and professional education and subject

specialization required for the particular endorsement as stated in the New Jersey Instructional Supplement to the Standards for State Approval of Teacher Education.

[5] National Association of State Directors of Teacher Education and Certification (NASDTEC), *Standards for State Approval of Teacher Education* (1971) pp. 3-4.

[6] Wallace M. Maurer, "CBTE Program Director in Pennsylvania Responds to Arguments in Freeman's Article," *Study Commission Newsletter* (May, 1974) pp. 15-17.

[7] Nebraska Guidelines for Teacher Training Program Approval, *Policies and Criteria for the Approval of Teacher Education Programs and Institutions in Nebraska, 1974*, p. 2.

[8] Illinois Guidelines for Teacher Training Program Approval, *A Manual of Procedure for Approving Illinois Teacher Education Institutions and Programs*, January, 1974.

[9] National Council for the Accreditation of Teacher Education (NCATE) Regulations, introduction.

[10] Harold Orlans, N. Jean Levin, Elizabeth W. Bauer and George E. Arnstein, *Private Accreditation and Public Eligibility*, Vol. II (1974), p. 556.

[11] Paul L. Dressel, quoted in *Financing Postsecondary Education in the United States* (Washington, D.C.: National Commission on the Financing of Postsecondary Education, U.S. Printing Office, 1973), p. 172.

[12] Frank G. Dickey and Jerry W. Miller, *A Current Perspective on Accreditation* (Washington, D.C.: American Association for Higher Education, 1972), p. 57. (Also quoted in *Financing Postsecondary Education in the United States*.)

[13] *Chronicle of Higher Education*, August 19, 1974.

[14] Orlans, *et al.*, Vol. II, p. 556.

[15] NCATE Regulations, document prepared pursuant to Contract No. OEC-3-8-080248-0030(010) with OE, standards, accepted 1970, p. 1.

[16] NCATE Regulations, pp. 4-5. Current NCATE Standards, 1970. These standards were prepared under OE Contract No. OEC-3-8-080248-0030(010) with USOE, HEW.

[17] Murray L. Wax in his article "How Should Schools Be Held Accountable?" (*Education for 1984 and After,* Study Commission, 1972, pp. 64-65) underlines this point when he mentions "isolated one room" reservation schools where despite all that conventionally-trained teachers can do children do not learn conventional subject matter in the conventional mode of "individual effort" and "individual student responsibility," and *also* despite all that teachers do to discourage "collaborative work" ("cheating"), the children *do* learn, in a "group" way, teaching each other and assisting each other with problems or examinations. Wax mentions that one such conventional teacher admitted sadly that "although he taught for a school year in this particular school, he did not know at the time that he left what were the real levels of performance of most of the Indian pupils"; Wax's comment is that although this situation shocks most educators, "I would argue that it exhibits something of great value which we have lost by structuring our schools as if they were factories to process young children in identical blocks."

[18] Rolf W. Larson, chief administrative officer of NCATE, has recently written *Accreditation Problems & the Promise of PBTE* (November, 1974) calling for accreditation team respect for institutional differences, substance rather than form, assessment of actual qualifications of the graduates, including effects on common school students, and *"the need to determine the focus or function of accreditation"* [emphasis added]. The report contains no proposals for validating the standards applied to graduates in terms of post-Griggs decisions or for including lay audiences in determining licensing and/or accreditation standards. The paper makes an appeal to the notion that accreditation is extended to an institution when "its produce met acceptable societal demands" (elsewhere "the public as a whole"), but it describes no mechanisms for doing this and makes no proposals for determining when societal demands have been met. No way of answering the need of the "dissatisfied consumer" is described other than the profession's calling together "its best professionals" to modify the standard (pp. 24-25).

[19] Letter in Study Commission files is a copy dated March 1, 1975, of an official notice from Bell to Dr. Rolf W. Larson, director of NCATE, regarding the action of the Advisory Committee on Accreditation and Institutional Eligibility at its meeting January 22-24, 1975.

[20] Information on procedures and philosophy can be obtained from Hector Burke or Rafael Poblano at the California offices of the State Commission for Teacher Preparation and Licensing.

[21] Hazel Henderson, speaking recently to members of the World Future Society, expressed the Study Commission view nicely: "We continue to reward the 'disciplines,' while all the interesting problems bubble up at the interfaces." (Ms. Henderson, author and social critic, and June Thomas, a black Ph.D. candidate at the University of Michigan, were last-minute additions to the list of speakers at the society's plenary session in Washington, D.C., June 3, after women and minority

representatives complained that the conference was dominated by what John Platt, another speaker at that session, said his wife called "WASOAM's"—White. Anglo-Saxon, Old, Affluent Males.)

[22] NCATE Reports (Pittsburgh); see also School of Education, University of Pittsburgh Report to NCATE (1972-73), p. 44.

[23] John G. Merrow II, in a report on "The Politics of Competence: A Review of Competency-Based Teacher Education," from the Basic Skills Program on Teaching, National Institute of Education (Washington, D.C., 1975), p. 5, comments on the lack of evidence:

> There is simply no good evidence equating any specific training steps with subsequent teaching behavior and student performance. Let's go backward from the desired student performance, say, higher reading scores. There is no conclusive evidence that one way of teaching is better than another for producing higher test scores. (There is some evidence that one approach works well with some kids, another approach with others.) The link between training methods and actual teaching practices is also weak. Even if one method works there is no guarantee that training teachers in the use of that method would actually cause them to *use* it in the classroom.

[Merrow recommends the following research for background information:] (1) B. Rosenshine and N. Furst, "Research on Teacher Performance Criteria," in B.O. Smith (ed.), *Research in Teacher Education: A Symposium* (Englewood Cliffs, N.J.: Prentice Hall, 1971); (2) B. Rosenshine and N. Furst, "The Use of Direct Observation to Study Teaching," in R.W. Travers (ed.), *Second Handbook of Research on Teaching* (Chicago: Rand McNally, 1973); (3) M.J. Dunkin and B.J. Biddle, *The Study of Teaching* (New York: Holt, Rinehart and Winston, 1974); (4) C.S. Jencks et al., *Inequality: A Reassessment of the Effect of Family and Schooling in America* (New York: Basic Books, 1972); (5) H. Featherstone, "Cognitive Effects of Pre-School Programs on Different Types of Children," (Huron Institute, Cambridge, Mass., 1973); (6) M.S. Mith and J. Bissel, "Report Analysis: The Impact of Headstart," *Harvard Educational Review*.

[24] *National Policy and Higher Education* (U.S. Department of Health, Education and Welfare: Special Task Force—Second Newman Group), Recommendations, draft, p. 118.

[25] Benjamin Shimberg, *Occupational Licensing: Practices and Policies* (Washington, D.C.: Public Affairs Press, 1972), p. 1.

[26] Albert Maslow, *Licensing Tests—Occupational Bridge or Barrier?*, Proceedings, Third Annual Conference, Council on Occupational Licensing, Inc. (July, 1971), from Shimberg, p. 208.

[27] 401 U.S. 424 (1971).

[28] *Griggs v. Duke Power Company*, 401 U.S. at 433.

[29] See, e.g., *Baker v. Columbus Municipal School District* 329, F. Supp 706 (N.D., Miss, 1971), aff'd 462 F. 2d 1112 (5th Cir., 1972); *Armstead v. Stakville Municipal Separate School District,* 325 F. Supp. 560 (W.D., Miss., 1971); *Walston v. Nansemond County School Board,* 492 F. 2d 919 (4th Cir., 1974); *Chance v. Board of Examiners,* 330 F. Supp. 203 (S.D., N.Y., 1971), aff'd 458 F. 2d 1167 (2d Cir., 1972).

[30] *Chance v. Board of Examiners,* 330 F. Supp. at 216.

[31] *Chance v. Board of Examiners,* 330 F. Supp. at 220.

[32] *Walston v. Nansemond County School Board,* 492 F. 2d at 926.

[33] See the *amicus curiae* brief for the National Education Association (NEA) in *Walston v. Nansemond County,* Nos. 73-1492 and 73-1493, p. 40.

[34] The successful attack upon the examination system for supervisors in New York City has recently been followed by a more broad-based challenge to the examination procedures for the city's 60,000-man teaching force. *Rubinos v. Board of Examiners,* Cir. No. 74-2240 S.D. N.Y. (filed May 23, 1974).

[35] Education personnel represent the largest single occupational group that is subject, in every instance, to licensing criteria and procedures, and prospective education personnel represent the largest category of undergraduates preparing for a licensed occupation. The most recent and authoritative statistics available to the Study Commission indicate that there are approximately 2.3 million licensed teachers; that in 1971, 21 per cent of all bachelor's degrees conferred in the United States were in education (37 per cent of all B.A.'s are eligible for a license), 33 per cent of all master's degrees, and 20 per cent of all doctorates. No other area accounts for such a substantial portion of higher education's total resources. Presently, there are about 1.5 million college students intending to teach, and according to a recent Gallup Poll (reported April 25, 1974), 34 per cent of all college students intend to teach at some level, the largest group among students questioned about their plans. Thus, the number of people affected by questionable "equal opportunity" or "consumer-protective" licensing in education is enormous; moreover education is a "lighthouse" profession, reform of which would serve as a model for the entire workforce.

[36] At least one federal court has specifically held that parents and children as "consumers" have a right under the equal protection clause of the Fourteenth Amendment to require the state to provide adequately educated teachers who are

qualified in fact for their profession. In *Hunnicutt v. Burge* (M.D. Ga., 1973), the court found that the program at a predominantly black state college appeared "academically inferior" and since graduation from this below-standard institution would automatically entitle a graduate to a teaching certificate, both the plaintiffs (students, faculty and potential students of the college) and public school parents and children as "secondary beneficiaries" were entitled to an order requiring the State Board of Regents to revise and improve the curriculum and character of the school.

[37] Donald P. Mitchell and Anne Hawley, *Leadership in Public Education Study: A Look at the Overlooked* (Academy for Educational Development, 1972), p. 33.

[38] Michael Rebell, *Teacher Credentialling Reform in New York State: A Critique and a Suggestion for New Directions* (Lincoln, Nebraska: Study Commission, 1974), *passim.*

[39] Rebell, pp. 96-97.

[40] William L. Robinson, "The Power of Competency-Based Teacher Education: Views of a Civil Rights Lawyer," Appendix I to *The Power of Competency-Based Teacher Education*, Report of the Committee on National Program Priorities in Teacher Education (Boston: Allyn and Bacon, Inc., 1972), pp. 276-80.

[41] For studies of ethnic and class-related cultural factors which affect learning, see: Courtney B. Dazden and Vera P. John, "Learning in American Indian Children," in *Anthropological Perspectives on Education,* edited by Murray L. Wax, Stanley Diamond and Fred O. Gearing (Basic Books, 1971); Susan Philips, "Acquisition of Roles for Appropriate Speech Usage," in *Language and Cultural Diversity in American Education,* edited by Roger Abrahams and Rudolph Troike (Prentice-Hall, 1972); Geneva Gay and Roger Abrahams, "Black Culture in the Classroom," in *Language and Cultural Diversity in American Education;* Luther X. Weems, "Racial Differences and the Black Child," (unpublished paper, 1974); Manuel Ramirez III and Alfredo Castaneda, *Cultural Democracy, Bicognitive Development and Education* (Academic Press, 1974); Susan Stodolsky and Gerald Lesser, "Learning Patterns in the Disadvantaged," *Harvard Educational Review* 37(4), 1967, pp. 546-93; Rosalie Cohen, "Conceptual Styles, Culture Conflict and Nonverbal Tests of Intelligence," *American Anthropologist* 71 (1969), pp. 828-56.

[42] *College Composition and Communication* (October, 1972), p. 325.

[43] Civ. 4002 (S.D. N.Y., August 29, 1974).

[44] United States Commission on Civil Rights Hearing held at San Antonio, Texas, December 9-14, 1968, U.S.G.P.O. Washington, D.C. See also United States Commission on Civil Rights: Mexican-American Education Study. Report III:

The Excluded Student (May, 1972), U.S.G.P.O. Washington, D.C., pp. 13-20.

[45] *The Education Professions 1968,* U.S. Department of HEW, Office of Education, p. 42. In California in the school year 1972-73, there were 47,508 children of non-English speaking capabilities and 140,651 limited English speaking children, grades K-12. The figures are probably very conservative because of the identification process. This includes 64 identifiable language groups. In 1970 (census data), 9.6 million persons were of Spanish language dominance. Public Advocates, Inc., suspects it could be 15 per cent higher (statistics furnished by Jeanne Guertin of California State University in Los Angeles).

[46] A recent issue of The Student NEA newspaper, *Student Impact,* estimates that "of America's five million public school children whose native language is other than English, less than three per cent were in bilingual education programs during 1974" ("Bilingual Education: We're Not There Yet," March-April, 1975), p. 7.

[47] A more complete version of the dissenting opinion can be found in the *Study Commission Newsletter* (May, 1974) Supplement.

[48] The accreditation difficulties encountered in the state of New York by the only predominantly Puerto Rican institution on the mainland United States, the Universidad Boricua, are a case in point here.

[49] See, e.g., *Parsons College v. North Central Association,* 271 F. Supp 65 (E.D. Ill., 1967).

[50] As Betty J. Anderson, attorney for the American Medical Association, recently observed: "There are three basic areas that may cause legal concern for organizations or associations that conduct accreditation programs: (1) possible liability under the federal and state antitrust laws; (2) liability to consumers or individuals who rely upon the accreditation; and (3) possible liability for injury to business . . . such as actions alleging unfair competition. . . . The Antitrust Division of the Department of Justice and the Federal Trade Commission are suspicious of standards because of the use made of them as a means of restraining trade by allocation of markets and agreements to market only standardized items. . . . Accrediting agencies . . . have a more visible ability to restrain institutions from attracting students today than they have ever had before. . . . The public reliance and the monopolistic role of educational accrediting agencies strips away their cloak of voluntariness and gives them the characteristics of governmental agencies." Quoted from Harold Orlans, *et al., Private Accreditation and Public Eligibility* (February, 1974), I, p. 178.

[51] National Commission on Accrediting (NCA) Constitution.

⁵²See, e.g., *Associated Press v. United States,* 326 U.S. 1 (1944), *Silver v. New York Stock Exchange,* 373 U.S. 341 (1963).

⁵³*AMA v. United States,* 130 F 2d 233, 237 (D.C. Cir., 1942), aff'd 317 U.S. 519 (1943).

⁵⁴302 F. Supp 459 (D.C. D.C., 1969), rev'd 432 F 2d 650 (D.C. Cir., 1970).

⁵⁵Orlans, *et al.,* Vol. I, p. 34.

⁵⁶"Antitrust and the Non-Profit Organization," *Non-Profit Report* (March, 1973), p. 17.

⁵⁷See, e.g., Chaffee, "The Internal Affairs of Associations Not for Profit," 43 *Harv. L. Rev.* 993 (1930); Kaplin and Hunter, "Comment: The Legal Status of the Educational Accrediting Agency," 52 *Corn. L.Q.* 104 (1960); "Developments in the Law: Judicial Control of Actions of Private Associations," 76 *Harv. L. Rev.* 983 (1963); *State of N. Dakota v. North Central Association,* 23 F. Supp 694 (E.D. Ill., 1938), aff'd 99 F 2d 697 (7th Cir., 1938); *Parsons College v. North Central Association,* 271 F. Supp 65 (E.D. Ill., 1967).

⁵⁸See, e.g., *Falcone v. Middlesex County Medical Society,* 170 A 2d 791 (1961).

⁵⁹Cf. William A. Kaplin and J. Philip Hunter, "The Legal Status of the Educational Accrediting Agency: Problems in Judicial Supervision and Governmental Regulation," *Cornell Law Review Quarterly* 52:104-31 (Fall, 1960).

⁶⁰Orlans, *et al.,* Vol. I, p. 37.

⁶¹*Boddie v. Connecticut,* 401 U.S. 371, 375 (1971).

⁶²Quoted in Orlans, *et al.,* Vol. I, pp. 177-78.

⁶³See Orlans, *et al.,* Vol. I, pp. 179-80. The Court of Appeals ruling in *Marjorie Webster,* one notable reported decision which upheld an accrediting agency in a due process challenge, did not involve a frontal attack on evaluation procedures, but only the specific issue of whether an agency rule automatically excluding proprietary schools was arbitrary. The court held that the profit motive might subtly influence educational goals and that, in any event, Marjorie Webster was not significantly harmed by the exclusion and was in a position to form an accrediting association of proprietary schools. It is interesting to note that although Marjorie Webster lost on appeal, the accrediting associations are apparently now considering accepting proprietary schools for accreditation (Orlans, pp. 40-41).

⁶⁴Orlans, *et al.,* Vol. I, pp. 179-80.

⁶⁵Two-tier or two-step licensing systems of different sorts have been proposed by others. See Public Education Association of New York City, "Memorandum Regarding Reform of Personnel Selection Procedures for New York City Public School System By Establishment of a New Two-Step Performance Based Certification System" (memorandum prepared at the request of the New York State Assembly Education Committee, Constance Cook, Chmn., September 15, 1973); and see Metropolitan Research Center, *A Possible Reality of High Academic Achievement for the Students of Public Elementary and Junior High Schools of Washington, D.C.* (1970), reprinted in Committee Print, Select Committee on Equal Educational Opportunity, U.S. Senate, 91st Congress, 2nd Session, September, 1970. The two-tier approach is also being seriously considered by the federal court which is in the process of fashioning a permanent new licensing plan for New York school supervisors in *Chance v. Board of Examiners.*

⁶⁶"Human Nature and the Scope of Education," in *Philosophical Redirection of Educational Research,* 71st Yearbook of the National Society of the Study of Education (Chicago, 1972), pp. 301-03.

CHAPTER IV

GATHERING INFORMATION ON

THE PROCESS OF EDUCATING TEACHERS

The basic structures of education, legitimized by state and federal licensing and accrediting procedures, are actually run by governance and information systems. *Governance arrangements,* whether federally or locally developed, seek to answer the question: "Who decides what, in general, will be done in the education of our children and their teachers? What will be our policy?" *Information systems* answer the broad implementational questions as well as the numerical questions: "What do people (teachers) do on a day-to-day basis to carry out the policy previously set? What information is gathered on the growth, development, education of our children? How is that information used? How will we implement our policy?"

Questions about both policy and implementation are asked in "bush schools" working with two to twenty students and in the highly sophisticated state university systems working with forty or sixty thousand students. Everywhere there are those "managers" who ask about how education is developed and administered as well as about content and quality. People who govern usually endeavor to do so on the basis of some kind of data, formally or informally gathered. To a considerable degree, the kind of future society we create will depend on our processes of selecting and continuously educating those who teach our children and youth—on our management of teacher education. The formal education of teachers is difficult to manage, for it relates not only to the schools of America but also to the diverse social realities outside those schools. The "glasses" (information systems) through which we see and interpret formal and informal education—as much as who manages or governs it—will partly determine what kind of society we are to have in this country.

Recently the U.S. Office of Education and subcontractors of the office have developed a number of model governance and information systems. Many of the governance plans are designed as parts of Title I (Parent Advisory Committees), Teacher Corps, and Bureau of Educational Personnel Development (BEPD) training programs. Information systems, on the other hand, are represented by testing and assessment schemes of the Higher Education General Information System (HEGIS), the National Center for Higher Education Management Systems (NCHEMS), and some less well-known systems designed for smaller federal projects or subsystems. Both governance and management systems reflect some degree of federal intervention, and while there has been a continual urging for over a hundred years that they become more effective and more efficient,[1] they have not yet produced the diversity which might make them so.

Governance

The Study Commission position on "Who decides what?" is set forth in detail in our first chapter. We strongly assert that those who are the clients and constituents of the educational process must have a primary role at every level in formulating educational goals. If parents are to be held responsible for the general care, character and growth of their children, then they have to have a major role in the selection of who will teach their children outside the home and how these teachers will be taught. If communities are expected to create their own futures, they must have a say in what their children learn and how they learn it. This can happen through formal governance processes which give parents and communities a major role in the education and certification of teachers and in determining the role of the schools in the community and the community in the schools.

The federal government has not, in the main, intervened in the governance process save to encourage parent advisory councils in Title I (ESEA) (which puts a good deal of money into teacher training) and in Title VII (which limits its advisory committee to parents of the non-English and limited-English-speaking children) and to encourage similar kinds of "parity" councils in many of its temporary teacher education programs: Training Teachers of Teachers, Teacher Corps, Career Opportunities Program, and so forth. Few of the teacher education projects appear to have developed strong parent "advise and consent" systems. Fewer yet of the conventional state or private systems for choosing and educating teachers pay any attention to parents and their communities (in Chapter II, we looked at a few which do). And very few of the permanent systems have been affected by federal "temporary systems" money. Federal talk of local and neighborhood control has not produced collateral federal action to secure it. This, in part, derives from an element of cynicism which appears to have crept into Washington lobby negotiations over parent rights in the development, assessment, and monitoring of the education of their children and of those who will educate them in the future. Harry Summerfield writes in *Power and Process: The Formulation and Limits of Federal Education Policy* of the lobby fights over Title I governance procedures in 1970. First, the minority lobbies demonstrated that Title I funds were not being properly spent and argued that local parent councils were needed at all Title I sites to insure effective targeting of the money:

> The Washington Research Project [a lobby representing primarily minority interests], basing their protest on their own research drawn in part from published government reports, published a so-called "Martin-McClure Report." In it they presented evidence that administration of Title I dollars failed to comply with regulations and guidelines requiring rigorous federal enforcement of targeting of dollars to the poor. The Martin-McClure Report cited instances where Title I money was used for general aid to school systems benefiting all children, not just the poor. To ensure closer control of the dollars—local enforcement to supplement weak federal enforcement—the group proposed a guideline change to require creation of parent councils in every school with power to review and determine Title I expenditures.

Then the education lobbies moved and forced a compromise which gave parent councils the appearance of power without real power:

> Visions of "community control" and administrative agony in the local schoolhouse prompted the large education lobbies into aggressive opposition to the Washington Research Project move. Ostensibly a compromise was reached between the civil rights advocates and the lobbies by changing the guidelines to require parent councils on a school districtwide basis with symbolic but not real review and control authority of Title I. In this way the big lobbies could be in favor of "local control" of education while continuing to focus power on education professionals.[2]

Recent evaluations of model governance practices developed under federal programs such as the Teacher Corps suggest a similar tokenism in the federal commitment to real lay and parent input to the program. If the federal government is to intervene to develop or encourage local culture-based responsibility systems, let it do so with full energy and candor and not with guidelines which seem to promise people a power they do not have and give them responsibilities which are not real.[3]

Information Systems

Though the federal government has developed or pushed some governance schemes which carried the promise of making parents more directly responsible for the education of their children and their children's teachers, it has intervened most vigorously in the creation of national assessment and information gathering processes which putatively can be used with any governance scheme. While these processes were partly devised to return education to the public, they have served to nationalize and standardize both the schooling and teacher education process.

From our perspective, for an information (or "management information") system to be effective, the information gathered has to be crucial to the educational process. It has to represent what has been learned or created by the process. Its information must be available to all decision-makers and all clients or constituencies. It must also recognize that different accounting procedures exist in different groups, and that these procedures change continuously. To be useful to the school's clients, the ways of gathering information must be local enough to mean something to the people from whom, and about whom, the information is gathered; yet, this same information, if federally gathered, must somehow be sufficiently translatable into national statements to assist people who bear responsibility at a national level—such as the Assistant Secretary for Education, the Commissioner of Education, the Congress, and so forth. Ways of gathering information exist at federal, state, institutional, and private levels—from the federally-supported Higher Education General Information Systems (HEGIS) to gossip. Each of these ways serves a different master, but most of them claim the creative function of bringing order out of chaos.

The original impulse for clearly-defined ways of gathering information about education and for clearly-spelled-out ways of running the enterprise was precisely the same as one underlying this report: "to return education to the people." Fortunately or unfortunately, those segments of business and industry interested in keeping close track of the public tax dollar, efficiency experts, and some legislators have for a long time wanted to keep close tabs on what education was doing with its money. Some even wanted to turn the schools into what James O'Toole has called "an anticipatory mirror, a perfect introduction to industrial society."[4] Of course, education could not fully be this. Its management, "marketing" and change aspects, located as they are in the grants economy rather than the exchange economy, depend only to a minimal degree on free choice decisions by consumers.[5] For taxpayers and consumers, education has always depended on a "good faith" relationship—a sense of community between the person who pays and the person who receives benefits from the educational process. Nevertheless, as education in the sixties came to command the largest section of the grants economy, many ordinary taxpayers came to feel that educational services which were "better" could be "purchased at the same price" ("accountability" was a popular word even in the rhetoric of ghetto school reform, though the "accountability" meant was different from that meant by management specialists). Other authorities claimed that, with better information, services which were "just as good" could be "purchased more cheaply." The original HEGIS director (Theodore Drew) claimed that the system he was developing for finding out about higher education was part of a general managerial revolution—permitting states to control higher education in their boundaries, permitting local governments to know education in their own jurisdiction, and permitting both to make education as responsible to the public as possible.[6]

Looking back on the push for management and information systems in education, the National Commission on the Financing of Postsecondary Education could persuasively argue that the movement to get information about per-student costs symbolized to members of Congress, state legislators and governing board members: (1) that their selected administrators knew what their own institutions were doing and that they as arbiters among institutions had sufficient comparable data from other institutions from which to pick and choose, (2) that they could know enough to arbitrate any competing demands among special interest groups in an arena where the discretionary money available usually constituted about 25 per cent of the available federal or state dollars, and (3) that they could find out which programs were most "effective," which had most pressing financial needs, etc., a knowledge which would permit them to make wise decisions.[7] Producing common cost information in like institutions would also supposedly permit sloppy institutions to discover how they could meet their basic objectives at minimum cost through more careful work. At the beginning what was computed was the cost of fulltime students per major, cost of each "credit hour" in various kinds of courses, costs of various kinds of faculty salaries, and costs of facilities. The "product" of the higher education was "graduates," and so earned degrees conferred were counted. The aim was to let the public governing bodies know. Yet, somehow the public at large never became part of the act—they either did not receive the information or did not act upon it.

It is logical that "costs" and "management" were issues in the 60's, when larger numbers (the post-war "baby boom") and higher percentages of students were going to college. But it also seems probable that the growth of more explicit external information systems came from the increased power of "professional society" lobbies and of accreditation organizations which embodied "professional" values and made an "inside" assessment of whether higher education was doing its job. A legislator faced with a budget justification which stated, "Either the chemistry department gets a new building or it will lose its accreditation," or "The School of Education must add several members trained in professional education to its secondary education department or it will lose its accreditation," may well have wondered whether the "accreditation" or "profession-related" demands served the public interest.[8] Or he may have said, "If the state is to provide these items in order to fulfill professional or accreditation criteria which the public did not create and cannot understand, then the college or department receiving the items will have to be willing to accept more students," or "provide more graduates," or "place more graduates in the state" or whatever. Information-gathering by accrediting organizations was then, in one sense, used for lobbying and, in some sense, still is.[9]

As professional power and the number of students increased, the federal government "assisted" the states, school systems, and institutions of higher education to find out what was going on in their midst by establishing:

    1. The Higher Education General Information System (HEGIS), which is part of the National Center for Educational Statistics and which collected information yearly about institutions

of higher education, putatively to serve Congress, the executive branch and the higher education community;

2. The Elementary and Secondary General Information System (ELSEGIS), which did for elementary and secondary education what HEGIS did for higher education;

3. The National Center for Higher Education Management Systems (NCHEMS), which was developed with federal support by the Western Interstate Commission on Higher Education (WICHE) and which is now being used by a growing number of IHE's—either voluntarily or at the behest of state legislatures;

4. Federally-supported testing and assessment devices, such as the National Assessment of Educational Progress done by the Education Commission of the States (ECS), which has been proposed as a management device in teacher education and other education policy arenas and seems likely to be not only a "managerial" device but also a "resource allocation" one;

5. In addition the states and school districts have adopted— sometimes with federal financial help—a number of private national assessment devices and certifying instruments to determine "what ought to be done" in education, such as the National Teacher Examination (NTE) and various state manpower information systems bearing on teacher education.

Together these constitute a many-mirrored device through which the process of selecting and educating the leaders of America's children may be scrutinized. As we look at federal or federally-supported management and data systems, we should ask at every stage of the way, "Are these the best and best-executed systems for directly serving the people?"

If the ordinary citizen were confronted with the welter of data available on schools, school performance, teachers and teacher education, he would surely wonder, "If we know all that much, why can't we solve our problems?" But solving our problems involves knowing the right things in the right order at the right time to make solutions possible—being able to act on the knowledge we have. It is surprising how little of what we know really tells us what we are doing in educating children or in creating our successor societies. For example, one describer has written of the HEGIS schedules (the government's most ambitious official data-gathering effort on higher education) that they will tell one that every institution of higher education has certain "countable" characteristics: buildings, books in a library, faculty members, and students; and that it "awards degrees, with all students having majors"; but neither HEGIS nor the other schedules will tell one whether any teachers-to-be were recruited on intelligent grounds for real needs, whether they learned anything while money was expended and hours accumulated, whether they changed as they were "educated," or whether they can be of more benefit to children as a consequence of their undergraduate education.

One can learn cost per student and per credit hour from HEGIS and NCHEMS; one can compare program costs, etc. But one cannot really say anything about the "effectiveness of individual programs." If effectiveness is to be measured in anything more than head counts of graduates—if it is conceptualized as involving what futures the graduates have been empowered to create, how they have been affiliated to the survival changes of their peoples—then we know nothing. Too often even the head counts come too late. Not only the what and the when of information about teachers and teacher education need to be changed but also the how and the who of it.

The What and When of Information About the Education of Teachers

If we are to collect data on a national basis about who educates our children and how they are readied to do so, we ought to know some basic matters and we ought to know them early enough so that we can anticipate crises, adjust policy when legislative bills come up for renewal, and alter budgetary and institution-building policy if it needs altering within the framework of annual or biennial state and federal budgets. For instance, we need to be able to answer such questions as:

    1. What is the general effect of the federal teacher education programs and what do they cost;

    2. Roughly how many teachers and what kinds are we likely to need now and in the foreseeable future? What kinds of teachers-to-be are being recruited to be able to fulfill public school policy—at the local, state or national level?

    3. What is the cost and the effectiveness of the fieldwork

component, where teachers-to-be may find out whether they can really teach?

Steps are now being taken to answer some parts of these questions. They have not been well answered in the past.

Federal Teacher Education Dollars

The federal government obviously operates a great many teacher education programs—pre-service or in-service or both. The programs come out of several branches of HEW, as well as from the National Science Foundation (NSF), the Department of Defense (DOD) and from other agencies. During the period when the Study Commission was assisting the Newman Task Force with the research on a possible report on the education of teachers, the Study Commission decided to ask what the total federal spending on teacher education was. Surprisingly, the Newman researchers could not readily find out. In its preliminary paper on teacher education policy circulated internally in the Office of Education, the Study Commission wrote about the apparent "chaff-in-every-direction" effect which results from the placing of federal teacher education funds "all over the place" without general information on the placement and without flexible general strategy as to their purpose.

The present federal teacher education support system's effect on the campus is more to fragment than to unify. A single institution of higher education having an enterprising faculty may find itself with an NSF teacher-training project, a University-Year-in-Action project involving 50 per cent teacher trainees, a Teacher Corps project for students who have completed their bachelor's, a COP project preparing paraprofessionals and degree teachers from low-income areas, and an NIMH teacher-training project working on issues of school mental health—all temporary systems with predominantly temporary faculty.

Each of these projects may receive its leadership through different departments. Some work through different colleges. None will have, or be expected to have, a major impact on the university's or college's permanent system for educating teachers. In many of the projects federal money may provide the faculty and training program, recruit the students, and provide the stipends—all three. Because federal funding for most such projects is done on a year-to-year basis and because they exist in a kind of limbo separated from internal governance systems in the schools, they seldom have the institutional effect which their proponents hope they will have.

They do have deleterious effects. Projects divert universities from mission. They split responsibility. They divert the faculty and administration from asking what they can do with the local money they control. Indeed, the present system magnifies in the federal sector the faults and tensions of the local system and substitutes a sort of fumbling in every direction for a coherent policy.

... The money is all over the place. It is not possible to find any thread which runs through all of these programs. Many of them individually are encouraging hopeful developments. Some emphasize the disciplines, some professional education, some emphasize new courses, some field experience. None appears to emphasize committing the responsibility system of the total permanent institution in a meaningful way as did the NSF Science Development Grants.[10]

Later, in a 1973 report, the General Accounting Office (GAO) came on strong on the need for a central source of information:

At the beginning of our review, we intended to obtain an inventory of federal programs which affected the supply and demand of new elementary and secondary teachers. Although OE would appear to be the logical place for this information, it did not have it; we learned that no central source of such information existed.[11]

The GAO report indicated that the teacher surplus was becoming worse and that federal programs for offering incentives to people who went into teaching were continuing. Evidence gathered by the GAO indicated that OE administered $75 million per year in four programs exclusively for teachers (Teacher Corps, Career Opportunities, state grants, and vocational education). It administered $175.6 million per year in programs that had teacher training as one of several objectives. Other bureaus and departments of the federal government (National Endowment for the Arts, Smithsonian, Environmental Protection Agency, National Endowment for the Humanities, National Aeronautics and

Space Administration, National Science Foundation, AEC, Department of Defense), administered $13.3 million. All in all, 39 programs were involved in some sort of support for teacher education. Moreover, the Office of Education spent $965 million per year on student aid (e.g., student loans, work study, and educational opportunity grants). It insured over a billion dollars in loans. Under the Veterans Administration it provided $1.7 billion yearly in assistance and loans to veterans and servicemen. The Social Security Administration spent $768 million for expenses of student dependents or survivors of social security beneficiaries between 18 and 21. Since we know that in the past several years more than 20 per cent and in some years more than 30 per cent of our undergraduates were teachers-to-be, we can estimate that between 20 and 30 per cent of the $3 billion provided to students had to go to some aspect of educating teachers. If one adds to this figure ($750,000,000), the $175 million spent yearly on teacher education-related programs and the $75 million spent on teacher education programs, the GAO report appears to suggest that roughly one billion dollars in federal monies was being spent annually to create further surpluses in a surplus market and to maintain a series of fragmented approaches to in-service and pre-service education.[1,2]

The GAO's final recommendation was like the Study Commission's recommendation to the Newman Task Force: the federal government should centralize all its data about all federal programs affecting teachers, maintain feedback on areas of study undertaken by recipients of federal education funds, and use that feedback to coordinate the money spent with money given by other federal agencies for supporting education programs. Finally, OE and the Bureau of Labor Statistics were advised to improve coordination of their joint effort to provide a basis both for dissemination of supply and demand information and for projection and description of the job market for potential college students. In turn, states, colleges, and universities were advised to develop better student counseling programs concerning the surplus and to direct retraining efforts for prospective and in-service teachers needed in shortage fields. Fortunately, the federal government, in its written reply from an HEW official, was generally receptive to the GAO's recommendations, and if HEW action follows the direction of this reply, the country may soon have the sort of unified information on federal teacher education programs which the GAO was asking for.

Keeping tabs on federal teacher education program money may avoid wasteful duplication. However, a proper kind of local needs-assessment and follow-up on evaluation findings are also needed. This information could lead to targeted teacher education programs for specific cultures and communities. However, present data-gathering systems do not collect information on this basis. For instance, once "drug education" had become a federal program, teacher education for drug education became a national effort—done in similar ways everywhere and not very profoundly in many places. Drug data everywhere look about the same. But common sense should tell us that drugs used and causes of drug use and addiction vary from community to community and are as different as the varying forms of social disorganization which afflict us. The same devices which tell us how many and what kinds of teachers are needed may also tell us what kind of teaching is needed in areas like drug education, if the devices probe deep into the roots of the specific community which they assess. It will also be necessary to distribute widely the results of evaluation of federal programs, since a great deal of money is spent on that aspect (often 10 per cent out of the budget is set aside for evaluation), and since parents, communities, and older students need the information to tell how well a particular federal teacher education intervention in a specific community has worked. (Various groups may want to use specific evaluation reports to fight for the continuation of a project or to recommend drastic revision or closing of a project.)

The Employment Situation in the Teaching Profession

Getting manpower information also involves (1) getting information in time to use it effectually for present program needs, (2) getting information that is not so mechanically gathered as to have no particular use for policy, and (3) disseminating that information broadly and promptly. Recently we have heard a great deal about the "teacher surplus." Some of that surplus may have been created by inappropriate federal action. By the late 60's, almost one third of higher education was teacher education, and the Bureau of Education Personnel Development (BEPD) had in part been formed and supported to deal with critical shortages of teachers in important areas. BEPD associate commissioner for planning and evaluation Joseph Froomkin warned in a 1967 monograph, *Education for the 70's,* that the 1967 shortage would quickly be replaced by an overall teacher surplus.[13] This view was not generally adopted by BEPD, and the commissioner's report on the education professions *(The Education Professions: 1968)* states, "There was a teacher shortage in 1967-68. Were we to try to meet minimum standards as defined by the National Education Association, we would have needed nearly 400,000 additional teachers." The report does not make clear the distinction between NEA statements of "minimum standards" shortages, a fictitious number based on conceptions of more ideal student-teacher ratios than we presently have, and the actual jobs-to-graduates ratio. Later editions of the commissioner's report were a little more uncertain about the existence or scope of the surplus. Nonetheless, much BEPD policy in 1967-71 went ahead under the spoken or unspoken premise that shortages existed. Not so in 1971-72. Everyone knew by that time that people in graduate programs related to education were having a hard time finding jobs in schools and colleges and that those recently graduated with baccalaureates were having a very difficult time. The OE-BEPD mission statements emphasized quality, renewal, in-service—everything but quantity—[in their program statements prepared for educational revenue sharing, teacher centers, Undergraduate Preparation of Educational Personnel (UPEP), and Teacher Corps]. The uncertainty in this and other data areas led to uncertainty in Congress and the executive branch, to Congress's concern about lack of data as it passed the Education Amendments of 1972, to the Newman Committee's blast directed at NCES's preparing data which was late and policy-useless, and to the GAO report on the teacher supply and demand situation which indicated that neither NCES nor the Bureau of Labor Statistics could state with confidence what the teacher supply and demand situation was. The GAO itself found that there was a gross surplus of teachers in relation to the available jobs except in a few areas, such as vocational education and special education. At about the same time the Study Commission and other groups had noted that the predicted million and a half person teacher surplus would probably not materialize, since only four to six of each ten teacher candidates in the early 70's planned to teach in the common schools.[14] [The most recent development in this history is the belated recommendation of the National Advisory Council on Education Professions Development that the EPDA (Education Professions Development Act) authority be renewed as an organization which would be concerned only with in-service education of teachers and school officials.]

The net result of the history of federal data gathering in the late 60's and early 70's is that a lot of money was spent by NCES and other agencies to gather information that came in too late to affect student choices appreciably, too slowly to affect federal or state legislative decisions as it ought to have, or without sufficient focus to direct the spending of money toward some continuing need areas. It may be that NCES's goal of collecting and publishing data which have been scientifically edited (a process which takes, in some cases, years) may have to be sacrificed in the interests of developing rougher, earlier data. Some such system as that developed in Florida ought to be tried. There the education manpower system is so arranged that the school districts report their monthly vacancies in all areas—elementary, secondary, vocational-technical-adult, and community college instructors. The automated system is regularly updated and printouts are available twice each month. At the end of each month, the data are organized in booklet form and forwarded to all Florida Institutional Career Planning placement centers and to all institutions in the nation approved for teacher training. In assisting in the development of this, the Florida State University system has also developed a set of user-data "value postulates" which assert, among other things, that the data-gathering activity must be governed by such notions as (1) the campus should be extended into the community, and (2) the university should serve needs defined by people in society. Data which shed light on the extent to which these "value postulates" are being fulfilled are treated as priority data. Were these postulates interpreted to include the notion of gathering data on teaching jobs unfilled—along with "job descriptions," as these are developed by parents and their communities or by negotiation with professionals, a more useful system might emerge. And were we to extend our assessment of community systems—agencies, industries, businesses, neighborhood organizations—we might not suffer the constant trauma of having too few school teachers and other community workers and then too many as population curves rise and fall. Teachers who teach reading to high school students probably could meet the criteria for teaching adult literacy; elementary teachers may need the experience of a day-care center job; junior high and high school social studies teachers could teach civic literacy to adults. "In-community" education might crest and fall off in waves complementing "school" education. Presently few of the "in-community" teaching jobs seem to be handled by persons trained to educate in the schools—to the detriment of the educator's sense of community need and to the community's loss of connection with the schools. The University of Michigan School of Education has begun exploring ways of training people to work in a variety of educational settings: museums, corporations, social service agencies, public television, recreation centers, voluntary organizations, health agencies, and industrial firms. A data system which coordinated the crests and troughs of the birth rate as these affect schools with the crests and troughs of adult populations having need of educational services would do much to assist in the rationalizing of educational manpower policy and the relating of work and education, a goal of Chinese education which President Ford recently observed to be worthy of American emulation. What we are really advocating is the replacement of the surplus-shortage data systems with employment assessment systems.

If we are concerned to assess employment possibilities in our design of manpower systems, we ought also to be concerned about quality shortages. Chapter II displays data from 1970 about the teacher-to-be pool in that year—one of the years when the supply and demand situation was at its most favorable for our developing a good recruiting policy. By any "management information standards," we did not recruit very successfully at that time. We did not recruit teachers who were particularly racially sensitive or committed to justice or to the life of the mind, or even teachers hopeful about the educational process, its possible integrity and creative functions. We may have a few somewhat favorable "surplus" years left in which we can pick and choose. It is essential that data are distributed to (1) students as consumers, (2) deans as recruiters, and (3) administrators and their communities as the hirers of teachers.

Recruitment-management systems may be required to protect both public funds and students. At present, Deans of Education, such as George Denemark at the University of Kentucky, who have pushed for teacher and administrator recruitment targeted to social needs identified by minority social cultural groups or to data system descriptions of need, have generally not been well supported by other (higher) administrators facing "declining enrollments" and other threats to university budgets.

Fieldwork and Other Non-Traditional Education

For at least a decade, federal programs in teacher education and the rhetoric of teacher education "reformers" have emphasized "fieldwork," "clinical schools," "educating teachers in the kinds of classrooms where they will actually perform," and simulations of classroom interaction—whether video-taped or otherwise recorded and interpreted—as recruitment-by-trial devices and as alternatives to the often impractical "theory" conventionally offered earlier in the higher education preparation of teachers. However, a fairly recent (1968) Bureau of Research survey suggests that, in most conventional institutions of higher education, fieldwork and community work still get "bottom of the barrel" treatment: In 1968, 38 per cent of reporting institutions of higher education had written contracts with cooperating schools, and only 19 per cent paid the school systems for the services provided; 44 per cent paid cooperating teachers, but the national average was only $58 per cooperating teacher per term with the amount ranging from $29 in Arkansas to $150 in Pennsylvania.[15] Recent Study Commission site visits to a variety of teacher education field-based programs suggest that the support is not much better or more systematic in most places now. Schools such as Northwestern, which have clear school/college contracts, or states such as Wisconsin, which have ear-marked funds to pay interns-in-training, are the exception rather than the rule. Though an enormous amount of temporary federal funding has created field-and-community structures for educating special kinds of teachers (Teacher Corps, COP, TTT, etc.), little has been developed to measure the effects of federal efforts on permanent systems in the colleges and universities. Fieldwork is still an undersupported, limp-along enterprise.

The reasons for the underfunding of fieldwork in teacher education are rooted in the character of our information systems. Let us illustrate. Clinical hospitals giving in-field and in-institution practice to would-be doctors are enormously well-supported. We also have pretty good information on these hospitals. The HEGIS survey contains full provisions for finding information about them: number and kinds of employees, kinds of hospital facilities (classrooms, labs, research, special uses, etc.), sources of their fees. Thus, when a particular state's medical school or schools have a problem in their clinical hospitals, they can present comparative data in their state legislatures about the probable causes of the problem. Indeed, the information available is gargantuan.

In contrast, neither the HEGIS nor the ELSEGIS surveys contain space for comparable information about the practical aspects of the training of teachers—perhaps because the "practical education place" for teachers falls between the higher education system and the school system and is commonly equipped and staffed by both. Staff costs for fieldwork would probably be represented under course costs in HEGIS; from ELSEGIS one can learn something about costs for the number and kinds of teachers and students in school systems, about secretaries, psychologists, psychometricians, custodians and bus drivers, even something about supplementary educational centers (Title III). But nothing is available on centers for in-service or pre-service training nor on the specific costs and equipment of such centers. No categories are available which would permit the surveys to assess data as to the populations underserviced by teaching systems, the availability of teachers to meet needed teaching services, or the experiences offered to meet various needs. So far as we know, only the Fleischmann Commission report done for the state of New York gives serious attention to estimating what community-school practical work for teachers-to-be would cost (roughly 100 million dollars annually in New York),[16] and the "Lighthouse School" recommendations in that report have so far been ignored. Fieldwork and community work have not generally been decently represented in any conventional management schedules precisely because the "credit hour," "the classroom contact" hour, and the "fulltime student" (i.e., in classroom contact hours)—the main units of education production measured by such schedules—are "within-walls" educational concepts. On the other hand, fieldwork in education is an amorphous, nonlinear enterprise, often asking for work in the streets and requiring extensive organization, a good deal of money for planning and assessment, and peculiar non-academic genius in the teacher. Field-based and interdisciplinary educational institutions such as the University of Wisconsin at Green Bay, Evergreen State, the Native American institutions, and the Center for Teaching and Learning in North Dakota have all found themselves in jeopardy because they could not or chose not to produce conventional information in credit hour terms. The University of Kentucky College of Education faculty, seeking more in-community and in-field work, increased the amount of time spent on such matters from the time which it would take to educate 38 "fulltime equivalent" students (1972) to the time it would take to educate 404 fulltime equivalent students (1973); yet, Kentucky, like most universities, had no machinery for "counting" that kind of activity in its official statistics. George Denemark, Dean of the University of Kentucky's College of Education, in a letter to his university officials[17] remarks on the extent to which the official statistics' failure to count off-campus, non-credit, non-degree fieldwork activity discourages the development of in-service and continuing education missions for colleges such as his. (At the same time, no one seems to ask for an accounting of all the tuition money paid in for courses in student teaching. Does the school or cooperating teacher get compensation for time spent, use of the classroom, janitorial services, etc.?)

The extent to which the conventional credit hour and FTE concepts embedded in federal regulations discourage fieldwork, in-community education, and almost all sorts of non-traditional education is cogently displayed by L. Richard Meeth in his paper on "The Impact of State and Federal Funding Regulations on Non-Traditional Post Secondary Education":

> Meeth's report, based largely on a nationwide survey of administrators of nontraditional programs, points up nine ways in which [federal and state] budgeting formulas and guidelines restrict non-traditional programs. Some of these problems include: (1) many non-traditional programs don't use the credit hour as a measure of productivity, although most formulas are based on it; (2) in states with direct grants for private colleges, almost all funds are based upon fulltime study on campus, although many "new" students—workers, housewives, etc.—only attended part-time; and (3) external degree programs operating regionally or nationally have great difficulty getting direct state aid or even state grants for students who are residents of those states in which the regional center is located. Meeth's study goes on to suggest a number of full or partial remedies, including: (1) flexible interpretation of guidelines by state officials, (2) increased overtures to policymakers to change funding bases, (3) entirely new formulas or (4) abolition of formulas altogether.[18]

To the degree that federal formula funds administered by the state are part of the picture which Meeth draws, they contribute to the confinement of the education of teachers and other educational personnel to the fulltime, on-campus student and discourage work in teacher education institutions by industrial workers or other persons with standard daytime obligations in community life.

In general, the "what" and "when" of data must be considered if the policy which relates federal "soft" money to state "hard" money is to be effective. If the federal government is going to have programs to get rid of shortages, it ought to know whether and where these shortages exist. If it is to have temporary programs to move teacher education to the "field," "school," "community" (such as the Teacher Corps, COP, etc.), then its reporting systems need to show what the states are doing with their hard money in the same area. Sometimes the discrepancies are blatant. The 1973 OE commissioner's report on the education professions announced as OE's priority "that educational personnel for children from low income families will continue to be a major focus of Education Profession Development Act efforts" and specified that virtually all EPDA teacher personnel programs would concentrate on low-income, Spanish, Indian or minority issues. At the same time, in preparing for the 1973 HEGIS survey, the HEGIS advisory board (made up largely of representatives of education lobbies) really rejected data-gathering on all areas relevant to these priorities. They accepted gathering data on "institutional" characteristics, opening fall enrollment, financial characteristics, and on IHE's average faculty salaries. They, however, assigned less than top priority to earned degrees, students enrolled for advanced degrees, characteristics of employees, higher education facilities, residence and migration of college students (which meant that these categories were left out of the 1973 HEGIS survey). They did not assign any priority to any of the following which were proposed for consideration: instructional resources, student characteristics data, or so-called input-output data. Student characteristics would have included information on the abilities, socio-economic status, race, sex, career objectives, and educational objectives of students. "Output" would have included information about the outcome of the educational process. Thus while special projects for minority and low-income people were made a priority, the actual data systems for providing vital information on what higher education was doing with minorities on regular funds, and the interpretation of such data, were left untouched.[19]

The How and the Who of Gathering Information

If one begins with the perspective that information gathering should serve the people of the United States, it may at present be impossible to spell out exactly how an information system which first serves the people would work. However, it is possible to suggest some of the more obvious characteristics which it would have.

The Reality Maps of the Clients

First, the information system used would, in at least one of its forms, respect the "reality" map of the clients of the schools. The genius of the present data systems is that they permit comparison among distant situations and allow one to make judgments among unlike structures. But if the situations are really unlike, the gathering of like data may not be so much a diagnostic as a destructive act.

A tool which has been proposed as a useful diagnostic instrument in the reform of teacher education and in educational renewal generally is the National Assessment of Educational Progress (NAEP). The NAEP, originally the product of no public debate, was initiated by a combination of one million dollars in USOE funds and private foundation funds. The administering agency is now the Education Commission of the States. One schedule of that assessment, one which probably symbolizes its general view of the function of education, is The National Assessment of Musical Progress, a criterion-referenced test for determining the extent to which young people in America are achieving certain "musical objectives," "compiled by musical professionals in 1965." The test's "professional" (that is ethnocentric) criteria make up its reality map of music. The test exercises constructed ("criterion referenced") include singing familiar songs, e.g., "America" and "Are You Sleeping"; repeating unfamiliar musical material; improvising; performing from notation, and performing a prepared piece. Precise criteria for judging each performance were developed. For example, in singing "America," "pitch" was judged unacceptable if a pitch was closer to the next half step than to the right original pitch; four or more pitch errors led to classifying a response as unacceptable. In improvising melody, an acceptable response had to begin "within two measures of the end of the stimulus, must not have deviated in tempo by more than 10 per cent and must have not contained more than two unidentifiable pitches." And in sight-singing, "a pitch was considered to be incorrect if it was closer to the next half step than to the right pitch. Three pitch errors and one change of key were allowed in an acceptable performance. However, if one of the major second intervals were maintained consistently, the other interval may have been sung at a minor second interval without causing the responses to be scored unacceptable."[20]

Nowhere in the materials that have been examined is there an explicit statement about the social and cultural function of music. The performance of music is seen as an extremely technical process, with the standards derived almost exclusively from Western European music and Western European conceptions of pitch, tonality, harmony, and performance-timing.

Nowhere does one get the sense that music is seen as an outlet for imaginative expressions, as fun, or as a means for expressing and elaborating a perceived world order or social order. One contrasts the examination's expressed view of music and its role in society with the diversity in the American musical heritage—ranging from black worksongs and spiritual songs, to pietistic and evangelical hymnody (owing much to Dwight L. Moody), to Appalachian folksongs, from music associated with labor movements to that in which Calvinistic tendencies severely limit the repertoire, to Native American songs employed on occasions of love, death, honoring, religious ceremony, etc.

Respecting "the reality map of the particular clients of the schools" would mean assessing people first on the "mournful melodies" that are their own, and only using national standards as a secondary device, if they are used at all.

The notion that such tests as those constructed by the National Assessment—or similar national standards criterion-referenced tests—ought to be basic in federal management systems including teacher education was proposed by Representative Albert Quie in hearings having to do with the Education Amendments of 1974. Title I has traditionally paid hourly salaries for undergraduate pre-service teacher education students—those in the Career Opportunities Program—and it now has authorization to pay for the in-service education of teachers also. It has always been a kind of revenue-sharing program, posing as a special program "to aid those of disadvantaged culture." However, no really serious analysis of human cultures has ever been required in Title I programs (the very concept of "deprived cultures" or "cultural" as opposed to "economic" deprivation would be called into question by many scholars). In recent years, the program has served well enough as a species of semi-categorical program, half-way between revenue sharing and strict categorical programs. This kind of program pumps some money into low income school districts and schools until such time as the Supreme Court's word to the states (as in the *Rodriguez* case)— that they (the states, not the Court) should be concerned about the unequal support of education given children—is heard. Congressman Quie's notion, probably correct, was that Title I should not be a substitute for a bad taxing system, but that it should feed money in wherever it appeared people were not learning—whether in low, middle or upper income schools—and that the determination of this matter should rest with criterion-referenced tests in mathematics and reading which would control the allocation of funds to bring students "up to the expected level." The notion would be a cogent one if all Americans were asking the same thing (the same sort of "expected level") from their schools and if the courts had held that responsibility for the schools of America does not rest on the parents, the neighborhoods, or the local communities.

But clearly neither of these is the case. Though the Quie amendment did not succeed in 1974, it is still under study. The authors of one follow-up study[21] done for the Assistant Secretary for Education show that, if a criterion-referenced test did not assume that all students had studied the same thing, it would be like an IQ test; that if it were based on "current curricula," it would resemble an achievement test; and if it used only "dominant curricula," it would be invalid for use with pupils who had had different curricula. The authors then ask, "Should a single standard be imposed, or should we adopt standards which vary according to region, locality, and curriculum?" (The Study Commission would add "culture" and "sex" in certain instances.) Accepting all of the authors' reservations about the costs of differing performance standards for different locales, the Study Commission would still argue that different "performance standards" make sense to the degree that "life curricula" of the places where children are growing up are different, to the degree that the language and survival demands of various places—and so their performance demands—are different. Needs for children and youth exist first as needs perceived by parents and families, unless the state is seen as the first guardian of children and youth. Paulo Freire's research suggests that people learn to read best in their own language and in relationship to their developing sense of survival and political needs; Yetta and Ken Goodman, in their "miscue" research on reading in Appalachia, demonstrate that children there read best their own language and the stories which have first fulfilled their own culture's needs. The use of reading and mathematics in relation to those specific "close-to-home" needs must be assessed first in determining how teachers and schools are to act, if assessment and information are not to deprive education of meaning and function.

Change-Oriented Data Systems

Second, data systems should focus on how institutions change, the effects of decentralization, and parents' perceptions of effective teacher capabilities.

By using industry-derived conceptions of input-output, cost effectiveness, and resource allocation, while continuing to accept the fundamental units of measurements of traditional higher education (the credit hour, the department, the full professor, the fulltime student and part-time student, the degree), the conventional information systems give useful tools to those who are asking what an institution is spending and on what. It gives few tools to those who might want to ask whether another way of doing things might be better—both as to educational strategy and as to who is in charge and whose interests are being served. It has been argued by some Study Commission researchers that the development of publicly supported data systems which make it easier for those who allocate funds and make "day-to-day" decisions to "look out" than for parents, students and ordinary citizens to "look in" is a consequence of the founding of the data systems in "structural-functionalist" sociology. This form of analysis of society tends to picture human institutions as like permanent scaffolds—a series of static structures each of which has a fixed function necessary to society. If the functions are both necessary and static, any deviation in the institution can properly be regarded as "temporary stress" which the structure will absorb. The function of statistics-gathering, then, is to find out how to maintain the system as it is by absorbing temporary stress. In such a view, matters of floor space, faculty salaries, degrees conferred, jobs available and persons-to-fill-jobs are important to know, because misjudgments in such matters may cause social stress. If intense racial unrest appears in the country, racial statistics may come to be important for the same reason. But if a group desires a new institution, creates a new consensus, envisages a mythical nation of Aztlan which requires new institutions, if a group wishes not only to articulate the stress which it feels but to take responsibility for making things different, neither a sociology which conceives of society as a grand scaffold held together from the top nor a management and data system which views data from the same perspective is likely to be adequate. As one writer has put it:

> . . . [T]here is a compelling tendency to conceive of systems as things that have interdependence and have equilibrium, and thus to miss that these are the positive values of dimensions. . . . To conceptualize systems in terms of their interdependence, as [Talcott] Parsons does [and as conventional management information systems do], tends to focus primarily on the 'whole' and on the close connectedness of the parts. . . .

Such an analysis both ignores the pressure of many parts of a social group to move toward autonomy and tends to make efforts to thwart such moves into a simple sustaining of the system. What structural-functionalism tends to see as fundamental to society or to an institution is:

> . . . the tendency of the system itself, or more accurately, of those

parts that are charged or identify with system management, to strive toward fuller integration, reducing the autonomy of the parts and increasing their submission to the requirements of the system as a whole....[22]

Structural-functionalism is interested in "how the [dominant] social system as such maintains its own coherence, fits individuals into its mechanisms and institutions, arranges and socializes them to provide what the system requires."[23] Its sociology leaves little room for the notion of social institutions as constructed—sometimes on an *ad hoc* basis—by collaborative efforts among individuals. Nor does it allow for portrayal of the subjective feelings, the deviations of feeling, or the momentum for change which exists, active or latent, within individuals. Finally, such sociology has little capacity to represent the process according to which institutions having historical continuity and weight are dissolved—though their functions remain—or how structures remain when their functions have long since ceased to be. By denying the forces which might create change, the information systems may preclude movement, particularly movement toward new institutions, toward culture-based higher education and toward parent-controlled community schools for educating teachers, or it may force such movement into exile in underground institutions. New priorities for data collection might be ranked by (1) local needs, (2) district goals, and (last) national or aggregate needs. (Collectors of local data might be trained to expect some "snobbism" at various levels and be warned not to be intimidated by it.)

Consumer-Oriented Data Systems

Third, the data-schedules would, as we have suggested, be composed in the presence of consumer representatives, and disseminated widely in an understandable form. Too often information—when it is popularly circulated—is not in a form which permits citizens to judge how they are to take the data or how they are to separate the "facts and figures" offered by one information gatherer from those offered by another. How is the ordinary citizen to respond to information systems that present the following kind of analysis?

In Nebraska, the projections of enrollment for the next five years are conflicting. The Nebraska legislature's fiscal analyst's office estimated college and university enrollment would drop 17.7

per cent between 1970 and 1979. That figure was based on the continuance of a downward trend in the percentage of Nebraska high school graduates going on to college. University of Nebraska officials disagreed and predicted that the university system would increase its enrollment 10 per cent in the next five years. The University officials based their projection on a 10 per cent increase in high school graduates by 1979 and a belief that the decline in the going-to-college rate has hit bottom.[24]

The citizen has to know about the two different methods used and that the data collected—and the way in which they are presented—depend on the fact that two sets of officials are seeing the budget from opposite ends—the dispersing end and the receiving end. **Federal information systems will be doing their work well when the data they generate are being used by citizen consumer groups, by parents, by students and teachers-to-be to help determine who should be recruited to teaching, what the processes of teacher education should be, what forms of teaching and teachers "our children" should have—given "our plan" for our community's future. If the data are presented in a simple, straightforward and honest way, and if the doors of the teacher education institutions and of the schools are kept open, parity governance can be achieved.** In the New Rochelle, New York, school district, parents school-by-school have full access to all school "MIS" data gathered and determine fully the school budget allocation and policy—a style of asking parents to assume responsibility which could be emulated by teacher education centers everywhere. Under this sytem, the New Rochelle schools have improved on a "barebones" budget.

There are other hopeful signs that we may eventually get consumer-useful data. Though the older NCHEMS schedules tend to reinforce the conventional notion of how the university or college should be divided and run, new schedules now being developed may be very useful to teacher education. These include assessments of student growth and development, specialized knowledge, critical thinking, creativity, social development, social leadership, racial/ethnic attitudes, personal ethics, social conscience, cultural interest, change/stability attitudes, self-concept, career preparation, development of new knowledge or its application, and community development. Some of these new schedules reflect the limitations of ordinary standardized testing but others are based on relatively inobtrusive measures which allow one to look at "what actually happens."[25] These measures should be further developed, bearing in mind their possible limitations. They should not replace community created needs assessments and norming processes.

Recently, the National Center for Educational Statistics let a Request for a Proposal (RFP) for a very thorough management study of American teacher education related to its present conditions and the ways in which more appropriate management information systems might be developed. The design recognizes the community factor in the management of teacher education programs. We quote from the request:

> For at least the past decade American public schools have been the subject of much criticism relating to the preparation of teachers. The passage of the Educational Personnel Development Act in 1967, designed to upgrade the level of instruction of elementary and secondary teachers, is perhaps the most dramatic Federal response to this criticism. Although there have been a number of other Federal, State and local efforts aimed at the problem, the criticism continues and has perhaps increased. Simultaneously, the new resources available to Federal, State, and local levels to reform American education in general and teacher education in particular, seem to be diminishing.
>
> The general direction which future education is likely to take in response to existing concerns and criticisms is both implicit and explicit in judicial opinion as well as in a number of recent studies and recommendations. In the recent case of *Wisconsin v. Yoder* the Supreme Court articulated a wider definition of education than has ever been advanced by the high court, a definition that is likely to be expanded further by the courts. The concept of relating education and work has recently been voiced by a Special Task Force to the Secretary of HEW (Work in America). "It might be worthwhile to view schools as work places, as much in need of job redesign as other work places, and to understand that the proper prerequisite to satisfying work is a satisfying education."
>
> With respect to higher education, the *Newman Report on Higher Education* outlines the need for considerable redesign of institutions of higher education. The recent creation of the Fund for the Improvement of Postsecondary Education is further indication of the trend to broaden the operative notion of education

and consequently of "teacher" and "student."

A redefinition, of the terms "education," "student," and "teacher," is taking place through a growing number of specific programs and institutions. Parkway School in Philadelphia and Metro High School in Chicago are only two examples at the secondary level; at the collegiate level, there are the renowned New School in New York City, the University of Wisconsin at Green Bay and Evergreen State to name but a few. Literally hundreds of similar programs or colleges exist and have been supported in the past by Federal efforts such as the ACTION and Teacher Corps programs. Changes in teacher certification procedures and requirements are, in a similar way, moving from a "program" base to a "competency" base.

Finally, there is growing recognition that a large number of persons are participating in educational programs not operated by nor generally supervised directly by State agencies. Present projections suggest that adults engaged in such programs will soon outnumber those enrolled in conventional collegiate programs. Other data leads to the conclusion that the education of teachers is becoming more intersystemic, involving a growing number of institutions, colleges and schools, and departments other than education.

The results of the study to be designed under this contract would assist in developing an understanding of the present status of undergraduate preparation of educational personnel in the U.S., and would contribute to the development of more refined systems for collecting information regarding it.[26]

The RFP also recognizes, by implication, that present teacher education is not meeting, or may not be meeting, the particular needs of local cultures in local schools and asks the investigation to ask on a preliminary basis:

    1. What is the content of teacher education programs, i.e., the disciplines, settings, programs, methods, including those which are recent developments in the field?

    2. What effect has the critical financial crisis at many institutions of higher education had on teacher education programs?

3. What kinds of students are now being recruited for teacher education programs?

4. What adjustments are being made by institutions of higher education in response to the current teacher surplus?

5. What are the costs of undergraduate preparation of educational personnel?

6. What kinds of teaching roles are, or are not, being properly filled by present training procedures?

7. What has been the impact of the State-mandated performance-based teacher education?

8. What efforts are underway to assure that future teachers will be trained to **meet the particular needs of local schools?**[27]

At its best, we can hope that such a study will clarify a number of things, such as: (1) differentiations in data gathering modes appropriate to different age levels and cultures and possible data-translations; (2) possibilities of establishing continuous systems of education for teachers who work in community systems and "schooling" or "with walls" systems; (3) differentiations in personnel skills needed and kinds of teachers needed in prototypical national environments. We can hope that such a study will (1) include ample input from parents and students, (2) lead to ways of getting information which will respect what people say about what they want, and (3) permit the development of different tools for gaining different kinds of information on places and children. "Eagle chasing at Jemez, New Mexico," is not "surviving among pushers at First Avenue and 104th Street," and neither skill, necessary to survival in its context, is presently attended to in the gathering of information.

Education, like other great enterprises, seeks more and more to describe itself through the vocabulary of numbers in place of words. Of course, it is important to get good counts of persons, places, plans and procedures in education. Our principal argument indeed stands in favor of clarification and articulation of the critical features of education that are possible only through numbers. There is a further task, however, in information gathering on education. This task can be accomplished mainly through words. We need to know what is happening in education, wherever things are indeed happening. We need to be told in so many words how education makes up circumstances in the life of students and their parents, of teachers and administrators in the schools and, of course, of persons preparing to be teachers. In the social sciences, particularly in sociology, there is a strong development of what may be described as ethnographics or a deliberate concentration on the stories of people. Ethnographics celebrates actualities, the direct experience of actualities and the careful interpretation and appraisal of actualities as experienced.

Balancing the collection and analysis of data which, by and large, consists of assembled counts of numbers, there could be outright attempts to assemble ethnographical accounts put largely into words. A good place to start in this special effort is in fact in the work of educating teachers. A good report on this work would call upon prospective teachers to tell their stories, to provide their interpretations and evaluations of their own involvements and preparations for involvements in education.

In this chapter we stress the need for a *quantum* leap in information gathering on the education of teachers. We state further that there is required a *qualis* leap, a clarification of the qualities of what is there in education, a careful accounting of what is happening there as that clarification is put into terms that we all can understand.

SPECIFIC RECOMMENDATIONS

Recommendation I:

Governance

All federal and state programs which have teacher-training components should require community (parent and student) control which goes beyond mere tokenism. Parent and student rights in the development, assessment, and oversight of the educational process ought to be fully supported. Where formal bargaining arrangements exist, parent and student groups should be a party to the negotiations. In addition, whenever and wherever federal programs are evaluated, results of the evaluation should be widely disseminated to interested parties, including parents and students.

Recommendation II:

Federal Dollars

The National Center for Higher Education Management Systems (NCHEMS), the Higher Education General Information Systems (HEGIS), or Common Core of Data Collection (CCDC) should be improved to include schedules on the costs and effects of school-community teacher education centers attached to institutions of higher education. Efforts should also be made by these organizations to develop cost-analysis systems for non-university centered, truly field-based programs. (See also Recommendation IV.)

Recommendation III:

Employment Information

The National Institute of Education (NIE) and other appropriate federal agencies should support the formulation of job descriptions for education personnel needed by all sectors of society. All information gathered should consider the perspectives of the specific groups for which information is being gathered and should allow for talk, gossip, community protest statements, and other informal methods of symbolizing what is needed as well as the formal statistics.

Recommendation IV:

Fieldwork

NCHEMS should be encouraged to develop instruments that assess what students have learned in relation to community-articulated needs. The effects of conventional management systems—using departments, credit hours and full-time equivalent (FTE) mechanisms—in handicapping non-traditional institutions should be studied to verify or refute Newman Commission and Study Commission assertions. Schedules which account for field-based activities in teacher education should be at least as full as those which give an account of medical fieldwork activities.

Recommendation V:

Reality Maps of the Clients

The federal government should direct funds toward developing community-specific assessment instruments for teachers, schools, and the children they teach. The federal government should also direct more of its efforts at helping the states to gather and analyze information about their educational needs and to plan the use of their resources in ways which promote diversity in teacher education.

Recommendation VI:

Change-Oriented Data Systems and Consumer Interests

NCHEMS and HEGIS should work with student and citizen participant groups having strong bases in third-world, poor-white and student communities to develop priorities for data schedules as well as to develop methods of representing higher education management data so that issues become a matter of public discussion. We would make the same recommendations to NIE as it develops its research.

FOOTNOTES

[1] Donald R. Warren, *To Enforce Education: A History of the Founding Years of the United States Office of Education* (Detroit, Michigan: Wayne State University Press, 1974), pp. 77-87 and 204.

[2] Harry L. Summerfield, *Power and Process: The Formulation and Limits of Federal Educational Policy* (Berkeley, California: McCutchan Publishing Corporation, 1974), p. 156.

[3] For example, see Ronald G. Corwin, *Reform and Organizational Survival: The Teacher Corps as an Instrument of Educational Change* (New York: John Wiley, 1973), p. 121, which talks about how early Teacher Corps programs, despite their community participation rubrics, were introduced from the top; cf. pp. 24, 72-73, and pp. 146-51 for an account of the disparity between the rhetoric of Teacher Corps projects about the importance of community fieldwork and participation and their actual performance in this area. Teacher Corps interns tended to see work in the community as concerned with the total health of the community including civil rights, housing, and jobs, whereas classroom teachers and team leaders tended to regard community work as primarily concerned with improving in-classroom teaching skills. The Study Commission's committee for "Evaluation of Impact of Federal Intervention on Higher Education," which did a study of the effect of the Career Opportunities Program, found that in most instances involving program creation or change (e.g. selection of faculty, initiation of new or modified courses, etc.), the COP Community Advisory Boards had little impact on the development of the Career Opportunities Program (COP). At the same time, both Project

Directors and IHE coordinators generally saw the Community Advisory Boards as facilitating changes needed by the COP program (54.6 per cent of COP project directors and 55.8 per cent of COP-IHE directors). Not every culture in the U.S. has mechanisms for developing group direction through discussions and voting. For example, Hopi holy men may make decisions affecting a third of mesa life based on data which is not statistical and which is gathered in non-ordinary ways. The decision-making system does have community sanctions. Any governance system developed needs to respect such sanctions.

[4] James O'Toole, *Work in America,* p. 142.

[5] Kenneth Boulding, "Education and the Economic Process," in Lew Pino, *Nothing But Praise* (Lincoln, Nebraska: Study Commission Publication, 1972), pp. 64-67.

[6] Theodore and Sheila Drew, "HEGIS: A Report on States and Plans," *Management Information Systems in Higher Education* (Durham, 1969), p. 80.

[7] Donald E. Leonard and others, *Financing Postsecondary Education in the United States* (Washington, D.C.: GPO, 1973), pp. 323-24.

[8] The Study Commission directorate has examined several appeals for budget increases directed to state legislatures in which part of the appeal is a mention of a threat to the institution's accreditation standing if further funds are not provided.

[9] The accreditation agencies, by accrediting black colleges on a separate and "lower standard" basis (not a basis differentiated by cultural considerations), denied the black colleges a major tool in lobbying with state legislatures. Had that not been the case, the "Developing Institutions" program for black colleges then already accredited and fully supported by the states would not have been necessary. These valuable colleges would in all likelihood have been supported at a first-rate level because accreditation groups would have demanded that they be equal. State legislatures which cared for justice would have been under strong pressure to respond to the threat of accreditation cut-offs as they did in the case of white colleges and universities. Paul Mohr, Dean of the College of Education, Florida A & M State University, in letters to the Study Commission, documents this process.

[10] Draft chapter on teacher education for the Newman Commission, on file with the Study Commission and dated November 16, 1972, pp. 34-36.

[11] GAO Report, *Supply and Demand Conditions for Teachers and Implications for Federal Programs* (Washington, D.C., 1974), p. 8. (The report was in draft form in August, 1973).

[12]GAO Report, p. 7. Cf. letter from Patrick E. Daly of the GAO dated September 11, 1974, giving a list of all federal programs bearing on teacher education and their budgets, gathered by the Federal Interagency Commission on Education (available, Study Commission files).

[13]"Decision Making in the Bureau of Education Professions Development," Ch. II, *The Role of Evaluation in Federal Education Training Programs,* Center for Educational Policy Research (Harvard University, December, 1971), p. 14 (Xerox).

[14]*Study Commission Newsletter* (December, 1973), pp. 2, 33-34.

[15]James A. Johnson, *A National Survey of Student Teaching Programs* (July, 1968), USOE Project No. 6-8182, pp. 58, 67-68.

[16]*Report of the New York State Commission on the Quality, Cost and Financing of Elementary and Secondary Education* (Fleischmann Commission), 1972, Vol. III, Ch. xiii, p. 4.

[17]Letter from George Denemark on file with the Study Commission. Lew Pino suggests that this kind of activity can be more easily built into the "Master of Teaching Arts" concept; cf. December 5, 1973, memo from David K. Blythe, chairman, Ad Hoc Committee for Standard Nine, Southern Association of Colleges and Universities, to Dr. Lewis Cochran, vice president, University of Kentucky, concerning accounting for continuing education and public service functions of the university.

[18]Institute for Educational Leadership, "News of the Convening Authority," *Monthly Memo* (April, 1975), p. 4.

[19]Cf. report on the HEGIS VIII planning conference in the Study Commission files and the subsequent Study Commission correspondence with HEGIS planner, Maureen Byers of NCHEMS (March 12, 1973); *The Education Professions: 1971-72* (Washington, D.C., 1972), pp. 61-64. The report was released in December, 1972, and describes 1973 priorities.

[20]Frank W. Rivas, *National Assessment of Musical Performance,* published by National Assessment of Educational Progress (February, 1974), pp. 3-5, 15-17 and *passim.*

[21]John A. Emrick and James W. Guthrie, *The Use of Performance Criteria to Allocate Compensatory Education Funds* (Menlo Park, California: Stanford Research Institute, 1974), I, pp. vi-vii, 22-23.

[22]Alvin W. Gouldner, *The Coming Crisis of Western Sociology* (New York: Basic Books, 1970), pp. 214-16.

[23] Gouldner, p. 143. This work is extended by Eric Margolis' analyses for the Academic Disciplines Committee of the structural functionalist assumptions of standard management information systems used in education; Margolis' draft manuscript is in the Study Commission files and will be published soon in Ed Rose, *The Academic Disciplines and the Structure of Education* (in press, Study Commission Publications).

[24] *Chronicle of Higher Education* (November 18, 1974), p. 5.

[25] For example, Robert Wallhaus and Sidney Micek, "Inventory of Higher Education Outcome Variables and Measures," *Program Measures,* Technical Report 35 (Boulder, Colorado: NCHEMS, 1973), pp. 202-03.

[26] NCES RFP 74-37, "Design a Study of the Preparation of Education Personnel in the United States," pp. 4-5.

[27] NCES RFP 74-37, p. 2.

CHAPTER V

THE FEDERAL ROLE IN TEACHER EDUCATION

While federal involvement in education goes back to the early days of the republic, the years since World War II have seen the initiation, growth, and decline of an amazing number of new and essentially uncoordinated federal initiatives in response to new sets of realities. During this post-war period, America's schools and colleges were perceived to be responsible, in part, for this country's loss of international advantage in science, technology, and commerce. Internally, there were growing demands for greater social, political, educational, and economic equity within a society which was beginning to appreciate its cultural diversity and pluralistic origins. With a few notable exceptions, however, the national record of accommodating cultural diversity in the schools has been poor. And collegiate programs for preparing personnel to educate America's poor and minority cultures have been spotty and inadequate.

We recognize that the primary responsibility for providing support for public and private educational systems at all levels will continue to reside at the state and local level; however, we believe that certain tasks are best handled at the federal level if the mission of aiding "the people of the United States in the establishment and maintenance of efficient school systems" is to be fully carried out. We do not call for massive new federal programs to support teacher education and to lift it from its undersupported state. Rather, we call for federal leadership and advocacy for good state support of teacher education and for federal support of some developmental efforts to create the new forms envisaged.

We began this study with the firm conviction that the role of federal agencies dealing with children and with teacher education ought to be one of helping people build and maintain effective school systems. This conviction is supported and given some direction in the Department of Education Act of 1867 which created what is now the U.S. Office of Education (USOE):

> Be it enacted by the Senate and House of Representatives of the United States of America in Congress assembled, That there shall be established, at the city of Washington, a Department of Education, for the purpose of **collecting such statistics and facts** as shall show the condition and progress of education in the several States and Territories, and of **diffusing such information** respecting the **organization and management of schools** and school systems, and **methods of teaching**, as shall **aid the people of the United States** in the **establishment and maintenance of efficient school systems**, and otherwise promote the cause of education throughout the country. [Emphasis added.] [1]

The argument of the Study Commission's report is that, in the federal policy area, we have lost sight of the notion of direct service to "the people of the United States." In addition, our definition of what constitutes "efficient education" has been too narrow in that it has allowed for education which severs people from their kin and community, from their traditions of work and play. Moreover, what constitutes the "cause of education" has been too largely circumscribed by definitions developed by the profession. In this chapter we want to discuss in some detail several impediments to effective federal intervention in teacher education. We also want to examine what we feel the federal role in teacher education ought to be. This section is not meant to be exhaustive, but merely to highlight some problems and solutions which we see as important.

Impediments to Effective and Efficient Federal Intervention in Teacher Education

The Power of Educational Lobbies

Higher education receives a great deal of support from categorical grants administered directly from Washington. Theoretically such a grant program is supposed to begin—after the bill has been passed and a budget assigned—with the devising of guidelines, the publication of the guidelines in the Federal Register, a call for proposals and the reviewing of proposals in terms of guidelines by a panel. The choices of the panels are usually accepted unless compelling evidence indicates that, in one or another choice, the panel has not observed the published guidelines. (Lewis Pino, in a Study Commission report, has pointed out the weaknesses of this system of funding.[2]) It is not, in essence, a public system—each federal fund-granting agency is limited by the exclusive nature of the guild which supports it; each categorical program has a clientele which consists of a specific academic community; and this special interest lobby defines the problems, determines need, designs solutions, and in the end receives the actual benefits of a particular program. People from this special interest group serve on reviewing panels, act as consultants, make up the very staff of the agency and finally receive the funds. Nothing conspiratorial is intended. The developing and granting is all done politely and well in the name of professionalism. The special interest groups' power is possible because of their presence in Washington, their inside contacts, their wealth of information, and the number of relatively powerful constituents they represent.

One of the most powerful present lobbies is the American Vocational Association (AVA). It had, according to the testimony of a recent book, control over federal vocational efforts until the mid-60's and it more recently has had, according to its own testimony, a major role in the development of the present efforts to change the ethos of the whole of education from elementary school through college in its shaping of career education.[3]

Though most of the education lobbies—higher education, public education, public schooling, and the professional associations—are not actually registered as lobby agencies (most are listed as 501.C.3 charitable organizations), they do in fact exercise great influence on Congress and on the executive branch, particularly on middle level bureaucrats.[4] It would not be realistic to expect special interest groups to act in ways contrary to their own concerns. However, these groups do not represent "the people of the United States" in their roles as representatives of the professions. We believe that bona fide consumer groups such as PTA, the groups represented in the Institute for Responsive Education's bibliography of "citizen participation" in education, the National Student Lobby and similar groups from the minority and women's sectors, should receive at least as much attention as the professional "producer" interest lobbies. The definition of "what needs to be done" or what information should be gathered in OE hearings, briefings, proposal readings, and guideline development projects should be determined by panels which include representatives of consumer groups in education—particularly parents and students. And of those groups, those having the most problems within the present system should have clear, vigorous, articulate representation. The problems ought to be articulated by the people having the problems—not by the professionals dealing with the problems. The Office of Education ought to be returned to "the people of the United States," because the present state of affairs gives too much power to educational lobbies and causes the expected diffusion of resources.

Diffusion of Federal Policy in the Proliferation of Programs

President Ford, in a commencement speech at Ohio State in 1974, indicated the need for some kind of coherent federal approach to higher education:

> Oftentimes our federal government tries to do too much and unfortunately achieves too little. There are, for example, approximately 380 separate federal educational programs beyond the high school level, some duplicating others, administered by some 50 separate executive agencies. The result inevitably is a bureaucracy that often provides garbled guidelines instead of taut lifelines to good and available jobs.[5]

In an attempt to gather information, the General Accounting Office (GAO) contacted the Federal Interagency Committee on Education to put together a list of all federal education programs. That listing showed that the federal government in 1973 had 39 programs directly educating teachers or bearing on their education; spent 250 million dollars in direct federal funding of teacher education programs; and in addition, had spent more than 750 million dollars in student scholarships, or scholarship-like monies which went to teacher education candidates.[6] All this took place when publicity on the teacher surplus could hardly be labeled minimal and when many programs were supposedly being cut.

Congress, in passing the Education Professions Development Act in 1968, hoped to consolidate many of the existing programs in teacher education to give them some focus and direction. In the summer of 1973 Commissioner Ottina of OE indicated that the Teacher Corps was to be the sole agent of teacher education development in the federal establishment.[7] The most recent chapter in this story of consolidation and coordination can be easily read in the Amendments for 1974 signed into law in August of 1974 and effective for four years. Without complete or consistent data about the supply and demand conditions within the teaching profession, Congress has written into law the following programs having as part of their mission the provision of pre-service and/or in-service training for education personnel:

a. bilingual
b. gifted and talented children
c. community schools
d. career education
e. consumer's education
f. women's equity in education
g. adult education
h. national reading improvement
i. Title I
j. Teacher Corps
k. Indian education
l. education for use of metric system
m. elementary and secondary school education in the arts

We cannot lay the entire blame for this diffuse approach to teacher training on the professional societies and their lobbyists, although they do share the blame. What also enters in here is the political aggressiveness of the members of Congress, their understandable desire to create programs which can strengthen their position. As a case study of this, Harry Summerfield traces the development of the Environmental Education Act and shows how teacher education is "added on" to federal policy in areas outside of education. Summerfield examines the memos written to Congressman Scheuer (N.Y.) by this staff prior to the development of the legislation:

> ... The LA (legislative assistant) thought, "Bottles, cans, and abandoned autos are good issues, but what can a member of the Select Education Subcommittee of the House Education and Labor Committee do both to help education and to capitalize on coming political opportunities on the environmental issue?" . . .

> At this point Mr. Scheuer's situation began to congeal. He wanted a dramatic issue for publicity purposes; he needed a reform issue because of his ideology; he was convinced that environment was a coming issue, and he was already dabbling in the area with bottles, cans, and automobiles. However, none of this had anything to do with education. Suddenly, the proper synthesis emerged, and it became obvious that Mr. Scheuer should "author" legislation entitled the Environmental Education Act. . . .

At this point the legislative assistant drafted a policy memo to Congressman Scheuer:

RE: A Potentially High Payoff Angle to Environmental Pollution

On the question of environmental pollution and the approach you should take, several formats have been suggested during the last few weeks:

   a. Make yourself an all-around, generic "expert" on environmental contamination, . . .
   b. You could dabble in pollution with items like the bottle bill, junk autos, or others. . . .
   c. You could sponsor a serious bill which will get hearings. Preferably, the hearings would be on one of your subcommittees where leadership on the issue would be acknowledged to be yours. . . . (This is the route I recommend.)

The Plan

There is a need for a strong public education program on pollution and environmental abuse. The demand first comes from industry, which eschews regulation and would be eager, very eager, to support public education approaches. Secondly, there is a great deal of political mileage because no one is opposed to environmental protection particularly at the level of public education . . . a government public education program can be easily and eagerly absorbed.

The Plan for a *Public Education on Environmental Contamination Act*

The legislative format could include a range of public information programs: *classroom curriculum* and *materials development; educational professional development* along the lines of *summer institutes;* grants for university course development; university *research grants* for development of *teacher education.* . . .[8] [Italics ours.]

The federal government should not—as was attempted in this instance— use federal programs for educating teachers as a substitute for needed federal action in an area outside education.

We want to make clear that we are not arguing for a uniform nationalized approach. What we are talking about is structures which come out of priority planning and which are focused to meet serious educational needs rather than the present impotent and proliferated programs, heavily influenced by the winds of powerful lobbies. We ask for a coherent flexible federal policy which includes the targeting of federal dollars to the districts where the need is most intense, either assessed in educational or economic terms or both, and controlled or monitored by the parents of children having the intense needs.

Too Limited a System for Anticipating, Clarifying and Disseminating the Implications of Court Decisions on Teacher Education

That the federal government in the executive branch has been slower than it might have been to educate itself and the people with respect to the meaning of judicial decisions, particularly Supreme Court and circuit court decisions having a high authority, has come to be something of a bromide now. This has been observed particularly in the *Brown v. Board of Education* matter. But it is also apparent with respect to other cases having more direct bearing on teacher education: the *Tinker* decision and others bearing on student rights; the *Griggs* decision and related decisions (e.g., *Chance and Mercado*) having to do with rights of licensing and employment in labor and the professions; the *Lau* decision, *Portales,* the *ASPIRA* decree, and others having to do with the provision of bilingual and "culturally pluralistic" education to minority cultures. While Congress and the Office of Education have, since the late 60's, sought to develop bilingual programs, no clear nationwide contingency plans for teacher education in this area were developed comparable to those developed by OE in the wake of *Serrano* and *Rodriguez*. When, in 1974, San Francisco's failure to provide special language instruction to some 1800 non-English-speaking Chinese students was found to violate the 1964 Civil Rights Act, it was no coincidence that President Nixon at the same time was pushed to increase his bilingual budget (1975) from $35 million to $70 million. HEW Secretary Casper Weinberger, in defending the awarding of a $1.1 million bilingual evaluation contract, cited the San Francisco *Lau* decision as the impetus for his creating a mechanism to determine compliance and to find ways of meeting the needs of non-English-speaking children.

While it is clear that a variety of legal decisions affect how HEW and the Congress behave, the effect on their behavior is likely to vary depending on whether the court's appeal is to the Constitution (as in *Brown* or *Griggs*), to a federal law (as in the various court fights which have developed over the intention of ESEA Title I), or to a set of federal guidelines under which a school system or IHE accepts contractual obligation (as in *Lau,* though the *Lau* decision also appeals to the Constitution). Bills are likely to be written on the basis of Constitution-based decisions, but when decisions involve the application of the principles of bills or guidelines, the congressional or administrative question is much more likely to be, "Do we accept the application or do we revise the guidelines or bill?" Federal legislative and executive policy **creates** court enactments (in attempts to determine the extent to which a program may have departed from its guidelines) as well as **responds** to court enactments (in attempts to correct court-declared grievances—as in the *Lau* case).

The Los Angeles City case is an interesting case of how policies and court cases cross each other. The Office of Civil Rights did not approve the school district's voluntary plan of desegregating school staffs. Yet the few bilingual teachers they have (2 per cent) will be affected by this plan; i.e., the Spanish-surnamed teachers are concentrated in Spanish-surnamed schools. When desegregated they will deprive Spanish-speaking children of appropriate instruction as defined by *Lau vs. Nichols* which itself was based on an Office of Civil Rights policy.

We are not arguing here for the correctness or incorrectness of any court decision. Rather we believe that as the courts resolve disputes between legislative bodies and executive branches of government or between citizens and the executive, or between citizens and school boards, there is a need for collection, analysis, and dissemination of these judgments within the government itself, to concerned state and federal officials, and to educational consumers. In this regard the Study Commission feels that Congressional hearings on bills relating to education always ought to involve literature searches on prior court decisions germane to the legislation; and that HEW and OE, which have specific components that engage in legal research and give legal advice in the formation of contingency plans, legislation, programs, and their implementations, should stress the anticipatory nature of the legal research— to avoid problems later. Relevant legal issues and specific court decisions should also be listed in actual legislation, RFP's, guidelines, and program guides, and follow-up on guidelines is essential. HEW should take the initiative, seeing to it not only that its guidelines are being followed, but that germane court decisions are understood and observed, anticipating and avoiding lengthy and costly court actions. We believe that a good deal of impetus toward such collection, analysis, and dissemination would be provided by the comprehensive education law reporting systems called for in Recommendation III at the end of this chapter.

Improving the Federal Role in Teacher Education

The protection of the interests of the people may require intensive federal leadership to revitalize the functions of teaching and learning. As we mentioned in Chapter II, though teacher education accounts for about one third of America's college students at any given time, it receives less than 9 per cent of the support given to higher education. Education departments in humanistic and fieldwork areas receive less per credit hour than conventional departments in other colleges of most institutions. Teacher education in 1972-73 received $1,300 to $1,500 per FTE (full time equivalent) as contrasted with expenditures considerably higher in other professional areas, particularly in the junior and senior years. Sixty-five per cent of the teacher education students in the country went to "low quality" institutions as rated by the Carnegie Quality Indices. (See Chapter II, footnote 50.) And federal teacher education projects were all temporary systems "training grant" style projects providing soft money, often on a one-year or one-to-three-year basis. Now teacher education is being cut back in many states because of the surplus. The reforms we propose will cost money. They cannot be paid for with hot air and good intentions or with money scattered to every possible cause. It is the Study Commission's argument that the provision of a high quality staff for educating the youth of America would be one of the most important things—perhaps the most important thing—that higher education and the schools could do. Specifically, we urge support of the following areas:

Research and Development

We believe that the federal government must continue to be the major source of support for research and development aimed at improving our understanding of the mechanisms of human learning.[9] To this end we recommend that funding for basic and applied research and for the testing and demonstration of research results be enhanced and stabilized. In particular, we call for greater federal recognition—not only in the executive branch, but in the halls of Congress—that studies on the teaching and learning process and related work in general human development are important. As in the cases of student support and teacher training, federal support for educational research ought to reflect the government's commitment to educating a diverse America. This would mean that the government would encourage and support research which is directed toward assisting specific cultures rather than toward assisting the generalized country where Everyman is thought to dwell. It would mean that members of diverse cultures would participate in the selection of research proposals to be funded. The specific kinds of research we encourage are described in the recommendations for Chapters II and III.

Required here is the involvement of the very best minds we can muster, combined with a research training effort which can recruit and develop an ever-expanding cadre of talent. The efforts currently going on, not only in the Office of Education but in agencies such as the National Institute of Mental Health, the National Institute of Child Health and Human Development, the National Science Foundation, and the National Institute of Education should be fostered, coordinated, and funded at adequate levels.

The lag between the publication of tested research results and their incorporation into programs for the pre-service and in-service preparation of teachers of all levels should be minimized—as we discussed in Chapter IV. A major hope for the future is that better understanding of the nature of human learning and human behavior within varied cultural contexts can be and will be adapted quickly for field use. We believe that the federal government, through appropriate agencies, must assume a major responsibility for the dissemination of research results, so as to improve both the processes of teaching and learning and the processes of measurement of the outcomes of instruction. We believe that several models for the dissemination of research findings exist: the extension agent model; the cooperative, as in the REA; the demonstration, as in the experimental schools program, and others. We would argue for giving serious trials to each of these to test their speed and efficacy in accomplishing the needed reform.

Institution Building

The last few years have seen a number of federally-supported projects intended to test and demonstrate various experimental approaches to education and training. We believe that the coordination of these efforts in comprehensive programs for the initiation and development of responsive institutions is badly needed. (We describe these kinds of institutions in Chapters I and II.) The federal government should establish, at adequate levels of funding, a series of developmental programs which can make tangible in new and improved institutions the results of the best that is known on the processes of teaching and learning. It is particularly important that the needs and aspirations of individual communities be reflected initially and continuously in the planning of new and revitalized institutions, as in the Universidad Boricua, a Puerto Rican community project. Paramount in accomplishing this end is both the establishment of new institutions and of new "alternative institutions" and the reshaping of more traditional institutions such as is presently being carried ahead at the University of North Dakota, the University of Vermont, the University of Kentucky, and Oregon State University.

We believe that this sort of developmental effort must be at the core of the federal role in education. Only such a stance can assure the growth over time of a wide range of diverse and effective institutions for the education of our citizenry. A developmental approach assumes that the federal government will bear the bulk of the developmental cost of new and alternative institutions, as well as the cost for conversion of existing local educational agencies and institutions of higher education to more responsive patterns. There is some experience now, not only in the Office of Education but in the National Science Foundation and the National Endowment for the Humanities, to show that support for start-up and transitional costs for periods of up to five years in individual cases can be instrumental in converting local aspirations to viable, strong, and effective institutions. Once launched, new, alternative, and reformed institutions can appeal to non-federal sources as well as federal sources for continuing support in the expectation that those which truly respond to community needs will prosper.

Federal program units concerned with developmental funding must be staffed by especially competent and sensitive professionals who can assist local communities in the development of sound plans and realistic budgets. A federal policy of prospectus solicitation leading to a formal proposal after informed consultation, seems to be called for. Also needed, of course, is careful and open evaluation both of proposals and of the effectiveness of institutions established or modified by this means. And local community members should definitely be included in evaluation teams. The dissemination of evaluation reports should be encouraged—to assist communities in drawing on the experience of others.

Carefully planned and coordinated federal support for the development of new, alternative, and improved institutions of learning at all levels can, if thoughtfully done, help to strengthen and revitalize local community life. In order to be strong and viable, a community must not only reach general agreement on goals and life styles but it must also be able to retain an ever-renewed supply of young people who are aware of community roots and who can contribute to realization of community aspirations. We argue, then, for the application of our uniquely American pragmatism to the development of greater diversity in our educational institutions based on community needs and community hopes for the future.

We are not suggesting that the quality of learning be ignored, but rather we are calling for recognition that each community, if it is to prosper, needs a voice in the definition of desirable educational outcomes for its youth. In the long pull, this effort to diversify as well as improve institutions of learning can only contribute to the total richness of our civilization.

Information Collection, Analysis, and Dissemination

We have mentioned the 1867 Act creating the Office of Education, whose office was to be "collecting such statistics and facts . . . as shall aid the people of the United States in the establishment and maintenance of efficient school systems, and otherwise promote the cause of education throughout the country."[10] Chapter IV in this report goes into specific detail in the area of data-gathering usage and should be regarded as the prologue to this particular section. Federal agencies dealing with education must be responsive not only to the needs of professionals working in the field but to individual students and parents, as well as local community groups concerned with the effectiveness of particular institutions. The exchange of accurate information requires that effort be devoted to the standardization of definitions and the collection of data in ways which permit valid and timely comparisons to be made. Only in this way can students, parents, and the general public make fair evaluations of the efficacy of local schools and of institutions dedicated to postsecondary education. At the same time, provision for the representation of local perspectives should be made in the schedules. The call for greater precision in definitions, however, should not be translated into a call for greater uniformity in institutions. As we have indicated earlier, we see a major federal responsibility in promoting diversity and responsiveness to local aspirations in our institutions of teaching and learning. Congress has recently recognized the growing importance of the National Center for Education Statistics. We share this view, while at the same time calling for greater public access to the work of NCES.

Enhancing Access

In Chapter II we call attention to the small number of minority students in the ranks of teachers-to-be. In this connection, Section 801 of Public Law 93-380, the Education Amendments of 1974, bears quoting in full:

> Recognizing that the nation's economic, political, and social security require a well educated citizenry, the Congress (1) reaffirms as a matter of high priority the nation's goal of equal educational opportunity and (2) declares it to be the policy of the United States of America that each citizen is entitled to an education to meet his or her full potential without financial barriers.

It is clear that this goal is directly related to service "to the people of the U.S." It is also clear that education to full potential is not available for many groups of prospective teachers at present; it is not the case for visible minorities, it is probably not the case for "unmeltable ethnic" minorities; and it is clearly not the case for women seeking administrative responsibility or work combining administration and teaching.[11]

We call on the federal government to support a new, more just policy for funding through such means as:

a. **A diverse system for support of students, especially at postsecondary levels, with proper funding and stable administrative procedures to promote access to educational opportunities and, in particular, to assure culturally diverse student bodies in teacher education programs at the undergraduate and graduate levels.**

We call for increased funding devoted to direct support of students through grants and cooperative education programs, rather than loans, as the means most likely to attract a full range of students from various economic and cultural groupings. A stable and fully funded system, incorporating the elements of Basic Educational Opportunity Grants (BEOG), Supplemental Educational Opportunity Grant (SEOG), College Work Study, National Defense Student Loan (NDSL), Federally Guaranteed Student Loans, State Scholarship Incentive Funds, and Cooperative Education, would provide the sort of framework which recognizes the full needs of our pluralistic society. We would hope to see greater recognition of the needs of part-time students and of mid-career professionals, including in-service teachers.

    b.   **Increased efforts, such as exemplified by the TRIO Programs, to bring together in a coordinated way related program elements (e.g., Talent Search, Upward Bound, and Special Services) designed to enhance both access to and retention in educational institutions at all levels.**

In many instances, access is not limited simply by financial constraints but by failure of our educational institutions to provide appropriate environments for learning. Enhancement of access must be defined broadly to include those sorts of responsive and sympathetic support services needed to serve individual and group needs and to provide cogent learning experiences. Opening up and strengthening of our total educational capability is badly needed if we are, in fact, to assist each citizen in meeting his/her full educational potential. Specifically, enhancement of access would include support of personnel knowledgeable about and sympathetic to non-mainstream cultures; precollegiate and collegiate educational programs which build upon the students' cultural strengths, while broadening their exposure to mainstream cultural and educational opportunities; and social and psychological services rendered by culturally sensitive professionals. Such access may be offered by new small institutions serving specific constituencies or by small mission-oriented units created within large institutions; but in any event, treatment of TRIO awards as developmental funds aimed at permanent improvement is clearly desirable.

    c.   **Development of an accurate and timely public information service which can describe in realistic terms the career opportunities available to students completing educational sequences and the needs which neighborhood community groups and parents express as to educational resources and services needed.**

We believe that, in general, this particular function should be carried out by the federal government, since this information could be used to match a surplus of trained manpower in one area against a shortage in another region of the country and to assist areas having similar problems, needs, or cultures to identify persons who fit their needs. Further, such an information service would be a guide for students at the undergraduate level, leading them away from pursuit of areas of oversupply, such as social studies and English, to areas of need, such as special or bilingual/bicultural education. The service would also be helpful to graduate students and in-service teachers who prepare for mid-career re-tooling. The logic of the sorts of local and national information systems which we envisage as most useful is set forth in Chapter IV.

We also believe it is important that existing federal authorities such as those embodied in the Education Professions Development Act, including the Teacher Corps titles, should be maintained and strengthened so that the federal government can respond in timely and appropriate ways to needs for recruitment and training of specialized education personnel. We have seen, for example, in recent legislative and court actions, calls for improved educational opportunities for the handicapped and mentally retarded. Federal actions to assist in increasing the supply of qualified education personnel in selected areas are clearly appropriate. Equally appropriate federal actions ought to be taken to increase the numbers of professionals qualified to teach blacks, Puerto Ricans, Chicanos, Native Americans, Asian people, and Southern mountaineers.

    d.   Initiation and continuation of a stable, coherent, and flexible set of local, neighborhood, culture-specific but federally assisted in-service and pre-service professional development programs for teachers at all levels.

The federal involvement in the improvement of pre-service and in-service opportunities for education personnel goes back to the Smith-Burton Act of 1917 and before. The bewildering variety of federal efforts begun in recent years, many of them overlapping and providing funding at less than full cost, suggests that it is time for regrouping and evaluation. It is our belief that the enhancement of access for students requires a firm and continuing commitment to improving the capabilities of school and college faculty and staff. While much of this effort may be subject-oriented, the agencies involved must also emphasize the development of emotional capabilities to respond to the culturally pluralistic student bodies of the nation. Included here as well is the expectation that training opportunities for faculty and staff will recognize local aspirations for institution building. These training opportunities must be geared not only to the potential of an individual and his or her personal and career aspirations but also to the needs of a particular college or a particular environment which can contribute both to educational effectiveness and to economic efficiency (cf. Chapter II for examples). If we are to justify the continuation of university-controlled, university-centered programs, then let those programs be based largely in schools and communities and let their substance be the life needs, emotional needs, and cultural needs, as well as the more traditional educational needs, of the children.

Conclusion

We believe that the goal of a permanent, comprehensive, coherent, and unified federal role in teacher education—which emphasizes local decision-making—can be achieved, largely because there is growing public recognition that the strength of our educational enterprise is fundamental to the realization of the full potential of a pluralistic society. We have seen, in recent years, the results of a national failure to allocate resources in ways which are responsive to fundamental national needs, and we are quite certain that the growing public demand for greater accountability in legislative actions and agency responses will not be unheard by those who see the disparity between community aspirations and governmental responses.

We are in a time of change and hopefully in a time of movement toward improvement in access to opportunities for personal and community growth. If our vision of the future is correct, and if it can continue to enlist the concerns and the energies of a growing part of our citizenry, we could be on the way to the sort of America our ancestors hoped to see.

SPECIFIC RECOMMENDATIONS

Recommendation I:

Consumer Access to Policy Making

Consumer interest groups representing the needs of students, parents, and local community groups ought to be involved at least as much as are professional interest groups in decisions on matters of educational importance, particularly on panels designed to advise Office of Education and state agencies as to community plans and teacher education needs, strategies, and ways of gaining parent and community parity at the local level. This recommendation is supported and expanded by

Recommendation VI of this chapter and Recommendation VI of Chapter IV.

Recommendation II:

Proliferation of Programs

All of the chapters in this report argue for a unified, comprehensive, and flexible, yet decentralized, national strategy based on a clear sense of national priorities. More specifically, we feel that the federal government must continue to have and use its authority to intervene in response to manpower deficiencies as they may arise. Existing legislation (e.g., EPDA) could be used to create a responsive and flexible stand-by authority to provide funds for the expansion of opportunities in the recruitment and preparation of needed education personnel; beyond this, we call for an institution-building program as a major component of the strategy (cf. V, below). A recent report of the National Advisory Council on Education Professions Development, *Staffing the Learning Society: Recommendations for Federal Legislation* (April, 1975), pp. 41-55, proposes "a new EPDA" based on recommendations independently arrived at but essentially parallel to those of the Study Commission.

Recommendation III:

Court Decisions

The federal government should provide support for the development of a comprehensive education law reporter system (involving issues in early childhood, elementary, secondary and postsecondary education). Such a system should build on current law reporter systems addressing limited audiences and issues, and should recognize the fast-growing importance of access to the legal system in issues of access, financing, accreditation and eligibility, licensing, and public disclosure in education. It is important also that federal programs be checked by these law reporters to be certain that court decisions referred to in RFP's and guidelines are being followed.

Recommendation IV:

Research and Development

The federal government must continue to be the major source of support for educational research and development. To this end it is recommended that research funding be stabilized and the management of the research and development activities of HEW be developed to permit both adequate evaluation of research proposals and of the results of research grants. In particular, it should be recognized that research and development in education, including the education of teachers and other school personnel, is a long-term process.

Fundamental to the improvement of programs in teacher education is a better understanding of the nature of human learning and behavior within cultural contexts. These findings will have only limited value until they are adapted to the education of teachers and to their performance in the classrooms of the nation's schools. Federal agencies must assume major roles in the conversion of research data to demonstration projects, to dissemination of proven methods and to improved means for evaluation of teacher and student performance. Particular priority should be given to research needs described in the recommendations of Chapters II and IV.

Recommendation V:

Institution Building

The federal role in supporting exemplary projects should be expanded and coordinated, both with the results of research and development and with the needs of communities as they are identified locally and communicated to the national level.

The federal government should establish and maintain a centralized developmental grant program with adequate and stable funding to permit the widest possible range of traditional and alternative institutions of higher education, schools, communities and other agencies to demonstrate effective training of school personnel. These pilot models should be continuing, anticipatory and widely varied in thrust. The institutions envisaged include the kinds described in Chapter II as well as institutions supportive of these, such as centers for the study of occupational licensing, examining schools, community-based futures studies centers, and community data-gathering centers (cf. Chapters I-IV). Provision must be made for the institutions to be vulnerable to community pressure and participation, as in some Title I and Title VII programs and in child care legislation (parent councils, etc.).

Recommendation VI:

Information Collection, Analysis, and Dissemination

The federal role in collecting and disseminating educational information must be strengthened and developed so that all Americans may have access to cogent, accurate, and timely data and information. The needs of individuals and local community groups for information must be dealt with in an appropriate manner by NCES.

In order to provide for the exchange of information among the various parts of the domain of teacher education, greater efforts should be made to standardize definitions and to collect data so that valid comparisons can be made. The students, their parents, and the general public need access to data and information that permits a fair evaluation of the efficacy of local schools and institutions of higher education.

Recommendation VII:

Enhancing Access

The current multiple system of student financial assistance is desirable and should be continued and expanded. The diverse support system of BEOG, SEOG, college work study, NDSL, federal guaranteed student loans, state scholarship incentive funds and cooperative education is one that is most likely to promote access and achieve a culturally diverse student body in teacher education programs. Increased funding should be concentrated in grant and cooperative education programs (rather than loans) as the means most likely to promote diversity and to get the percentage of minority candidates for teaching up to parity levels.

The federal government should continue and expand the support of such programs as **TRIO** (Talent Search, Upward Bound, Special Services) and others which may be designed to enhance access into and retention in institutions of higher education of persons whose access would otherwise be poor or limited.

Information describing, in realistic terms, the opportunities available in the school-related professions should be prepared in timely fashion and widely disseminated to potential students in teacher education programs.

The provision of a portion of the funds available under various titles of ESEA for the pre-service and in-service education of personnel for schools is a desirable action and should be continued in coordination with related legislative and agency authorities and programs, with modifications as suggested in this report.

FOOTNOTES

[1] Donald R. Warren, *To Enforce Education: A History of the Founding Years of the United States Office of Education* (Detroit, Michigan: Wayne State University Press, 1974), p. 204.

[2] Lewis N. Pino, *Nothing But Praise: Thoughts on the Ties Between Higher Education and the Federal Government* (Lincoln, Nebraska: Curriculum Development Center, 1972), pp. 20-33, 39-46.

[3] "Since 1917 when the Smith-Hughes Act first established a federal role in vocational education, policy had been controlled mainly by the American Vocational Association (AVA) working closely with Congress. (Secretary Gardner once cited AVA as one of the most effective lobbies in Washington, competing in effectiveness with the best defense lobbies.)" Harry L. Summerfield, *Power and Process: The Formulations and Limits of Federal Education Policy* (Berkeley, California: McCutchan Publishing Corporation, 1974), pp. 140-41. See also the chapter on the AVA in the Study Commission study document on professional societies, Rosemary Bergstrom, *et al., A Time Half Dead at the Top* (Lincoln, Nebraska: Study Commission Publication, 1975), pp. 209-15.

[4] NEA has recently voluntarily given up its tax-exempt status in order to act openly as a lobby. We urge other professional "lobbies" to come out of the closet.

[5] *Chronicle of Higher Education* (September 16, 1974), Vol. VIII, No. 42, p. 6.

[6] GAO Report, *Supply and Demand Conditions for Teachers and Implications for Federal Programs* (Washington, D.C., 1974), pp. 1-2. (The report was in draft form in August, 1973.) (See Chapter IV.)

[7] This information was distributed at a Teacher Corps conference conducted in August, 1974, at the Belmont conference center.

[8] Summerfield, pp. 49-50.

[9] Cf. Pino, *Nothing But Praise,* pp. 51-56.

[10]Warren, p. 204.

[11]David Rosen, Seth Brunner, Steve Fowler, *Open Admissions: The Promise and the Lie of Open Access to American Higher Education* (Lincoln, Nebraska: Study Commission Publication, 1973); cf. the three case studies on Nebraska (pp. 11-35), California (pp. 35-53), and City University of New York (pp. 53-166).

CHAPTER VI

AN ALTERNATIVE REPORT

The following letter from George Denemark of the University of Kentucky is his statement of non-endorsement of this report. Mr. Denemark was a full member of the Study Commission throughout its life and made a significant contribution to the development of its position. The final position of the Commission, however, differs from Mr. Denemark's position in important particulars. The position which Mr. Denemark has set forth should be taken very seriously as an alternative to the Commission's position. It seems probable that the debates over federal, state, and local policy with respect to teacher education will turn on the issues formulated by Mr. Denemark and the Commission. Mr. Denemark is the Dean of Education at the University of Kentucky and past president of the American Association of Colleges of Teacher Education.

• • • • • • • • •

I am writing in response to your letter of March 27 soliciting reactions to the revised report and recommendations of the Study Commission. Your letter requested both the notation of errors or bad prose and a statement of disagreements with positions which would warrant notation or revision before a Commission member's name was attached to the report. It is this latter element that has caused me to delay my response until now. Examining my notes growing out of a reading of the manuscript, I have come to the conclusion that my concerns with significant portions of the report are so fundamental as to require either a major recasting of the report or a deletion of my name as a concurring Commission member. Since time deadlines and the massiveness of the task do not permit the former alternative, it seems clear to me that I must ask you to remove my name as one who endorses the report and its recommendations.

My decision was reached only after several hours of agonizing appraisal. The judgment was made especially difficult because I believe the report to be in many respects a splendidly provocative statement of positions which should receive major discussion and debate in our society. It is, however, precisely in these terms that perhaps my most fundamental concern needs to be understood. The ideas and alternatives which the Commission or its various sub-groups have discussed over the past several years are clearly worthy of study and discussion. So long as the Study Commission was playing that role, that is, one of study, debate and analysis, I felt that every idea seriously proposed was a potentially useful stimulus for improved practice Now, however, the Commission in concluding its life is proposing a series of quite specific recommendations, the function of which is not to continue or enrich debate and discussion, but rather to persuade members of executive and legislative branches of government at federal and state levels to endorse, legislate and fund certain proposals. At this point the Study Commission relinquishes its study charge and becomes, in effect, a lobby or advocate.

My own personal commitment to reflection and debate on educational alternatives is unequivocal. I believe, however, that the final report of the Commission in the form in which it is proposed seeks to end reflection and debate and instead to spur action on its recommendations. Those critical of my reaction to the manuscript will doubtless suggest that I am behaving like a typical professor, willing to debate endlessly but never to reach a conclusion or take a position. I sincerely believe that not to be my position, but instead view it as representing a conviction that the issues identified merit lengthier and more broadly representative consideration before governmental solutions are advocated.

A further general concern of mine relates to the representativeness of the Commission participants when we turn from a task of illumination to one of advocacy. Where proposals for study and discussion are involved, the representativeness of the proposing body is not as critical as when the group's charge turns to efforts to generate legislation and executive policy. As you well recognize, those of us participating on the Commission have not done so as formal representatives of a particular constituency (i.e., Land-Grant Education Deans, AACTE Board members, etc.) but rather as individuals interested in the ideas under discussion. So long as the agenda dealt with alternatives worthy of consideration there was no problem. When, however, we move to formal recommendations, it is likely that our institutional and organizational ties will be interpreted by recipients of the report as endorsements by such agencies, endorsements which, in fact, are not intended. Were I to have been asked to reflect the thinking of the AACTE Board of Directors or the Land-Grant Education Deans, I would have had to play my role in a very different manner and the report from the Commission would likely have been quite different in character.

With this somewhat extended expression of generalized concern, let me next note several specific concerns which provide the basis for my decision that I not be identified among the endorsing members of the Commission. First, let me express my strong opposition to the proposal for "deprofessionalization" of teacher education. I believe the recommendation is at odds with reality since we have never truly achieved professional status for teaching nor come to view teacher education as the training arm of the profession. The report, therefore, seems to be calling for the breaking down of something we have never succeeded in establishing. In my judgment, many of the problems in education and teacher education today result from our inability to recognize the essential elements of a profession and to incorporate these into the field of teaching and related specialties. In many respects the task of the teacher is more complex, more sophisticated, more demanding than that of any other profession. Yet this report would call for a dismantling of the mechanisms and structures designed to increase the effectiveness of teachers as professionals. I continue to believe in the fundamental involvement of parents and other citizens in the identification of the objectives and values toward which they wish their children educated. I believe just as strongly, however, in the importance of a profession exercising appropriate controls over entry to its membership and maintaining concern for the quality of performance by teachers consistent with the broad educational goals identified by parents and other concerned citizens. Teachers need to be *professionalized* rather than deprofessionalized, for they have never achieved a status that enables them to provide the educational leadership our society demands.

A second fundamental concern with the report lies in its serious oversimplification of the concept of community and its uncritical endorsement of culture-specific or community-specific teacher preparation programs. Implicit in the document at several points is a naive assumption that local communities, left to their own resources, will reflect the best and finest of human aspirations. In fact, many examples come to mind which suggest that decentralization often results in racist, sexist, or social class biases that constrict rather than enlarge educational opportunity for children and youth. While the report rejects such developments as antithetical to its objectives, it does little to suggest how narrow, provincial, and bigoted community values can be prevented from self-perpetuation through a biased community power structure control over teacher employment, training, and instructional program matters. The report, calling for the integration of the school with other organizations of society, concludes, "We want the schools to be so integrated provided that the society to which they are integrated is a good society." That, of course, is precisely the problem: How is the good society to be defined and who defines it? It appears that the Commission members may be willing for a local community group to have total control so long as its values conform to those judged appropriate by the Commission members. I strongly believe our larger society has an obligation to seek deliberately the enlargement of shared values among a broader circle of our citizens and to insure that core values and freedoms are guaranteed individuals. The report falls into the familiar trap of assuming that freedom is the absence of control rather than viewing certain kinds of professional or governmental controls as enhancing and enlarging the degrees of freedom available to individuals. In some Appalachian communities, for example, the absence of accreditation or certification controls might not result in the employment of teachers and administrators more sensitive and responsive to local community concerns. Instead, the result might be employment decisions based upon kinship, friendship, or other factors totally unrelated to teaching competence or community needs.

Another gnawing concern of mine stems from the seeming preoccupation with the virtues of smallness implicit at many points in the report and noted particularly in Chapter I. Recent developments in the education of handicapped children, for example, suggest the need to think of such children in the broadest context rather than in oversimplified subdivisions of exceptionality. Currently we are moving toward the concept of mainstreaming as a means of relating such children's learning experiences wherever possible to others without such handicaps. If we are to prepare teachers to relate to a broad range of exceptionality and yet maintain a high level of specific functional teaching competence, we are unlikely to do it in preparation programs staffed with one or two persons.

At the heart of many of my concerns is the seemingly simplistic view of teaching, of community, of culture, etc., reflected in the report. The frustrations arising from our need to deal with the realities of a large, complex, urban society have seemed at times to elicit nostalgic yearnings for a return to the simpler and smaller "good old days"—days of town meetings, one room schools, and city teachers' colleges. But as the Rockefeller report, *Pursuit of Excellence,* observed:

> The notion that we might escape the complexities of modern life by returning to some simpler form of existence is sheer romancing. The inter-locking complexities of modern society are an inescapable part of our future: if we are to nourish individual freedom we shall have to nourish it under these circumstances. If we are to maintain individual creativity we shall have to learn to preserve it in a context of organization.

Oversimplification is again evidenced in the statement in Chapter I which speaks of *"the* language and culture of children." The reality of many communities and neighborhoods is one of *multiple* languages and cultures. Our task then is one of helping teachers develop the capacity to work with children representing a variety of languages and cultures rather than relating to only a single variation from the dominant culture.

The above point strikes at the heart of my view of the difference between a professional and a technician in the realm of teaching. In my thinking a technician can be provided with a battery of situation-specific skills which he or she applies in a generally repetitive and routine fashion. A professional, on the other hand, is expected to develop the capacity to assess needs, diagnose difficulties, and prescribe alternative measures appropriate to those needs. Those qualities demand a broad-ranging, multi-cultured preparation rather than a narrow, provincial, monolithic experience. This conviction causes me to emphasize the distinction between community-*responsive* and community-*controlled* teacher education paralleling the distinction I would draw between field-oriented and field-based teacher education. We need teachers who are *sensitive* and *responsive* to community concerns but if they are truly to become professionals, I believe they *cannot be controlled* by single communities unless we use the term community in its broadest societal or cultural sense.

The report identifies a number of generic teaching skills or competencies judged important by the Deans' group. I concur in those and suggest that other portions of the report are inconsistent with such views and instead suggest a much narrower, more provincial view of the teacher and of the community.

At another point the report calls for a rejection of the influence of voluntary accreditation of institutions by peers in favor of a plan which would permit federal agencies to establish their own criteria for funding institutions and agencies. I strongly oppose such a move for I believe that we have a no more responsible base for determining eligibility for funding than the broad circle of agencies and institutions committed to the review and reexamination of their own efforts. Why are we to suppose that federal establishment of governmental criteria will result in anything other than rewarding sycophants skilled in developing proposals which suit the preferences of a much narrower and less responsible group of bureaucrats? Nongovernmental accreditation is far from perfect but I would much prefer it to establishing a small appointive group of Washington bureaucrats as the determiners of criteria for including or excluding institutions from grants designed to improve their effectiveness.

Still another area for concern relates to the report's endorsement of the skill-specific voucher system which, in my judgment, would encourage a variety of agencies, some of them profit making agencies, to contract for one or more isolated tasks of education in specific skill areas without assuming any responsibility for the integration of those areas in a broader development of children and youth. I believe the skill-specific voucher plan would be disastrous to the educational experiences of many young people. Indeed, the evaluations of earlier efforts in this regard would, I believe, support my concern.

I could continue the identification of many more specific items in the report which have caused me concern but this letter has already stretched far too long. Let me conclude by reaffirming my enthusiasm for the work of the Commission *as a document designed to stimulate discussion and debate.* At the same time I must *reject it as a prescription for the solution* of our nation's teacher preparation problems. There are many exciting and important ideas included in the report that I believe merit spirited discussion by professional and lay groups throughout the land. Many of the conclusions, however, I find it impossible to advocate.

Let me finally reaffirm my admiration for your effectiveness in and commitment to this important assignment. My decision to separate myself from the Commission's recommendations in no way changes my respect for your efforts to make the study a significant one.

Sincerely,

George W. Denemark

DEFINITION OF CULTURAL PLURALISM

Early in the Commission's life (August, 1972), the chairperson of the Cultural Pluralism Committee, Antonia Pantoja, presented to the Study Commission a definition of "cultural pluralism" which was accepted by the full Study Commission at its August, 1972, meeting. This statement has guided the Commission's actions vis-á-vis "cultural pluralism" since. The statement is as follows:

The educational system of this country fails to educate all its students, especially non-white students. Students are not taught to apprehend concepts, to understand, analyze and digest, and most important, to question. The goal of the school system is the maintenance of the status quo with respect to cultural, racial, sexual, and economic class, superiority-and-inferiority relations. Too often, America's school systems promulgate the erroneous theory that some people are better than others—that homogeneity is better than heterogeneity. The theory that some culture's forms of behavior are better than others, that one sex is superior to the other, is transmitted to the student body through the selection of curriculum content, books, texts, and symbols, and school personnel (including administration). The family, the general environment of the community, TV and media also disseminate the idea.

The aim of this pressure so created is to shape all Americans into what people recognize as an "Anglo Saxon Protestant" model—to force upon women roles of passivity, dependence and fear of aspiration. The schools, in looking among different races, cultures, life styles, and personal identities, have never recognized that each is as valuable as the other—have never attempted to accommodate these differences in their curricula, staffing, and governance patterns.

The creation of a model "Preferred American" from the variety of people who form the U.S. requires a process which melts away all differences in languages, life styles, religions, and any other cultural characteristics. For those whose skin color or other characteristics will not permit melting into the preferred group, the process penalizes and stigmatizes. The school has the primary responsibility for transmitting the model to each generation. The rest of the institutions of society including the mass media, politics, religion and industry reinforce and reward adherence to the model.

Two centuries of indoctrination in the "preferred/unpreferred" ideology have resulted in a substantial assimilation of many white European immigrants who are not from northern Europe and the development of other "minorities," both the visible minorities and Eastern European ethnics who carry a language or other visible characteristics. The very serious negative results of the model are evidenced in the United States:

    1. The development of a preferred group whose members enjoy "equality," "justice," "democracy" and the rights and privileges which the American dream promises with the exclusion of the unpreferred;

    2. The loss of the country's variety of cultures and the enrichment which might have resulted for the country;

    3. The emergence of marginal people with the resulting alienation;

    4. The development of competition and hostility among ethnic groups;

    5. The perpetuation of religious discrimination;

    6. The movement toward a mono-lingual country.

Although the majority society demands conformity from the minority, it does not permit them entry into the mainstream. More perversely it places the blame and guilt for these peoples' failures on the victims. The perversion is further compounded when the efforts of the minorities to separate in order to find their own strength is met with alarm, anger and hostility. The results of this paradox have been the development of:

    1. An economic system where minorities are unemployed or hold the least desirable jobs;

2. A number of groups called by the majority society "the poor," "the disadvantaged," "the culturally deprived," etc.;

3. The civil rights revolution of the sixties when oppressed minorities, particularly blacks, Puerto Ricans, Chicanos, and Indians, gained an awareness of their victimization;

4. An attitude of rejection and anger in the "unpreferred" towards the educational system and their conclusion that they must either control the school systems or establish alternative systems.

Meaningful pluralism requires a situation in society where individuals and groups can function successfully in one, two, or more languages and cultural styles and where individuals can abide by and function successfully adhering to different customs and religions, and to less crippling class and sexual stereotypes than those accepted today. It requires a society where no one race, sex, culture, or class is preferred over another. Certain conditions must be set before we can endeavor to reach the ultimate goal of the kind of pluralism sought here:

1. A period will be needed to develop the conditions where cultural pluralism will be successfully established;

2. There must be a rejection of all concepts and theories of "conformity to the preferred model";

3. Opportunities must be offered and supported, financially and morally, for "unpreferred groups" to come together for the purpose of undoing the damage caused by their being constantly placed in positions of "unpreferredness." They will need the time to put their "houses together," to eradicate self-hate, and to acquire a positive self image. If and when these groups wish to resume relationship with a pluralistic national environment they can do so from a position of strength; those who wish to remain separate must be respected in their decision.

4. Opportunities must be created for "preferred groups" to confront their illusions of "being better" and to realize the evil of their arrogance. They must learn to deal with their prejudices and acquire a healthier self image. They, as members of the

majority, must behave in congruence with American declarations of "democracy," "law," and "justice" for everybody.

Cultural pluralism can be made a reality if the school system is used as a positive tool to teach it through its educational efforts and behaviors:

1. Educational personnel (administrators, teacher-trainers, teachers, guidance staff) must be oriented away from treating people as "preferred" and "unpreferred" toward a vigorous encouragement of pluralism. Behaviors and attitudes which move in this direction should be rewarded.

2. Educational philosophies, curricula, materials and methods must be developed to create and encourage a pluralistic attitude in existing institutions of teacher training.

3. At the same time, new institutions must be created— based on the concept that all cultures in the U.S. have a right to institutions which reflect their values, language, authority system and way of life.

4. "Consubstantiality" between the school and the community must be made a reality. That is, the interests, goals and chemistry of the schools and the home must reflect each other in a way which enhances each. (The use of religious terminology which suggests two individuals "having the same substance" is deliberate. School and home, clan, or whatever the agent of informal education is, should be "of one substance.")

5. Where "unpreferred" groups constitute a majority of a school district, they should control the schools. Legislation should ensure and support respect for this concept.

6. In instances where unpreferred groups must develop their own alternative schools, revenue monies and financial support must be made available for such schools.

7. The need for ethnic "consubstantiality" between client and professional in helping relationships (teacher-student, counselor-student, psychiatrist or psychologist-client, social worker-client) must be accepted. The acceptance of "help" is not possible when the client or learner is a member of the "unpreferred" group and views the "helper," who is a member of the "preferred" group, as a part of the oppressive system.

It is the right of every child to acquire basic educational skills in his own language—and, in so doing, utilize the cognitive and value systems underlying that language. At the same time, non-pluralistic views of language exist in both the American school and general society. For this reason, many linguists have asserted that the control of English, at least as a tool language, is desirable for survival within the present social, political, and educational systems of the United States. Any real pluralist will strongly support the concepts of bilingual and bidialectal education within the general framework of multicultural education. Indeed, bilingual, bidialectal-multicultural education is perhaps the greatest present-day educational priority in communities containing a substantial number of minority group members. This type of education is neither "remedial" nor "compensatory" and does not presume to make up "deficiencies" in children, but rather recognizes the legitimacy of their differences. Further, it views bilingual children as **advantaged** not **disadvantaged**, and seeks to develop bilingualism as a precious asset and not a stigmatized behavioral characteristic.

If the nation wishes to implement an enlightened bilingual program, it will do the following:

  1. It will encourage speakers of other languages and dialects, if they wish, to attend schools where Standard American English can be acquired as a "second" or "tool" language or dialect. The form of English to be expected ought to reflect the influences generated by the "home" language or dialect. Several approaches may be used for achieving this goal; however, the precise approach to be used in a given school or community ought to be determined by linguistic data and parent wishes.

  2. Speakers of Standard English dialects ought to be able to attend schools where they (or their parents) will be able to exercise the option of requesting the acquisition of other languages or dialects as a second language. This goal is not best accomplished in the same physical settings as those where goal 1 above is being pursued.

  3. Teachers in bilingual, bicultural schools ought to possess

a bilingual, bicultural background, having shared the life chances of the group(s) that they teach (state and federal funds must be designated for the training of bilingual teachers and the development of bilingual curricula).

4. Parents should be involved in a decision-making role in the development of all phases of the bilingual, bicultural program, specifically in the design, implementation and evaluation of the program.

5. Poverty must not be a criterion for the use of the funds or for participation in these programs.

LIBRARY OF DAVIDSON COLLEGE

Books on regular loan may be checked out for **two weeks**. Books must be presented at the Circulation Desk in order to be renewed.

A fine is charged after date due.

Special books are subject to special regulations at the discretion of library staff.